SPATIAL MICROECONOMICS

ECONOMISTS OF THE TWENTIETH CENTURY

General Editors: Mark Perlman, *University Professor of Economics, Emeritus, University of Pittsburgh* and Mark Blaug, *Professor Emeritus, University of London; Professor Emeritus, University of Buckingham and Visiting Professor, University of Exeter*

This innovative series comprises specially invited collections of articles and papers by economists whose work has made an important contribution to economics in the late twentieth century.

The proliferation of new journals and the ever-increasing number of new articles make it difficult for even the most assiduous economist to keep track of all the important recent advances. By focusing on those economists whose work is generally recognized to be at the forefront of the discipline, the series will be an essential reference point for the different specialisms included.

A list of published and future titles in this series is printed at the end of this volume.

Spatial Microeconomics

Theoretical Underpinnings and Applications

Melvin L. Greenhut

Abell Professor Liberal Arts and
Distinguished Professor of Economics Emeritus
Texas A&M University, US

ECONOMISTS OF THE TWENTIETH CENTURY

Edward Elgar
Aldershot, UK • Brookfield, US

Published by
Edward Elgar Publishing Limited
Gower House
Croft Road
Aldershot
Hants GU11 3HR
UK

Edward Elgar Publishing Company
Old Post Road
Brookfield
Vermont 05036
US

British Library Cataloguing in Publication Data
Greenhut, M.L.
Spatial Microeconomics: Theoretical Underpinnings and Applications. – (Economists of the Twentieth Century Series)
I. Title II. Series
338.5

Library of Congress Cataloguing in Publication Data
Greenhut, Melvin L.
Spatial microeconomics : theoretical underpinnings and applications / Melvin L. Greenhut.
p. cm. — (Economists of the twentieth century)
Includes bibliographical references and index.
1. Space in economics. 2. Pricing. I. Title. II. Series.
HB199.G727 1995
338.5—dc20 95–7198
CIP

ISBN 1 85898 137 9

Printed and bound in Great Britain by
Hartnolls Limited, Bodmin, Cornwall

Contents

Acknowledgements

The publishers wish to thank the following who have kindly given permission for the use of copyright material.

American Economic Association for articles: 'Monopoly Output Under Alternative Spatial Pricing Techniques' with H. Ohta, *American Economic Review*, **LXII**(4), September 1972, 705–13; 'Monopoly Output Under Alternative Spatial Pricing Techniques: Reply', with H. Ohta, *American Economic Review*, **LXIX**(4), 1979, 680–81; 'Related Market Conditions and Interindustrial Mergers' with H. Ohta, *American Economic Review*, **66**(3), June 1976, 267–77; 'Related Market Conditions and Interindustrial Mergers: Reply' with H. Ohta, *American Economic Review*, **68**(1), March 1978, 228–30; 'Vertical Integration of Successive Oligopolists', with H. Ohta, *American Economic Review*, **69**(1), March 1979, 137–41; 'On the Basing-Point System', with Bruce L. Benson and George Norman, *American Economic Review*, **80**(3), June 1990, 584–8; 'On the Basing-Point System: Reply' with Bruce L. Benson and George Norman, *American Economic Review*, **80**(4), September 1990, 963–7.

Aoyama Journal of International Politics, Economics and Business for articles: 'Theoretical Error, Economic Space, Price Theory and Data' with John Greenhut and Hiroshi Ohta, First Issue, 1984, 181–97; 'Price and Market Space Effects of Bank Mergers' with John Greenhut and Hiroshi Ohta, 1990, 153–75.

Blackwell Publishers for articles: 'The Decision Process and Entrepreneurial Returns', *Manchester School*, September 1966, 247–67; 'Spatial Price Discrimination, Competition and Locational Effects' with John G. Greenhut, *Economica*, **42**(168), November 1975, 401–19; 'Spatial Pricing in the United States, West Germany, and Japan', *Economica*, **48**, 1981, 79–86; 'Impacts of Distance on Microeconomic Theory', *Manchester School*, March 1978, 17–40; 'Mr. Dorward and Impacts of Distance on Microeconomic Theory', *Manchester School*, September 1981, 259–65; 'A Theory of Oligopolistic Competition' with W.J. Lane, *Manchester School*, **LVII**(3), September 1989, 248–61; 'Reverse Dumping: A Form of Spatial Price Discrimination', with H. Ohta and Joel Sailors, *Journal of Industrial Economics*, **XXXIV**(2), December 1985, 167–81; 'Basing Point Pricing and Production Concentration' with Jean B. Soper, George Norman and Bruce L. Benson, *The Economic Journal*, **101**, May 1991, 539–56; 'An Anomaly in the Service Industry: The Effect of Entry on Fees' with C.S. Hung, G. Norman and C.W. Smithson, *The Economic Journal*, **95**, March 1985, 169–77.

Cambridge University Press for article: 'Appendix A to An Efficient Long-Run Allocative Equilibrium' with G. Norman and C.S. Hung in *The Economics of Imperfect Competition*, 1987, 334–40.

Cato Institute for article: 'Interest Groups and the Antitrust Paradox', with Bruce L. Benson and Randall G. Holcombe, *The Cato Journal*, **6**(3), Winter 1987, 801–17.

The Econometric Society for articles: 'Observations on the Shape and Relevance of the Spatial Demand Function', with M. Hwang and H. Ohta, *Econometrica*, **43**(4), July 1975, 669–82; 'Nonlinearity of Delivered Price Schedules and Predatory Pricing' with John Greenhut, *Econometrica*, **45**(8), November 1977, 1871–5.

Elsevier Science Publishers for article: 'Spatial Discrimination, Bertrand vs. Cournot: Comment', with C.S. Lee and Y. Mansur, *Journal of Regional Science and Urban Economics*, **21**, 1991, 127–34.

Houston Law Review Inc for article: 'An Economic Theory for Use in Antitrust Cases', *Houston Law Review*, **7**, 1970, 318–40.

The Institute of Management Sciences for article: 'Mathematics, Realism and Management Science', *Management Science*, **4**(3), April 1958, 314–20.

International Journal of Transport Economics for article: 'Financial-Economic Aspects of Airline Deregulation' with John Greenhut and George Norman, **XVIII**(1), February 1991, 3–30.

Kluwer Academic Publishers for article: 'Industrial Structures Components of Finance Theory's CAPM' with John G. Greenhut, *Review of Industrial Organization*, **7**, 1991, 361–73.

MIT Press for article: 'Spatial Pricing Patterns in the United States' with John Greenhut and Sheng-Yung Li, *Quarterly Journal of Economics*, **XCIV**(2), March 1980, 329–50.

Nuova Casa Editrice L. Cappelli di GEM s.r.l. for article: 'The Pricing Policies of a Spatial Monopolist' with Ralph W. Pfouts, *Metroeconomica*, **IX**(3), December 1957, 153–66.

Pion Press for article: 'On Demand Curves and Spatial Pricing' in *Spatial Pricing and Differentiated Markets*, (ed. G. Norman), 1986, 65–76.

Review of Regional Economics and Business for article: 'Economic Theories and Economic Policies', October 1984, 29–35.

The South African Journal of Economics for article: 'Hypotheses in Science and an Evaluation of Normative Microeconomic Theory', **35**(2), June 1967, 134–44.

Southern Economic Journal for articles: 'A General Theory of Maximum Profits', **XXVIII**(3), January 1962, 278–85; 'Output Effects of Spatial Price Discrimination Under Conditions of Monopoly and Competition' with Hiroshi Ohta, **46**(1), July 1979, 71–84; 'A Theoretical Mapping from Perfect Competiton to Imperfect Competition', **XLII**(2), October 1975, 177–92; 'Free Entry and the Trade Mark-Trade Name Protection', **XXIV**(2), October 1957, 170–81.

Springer Verlag for articles: 'Differences in Spatial Pricing in the United States: A Statistical Analysis and Case Studies' with M. Hwang and S. Shwiff, *Annals of Regional Science*, 1984, 49–66; 'Alternative Uses of Spatial Microeconomics' with John G. Greenhut, *Annals of Regional Science*, **26**, 1992, 257–67.

University of Pennsylvania Press for article: 'Spatial Pricing with a General Cost Function: The Effects of Taxes on Imports', with George Norman, *International Economic Review*, **27**(3), October 1986, 761–76.

Weltwirtschaftliches Archiv for articles: 'Discriminatory and Nondiscriminatory Spatial Prices and Outputs Under Varying Market Conditions' with H. Ohta, Band 111, Heft 2, 1975, 310–31; 'Mr. Gripsrud and a Theory of Oligopoly', **110**(3), 1974, 518–24.

Every effort has been made to trace all the copyright holders but if any have been inadvertently overlooked the publishers will be pleased to make the necessary arrangements at the first opportunity.

Introduction

The Elgars offered me the opportunity to include some autobiographical materials here and in the companion book, *Location Economics*. How can one resist the opportunity to re-examine and classify certain events in one's life? I shall do this chiefly over the early pages of this Introduction. In fact, its initial pages correspond basically to the initial pages in the companion book on location economics. Those who may have read that book's introduction can therefore turn their attention directly to the first complete paragraph on page xvii of this Introduction where I begin to recall the most recent 30 years of my life in academia, chiefly the opportunities and advantages given me at Texas A&M University. Or, the reader may want to turn to page xix where my description of the contents of this book begins.

I will profess to having been essentially a product of the Depression years, during which time my father worked as a part-time policeman, a window washer, and probably at many other tasks I was sheltered from knowing about. This bleak history, combined with my mother's work in a factory and their insistence that I acquire at least a high school education (which neither of them had), played on my mind throughout my young life. The little I recall of my pre-teen years at home was highlighted by the fact that my father was a prankster and rather proud of it. In particular, in between admonitions that nothing in life comes free, and that I should put my mind to studies and the value of education, was his 'happy-tale' about being kicked out of elementary school for putting limburger cheese on a radiator during a bitterly cold, wintry day. If the United States Army had learned of a stunt I pulled umpteen years after my father's prank (probably in indirect honour of him), I would possibly still be in the proverbial 'hoose-gow' without the opportunity to recall the bittersweet days of yesteryears.

It was probably the fact of being poor, never owning a bicycle nor even a baseball glove, i.e., until my father learned I played a game in right field using a friend's catcher's mit, which surely served as the sources of a personal drive I have had. Most importantly, my father and mother were inspirational to me. Their stick-to-it policy of work, work, work, and take care of yourself, stands in stark contrast to the 'perhaps excessive and unending' welfare gratuities of today. I can easily add at this point the fact of inspiration derived later on in life from my Father- and Mother-in-law, Evan and Huldah Griffith, each of whom lived by the same take care of yourself ethic.

Throughout the Depression years, I wondered why an Army of Unemployed – as large in number as the combined American Army, Navy, Marine Corps, and Coast Guard of World War II – had to exist. What was wrong with Economists? What did they know? What did they do? I rather imagine most economists of ages 65–80 today, regardless of family wealth during the 1930s, were motivated to study our science because of the real economic crises that prevailed back then.

But enough of these personal reflections about the dark ages. Allow me to insert below a few statements by Hiroshi Ohta that were based on information my son, John, had provided him for a book he was coediting with Jacques Thisse.* Because this book was brought to my attention only after its publication, I have corrected a slight error and added minor updating to Professor Ohta's remarks to reflect a change in my University position which had taken place but which had not been publicized at that time. After the insertion, I shall sketch in personalized form what some of my years as an academician were like, as well as a few immediately preceding ones. After these sketches are complete, I shall provide a brief summary of the articles included in this book. Perhaps the personal sketches will offer a meaningful interpretative background for the articles included herein. Incidentally, I should repeat at this point that I am using the same initial introductory pages in the companion volume to the present book in belief that many readers of that other one will not necessarily be interested in the contents of this book, and, may I also say, vice versa.

> For readers who are not completely familiar with Mel Greenhut's career, we take a moment to provide the following brief sketch. Mel received his PhD degree from Washington University in 1951. His first professorial position was at Auburn. He was side-tracked into administration as Associate Dean at the University of Richmond, during which time he consulted extensively with AT&T (American Telephone and Telegraph) and research companies located in Washington, DC. He was consulting editor to *Industrial Development*, and also served on the National Economic Policy Committee of the US Chamber of Commerce and the executive committee of the Southern Economic Association. He was on the board of editors of the Association's journal and a professor at Florida State University for many years. Since 1966, he has been at Texas A&M University, initially as Professor and Department Head, and from 1969 up to the present as Distinguished Professor of Economics; in 1986 he also became the George and Gladys Abell Professor of Liberal Arts, and in 1992 the title of emeritus was added. For many years, Mel Greenhut served as Adjunct Distinguished Professor at the University of Oklahoma and at the University of Karlsruhe, in Germany. He has lectured extensively throughout Europe and the Orient, besides the United States. Summer visiting appointments included Michigan State University and the Universities of Cape Town and Pittsburgh.
>
> His publications consist (at present count) of a dozen books, and articles numbering in the three digits. His latest interests include work in fuzzy mathematics. He is a contributor to *The New Palgrave* and to the latest *Encyclopedia of Economics*, under publication by McGraw-Hill. He was listed in the initial 1981 *Who's Who in Economics* and the editions that have followed.
>
> On a personal side, he is married to Elmara Griffith Greenhut, has four children – Peggy Chase, Pam Blaylock, John Greenhut, and Pat Thomsen – and ten grandchildren. He served actively and in the US Army reserve, obtaining the rank of major. He has been listed in *Who's Who in the United States* for more than 30 years.
>
> 'Drop everything else.' This is one of the colonel-like orders Professor Greenhut would give to his students. But they knew that he was a decisive and conscientious teacher who cares. He cares about any fuzzy idea a student may bring forth. The caring teacher would then say, 'Sounds great!' The decisive colonel would hasten to add, 'Let's work out a paper. Drop everything else.' The conscientious teacher would then sweat on working *for* and *with* the student repeatedly for improvement of the output. Upon completion of the work, Mel would finally say, 'Well done. Have a day off this weekend. Well, make it a half.'

* *Does Economic Space Matter*, London: Macmillan Ltd, 1993, see pp. 2, 3.

In many ways, the second leg of my professional career started with Hiroshi Ohta. But well before Hiroshi Ohta, I had visualized my field of specialization in the form of the old and new location economics, indeed much as Hisao Nishioka described in the Ohta-Thisse book over its pages XVII–XX. This Professor Nishioka, formerly a President of the Aoyama Gakuin University in Tokyo, knew as well as I did my views on location economics. This gentleman had translated my *Plant Location* book into Japanese besides also an article of mine included in the companion volume to this book. I had become interested initially in location economics because a new head (Werner Hochwald) took over the economics department at Washington University; I believe it was in 1948. He quickly advised me that because a senior professor who I virtually idolized, Orval Bennett, was retiring in a year or so, and because I was moving to Auburn University (then called the Alabama Polytechnic Institute), I *had better* select a different dissertation subject than the Antitrust Laws (Professor Bennett's field of specialization). Professor Hochwald recommended Industrial Location and the Southern Economy.

One thing any military experience can teach is the reality that if you are unwilling to go it all by yourself, take the order and swallow your pride (or desires, is it?) until you can say to hell with everyone and everything. Until then, do it the Army, Navy way, as the pilots who were then all in the Army or Navy Air Force had often been told. So although I had happily volunteered three times for certain duties during my days in the Army – probably the only thing that looked special on my Army records – and regardless of whether the good Lord decided against me on those occasions in order to protect me and/or my comrades in the service, I did not think during my graduate student days that I should go it my own way. So I forthrighteously and independently 'volunteered' to write on *Industrial Location in Alabama*. Because back then the PhD was dragged out by professors even more mercilessly than today, I later on left out of the dissertation the main cogs of my thinking at that time, my 1952 papers on *Location Theory*; in effect, I left my dissertation essentially restricted to a rehashing of early-accepted location theory along with some data on the location of industry. My conformist decision, and by this stage of my life I had a wife and three very young offspring to support (so I really had to conform), enabled me to convert my dissertation a few years later to a better manuscript, a book entitled *Plant Location in Theory and Practise*.

To my way of thinking, the main contributions in the book were to convert the von Thünen–Weber school of thought via Lösch into a new location economics. This belief was highlighted by the papers I wrote in the early 1950s and 1960s that are recorded in Part II of the companion book. Permit me to recognize that the good Lord had sent a young German to study at Auburn in addition to the many other blessings He had given me. Since the Lutheran Church in Auburn, for which I had the honour to serve as a trustee, was sponsoring this student, I had the good fortune to be with him often. In what I can call a partial – but unfair to him – exchange, this young student helped me with my attempts to read German while I helped him in his studies in the principles of economics course at Auburn. (For those unfamiliar with the PhD requirements of yesteryears, reading skills in two foreign languages were required, and German was my second choice.) The book that *we* worked with, not yet translated into English (nor for that matter until many years later), was

August Lösch's *Die räumliche Ordnung der Wirtschaft*. Talk about good luck, good fortune, or *God* given breaks in life, I had them!

My late 1940s, my 1950s, and early 1960s were dotted with diverse academic positions, including an associate deanship that subsequently led to an offer of a full deanship which I most fortunately rejected. During this period, I worked essentially in the field of what I would call the old and the new location economics, including their applications. This emphasis took place in partial conjunction with some writings, actually a couple of books on macroeconomics. My side interest in macroeconomics probably reflected the Depression years effect on me to become a do-gooder economist.

If good luck, or frankly more to the way I truly feel, the great fortune of having had *God* protecting me was ever in doubt in my mind, this possibility had been dispelled in very late 1950, a half-year or so before my dissertation was completed and the PhD awarded me. As many reservists feared during the Korean War, I received a military service recall (and this clearly, by coincidence) to the division that I had been with about six and a half years previously, the 87th (Acorn) Division. But the recall notice (including about 80 other Alabamans) had been misdelivered to each of us. Without this particular knowledge of misdelivery, when I learned about being recalled from my tearful wife *at the front door of our home in Auburn*, I was truly shaken. Because I hated goodbyes, my wife was convinced that I had deliberately failed to tell her I was going back on active duty. She expected me suddenly to be packed up and announce I had been recalled to service as I walked out of the front door to a waiting taxi.

If you are familiar with Special Orders of the Military, you can appreciate the fact that my wife misread the orders. The order I had received was a cancellation order, a cancellation involving about 80 men who had never shown up for duty at the posts they were assigned to. Indeed, though I was familiar with the cryptic language of Special Orders, I will admit that I was so nervous and upset about the order she had shoved at me, along with my sudden thoughts of having to leave my family and in all possibility never getting my dissertation completed nor approved nor the PhD awarded, that I missed for at least 30 minutes the fact that what we had received was a cancellation. Having once quivered at the door of a military plane fearing possible bail out orders, I have ever since that day in Auburn wondered which of these two events gave me the shakier knees. When a couple of years later, towards the end of the Korean War, our military establishment offered reservists with some (unrecalled) combined number of years of active and reserve service the option to go standby, I jumped at going standby. This status meant no future reserve duty pay nor in-line active training service that would lead to promotions in the reserve, but among other benefits the opportunity to still feel patriotic by remaining in the reserve. Most vitally, the great advantage of standby status was the fact that only Congress in a declaration of war could henceforth immediately claim my services in place of the very happy, pleasant, and safe days I was having as an academician. Of course, when I say 'safe days as an academician', I am recalling that back then students were not as violent as we somehow or other have permitted them to be today.

A few final words about *God* provided grace and good fortune are warranted before I can turn my attention to certain events in the 1960s which serve as direct background to the contents of this book. First, back in the servile days when I was still a graduate student, I was fascinated by the underlying theoretical framework of the writings of von Thünen, Weber and followers. This fascination led me to construct my two 1952 articles in the *Southern Economic Journal*. Why that journal? Well, the editor was Gus Schwenning, a delightful individual of German ancestry. He knew and virtually worshipped the writings of August Lösch much as I, the latter condition to be readily apparent to readers of this book. More germane to present statements about good fortune, if ever anyone meets a journal editor more interested in the author's subject than I did in meeting Professor Schwenning, I would like to hear of it. Our joint fascination with the German writers on location economics, combined with my early contacts and discussions with Professor Schwenning, had led me to the philosophical interests about thought frameworks which led me to my specialization in the economics of space.

During the late 1960s, I had the exciting challenge to develop a top-quality department of economics at Texas A&M. I leaped at the opportunity partly because of my frustration with the growth of our department of economics at Florida State University (FSU). Two top quality economists, Jim Buchanan and Charles Ferguson, had expressed interest in relocating at FSU in the middle 1960s, in Jim's case to return to FSU. However, between our faculty, its head, and the Dean of the College, their joining us fell through the cracks.

Alas, I had long wanted to be in an economics department which had many research-leading economists. This appetite had been whetted by a summer visiting professorship and possible permanent stay that I had at Michigan State, as well as opportunities to go to Berkeley and College Park, among other exciting places. I had turned down these overtures because of my wife's *strong* desire to remain in the southern part of the United States. So, when Texas A&M invited me to give a few lectures and subsequently offered me a veritable *carte blanche* to build a top quality department, I had little reason not to move.

The President at that time of Texas A&M University was Earl Rudder, a general in the US Army Reserve, a graduate of A&M, and a former Light Colonel who had led the charge of our forces in scaling the heights at Pointe du Hoc. He was also a close friend of Larry Fouraker, then Dean of the Harvard Business School. Rather interestingly, Larry, an A&M graduate, had been on the faculty at Penn State and had been responsible many years prior to the 1960s in having his department enquire as to whether I would be interested in moving from Auburn, Alabama to College Park, Pennsylvania. Larry, by the way, has long been interested in multinational corporate oligopolies, and my own writings from the early days had heralded the importance of oligopolistic markets. Mr. Rudder, who dearly loved A&M, as do most of its former students, was a close friend of Governor Connally. The University was then a male-only institution, half of whom were in the Corps of Cadets with the other 3 000 having interests outside of the military in their minds for the years following graduation. Earl Rudder wanted another University of Texas type for his A&M. But during his early days as President of A&M, he had learned to his deep regret that, beyond the military accomplishments of its graduates plus the rather selective albeit limited research accomplishments of its faculty, the University had not achieved the status among the elites of academia that he wanted.* Need I say that Larry Fouraker recommended me to Earl Rudder.

I received a blank cheque from Earl Rudder to develop a top-quality department which would offer the PhD degree. The blank cheque included ten secretaries for ten faculty members when I first moved there in 1966,** plus first class airline passage for me anytime I felt there was advantage in my traveling to DC or elsewhere. Within three years, we had converted a faculty of four PhDs and seven with masters degrees only to a faculty of about 24 PhDs and three or so without. Our seven MA student candidates had become some unremembered number, several times the original; and we had up to 40 PhD candidates walking our corridors by 1969.

Professors Ferguson, Basmann, Furubotn, Saving and many other very well-known men today were part of our new faculty, including, for example, Bob Ekelund, Horst Siebert, Phil Gramm, Ray Battalio, John Kagel, Chuck Maurice, Phil Rahbany, Steve Pejovich, Rufus Waters, Bert Bowden plus others. Oskar Morgenstern was a regular visiting adjunct professor with us for a few years and Herman Hartley, J.N.K. Rao, Ron Hocking, and Rudy Freund of the TAMU Institute of Statistics provided teaching and related support to our department. Our other faculty, including Al Chalk, its former head, and Irv Linger, a long-time faculty member, carried diverse administrative responsibilities and heavier teaching loads than those who were specifically mentioned above. They were primarily responsible for trying to maintain the teaching excellence that had characterized the department prior to my joining it. This, by the way, was the hardest, and in some respects the impossible, target for a publish-perish group interested chiefly in working with graduate students.

Among our PhD students was Hiroshi Ohta. My good friend Hisao Nishioka, who had had the courtesy of visiting me and my family in Tallahassee years earlier with his wife and daughter, had recommended Hiroshi, his brightest student, to me. Hiroshi, the nephew of a World War II Kamikaze crewman, was as challenging to me as a student as had been Professor Nishioka when he was translating (and questioning me regularly about) my *Plant Location* book. After a few years at A&M of rounding out my own prior efforts to advance the integration of location interdependence and market area theory with, may I call it, the old location theory, Hiroshi joined me in seeking to integrate location economics with general microeconomic theory. Manifestly, for one who lived in Texas, spatial distances had their impacts on production and consumption. Also quite clear *to our way of thinking*, space must be integrated with time in order for any truly meaningful advanced theory of microeconomics to arise.

* Interestingly, George Patton is said to have stated, 'Give me an Army of West Point graduates and I will win a battle; give me an Army of Texas A&M Aggies and I will win a war.' That there were more officers in the Army during WWII from Texas A&M than from the Point may help buttress this claim.

** My severest personal constraint up until my move to A&M was in not having sufficient secretarial support to counterbalance my poor handwriting and writing skills and hence the multiple rewriting attempts I found necessary for improving the prose of my papers.

Part I of this volume, in counterpart to Part I of the companion book on location economics, provides the philosophical roots which support my conception of spatial microeconomics. I had felt for many years that the standard neo-classical spaceless microeconomics must be subsumed within a thought framework that included distances. The articles in Part I call for greater realism, such as I had believed was needed for the old location economics. In particular, Part I provides a general theory of maximum profits which fits a spaceless as well as the spatial microeconomic world. To buttress this writer's belief that classical spaceless microeconomics is both inadequate as well as irrelevant *per se*, the next paper in Part I returns to the subject of realism in tracing the mathematical properties and restrictions which then applied to the theory of business management. It is further in order for me to propose at this point that all of us in academia are pompous, perhaps because if we lacked strong belief in our own way of thinking and in our subject matter specialization, we could not teach nor write with the conviction that is necessary for self-fulfilment. If I were writing that same paper today, I would now – in conformance with the preceding statement – have to include my own beliefs of the inadequacy of the crisp number mathematics which we apply in the form of the calculus *vis-à-vis* the more realistic logic of (and need to use) fuzzy math. Indeed, towards the end of the Introduction to this book, I shall include further words, and even specifications about fuzzy math, especially in the context of oligopoly markets.

More to the point of the papers in Part I of this book, it follows naturally from my theory of what maximum profits portends *and* my belief that more realistic mathematics is needed to explain how most entrepreneurs resolve their decision problems that further words of philosophical order are required, as in the third paper of Part I. Finally, because all of us who have been attracted to the science of economics have some 'do gooder' in our make-up, I chose as a fundamental closing point for Part I my 1967 paper on normative microeconomic theory. How things ought to be is a captivating subject which involves complex postulational roots to support any meaningful normative theory.

The four papers noted above help frame the overall philosophical basis which led me to probe further into the field of economic space, and especially into what I call spatial microeconomics. This extension of my early thoughts on the subject of industrial location opens up a new thought system which, in my opinion, includes as a sub-part the spaceless microeconomics that many of our Veblenesque economists of today insist on maintaining. Why not move closer to the real world, I keep wondering? Perhaps the papers in Parts II and III of this volume will convince a few readers of the applicability and inclusiveness of spatial microeconomics.

Part II's papers stem chiefly from interactions I had with graduate students at Texas A&M, with my son, John, now a Finance Professor at Arizona State University West, and with George Norman. Recorded initially in this section is, however, a paper I wrote many many years ago with Bill Pfouts, a paper that probed into the pricing policies of the *spatial* monopolist. This early jump start, as it were, on a topic that has continued to fascinate me over the years led among other papers to my first paper with John, the second paper included in Part II of this book. In that paper, we probed theoretically into the different price schedules and location effects that competitive firms at alternative production centers would have over both their local and their distant markets. As one might expect, that paper next required evaluation of how firms actually do price in free enterprise countries. Included among those that were studied are the US, then West Germany, and Japan, recorded also in Part II.

One extension of different pricing policies is to compare the *output* effects of monopoly and competitive f.o.b. pricing with spatially discriminatory pricing. These particular roots of space microeconomics are themselves just part of the panoply of differences that is brought about by conceiving of a microeconomics which includes the spatial dimension. My papers along these lines that we included in Part II also relate to a paper entitled 'Impacts of Distance on Microeconomic Theory'. That particular paper brings into focus the full spatial picture I had visualized during the late 1970s.

Perhaps the most general and pervasive impact of the spatial phenomenon is that it points to the oligopoly market type as the *only* realistic market entity. It follows that whether or not oligopolistic markets can be revealed as having deterministic solutions in the short and long run becomes critical subject matter. This is especially the case for those of us who believe that greater realism is needed in economic theory. Two of the papers in Part II which followed my conception of a deterministic theory of oligopoly involve disclaimers by certain readers and my reaction to their critiques. In concert, they required my inclusion in this book of an appendix that I had written with George Norman and C.S. Hung in our *The Economics of Imperfect Competition*.* Beyond the aforementioned thoughts, it warrants in my final reference to Part II the claim that the subject of economic space has no greater requirement than appreciating the impacts on it of different demand functions. These impacts are not only central to spatial economics *per se*, but provide insights into the long-run determinancy of oligopoly markets. Indeed this analysis also points to the legal and other applied spin-offs from the theory of spatial microeconomics that are included in Part III of this volume.

Part III concludes this book. Its first paper discusses errors we economists are subject to, especially if we ignore space as a dimension to be included with time. But space is much more than just a needed dimension. The very recent papers with John Greenhut that are then set forth in Part III demonstrate alternative uses for the spatial framework of thought; i.e., uses beyond those stressed in Part II. For example, the portfolio theory and CAPM model of the recent Nobel Laureates in finance economics, namely Markowitz and Sharpe, can be evaluated and extended under the spatial framework. Indeed a basic reason for being more realistic in economic theory is that the theory of pure competition and its simple monopoly alternative offer restricted applications of economic theory. Whatever the specific uses, especially those which would involve trial lawyers, requires that we be cognizant of interest group impacts; moreover, we must be able to distinguish between non-predatory and predatory pricing, both within a nation and between nations. The spatial framework provides a helpful vista. In fact, as one focuses on the international scene, the impact of taxes becomes clearer when viewed from the perspective of spatial micro theory. All of these areas of study are evaluated in papers included in Part III.

* Cambridge: The Cambridge University Press, 1987.

Furthermore, they are central to the policies legislators have practiced in the past and may practice in the future.

What merger constraints, among other legislative enactments, are really desirable from the consumer welfare standpoint is also clarified in my opinion when constructed on the foundations of spatial microeconomics rather than the classical spaceless microeconomics. Several papers along these lines are accordingly set forth, including analysis of the base-point pricing system. Applications of spatial microeconomics are next shown to reflect the relation between free entry conditions and the legalized trademark support of product differentiation. Most vitally, conceiving of differentiated products along a line is but a simple carry-over from the line focus of location economics. That spatial microeconomics even answers such classic problems as why and how the fees of MD's have been found to increase with an increase in their supply *ceteris paribus*, in complete denial of elementary demand, supply economics, is explained as we approach the end of the section. Finally, selected aspects of airline deregulation are considered in the backlight of spatial microeconomics.

As was my practice in the companion volume, may I now observe that this book is more concerned with topical (thematic) ordering of papers than a strictly chronological development. I selected this path in belief that a side interest of any reader would be to witness how another person's thought system has evolved on a given subject, *and perhaps* how it was also contradicted at diverse points in time.

It should be evident from my previous sketch of the contents of this book that the same type of observation Mark Blaug entered about the classical English economists being reformers who addressed themselves to the *economic policy issues of their day** also applies to spatial price theorists. Most important to many of us in this field of study is the need to determine whether overall efficiency characterizes the economic landscape. A by-product of this need is well evident in the Part III papers dealing with mergers, delivered pricing systems, and *in general* antitrust policy.

On a somewhat different level of thought, may I also mention the obvious fact that mathematics has been used as extensively in the field of spatial microeconomics as it is in all of present-day economic literature. One future difference may stem from our natural emphasis on oligopolistic industries, which industries point directly to the importance of game theory *and fuzzy math*. I will accordingly later propose that the uncertain action-reaction decisions of oligopolists involves fuzzy numbers, not crisp ones. I further predict that fuzzy math must (and will) become a vital topic in the future. But first, let us turn to some thoughts about game theory, *viz.* locational interdependence.

Present day location theory, unlike that of von Thünen, Weber and their followers, has focused to no small extent on the locational interdependence of firms. The writers who were interested in locational interdependence, including H. Hotelling, A. Smithies, M. Copeland, A. Lerner, H.W. Singer, and E.H. Chamberlin, among many others, stressed duopoly-oligopoly markets pursuant to their central interest in imperfect competition economics. This school of thought also had roots in game theory, and as noted in my writings on location theory proved to be integrateable

* See his *Economic History and the History of Economics*, New York: The New York University Press, 1986, p. VII.

with the classic location economics of von Thünen and Weber. In substance, the writers on locational interdependency, and more recently present-day location, price (quantity) game theory, considered all feasible location alternatives while, in effect, selecting the best prices (quantities) for each location. In substance, price became the proper sub-game.

Consider in the game theory context a perfect information game, which means that the players (firms) know the history of the game, i.e., they know all of the past moves of the game. Any of the players can, accordingly, reconstruct the game, starting from any point in the game. This corresponds to assuming that two chess players have such perfect recall that if, because of an earthquake, the chess board were to fall to the ground, either of the players can reconstruct the game and arrive at the positions that existed prior to the quake. The perfect information game requires each player to know meticulously the history of competition in his/her market. Simply put, the past is an open, well documented book.

A multi-stage game commits the participants to playing the game in stages (sub-games). If the payoffs (profits) are distributed to the players at the end of the last stage, then rational players must commit themselves to playing all of the sub-games. A common application of multi-stage games to the space economy was the two-stage game. Here, the firms determine all of their feasible locations in the first stage, and then confirm their profit maximizing location via the equilibrium price (output) that is next derived. In substance, they determine their profit maximizing prices (outputs) given all potential profit maximizing (optimal) locations (capacities). One can recognize that the full game is solved recursively, i.e., the last stage, when solved, proves the feasibility of the location that was expected to be the best in the first stage.

It is manifest that the relevant sets of strategies are virtually infinite in each game. Locations are practically countless and so are the prices. Nevertheless, the theory of games points to a Nash equilibrium provided the strategies are finite. In order to invoke Nash's theory, economists close the location (capacity) and price (output) spaces by making them bounded and convex. Thus the location is set at a point in a closed interval (or over the circumference of a circle) while the price is bounded by a reservation value from above and by 0 from below. We have in reverse order $0 \leq P \leq$ reservation price, with output greater than or equal to zero, and restricted by the length of the interval (or the circumference of the location circle). To repeat, the location is synonymous with capacity. With sufficient abstractions, including explicit capacity constraints, a location, price equilibrium pair could be obtained for each firm. Most significantly, the theory of games does not tell us *per se* which equilibrium results when there are many equilibria, nor does it tell us how to play the game.

At an opposite end of the same spectrum as game theory stands a new sub-field of mathematics, fuzzy sets, in which a former student of mine, Dr Yusuf Mansur, and I have been 'playing'. Where game theory requires multiple abstractions, fuzzy sets can model and process *generalizations* as its special form of abstracting. For example, taste cannot typically be specified precisely, but it can be identified as slightly differentiated among all buyers; *or* elasticities of demand and supply cannot be precisely numbered, but they can be approximated as being more elastic for a certain good than another; *or* products which cannot be said to be identical or to differ from one to another on a scale of one to ten can be defined as just being similar; *and* market boundaries which cannot be said to be 1.427 miles in all directions from St Louis can be defined as being at varying distances within the market space of a St Louis firm. All of these statements, along with the locations of competitors, relate to fuzzy sets. For further example, the locations of rivals can be distinguished by the semantic that they are proximate to our production centre ABC, or that they are somewhat distant from ABC, or that their location is very distant from ABC, etc. In other words, we can model vague or incomplete knowledge via fuzzy sets to replicate empirical phenomena. And this is the way you and I actually consider most real-life alternatives, especially those involving our own actions and reactions to the actions and reactions of others. One must in contrast severely violate reality in employing crisp number game theory.

Perhaps a still more precise statement of the use of fuzzy mathematics in spatial economics requires inclusion here. Consider a firm that *competes* with five other firms in a *large* market, each member firm of which produces products *similar* to those of the others. Not all of the firms need be full competitors; rather, each firm may compete with the representative firm at a different level of interdependence. Their market sizes may be estimated subjectively by approximations, and the similarity of their products may be designated to varying extents, such as very similar, basically similar, not too similar, etc. May we say that the heterogeneous economic space which characterizes their competition can be described realistically. In fact, it can be described in a manner consistent with human cognitive processes and devoid of totally unrealistic abstraction, such as assuming (explicitly or implicitly) that all buyers and/or all sellers are located at a single point in space, as in the theory of perfect competition.

May I sum up my thoughts about game theory, spatial microeconomics, and fuzzy math as follows: The classic spaceless economy solutions of oligopoly that are so well-known from the writings of Cournot, Bertrand, Stackelberg, Chamberlin, Robinson, and countless others can be easily extended to the spatial economy.* In similar manner, game theory can be applied to location economics. Most vitally, any microeconomics inclusion of costs of distances brings oligopoly firms into focus and these interdependent sellers run smack into fuzzy concepts. The fuzzy number reality of their economic decision making process colours the game that one would ascribe to these sellers. By what are called alpha cuts, along with the use of selected fuzzy-math principles, much is nevertheless salvageable. The only basic problem that remains lies in the fact that applications of fuzzy numbers signify that a band of solutions obtain rather than a single crisp number result. Of course, this condition places significant limits on the information which game theory can provide, as must next be emphasized.

In the long run a precise microeconomic solution obtains given a world of fuzzy (oligopolistic behavioral uncertainty) relationships. The long-run precision I claim

* For example, I included a direct spatial take-off of Cournot over pages 111–13 in my 1970 book *A Theory of the Firm in Economics Space*, as reproduced in 1992 (Aldershot: Gregg Revival Series, Gower House). This spatial take-off was done under the sub-heading 'Introducing Economic Space into Cournot's Model: Buyers Distributed Over the Space'.

will hold is proposed in several papers of Part II.* Correspondingly, it is only in reflection of a precisely determined long-run optimal space economy solution that any definitive game can arise; this is so because the characteristic function and other game parameters can be *prespecified* only for that point in time *as a spin-off from* the unique equilibrium which that microeconomic theory will provide.** It follows that a deterministic (unique-equilibrium) game theory derivation can stem only from a microeconomic theory of the long run, for it is in that period alone that crisp numbers do obtain. In this respect, game theory is therefore a sub-discipline within the general confines of spatial microeconomics.

This writer thus proposes that a uniquely determinate crisp number Nash equilibrium game can obtain only in the long run of the space economy. In the short run, subjectively altered crisp numbers prevail or, more precisely, fuzzy numbers apply. Moreover, with respect to the more recent game theory which recognizes the existence of multiple oligopolistic equilibria alternatives *and* the use of subjectively weighted probabilities, the need to employ and advance fuzzy mathematics is quite evident. In sum, it is my belief that fuzzy mathematics will soon rise to the forefront in economics, including the present-day game theory which has been centring its attention more and more on the behaviourally uncertain actions and reactions of oligopolists.

As I point towards the conclusion to this Introduction, I would like to repeat certain 'political-type', and personal remarks that I had set forth over the last two pages in the Introduction to my companion book, *Location Economics*. I should note initially that I have never kept a personal diary. So the challenge given me by Edward and Sandy Elgar to include autobiographical materials has stirred up thoughts about academic politics which, in time, would probably have been forgotten. Specifically, about ten years after I had received my PhD, I was busily engaged in side-line consulting work with the Amerad Research Co., and with an executive committee of AT&T, and with other organizations. I was offered the President-Elect position of the Southern Economic Association, but turned it down then because I was just too busy. A decade and a half later, I was again honoured that way by the association, but rejected it again. This time I wanted the Dean of the Liberal Arts College at Texas A&M to provide me with an *extra* secretary who would handle all of my added needs. He told the department head (Bob Tollison, I think it was then) that Mel will take the honour without my having to give him *extra* secretarial support; he already 'consumes' too much help. I surprised him. The honour of being president of an economics association was not a personal goal. Over the last 20 plus years, I have in fact tried my best to stay outside of the glad-handing fraternity. We academicians, to my way of thinking, often act too much like politicians, and that is such a low form of behaviour that I have preferred to limit my days of attendance at conventions. This has bothered my son, John, who has frequently critiqued me for this, while often telling me about meeting someone who said, 'I know of your Dad but never met him, never ever saw him, what is he like?' I guess the final answer might be

* See the 12th through the 15th essays in Part II.
** Again see essays 12–15 in Part II.

I am a recluse, except I do enjoy tennis, I used to be an avid golfer, and I find going to good parties and dances among the best events of life.

I must now conclude this volume by expressing my deepest gratitude to all of the many students, colleagues and friends in academia with whom I have had the good fortune of working and knowing over the years. I dare not provide the names of many of them because if I did I would also omit many who I would like to include if space was unlimited and memory impeccable. I must therefore confine final – and special – references to Hiroshi Ohta, Jacques Thisse, George Norman, Hisao Nishioka, Yusuf Mansur, Roy Gilbert, a current graduate student, Shawn Carter, Ms Dymphna Evans and Ms Jo Perkins of Edward Elgar Publishing, and a top-quality secretary of several years, Ms Tamara Ariens. All mentioned here have helped me so greatly and directly on preparing this and the companion book currently under publication that a somewhat substantial effort has been reduced to a most enjoyable one.

I would also at this point like to include my thanks to Tim Gronberg who provided most vital departmental resources to me. Also I must thank the many friends who induced me to visit them and their universities, typically as a visiting professor, lecturer, or even adjunct, in Karlsruhe, Münster, and Münich, Germany, besides Taipei, Taiwan, Tokyo and Kyoto, Japan, Cape Town, South Africa, and a dozen or more universities in the United States *and* several in Great Britain. Hopefully, these generalizing words point sufficiently to the many I have in my mind. Finally, and surely most importantly, I dedicate this book to, and express my deepest gratitude and love to my wife, Marre, of 50 plus years (need I say more), and to my immediate family recorded below.

Offspring:
- Margaret Lee Chase
- Pamela Jo Blaylock
- John Griffith Greenhut
- Patricia Lynn Thomsen

Daughter-in-law:
- Karen Scoggins Greenhut

Sons-in-law:
- Ronald Wilburn Chase
- Glenn Watts Blaylock

Grandchildren:
- Richard Michael Hare
- Krista Dawn Hare
- Jeffrey Todd Chase
- Tyler Michael Chase
- Michael Thomas Senter
- Chad Talbot Thomsen
- Corey Lynn Thomsen
- John Austin Greenhut
- Susan Leigh Greenhut
- Kimberley Gayle Greenhut

Step-Grandchildren:
- John Southern Blaylock
- Elizabeth Blaylock McManus

Step-Great Grandchild:
- Stephen John McManus Jr

PART I

THE PHILOSOPHICAL FRAMEWORK

Reprinted from The Southern Economic Journal
Vol. XXVIII, No. 3, January, 1962
Printed in U. S. A.

A GENERAL THEORY OF MAXIMUM PROFITS*

MELVIN L. GREENHUT

University of Richmond

INTRODUCTION

Hurwicz, Luce-Raiffa, Savage, Wald and others have distinguished between decision making under conditions of certainty, risk, and uncertainty. But other than for discourses such as Knight's, which was concerned with comparing reality and theory, writings in the field of pure competition economics were centered on conditions of certainty, though, more recently, extended to include the state of risk. But what about uncertainty? If we assume that it is basic to certain economic markets, would it be possible to include it as part of general economic theory in much the same way that decision making theory includes uncertainty as part of its framework? We shall contend that it *is*, first by accepting a simple transformation which combines risk and uncertainty, then by formulating a general theory of maximum profits.

Our initial task is the most elementary and hence easiest to fulfill. We need observe only the well established thought that risk differs from uncertainty in the sense that mathematical probabilities are assignable to the former but not the latter. It follows in the literature that when uncertainty prevails the decision maker must select some criterion which, in effect, enables him to apply *his own* a priori probabilities distinct from the statistical or analytic probabilities on which all may agree. He is able to do this on the basis of some criterion; e.g., the criterion of regret, or optimism, or, say, the Laplace criterion where each unknown is considered to be equally likely to happen and where, accordingly, the probabilities are equal and the given strategy takes the form $1/n$ (Payoff 1 + Payoff 2 + $\cdots$ + Payoff n). For our purposes, we should note that once the criterion is given—a pre-condition establishable by the individual household or business unit—any payoff matrix will appear the same as that under risk. It follows further that the general theory of maximum profit which we will formulate—and which speaks in terms of probabilities—includes the statistical or analytic probability relevant to decision making under risk, or the probability selected under uncertainty on some personal basis, such as hunch, fear, or, let us say, reason.

One more preliminary should be observed. We accept the premise that a general profit theory not only will have good use in "pure economics," especially the kind in which a closer approximation to realism is fruitful[1] but also applied economics. In fact, to help form a framework for our theory, we will refer to an empirical study in economics which requires this particular kind of realism. Our approach (and objective) is to suggest the importance of a general theory of maximum profit, and, of course, to form this kind of theory.

Survey Findings in Florida On New Industry Location

Recently a survey was conducted in Florida by Professor Colberg and myself which was supposed to uncover the reasons for industrial location in the state. Among the major problems in this kind of survey are: (1) the frequency of claims by many company officials that their location was selected because of a personal preference to live in the subject area. (2) The often asserted view by officials that they expected smaller profits for a few years at the selected location but larger profits in the long-run, because, for example, they anticipated a greater potential growth in the area selected than elsewhere. (3) The still more frequently expressed argument that the locators were forced to choose between extremes; that is, one site appeared to offer greatest profits or greatest possible losses, given alternative kinds of market area expansion, whereas, at another place, the profit potential was less favorable while the loss possibilities were more favorable under equivalent developments. But which site is the maximum profit location, the one that proffers greatest possible

* The author wishes to thank M. Colberg, A. Alchian, G. Tintner, and T. Berry for their helpful suggestions.

[1] See the writer's "Mathematics, Realism, and Management Science," *Management Science*, V (1958), pp. 225–228.

gains *or* losses, or the one that proffers a smaller set of values? Does resolution exist to any of the above problems which indicates that they are proper subjects for theory to consider?

Our survey uncovered a significant amount of indecision among company officials concerning this matter of profits. Most prevalent, it seemed, was the situation where locators visualized different potential ranges of profits and losses at alternative locations and then selected their site because some range of returns appeared more appealing to them considering their financial resources, their desires for the future, some unknown probabilities, and the criterion for behavior which governed their actions. In fact, it was found that even where the personal factor was cited by company officials, it was really not that we had an example of a location dominated by non-profit personal considerations but a selection attributable to, say, individual conservatism based on existing assets. This combination often forced the choice of a site that promised smaller potential gains or, if the good breaks did not occur, smaller possible losses. At the least, one could easily see that the economic and near psychic factors overlapped in many instances.

It is manifest that the kinds of situation described above have no place in the long-run theory of pure competition. That they could belong to a profit theory formed on the basis of continuing uncertainty is, on the other hand, inherently evident. We will see this most clearly by first setting forth our model in rough terms and then briefly scanning the existing literature. After this is done the details of our theory will be examined.

Risk and Uncertainty: Certain Preliminaries

Whenever there are only a few sellers in the market because either technocracy or space restricts their number, an entrepreneurial belief tends to develop that each is important. In turn, a "watchful waiting" business policy arises under which sellers form uncertain conjectures about the policy and reactions of their rivals. It is small wonder that decision making in this kind of market is complex. The prevalence of risk causes a range of probable profit or loss values to arise while the element of uncertainty—attributable to stochastic and unpredictable behavior patterns—yields again a set of alternative ranges of profit or loss. Company officials are therefore subject to a double-edged problem: (1) selecting the maximum under existing conditions of risk, and (2) selecting the best set under existing uncertainties.

TABLE I

MEAN PROFIT RETURNS UNDER RISK

(Location at Site 1 With Price Set by Firm B)

	1% Flaw Factor	2% Flaw Factor	3% Flaw Factor
Process A	70	20	5
Process B	50	35	20

The Risk Matrix: A very simple matrix will serve our introductory needs most effectively. Assume a location, a commodity, and consider two alternative processes of manufacture, *A* and *B*. Production carries a well designated risk, as the raw materials which are used tend to vary slightly in quality. The effect is that, if a one percent flaw factor prevails, Process A yields the highest profit; while, if a two or three percent (the maximum possible) flaw factor holds, Process *B* is best. Table I records the assumed data. Which process should be selected?

To solve the problem a set of probabilities is needed. For example, if the probabilities are fifty percent that raw materials will be used which have a 1% flaw factor, and forty or ten percent respectively for 2% and 3% flaw factors, we have as the value of the alternative strategies:

Strategy $A = 70(1/2) + 20(2/5) + 5(1/10) = 43.5$
Strategy $B = 50(1/2) + 35(2/5) + 20(1/10) = 41$

Manifestly, Strategy *A* (i.e., Process *A*) is the maximum and will be used by the company. Should probabilities of raw material flaws change to thirty—fifty—twenty percent, the alternative process (Process *B*) would offer the greater profits.

Selected Literature: To explain further decision making under risk and to move toward decision making under uncertainty, let us record some ideas and statements of others, with a warning that this may be partly out of context. This warning is necessary because it is not the present purpose to offer the full thoughts or conclusions of those who are to be mentioned here. Rather, what we seek is to find a melting pot which relates directly to our own model and into which their thoughts and words *might* fit. To be sure, this melting pot is probably not the one which each or any of these writers would design for himself—a condition irrelevant for our purposes.

Machlup[2] compares a motorist with an entrepreneur. The motorist may drive has car between two towns at an average speed of 100 m.p.h. or 60 m.p.h. or 20 m.p.h. His risk of injury is greatest at the initial speed, average at the in-between speed, and least at the lowest speed. Which is the optimum? Is not the risk of too rapid a speed so vital that it must be included in the concept?

Others stress the matter of risk and its effect on the profit and loss computation in a slightly different way. For example, they suggest that sellers will conjecture about a profit and loss amount each of which is not a sum certain but rather extends over a range of values. Under this condition, sellers may give varying emphasis to the highest mean or even the variances around that mean for, among other combinations, the question arises whether a higher mean with a larger spread is the maximum compared to a lower mean with a smaller spread. Selecting an action whose outcome is preferable may well not be a case of maximizing the mean.[3] Indeed, which mean is relevant, a short-run or long-run mean?[4]

Means and Variances: The activity in question, or let us say the risk in question, may be of the type that when things go well they go very well. In contrast, when things go wrong they are very wrong. The quantitative reflection of this kind of risk ranges from very high positive values to very large negative values. The statistical mean may prove to be positive but, in any case, the variance will be large. Clearly, different activities may offer different risks such that a smaller set of values, both positive and negative, will obtain. The means may be positive and the variances may be small.

The true concept of maximum profit under risk points not to the greatest possible profits (e.g., the analogy of 100 m.p.h.), but to the largest mean value with the smallest variance. By definition, the possible losses from the activity are thereby considered and the foolish or pure "let us do it or die policy" is laid to rest as exceptional. But what about the near gamble, or should we say, what about the large mean when it is associated with a large variance in contrast with a smaller (yet large mean) associated with a smaller variance? Which of these is the maximum?

It is clear that an individual's position in life tempers or, better yet, designates what his maximum will be. Thus he who has a large amount of reserve (either in cash or in the form of smaller responsibility) will be likely to seek the greater mean with the larger variance, and contrariwise for an oppositely situated person. While it may be that some of the "force is lost," the concept of maximum profit applies to either case and "remains formally valid."[5] In either case, the seller will seek to equate marginal revenue with marginal cost and in the process to maximize his selected return.

We obtain comparable results to the above if we assume a difference in desires among sellers to protect their future returns (near or distant). The quest for some security of a future position can readily be seen to modify, at best, the present outlook. It limits and defines in its own way the maximum that the entrepreneur seeks to attain.

The Uncertainty Matrix: It is a relatively simple step to move toward bringing uncertainty into our analysis. First recall Table I and observe that when the individual's position in life (i.e., either his financial resources, personality makeup, etc.) causes him to select a given program,

---

[2] F. Machlup, *The Economics of Sellers Competition* (Baltimore, Md.: The Johns Hopkins Press, 1952), p. 53.

[3] See A. Alchian, "Uncertainty, Evolution and Economic Theory," *Journal of Political Economy*, LVIII (1950), pp. 211–221; J. Marschak, "Rational Behavior, Uncertain Prospects and Measurable Utility," *Econometrica*, XVIII (1950), pp. 111–141; and originally G. Tintner, "Theory of Choice Under Subjective Risk and Uncertainty," *Econometrica*, XIV (1941), pp. 298–304, and "The Pure Theory of Production Under Technological Risk and Uncertainty," *Ibid*., pp. 305–311.

[4] N. W. Chamberlain, *A General Theory of Economic Process* (New York: Harper & Bros., 1955), pp. 67–69, notes concern with the usual abstraction from time in the maximizing concept, and M. Bronfenbrenner, "Imperfect Competition on a Long-Run Basis," *Journal of Business*, XXXII (1950), pp. 81–93, asserts that business men price on a long-run basis and not in close response to all short-run changes.

[5] For another form in which this same question appeared, see W. J. Baumol, "Discussion," *American Economic Review*, Papers and Proceedings, XLIII (1953), pp. 415–416. Also see J. Marschak, *op. cit*., p. 131. And in this connection, let me note the suggestion by Armen Alchian that the analysis system proposed here might relate improved expectations to increased utility while increased variance "could" then be regarded as reduced utility.

he may be complying perfectly or not with the mean value derived from the table. If he is not, it does not signify non-profit-maximizing behavior. Rather, it signifies only that "his utility for dollars cannot be measured by the dollar amounts."[6] In effect, the values in the matrix must be re-designated to account for, say his fear of a low profit or a large loss, or the extra utility he derives from an extremely large profit. Given the relevant redesignations, if any, the matrix value can be determined and the accepted behavior indicated.[7]

Uncertainty appears in the picture presented by Table I when we remember that the mean value for Process *A* and Process *B* holds only at a given location. If we consider the feasibility of alternative market areas, a logical extension would be to assume that diverse kinds of competition may take place in the alternative markets. Possibly the degree of competition is predictable on the basis of probabilities; if so, the decision making process is still that of selecting an outcome under conditions of risk. But as is suggested by Table II, the matrix may not involve known probabilities, for in each market area there may be different firms, different historical backgrounds, or, in general, different situations.

TABLE II

Mean Profit Returns Under Uncertainty for Firm A

	Price Following with Price Set by A	Price Following with Price Set by B	Competition in Price
Location 1	60	43.5	25
Location 2	90	40	35
....	...	...	...
Location n	80	41	32

To select the profit maximizing location now entails the subjective creation of probabilities. How individuals may assign their own probabilities to each event is of no concern to us. As noted in our introductory remarks, it may be done on the basis of some criterion: optimism, regret, rationality or others. For those who have not read the developing literature in operations research on decision making under uncertainty, we might illustrate by reference to the simplest criterion, the so called criterion of pessimism. This criterion holds that if the individual always expects the worst, he will look for and select the maximum of his minimum payoffs. In the subject case of Table II, this would be found at Location 2, Value 35.

It is manifest that regardless of the particular criterion followed by the individual, he is actually engaged in a decision making process, which, in matrix *form*, is identical to that of decision making under risk. And though the market type which we will emphasize in this paper is one marked by uncertainty, a full understanding of maximum profit under risk is therefore basic and must be stressed. Indeed, because the very definition of uncertainty signifies that all true unknowns are equally likely, the acceptance of one or another criterion by an individual cannot be construed as noneconomic. Noneconomic behavior must relate only to market situations where probabilities or certainties exist. What really remains is simply to sharpen the meaning of maximum profit under risk, and to distinguish the business behavior pattern which is and is not economic. Once this is done, our general theory of maximum profit under risk and uncertainty (and of course certainty) will have been completed.

SPECIAL ASPECTS OF THE THEORY

Non-Maximum Profit Seeking Behavior

We include in the category of non-maximum profit seeking activity (A) the case of a "hell-bent" gamble, and (B) the case where the risk is deliberately minimized or unduly avoided by seeking the security of some acceptable minimum; in effect the decision is governed by psychic satisfactions which revalue the mean and the deviations around the mean, thereby eliminating the extreme.[8]

Maximum Profits vs Rent and Risk

By maximum profit we do not mean the quest for the largest possible profit. Rather, we have

[6] Miller and Starr, *Executive Decisions and Operations Research* (Englewood Cliffs, N. J.: Prentice-Hall, 1960), p. 84.

[7] The reason attainable ends tend to differ among people ties up often with the difference in their present resources. Alternatively, in economic theory, we speak of rent differentials among firms.

[8] Elsewhere this quest has been called purely personal considerations. Unfortunately, whether it determines an action all by itself or is an inseparable part of some definite pecuniary reward has often been ignored. And see note 14.

seen that a distribution is conceived to exist which indicates that any activity involves possible losses as well as profits. Let us observe in a technical sense that not only must we consider a series of possible and probable net returns, positive and negative, and of means and deviations around the mean, but we must also recognize—and by subtraction eliminate—the element of risk. Risk, we know, is a cost, and the returns for it cannot be profit. They appear in the form of differential rents to be received by resources which are scarce. Profits, on the other hand, relate to uncertainties and indivisibilities, and hence form a vastly different kind of receipt. It follows that when scarce resources are applied, they carry a rent that reflects entrepreneurial risk. By convention, this rent may be thought of as part of the overall profit motive. In turn, a sum exists on top of this to cover the uncertainty and indivisibilities that prevail. It is this sum which is truly profits. It arises when existing resources do not move into the industry for production, because some market condition limits their entry.

MAXIMUM PROFIT: SUMMARY TO THIS POINT

Different leadership in different enterprises with diverse reserves produces different incentives, fears, and drives. Accordingly, an action that offers a high mean among possible outcomes with a large variance around that mean may possess greater appeal to one person than an action that proffers a somewhat smaller mean with a smaller variance, and vice versa. The ends that are sought by two enterprisers may be the same (example, the best possible economic position) but the means or actions they select may differ because their expectations over time differ or because the ends that are attainable by each may differ.[9] In any case, one can hardly disclaim the relevance of maximum profit in the selection of an economic activity, though, of course, the bundle in which the concept may be packed is bulkier than we would like.

Moreover, let us not forget that non-maximum profit seeking situations may exist, such as (1) the "go for broke" individual who is a gambler, not a business man, and (2) those who want security in the form that available opportunities elsewhere with their associated risks are bypassed in favor of the smaller risk with attendant psychic satisfactions. Significantly, these are not examples of preferring a smaller (larger) mean with a smaller (larger) variance because of one's economic position, instead they illustrate the case where the smaller (larger) mean and variance are wanted solely to satisfy a psychic income desire.

Quantifying our Concept of the Maximum Profit: In General Terms

One may ask, of course, how a distinction can be drawn between a "go for broke" gamble and a quest for maximum profit. Oppositely, one may ask how a maximum profit activity which involves some noticeable business conservatism, for example, because cash is low, can be distinguished from a psychic income obsession that appears in the form of a drive to be secure in one's home environment. Our distinctions admittedly must be fuzzy. Perhaps the juridical type of approach which would speak in terms of the reasonable man or the average man is the best available. However, even this can be sharpened by quantifying our judgment of reasonableness so that the subjective factor does not dominate the selection. We achieve this as follows.

[9] We might observe here in note that in our prior remarks we were examining the maximum profit concept chiefly from the standpoint of its ability to explain the "means" taken to accomplish an "end." For example, the good life is desired and activity A at location X is selected to provide this life. When, on the other hand, the "ends" are in focus, which in many ways can be accepted as the basis for the present discussion, the all-inclusiveness of the concept depends upon whether we decide to permit an adjustment for psychic income or exclude such case. Borrowing from Alchian (note 3), who, for example, would say that society adopts successful firms and rejects the unsuccessful, we could hold that the economically profitable firms survive and are of singular interest to us, or, if we want, among our survivors we may also include those whose psychic income gains offset whatever monetary deficiencies may prevail.

For other writings on this general subject, see notes 3 and 4 and Stephen Enke, "On Maximizing Profits: A Distinction between Chamberlin and Robinson," *American Economic Review*, XLI (1951), pp. 566–579; J. von Neumann and O. Morgenstern, *The Theory of Games and Economic Behavior* (Princeton, N. J.: Princeton University Press, 1944), p. 95 ff.; M. Friedman and L. J. Savage, "The Utility Analysis of Choices Involving Risk," *Journal of Political Economy*, LVI (1948), pp. 279–304; and Edith Penrose, "Biological Analogies in the Theory of the Firm," *American Economic Review*, XLII (1952), pp. 805–819.

Between profit seeking and non-profit seeking stands a line. Better yet, shall we say, a tolerance exists for different actions. This line or tolerance is determinable on the basis of an approved number of variances or standard deviations around the mean; *for present purposes*, let us say three standard deviations.

Specifically, when the redesignation of matrix values is *determined* by an unusual return lying above the limit set by the third standard deviation, then, we assert, the thrill sought by the gambler has dominated. The decision does not reflect, at least generally, the policy of the business man. In opposite contrast, when an otherwise superior mean and deviation is rejected because the payoff matrix values are altered as a direct result of a loss (or small profit) possibility falling below the lower limit of the third standard deviation beneath the mean, which loss (or small profit) exceeds (or is less than) that of the accepted alternative, then, we hold, a passion for security has dominated the decision.

The Confidence Limits: Our theory recognizes that a given enterpriser may select an activity strictly on the basis of the highest objective mean available. Or, he may redesignate the values of one activity compared to another on the basis of the alternatives which fall within one standard deviation of the mean. (Example, where before adjustment an activity *A* offers values of 70–100 and an activity *B* offers 80 to 95 and the probabilities leave *A* with the greater payoff, the conservatism of the individual may cause a redesignation of values such that the strategy actually selected is *B* not *A*). Or, he may regard the values set by two standard deviations around the mean. (Example, we may find one sigma values redesignated as 50–70 for *A* and 60–70 for *B* . . . and that on this basis, *B* would be selected; between two sigmas, the redesignated values might be 40–80 for *A* and 55–75 for *B* . . . and on this basis *B* might be selected, though possibly *A*, depending on the probabilities). Or, of course, three standard deviations may mark the relevant range of values, etc.

Shall we say, for armchair speculation, that the custom of the trade can be imagined to govern; that is, the more hazardous the business, the lower the spread—hence confidence—probably demanded by the business man who engages in the activity, and contrariwise. For empirical studies, the opinion of the subject person is probably the best key to the problem.[10] Of course, if the home environment (or some other purely personal factor) governs the action, the individual's opinion that this condition is the case establishes in itself the fiducial limits for interpreting the action.[11] We may sum up by saying that the security motive or the pure gamble instinct prevails when an extreme value or group of extreme values exist that unduly disturb the person and cause him to violate the specification that he and/or others ordinarily tend to establish.

---

[10] In no case should an extreme value beyond three standard deviations of the mean control the decision under risk. In fact, confidence limits of .95 are generally thought to be suitable for most problems and are typically used. E.g., see J. S. Freund, *Modern Elementary Statistics* (New York: Prentice-Hall, 1952), pp. 162, 165. And for this intervals use in explanation of the concept, see G. Tintner, *Mathematics and Statistics for Economists* (New York: Rinehart & Co., 1953), pp. 251–253. Our designation of three sigmas is, if anything, very conservative.

[11] One must, however, be sure that the personal factor really exists apart from the economic factor, and in many situations an interviewee misjudges his own act. Example: Suppose an individual admits to conservatism in all respects, that is, he must know the probable outcome of an economic activity with substantial assurance and he cannot afford a bad payoff or two. In such case, three sigmas are probably indicated. Assume alternative opportunities offer a 40–100 and 55–75 spread. We have a simple example of economic decision making under risk if the derived mean of the second—and accepted—payoff is larger after the values are redesignated to conform to the individual's short cash and conservative position and the given probabilities are assigned. What, in contrast, would it mean if the so-called "security" motive prevailed? To answer this, suppose we add to the above situation the fact that a 60–75 spread exists elsewhere with probabilities identical to the 55–75 spread but that the superior payoff of this alternative is rejected because a chance for a value of 20 exists whereas the lowest sum conceivable in the 55–75 spread is, say, 45. Equivalently, suppose it is rejected just because of the extra satisfactions that are gained in living at the place of the 55–75 spread. In these instances we would have clear cases of non-maximum profit seeking. They are distinguishable from the related situation where, because of working in a given community where the family resides, better business contacts due to the family background lead actually to a 60–80 rather than a 55–75 spread with equal probabilities. We will see later that conditions of uncertainty do not affect our present statements.

From A Risk to Uncertainty Matrix

Some readers may wonder whether we are not double-counting when we add uncertainty elements on top of risk. For example, they might conjecture that conservatism on the part of the entrepreneur might cause him to redesignate the matrix values normally to be expected, and then, in addition, when uncertainty prospects are added, the criterion of pessimism might be applied anew. This would suggest that we are double counting the practice of being conservative. However, as will be apparent from Tables IIIA, IIIB and IV, the conservatism of the individual affects each matrix value in Table III that finds its way into Table IV. As such, Table IV is independent of particular and special bias.

We may observe in a similar key that noneconomic motivations may be viewed only in conjunction with a risk, not uncertainty, matrix, for, by the very meaning of uncertainty, all alternatives are likely. Moreover, realize that if noneconomic motives dominate the risk matrix, the decision maker is either a security minded extremist or a gambler. It follows that the uncertainty criterion he would select must be either the conservative maximin or the daring maximax criterion. The consequence is that the uncertainty matrix values (see Table IV) which are "considered" by the noneconomic decision maker would be those at the extreme of the matrix (low or high, as the case be). And significantly, only the extreme values are redesignated in the risk matrix. Hence our theorem follows that noneconomic decision making under risk appears the same when uncertainty conditions *also prevail*. Alternatively, economic decision making under risk carries forward to include uncertainty, but does not work backward.[12]

TABLE III
MAXIMUM PROFIT UNDER RISK
(Location j: Price Leadership by x; known probabilities)

	A Original Mean Values Weather (Probabilities are Known)			B Mean Values redesignated by limited reserves and the conservatism of the company officials Weather (Probabilities are Known)		
	Good 30%	Fair 30%	Bad 40%	Good 30%	Fair 30%	Bad 40%
Activity 1	90	50	10	90	50	4
Activity 2	70	40	30	70	40	27.5
Highest value of payoff (Activity 1) = 46				Highest value of payoff (Activity 2) = 44		

TABLE IV
MAXIMUM PROFIT UNDER UNCERTAINTY
(n locations)

	Price Leadership by Firm x	Price Leadership by Firm y	Competition in Price by All Firms
Location a	50	32	6
....	..	..	..
Location j	44	30	14
....	..	..	..
....	..	..	..
Location n	37	26	10

SURVEY FINDINGS IN FLORIDA: FINAL THOUGHTS

Assume an interest in the forces which cause a plant to locate in a particular state. Consider the fact that many company officials will describe factors which make the state (or some wide area within the state) most attractive, and, in addition, designate others as responsible for inducing the location in a particular city or town within the state. Quite likely, one will find that in only a small number of cases is there a single factor or factor set which attracts the firm to both the state and the particular locality.

It was found in the Florida survey,[13] and under the theory of maximum profit described here, that there was not a single case of a new firm locating in the state because of the purely personal factor. Rather, it was found that whereas many respondents to the questionnaire may have checked this factor as the number one force, they

[12] W. Baumol, *Economic Theory and Operations Analysis* (Englewood Cliffs, N. J.: Prentice-Hall, 1961), p. 384, observes in comparable key that there is a conflict between maximin strategy and the von Neumann-Morgenstern cardinal utility theory as the maximizer views only the worst possibility payoffs whereas the utility "calculator" takes all payoffs into account.

[13] For certain details about the survey which was jointly undertaken with M. R. Colberg, see the writer's "An Empirical Model and a Survey: New Plant Locations In Florida," *Review of Economics and Statistics*, XLI (1959), pp. 433–438.

agreed during a follow-up personal interview that they preferred the profit range prospects in Florida to all alternative non-Florida locations that had been considered. Not one would aver that he was so imbued with love for Florida living that he would have located in the state if he were convinced (*let us say* to the extent of 3 standard deviations around the mean) that he could not do better in Florida over the time-period that he considered in formulating his decision. May we say, in effect, that *the matrix values* which would form such a Table as IIIB were *unaffected by extreme items*. Accordingly, what started out in many cases to be statements of undue preference for Florida finished up in the form of a profit range that proffered neither as great a maximum nor as a low a minimum as elsewhere. Under our theory, the locators of new businesses in Florida in 1956 and 1957 were profit-seeking individuals.[14]

The same result did not hold with respect to the selection of specific communities. In many cases (approximately ten percent of the 752 plants that were surveyed), the spokesmen asserted that while they preferred the likely profit range at the Florida location to non-Florida locations, they rejected alternative Florida locations which proffered a better likely profit range simply because of their personal preference for the locality or section actually selected. This is the way that the purely personal (psychic income) factor *was governing*.

It is perhaps significant to mention briefly that several companies (approximately fifteen percent of those surveyed) were strongly influenced by the thought that skilled labor and research personnel would be attracted readily to certain places in Florida because of purely personal considerations and hence located in the designated area. Of course, from the company's viewpoint, the location is economic. Similarly, officials of nearly ten percent of the plants surveyed expressed the thought that their existing personal contacts in the area would inure to their advantage and were induced by this to locate where they did. Again, maximum profit (as defined) reigns supreme.

It is thus the case under our theory that while the personal factor may be prominent in business decisions, it rarely proves to be dominant if carefully defined in a world of risk and uncertainty. The effect is that the psychic income or personal factor under the economics of risk and uncertainty actually ties up with such other business determinants as existing cash and fixed asset positions, general business and specific product forecasts, and their like. And note, all this is not to say that *purely personal* activity choices can not be found in practice; rather it is to say that the number of instances in which the economic man concept is not relevant is substantially less than many economists have suggested to be the case to their students. Our fundamental theorem and conclusion must therefore be just this: the concept of economic man is both significant in the theory of oligopolistic competition as well as pure competition; similarly, it is usable in applied economic research.

[14] Realize that oftentimes a person may wish to live in a certain place and selects as his activity a business that fits the area.

SUMMARY

Our concept of maximum profit is a more liberal one than that which many economists tend to maintain. It includes, among other things, the effect on a firm's behavior of such items as the firm's financial resources (including here its past and present asset policy), its willingness to take chances, to subject itself to federal investigation and anti-trust counts, its desire for some security, and its expectations of the future.

Maximization under conditions of uncertainty is basic to our concept. Maximization over time and not maximization at a moment is also fundamental. Our concept retains original economic terminology, reflects traditional economic meaning, and is readily usable in empirical work because it ties itself to risk and uncertainty rather than to perfect knowledge.

Our general theory of maximum profits is available for use in complex market models as well as simple. Significantly, it permits differences in individual goals and in resources and daring. On the other hand, it does not permit or include the gambling instinct or those extreme cases where ultra conservatism dominated the business activity. It is fully general, for it may be used in basic theory, such as pure competition economics and in oligopolistic competition economics. Also, it may be used in applied economics.

Reprinted from MANAGEMENT SCIENCE
Vol. 4, No. 3, April, 1958
Printed in U.S.A.

MATHEMATICS, REALISM AND MANAGEMENT SCIENCE*†

MELVIN L. GREENHUT

Florida State University

I. Introduction

In a paper which appeared in the 1957 edition of this journal,[1] Professor Weinwurm suggests that the use of mathematics in management science may so dominate a given model as to cause the disregard of vital human values. He cites Professor Bodenhorn who warns that the trend toward mathematical frameworks in economics may be associated with an application of good mathematical assumptions but poor economics.[2] In some dispute with Professor Flood's philosophy,[3] he feels that we cannot ignore the nonquantitative factors in human relations.

This whole matter of how "mathematical" a model may be in the social sciences without losing contact with reality has been a long standing problem. In my own field of special interest, location theory, its significance has appeared in the form of a dispute over whether we should assume the quest for maximum profits by individuals or else substitute in its place the more general and realistic hypothesis of a quest for maximum satisfactions. If what we seek in the social sciences are hypotheses which most closely reflect reality, then one wonders why such strong disagreement exists over the merits of the unrealistic maximum profit postulate. Perhaps it is in fact the case that both sides are right, or may I say that Professor Flood is correct when he contends that fancy new electronic calculators might "... routinize a bargaining procedure that is now highly charged with emotional and rational uncertainties,"[4] while Professor Weinwurm is also correct when he states that "A mathematical model which fails to reflect reality is inadequate and needs to be replaced by a better and more adequate one."[5]

This paper contends that in static models the assumptions may fail utterly to reflect reality and yet be superior to others founded on realistic human values.

* Received October 1957.

† The author wishes to express his thanks to Professors Mehren, Dewey, Pfouts, and Machlup for their most valuable suggestions.

[1] ERNEST H. WEINWURM, "Limitations of the Scientific Method in Management Science," *Management Science*, April 1957, pp. 225–233.

[2] DIRAN BODENHORN, "The Problem of Economic Assumptions in Mathematical Economics," *Journal of Political Economy*, February 1956, pp. 25–32.

[3] MERRILL M. FLOOD, "The Objective of TIMS," *Management Science*, January 1956, pp. 178–183.

[4] *Op. cit.*, p. 182.

[5] *Op. cit.*, p. 231.

Generally, this holds true in dynamic models where again a mathematics which ignores certain values may well be used. In theories dealing with the "ideal", however, the realistic assumption gains its most vital role. In substance, both Weinwurm and Flood are correct. The fact is that often we speak with different theories in mind when we approve or disapprove of mathematics. To demonstrate this claim, let us note first what a theory is and what kinds of theory exist. To facilitate our discussion, we use the postulate of maximum satisfactions vs. maximum profits as a convenient reference point to the matter of reality and mathematics.

II. Formation of a Theory

A theory might be defined as an abstract system of thought which is formed on the basis of certain working rules of procedure.[6] These working rules relate essentially to approved methods of analysis. In turn, the approved methods of analysis are those which scientific inquiries have shown to yield knowledge. One might say that that which works is proper methodology; less debatable is it to say that properly formed inductive or deductive reasoning serves essentially as the cornerstone to a theory.

The vital part of any theory is then the method by which it is derived or shall we say its framework. Was the consequent of the theory induced or deduced?

Under inductive procedures, some correlational matter must be evidenced. In the words of Northrop,[7] an epistemic correlation may be cited, such as inducing the conclusion that it is one's nose which "can be" seen when single eye vision takes place. Or, a more elegant system such as statistical probabilities may be applied to support the induction. In sharp contrast, it is probable that many will argue even for simple agreement among experts, formed on an intuited or introspective basis, as a sufficient foundation for an induction.[8]

When a deductive system is used, the proof of the pudding must be either on the level of the postulates or on the level of the consequents. We may confirm the theorem through a test of its assumptions or through a test of its consequents.[9] Under the latter technique, we, in effect, superimpose an inductive system on a deductive one. Verification through a test of the consequent involves the fallacy of the hypothetic syllogism; that is, if A then B, and if B is proven to be the case therefore A stands . . . but, clearly other data may really explain B not A. All that which has been done is to have proven that A "might be" correct. The

[6] See *Webster's New Collegiate Dictionary*, 2d ed (Springfield; Funk and Wagnalls, 1956) . . . the analysis of a set of facts. . . or *abstract* principles (italics mine). And see G. Stigler, *The Theory of Price* (N.Y.: Macmillan and Co, 1947), Chapter 1.

[7] F. S. C. Northrop, *The Logic of the Sciences and the Humanities* (N.Y.: Macmillan and Co, 1949), p. 117.

[8] F. Machlup, "The Problem of Verification in Economics," *Southern Economic Journal*, XXII, 1953, 1–21, holds that those who accept introspective findings may contend that constant verification exists.

[9] M. R. Cohen and E. Nagel, *An Introduction to Logic and Scientific Method* (N.Y.: Harcourt Brace, 1934), p. 207.

null hypothesis prevails. The test of the consequent has not proven the postulates to be wrong. In contrast, a test of a theory by direct empirical examination of its postulates leaves a verified system that does not involve a broader conclusion than its parts.[10] Unfortunately, this method is ultra-empirical. The science remains within the immediately apprehended. One understands so much that one understands practically nothing. To avoid this Aristotelian limit, the postulated correlates of verified data may be substituted for the immediately apprehended knowledge in the forming of a theorem. Should the deduced theorem not be directly testable (as is often the case in the social sciences and always the case when ideal social systems are being imagined), one nevertheless has a verified theorem because its fundamental parts (the assumptions) were directly confirmed. To be sure, the verification is of an inductive order, similar to the case where the postulates are "allowed" because their consequents have been proven. The difference between advanced deductive theories lies in the method of confirmation. In some cases, the raw postulates are more easily verifiable; in others, it is the end theorem.[11]

III. Types of Theory

There appear to be three main varieties of theories. Those which seek to explain certain relationships within a structure in which time is not a variable (static theory), those which designate the path of variables over continuous time (dynamic theory), and those of static or dynamic nature which seek to form ideal systems for possible substitution in place of the prevailing. The last type of theory can be dispensed with quickly at this point in the paper. If the maximum satisfaction vs. maximum profit hypothesis is tied up with a normative social theory that is to be applied (and if the application is significant and costly), the most realistic assumptions that could be grasped and controlled should be sought. This requirement of realism reflects the fact that any test of the consequents in advance of application would be impossible.[12] With respect to dynamic theory, that too can be discussed rather summarily at this point. The specification of the microscopic *details* of future states over a continuous path of time may or may not be in issue. The matter of how realistic the assumptions must be depends upon how specific one wants to designate the details of the future state.

[10] R. W. SELLARS, *The Essentials of Logic*, Rev. Ed. (N.Y.: Houghton Mifflin, 1945), pp. 135ff, especially 138. Also see Northrop, *op. cit.*, pp. 108, 109.

[11] SIR JAMES JEANS writes on p. 52 of his *Growth of Physical Sciences* (Cambridge, Eng.: University Press, 1951) that "Nearly 2000 years were to pass before the deductive methods of Aristotle were discarded in favor of inductive methods . . . . and then progress became rapid indeed."

[12] Let it be noted that many ideal systems theories may be simple and unimportant or else they may embrace such vital data as the establishment of a new economic, social, or political system. In the case of significant ideal systems, the verification of the theoretical system must be made in advance. But if the significant ideal system is designed simply as a point of reference (that is, as a departure point for more relevant analysis), its assumptions may be unrealistic and utterly false. The sole factor of import here is its explanatory value.

And last, with respect to a theory that describes the existing "in a static framework", it is asserted that one wants as realistic an assumption as is discoverable, though useability, indeed final consequents, is even more important. "Of all the models that might explain the result, we choose the one that works with the assumptions that we believe conform most closely to observed reality. Models with more realistic assumptions but not yielding results conforming to observed reality are disqualified".[13]

It is of course questionable whether the direct inclusion of a maximum satisfactions postulate (or may we say the inclusion of all human values) would yield valuable theories which conform with and explain observed reality. To some large extent, such inclusion would reduce the simplicity of our models. And it has been noted that this would not be desirable because the criterion for selecting from among alternative theories which "explain all of the facts equally well" is "simplicity—which is not a simple notion."[14] Inclusion of a maximum satisfactions postulate, or its like, to borrow again the applicable words of another, "may cause confusion by 'cluttering up' the model with irrelevant details." "A complaint of unrealism . . . should be taken seriously only if the critic can prove that the missing parts in the model essentially change the end results of its operation and that a 'more complete' model yields results much more closely conforming to generally observed or experienced reality."[15] If a theorist is not concerned with an ideal system, and if he is not concerned with setting up a dynamic theory that would predict particular positions over time, the maximum satisfactions or like postulate may be rejected under the claim that it would not add to the presented theory. Indeed, the view could be offered that the dynamic qualities of social science are restricted to general relations and that maximum satisfactions and like postulates would, therefore, not be generally advantageous. It would only be where a maximum satisfaction type of postulate ties up with a different entrepreneur's risk-aversion scheme, so that dynamic models without this postulate would yield consequents that offer realistic results on a purely fortuitous basis, that such models would have to be supplanted by more high-powered ones. The improved theorems would not only yield realistic results on a regular and consistent basis, but they would also have an explanatory value far greater than the supplanted theorems. Whether or not risk-aversion preference schemes are reshaped by particular subjective considerations is of high influence in determining the degree of realism required of the assumptions.[16]

[13] F. Machlup, *The Economics of Seller's Competition* (Baltimore: Johns Hopkins Press, 1952), p. 8.

[14] Stigler, *op. cit.*, p. 8.

[15] Machlup, *Seller's Competition*, *op. cit.*, pp. 7 and 8.

[16] See G. Tintner, "The Pure Theory of Production Under Technological Risk and Uncertainty," *Econometrica*, IX, 1941, pp. 305–311, and also "The Theory of Choice Under Subjective Risk and Uncertainty," *Ibid*, pp. 298–304. And F. Machlup, *Seller's Competition*, *op. cit.*, pp. 54, 55.

IV. Conclusion

We have noted that three main kinds of theories appear to exist. Those which are concerned with the existing and use a static framework, those which specify future states over a continuous path of time, and those which define the ideal.

The assumptions of a significant ideal theory that is proposed for future use must be realistic. Also, they must be understandable.[17] Any confirmation of this kind of social theory in advance of its full application depends upon the verification of its hypotheses. With dynamic theories, however, the assumptions need not always be realistic. The consequents of the theory may often be tested over time without great cost so that the assumptions need not be verifiable. It is even possible that a broad set of relevant yet unrealistic assumptions may yield a dynamic theory that *specifies particular positions*.[18] But though a future state may be deduced and subsequently verified, the variability of human wants and expectations suggests that it would be a rare case indeed when "this kind" of dynamic theory yields in a consistent fashion and without error the data of specific nature from one period to another. More likely it is that a dynamic theory formed on unrealistic assumptions will outline a general future state and only in an exceptional case specify the particular positions.[19] And even should this type of theory predict a future state which includes particular positions, its verification through the confirmation of its consequents would be limited to the period then concluding. To hold up again in specification of a still future state would probably require more than a simple change in the numerical data that form the theory. The variability of individual behavior suggests that a dynamic theory which predicts continuously the data of specific nature must be formed on specific, detailed and realistic assumptions. Finally, with static theory the need is only for relevance of assumptions. This need stands alone. Any verification of the theory for once and for all can be made by testing the consequent. This theory allows often for incomplete or unrealistic assumptions. The designation of the static problem in readily answerable terms in as simple a model as can be gained becomes of prime end.

The degree of realism that is required of the assumption thus depends on the type of theory in question. Static theory sets up predictions in general terms. It can explain, or predict if you will, the outcome of a past event, a present event, or a future relation. It is discontinuous with respect to time and general in formulation. The realism of its assumptions is clearly unnecessary. We may

[17] And see A. Schuetz, "Concept And Theory Formation in the Social Science," *The Journal of Philosophy*, LI, 1954, pp. 257–273, 264–265, where the author proposes understanding as a vital part of social science theory. Especially is this true for ideal systems.

[18] One needs merely to construct a theory in such a way that for given changes in the magnitudes of determinants, the given set of relations would change in some systematic manner.

[19] May we say, a dynamic theory of location formed on limited postulates may predict a future shopping district with x number of food stores, y number of five and ten cent stores, *etc.* It would be a rare event when in addition it would be able to specify consistently the particular food stores and five and ten cent stores that will be located at the given site.

say in sum that the permissible falsehood of any assumption varies in accordance with the type of theoretic formulation that is being offered. With static theory, the assumptions may be very false.[20] With dynamic theory, the degree of falsehood depends upon the specificity sought by the theory. With an ideal system theory that is designed for application rather than just for comparison, the approximation to reality must be closest of all. It follows that uses and nonuses of maximum profits or of like postulates depend essentially upon the objectives which form the theory. Disagreements as to matters of validity and realism should lie properly on the level of disputes as to the value of the theoretical objective. If so assigned, there probably will be much less concern in the future than in the past with the merits and demerits of realistic hypotheses.

These above conditions determine the extent to which mathematics is useable in the social sciences—and in particular in management science.[21] Thus, we found that when a significant system about an ideal is being formed, which system is planned for application and not as a departure point for other analysis, the important specific items in the system must be designated and verified in advance. Realistic assumptions must be used for these items. However, these assumptions do not lend themselves readily to mathematical form *when they are tied to matters of individual behavior*. A mathematics of human behavior tends to generalize not particularize. Ideal systems of this kind find limited use for mathematics.

In comparable manner, a dynamic theory that seeks to designate the specific positions of individuals requires realistic assumptions. But because these assumptions are tied to human behavior, mathematics cannot well be used. A paradox exists. Our mathematical equations which make time a variable cannot specify individual positions. A dynamic theory that seeks to specify particular positions at a designated point of time cannot relate therefore to individual behavior. We may predict through mathematics the position of things in the future, but not of individual persons. Our mathematics generalizes. In this respect it is incomplete and not completely realistic. On the level of dynamic

[20] See M. FRIEDMAN, *Essays in Positive Economics* (Chicago: Chicago University Press, 1953), particularly p. 14, where to attain the end of simplicity it is noted that: "A hypothesis is important if it 'explains' much by little . . . . ", and "To be important, therefore, a hypothesis must be descriptively false in its assumptions."

[21] We might add that methods alike for all sciences (natural and social), there are nonetheless significant differences apart from the obvious distinctions in subject matter. Obedience to laws of conservation permits the natural sciences to take on a more generally dynamic tinge than do the theoretical frameworks (and equations) of the social sciences. Moreover, their dynamic tinge relates to particular positions in contrast with the rather general positions that are predicted through the dynamic theories in the social sciences. In related manner, the natural sciences investigate the ideal workings of the universe in a context which takes the ideal as a datum to be observed; while, in the social sciences, the ideal is to be determined not from a de facto condition but through imaginative references to that which cannot yet be observed. The social scientist therefore finds himself among three kinds of theories: the mathematically static, the mathematically dynamic, and the ideal that does not exist.

theories that relate to human behavior, generalizing assumptions may just as well be used unless we can imagine a dynamic social (nonphysiological) theory of real substance which may particularize and does not require mathematics.

Finally, let us recall that static theories do not require realism. Also, general-probabilistic pictures often suffice in this realm of thought. Mathematical postulation may readily be used. Indeed, even if realistic assumptions about behavior are, for some reason or other, intended for use, a mathematical postulation may be employed. This combination means a transmutation of the realistic assumption to the level of generalities not particulars. We hold then in sum that mathematics is readily useable in the social sciences. Only ideal and dynamic systems *that are tied to individual behavior patterns and that are based on the individual positions that may exist* cannot avail themselves of mathematic postulation. In the former case, nonmathematical models must be designed. The latter system lies fundamentally outside of man's domain.

The Decision Process and Entrepreneurial Returns*

The objective of this paper is to place oligopoly and decision theory together in a single model which reveals the existence of an hierarchy of profits among industries much as we conceive of the distribution of differential rents under perfect competition. We shall see that notwithstanding the complexities of the decision process and the different personalities and asset positions of decision makers, a consistent pattern and order arises over time from industry to industry. Our investigations will cause us to resolve the dichotomy between profits as a return for the entrepreneurial "function" or as an incident (i.e., residual) in the economic process in favor of the former.[1]

We shall set forth a concise picture of decision theory in Section II of this paper, and, in turn, present some key properties of our model in Section III. Sections IV and V then discuss the basic economic relationships underscored by the model. These last two sections of the paper will show, in effect, that the essential properties of perfect (or pure) competition in the long run are fully applicable and relevant to an oligopolistic economy. But, first, we must establish certain features of oligopoly economic theory and contrast them with their counterparts, as they are set forth by the classical theory of pure competition. This is the subject matter to which Section I is devoted. Incidentally, our conception of oligopoly will carry spatial properties as set forth

* This paper was first presented in a somewhat different form at the first annual conference of the Industrial Development Research Council in the Roosevelt Hotel, New York City, October 25, 1961, under the title : "A Theoretical Base for Planning Industrial Expansion". Acknowledgement of thanks to W. Baumol, R. Johnson, R. Kavesh, S. Grable, L. T. Wallace, D. Ekey, C. Ferguson, and R. Cavendish for helpful comments and critiques is further in order.

[1] J. Fred Weston, "A Generalized Uncertainty Theory of Profit," *American Economic Review*, Vol. XL, (1950), pp. 40–60, 46 claims that uncertainty results in a deviation between expected and actual returns, and defines profits as the difference between ex ante and ex post incomes. Following a long line of theory, this concept gives profit no unique role in the system. It appears simply as an incident (*not function*) in the allocation process.

elsewhere[1]; here, without any loss, we shall accept them as already having been defined.

I. Economic Theory : Extending Some Tradition

Consider a space economy over which resources, people, and economic units are dispersed in some unspecified order. Because of spatial limitations, uneven resources distribution, and the tendency of some people to agglomerate, a series of markets and market areas develop each linked to others to varying extents and combinations.

There exists in the economy a limited number of sites at any production center, a substantial expense in transporting most goods over distance, a chain linking of markets, and an overall industrial pattern in which the use of branch plants in certain industries is practical. The aforementioned physical conditions combine with modern technology to yield, in fact, the large size plants and firms of today. In the system, the large plants and firms (speaking either absolutely or comparatively in so far as a given market area is concerned) are mindful of each other and cognizant of the effect of their policies on the total market. They do not behave atomistically.

The conception of economic relations taking place over space, where firms seek to overcome the friction of distance, and where there are large enterprises produces nonclassical conclusions. First of all competitors have their eyes on each other and their ears directed toward the nation's capital. Second and more importantly, long-run profits become inevitable consequences of the market pattern. We visualize, accordingly, a sharp difference in the incomes received by oligopolists and pure competitors, as the differences in skills and risk, which alone restrict entrepreneurial activity in pure competition, are not the only "natural" factors limiting economic activity in complex (oligopolistic) markets. In the complex markets, the scarcity of entrepreneurs, and of entrepreneurial activity, is attributed to some combination of *three natural forces* : (1) the nonexistence of skills, or, let us say, abilities, (2) risk, and (3) uncertainty. That resources and abilities may exist and yet not move into the market because of uncertainty

[1] M. L. Greenhut, *Microeconomics and the Space Economy* (Chicago : Scott, Foresman and Company, 1962).

is the vital cornerstone of our space economics. That each firm in the market tends to have a chance for profits, both in the present and the long run, follows in turn.

In classical economics, all firms in a given industry are considered to have similar costs. This conclusion recognizes the fact that different skills and risks exist among firms and entrepreneurs, and that they yield differential rents. In effect, classical economics assumes a state of natural scarcity among the factors of production, and holds that this condition brings about different returns attributable to the differences in the skills and risks of doing business. A space oligopoly market theory accepts this concept, but then goes one step further. It asserts that, over and above costs, firms are entitled to a long-run return in the form of profits, a return which measures the uncertainty conditions in the market. The answer to the question why we include uncertainty as a basic force in a space oligopoly market, but not in a purely competitive market, demands our immediate attention.

When economic units are atomistic, market price is the resultant of an extremely large number of independent decisions. No firm or group of firms is important enough in the classical model to have discernible influence, and, hence, control over price. In space economics, however, firms may be large in size, absolutely or comparatively in any market area. Such firms are capable of influencing and controlling price. The market pattern which emerges differs, as a consequence, from the traditional.[1]

In complex markets, the act of a representative firm does not generate a fixed determinable response on the part of each and every competitor, chiefly because a firm's behavior is not limited to accepting the established market price and equating the market determined average revenue with marginal cost. Instead, market reactions and policies are unknown, and sometimes capricious. Except in the case of collusion, firms may predict specific policies of rivals only under a fortunate mixture of guess and luck. Alternative *pricing systems*, among other special characteristics and unique phenomena, are intrinsic to complex markets and predicted for any time and place in a rough way at best.

[1]Indeed, one of the basic objectives of oligopolistic entrepreneurs must be to change (improve) the market's structure. See Jean Marchal, "The Construction of a New Theory of Profit," *American Economic Review*, Vol. XLI, (1951), pp. 549–65.

When objective probabilities are applicable to the possible alternative states which confront a decision maker, the condition of risk is defined to hold ; when, however, these probabilities cannot be assigned, because history is an insufficient or inadequate guide to future practices, the condition of uncertainty is defined to hold.[1] Over any period of time, such as a decade, certain pricing alternatives may have been recognized by large size competitors. When, however, history cannot be expected to serve as an adequate guide to the particular price system that may prevail in the market at a given time, the several price patterns of oligopolists appear as different states of the given uncertainty condition.

It is of critically vital importance for us to observe here that in the purely competitive economy of classical and neoclassical theory, business units were conceived to be subject in the long run only to objectively measurable and predictable alternatives. As a result, they were subject only to risk and skill differentials. In complex markets, however, the number and size of firms are such, and the kind of competition they experience so different that the impersonal market forces of classical theory are joined and/or altered by personalized relations which are unpredictable objectively. Because these forces lack objective predictability, they are distinguishable from those typically considered in economic theory.[2]

As a working postulate, then, we propose that the atomistic firms of long-run pure competition theory are subject only to risk, and that risk differs from uncertainty since objective measurement of the one but not of the other is possible.[3] This objective

[1]I am employing the terms risk and uncertainty somewhat as did Frank Knight. See his *Risk, Uncertainty and Profit* (Boston : Houghton-Mifflin, 1921) ; also see J. R. Hicks, "The Theory of Uncertainty and Profit," *Economica*, Vol. 11 (1931), pp. 170–9 and A. G. Hart, "Risk, Uncertainty, and Unprofitability of Compounding Probabilities," in O. Lange, F. McIntyre, and T. O. Yntema ed., *Studies in Mathematical Economics and Econometrics*, 1942, pp. 110–18. At the moment, I am following the operations research practice of considering risk as an objectively measurable phenomenon and uncertainty as an objective unknown.

[2]Hart, *op. cit.* Uncertainty proper cannot be insured against. Knowledge under uncertainty is quite imperfect.

[3]Knight, Hicks, Hart and others. And see Miller and Starr, *Executive Decisions and Operations Research* (Englewood Cliffs : Prentice Hall, 1960), pp. 79–98.

measurement requires reference to statistical probabilities[1]; let us say a risk pattern prevails among industries which distinguishes one from another. It may be that one industry is influenced more strongly by weather conditions than another. Therefore, it has risks related to the "probable" adversities of mother nature. Obviously, the importance of weather, or more generally of any other probabilistically determined business component differs from industry to industry. Decision-making in deference to this kind of business factor involves selection among the alternative payoffs designated by the probabilistically based components. The alternative payoffs are, then, the risks of the trade. If these risks are great, the market must provide large enough payoffs. If the market returns are excessive, new firms will enter and normal returns will result. If market returns are inadequate, old firms will leave the industry and normal returns will ensue. A fair-return competitive equilibrium tends to arise in time.

Under pure competition, the economy guarantees long-run differences in net returns *within any given industry* on the single basis of rent differentials attributable to differences in skills.[2] As between industries, long-run differentials relate only to risk. The rents for skill and risk are, in classical economics, costs of production. In the long run, the purely competitive system guarantees to its enterprises that all costs of surviving firms will be covered.

A space economy, as noted, adds uncertainty to risk and skills. It does this by holding that uncertainty is tied to competition from identifiable rivals who, by the very nature of our

[1]See C. W. Churchman, *Prediction and Optimal Decision* (Englewood Cliffs : Prentice Hall, 1961), p. 170, where he observes that under "uncertainty" the past is unknown, and, hence, we have two choices : (1) turn our backs on the situation, or (2) attempt to do something about it. In effect, the attempt involves converting subjective values into similar "form" as the objective probabilities one finds under risk. Earlier F. Ramsey, "Truth and Probability", in *The Foundation of Mathematics and Other Logical Essays*, London : Kegan Paul, 1931, had contended that subjective probabilities could always be assigned. But Knight, A. Wald *Statistical Decision Functions* (New York : John Wiley and Sons, 1950), and others did not accept this idea fully.

[2]A Marshall, Principles of Economics, 8th Edition (London : Macmillan, 1938), pp. 613–14 . . . in trades where the work of management consists chiefly in superintendence, the earnings of management follow closely the amount of work done.

definition of indentifiable rivals, cannot be atomistic. These rivals are significant, at least in their market areas, limited as they are by transport cost, availability of sites, and other geographical features.[1] They must produce similar or at least competitive products. Most important, the type of competition we visualize is not predictable ; there are no objective probabilities available to the decision-maker to help him in selecting among his alternatives.[2]

Where the inroads of competitors are likely to be substantial, where the market frequently degenerates into a "dog eat dog" affair, where the spatial market pattern is such from one market area to another that the particular regional economy in which a would-be efficient firm must operate might degenerate chaotically at any moment,[3] uncertainty is at its highest. Between industries, then, firms are entitled to returns commensurate with whatever risk and uncertainty patterns may be found to exist. Of course, the risk any firm may be subject to could be great while its uncertainty might be small, or *vice versa*.

It is a fair question to ask whether or not some uncertainty is present under pure competition. In this connection, it is appropriate to recall that Knight dealt primarily with a competitive situation in his discussion of uncertainty. In similar vein, it would also be fair to claim that the mercurial tastes of consumers are surely not all measurable in terms of known probability distributions, and yet they play an important role in classical economics. How can we reconcile these observations with our previous discussion ?

In answer, we suggest that the existence of a chaotic demand for a particular product is chiefly a short-run phenomenon. Companies with a long history are able to forecast their sales

[1]E. Chamberlin, *The Theory of Monopolistic Competition*, 5th edition (Cambridge : Harvard University Press, 1946) Appendix C ; and J. Robinson, *The Economics of Imperfect Competition* (London : Macmillan and Co., 1934), Book III.

[2]F. H. Hahn, "A Note on Profit and Uncertainty," *Economica*, N.S., Vol. XIV, (August, 1947), pp. 211–25, 211. . . . The organizational function includes planning output, setting price policy, and deciding among policies which involve a great deal of uncertainty. If not for these, management could be delegated entirely to a salaried employee.

[3]The economic upheaval suggested here for a given market area is not to be confused with the cycle behavior of the economy which may be predictable.

fairly well on the basis of anticipated disposable income and other projections. In effect, a sales function becomes discernible. Moreover, the policies and practices of *atomistic competitors*, in response to varying demand, can be forejudged, whereas in complex oligopolistic markets competitive responses remain basically unpredictable. Whatever uncertainty may be defined to hold in pure competition must, therefore, have exclusively short-run status and fail to have any roots in what may be styled the unpredictable policies and reactions of firms. They can have roots only in demand and here too the theory ruled uncertainty out. This is, of course, not equivalent to saying that classical theorists and their followers did not consider the likelihood or possibility that demand may sometimes practically disappear in pure competition or rule out the possibility of its reaching hithertobefore unimagined magnitudes. It is simply to say that if tastes for a product and/or the policies of firms prove to be extremely variable, the state is either one of risk or uncertainty, depending upon whether or not significant probability values could have been assigned to the state affected by these forces before these forces occurred. *In practice, classical economics assumed that these probabilities prevailed.*

II. The Decision-Making Process

Economic activity takes form at a certain place over a given time. The productive process used is frequently a function of "the" place and "the" time. The risks of engaging in the activity are known ; the prevailing uncertainties are, in a sense, unknown. Under these, business men estimate their future payoffs.

Consider first the state of risk at a given time, and assume that alternative processes and locations are available.

In Table I we visualize locating the plant in a particular place. There are h alternative production techniques (processes 1, 2, 3, . . ., q) under consideration. There are $j = 1, 2, \ldots,$ k states of risk. Each of these processes involves the use of slightly different material and factor combinations, and each yields conjectures of different net profits, depending, as the case may be, on general forces affecting business. These forces, which may be called exogeneous forces, are readily identifiable and have known probabilities. They may, for example, relate to weather conditions

TABLE I

MEAN PROFITS AT LOCATION X (a_{hj} PAYOFFS PROJECTED) UNDER A GIVEN RISK WITH j STATES, EACH STATE BEING OBJECTIVELY MEASURABLE

h Processes	Risk State 1	Probability	Risk State 2	Probability		Risk State k	Probability
Process 1	a_{11}	p_{11}	a_{12}	p_{12}	......	a_{1k}	p_{1k}
Process 2	a_{21}	p_{21}	a_{22}	p_{22}	......	a_{2k}	p_{2k}
Process 3	a_{31}	p_{31}	a_{32}	p_{32}	......	a_{3k}	p_{3k}
....	..	..	..	..	......	..	..
Process q	a_{q1}	p_{q1}	a_{q2}	p_{q2}	......	a_{qk}	p_{qk}
	j states of risk						

(fair weather, rain, snow, *etc.*), to strikes in nearby supplying industries, or to the number or extent of forest fires. They *may* refer to economic development, growth rates and distribution of population, length of expansion and contraction periods in the business cycle, extent of innovation and obsolescence in the subject industry, and similar phenomena. There are a_{hj} payoffs.

Given the external risk (e.g. weather), the projected net profits at location X under any process may involve a range of likely values for any one risk state, or else be a specific sum, as we are suggesting it to be in the table. The particular payoff or range of payoffs reflects the actual exogeneous force under examination. But though a mean profit figure for the state is identifiable and alone is used in Table I, we shall be obliged very shortly, indeed in the next paragraph, to emphasize the distribution of values under any state of risk. It suffices, however, to consider at this point only the mean value for a risk state, such as for good weather, as shown, let us say, in column 1 of Table I. By taking the mean profit and multiplying it by the probability of the condition, and then performing the same operation for each alternative state of the risk, we obtain as a sum of all of these values the expected payoff for the process. Alternative payoffs apply, however, to different risk situations (e.g., strikes compared to weather). In fact, the risks that are relevant will interact such that weather would combine with the number of days lost by strike, the number of machine breakdowns, *etc.*, in various combinations. As we shall see later on, each possible combination of risks proffers a payoff and related probability, and all payoffs and probabilities yield a mean for the given process and location. For a while, we will continue to limit our thinking essentially to one risk (e.g. Table I), though, if preferred, a given risk state could be considered as a particular combination of risks ; over a shorter reading span, we shall confine our thinking to one location.

Let us imagine that among rival sellers one enterpriser has less cash than the others, *ceteris paribus*. This seller notes that a likely (but not the mean) value for a particular process under a certain risk state is extremely low, and realizes that, even though this result is not an average result, its chance of occurrence is sufficiently possible to warrant its being considered.[1] Accordingly, he might reduce the a_{hj} value shown under this state and process, and again for any other condition or process that might be affected similarly.[2] Comparably, values at the top end of the scale might be adjusted if special benefits were visualized.[3] Given these redesignations, we might find that different processes offer the best return at different locations. We could extend the same thought system to include concern with "unlikely" low or high returns, in which event any adjustment of matrix values would reflect "a purely personal or noneconomic location decision".[4] Most important, any redesignation of payoff values to reflect differences between utility and dollar amounts causes a separation between objective and subjective measurements of risk. When, however, the redesignation reflects economic decision making rather than purely personal considerations, the redesignated values, just as the original numbers, will be considered to be "objectively based" and not a subjective value. We shall discuss the significance of this matter at a later point, at which time we shall also note that decision making under uncertainty automatically involves what we shall call "accepted objective" values.

[1]We may accept, for example, any value falling within three standard deviations of a mean payoff as a likely return, and any value falling outside these limits as unlikely.

[2]The revaluation of matrix elements reflects the failure of utility to be identical to dollar amounts. And see W. Baumol, *Economic Theory and Operations Analysis* (Englewood Cliffs : Prentice Hall, 1961), Chapter 17.

[3]The adjustments we propose here for dollar values are counterpart to the conversion of money payoffs to utility payoffs customarily made in decision theory. We favored the dollar adjustment approach rather than the use of a utility concept because one of our hopes is to set forth a model that would be meaningful to businessmen and jurists without undue misinterpretation. In either event, the tradition of expressing a_{hj} as real numbers if probabilities can be assigned is well established. J. von Neumann and O. Morgenstern, *Theory of Games and Economic Behavior*, 2nd ed. (Princeton : Princeton University Press, 1947) ; J. Neyman, "Outline of a Theory of Statistical Estimation Based on the Classical Theory of Probability," *Philosophical Transactions of the Royal Society*, Series A, Vol. 236 (1937), pp. 333–80, and F. Ramsey, *op. cit.*

[4]See M. Greenhut, "A General Theory of Maximum Profits," *Southern Economic Journal*, Vol. XXVIII (1962), pp. 278–85, 282, 283, for a discussion of what is an economic and what is a noneconomic decision.

TABLE II

MAXIMUM EXPECTED PROFITS AT ALTERNATIVE LOCATIONS UNDER "A" GIVEN RISK STRUCTURE

Location	Process	Profits
Location *F*	(process 3)	Z_4
Location *G*	(process 17)	Z_2
....	....	..
....	....	..
....	....	..
Location *X*	(process 2)	Z_1
Location *Y*	(process 1)	Z_7
Location *Z*	(process 3)	Z_{11}

Whether or not the mean values are adjusted by weight of likely or unlikely extreme items or are left unchanged, a set of returns such as is shown in Table II will obtain. To understand the implication of Table II, we need only observe that several alternative locations might be available, say at cities *F*, *G*, . . ., *X*, *Y*, *Z* and that for each possible site a best process and related expected payoff will exist for a given risk structure.

To complete the description of the basic elements of our model, we recall now that in addition to risk (as described in Table I by means of the objective probabilities), the market may be subject to uncertainty. For example, the degree and extent of competition at alternative locations and in different market areas may not be predictable. In one market area, there may be a possibility that company *A* will serve as a price leader, or even that hyper-competitive price practices may arise, or other possibilities may prove to be the case. Elsewhere, the alternatives may be different. In any event, a matrix must be formed which shows all of the uncertainty payoffs. Thus, we might find that Location *X* yields a maximum payoff value for a certain process under uncertainty state *F* (e.g., price leadership practice by the subject firm), whereas a different payoff value (and possibly a different process) holds for uncertainty state *M* (e.g., price competition). It suffices to say for the moment that an expanded table which corresponds to Table II but which has several columns, one for each uncertainty, will be obtained, and that, on the basis of some criterion (e.g., the equally likely criterion),[1] the decision will be resolved.

Recognizing, but not expanding here on, the matter of criteria, we are ready now to blend together economic and decision making theory. In the process, we might keep in mind such decision as the 1923 Bluefield Case (262 U.S. 679) where the United States Supreme Court held that a public utility is entitled to earnings comparable to those received by nonregulated enterprises which are subject to the same risks and uncertainties as the utility.

III. Some Key Properties of The Model

(A) Table II, as indicated previously, can be expanded to show the full set of payoffs expected under different risks and uncertainties given alternative locations, investments, types of plant, and so forth. In effect, we take the full set of prospective payoffs under the combination of risk probabilities applicable to each payoff at a given location, *etc.*, for a given uncertainty, and, in the process, obtain the expectations shown in Table III. For example, consider the set of elements, $a, b \epsilon R$ where "a" refers to all alternative payoff projections under all combinations of risk (e.g. good weather with 5 days of strike and, say, 6 months of recession with production index between 90 and 95 *etc.*), and "b" refers to the *compound* probability formed by multiplying together the individual probabilities relevant to each risk in one of its states. By taking the dot product of a,b (i.e. the projected payoffs times their related compound probabilities), we obtain a vector of weighted payoffs. The sum of these weighted payoffs yields the expected return. Then, if we consider only the ideal process, the best size of plant, investment, *etc.* applicable to a given location, and next evaluate in iterative manner the expected return of all locations under all uncertainties, the full set of expected payoffs shown in Table III is derived.

[1]Under the criterion, each uncertain alternative is considered to be equally likely and any decision maker would select the location and process offering the highest expected payoff of all uncertain payoffs averaged together. Alternative criteria proposed by Savage, Wald, Hurwicz, and others may be applied and can be found readily in the literature of decision theory. (See Miller and Starr, *op. cit.*)

TABLE III

MAXIMUM EXPECTED PROFITS AT ALL LOCATIONS UNDER ALL RISKS AND UNCERTAINTIES

i locations, *j* uncertainty conditions ; $i = a, b, \ldots, n$; $j = 1, 2, \ldots, p$)

	Uncertainty 1	Uncertainty 2	....	Uncertainty P
Location *a*	Z_{a_1}	Z_{a_2}	....	Z_{ap}
Location *b*	Z_{b_1}	Z_{b_2}	....	Z_{bp}
....	..	..	....	..
....	..	..	....	..
....	..	..	....	..
....	..	..	....	..
Location *n*	Z_{n_1}	Z_{n_2}	....	Z_{np}

Assume that Location *b* is selected as the very best. Then recall that there exists a set $a \epsilon R$ such that related to each expected payoff in Table III is a set of individual payoffs, one projected payoff for each combination of risks that might occur. Finally, note that there exists *a particular combination of risks* at location *b under the best uncertainty* which yields *the worst payoff.* If the relevant probability for this bad payoff (i.e., the related element $b \epsilon R$,) warrants consideration (that is, a 1 per cent or better probability of occurrence applies), we can designate the difference between the expected payoff and this particular payoff as a rough measure of the risk.[1] In turn, we can take the difference between this low payoff (which, to recall, applies to the best uncertainty) and the lowest likely payoff under any other uncertainty as the basis for a measure of uncertainty. Manifestly, in any measurement of risk and uncertainty we must weight our lowest payoffs ; moreover, we might even use different yardsticks to measure risk and uncertainty than that proposed above, such

[1]The probabilities of receiving poor returns may differ, as is the case when two alternative investments promise the same lowest return but with a different likelihood for each. Then, if each alternative also happens to proffer the same mean, the venture which has the worst distribution will readily be seen to have the greatest risk, and, *ceteris paribus*, not to be chosen. By weighting the lowest return(s) by the *reciprocal* of its probability, we would cause that low return which is most likely to occur to carry the lowest weighted value. Or, we could use a variant of the von Newmann-Morgenstern cardinal utility index as our basis for identifying and evaluating the lowest likely return. In any case, consistency in "weighting" would alone be necessary.

Note further that instead of identical mean payoffs, one alternative might promise a higher mean but a smaller equally weighted lowest likely return than another. In this case, the most desirable alternative would not be indicated by the value assigned to risk since some companies want more risk (with a greater mean payoff expectation) than do others.

as, for example, to measure uncertainty as the difference between the mean payoff under the best uncertainty and the mean payoff under the worst uncertainty.[1] For present objectives, full specification and discussion is unnecessary, for, as we shall see, our interest centers on the different bases for decision making by firms and industries and the composite effect of risk and uncertainty on competition and rates of return, not on empirical measurements of each.

(B) Risk-uncertainty matrices of order n x p, we assert, underscore economic decision making.[2] Enlargement of the matrix order to include alternative processes or varying investment amounts and other elements may readily be included. Because we are considering decision making under uncertainty, the best location, the best process at the location, the optimum size of investment for the best process at the best location, *etc.*, are not self evident. Unlike in risk, where the highest expected payoff may be readily designated, there is no mean uncertainty payoff which stands out as the best expected payoff. Decision making under uncertainty, rather, requires the use of some subjectively applied criteria before one is able to select his course of action.[3] Thus, a firm which is short of cash, or, let us say, is conservatively

[1]O. Lange, "A Note on Innovations," *Review of Economic Statistics*, Vol. XXV, (1943), pp. 19–23 refers to the difference between the risk premium and expected receipts as "effective receipts". His concept approximates ours as in effect we shall relate the amount of risk to the expected receipts and argue that if they are not in line firms will enter or leave the industry. (See Section IV.)

[2]In line with previous illustrations, we let n stand for location and p for uncertainty states.

[3]This is why K. J. Arrow, "Utilities, Attitudes, Choices : A Review Note," *Econometrica*, vol. 26, 1958, pp. 1–23, p. 8 states that some method is needed for combining the pictures of utility and subjective probabilities of different individuals. However, this need holds only if economists are concerned with the choice itself distinct from the consequences of the choice, as in Georgescu-Roegen, "Choices, Expectations, and Measurability," *Quarterly Journal of Economics*, Vol. LXVIII (1954), pp. 503–36, and Tajas Majunder, "Behaviouristic Cardinalism in Utility Theory," *Economica*, N.S., Vol. XIX (1951), pp. 273–392. The more general concern in economic theory with the consequences flowing from decision making leads us to the realization that by the principle of survival of the fittest, as applied to economic society (See A. Alchian, "Uncertainty, Evolution, and Economic Theory," *Journal of Political Economy*, Vol. XVIII (1950), pp. 211–21), a natural selection is made. As is intrinsic to Section IV of this paper, the common bind between individual utilities and subjective probabilities is the market mechanism. Our main interest centers on the result of the choice and not the process of choosing.

managed, may lean towards a maximin decision.[1] A firm oriented differently may focus its attention on the best of all best possibilities, that is to say, a maximax type of decision. Among still other possibilities, the decision may be based on equally likely standards, or the so-called criteria of optimism or regret. Whatever the basis for the decision, economic irrationality cannot be claimed when one firm selects a particular set of returns different from that accepted by another. Such irrationality applies only under a risk matrix (or, of course, under a state of certainty), and then only when a decision-maker happens to ignore the objective data which prevail in the market.[2] Manifestly, it is only under risk or certainty that a maximum value holds for all. The concept of maximum profits is vastly different when applied to an economy marked by uncertainty than one marked by risk or certainty.

(C) It should be obvious that if one company continuously accepts a risk and uncertainty different from that of its rivals by, for example, taking an ultra conservative position, said company may fail to grow in step with its rivals. In time, it will be squeezed out by forceful competition. An *underlying accepted objective return, therefore, tends to be established for each industry, and this return, as related to the accepted risk and uncertainty, helps distinguish each industry from any and all others.* We will continue our examination of this matter at a later point.

IV. The Long-Run Adaptive Process

Decision theory focuses attention on the matter of alternatives, on states of nature, on unknown actions by competitors; more generally, it proposes ways in which company officials view and resolve the risks and uncertainties of doing business. Economic theory on its part speaks in terms of earned and unearned returns, of short run and normal price; it forms a picture of economic life which provides the reasons why things are produced the way they are.

[1]This decision, for example, would involve a search for the highest of all the worst *expected* payoffs. These worst *expected* payoffs are those payoffs which relate to the most unfavorable uncertainty state for the given alternative opportunities in location, investment, production, process, *etc.*

[2]Remember, the a_{hj}'s can be expressed as real numbers if probabilities can be assigned. And see K. J. Arrow, "Alternative Approaches to the Theory of Choice in Risk-Taking Situations," *Econometrica*, Vol. 19 (1951), pp. 404–37, on this point.

By borrowing from economic theory the idea of an hierarchy of returns for all industries, by recognizing from decision theory that objective measurement may be made by responsible officials of the risk and uncertainty visualized for a company, by considering at the same time the criteria which these officials may select in deciding the policy and practice of the company, a broad-view is gained of all business organizations. In the process, the basis for understanding intra-industry and inter-industry differentials will have been sharpened.

We propose that the objective risk and uncertainty payoff values a decision-maker visualizes range from a best uncertainty set of values down to a worst uncertainty set of values. But just as man's institutions and culture impinge on the underlying universe, so do his decision criteria alter the risk and uncertainty payoff range which prevails. Should the decision of one set of industrialists in one industry be of a maximining nature, a different decision (e.g. location and process types) will be approved than its counterpart borne out of a maximaxing character. The *accepted* risk and uncertainty of the one industry would, accordingly, diverge from the other, and an industry which in the purer sense is subject to a risk and uncertainty range greater than another might, in fact, have a smaller range in the light of the "accepted-objective" values it faces. Significantly, those surviving members of the industry would each face a comparable range of risk and uncertainty, albeit the differential skills within the industry would enable some (i.e., essentially single proprietors) to countenance higher payoff values (again with the same range) than others. This differential is the meaning economic theory gives to intra-industry returns, and it would be determinable similarly by the model proposed above in this paper.

We visualize, then, an hierarchy of industries where each member has a given range of risks and uncertainties. Each range reflects the risks and uncertainties accepted in the industry. In some cases the accepted range may relate to purely objective values, while in others it is determined by altered valuations. Within each risk and uncertainty classification returns differ; but these, of course, are just the classical differentials. Risk signifies a mean payoff which should be realized in time. What uncertainty means is that decision makers will differ—and objectively so—on the business policy which they would expect will optimize their position in the market, since any particular payoff need never be realized much less even approximated in a world of uncertainty.

Payoffs between industries must settle in time in proportion to risk and uncertainty. That is to say, somewhat higher payoffs would be required for higher risk if higher risk ventures are ever to have a chance of being selected.[1] Comparably, returns in a world of uncertainty alone will rise with increased uncertainty, though possibly not in a perfectly continuous form since no one activity can be understood by all to promise the best mean payoff ; hence, firms will tend to lean this way or that from time to time, changing their policies and practices for a while in an *ad hoc* manner. The fact of the matter is that competition alone serves to provide regularity and proportionality among firms and industries in a system marked by uncertainty. However, before examining in detail the significance of competition in our framework of thought, we must first note that, within any industry, different criteria may be followed by certain firms so that, in effect, they accept different risk and uncertainty ranges than is typically followed by others. These differences, as already indicated, help establish the differential returns within an industry, though an underlying common character for the industry is identifiable over time as new entrants or exits ultimately leave only the most successful firms—*and their imitators*—in the market. These similarly rooted organizations thereby characterize the industry.

The competitive impact on economic decision making under uncertainty may be visualized by taking the "industry" investment decision as given, and assuming that the range in the one industry (i.e., from the "highest expected" payoff under the best uncertainty combination to the very lowest "likely" payoff under the worst uncertainty arrangement) is greater than that applicable to another industry, but that most of its payoffs for different uncertainties are lower than the counterpart projections in the other industry. An explanation (or basis) for the assumption might simply be that the decision makers in the one industry are

[1]K. Arrow, "Alternative Approaches to the Theory of Choice in Risk-Taking Situations," *Economica*, Vol. 29 (1957), pp. 404–37.

"maximaxers" who seek the greatest possible return. This greatest possible return, we assume, unfortunately involves a location, a size of plant, and an investment which carries a greater range than that proffered by other criteria, and which, further involves a group of expected returns for all uncertainty states, other than the most favorable, which are lower in the maximaxing industry than in the other. As fate would have it, let us assume, the most favorable uncertainty state never seems to occur, and the profit receipts are, therefore, lower notwithstanding the great risk and uncertainty accepted in the industry. Of course, competition and dame fortune will eventuate in such pattern that the higher risk and uncertainty industry (which, we assumed, was offering in fact the lower profits) will gain an increase in its payoffs to the level commensurate with the risks and uncertainties accepted in the industry. This result stems naturally and directly from our definition of uncertainty, our interpretation of rational-economic decision making under uncertainty, and then, in turn, from the meaning of competition in economic theory. Significantly, the way the industry regards its risks and uncertainties determines the risks and uncertainties that are accepted, and the risks and uncertainties that are accepted in the culture must establish the basis for the returns that are to be earned.

Let us explore this vital matter somewhat further by asking the question why might the management of some company and industry adopt a maximin policy while the management in another industry which—at the same time—proffers the exactly same set of payoffs, risks, uncertainties, *etc.* does not ? By way of just one possible answer, we may suggest the possibility that the one industry might have a slow cash-flow cycle compared to the other. Then, if the worst expected return (i.e., the mean payoff under the worst uncertainty state) happens to occur regularly over time, and there is no firm which selected the maximin location, some firms in the one industry may fail while those in the other might be able to survive until a better combination of uncertainties takes hold.

Now, if we assume that because of the above possibility the industry with a slow cash-flow does follow the maximin criteria, and if we assume further that the full range of payoffs for the industry which adheres to "maximin" principles exceeds the payoff range confronting the "nonmaximin" deciding industry, and finally that most of its expected and lowest likely payoffs are less than those in the other industry, we *could* have on hand—depending upon dame fortune—the case where the greater risk and uncertainty spread proffers a set of returns over time which is less than that of the industry confronted by the lower risk and uncertainty total. If, then, the maximin management was pursuing policies inimical to the interests of its stockholders, these policies will be changed to restore the proper hierarchy between risk and uncertainty and net revenues. On the other hand, if stockholders are generally in accord with the policies of management, because the industry type indicates the propriety of these policies, any unduly low set of net revenues in the face of the accepted risk and uncertainties will, *in time*, lead to a relative decline of competition in the industry and hence increase the set of payoffs.[1] In sum, an hierarchy of returns tends to result which yields greater payoffs for greater risk and uncertainty.

We suggest, therefore, that a distinctive pattern (or character) arises among industries in an uncertain world. We propose that values may be altered when dollars and utilities are not identical, and also that economic decision makers will often differ in the way they analyze the problem of uncertainty. As a consequence, these decision makers cause different distinctive patterns to arise. We propose, in fact, that undue subjective revaluations may even arise, but that these so impinge on the culturally influenced economy as to convert an industry of one kind of risk and uncertainty *only temporarily* into one of another kind.[2] Acceptance of any state determines future entry and exit ; these

[1]Note that the slow cash flow tends to justify a maximin policy as it reflects, *ceteris paribus*, a more hazardous base. Of course, the fact of a more hazardous venture may not be revealed in the payoff projections that appear at any point in time, though ultimately they must rise.

[2]While we recognized what we shall call the "accepted-subjective" industry possibility, reasons similar to those presented earlier would suggest that this condition will be essentially short run in nature. In any industry, noneconomic decision makers (that is, those influenced by unlikely remote possibilities) tend to disappear. Let us say, following G. Debreu "The Coefficient of Resource Utilization," *Econometrica*, Vol. 19 (1951), pp. 273–92, that the stability conditions in economic society involve actions to increase payoffs.

ultimately provide a character for the activity which conforms with basic economic principles.[1]

V. Profits as a Functional Return.

Underscoring our theory is, therefore, the conception of profits as a functional, not residual return. That is to say, profits play the same role in an economy subject to uncertainty as do rents in an economy subject to risk.[2] The function is, of course, organizing under conditions of uncertainty ; hence uncertainty and organizing appear as parts of the same entity. Similarly, the ultimate coincidence between pure competition theory and oligopoly theory may be seen by noting the fact that special returns apply to selected functions in each system of thought.[3] Shall we

[1]It is significant to note that the "exclusionary effect" of risk and uncertainty is, *ceteris paribus*, independent of the amount assigned to risk and the amount assigned to uncertainty. That is to say, a 1 per cent risk plus a 5 per cent uncertainty constrains entry to the same extent as a 4 per cent risk plus 2 per cent uncertainty. This result relates to the very existence and meaning of uncertainty, for we just do not know which uncertainty state will hold, and hence we must—after as well as before the decision—contemplate the full range of payoffs promised by the activity. By altered valuations alone—which involve the application of subjective forces—do we give vent to differences in "labels" and personal positions. But this force bears impact either in specifying the value of the payoffs placed in the matrix (see note p. 256), or in determining the criterion selected to resolve the decision problem. In any case, once the decision maker has evaluated the payoffs and selected what would be his best position, he focuses his attention on the total payoff range from best to worst, and decides whether it is favorable enough to warrant positive action. Manifestly, he is indifferent to the part of the total range which economists may classify as risk or uncertainty.

[2]See R. M. Davis, "The Current State of Profit Theory," *American Economic Review*, Vol. XLII (1952), pp. 245–64, especially 256–62, for discussion of profits and imputed or unimputed returns.

[3]Such statement by Hahn, *op. cit.*, p. 211, that profit as a surplus over total cost does not enable us to distinguish between high and low, excessive or deficit profit, may, accordingly, be fully appreciated. By relating profit to the spread between the lowest likely return under the best to the worst uncertainty state (or, more generally, under the best to worst uncertainty combination), we realize that competition eliminates disproportionate returns as it raises or lowers the expected and lowest likely return while often leaving the range unchanged. Furthermore, we may realize that it is not the difference between actual and expected returns which regulates economic activity, but any existing imbalance between expected returns and the underlying range of uncertainty plus risk. Manifestly, a state of misallocated resources (e.g., profits in excess of, or short of, uncertainty magnitudes) contains its own stability conditions (Debreu, *op. cit.*). At the same time, we see that our system of thought denies the non-functional role that is claimed for profits by others. (See Weston, *op. cit.* ; and for other discussion on this point, see Davis, *op. cit.*).

simply say that unorganized oligopoly (i.e., a non-collusive oligopoly, open to competition, with free entry and exit) may be seen to be essentially similar to pure competition in so far as concerns its long-run returns.[1] The present paper points to the similarity only in terms of factor prices ; similar results, however, can be shown in the matter of resource allocation and consumer satisfactions.[2]

In conclusion, notwithstanding the myriad of alternative payoffs that confront the decision maker, and notwithstanding the diverse personalities and asset positions which produce differential profits in the short run as between *and within industries*, a common character of returns arises over time for any given industry. In the long run, differential rents alone mark intra-industry returns, even though in the short run differences in approach and attitude underscore the policies, practices and profit differentials of the members of an industry. The resultant—and ultimate—order that is brought about applies, let us remind, to long-run returns in economies marked by distance where, instead of a microscopic identity, rivals are able to identify their competitors. Even for this economy, characterized as it is by imperfect knowledge and the uncertain reactions of firms, *a common approach to decision problems* takes place within industries, and a long-run determinacy therefore results.

M. L. GREENHUT

Texas A. & M. University,
Texas

[1]Along this line, see L. McKenzie, "Ideal Output and the Interdependence of Firms," *Economic Journal*, Vol. LXI (1951) ; W. Baumol, "On the Theory of Oligopoly," *Economica*, Vol. XXV, pp. 187–98.

[2]And see the writer's *Microeconomics and the Space Economy, op. cit.*

[4]

HYPOTHESES IN SCIENCE AND AN EVALUATION OF NORMATIVE MICROECONOMIC THEORY

By M. L. GREENHUT*

ECONOMISTS WHO DABBLE in political economy typically *predict* a future state *or prescribe* for the future. All too often, however, they fail to realize that *certain* kinds of *predictions* and *prescriptions* involve the use of normative economics, and, accordingly, require models more realistic than, say, the classical one of pure competition. It is only with respect to statements of historical kind, or explanations which entail minor change in the basic institutions of the system (e.g., a slight change in tax structure) that the theorist though engaged in predictions or prescriptions, as the case be, is not dabbling in normative economics. In such case, i.e., in positive economics alone, he may employ unrealistic models without violating some rather elementary rules of epistemology.

This paper seeks to establish the claims just made. It attempts this by analyzing the situations under which economists must, or may use (1) models describable as containing a greater degree of realism than the model of pure competition, or (2) models of the kind founded upon such assumptions as an *infinite* number of *homogeneous* buyers and sellers who are located at a *point* in space and who operate under perfect *certainty*, complete *knowledge*, and the like. In the simplest, yet still a general sense, this paper seeks to substantiate the claim that normative economics requires more realistic models than pure competition, allowing for positive economics those models of very unrealistic order.

To fulfil our objective, we must establish a common understanding of some vital working concepts. So, let it immediately be agreed that when we shall speak herein of a scientific (economic) hypothesis, we may be referring either to the concepts, statements, or assumptions of the hypothesis, or, of course, the entire hypothesis. By the concepts included in the hypothesis, we shall have in mind the set of formally defined terms as well as the undefined terms which comprise the typical hypothesis. (By undefined terms, for example, we mean such concept as the number, the point, or the line, as customarily used in elementary mathematics.) Hypotheses in economics include known or accepted propositions from other disciplines, or the subject discipline; indeed, an accepted theory could be—and often is—availed of in making up part of a particular hypothesis. Finally, diverse assumptions, usually implicit, sometimes explicit, form the hypothesis. These assumptions almost invariably prove to be the properties of the hypothesis over

---

*Head, Department of Economics, Texas A&M University. The author wishes to acknowledge a great debt to Alfred Chalk, William Laird, Jack Melitz and John Moroney for their diverse kinds of help.

which the arguments about realism and unrealism rage. How they are part of the hypothesis, where they come from, what is and what is not realistic are matters requiring early discussion. But before going further, let us initially define (i.e., accept the definition of) the hypothesis itself as: "a theory of limited application."[1] And then let us develop our view of the hypothesis by recording the classifications and analyses of others in the next two sections of the paper, after which we proceed with our main theme.

II

The assumptions which make up an hypothesis are, according to Melitz,[2] divisible into two categories, generative and auxiliary. He defines the generative assumptions as those "which serve in deriving the hypothesis itself." The auxiliary assumptions are those "used in conjunction with the hypothesis in order to deduce predictions."[3] Typically the profit maximizing principle, he tells us, is generative. Through it, we may derive such formulation as the most efficient resource allocation possible for a given economy. In turn, the *ceteris paribus* principle is typically an auxiliary assumption. It holds constant other forces, in the process enabling the theorist to isolate and identify selected relationships that are vital to his interests.

We may appreciate Melitz' distinctions further by use of an example, specifically a thesis dealing with secular unemployment. For the purposes of illustration only, *let us accept* the hypothesis that if certain minority groups are becoming increasingly unemployed, because of the regular introduction of new products and technology, secular unemployment is occurring. If, however, their rising unemployment is attributable only indirectly to these forces, being directly related to regularly recurring business recessions which increase in intensity, the problem is *essentially* not a secular one but a cyclical one. In other words, for our purposes, *let us accept the hypothesis that the increase in the unemployment of persons belonging to certain minority groups, e.g., persons over 40 years of age, ties up directly with short-run business aberrations and is, accordingly, not a matter of structural unemployment.*

Now, among other possibilities, two groups of assumptions (implicit and explicit) may be identified in connection with this hypothesis. Generative (i.e., helpful) support may be found in the assumptions that older workers suffer no disadvantage (or quicker deterioration of skills) compared to younger workers. Any long run increase in their unemployment may, therefore, not be attributable to secular forces. Or, similarly, it may be assumed that members of selected minority groups are equally adaptable to jobs and as skilled as those not belonging to these groups, from which it might follow that a long run increase in their unemployment is due to nonsecular phenomena. Indeed, if we are able to find only a bias against older workers or minority groups which operates independently

1. "A hypothesis . . . is . . . a theory which has, at present at least, a limited range of application. It is promoted to the status of a theory if and when its range is deemed sufficiently large to justify this more commendatory appelation." H. Margenau, "Methodology of Modern Physics", *Philosophy of Science*, Vol. II, 1933, p. 67.
2. Jack Melitz, "Friedman and Machlup on the Significance of Testing Economic Assumptions", *Journal of Political Economy*, LXIII, 1965, pp. 37-60.
3. *Ibid.*, p. 42.

of secular problems, i.e., arises stochastically with respect to time, the nonstructural hypothesis presumed above might be tenable.

It is significant that the assumption of equal skills and adaptability, while not verifying the hypothesis in any way, does provide possible substance to it. We might, indeed, even posit a more highly theoretical-generative assumption than that of equal skills and adaptability. For example, we could aver that the economy under consideration is subject to regularly recurring business cycles which increase in intensity from cycle to cycle. And we could then claim that though the unemployment process is a random one, the comparatively limited rehiring pattern is not. This problem is initially cyclical. All of these assumptions, in particular the last one, would help to derive the hypothesis itself, and if selected tests might reveal the plausibility of the assumptions, these same assumptions would have served as generative of the hypothesis.

Auxiliary support to the hypothesis would be the *ceteris paribus* assumption. Another auxiliary assumption might be the statement that, if data are available, a significant correlation can be found between the increase in total unemployment and the relative rise in the unemployment of persons belonging to the group of persons over 40 years of age. (Note that this assumption would relate selected unemployment to an economic problem which goes *beyond* the possibility of inferior skills and adaptability, or, say, bias.) It is of significant importance in model building, as we shall next see, that the assumptions often point to a specific test.[4]

Melitz claims that evidence opposed to an auxiliary assumption "increases the ambiguity of test results" and from this statement we can see that the "realism of 'auxiliary' assumptions . . . is plainly relevant."[5] From our example, we can see that the hypothesis may still be true even if an auxiliary assumption is false, for surely diverse auxiliary assumptions, including those escaping our attention or perspicacity might apply. Be this as it may, the truth or significance of the hypothesis would be in doubt if statistical evidence failed to support the auxiliary assumption.[6] If the generative assumption is false, Melitz seems to feel an even

4. Our hypothesis of nonstructural unemployment is traceable to a recent paper by N. J. Simler, "Long-Term Unemployment, the Structural Hypothesis and Public Policy", *American Economic Review*, LIV, 1964, pp. 985-1001. The breakdown into generative and auxiliary assumptions is my own and is not designed to comply exactly with those which are implicit or explicit to Mr. Simler's paper. Correspondingly, the example used is simply designed to characterize the type of assumptions one finds in economic models: In no way do we wish to imply our belief in the hypothesis under consideration nor even to claim that it mirrors the views of Professor Simler. Our objective in its use is to repeat, simply illustrative of the properties of an hypothesis.

5. Melitz, *op. cit.*, p. 44.

6. Note that a nonstructural auxiliary assumption which ties up with the highly theoretical generative assumption posited above in the text would be that both total unemployment and the unemployment of older persons rose together in such unison as to yield practically the same ratio of the one to the other over time. Such evidence would suggest that the economic 'growth' problem was not attributable to minority group unemployment. But suppose instead that the minority group unemployment is revealed to have risen steadily over the years and at a great rate relatively speaking, yet failed to correlate with total unemployment which might have arisen stochastically. It would seem that structural unemployment *is* indicated by the failure of the statistical evidence to support the auxiliary assumption, for the low (insignificant) correlation would be suggesting that the rising minority group unemployment is carrying with it a rise in total unemployment. Nonetheless, the truth of the matter could just happen to be something else. For example (1) cyclical recessions might have become more and more severe, and (2) the *length* of recessions might have increased so greatly that with the emergence of revival(s) a new set of wants (tastes) tended to arise which just happened to be best produced in areas which happened to be inhabited by relatively few members of minority groups. Such assumption of new sets of wants taking hold periodically, *etc.*, would, of course, be generative to a nonstructural unemployment hypothesis, as the large unemployment of a selected group would be revealed actually to be of accidental design. In turn, for *this* generative assumption, the auxiliary assumption (and evidence) could be the low (insignificant) correlation of total unemployment with minority group unemployment. But note, the new generative assumption invokes a highly unlikely set of events. That it would not be readily acceptable should be kept in mind as one reads the next sentence in the text above.

greater loss for the hypothesis, observing that the probability of the hypothesis being true is reduced, if not notably undermined. We know from any inductive reasoning process that other explanations for a given result may exist than the one which first appeared to be the logical one. To say the least, the falseness of any assumption renders the hypothesis—and more generally any related construct of thought—less attractive and meaningful in the science. It points, at the same time, to the fact that any given assumption is not *ipso facto* established by any single test. Hence when we speak of relevance, truth and confirmation, we are, therefore, thinking essentially in terms of degrees. And it is this proposition—which at first blush may appear to be elementary, but which lies at the root of all methodological disagreements over verification of and types of theoretical formulation—that underscores the main thesis of this paper.[7]

III

Recall that we have so far used the term false at several points in our discussion. However, we employed this term by resisting repeated temptations to employ the word unrealistic instead. The term unrealistic, and its counterpart term realistic, have a very special meaning to us, a meaning which may best be approached by observing some selected use of the words by others. In the forthcoming discussion, we shall also employ the awkward expressions nonfalse and nondisconfirmed instead of the seemingly easier to handle terms true and confirmed. We shall follow this practice because failure to disconfirm an assumption is not identically equivalent to the confirmation of the assumption. The awkward expressions, in short, possess greater scientific precision.

Friedman infers that a fruitful hypothesis cannot have 'realistic' assumptions.[8] In similar terms, Machlup—in the Senior, Cairnes and Mill tradition—suggests that it is not the assumptions which are put to empirical tests but the predicted results; he then goes on to say that, if the assumptions are completely realistic and may all be tested directly, the scientist is limiting himself to raw empiricism, and, as a consequence, his work must remain within the immediately apprehended.[9]

Samuelson, on the other hand, observes that some realism, *per se*, may serve as a necessary check against those who would try to accomplish a great deal with too little information.[10] Robbins, somewhat less directly, avers that the basic

7. It is clear from our example that the test of the auxiliary assumption, i.e., the validity of the assumption itself, hinges on the particular form of the generative assumption. Thus, one generative assumption may point to a certain kind of auxiliary assumption, and find support in a given empirical finding; whereas, an alternative assumption—generative of the same hypothesis—would be denied by the same empirical results. Thus, in our example, a generative assumption which speaks in terms of regularly-recurring, more intensive recessions would find support for its nonstructural hypothesis by auxiliary evidence which points to an increasing ratio of minority group unemployment, where both minority group and total unemployment are rising; whereas, the same finding would support a structural unemployment hypothesis if its generative assumption and confirmation spoke in terms of technology and the lack of skills of selected peoples in the system.

8. M. Friedman, "The Methodology of Positive Economics", *Essays in Positive Economics* (Chicago: Chicago University Press, 1953), pp. 14-15.

9. F. Machlup, "The Problem of Verification in Economics", *Southern Economic Journal*, Vol. XXII, 1955, pp. 1-21.

10. P. Samuelson, "Theory and Realism: A Reply", *American Economic Review*, September, Vol. LIV, 1964, pp. 736-38.

postulates of economic analysis must conform to the facts of experience.[11] In effect, the main assumptions should be realistic.

By a realistic assumption one could have in mind simply a statement that describes a given event cogently and precisely in accordance with sensed data. On the other hand, realism could refer to an assumption that is confirmable directly or is otherwise well established in the discipline (let us call it a nonfalse assumption) and which may or may not carry descriptive implications. We shall employ the term in this second sense; that is, a realistic assumption is, to us, simply a nonfalse assumption.[12]

If a realistic assumption is confirmable directly, it has been so tested; if it is not confirmable directly, (a) it must not be disavowed, so indeed, if (b) it were possible to separate the assumption from the other elements with which it is inextricably mixed and to test it directly, one would expect that confirmation would result. The realistic assumption, therefore, does not have to be descriptively realistic, as is well evidenced by the assumption of a fourth or higher dimension in mathematics; and yet of course the assumption is realistic. The realistic assumption may even apply to a nonexisting institution; for example, free speech may serve as a realistic assumption in a model formulated by a theorist in a land where speech is not free, being realistic in the sense that it can be defined and demonstrated to have validity elsewhere under certain conditions. What we shall imply with respect to descriptive qualities is only this: If an assumption does happen to have a descriptive counterpart (e.g., the variation of freight rates as distance changes), the assumption must either duplicate or approximate (e.g., freight rates increase linearly with distance) the real condition in the economy to the extent that its existence and character (e.g., the cost of distance) is retained in the analysis. What is unrealistic is therefore: (1) An assumption or abstraction which violates its empirical base by presenting a false view of this base (e.g., freight costs decrease as distance increases). Or (2) an assumption or abstraction which denies or ignores the relevance of the phenomenon at hand. (Significantly, a denial might exist even though on the surface the identity in question is retained; for example, freight rates are defined to be linear with distance, but all buyers and sellers are assumed to be at opposite points in space so that in effect the assumption of space fails to add or subtract anything of substance to the derived

11. L. Robbins, *An Essay on the Nature and Significance of Economic Science* (London: Macmillan & Co., 1948), p. 75 where he observes that from an elementary fact of experience . . . the refined scales of relative valuations . . . we derive the theory of value; and on pp. 99-100; Economic analysis . . . "consists of deductions from a series of postulates, the *chief* of which are almost universal *facts of experience* . . ." (italics mine.) It is but a short step to T. W. Hutchison's position in his *The Significance and Basic Postulates of Economic Theory* (New York: Augustus M. Kelley, 1960 edition), p. 166 henceforth referred to as *Basic Postulates* that . . . "if one wants to get beyond a certain high level of abstraction, one has to begin more or less *from* the *beginning* with extensive empirical investigation." (italics mine.)

12. Friedman and Machlup often seem to view a realistic assumption as the equivalent of a readily observable event. (And see note 17.) Our category of realism does not require descriptive realism, though it will be seen to exclude the descriptively false.

theory.) In effect, the unrealistic assumption or abstraction is false,[13] even though from another standpoint, as we shall see, the model itself and the theory derived from it may well be valid.

IV

The question of realism of assumptions is basic to the much broader matter of types of theory and their uses. For our purposes, we shall distinguish between two kinds of theory, positive and normative. Positive theory, or more pointedly let us say positive economics, is designed to explain the existing and to predict the effect of changes in economic conditions (including small changes in prevailing institutions) on a given set of relationships. For its purposes, unrealistic assumptions may be used. Normative economics, on its part, is concerned with another economy, or, let us say more generally, with ideal nonexisting states; it formulates and describes the workings of that economy. Because it speaks of what ought to be, it has the double context of relating to the nonexisting and involving a use of value judgements or of quasi-value judgements, depending upon the speciousness of the theory and the viewpoint of its developers.[14] Significantly, normative economics may include the study of significant changes in the parameters (i.e., institutions) of an existing economy, such as a change from a fractional reserve banking system to one hundred per cent. reserves. We shall see that its interest generally demands as much realism in the assumptions as is possible.

It is unfortunately the case that positive economics has been stretched to include normative economics without recognition having been given to their structural differences. Because positive economics deals with the existing, or at best tends to predict states of the near-distant future, the validity of its predictions may be established, or soon established; hence the assumptions it uses may be

---

13. Assumptions may be classified as inspected or postulated, with the postulated association involving the elevation of an inspected concept to a more meaningful — or advanced theoretical — level. It is in jumping from an inspected concept to the postulated one that the scientist demonstrates his great ability. (See F. S. C. Northrup, *The Logic of the Sciences and the Humanities* [New York: The Macmillan Co., 1949], pp. 95 ff.). Now, the distinction between the assumptions is important to us because of the different degrees of assurance one may have with respect to each. Unlike the inspected concept, which, by the very meaning of the word inspected, is verifiable directly, the postulated assumption is never formally established quite so clearly. Thus, even when the consequence of the assumption is brought to test and revealed to be correct, we have on hand the system, if A then B, so if B *is* the case, all one might claim is that A has not been disconfirmed. Similarly, an alternative way for gaining faith in the postulated assumption, namely by verifying some concept which one might statistically correlate, or otherwise relate to it, cannot formally establish the validity of that postulated assumption. But, be this as it may, we can readily see that we may speak of realistic and unrealistic assumptions even if the assumption itself is a postulated one. Simply put, the postulated assumption is unrealistic when the empirical evidence stands contra to its correlated inspected concept.

Let us observe finally here in this note that if it were not for the prior use of the term false by others in connection with the inspected correlate, we would have preferred a more restricted and precise use of the term false. We would have preferred to employ the term false to refer not only to ignored data or to assumptions which have been disconfirmed, i.e., where the inspected concept or the inspected correlate is clearly at odds with the evidence, but to assumptions which are analytically misleading as well, i.e., the theorem derived from the assumptions is also disconfirmed. Again, we are not following our preference.

14. That positive science deals with what is and normative science with what ought to be is well established in the literature and I shall refer in this regard only to J. N. Keynes' *The Scope and Method of Political Economy* (New York: Kelley & Millman, 1955), 4th ed., p. 34. That normative science entails the use of value judgements to some greater or lesser extent is, similarly, well established, and T. W. Hutchison in his *Positive Economics and Policy Objectives* (London: George Allen and Unwin, 1964), pp. 40-41, states this idea capably by noting that: "Welfare economics developed as an attempt to make policy recommendations while dispensing with value judgements, or, at any rate, while reducing them to a minimum of one or two presuppositions generally acceptable by all reasonable men." F. S. C. Northrup, *op. cit.*, p. 287, possibly goes further by saying that normative science may actually involve a scientific-type of value judgement. ". . . theories designate a character of our universe . . . which go beyond the immediately sensed data . . ." and ". . . this *philosophical conception* in its epistemic correlation with the immediately apprehended data which provide its verification is to be *identified with* our *scientific criterion of* the correct *normative* social theory of culture." (Italics mine.)

unrealistic. For example, imagine with reference to our nonstructural unemployment hypothesis that because of contrasting data we cannot readily prove or disprove an increase in the severity of the business cycle, but we can show significantly high correlation over time between increases in total unemployment and the unemployment of a selected minority group, and we can predict, it would seem, total unemployment reasonably well on the basis of population growth. At best our generative assumption is not disconfirmed; it may actually be right or wrong. So, if our concern is less with explaining the basis for the minority group's unemployment than with describing its past and present unemployment, or predicting its unemployment in the near future, we may well be on safe grounds. But if we employ unrealistic assumptions in a normative way (e.g., should we apply our nonstructural unemployment hypothesis including its generative assumptions to a vastly different economy, say one which, *in fact*, because of its political—social—and economic institutions could not readily experience an increase in cycle intensities) not only may we become victims of false predictions,[15] but our policies will err. Indeed the true meaning of economic science tends to suffer from distortion as we become engaged in a play of art not science when we employ the methods of positive economics as if this economics were normative as well.[16] Let us see why this is so.

Consider, for example, Friedman's advocacy of flexible exchange rates and one hundred per cent. money, or the objections he raises to the Federal Reserve System in his volume on positive economics. Is he not espousing a 'policy set' based on nonexisting institutions, and does not this set really lie outside of positive science? If it does not, it would seem that positive economics includes normative properties, but then it would be anything and everything to all people. And if it is all inclusive, could it still be founded on unrealistic assumptions?[17] How can we confirm or disconfirm such kind of economic model, assuming the inherent logic of the argument?

Any system of economic thought allegedly based on models which work even though its assumptions are highly unrealistic must be confined—if it belongs

15. "Whatever the past success of H may be, should the hypothesis bear false contents, it may yield false predictions in the future." Melitz, *op. cit.*, p. 46.

16. W. Ross, *Business in a Free Society* (New York: Charles E. Merrill, Inc., 1966) presents this view and cites Joan Robinson, *Economic Philosophy* (Chicago: Aldine Publishing Co., 1962), pp. 13-14 in partial support.

In contrast, remember, in the positive economics of Friedman, Machlup, and others, indirect confirmation of the hypothesis supports the assumptions, which therefore may be empirically invalid. When, however, applying this method in normative economics — where the test of the hypothesis cannot be had — one is playing rather loosely with an unknown. So, if other things are equal, and an empirically valid assumption is available, it would seem that the theoretician would be better off using it. And see P. Samuelson, "Professor Samuelson on Theory and Realism: Reply," *op. cit.*

17. Friedman, *op. cit.*, pp. 14-15. "To be important, . . . , a hypothesis must be descriptively false in its assumptions; t takes account of, and accounts for, none of the many other attendant circumstances, since its very success shows them to be irrelevant for the phenomena to be explained."

Manifestly, reliable far-reaching hypotheses require considerable abstraction, and from this standpoint Friedman's willingness to have false assumptions may seem to be valid. But, see Melitz, *op. cit.*, p. 40 where he notes that: "In abstracting, we leave some facts out of consideration. This commits us to view that these facts do not matter, not to the assumption that the facts do not exist." And later on p. 41 — "Abstraction . . . does not necessitate the acceptance of false assumptions . . ." In our words, abstraction necessarily tends to yield unrealistic assumptions, implicitly if not explicitly too. And this natural condition is, of course, desirable provided what would otherwise be unrealistic assumptions actually do not matter; if, in fact, they do matter, error(s) will surely result. And see T. W. Hutchison, *Basic Postulates*, *op. cit.*, Chapter III where the idea permeates that beginning with too many highly simplified abstractions in hopes of raising the level of realism of a few of them tends to come to a dead end.

anywhere[18]—to the field of positive not normative economics. It is essentially by examining the predictions and/or the descriptive power of models in the light of past and present events that assurance of the relevance and validity of these models is gained. Without past or present test, either of exact or near duplicative order, relevance and validity cannot be assured. Now this is not to say that positive economics is unsuited for predicting any future state; rather, it is to say that positivism in our science is confined inherently to describing and explaining the past and the present and is able to predict a future state systematically if and only if the existing parameters (i.e., institutions) are left substantially unchanged.[19] Even here, let us reobserve, grave doubt has been cast on its use of unrealistic assumptions.[20] In any case, there is assuredly great need for history and the analysis of an existing system; more generally there is a vital place for positivism in science. But, what is being asserted is the related need for visualizing a noticeably different society than that which exists, and clearly the unrealism of the assumptions intrinsic to (and generally accepted in) positive economics limits sharply its predictiveness to societies for which the assumptions still work.

Positive economics, as suggested, has been used to evaluate and promote the nonexisting. This has been done via the use of *selected value judgements* which are so well accepted (or desired) that seemingly they no longer are considered to be value judgements.[21] Significantly, *to say the least*, value judgements designed to support *new institutions* may, at best, serve as the roots for a normative, not positive economics.[22]

Positive economics is made up of techniques of analysis which are claimed to yield testable, and hence refutable hypotheses. However, we have not seen 100 per cent. money in action in this century, nor observed the effectiveness of automatic controls and a world-wide system of flexible exchange rates as advocated by so many in the Chicago tradition. It would seem that we must establish whatever

18. Of course, writers in the Hutchison, Melitz, Samuelson tradition — and I might add here such economists as Myrdal and J. M. Keynes among many others — would dispute the acceptability of unrealistic assumptions in positive economics as well. They appear disposed in favor of the idea that the real base for positive economics is empirical validity of the important assumptions in the theory, as, for example, Samuelson, *op. cit.*, p. 1165, ". . . I only insisted that the validity of the *full* consequences of a theory implies the validity of the theory and so of its *minimal* assumptions." Since this matter is essentially vacuous to this paper's interest in normative economics, we shall carry the issue no further.

19. This matter of prediction via positive science raises some basic questions of an epistemological nature; e.g., how far removed from 'the real world' may a set of assumed conditions be and yet be acceptable in formulating scientific 'principles'? Thus we can *never* literally know the *precise* 'parameters' of the *present* economic world, for it is a trite, yet true, observation that the data with which we deal are *constantly* changing and our assumptions therefore *must* deviate to *some* extent, from 'real world' conditions. As a consequence, we perenially qualify our laws or 'principles' with the prefix, "*If* certain conditions exist, then certain consequences will follow." The degree of empirical relevance, therefore, usually depends upon the *closeness* of the correspondence between our assumptions and real-world conditions. So, as noted before, we are really speaking in terms of degrees of realism, more or less systematic predictiveness, and their like.

20. And again, see note 18.

21. Witness Friedman's introduction to his paper, "A Monetary and Fiscal Framework for Economic Stability," *op. cit.*, p. 134. The author states that: The basic long-run objectives shared, I am sure, by most economists are political freedom, economic efficiency and substantial equality of economic power." *But what does the last objective mean?* He goes on to derive as postulates certain propositions which he advises stem directly from these objectives, such as a monetary framework in a competitive order, a free market, however, that is defined, and the rule of the law. Then he analyzes 100 per cent. money, a related program of government expenditures, transfer payments and places emphasis on the personal income tax. What a curious twist of positive economics. To me, it seems much more like normative economics. And see T. W. Hutchison in his *Positive Economics and Policy Objectives* (London: George Allen and Unwin, 1964), p. 167 where he observes the frequent use of *well accepted* value judgements as if the science were denuded of our personal values.

22 M. L. Greenhut, *Microeconomics and the Space Economy* (Chicago: Scott Foresman Co., 1963), Chapters 4 and 12.

proof we can find for these normative systems by testing the validity of the other assumptions of the hypothesis and by being sure of the logic used in deriving any theory therefrom. Please observe, we do not go so far as to claim that one must be able to demonstrate directly the validity of all parts of the hypothesis, for surely the main operator in any model (e.g., the idea of 100 per cent. money) cannot be set forth as an accepted concept.[23] We do contend, however, that a substantial portion of the component parts of a normative hypothesis must be accepted. In other words, economists cannot tie a nonexisting institution (100 per cent. money) to *a set of unrealistic assumptions* which is part of a nontestable hypothesis that argues in favour of the new institution and have faith in the related policy.

V

Let us, then, consider positive economics as essentially an economics which explains as it describes, though defining it also to possess the ability to predict within the general confines of existing institutions. By its very nature and history, unrealistic assumptions, it is often claimed,[24] may be used. Let us regard normative economics as descriptive and predictive too, but unlike positive economics descriptive and predictive with respect to a set of nonexisting, usually desired institutions. By its very nature, the assumptions constituting the hypotheses of normative economics *must be* realistic,[25] or else they must be inconsequential to the hypotheses and, in effect, ignored via the process of abstraction. In the broad sense, of course, the matter of realism of the hypothesis is one of degree—*though certainly not taste.* But we must explain the full meaning of this vital idea and shall do this by reference to the theory of pure (perfect) competition.

On the postulational level, the proponents of pure competition theory select some undefined concepts, such as utility; they accept certain laws, such as diminishing returns, and develop them into demand and production functions which are treated as fundamental parts of the science; next they add some unrealistic assumptions to the developing framework, such as the existence of an infinite number of homogeneous buyers and sellers at a 'point' in space, with each possessed of perfect knowledge and free to enter or leave the market; moreover, capital and labor are assumed to be fully mobile, and prices are accepted as perfectly flexible, with no transport cost being defrayed or charged to anyone, *etc.* Now, from the standpoint of some economists who practice positive economics, these assumptions are valid, even though with respect to twentieth century

23. Such operator as 100 per cent. money approaches the role of a definitional assumption and following Machlup, *op. cit.*, p. 9 to this extent, we could consider it as a fundamental (heuristic) assumption that does not require individual or special test. Whatever we call it (e.g., the main operator as I have referred to it), it need not be realistic by way of reference to the existing society.

24. The recent disputes appearing in the *American Economic Review*, Volumes LIV, September 1964 and LV, December 1965, pp. 733-739 and 1151-1172 respectively, which involved Machlup and Samuelson and then Garb, Lerner, Massey and Samuelson suggest — even by the admission of Samuelson — that the majority of economists are probably still in the unrealistic camp. One would gather from Samuelson's references to physics that physicists have been leaning to empirical validating of assumptions. As we will later observe, if welfarists, and other like positive economists, would accept the obvious truth that they are really engaged in normative not positive economics, added argument to the cause of empirically verified assumptions will be seen to prevail.

25. T. W. Hutchison, *Positive Economics and Policy Objectives, op. cit.*, p. 192 " . . . normative-evaluative statements and theories are not in the relevant sense empirically testable and refutable . . . "

capitalism they are rather tortuously removed from reality. Do they explain, do they furnish hypotheses which work, do they yield an advanced science of economics; in short, what do we gain from the theory they yield?

Pure competition theory, we know, offers many descriptive and explanatory insights to capitalism. For selected issues, it predicts reasonably well, and, in fact, may provide focal points for prescription. In many respects (i.e., in the non-prescriptive sense), it is a branch of positive science by our definition, though during recent centuries Adam Smith's counterpart to our theory of pure competition was surely used as a norm for many lands. As we have seen, many of the assumptions of pure competition are false; especially today the fundamental properties of the theory are quite unrealistic, and, as we have suggested, there is great advantage in deriving other systems of thought.

Take the concept of oligopoly; in fact assume a well developed normative economics based along the lines of oligopoly theory. What would be (or might be) its points of difference with pure competition?

For one thing, it would contain a model which would include primitive (undefined) concepts, such as possibly 'the industry.' The model would be likely to utilize and hence include a vast body of accepted doctrine, such as the law of demand, a production function based on diminishing returns, and the like. Also it would employ a set of assumptions which compared to those in pure competition theory may be *more* realistic. We might find, for example, that a distance between people and institutions is hypothesized; moreover, advanced technology and limited demand may be postulated, with a less than infinite demand for the product of a firm being designated to reflect the fine line that distinguishes our present day set of differentiated and alternative products from the small group of standardized products one might well have found a century ago. Indeed, the aforementioned limited demand might be specified to reflect the poverty of some group of people (in fact, an underdeveloped nation could be our subject area of interest), or the limited demand might be said to reflect the spatial restrictions to markets that relate to the cost of shipment, the need for quick delivery (perishability), and their like.[26] Manifestly, the theory derived from this set of assumptions might well take issue with pure competition theory, at least in some respects.

It is fundamental that any alternative (new) theory must be checked against existing or past events, if said theory is 'positive' in nature. On the other hand, if the theory is so arranged as to refer to forces not *now* prevailing (e.g., assume that no undue artificial restraints on entry are conceived to prevail in the form of patent pools and extensions, or that no collusion at all is defined to be possible in any form, *etc.*), and the use of the theory is for normative purposes alone, then the related and derived theory would be more normative than positive, inveighing as it would in favour of what ought to be or might be. *Proof* of its consequences, validity, and applicability—apart from the need for proper use

26. M. L. Greenhut, *op. cit.*, Chapters 5-8.

of the tools of the discipline—would then depend on the direct acceptance or rejection of the assumptions which form the theory. And if the excluded assumptions (hence the unrealistic assumptions implicit in the model) happen to be critical, the normative theory would mislead. More specifically, because the consequences of the normative theory cannot be tested, since the model, itself, applies to the 'fanciful' not to the existing, any disaffirmation or failure to disconfirm must, *ceteris paribus*, be attributed to the component parts of the related hypotheses. Phrased somewhat differently, if the component parts (i.e., concepts, statements, and assumptions) of the hypothesis are accepted because they are realistic, the related normative theory, *ceteris paribus*, attains scientific status.

Stated as forcibly and directly, but yet as delicately as possible, it would seem that present-day myopia in economics involves the danger of misusing positive economics.[27] Most fundamental, when economists in economically advanced nations seek to apply a model which does not conform to the facts, and do so promiscuously even with respect to new nations which do not have the fundamental institutions, much less technology, demand, and non-space environment of classic theory, their application must often give misleading or irrelevant answers.[28] Let us recognize traditional competitive theory for what it really is: A body of early thought which helps light up the way so that someday economists will create new theories that *answer* the problems of *their day* sufficiently well to be understood and accepted by practically all.[29] As the chemist and physicist long ago realized, such scientific advances require willingness to place the old in a proper perspective, to challenge the old, and, in fact, to discard the simple and the false, whenever possible. The hope that such advance will someday happen in economics—in the fullest sense—not only underscores this paper but points to a change that is long overdue.

Texas A & M University.

27. The welfarists who believe they are able to apply value judgements of such genera lacceptability that they are still in the field of positive science are surely stretching their point (and see A. C. Pigou, *Economics of Welfare*, 3rd ed. [London: Macmillan, 1929], p. 5). Correspondingly, those who apparently believe they are able to postulate objectives and then discuss policy without indulging in persuasion are, in this writer's opinion, taking great liberties with positivism. The view expressed by F. S. C. Northrup, *op. cit.*, where he notes that value judgements may be taken outside of the plane of pure art and given scientific form "when correlated with the experimentally verified physical theories of nature" has intrinsic merit because he applies such theories and philosophical conception to the end of formulating "the correct *normative* social theory of all time," (p. 287; italics mine). If our labels were surer, our methodological disputes might be fewer.

28. M. L. Greenhut, "Needed — A Return to the Classics in Regional Economic Development Theory," *Kyklos*, Vol. XIX, 1966.

29. As Alfred Marshall observedi n his *Principles of Economics*, 8th ed. (New York: The Macmillan Co., 1920), p. 37, and I paraphrase: every age and country has its own problems, and new social conditions will be likely to require new economic doctrines.

PART II

SPATIAL MICROECONOMICS

METROECONOMICA

Vol. IX | Dicembre 1957 | Fasc. III

THE PRICING POLICIES OF A SPATIAL MONOPOLIST *

by Melvin L. Greenhut, Tallahassee and Ralph W. Pfouts, Chapel Hill (U. S. A.)

This paper examines several aspects of the pricing policies of a spatial monopolist. It determines the effects on freight absorption of the distribution of buyers within the trading area. It examines the effects on freight absorption of an extension of the monopolist's trading area that follows from reduction of freight rates. These theoretical arguments show how spatial dispersion of buyers conditions economic development. They lead to our final point that freight costs limit the pricing power of a monopolist and may lead him to adopt policies quite different from those usually ascribed to monopolists.

Throughout this paper we will assume that the monopolist wants to (or is forced to) sell at a non-discriminatory f. o. b. mill price. By this we mean that the seller's price at his mill is the same to all buyers, and all buyers pay full freight costs. It is well known that even with this uniform treatment of buyers by the seller there can be freight absorption.

I

To provide a background, we begin with a graphic demonstration of a simple case.

We assume the existence of two buyers for the monopolist's product. One buyer is situated at the monopolistic seller's mill and does not pay any freight charges; the other buyer is situated some distance from the mill and must pay freight charges. We assume further that the two buyers have identical linear demand curves for the monopolist's product, shown in Fig. 1 as the straight line Bq'.

Since the distant buyer must pay a freight charge, that we will denote by R, his demand curve is displaced downward a distance R in Fig. 1; i. e., it is the line Aq''. This downward shift of the demand curve reflects the fact that the effective price of the good to the distant buyer is the seller's price plus the freight cost per unit. Because the buyer near the seller does not pay freight costs, his demand curve is Bq'. Horizontal summation of the buyers' demand curves yields

(*) The authors are indebted to Professor Donald Dewey of Duke University for suggesting many improvements.

total demand. Fig. 1 shows this total in the form of the kinked line *BCD*. Marginal to this average revenue function is the discontinuous curve *BFGq*. In nonspatial conceptions, total demand takes the form

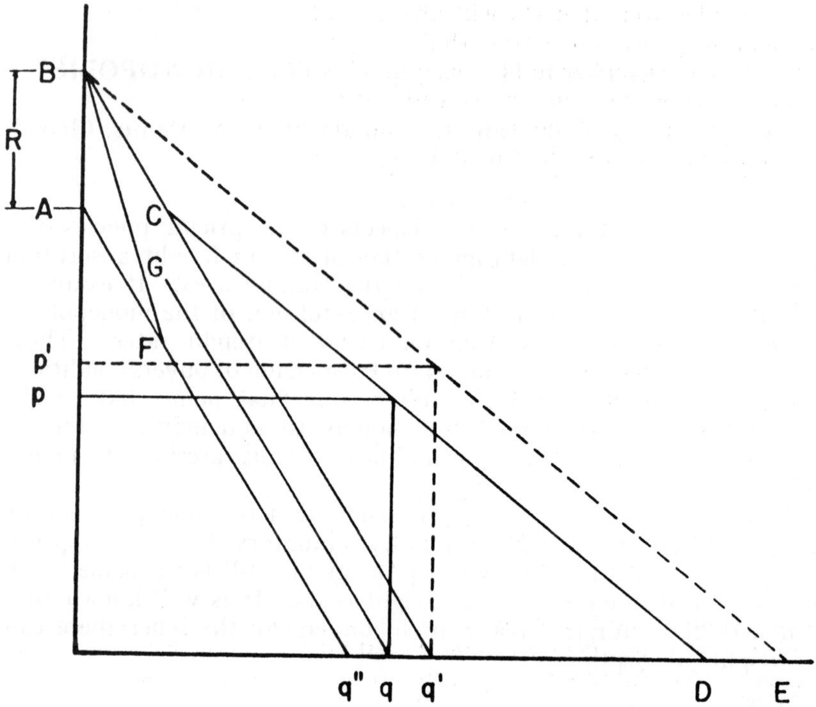

Fig. 1.

of the dashed line *BE*. With the seller and his buyers at the same point, the marginal revenue curve *Bq'* becomes relevant.

We ignore costs of production in the present illustration chiefly to keep the diagram uncluttered. This is a permissible omission because production costs do not require locational distinction in models concerned with general price policies. Under conditions of the diagram, monopoly price and output is established at the point where marginal revenue equals zero. For the actual demand curve this occurs at q; the corresponding price is indicated by p. For the hypothetical curve that would exist if there were not any freight costs, marginal revenue becomes zero at q'; the corresponding price is p'. It is clear that p is smaller than p', hence there is freight absorption (¹). Monopoly price is lower when spatial costs exist than

(¹) We use the term freight absorption to indicate the difference between net price with transportation costs taken into account and net price exluding all considerations of transportation costs. This is a different usage from that followed, for example, in basing point literature. In basing point discussions, freight absorption is said to exist if delivered prices in two markets differ by

when they are absent [1]. It is clear from Fig. 1 that a negatively sloped demand curve of decreasing elasticity will always cause freight absorption since the marginal revenue curve of the demand curve that includes freight costs will always fall below and to the left of the marginal revenue curve that does not take freight costs into account. This conclusion obviously holds in the general case in which [2] costs of production are considered?

The foregoing discussion may be restated by writing a linear demand equation for the buyer located near the seller as

$$p = a + bx' \text{ , or}$$

(1) $$x' = \frac{p - a}{b} ,$$

where $a > 0$ and $b < 0$. Here p and x' are price and quantity of the good, respectively, and a and b are constants in the demand equation. But for the distant buyer, a freight cost per unit of good, denoted by R, must be included. Hence we have

$$p + R = a + bx'' \text{ , or}$$

(2) $$x'' = \frac{p - a + R,}{b} ,$$

where a and b are the same as in and $R \leq 2a - 4p$ (1). This latter condition is included to preclude the situation in which the marginal revenue curve changes from positive to negative and back to positive again.

Then total quantity sold by the monopolist is

$$x = x' + x'' .$$

And his total revenue, since he does not practice price discrimination, is

(3) $$px = \frac{2p^2 - 2pa + pR}{b}$$

less than the unit cost of transportation between the markets. Our usage is similar to the concept of tax absorption in the literature of public finance.

(1) Cf. M. Greenhut: *Effects of Excise Tax and Freight Cost: A Geometrical Clarification*, « Southern Economic Journal », Vol. XXI (1954-55), pp. 330-335, where it is shown that, in the general case, the impact on monopoly price of spatial cost (freight cost) is greater than the impact on monopoly price of an equal amount of excise tax.

(2) But opposite results hold for the less realistic case of increasing demand elasticity as price falls. Cf., for example, D. Dewey: *A Reappraisal of F. O. B. Pricing and Freight Absorption*, « Southern Economic Journal », Vol. XXII (1955-56), pp. 48-54, especially p. 50. Also, M. Greenhut: *Plant Location in Theory and in Practice*, «Chapel Hill, University of North Carolina Press», pp. 50-57, 157-159, 309-311.

Consequently, the revenue-maximizing price can be found by

$$\frac{d\,(px)}{dp} = \frac{4p - 2a + R}{b} = 0\ , \text{ or}$$

$$p = \frac{a}{2} - \frac{R}{4}\,.$$

If there were no freight costs, R would not appear in the preceding equations and monopoly price would be $a/2$. Thus the freight absorption is $R/4$. It may be noticed that the freight absorption is not $R/2$, as has often been argued (4).

II

We will now consider a somewhat more general model of the buyer's market. We assume that all buyers have identical linear demand equations similar to (1). We also assume the existence of several towns or groups of buyers such that within a single town or group of buyers freight costs per unit are the same to all buyers. We let n_i indicate the number of buyers in the ith town or group of buyers. The quantitity of the good sold in the ith town or purchased by the ith group of buyers is thus

$$x_i = \frac{n_i p - n_i a + n_i R_i}{b}\,, \tag{5}$$

where R_i is the freight cost per unit paid by each buyer in the ith town, and

$$a - 2p \geq \frac{\sum\limits_i niRi}{\sum\limits_i ni}\,.$$

This condition corresponds to the condition

$$R \leq 2a - 4p$$

in the simpler case and serves the same purpose. It there are k towns, total sales are shown by

$$x = \sum_{i=1}^{k} x_i = \frac{p \sum\limits_{i=1}^{k} n_i - a \sum\limits_{i=1}^{k} n_i + \sum\limits_{i=1}^{k} n_i R_i}{b}\,. \tag{6}$$

(4) Cf. A. Smithies: *Optimum Location in Spatial Competition*, « Journal of Political Economy », Vol. XLIX (1941), pp. 423-439, especially p. 420. Also, D. P. Locklin: *The Economics of Transportation*, 3rd ed. (Chicago, Irwin, 1951), p. 22. Perhaps the emphasis on the case of spatial price discrimination by such writers as A. Lösch: *Die räumliche Ordnung der Wirtschaft*, (Jena: Gustav Fischer, 1944), p. 104, and E. Hoover: *Spatial Price Discrimination*, «Review of Economic Studies», Vol. IV, 1935-1936, pp. 182-191, has inadvertently fostered an incorrect view.

Total revenue is

$$(7)\qquad px = \frac{p^2 \sum_i n_i - ap \sum_i n_i + p \sum_i n_i R_i}{b} .$$

And the revenue-maximizing price is found by

$$\frac{d(px)}{dp} = \frac{2p \sum_i n_i - a \sum_i n_i + \sum_i n^2 R_i}{b} = 0 \text{ , or}$$

$$(8)\qquad p = \frac{1}{2}\left(a - \frac{\sum_i n_i R_i}{\sum_i n_i .} \right) .$$

From equation (8) it is clear that if there were no freight costs monopoly price would be $a/2$. Thus the amount of freight absorption is

$$(9)\qquad A = \frac{1}{2} \; \frac{\sum_i n_i R_i}{\sum_i n_i} :$$

i. e., the freight absorption is one-half of the weighted mean of per unit freight costs.

If we compare the absorption formula of (9) with the absorption in the case of two buyers considered in the previous section, the results of the simplified case agree with the more general formula. In the simplified case one buyer had no freight costs because he was situated near the seller, while the other buyer had a unit freight cost denoted by R. Hence one-half the weighted mean of the unit freight costs to buyers is

$$\frac{1}{2} \; \frac{0 \cdot 1 + R \cdot 1}{2} = \frac{R}{4} ,$$

and this is the result found directly in the simplified case.

The analysis of this section holds only for the case of identical linear demand functions for all buyers. It may be observed that a particular dispersion or locational pattern of buyers was not assumed in obtaining these results.

Inspection of (9) shows that distant buyers, with large freight costs, cause large freight absorption. Hence it is clear that the geographical distribution of the buyers within the trading area of a spatial monopolist is crucial to the determination of the amount of freight absorption. In a related manner, it is of vital influence on monopoly price formation.

The consequences of the principle of the preceding paragraph for economic development can be visualized by considering an example. Suppose the monopolist is situated in a metropolis surrounded by a relatively undeveloped hinterland. If most buyers are situated in or near the metropolis, there will be relatively little freight absorption (1). Low freight absorption in turn offers small inducement for development of the hinterland. Thus, if the buyer is near the seller freight charges and freight absorption are small and little incentive prevails to relocate at a distance. At distant sites, the buyer must pay heavy freight charges; freight absorption will be small if he is unimportant. Prospective developers of hinterland areas are limited in number and program by the influence of freight costs (2). The gregarious bent of people to locate near each other, so often noted in social theory, gains reinforcement from this economic force that retards dispersion.

Economic retardation of movement to hinterland regions need not continue indefinitely. Once the movement begins to the outer part of the monopolist's trading area, freight absorption increases. The associated reduction in delivered price to distant points serves to accelerate the movement into regions which previously offered inadequate economic position (3). The influence of freight costs on dispersion is thus wave-like in effect. Before the movement begins, low freight absorption retards location in the hinterland. After the movement has taken shape, spatial economic forces joint to make distant places desirable. As remote areas become populated the social force of gregarious concentration reapperars to support the movement into new areas. The spatial regularity of locations of individuals (4) has obvious influence on business and industrial location and other economic phenomena (5).

---

(1) A. Lösch, *op. cit.*, pp. 99-102, stresses the catering to local demand on account of greater numbers of these buyers as well as their stronger demand, *cet. par.* Patently, the impact of space on price is small in this type of market concentration of buyers in the city.

(2) E. Schneider: *Bemerkung zu einer Theorie der Raumwirtschaft*, « Econometrica », Vol. III (1935), pp. 79-101, demonstrates that the size of the market area is inversely proportional to the square of the freight rate.

(3) Cf. H. Ritschl: *Reine and historische Dynamik des Standortes der Erzengungszweige*, Schmoller Jahrbuch für Gesetzgebung, Vol. LI (1927), pp. 813-870, where the author stresses the impact of low delivered prices on market area extensions and the protective tariff nature of the high freight rate. A. Marshall: *Principles of Economics*, 8th ed. (London, MacMillan, 1920), pp. 273-277, stresses the industrial concentration effect on producers of low freight costs while correspondingly suggesting that with lower delivered prices buyers may move outward. And see G. Ackley's article on price policies, pp. 302-315 in the study *Indistrial Location and Natural Resources*, (National Resources Planning Board, Washington, D. C., 1943), where the practice of freight absorption through the equalizing delivered price system is indicated to encourage buyer location in the hinterland.

(4) G. K. Zipf: *Human Behavior and the Principle fo Least Effort* (Cambridge, Mass., Harvard University Press, 1949).

(5) P. Sargent Florence: *Investment, Location, and Size of Plant*, (Cambridge, Cambridge University Press, 1948); A. Lösch: *op. cit.*, Part IV.

III

The impact of freight costs on economic development has many aspects. Not only can we speak about the influence on freight absorption of a larger proportion of distant buyers within a fixed sales radius but we can also ascertain the effect on absorption of sales to still more distant buyers who are brought within the spatial monopolist's sales radius by a reduction of freight costs. We investigate the question whether freight absorption rises in this case in the same way as it does when buyers move away from the seller but remain in a fixed trading area. We will see that the relationship of distant buyers to freight absorption does hold here as it did before. Also, we will see that price policy depends on dispersion of buyers and on the amount of freight reduction responsible for the extension of the sales radius.

We hypothesize now the same conditions as in the linear model of the preceding section, except that the freight rate is assumed to be lower by an amount sufficient to reduce freight costs per unit by ΔR_i for each of the old buyers. New buyers previously beyond the trading area may now be brought into the trading area by the lower freight rate; the freight costs per unit to new buyers are indicated by R_j.

Before the freight rate reduction, freight absorption was given by

$$(10) \qquad A_1 = \frac{1}{2} \; \frac{\sum_i n_i R_i}{N_i},$$

where we use N_i to denote the total number of buyers in the old equilibrium. Applying the same formula to the new situation, we find that the freight absorpion is

$$(11) \qquad A_2 = \frac{1}{2} \; \frac{\sum_i n_i (R_i + \Delta R_i) + \sum_i n_j R_j}{N_i + N_j},$$

where N_j stands for the total number of new buyers, and n_j is the number of buyers in the jth.new town or group

To find the difference in freight absorption in the two cases, we subtract (10) from (11). When this subtraction is carried through we obtain

$$(12) \quad A_2 - A_1 = \frac{1}{2} \left\{ \frac{\sum_i n_j R_j + \sum_i \Delta n_i R_i}{N_i + N_j} - \frac{N_j}{N_i + N_j} \; \frac{\sum_i n_i R_i}{N_i} \right\}.$$

If the right member of (12) is positive, freight absorption increases with the extension of the trading area; if it is negative, freight absorption diminishes with the extension of the trading area. Equation (12) can be translated into the following form:

Change in Freight Absorption =

$$= \frac{1}{2}\left(\text{Average Change in Freight Costs} - \frac{2N_j}{N_i + N_j}\,\text{Old Absorption}\right).$$

There is no way to state definitely on the basis of (12) that freight absorption is either greater or smaller in the old as compared with the new trading area, but certain possibilities can be indicated.

One possibility is that only a small number of new buyers will be brought into the trading area by the freight rate reduction. In this case, if there was a large number of buyers in the old trading area, it would be quite possible for $\Sigma n_i \Delta R_i$ to be larger in absolute value than $\Sigma n_j R_j$, because of the small size of N_j. Since the ΔR's will be negative because they represent freight cost reductions, the first expression in the brackets in (12) can be negative. The second expression in the brackets in (12) will always have a negative effect since it consists of positive numbers but is prefixed by a minus sign. Thus if $\Sigma n_i \Delta R_i$ is larger in absolute value than $\Sigma n_j R_j$, There will be less absorption in the new trading area than there was in the old. The empirical reflection of this case requires that a relatively small number of new buyers be brought into the trading area by the freight rate reduction or else that the ΔR_i's be inordinately large as a result of large freight reductions to old buyers.

Freight absorption also decreases with expansion of trading area if the first expression in the braces in (12) is positive but smaller in absolute value than the second expression which will always be negative. Such a result could follow if the number of new buyers and their freight costs were not large enough to offset both the $\Sigma n_i \Delta R_i$ and the second term. If, however, expansion brings a large number of new buyers and high freight costs, freight absorption will rise. In this case $\Sigma n_j R_j$ would be larger in absolute amount than $\Sigma n_i \Delta R_i$ by an amount great enough to overcome also the second expression which is always negative. It is only in this last case that freight absorption will be greater in the new market area than it was in the old.

A simple illustration of this last type of case is found when a small manufacturer with purely local sales is able on account of freight reduction to expand his market area to include distant places. If there exist towns at many or all of the sides around the seller's plant, with numerous buyers in each town being drawn within the seller's market area, freight absorption will be great. The high importance of this large number of additional buyers accounts for this result. The effect of lower freight rates then would be lower net-mill price as the spatial monopolist responds to the stimulus of many new distant buyers with a price policy that seeks to keep delivered price to these buyers near the delivered price that would have been used if they were the only buyers ([1]).

In contrasting manner, if distant buyers are few and unimportant, freight absorption from lower freight rates will be slight and seller's net-mill price will go up. In these cases, where $\Sigma\, n_i\, \Delta\, R_i$ is larger or slightly smaller in absolute value than $\Sigma\, n_j R_j$, thus causing the first expression in (12) to be either negative or less in absolute value than the second, the distant buyers are so relatively unimportant that the delivered price to them will be much higher than it would have been if these distant buyers were the only buyers. This case (i. e., relatively even dispersion of buyers over an area) exhibits the fact that in spatial pricing the buyers nearest to the seller have the strongest demand, *ceteris paribus*, and consequently in fixing monopoly price, the seller caters more to these proximate demands than to distant ones. Under such spatial alignment, freight rate reduction leads to higher net mill price. The extension of sales radius that follows from lower freight rates is smaller than that which would arise when buyers are grouped in large numbers at distant places. Again it is clear that social proclivities work simultaneously with economic forces ([2]).

In summary it may be said that freight absorption decreases with expansion of trading area, if the number of new buyers and their freight costs are small. I. e., the first expression in braces in (12) is either negative or smaller in absolute value than the second expression because $\Sigma\, n_j R_j$ is small. It is only when the new buyers and their freight costs are sufficiently large in total that the freight absorption will be greater in the new trading area. I. e., $\Sigma\, n_j R_j$, the only positive term above the line in (12), must be large enough to outweigh the other terms. The principle that the more important the distant buyers the greater is the freight absorption, holds for expansion of the trading area as well as for movements within a trading area. This is true because $\Sigma\, n_j R_j$ is the only term in (12) that repre-

---

([1]) This price (which, of course, in also the same as would be the discriminatory price) can be visualized readily by reference back to Figure 1. If all buyers were located at the same distance, the aggregated demand curve that would compare with curve *BCD* would extend from point *A* parallel to the *CD* extension of curve *BCD*. Its associated marginal revenue curve would be Aq'' and its monopoly price (at abscissa point q'') equal to $\frac{1}{2}\, OA$. In contrast, monopoly price along curve *BCD* is (at abscissa point q) equal to $\frac{1}{2}\, OA$ plus one half of the distance between point *A* and imagined point *F* drawn by extension of *CD* to the vertical axis.

([2]) Of course, the grouped buyers at a distance may be located so far from the seller that any attempt to bring them into his sales radius without price discrimination would require such large freight absorption as to cause, through the associated lower net-mill price, a greater dollar revenue loss on sales to local buyers than is made up on sales to this distant group. In this extreme case of heterogeneous dispersion, sales radius could shrink clear back to the seller's locale, thus not being carried out so far as would have occurred if the distant buyers were spread out over the whole area.

sents the freight costs of the new buyers, and it is also the only term in (12) that can be positive and thus show increased freight absorption in the new trading area.

Returning to our example of a monopolist in a metropolis surrounded by an undeveloped hinterland, we see that the effects of freight costs are also likely to vary if an extension of trading area occurs. An extension which follows from freight reduction will decrease freight absorption when there are few buyers in the undeveloped hinterland. Delivered price to distant places stays high. This price result will defeat the high expectations of distant developers that were based on freight absorption in the old area. But again, once an outward movement gains momentum and distant buyers become more numerous, the rate of freight absorption will increase. In turn, the outward movement will be accelerated.

IV

The effects of spatial costs on the pricing policies of a spatial monopolist may be considered in a manner different from that of the preceding sections. In this new approach, we will not be directly concerned with the geographical dispersion of buyers but instead will work with general relations that ordinarily are either observed or assumed to be true. In this development we abadon the assumption of linear demand functions, and we introduce costs of production.

The first relation that we assume is a demand equation of the type

$$p = f(x, \bar{k}) \ , \tag{13}$$

where x, the quantity sold, is an independent variable, and $\bar{k}$ is freight cost per unit of good sold or average freight cost for all buyers, [1] given by

$$\bar{k} = \frac{1}{x} \sum_{i=1}^{m} r_i D_i x_i \ , \tag{14}$$

where i represents the various buyers served by the monopolist; r_i, D_i and x_i are the rate, distance, and quantity, repectively, for the ith buyer, and $x = \sum_i x_i$. In connection with (13) we assume that

$$\frac{\partial f}{\partial x} < 0 \ ; \ \frac{\partial f}{\partial \bar{k}} < 0 \ . \tag{15}$$

---

(1) It should be specifically noted that our concept of freight cost per unit of good sold differs from the system of mean freight rate used in section II. Here, our concept $\bar{k}$ refers to the freight costs that are allocated over each unit of good. In section II, we considered the mean freight rate weighted by the number of buyers at each rate.

The first inequality represents the usual assumptions concerning demand equations. The second inequality is best appreciated by recalling the suggestion of the preceding sections of the paper that the mean freight rate cost is a determining variable of demand in space. As such, this inequality represents the depressive influence of freight costs on price, i. e., it represents the fact that distant buyers regard freight costs as a part of the price of the good. In connection with (14) we observe that

$$\frac{\partial \bar{k}}{\partial r} = \sum_{i=1}^{m} \frac{\partial \bar{k}}{\partial r_i} = \sum_i \frac{D_i x_i}{x} > 0 ; \tag{16}$$

$$\frac{\partial k}{\partial x} = \frac{1}{x}\left(\sum_i r_i D_i \frac{\partial x_i}{\partial x} + \sum_i D_i x_i \frac{\partial r_i}{\partial x}\right) - \sum_i \frac{r_i D_i x_i}{x^2} = 0 .$$

These statements are obviously true. We also postulate a relationship between freight rate and quantity hauled,

$$r_i = g_i(x_i) \ , \quad (i = 1, \ldots, m) \ . \tag{17}$$

It must also be recognized that distance will affect the freight rate; i. e., the tapering principle that lower rates are associated with longer hauls is not rejected. But since distance is constant from the viewpoint of a fixed buyer, all distance effects in (16) are subsumed in the shape of the g-function. In connection with (16) we assume that

$$\frac{dr_i}{dx_i} < 0 , \tag{18}$$

e. g., carload lots travel at a lower rate than less-than-carload lots, or heavy traffic to a terminal reduces the rate. From (18) it is clear that

$$\frac{\partial r_i}{\partial x} = \frac{d r_i}{d x_i} \cdot \frac{\partial x_i}{\partial x} < 0 . \tag{19}$$

Finally we state total cost as a function of output:

$$C = h(x) \ . \tag{20}$$

The monopolist's profit is given by

$$\pi = px - C \ . \tag{21}$$

Then making use of equations (13), (14), (17), (20) and (21), we seek the monopolist's maximum-profit output by using

$$\frac{\partial \pi}{\partial x} = p + x\left(\frac{\partial f}{\partial x} + \frac{\partial f}{\partial k}\frac{\partial k}{\partial x}\right) - \frac{dC}{dx} = 0 ,$$

or more specifically

$$\frac{\partial \pi}{\partial x} = p + x \left(\frac{\partial f}{x} + \frac{\partial f}{\partial \bar{k}} \; \frac{x \sum\limits_i D_i x_i \frac{\partial r_i}{\partial r_i} \frac{\partial x_i}{\partial x} + \sum\limits_i r_i D_i \frac{\partial x_i}{\partial x}}{x^2} - \right.$$

$$\left. - \sum_i r_i D_i x_i \right) - \frac{dC}{dx} = 0 \, .$$

For simplicity of notation we write the preceding equation as

$$(22) \qquad p + x \left[\frac{\partial f}{\partial x} + \frac{\partial f}{\partial \bar{k}} - \left(\frac{\partial \bar{k}}{\partial r} \frac{\partial r}{\partial x} + \frac{\partial \bar{k}}{\partial x} \right) \right] = \frac{dC}{dx} \, .$$

When (22) is trasformed into elasticities we obtain

$$(23) \qquad p\,(1 + \eta_{xp}^{-1} + \varepsilon_{p\bar{k}}\, \varepsilon_{\bar{k}r}\, \varepsilon_{rx} + \varepsilon_{p\bar{k}}\, \varepsilon_{\bar{k}x}) = \frac{dC}{dx} \, .$$

In (23) η_{xp} is the elasticity of demand and is, of course, negative. The first of the four additional elasticities is $\varepsilon_{p\bar{k}}$, the elasticity of price with respect to mean freight costs; it is negative because of its dependence on the second inequality following (15). The second of the additional elasticities $\varepsilon_{\bar{k}r}$, the elasticity of mean freight cost with respect to freight rate, is positive because its sign depends on the first inequality following (16). The third elasticity ε_{rx} is the elasticity of freight rate with respect to quantity. It is negative because its sign depends on the inequalities in (18) or (19). Consequently, the third term in the parentheses in (23) is positive because it is a product of two negative factors and one positive factor.

The last term in parentheses in (23) is the product of the elasticity $\varepsilon_{p\bar{k}}$, already noted as a negative quantity, and $\varepsilon_{\bar{k}x}$, the elasticity of freight costs with respect to quantity sold. This last elasticity can be either positive or negative since it depends on the second inequality following (16). It is clear from observation of that inequality that a large responsiveness of freight rate reduction to an increase in size of shipment will tend to make $\varepsilon_{\bar{k}x}$ negative, and a small responsiveness will tend to make it positive. If it is negative, the last term in parentheses will be positive; if the elasticity is positive the last term will be negative. The righthand member of (23) is, of course, the marginal cost of production.

The next point which we want to establish is that the elasticities in equation (23) may limit the monopoly power of the spatial monopolist. To approach this point we begin by recalling that the equation [1]

---

[1] Cf. for example J. R. Hicks: *Annual Survey of Economic Theory: The Theory of Monopoly*, « Econometrica », Vol. III (1935), pp. 1-20, reprinted in « A. E. A. Readings in Price Theory », Stigler and Boulding, eds., (Chicago, Irwin, 1952) pp. 361-83, especially pp. 363-4.

$$p\,(1 + \eta_{xp}^{-1}) = \frac{dC}{dx}\,, \tag{24}$$

has often been used to demonstrate the exploitative power of a monopolist. It is clear from an inspection of (24) that a monopolist will sell only in an elastic portion of his demand schedule, because it is only in such a case that he can price above marginal cost. If η_{xp}^{-1} is a negative fraction, as it is when demand is elastic, the quantity in parentheses in (24) will be a positive fraction, and it will be possible for the monopolist to price above marginal cost. Thus any influence that introduces a positive numerical value inside the parentheses in (24) will reduce or overcome the exploitative powers of the monopolist, i. e., it will reduce or overcome his power to price above marginal cost.

As a consequence of the preceding paragraph, we observe that the ε's in equation (23) may serve to diminish the monopoly power of a spatial monopolist. Equation (23) differs from equation (24) by the inclusion of the last two terms in the parentheses ([1]). Of these two terms, the first, $\varepsilon_{pk}\varepsilon_{\bar{k}r}\,\varepsilon_{rx}$, has a positive sign because, as we have previously noticed, $\varepsilon_{\bar{k}p}$ is negative, $\varepsilon_{\bar{k}r}$ is positive, and ε_{rx} is negative. Then the term in question is the product of two negative factors and one positive factor and is itself positive. Hence this term militates against monopoly power.

The last term in parentheses in (23) is the product of the negative quantity ε_{pk} and the ambiguously signed $\varepsilon_{\bar{k}x}$. Thus the last term may be either positive or negative; if it is positive, it further reduces monopoly power; if it is negative, it works in favor of the monopolist. On purely theoretical grounds, it is not possible to assert that it is more probable that the elasticity in question will be either positive or negative. This is true because we can say nothing with finality about the relative sizes of the positive term $x\,\Sigma\, r_i D_i\,\frac{\partial x_i}{\partial x}$ and the the negative terms $x\,\Sigma\,\frac{\partial r_i}{\partial x}\,D_i\,x_i$ and $-\;\Sigma\, r_i D_i x_i$ in the inequality following (16).

V

Two inferences for economic policy may be drawn from the preceding discussion. The first inference is based on the observation that

---

([1]) Perhaps is should be pointed out that the elasticity of demand for a product will be different if transportation costs are present from what it would be if there were no transportation costs. This is due to the shifting of the demand curve as a result of freight costs. Thus, we do not merely add the new elasticities in going from (24) to (23); we also alter the numerical value of the elasticity of demand. Putting this point in another way, the elasticity of demand at a given output will be different if the demand equation is $p = f\,(x)$ than if it is $p = f\,(x, \bar{k})$.

it is quite possible, perhaps quite likely, that spatial influences limit monopoly power under non-discriminatory f. o. b. mill pricing. On this ground it would appear that economic policy should support this type of spatial pricing. There is nothing new about this recommendation, but it gains added theoretical support from our argument.

The second inference relates to sign of the ambiguous elasticity ε_{kr}. From the second inequality following (16), we observe that the derivitive $\frac{\partial r_i}{\partial x}$, since it is negative, adds to the likelihood of the inequality being negative, thus serving to make the term $\varepsilon_{p\bar{k}}\ \varepsilon_{\bar{k}.r}$ positive and hence helping to offset the monopolist's power. This derivative reflects our assumption that freight rates are lower for large lots than small lots. The larger the rate concession for large lots, the more circumscribed is monopoly power. Perhaps it is paradoxical that a price effect often regarded as a concession to strongly entrenched (monopolistic or quasi-monopolistic) shippers actually serves as a check on monopoly pricing power.

One's first impulse is to argue that this rate concession for large lots should be encouraged by public policy as a means of checking monopoly power. But there is an obvious danger in that kind of recommendation. Policy of this type limits freedom of entry into a monopolized industry. It lessens the possibility that small firms will ship on the same basis as the well established firm. In practice, it would cost the purchaser more in trasportation charges to buy from the small newcomer than from the large established firm. The circle completes itself because rating by carload lot protects the monopolist while at the same time limiting his pricing power. In this case, what space gives, it takes back-up to a point.

Regardless of specific policy recommendation, it is clear that there is strong liklihood that transportation costs generally serve to limit monopoly pricing power under a non-discriminatory f. o. b. mill price system. In a sense the preceding arguments show that monopolies or near-monopolies do not actually operate entirely on the basis of demand and cost of production. The operation of the monopolist are circumscribed by other considerations and very likely transportation costs are only one of several considerations. There are many, as yet unanswered, questions that one might raise about these additional circumstances that limit monopoly power.

Spatial Price Discrimination, Competition and Locational Effects

By JOHN G. GREENHUT and M. L. GREENHUT[1]

Spatial price theory has typically assumed homogeneous gross demand curves among buyers who are dispersed over an economic landscape. Subtracting varying costs of distance to their locations yields a set of heterogeneous net demand curves. Any spatial monopolist subject to these conditions faces separable markets which are characterized by different effective demands. As a result price discrimination is feasible, and in theory straight-lined delivered price schedules of less than unit slope per unit cost of distance are customarily derived. But do spatial competitors ever discriminate (or appear to discriminate) over economic space? And if they do, what is the form of their delivered price schedules? Would their schedules also be linear given the same demand conditions that generate linear schedules for a discriminating monopolist?

Without answering questions such as those raised above anti-trust regulations dealing with unfair price practices and, in particular, the determination of what is legal or illegal, ethical or not, cannot be readily accepted by economists. The present paper is designed to provide a basis for answering such questions by uncovering selected properties of spatial price discrimination under conditions of varying intensities of competition over an economic space. More generally, the paper is designed to determine the effect on prices of rival locations and the intensity of their competition. Sharp contrasts between spaceless and spatial price theory will thus be drawn, with competitive differences over the seller's trading area being revealed to generate differential discriminatory prices over the landscape.

I. ASSUMPTIONS OF SPATIAL PRICE DISCRIMINATION THEORY

Four assumptions are customarily used in the traditional theoretical formulation of spatial price discrimination theory: (1) a simple monopoly market, (2) constant marginal costs, (3) buyers distributed evenly over the space, and (4) identical gross (or spaceless) demands. (See Hoover (1937), Dewey (1955), Smithies (1941) or, more recently, Greenhut and Ohta (1972).) Assumption (1) will be discarded here in order for us to determine the effects of competition and competitor locations on delivered prices; moreover, assumptions (2) and (3) will

[1] The authors wish to thank R. Battalio, M. Hwang and H. Ohta for constructive critiques. This paper is based on research funded by the National Science Foundation.

be dropped so that the analysis will include varying cost conditions and non-homogeneous spatial distributions of buyers. Assumption (4) can easily be relaxed but is best maintained for the objectives of this paper.

Two other critical assumptions dealing with competition and demand will be maintained throughout this article. The first—on equilibrium output—will be shown to reflect spaceless competitive equilibrium (i.e., when there is no cost of distance). We begin with

$$(1) \qquad p\left(1-\frac{1}{em}\right)=\overline{MC}$$

where e stands for the elasticity of demand, m for the number of sellers, em, accordingly, for the point elasticity on the firm's demand curve and $\overline{MC}$ for the average of the m firms' marginal cost values. Implicit to $\overline{MC}$ is the requirement that $MC=\sum MC_i/m$, where MC_i is the marginal cost function of the ith firm, $i=1,\ldots,m$.

The vital relation given by equation (1) warrants detailed evaluation. Note initially its obvious origin in the profit-maximizing condition of the firm, as given by

$$(2) \qquad \frac{d(pq_i)}{dq_i}=MC_i.$$

For the moment assume $dp/dq_i=dp/dq$, where q is the total output of the m firms. A change in *any* firm's output, then, affects competitive market price at a point in space through its effect on total output there. For example, an increase in q_i corresponds to greater total supply and lower market price, *ceteris paribus*, given negatively sloped demand. So profit maximization by the ith firm is given by

$$(3) \qquad p+q_i\frac{dp}{dq}=MC_i,$$

which equation holds for all m firms.

Two conditions for general market equilibrium which stem from equation (3) are therefore

$$(4) \qquad \frac{MC_i-p}{q_i}=\frac{MC_j-p}{q_j} \qquad (i,j=1,\ldots,m)$$

and

$$(5) \qquad mp+\frac{dp}{dq}\sum_{i=1}^{m}q_i=\sum_{i=1}^{m}MC_i.$$

Dividing both sides of (5) by m, factoring p on the left-hand side, defining $e=-(dq/dp)(p/q)$ and observing that $\sum q_i=q$ and $\overline{MC}=\sum MC_i/m$ combine to re-establish the vital equation (1). Through that equation, pricing over competitive economic space can be determined. (Equation (1) can also be shown to obtain from Cournot's (1927) equilibrium condition of the competitive firm (equation (7), Chapter VII, p. 86).) And though other industry structures may be analysed via equation (2), e.g. price leadership situations can be evaluated by altering the relationship between dp/dq_i and dp/dq, the focus of this paper is confined to competitive pricing. It is in this context alone that equation (1) serves as our departure point for evaluating spatial prices.

It may appear surprising that a spaceless equilibrium equation such as (1) can be used in a study of *spatial* differentials in price. Not only may m vary from market point to market point, but, more significantly for the heterogeneous world of the space economy, contrasting MC_i must be taken as data. (The existence of heterogeneous oligopoly relations in the space economy is well established in the literature, and is thus assumed *a priori* in the model set forth in this paper.) Though it may not be intuitively clear that different MC values yield a price level determined by the average rather than the lowest marginal cost producer (see Appendix to this paper for a proof), it should none the less be recognized that a stable market equilibrium price is provided by equations (4), (5) and (1). Moreover, this particular type of pricing has many supporters in prevailing economic theory (see Leftwich, 1956, p. 241). And Bain (1953, p. 287) asserts: "There will be a range of alternative maximizing prices (all probably in the same general neighbourhood) among which the sellers must choose. Price agreements will require some compromise on a price not too far from the optimal price of anyone." Schelling (1960, Chapters 2 and 3) goes beyond this and contends that a tendency exists for alternative price choices to converge to some prominent value, without collusion or even communication taking place between the sellers, an obvious split-the-difference situation. Institutional constraints such as statutes, customer goodwill, etc., as well as transport cost differentials may also prevent the lowest-cost firm from setting the price. But perhaps most importantly, as is seen below, even if price is determined by the lowest-cost producer rather than the average cost firm our results are not significantly altered. The effect of equations (4) and (5) and hence (1), in terms of the space economy and the arguments raised in this paragraph, is simply to determine the levels and curvatures of delivered price schedules; the basic underlying relations scored herein are otherwise unchanged.

Equation (1) possesses two additional vital features which conform to well accepted economic principles. Through it we find: (a) an increase in competition increases the elasticity of demand for the firm's product; (b) economic market relations running from simple monopoly to perfect competition can be easily obtained. To illustrate (b), note that if $m=1$ or $m=\infty$, equation (1) respectively provides through (6) and (7) the classical equilibrium conditions of a monopoly or perfectly competitive market:

$$(6) \qquad p\left(1-\frac{1}{e}\right)=MC$$

$$(7) \qquad p=\overline{MC}=MC.$$

Note that, since all firms must have identical marginal cost levels in the long-run zero profit competitive equilibrium, there is no need for subscript i in equation (7). On all of the counts entered above, equation (1) thus serves well as a departure point for analysing profit maximization in separable markets, where the number of suppliers may vary from that of a single seller to that of innumerably many sellers each of whom may be subject to different production and transport costs.

Our second critical assumption is that spaceless market demand is, let us say, an exponential of the form

$$\frac{p}{\beta}=1-\left(\frac{q}{\alpha}\right)^x \tag{8}$$

where p, q, α, β and x are positive, and variables α and β respectively stand for the quantity and price intercepts. In particular, when $x<1$, the demand curve is concave from above; when $x=1$, the demand curve is linear; when $x>1$, the demand curve is convex from above. These demand curves may be described as well behaved functions which conform to *a priori* expectations. Most vitally, equation (8) contains the set of demand curves whose elasticity decreases more rapidly than price. Of course, demand curves may exist which are more concave than those belonging to (8); e.g., demand curves may exist whose elasticity decreases less than proportionately to the lowering of price, or demand curves of constant elasticity (e.g. the rectangular hyperbola) could be conceived of, or we may have demand curves of increasing elasticity (e.g. a portion of an ellipse). Inclusion of such types of demand curves is possible by letting our demand curve be given by $p=\alpha q^x+\beta$, where α is positive but x is less than or equal to zero. This particular assumption however, is not made here for the following reasons: (1) the resulting demand curves usually require price discrimination against distant buyers, an unlikely practice in light of repackage-resale possibilities (see Hoover, 1937); (2) price intercepts do not exist when elasticity increases less rapidly than price (which implies infinite size market areas); (3) we could not refer to α and β simply as the quantity and price intercept since they are not the intercepts when $x<0$; and (4) the cases of these special demands are extensions of the concave *v.* convex analyses of spatial pricing already possible within the range of demand curves assumed in (8).

Exponential demand of the order given by (8) is thus not only meaningfully general but desirably specific. Not only can the price intercept, the quantity intercept and "general concavity" of the curve take any economically relevant values, but varying αs, βs and xs can be applied. For the purposes of this paper, however, a consistent unishaped demand curve is alone required.

II. Generalized Competitive Model of Spatial Price Discrimination

The effect of distance on demand may now be readily evaluated. Define spaceless demand by $p=f(q)$ and, in turn spatial demand as

$p=f(q)-T$, where T is the transportation cost of shipping one unit of the good from the seller's site to the buyer. The spatial demand function, therefore, yields the average revenue received by the seller after all transportation costs have been paid. By charging discriminatory prices, a seller equalizes his marginal revenue on sales to every separable market. Thus varying demands because of varying distances immediately offer a seller the opportunity to discriminate in price; in the process, the spatial monopolist maximizes profits for all values of T as given by either

$$\text{(9a)} \qquad p\left(1-\frac{1}{e}\right)-T=k$$

or

$$\text{(9b)} \qquad p\left(1-\frac{1}{e}\right)=k+T$$

where the equilibrium marginal cost k is identical for all distances, i.e. k is constant for all values of T. It might be noted that Hoover (1937) based his article on equation (9a), where k equals an assumed constant marginal cost. Under other cost conditions, k can be obtained as the equilibrium marginal cost level, as in Battalio and Ekelund (1972). In that case k is determined at the point of equality between marginal production cost (MC) and the horizontal summation of the firm's individual market's marginal revenue curves (obtained in spatial economics from the net demand curve in each market). Thus the sum of the individual marginal revenues, referrable to as total marginal revenue, TMR, is equated with k (i.e. $k=MC=TMR$). It follows that k is constant for all T, which signifies in turn that marginal revenues in each market are identical, and that total marginal revenue equals marginal cost. It should also be seen that in (9b) spaceless marginal revenue (MR) is equated with the spatial firm's composite marginal cost made up of its marginal production plus transport costs.

Spatial competitors whose buyers are distributed over varying distances may also discriminate in price since their markets too are naturally distinguished by the different costs of distance, and hence their net effective demands differ, *ceteris paribus*. The equilibrium output condition in a competitive market was assumed in equation (1) to involve competitive marginal revenue equal to average marginal cost. Therefore, the market equilibrium condition for spatial competitors who discriminate in price is given by

$$\text{(10)} \qquad p\left(1-\frac{1}{em}\right)=\bar{k}+\bar{T}$$

where $\bar{k}=\sum k_i/m$, $\bar{T}=\sum T_i/m$, the subscript i relates to the ith firm selling to the market T_i dollars from its plant, and m now refers to the number of firms competing for a given buying point. Since elasticity of the exponential demand function equals

$$(11) \qquad e=\frac{1}{x}\left(\frac{p}{\beta-p}\right)$$

the "competitive marginal revenue" reduces to

$$(12) \qquad p\left(1-\frac{1}{em}\right)=\frac{1}{m}\{p(m+x)-x\beta\}.$$

Combining (10) and (12) yields

$$(13) \qquad p(m+x)=x\beta+m\bar{T}+m\bar{k}$$

so that the delivered price P_D may be set forth as

$$(14) \qquad P_D=\frac{1}{m+x}(x\beta+m\bar{k})+\frac{m}{m+x}\bar{T}.$$

Equation (14) establishes delivered price under conditions of spatial competition as a function of m, x, β, $\bar{k}$ and most importantly $\bar{T}$, the *average transportation cost* of shipping the product from the m firms' locations to that of a particular buying point. This function points to the perhaps surprising relationship between the firm's P_D schedule and the individual seller's transportation cost T_i. Call this relationship the firm's delivered price schedule, and denote it as *DPS*. Most significantly, we see from (14) that the *DPS* does not depend on the demand variable α (the quantity intercept of the demand curve at any given buying point), nor is it influenced by the distribution of buyers. Ceteris paribus, *delivered price to any one location is unaffected by the delivered price to any other location, given the individual firm's marginal cost k_i and the average marginal cost $\bar{k}$.* There are "real world" exceptions to our general statement which requires the *ceteris paribus* pound. For example, anti-monopoly laws, resale possibilities (which exist when delivered prices to adjacent markets differ by more than transportation costs) and the cost of administering a complex price policy often constrain a firm's spatial pricing system. But these exceptions need not be included in our model or mentioned again in light of present objectives.

The slope of the firm's delivered price schedule is given by

$$(15) \qquad \frac{dP_D}{dT_i}=\frac{d\left\{\frac{1}{m+x}(x\beta+m\bar{k})\right\}}{dT_i}+\frac{d\left(\frac{m}{m+x}\bar{T}\right)}{dT_i}.$$

Assuming x, β and m are constant over all T_i, i.e., assuming homogeneous demands and identical levels of competition everywhere, we obtain

$$(16) \qquad \frac{dP_D}{dT_i}=\frac{m}{m+x}\frac{d\bar{T}}{dT_i}.$$

Thus the slope of the *DPS* is determined by the change in average transportation costs when distances from the sellers increase. To appreciate fully the effect of the change in average transportation costs on the *DPS*, observe that if $\bar{T}$ is the same for all buyer locations (i.e., ΣT_i is everywhere identical), the slope of the *DPS* is zero and uniform pricing exists. Its slope is positive, however, when an increase in T_i results in an increase in $\bar{T}$. In order to evaluate any firm's delivered price schedule, the exact relationship between T_i and $\bar{T}$ must be determined. The analysis that follows is designed to ascertain this relationship by determining the impact of different competitor locations on discriminatory prices in the space economy.

III. Sellers' Locations and Their Competitive Impacts on the DPS

Based on the model set forth in Section II, the impacts on delivered price schedules of different sellers' and buyers' locational arrangements over space can now be specified. In particular, three main locational situations will be covered: (1) all sellers at the same production centre, (2) sellers located at different centres joined by a transport facility along which buyers are evenly dispersed, and (3) sellers again located at different centres, but where a given transport facility runs from only one centre (not each production point) *to all buyers*; in other words, the rival firm(s) in this alternative production centre case is located at a substantial distance from the initial set of sellers *and all buyers.*

III.1 *All sellers located at one production centre*

For the moment, assume that spaceless demands are identical and that all sellers are located at the same (given) production centre. Since each seller is subject to identical transport cost T, delivered price under the defined spatial alignment may be set forth readily via equation (14) as

$$P_D=\frac{1}{m+x}(x\beta+m\bar{k})+\frac{m}{m+x}T. \tag{17}$$

The mill price P_m of any seller is in turn

$$P_m=\frac{1}{m+x}(x\beta+m\bar{k}) \tag{18}$$

and the slope S of his delivered price schedule is

$$S=\frac{dP_D}{dT}=\frac{m}{m+x}. \tag{19}$$

Because $\bar{T}$ increases everywhere at the same rate as T, the *DPS* is linear with slope $m/(m+x)$, as illustrated in Figure 1. When $x>0$, the

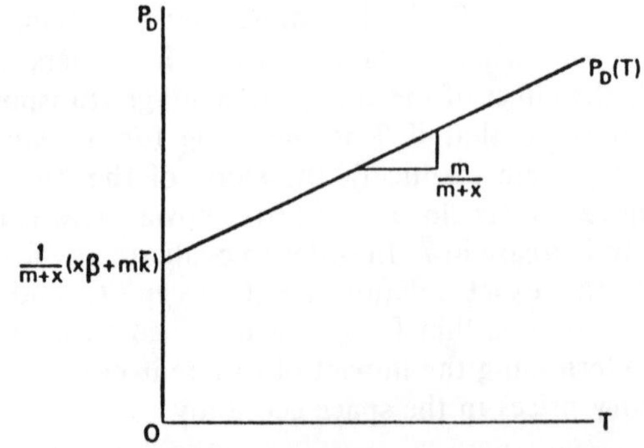

FIGURE 1 The DPS given one production point

slope is positive but less than unity; discrimination therefore proceeds in favour of distant buyers.

The effect on delivered prices of the number of competitors at the production centre is obtained by deriving selected partial derivatives. Consider the following:

$$\frac{\partial P_D}{\partial m} = -x\frac{\beta-(\bar{k}+T)}{(m+x)^2} < 0 \tag{20}$$

and

$$\frac{\partial S}{\partial m} = \frac{x}{(m+x)^2} > 0. \tag{21}$$

Important implications of (20) and (21) are that, the greater is m, *ceteris paribus*, the lower are prices but the steeper is the slope of the *DPS*. Figure 2 illustrates these relationships. The mill price approaches $\bar{k}$

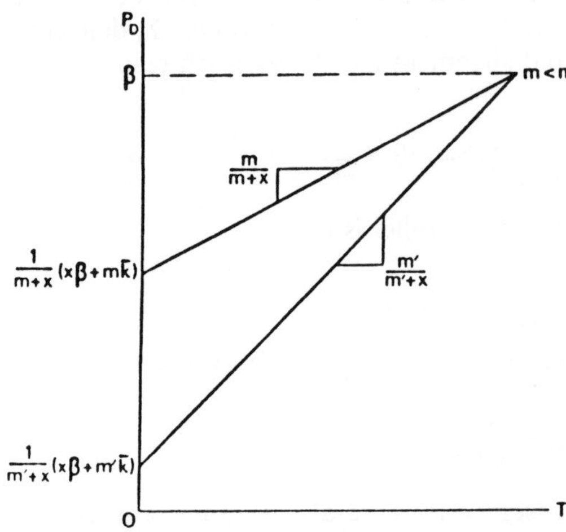

FIGURE 2 Effects of an increase in competition

and the slope of the delivered price schedule unity as m becomes increasingly great. Perfect competition culminates in a price schedule resembling non-discriminatory f.o.b. mill pricing. This offshoot of our theory conforms to Hoover's results; moreover, it has been verified by several "observations" of f.o.b. pricing (see Ackley (1943), Nelson and Keim (1940, pp. 299, 300, 303 and 315) and Dewey (1955)). Besides providing insights into spatial aspects of prices, equations (17) and (18) can yield the long-run spaceless equilibrium prices of free enterprise firms (Greenhut, 1974, Chapter 4).

III.2 *Sellers located at two production centres joined by the transport line*

Additional insight to spatial pricing under competitive conditions may be gained by conceiving of sellers located at *two* alternative production centres, each of which can serve a given market space. Assume further, for the moment, that the buyers in the space are distributed along a line that joins the two production sites, as illustrated in Figure 3. Let m_1 be the number of competitors at site (1) and m_2 the

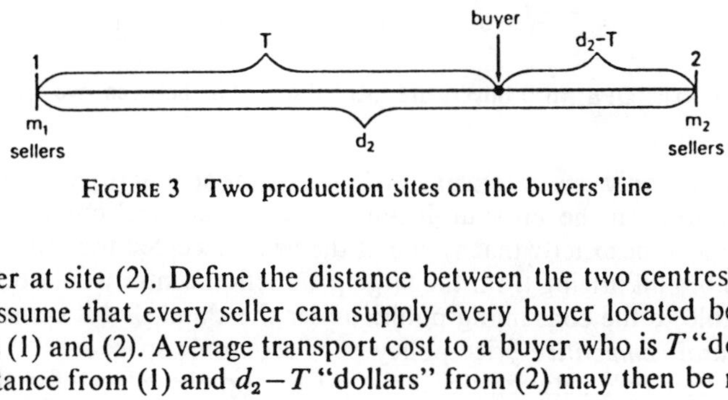

FIGURE 3 Two production sites on the buyers' line

number at site (2). Define the distance between the two centres as d_2, and assume that every seller can supply every buyer located between points (1) and (2). Average transport cost to a buyer who is T "dollars" of distance from (1) and $d_2 - T$ "dollars" from (2) may then be readily obtained from

$$(22) \qquad \bar{T} = \frac{1}{m_1+m_2}\{m_1T + m_2(d_2 - T)\}.$$

By utilizing $m = m_1 + m_2$ for simplicity and equations (14) and (22), the delivered price of each seller and the slope of the *DPS* of the sellers located at site (1) are determinable respectively as

$$(23) \qquad P_D = \frac{1}{m+x}(x\beta + m\bar{k}) + \frac{1}{m+x}\{m_1T + m_2(d_2 - T)\}$$

and

$$(24) \qquad S = \frac{m}{m+x}\frac{d\bar{T}}{dT} = \frac{1}{m+x}(m_1 - m_2).$$

Note that if all consumers were located at more distant sites from production centre (1) than production centre (2), the transport cost from site (2) would equal $T-d_2$ rather than d_2-T, and the slope S would be the same as when both sets of sellers were located at the same centre.

Equations (23) and (24) provide alternative delivered price schedules when different values of m_1 and m_2 are assumed. Figure 4 depicts three distinguishable and important schedules based on alternative m_1, m_2 ratios under the simplifying condition that total m is identically the same on each curve at each market point. The schedules are linear, as were the ones in Section III.1. One might propose on the basis of panel (a) of Figure 4 that, if several sellers are located at a production centre

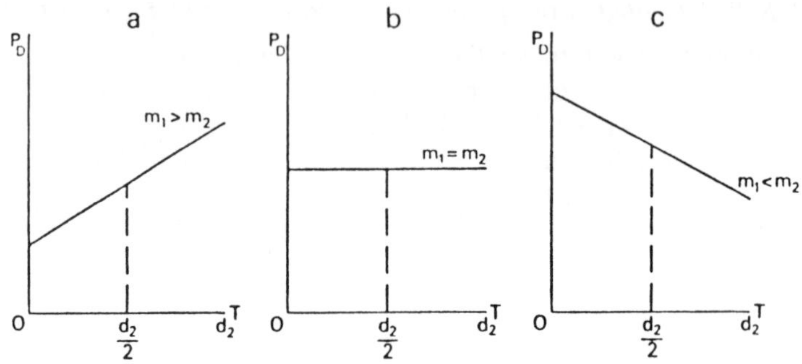

FIGURE 4 The DPS when buyers are located on a line between two sellers

and perhaps only one or two at a distant site, the spatial pricing schedule would approach the Pittsburgh plus of American steel companies; in fact it would be exactly that system if the firms accepted the proposition that f.o.b. mill pricing from the large production centre would be more acceptable to the consuming public under the claim that it constituted the *natural competitive* price policy over economic space.

A further link between delivered prices and the effect of a distant production site may be obtained by taking the partial of S with respect to m_2. This partial is negative, hence the incidence of an increase in m_2 is a decrease in the slope of *DPS*. Since delivered price rises by $ST=\{m/(m+x)\}T$ while freight costs rises by T, $(1-S)$ is the freight absorption rate. A most compelling implication is that, *the more competitive the distant location (i.e. the larger is* m_2), *the greater will be the freight absorption rate of the firms located at site* (1).

One special result of distant competition can therefore be uniform pricing. This common price practice in the United States would arise, *a priori*, when competition is of the same weight at alternative production centres (as in panel (b) of Figure 4, where $m_1=m_2$), and hence total transportation costs are the same to all buying points in the market. Although products advertised nationally are often subject to low freight cost and thereby are readily adaptable to uniform pricing, our theory indicates that even distribution of sellers is another important force behind the existence of uniform price schedules. It may in fact be the case that, when a product's price is advertised nationally rather than region by region, such policy itself is attributable to the state of even weighted production centres.

III.3 *Two production centres, one located at a distance from all buyers*

This section summarizes selected findings whose proof will be provided to interested readers upon request. Most significant in justifying only a brief summary here of our findings is the fact that the main objectives of this section of the paper have been (1) to examine the impact of seller and buyer locations on $d\bar{T}/dT_1$ (see equation (16)), and (2) to illustrate techniques that may be used in determining the exact T_1, $\bar{T}$ relationships, which objectives have, in many ways, already been fulfilled. The basic reason for analysing the impact of the particular spatial distribution to be discussed here is that it gives rise to a non-linear rather than linear price schedule under identical demand conditions which otherwise would generate the linear *DPS*. In effect, the analysis below focuses attention on the errors that may stem from the "use" of spaceless economic theory in formulating policy designed to regulate real-world (distance) pricing. To be specific: classical economic theory suggests that monopolists may discriminate in their prices. Such laws as the Robinson–Patman Act in the United States typically reflect the assumption that monopolists discriminate over space. However, when reality is confronted, competitors are found to discriminate. So, given an inadequate economic theory, and the need to be practical in dealing with spatial price practices, legal experts have developed the thesis that sporadic meeting of competitor prices at selected buying locations (*distinct from systematic matching*) might be "good faith price discrimination", hence acceptable under the statute. But this type of law and interpretation reflects the limited vision that has resulted from the lack of a body of price theory applicable to conditions of *spatial* competition. We shall see below that non-uniform freight rate absorption over space, which itself relates to non-linear delivered price schedules, and in turn to what may appear to be a form of predatory pricing, can in fact be competitively ordered *even if systematic*.

It can be shown that delivered price schedules may assume diverse slopes when a rival firm is located elsewhere in a plain than along the transport line of rival firms, as in Figure 5. Exact answer to curvatures may be obtained by utilizing the trigonometric law of cosines, which expresses T_2 in terms of d_2, A_2 and T, and then employing the differential calculus to show the dependence of curvature on the location of the rival production centre. If, for example, the rival centre is located at site (2) in Figure 5, and all buyers are located along line T, the *DPS* will curve upward as buyer distances from site (1) increase. Thus, even if the economic space is homogeneous with respect to competition and demand, a non-linear *DPS* will frequently be evident. Full identification of competitive locations and the levels of this competition, along with a determination of what the *DPS* schedule would be (and could tend to

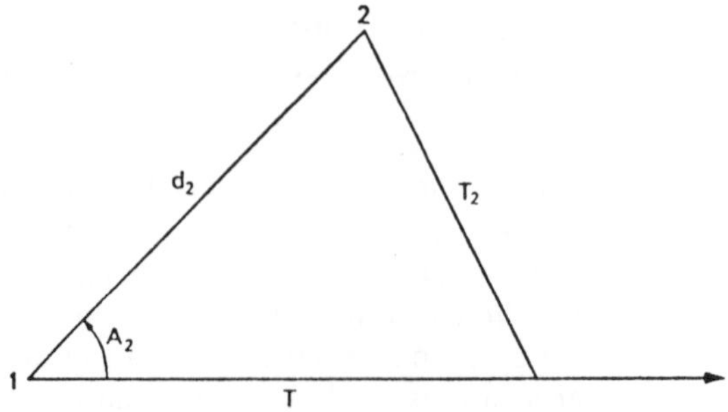

FIGURE 5 A simple seller distribution case

be), are clearly necessary for any evaluation of the spatial price practices of firms. It is sufficient for our purposes to recognize the obvious fact that a myriad of locational competitive possibilities exists, and that individual cases must be evaluated in conformity with the facts of each case.

IV. HETEROGENEOUS SPACE

Two vital results stemming from our preceding analysis are: f.o.b. pricing arises when perfect competition exists at a single production site, and uniform pricing obtains when buyers are distributed between production centres of equal competitive weight. It may further be recalled that, though these pricing patterns as well as the linear delivered price schedules related to them were derived from the assumption of homogeneous demands and competition, competitive locations could be of such pattern that the *DPS* becomes non-linear even when the economic space is of homogeneous order. But this possibility brings us to the special interests of the present section of the paper, where variations in competition at different market points can easily be shown to yield, among others, an f.o.b., uniform or non-linear price schedule.

Recall in this context that discriminatory pricing involves the maximizing of profits at each location independently of any other buying point. Thus the *DPS* under varying degrees of competition may be viewed as a combination of schedules for which competition is constant. Instead of assuming that firms at two production centres compete for sales at all points between them, as we did in Section III.2, consider now the possibility that market areas do not always overlap completely since distances may exist over which the rivals' delivered price would be less than the subject firm's cost of selling; i.e., in many instances a competitor's delivered price is less than the subject firm's cost of production and transportation to a given buyer. Sellers at any location may therefore experience differential competition from distant rivals on some distant sales. One might expect this situation to be frequently seen in markets where distant producers are simply unable to compete for buyers located nearest another seller. The effect of this competitive structure is that equation (17) determines the delivered price over the markets proximate to the seller's site, while equation (23) applies to the more distant markets of the firm which are subject to competition from another production point. Thus the delivered price schedule may involve a union of schedules, such as the two given in panel (a) of Figure 6 and in turn combined in panel (b); note that distances Y and Z stand for the locations between which the firms at both centres can sell profitably. The specific limiting values of Y and Z can be determined by finding the distance T at which the delivered price schedules given by equations (17) and (23) respectively intersect the lines $\bar{k}+(d_2-T)$ and $\bar{k}+T$ (which lines show the zero profit prices). The caveat applies that in constructing this figure, m_1 was assumed greater than m_2.

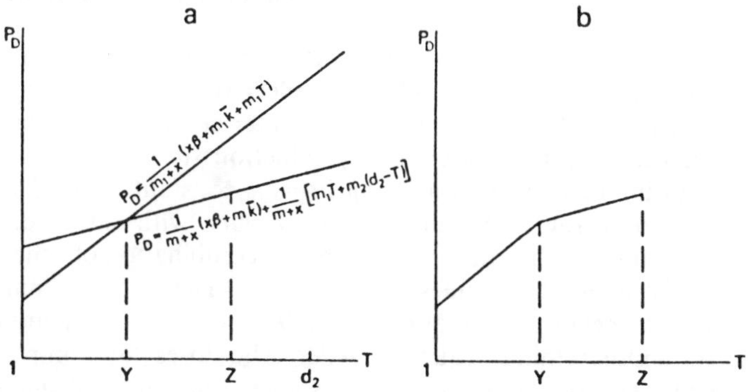

FIGURE 6 The combined DPS of a firm at production centre (1)

Diagrammatic representation of the *DPS* under conditions of heterogeneous competition over the space involves the following principles: all schedules generated by various competitive conditions in the space are so conceived that the delivered price at each distance T is obtained from the particular *DPS* applicable under the competitive conditions prevailing at that site. For example, let the number of firms competing at distance T_0 in Figure 7(a) be given by m', and assume that all sellers are located at the same production centre. Then, the delivered price at T_0 is obtained from the *DPS* for which the number of sellers is m', namely, $P_D(m')$. In this manner the combined *DPS* is specified.

We assume in Figure 7(a) that the number of sellers competing for distant markets happens to decrease in such pattern that f.o.b. pricing would prevail over a large part of the market area. Rather than adopt a complex price policy in which f.o.b. pricing is practised over most of the market and discriminatory pricing over the remainder of the market, a seller may price only f.o.b. mill in order to reduce administrative costs and maintain consumer goodwill. Figure 7(b) depicts, in turn, the case where competition from distant sellers increases continually with distance, while, as in Figure 7(a), the number of "local" firms

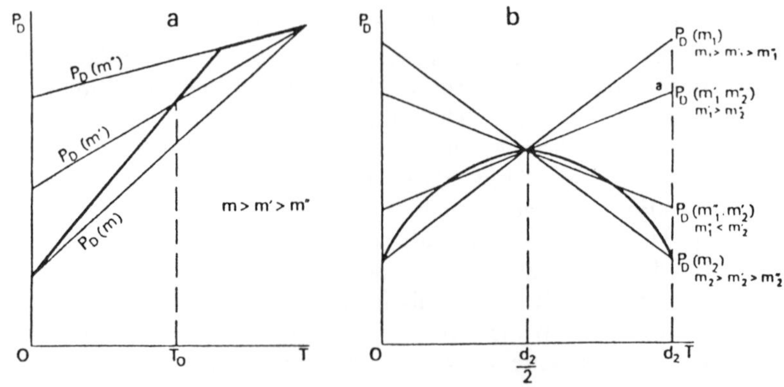

FIGURE 7 Construction of the DPS when competition is heterogeneous

competing for more distant markets decreases. This case not only applies to variations in the number of sellers but may also apply to pricing when distant sellers have vastly greater competitive impact on sales to markets located nearer their production site. In other words, even though the number of competing firms is constant over all T, the competition occurring between firms may vary with distance. The concomitant effect is that the *DPS* becomes a combination of schedules applicable for alternative values of m_1 and m_2. The rate of change of m_1 and m_2, and hence the curvature of the *DPS* may vary from industry to industry. Other things equal, a seller who loses his competitive advantage rather rapidly as his cost of distances increases will employ a sharply concave downward *DPS*; in contrast, a seller whose competitive advantage continues over distances proximate to his plant will derive a *DPS* that tends to curve downwards only over more distant market points, e.g. near the midpoint of their market areas; in this case the delivered price schedule will be of almost constant positive (or negative) slope over distances quite proximate to (distant from) the firm's production site, reaching a peak at the midpoint of its market area. Other schedules, e.g. uniform pricing, may similarly arise in a space characterized by heterogeneous competition.

One important principle standing behind Figure 6 was pointed out by an anonymous referee. He observed that our system will not be in long-run equilibrium if cost conditions are roughly similar and $m_2 < m_1$ since the rate of profit will be higher for the firms located at (2) as a result of the higher prices prevailing there. A tendency will thus exist for production to increase at (2) relative to (1) with long-run equilibrium occurring when profit rates are equalized; "in the process of adjustment, the delivered price schedule will become more uniform".

V. ALTERNATIVE FORMULATIONS

All previous results were derived as a direct consequence of assuming that price is fully determined by equation (1). But equation (1) may not adequately represent competition in an imperfect market. Adjustments can be made to our equations, however, in order to better describe imperfectly competitive market relations. For example, a convex from above demand curve where $x>1$ can be used to approximate a kinked demand curve assumption that might appear to be relevant. By utilizing equation (19) one would find that $(\partial S/\partial x)<0$. Thus, the type of competition among oligopolists that is reflected in our model by an $x>1$ results in a flatter delivered price schedule than would otherwise prevail.

Other conceptions of particular market relations may be made by assuming $dp/dq_i=\gamma_i(dp/dq)$. If $\gamma_i=\gamma$ for all i, then equation (1) becomes

$$p\left(1-\frac{\gamma}{em}\right)=\overline{MC} \tag{25}$$

yielding the delivered price equation

$$P_D=\frac{1}{m+\gamma x}(\gamma x\beta+m\bar{k})+\frac{m}{m+\gamma x}\,\bar{T}. \tag{26}$$

The basic underlying relations developed in this paper between spatial discriminatory pricing and the location and number of sellers clearly remains unchanged by letting $\gamma\neq 1$. Alternatively, price leadership may be specified by assuming $\gamma_i=0$ for all i except $i=1$, where firm number 1 is the price leader. $MR=MC$ therefore yields $p=MC_i$ for all $i\neq 1$ and $p+\gamma_1 q_1(dp/dq)=MC_1$ for $i=1$. Market equilibrium in turn requires

$$p\left(1-\frac{\delta}{em}\right)=\overline{MC} \tag{27}$$

where $\delta=\gamma_1(q_1/q)$. Equation (27) is, of course, similar to equation (25). The only difference is that, even though γ may be constant for all distances, δ may vary since (q_1/q), the market share of the price leader, generally varies with distance. Equation (26) points out a technique with which to analyse non-constant γ or δ. Notice that a change in γ or δ has the same impact on price patterns as does a change in the demand parameter x. A fundamental key to the relationships between spatial pricing and price leadership may thus be gained by theoretical examination of the values of x over all distances. Owing to space limitations, however, this and other competitive relations cannot be specifically dealt with in the present paper.

The diversity of spatial price relationships and patterns shown above reflects the importance of competitive structures for spatial prices, where by structures we have in mind the location, type, number and interdependencies of firms over the space. Individual judgment in evaluating and classifying competitive structures is therefore critically important to any theoretical or empirical inquiry into spatial prices. Full identification of competitive locations and forces, along with application of the *DPS* schedule derivable under our model, would correspondingly be necessary in any evaluation of the price practices of firms subject to unfair practice charges. Indeed, location theory itself is empty without considering the spatial pricing practices of firms.

VI. Summary and Conclusions

The effects of competition on spatial prices may be readily summarized by initially assuming a production centre (1) in Figure 8 in which $i=1, \ldots, m$ *homogeneous* firms are located. If demand is of the exponential order previously proposed, these firms would be pricing in accordance with equation (17) up to distance B. The mill price and *DPS*) of each firm would be of a lower value (and level) than that of the simple spatial monopolist; and the slope of the *DPS* would in turn be steeper. With each new entry of a competitor at (1), mill price falls and the slope of the *DPS* increases.

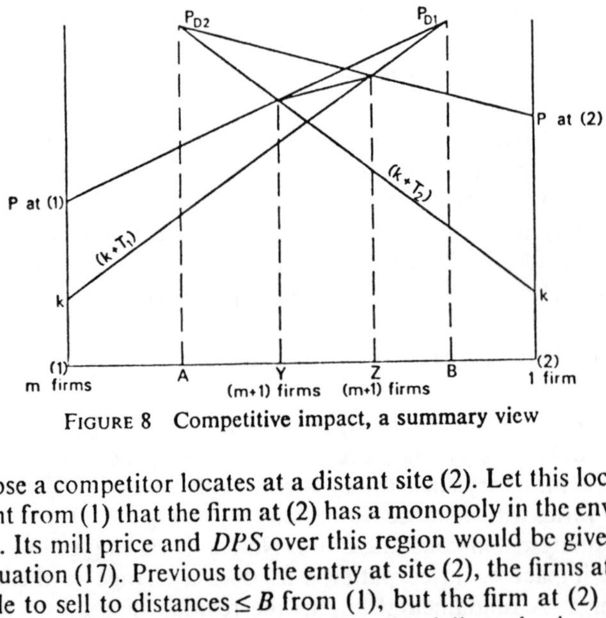

FIGURE 8 Competitive impact, a summary view

Suppose a competitor locates at a distant site (2). Let this location be so distant from (1) that the firm at (2) has a monopoly in the environs of its plant. Its mill price and *DPS* over this region would be given by the same equation (17). Previous to the entry at site (2), the firms at (1) had been able to sell to distances $\leq B$ from (1), but the firm at (2) can also supply many of these points. In particular, the delivered price of a seller to any and all locations must be equal to or less than the intercept limit price of the buyers, greater than or equal to the seller's freight plus marginal production cost, and less than or equal to the price of rivals. Given these conditions, the firm at (2) can compete for locations falling between Y and the monopoly limit point B of the sellers at (1).

The existence of the competitor at (2) increases the number of rivals for the firms at site (1) on sales between these markets. The positive slope of the *DPS* of the firms falls between Y and B as, let us say, equation (23) replaces equation (17). In fact, the market of the firms at site (1) is compressed to the new limit distance Z. A dramatic increase in competition actually takes place with respect to the firm at site (2) for market points located beyond its monopolized limit point Z; the result is a negative slope of its *DPS* for all buying sites located beyond that market point. For the firm at (2), the negativity of its *DPS* slope signifies that a distant buyer's intercept price does not determine the extent of its market. Correspondingly, the monopoly market limit point A, in effect, is shifted by competition to an effective distance much closer to location (2), as given by the equality of the marginal production cost k plus freight cost T_2 of the firm at site (2) with the *DPS* of the firms at site (1). Simultaneous solution of the two prices schedules involves the principles previously set forth. In this context, note that the increased number of competitors $(m+1)$ combine with the lower average transport costs in the environs of Z to promote a lower *DPS* than previously existed.

Additional entry at site (2) would cause mill price at (2) to fall and the related *DPS* slope from that location to increase. The firms at (1) would no longer be able to compete for sales at site Z since their marginal production plus transport cost must now exceed the lower delivered price from the firms at production centre (2). The shift, let us say, of Z closer to location (1) reflects an increase in the number of firms selling to all overlapping market points, which causes the positive slope of the *DPS* of the firms at (1) to fall further between the new points of competition. If, in time, the same number of homogeneous firms are located at site (2) as at site (1), the mill prices would be identical, the slopes of the *DPS* over the monopolized areas from each centre would be identical and all overlapping points of competition (i.e., where $k+T_1$ and $k+T_2$ are less than P_{D1} and P_{D2}) would involve uniform prices. In a sense, the distance Y to $\dot{Z}$ would be much closer together than was originally the case after the entry of the initial firm at site (2).

One last alternative set of situations requires recall and final specification. If the sum of the marginal production and freight cost is less than the mill price at sites (1) and (2) over all points in the entire market space, and if a long-run (equal profit) identity in the number of homogeneous firms applies to each centre, the *DPS* would be uniform throughout the market, as complete overlapping of trading areas exists. Effects of varying the weight of competition at (1) and (2), or of moving the location (2) off of the line of sales from (1), are readily determined, as we have seen. Other variants of the situations summarized above can also be effected readily. The upshot of spatial competition is, in any (every) case, sharply manifest. Delivered price schedules in a homogeneous space are linear of positive slope when firms at the same production centre are in competition (or in collusion) and no distant competitor is able to sell in the monopolized market. And they are linear of positive slope when firms in rival centres abstain from competing for markets between their centres. Otherwise, they are of zero slope or non-linear. Those who enter the clarion call in favour of f.o.b. pricing are acting in complete disregard of the implications of competition on spatial pricing.

Texas Tech University
Texas A & M University

APPENDIX

This appendix is designed to demonstrate individual firm profit maximization at a single-market price when firms are not identical in size. For simplicity, a duopoly industry is assumed in which the two firms have marginal costs MC_1 and MC_2, respectively. Profit maximization by the individual firm requires $MR=MC$ as given above in equation (3). Thus if price $\hat{p}$ is the industry equilibrium price level and $\hat{q}$ denotes the total quantity at $\hat{p}$, three equilibrium conditions must hold:

(i) $$\hat{p}+q_1\frac{dp}{dq}=MC_1,$$

(ii) $$\hat{p}+q_2\frac{dp}{dq}=MC_2,$$

and

(iii) $$q_1+q_2=\hat{q}.$$

These equations, when satisfied, result in

$$2\hat{p}+\hat{q}(dp/dq)=MC_1+MC_2,$$

which in turn leads to equation (1) for the duopoly market, $m=2$.

To determine whether or not price $\hat{p}_0$ in panel (a) of Figure A1 is the equilibrium price level, we construct the schedule

(iv) $$EMR=\hat{p}_0+q\frac{dp}{dq},$$

where EMR is an analytical operator which tests the stability of a particular price and for our purposes may be referred to as equilibrium marginal revenue. This line has price intercept $\hat{p}_0$ and slope dp/dq, which is the slope of the demand curve. The intersection of EMR with MC_1 and MC_2 respectively determine profit-maximizing outputs q_1 and q_2 given price $\hat{p}_0$. Production of these quantities at price $\hat{p}_0$ assures satisfaction of conditions (i) and (ii) above. But, for $\hat{p}_0$ to be the equilibrium price level, condition (iii) must also hold, i.e. q_1 and q_2 must add to $\hat{q}_0$. From the figure, it is obvious that

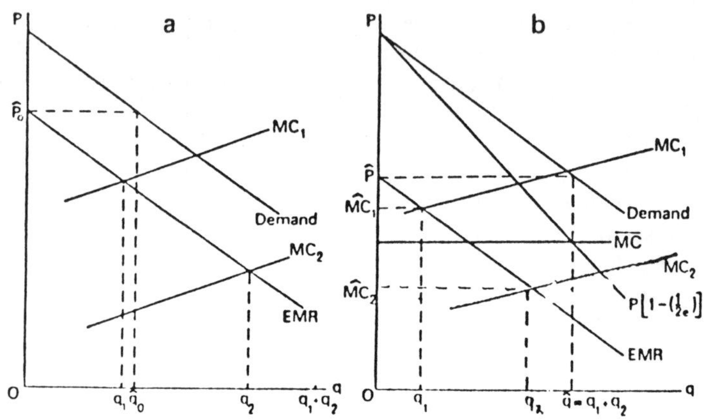

FIGURE A1 Illustration of equilibrium in a duopoly market

firms attempting to maximize profit under price p_0 would produce q_1+q_2 which exceeds $\hat{q}_0$. The industry supply is too great, which suggests that a lower price and lower output by each firm are required if equilibrium conditions (i), (ii) and (iii) are to be satisfied.

Price $\hat{p}$ in panel (b) of the figure yields output $q_1+q_2=\hat{q}$. All three equilibrium conditions are met when this price is charged so that we have

$$\text{(v)} \qquad \hat{p}\left(1-\frac{1}{2e}\right)=\overline{MC}$$

at related output $\hat{q}$. Observe that firm 2, the lower marginal cost firm, is equating MR with its MC and produces an output greater than its rival. Also observe that $\overline{MC}$ is the average of the equilibrium marginal cost levels, MC_1 and MC_2.

REFERENCES

ACKLEY, G. (1943). Price policies. *Industrial Location and Natural Resources*. (National Resources Planning Board). Washington DC: US Government Printing Office.

BAIN, J. (1953). *Pricing, Distribution and Employment*. New York: Holt, Rinehart.

BATTALIO, R. and EKELUND, R. (1972). Output change under third degree discrimination. *Southern Economic Journal*, 39, 285–290.

COURNOT, A. (1927). *Researches Into the Mathematical Principles of the Theory of Wealth*. New York: Macmillan.

DEWEY, D. (1955). A reappraisal of f.o.b. pricing and freight absorption. *Southern Economic Journal*, 22, 48–54.

GREENHUT, M. L. (1974). *A Theory of the Firm in Economic Space* (2nd Printing). Austin: Lone Star.

GREENHUT, M. L. and OHTA, H. (1972). Monopoly output under alternative spatial pricing techniques. *American Economic Review*, 62, 705–713.

HOOVER, E. M. (1937). Spatial price discrimination. *Review of Economic Studies*, 4, 182–191.

LEFTWICH, R. (1956). *The Price System and Resource Allocation*. New York: Holt, Rinehart.

NELSON, S. and W. KEIM (1940). *Price Behavior and Business Policy*. Monograph No. 1 (Temporary National Economic Committee). Washington DC: US Government Printing Office.

SCHELLING, T. (1960). *The Strategy of Conflict*. Cambridge, Mass.: Harvard University Press.

SMITHIES, A. (1941). Monopolistic price policy in a spatial market. *Econometrica*, 9, 63–73.

SPATIAL PRICING PATTERNS IN THE UNITED STATES*

JOHN GREENHUT
M. L. GREENHUT
SHENG-YUNG LI

This paper is an empirical extension of spatial price theory with results being established by selected statistical approaches, namely multiple linear regression and Chow's test. The locational pattern of competitors as well as varying intensities of competition at different spatial market points are found to play dominant roles in determining the pricing patterns of American firms. Differences in the price practices of firms of different states are identified, and price discrimination over geographic space is found to be the most prevalent pricing technique.

I. INTRODUCTION

The economics of space, particularly the theory of spatial pricing, has remained largely outside the basic structure of microeconomics. This isolation stems from the fact that most of the literature on the theory of commodity and factor pricing has been formulated on the basis of perfect competition. The cost of transportation has thus been either totally ignored or simply taken as a cost addition to production cost. The consequence is that the fundamental *significance* of the "space factor" has been overlooked [Eaton and Lipsey, 1977; and Capozza and Van Order, 1977a, 1978].

Corollary effect applies to the theory of price discrimination which, in its traditional spaceless format, *requires* the assumption of separable markets.[1] Market separation is, however, natural to the space economy; hence a necessary condition for price discrimination is intrinsically fulfilled. It is further an a priori likelihood that the world of economic space is marked by heterogeneous markets. This likelihood implies the existence of different demands and levels of competition at various market points. It is in the backlight of a heterogeneous landscape that the underlying determinants of prices and price patterns in the space economy must be determined.

This paper will investigate the spatial pricing structure of firms in selected states in the United States. It thus probes, in effect, into the relevance of the prevailing theory of spatial pricing, which theory

* The authors wish to acknowlege their thanks to Roy Gilbert for his valuable critiques and suggestions, and the National Science Foundation for helpful funding of this research.

1. Of course, separation of markets does not necessarily signify price discrimination. See Robinson [1933]; Watson [1968]; and Greenhut and Ohta [1972].

The Quarterly Journal of Economics, March 1980 0033-5533/80/0094-0329$01.00

establishes discriminatory pricing as the concomitant of spatial heterogeneities. Similarities as well as differences in the spatial pricing structures of firms in selected states are identified.

In order to fulfill our objectives, Section II will review very briefly the prevailing theory of spatial pricing. Section III will point toward an operational model that can be used in empirical investigation. The model and data obtained from a survey of pricing patterns of firms in the United States will be discussed in Sections IV and V. An Appendix providing selected details of our model concludes the paper.

II. A Brief Review of Spatial Price Theory

We utilize the usual $MR = MC$ rule for a competitive seller in the space economy:[2]

$$P_{D_j}\left(1 - \frac{1}{e_j c_j}\right) = \bar{k}_j + \bar{T}_j,$$

(1) $$\bar{k}_j = \frac{1}{c_j}\sum^{c_j} k_{ij},$$

and

$$\bar{T}_j = \frac{1}{c_j}\sum^{c_j} T_{ij},$$

where P_{D_j}, e_j stand, respectively, for the delivered price and the demand elasticity, while c_j represents the number of sellers that are competing with the ith firm in its jth market; in turn, $\bar{k}_j$ and $\bar{T}_j$ stand, respectively, for the average marginal and average transportation cost on sales to the jth market, as justified in Greenhut and Greenhut [1975] *and* applied in Phlips [1976, 1977].

Suppose that the spaceless market demand conditions are given by

(2) $$P_{D_j} = a - bq_j^x, \quad j = 1, \ldots, n,$$

which was shown to be a general form in the 1975 paper cited above. Note in particular that by spaceless we mean the gross demand in each market $1, \ldots, n$, i.e., the demand that would prevail if distance was costless. Substituting for e_j in (1) the elasticity of demand for equation (2), i.e., $P_{D_j}/x(a - P_{D_j})$, yields the delivered price schedule over economic space in terms of the market parameters a, x, c_j, $\bar{k}_j$, and $\bar{T}_j$.

2. See Greenhut and Greenhut [1975] for detailed proof of the relationship expressed here as equation (1).

This is given by

(3) $$P_{D_j} = [1/(c_j + x)](xa + c_j\bar{k}_j) + [c_j/(c_j + x)]\bar{T}_j.$$

Equation (3) establishes the delivered price schedule under conditions of spatial competition as a function of the distance cost $\bar{T}_j$. More specifically, the schedule is influenced parametrically by the spatial demand factors "x" and "a", by the spatial competition factor "c_j", and the marginal cost of production "k_j". As we shall later see, the gross demand given by (2) is not necessarily the demand allocable to the individual firm nor are the "x" and "a" parameters necessarily identical at all market points.

There are two main forms of spatial competition derivable from (3), each of which corresponds to a particular assumption that describes the locational pattern of competitors. Assume initially in this context that *all* sellers are localized at one production center. Then equation (3) becomes

(4) $$P_{D_j} = [1/(c_j + x)](xa + c_j\bar{k}_j) + [c_j/(c_j + x)]T_j,$$

since each seller is subject to identical T_j costs of transportation. The slope of the delivered price schedule is then given by

(5) $$\frac{\partial P_{D_j}}{\partial T_j} = \frac{c_j}{c_j + x}.$$

Note that under f.o.b. mill pricing $\partial P_{D_j}/\partial T_j$ is unity as individual market demands are aggregated and a unique mill price plus full freight cost obtains. In contrast, discriminatory delivered prices are affected by equation (3) parameters, as given by

(6) $$\frac{\partial P_{D_j}}{\partial c_j} < 0,$$

with c_j subject to

$$\frac{xa + c_j\bar{k}_j}{c_j + x} > \bar{k}_j,$$

(7) $$\frac{\partial P_{D_j}}{\partial a} > 0,$$

(8) $$\frac{\partial P_{D_j}}{\partial x} > 0,$$

(9) $$\frac{\partial}{\partial c_j}\frac{\partial P_{D_j}}{\partial T_j} > 0,$$

(10) $$\frac{\partial}{\partial x}\frac{\partial P_{D_j}}{\partial T_j} < 0.$$

The following theoretical results provided by (6)–(10) warrant stress:

(1) The greater is the number of competitors over a spatial market, the lower are prices, but the steeper is the delivered price schedule.

(2) The delivered price is greater, the greater is the ("a") price intercept of the spaceless demand. This result applies even though the slope of the delivered price schedule is not affected by the price intercept.

(3) The more convex from above is the spaceless demand curve (i.e., the larger is "x"), the higher are the prices, but the flatter are the slopes of the delivered price schedules.

Assume next that sellers are located at two alternative production centers with all buyers being distributed over a transport route (line) that joins these production sites. Let c_1 and c_2 be the number of competitors at sites 1 and 2, respectively, and let the total distance between 1 and 2 be given by d_2. The delivered price schedule to all buying points is then designated by

$$P_{D_j} = \frac{(xa + c\bar{k}_j)}{c + x} + \frac{1}{c + x}\,[c_1 T_j + c_2(d_2 - T_j)], \tag{11}$$

where $c = c_1 + c_2$. Note further in this connection the relation given by

$$\frac{\partial P_{D_j}}{\partial T_j} = \frac{1}{c + x}\,(c_1 - c_2). \tag{12}$$

This equation indicates that the slope of the delivered price schedule for each firm at site 1 is influenced sharply by the number of competitors located at the distant site 2. In fact, as a limit case recognized in Greenhut and Greenhut [1975] and Phlips [1976], uniform (discriminatory) prices apply to a set of homogeneous markets situated between two equally weighted production centers.

III. Toward an Operational Model

Varying degrees of competition or types of demand at distant points have divergent effects under discriminatory pricing. From equations (1) through (10), we see that as competition increases at the established production center, or demand convexity at all market points decreases, the *DPS* I (i.e., the delivered price schedule) of panel(a) in Figure I gives way to *DPS* II. In somewhat similar fashion, changes in competition or demand concavities *at selected market*

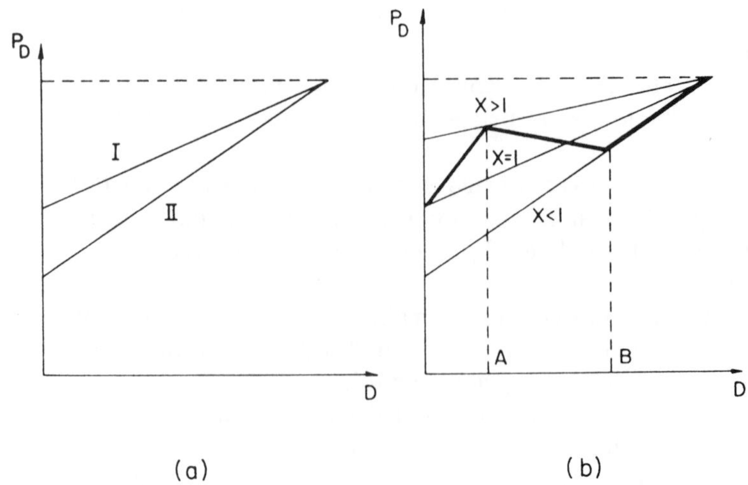

FIGURE I

points, e.g., convex, not linear, demand in and around the environs of distant point A, would generate a sharp change in price. It would, in particular, raise the price around A, as in panel (b), whereas more concave demands at points beyond A toward B will lower the price.[3] Because variations in competition or demand concavity have similar theoretical effects on the *DPS*, and correspondingly because businessmen may be expected to view the two together as one effect, we did not attempt to separate the "c" and "x" variables in our empirical work. We asked businessmen instead to view competitive effects in terms of the number and location of rivals, to rank the extent of the competition, and to classify broadly the demand patterns they faced as separate determinants of price. Our model, *as described later*, and attendent questionnaire thus provided a several-fold dimension of impacts of rival firms (and *indirectly* the effect of the value "x").[4]

Breaks in the *DPS*, which under the Robinson-Patman Act in the United States generally require demonstration by defendants of good faith price matching, appear in our theory to be justifiable either on the basis of different levels of competition or different underlying

3. We can propose that in a market space characterized by heterogeneous competition and demand, the profit-maximizing *DPS* could be a discontinuous schedule. Contrasting effects apply to f.o.b. mill pricing as only the level of the *DPS* is altered, the slope always remaining unity with respect to freight cost. (Also, see Smithies [1941], Ackley [1942], Dewey [1955], Beckmann [1970], Greenhut, Hwang, and Ohta [1975], and Capozza and Van Order [1977b].)

4. Part of the demand effect was included directly in our model via an estimate of the level of demand, i.e., the parameter "a" of equation (2).

demand conditions. Simply put, in the absence of constraining statutes and undesirable effects on consumer goodwill, profit-maximizing pricing could be expected to produce nonlinear, dip-bump types of price schedules over greater distances in a seller's market space.[5] We shall ascertain below whether such price schedules do prevail in the United States.

The empirical results we obtained relate to the theory outlined above. The following section of the paper contends that spatially discriminatory pricing is prevalent in the United States but that in general some differences characterize the pricing structures of firms in the sampled states. Section V extends the analysis in tests of the *specific properties* of our model.

IV. General Results

Our present discussion will *not* account for discontinuities in the *DPS* nor even indicate the extent to which sharp slope changes in price schedules occurred. Such particularization is left instead for Section V of the paper, where the particular properties of our regression model are explained and, in turn, specific data evaluated. For the present, we shall provide a bird's eye view of the data, in particular to indicate that pricing differences prevail among the sampled states. Whether these differences are due to contrasting reactions to some variable(s) in the different states will then be determined later in the paper after our operational model has been set forth. For the present, interstate comparisons of our data are recorded in summary form in Table I. We found the following:

(1) Firms in the United States generally price discriminatorily. Out of 174 sampled firms, less than one-third simply added the full freight cost to a unique f.o.b. mill price, i.e., priced nondiscriminatorily over space. More than two-thirds of the sampled firms priced discriminatorily, either everywhere over their market spaces or over some part of their market space.

(2) The contents of Table I provide the basis for a χ^2 test that can determine whether the distributions of the surveyed firms in the sampled states are the same or are different. The null hypothesis for the χ^2 test is

H_0. The firms in the five states recorded in Table I do not price differently. The alternative hypothesis is then

H_A. The firms in the five states recorded in Table I do price differently. We obtained

5. See Greenhut and Greenhut [1977].

TABLE I

COMPARISON OF PRICING STRATEGIES AMONG DIFFERENT STATES*

Region	Nondiscriminatory F.O.B. mill pricing	Discriminatory: Uniform pricing only	Discriminatory: Discriminatory pricing only	Discriminatory: Mixed f.o.b. and discriminatory pricing	Total
California	5 (13.5)	10 (27.0)	8 (21.6)	14 (37.8)	37
Florida	18 (52.9)	5 (14.7)	5 (14.7)	6 (17.6)	34
Missouri	18 (47.3)	5 (13.1)	5 (13.1)	10 (26.2)	38
Nebraska	5 (14.2)	11 (31.4)	7 (20.0)	12 (34.2)	35
Texas	11 (36.3)	6 (20.0)	3 (10.0)	10 (33.3)	30
The U. S.	57 (32.7)	37 (21.2)	28 (16.0)	52 (16.0)	174

* Each sampled firm reported a 5 percent or greater freight cost-delivered cost burden. Note further that the numbers in parentheses represent the percentage of firms sampled in each state practicing the given spatial price policy.

$$\chi^2(12) = 174(1.1367) - 1) = 23.80,$$
$$\text{hence } Pr[\chi^2(12) = 23.80 | H_0] < 5\%.$$

This χ^2 indicates that the null hypothesis should be rejected, and the conclusion established that the firms in the five states in Table I differed in their pricing structures. There remains, accordingly, the need to determine the behavioral reactions to the variables of the model that would account for the pricing differences in the sampled states.

It warrants mention that in another paper it will be shown that American firms price differently than do West German firms and Japanese firms. In a form corresponding to H_0, however, it will be shown that the West German firms price similarly to firms in Japan, with discriminatory pricing in the two countries being reflective of the same determinants and of the same general order. In fact, the discrimination is much more complete in those countries than in the United States as delivered prices are often lowered over great distances to values less than those charged to buyers located closer to the seller. This type of discrimination was *not found in the United States.* The data recorded in Table I thus reflect what can be styled as a comparatively moderate form of price discrimination. We probe more deeply into the American spatial pricing structure below.

V. The Regression Model and Specific Determinants of Spatial Prices

The model used in our survey required particularizing of the explanatory variables that constituted the theory of Section II. To view the requisite transformation, consider the implicit form given by

$$F = f(c,d,f,o), \tag{13}$$

where c represents the competition factor, d the demand factor, f the freight cost, o the other forces observed in spatial markets, and F the freight absorption reflective of the particular pricing policy adopted by the spatial firm. The regression equation that corresponds to (13), and that further helps evaluate the individual firm's pricing practice is then given by

$$F_{ij}^s = \beta_0^s + \beta_1^s NC_{ij}^s + \beta_2^s RC_{ij}^s + \beta_3^s RI_{ij}^s + \beta_4^s RD_{ij}^s + \beta_5^s LC_{ij}^s + \beta_6^s DP_{ij}^s + \beta_7^s SF_{ij}^s + \epsilon_{ij}^s, \tag{14}$$

where the superscript "s" stands for the sth state and the subscript "*i*" the *i*th firm in that state. A *detailed explanation* on the construction and interpretation of the dependent and explanatory variables comprising (14) is provided *in the Appendix to this paper* to which we also attach the questionnaire that was used. We record at this point only a brief explanation of the meaning of these variables.

F^s_{ij} stands for the freight absorption rate, which, in our operational model, serves to characterize the firm's spatial pricing policy. This dependent variable F^s_{ij} is influenced by NC^s_{ij}—the number of competitors the firm has at different market points, RC^s_{ij}—the rank (or extent) of the competition assigned by the seller as applying to his different markets, RI^s_{ij}—the importance of the given market to the seller, RD^s_{ij}—the dominance he claims his firm possesses over its rivals in a given market, LC^s_{ij}—the locational pattern of competitors, for example, a distribution in which the intensity of competition from rivals is significantly greater as distance increases, DP^s_{ij}—the spatial demand pattern, e.g., spaceless (local) demands that are homogeneous in all markets, and finally SF^s_{ij}—the level of the firm's freight cost burden in selling to its several market points.

Figure II helps tie up spatial price theory with our regression model. It assumes a unit freight cost per unit of distance D along its horizontal scale, while the linear delivered price schedule BB' implies a set of homogeneous markets over the firm's market space. Note in particular that the line BB' depicts discriminatory pricing, since it is drawn at less than unit slope; in contrast, the dotted line containing dips and bumps at market points 1 and 2 reflects not only discriminatory pricing but special impacts from equation (14) factors that are promotive of varying rates of freight absorption from market point to market point.

Consider in the above context the variables NC (number of competitors) and RI (market importance) in equation (14). Their β coefficients, β_1 and β_3, should, respectively, be positive and negative. β_1 should be positive because NC implies that the greater the number of rivals selling in a market, the lower will be the delivered price in the environs of that market, and in turn the greater will be the value assigned to the freight absorption rate F^s_{ij}. A positive β_1 thus combines with more competitors in increasing F^s_{ij}. But take RI. Because—as explained in the Appendix—our questionnaire assigns a high number to less important market points, such as market point 2 in Figure II, a negative β coefficient applies in order to lower the freight absorption rate. In corresponding manner, our model assigns a positive (negative) *LC when competition decreases (increases) at more distant market*

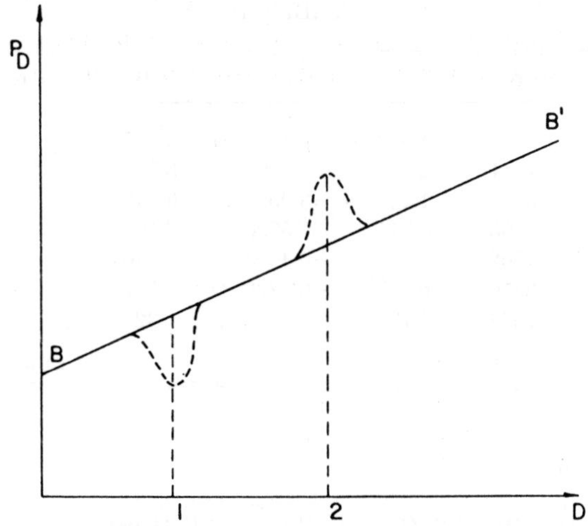

FIGURE II

points. Thus β_5—as with β_3—should normally be negative in reflection of the lower (higher) freight absorption rate that would apply when distant markets are subject to less (greater) competition than the proximate markets.

Test of Multicollinearity

Before presenting our regression findings *and* evaluating each factor's influence on the shape of the delivered price schedules of the sampled firms, the possibility of multicollinearity applying to the model requires brief discussion. Indeed, we stress that even though the estimated regression coefficients in the presence of multicollinearity will remain *BLUE*, a test for it is still in order. Utilizing a method reflective of Frisch [1934], as set forth by Toro-Vizcarrando and Wallace [1968], we found the differences between the sum of the incremental contributions of each variable and the R^2 to be less than 20 percent for all sampled states. We record in Table II our findings for the state of California.

The obtained index of multicollinearity M is given by

$$M = \sum_{2}^{8} \theta_j - R^2 = 0.3703 - 0.2621 = 0.1082, \qquad (15)$$

which suggests that existence of multicollinearity with respect to the California data was not severe. Using the same procedure, we note that similar results apply to the data of the other states.

TABLE II

Variables	β	σ	t	F	$\theta = (1 - R^2)F/n - k$
NC	2.4638	1.31	1.8807	3.5372	0.0435
RC	−7.1911	2.34	−2.9593	8.7574	0.1077
RI	−3.3902	1.12	−3.0081	9.0490	0.1112
RP	0.6395	0.24	2.5890	6.7032	0.0824
LC	−0.1502	0.32	−0.4693	0.2203	0.0027
DP	−0.3376	0.46	−0.7229	0.5226	0.0064
SF	0.1578	0.13	1.1718	1.3267	0.0163
	$n = 68$ $k = 8$ $R^2 = 0.2621$			Sum	0.3703

Specific Factors

Table III summarizes our regression findings for all sampled firms. Evaluation follows of each factor's influence on the slope of the delivered price schedules of the sampled firms.

The Competitive Factor

There are two factors in our model, *NC* and *RC*, which, respectively, provide objective and subjective measures of the intensity of competition to which the firm is subject. We see from columns (1) and (2) of Table III that in general these measures are statistically significant and that their signs conform to theoretical expectations. More specifically, whenever competition is severe, the firm's delivered price tends to be lowered and vice versa.

Figure III indicates that California firms were particularly influenced by *NC* and *RC*. To understand this result, recall that a line such as *BB′* was proposed to prevail when spatial markets are homogeneous with respect to demand and competition. In turn, the dip-bump shaped *DPS* was proposed, for example, under conditions of varying levels of competition over space. Observe that columns (1) and (2) of Table III suggest that American firms generally respond to changes in competition, and adjust their delivered price accordingly. This reaction is sharply indicated by the high level of significance obtained in most sampled states for *RC* (column (2), Table III). In fact, this particular (subjective) measure of competitiveness (see questionnaire, item 5d) helped distinguish Texas sellers from others since—unlike others sampled in the United States—officials of Texas firms apparently downgraded *RC* while claiming that a simple change in the number of competitors (column (1), Table III) was the dominant *competitive* consideration controlling their prices at different

TABLE III

SUMMARY OF REGRESSION RESULTS

States	Variables (1) *NC*	(2) *RC*	(3) *RI*	(4) *RD*	(5) *LC*	(6) *DP*	(7) *SF*	
California	2.4638	−7.1911	−3.3902	0.6395	−0.1502	−0.3376	0.1578	R^2 = 0.2601
	(1.31)*	(2.34)***	(1.12)***	(0.24)	(0.32)	(0.46)	(0.13)	F = 2.0446*
Florida	0.3840	−3.5206	−0.1299	1.4936	0.3247	0.2297	1.2387	R^2 = 0.1847
	(0.21)*	(1.67)**	(0.12)	(1.57)	(0.29)	(0.26)	(1.65)	F = 4.3846**
Missouri	−2.3224	−9.9996	6.9898	7.2208	−0.6529	0.8154	1.7583	R^2 = 0.1165
	(4.44)	(4.65)**	(4.79)	(3.81)*	(0.46)	(1.40)	(2.40)	F = 1.3556
Nebraska	1.2041	−0.4323	−1.8725	0.9324	0.2506	0.3565	0.7104	R^2 = 0.2705
	(0.68)*	(0.19)**	(1.24)	(1.03)	(0.33)	(0.45)	(0.72)	F = 3.1074**
Texas	1.1304	−0.7456	−1.3724	0.3820	−0.7653	−3.4826	1.0215	R = 0.2158
	(0.53)**	(0.65)	(1.78)	(0.22)*	(0.45)*	(5.80)	(0.73)	F = 2.1865*
The U.S.	1.4743	−0.1203	−0.4506	0.3203	−1.2754	−0.8706	0.7358	R^2 = 0.1450
	(0.86)*	(0.04)***	(0.22)**	(0.18)*	(0.74)*	(0.96)	(0.62)	F = 11.25***

a. The regression coefficients and their corresponding standard deviation are recorded under each explanatory variable, with standard deviations provided within the parentheses. As explained in the Appendix, only the signs are statistically meaningful at the significance levels.

b. We use *, **, and *** to denote, respectively, a two-tailed test that is significant at the 10 percent, 5 percent, and 1 percent level.

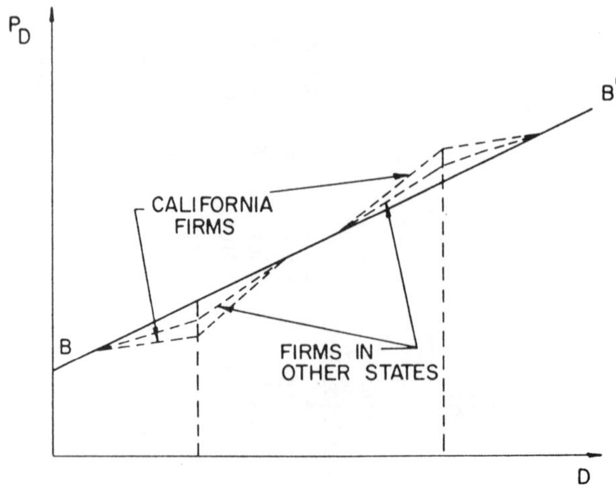

FIGURE III

market points. (Comparing the significance levels in columns (1) and (2) of Table III indicates that firms in the United States were generally more responsive than Texas firms to the rank they assigned competitive impacts compared to the number of competitors they faced at different points in their market space.) On the other hand, California officials appeared to react the most to competitive impacts, and in particular to the rank of importance they assigned to a particular market, column (3). Columns (1), (2), *and* (3) of Table III thus combine to imply that sharper dip-bump *DPS* schedules would apply to California firms because of competitive impacts vis à vis the firms sampled in the other states.

The Location Factor

We also found significant responsiveness in the *DPS* of firms in the United States to the location of their competitors (see column (5) of Table III). At the same instance, the dominance a firm may have possessed at different market points, i.e., column (4), tended to be a more important factor (in the sense of statistical significance) in determining price than the locational pattern of competitors, column (5). This result is not surprising if it implies competitive pricing. Moreover, since officials of most of the very large firms we sampled in the United States indicated that they priced f.o.b. mill, perhaps in recognition of Robinson-Patman constraints, dominance in a market did not necessarily tie up with price leadership (i.e., pricing

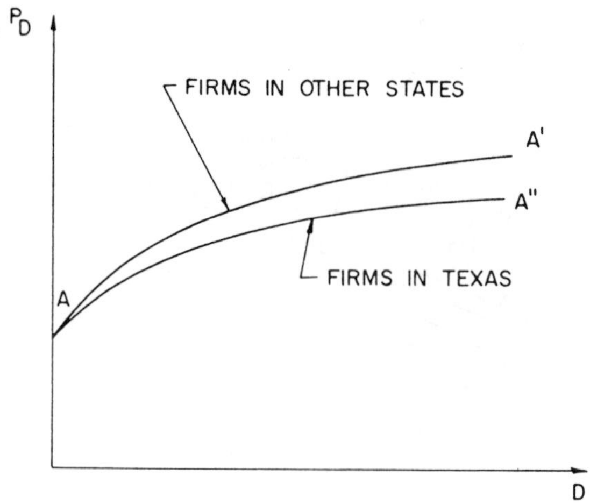

FIGURE IV

up or down freely as leadership opportunities arose). (We might observe parenthetically that this dominance factor *RD* was of significantly greater importance among the less constrained [by law and mores] firms of West Germany and Japan vis à vis their American counterparts.) Related speculation applies to the fact that Texas-based sellers tended to emphasize the importance of the location of rival firms *LC* more than did other American firms; in fact, the mere existence of locationally differentiated rivals tended to have a noticeable downward impact on the prices of Texas firms as their market distances increased (see Figure IV and equation (12)).

The Demand Factor

Our theory predicts a dip-bump schedule in the slope of *DPS* whenever spatial demands are heterogeneous. However, our statistical data uncovered only slight relationship between the shape of the *DPS* and the intensity of demands over space. In other words, our findings suggest a low responsiveness in pricing policy among American firms to changes in the gross demands that prevailed at different market points. This situation is understandable in the sense that though the antitrust laws in the United States permit "good faith" price matching, geographic adjustments in price—due to what may be considered temporary (or not readily identifiable and supportable) differences in demand—do not warrant adoption by firms of what might be considered in the United States as questionable pricing patterns over distance.

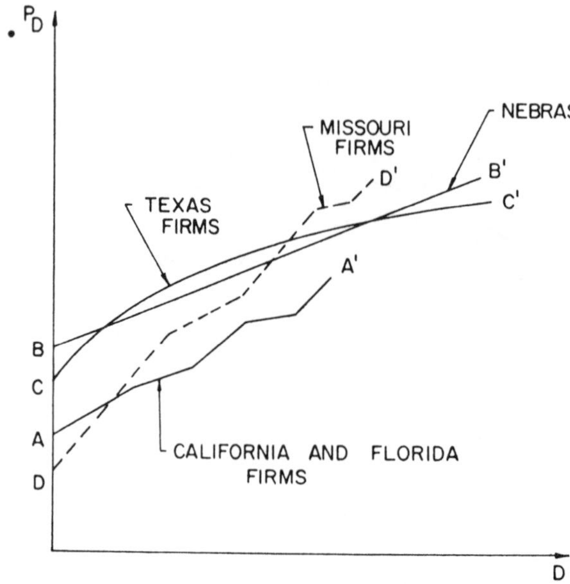

FIGURE V

Other Factors

Our model included other explanatory variables in addition to those noted above. These include the spatial friction (distance cost) factor *SF*, and the error term. Our findings indicate that the significance level of the *SF* factor was of a low order.

Interaction of All Factors

If we let all factors change at the same time, the several *DPS* would contrast noticeably from each other. We can nonetheless readily identify basic patterns among sampled firms and states, and utilize Figure V for this purpose.

We propose that California and Florida firms tend to have a bump-dip *DPS* in the nature of schedule *AA′*. In contrast, Nebraska firms are generally characterized by a straight-line discriminatory *DPS* of the form given by *BB′*. Texas firms, on the other hand, tend to be characterized by the concave downward delivered price schedule *CC′*. Missouri firms, in turn, are generally depicted by the *DD′* schedules. The reason we propose these patterns for the states in question is partly due to the finding that the statistical significance of competitive factors is somewhat greater in California and Florida than in the other surveyed states; more frequent changes are projected

TABLE IV

CHOW'S TEST

	California		Florida		Pooled	
	d.f.	*s.s.*	*d.f.*	*s.s.*	*d.f.*	*s.s.*
Regression	7	37.0078	7	7.8058	7	37.7143
Error	88	104.1851	76	33.3157	172	144.6369
Total	95	141.1930	83	42.1215	179	182.3512

Variance due to	*d.f.*	*s.s.*	*m.s.*	*F*
Pooled total	179	182.3512;		
less: pooled reg.	7	37.7143		
Pooled error;	172	144.6369		
less: separated error combined	164	137.5008	0.8384	1.03
Difference	8	6.9361	0.8670	

to take place in their *DPS* slopes with distance than for firms in the other sampled states (see Table III). As already observed, respondents for Texas firms expressed concern over the spatial location pattern of rivals, with the number of competitors proving to be statistically significant at the 5 percent level. In further contrast, we propose the *BB′* schedule in Nebraska because respondents indicated that homogeneity of competition characterizes the seller's industry, and further that they were not unduly influenced, as it were, by firms located at more distant market points. The comparatively large use of f.o.b. pricing by Missouri firms combined with the importance of the *RC*, *RD* factors provide the basis for our proposing a schedule steeper than *BB′* with occasional dips and bumps.

Chow's Test

A more precise basis for measuring the similarities or differences between the states is in order, especially since rather different price determinants were suggested above to dominate the pricing patterns of the sampled firms in different parts of the United States. We use here Chow's [1960] test for determining these differences.

Recall initially that the data obtained from California and Florida firms appear to be of rather similar order; therefore, these two states readily provide a basis for Chow's test, as recorded in Table IV. The F-statistic that was derived is $F = 1.03$, which is *not* significant even at the 20 percent level. We accordingly accept the hypothesis that the samples of California and Florida firms are drawn from the same universe, and hence that their respective *DPS*'s should be of the same type. Since there are five selected states at our disposal, ten different combinations obtain with tests of each of them applicable. Suffice it to say for our purpose that all of the other nine pairs provided significant differences. It was actually in light of this finding that the different *DPS* patterns of Figure V were drawn, with reasons previously entered providing our interpretation of Chow's test results.

APPENDIX

Data were obtained through mailed questionnaires and personal interviews, and the following regression model was used:

$$\text{(A1)} \quad F^s_{ij} = \beta^s_0 + \beta^s_1 NC^s_{ij} + \beta^s_2 RC^s_{ij} + \beta^s_3 RI^s_{ij} + \beta^s_4 RD^s_{ij} + \beta^s_5 LC^s_{ij} + \beta^s_6 DP^s_{ij} + \beta^s_7 SF^s_{ij} + \epsilon^s_{ij}.$$

This Appendix provides a detailed discussion of the model in order to explain the construction and meaning of each variable.

Define F^s_{ij} for the ith firm in state s as

$$\text{(A2)} \quad F^s_{ij} = 1 - (P^s_{i,j} - P^s_{i,1})/(D^s_{i,j} - D^s_{i,1}), \quad i = 1,2,3, \ldots, n_s; \; j = 2,3,4,5,$$

where F^s_{ij} stands for the rate of freight absorption on unit sales to the jth market by that firm and n_s provides the number of firms in the sth state. Likewise, $P^s_{i,1}$ and $P^s_{i,j}$ are the delivered prices the subject firm charges, respectively, in the 1st and jth markets, while $D^s_{i,1}$, $D^s_{i,j}$ are, respectively, the freight cost on unit sales to the 1st and jth markets.[6]

Now the explanatory variables of equation (14) in the text, repeated above as (A1), are defined below:

NC^s_{ij}. This measure provides the ratio of the number of competitors the subject firm has in its jth market to the total number of rivals it confronts throughout its market space.[7] On the basis of our theory, prices are lowered via increased freight absorption as the intensity of competition increases. Hence the NC^s_{ij} coefficient should bear a positive sign in our multiple regression analysis.

RC^s_{ij}. This measure provides a subjective ranking of the intensity of competition the firm faces in its jth market.[8] This measure

6. The rate of freight absorption is defined in our study as the portion of freight cost that is absorbed by the seller in his delivered price and hence not paid by the buyer.

7. Instead of defining NC^s_{ij} as $NC^s_{ij} = m^s_{ij}/\Sigma_j m^s_{ij}$, it could be defined as $NC^s_{ij} = (m^s_{ij} - m^s_{i,j-1})/\Sigma_j m^s_{ij}$. However, the definition utilized in this paper provides a better fit, as was indicated by the stepwise procedure we used in our preliminary model building stage.

8. A generally accepted measure of "intensity of competition" or "degree of competitiveness" does not exist. We, therefore, used *NC* and *RC*, respectively, to serve as an objective and subjective measure of competition.

is defined as the ratio between the subjective ranking assigned the jth market to the sum of all ranking numbers the firm is subject to throughout its market area. A small number indicates intense competition, since the ranking system used in the questionnaire utilizes the numbers 1, 2, 3, 4, and 5 to indicate strongest, next strongest, etc., competition the firm faces in each of the five markets for which company officials were asked to provide data. This coefficient should thus bear a negative sign because assigning a small number to RC^s_{ij} associates with the belief that competition is sharp at a given market point; in turn, the small subtraction yields a high rate of freight absorption for that market.

RI^s_{ij}. This measure provides the subjective ranking by the reporting official of the importance of the jth market to the seller. The calculation and interpretation of this measure is similar to that of RC^s_{ij}, numerically opposite to NC^s_{ij}. Thus, we expect a negative coefficient for this variable, since a small number in RI^s_{ij} reflects a very important market, and hence substantial freight absorption by a seller wanting to maintain a foothold in that market.

RD^s_{ij}. This measure provides the subjective ranking by the reporting official of the impact on prices that the subject firm has in its jth market. Market dominance in our model establishes a small RD^s_{ij}, so a positive coefficient is expected because dominance resulting generally from locational advantage suggests that only a low freight absorption rate will be necessary.

LC^s_{ij}. This representation provides an explanatory variable standing for the location of competitors at each reported market point. We use formula (A3) to determine the value for LC^s_{ij}:

$$\text{(A3)} \quad LC^s_{ij} = (LP + CP) \times (j - 1); \quad \begin{aligned} LP &= 0.1, 0, -0.1 \\ CP &= 0.1, 0, -0.1 \\ j &= 2, 3, 4, 5. \end{aligned}$$

In (A3), LP stands for the locational pattern of the subject firm's competitors. It equals 0.1, 0, −0.1, respectively, when the subject firm's competitors are located at its production site, dispersed evenly over the firm's entire market space, or located together at a distant center. The symbol CP relates to the subjective evaluation of the competitive pattern of rivals, i.e., the intensity of competition at different distances. It equals 0.1, 0, −0.1, respectively, when competition decreases, stays the same, or increases with distance from the subject firm's plant site. Note further, for example, that if the ith firm in the sth region reported localization of all of its competitors at the same point as the subject firm (LP = 0.1), and if in addition the intensity of competition decreases as distance increases (CP = 0.1), we would obtain the large positive values given in Case I below. However, if rivals were uniformly distributed ($LP = 0$) and the extent of competition increased with distance ($CP = -0.1$), the Case II values obtain:

Case I	Case II
$LC^s_{i2} = (0.1 + 0.1) \times (2 - 1) = 0.2$	$LC^s_{i2} = (0 - 0.1) \times (2 - 1) = -0.1$
$LC^s_{i3} = (0.1 + 0.1) \times (3 - 1) = 0.4$	$LC^s_{i3} = (0 - 0.1) \times (3 - 1) = -0.2$
$LC^s_{i4} = (0.1 + 0.1) \times (4 - 1) = 0.6$	$LC^s_{i4} = (0 - 0.1) \times (4 - 1) = -0.3$
$LC^s_{i5} = (0.1 + 0.1) \times (5 - 1) = 0.8$	$LC^s_{i5} = (0 - 0.1) \times (5 - 1) = -0.4.$

Given this construction for LC, the related β value is always negative, since a small amount of freight absorption is associated with decreasing competition over distance (i.e., a numerically high positive LC) in contrast to the substantial freight absorption associated with increasing competition over distance (i.e., negative LC).

DP^s_{ij}. This representation provides a dummy variable for the demand pattern over distance. We use (A4) below to determine the value for DP^s_{ij}:

$$\text{(A4)} \qquad DP^s_{ij} = (RD) \times (j - 1), \quad RD = -0.1, 0, 0.1 \quad j = 2, 3, 4, 5,$$

where the expression RD stands for the reported demand pattern the subject firm faces. This RD is defined as -0.1, 0, 0.1, respectively, for smaller, identical, or greater demand in more distant markets. The assignment process that provides the DP^s_{ij} value is therefore similar to that of LC^s_{ij}, and a negative coefficient β_6 should obtain to yield the appropriate freight absorption effect.

SF^s_{ij}. This representation provides the measure of spatial friction that applies to each market considered individually. It is defined as

$$\text{(A5)} \qquad SF^s_{ij} = D^s_{ij}/P^s_{i,m}, \quad j = 2, 3, 4, 5,$$

where D^s_{ij} and $P^s_{i,m}$ stand, respectively, for the reported unit freight cost to the jth market and the price quoted at the mill. A positive β_7 coefficient should be obtained because the greater is the cost of distance, the more leverage a firm has in adjusting its price. Also, a large measure indicates that the firm is approaching its market extremity; hence there exists a greater need for the firm to absorb even more freight than otherwise.

Special characteristics were assigned the explanatory variables. In particular, the variables RC^s_{ij}, RP^s_{ij}, RI^s_{ij} are of simple ordinal scale while variables LC^s_{ij}, DP^s_{ij} are of weighted binary form. Accordingly, the interpretation of our statistical findings is both affected and restricted by these characteristics with ordinal scaling limiting the objects in a class to "order" and "rank." Quite importantly, the numerals assigned are subject to monotonic transformation without losing their order, though the magnitude of many numerals, hence the differences between them, has no significance at all [Caws, 1959; Ackoff, 1962]. Statistical interpretation of our data must, therefore, be restricted to sign [Conover, 1971].

It warrants final mention that not only did the results recorded previously in this paper prove to have high levels of significance, but the basic assumptions of the linear regression model were not violated. In fact, recall that multicollinearity was expected to apply to numerical specifications of competition and demand magnitudes at different market points. Yet the comparison we effected of the incremental sum of squares of our predetermined variables with the R^2 values of all variables treated simultaneously revealed only slight multicollinearity of the data.

The questionnaire used to generate the data required in our study follows.

QUESTIONNAIRE

Firm Name ________________ Telephone Number ____________
Official Supplying Data ______________________________

1. Classify your activity by selecting a standard product or service below.
   The good manufactured is ______________; the service supplied is ______________; or the good distributed is ______________.
2. Is the item in question (check one):
   a. substantially different, b. slightly different, c. identical to competitors' products.
3. How do you typically transport a. by highway, b. rail, c. water, or d. air. (check appropriate answer)
4. Do you typically use your own transport facility a. yes, b. no. (check one)
5. Please describe below a typical shipment of your product (or service) from your facility in ______________________ to five different buying locations:

	1	2	3	4	5
a. Specify the buyer's location (e.g. Chicago, Ill.)	_____	_____	_____	_____	_____
b. The delivered price at the buyer's location is	_____	_____	_____	_____	_____
c. The number of competitors is	_____	_____	_____	_____	_____
How would you rank your competition at					

these buying points? (1) the greatest your firm faces, (2) the next greatest, (3) etc. (Possibly you will assign the same number to several customer buying points.) ______ ______ ______ ______ ______

d. Approximate the percentage of your total sales that your company sells to each of the locations ______ ______ ______ ______ ______

e. Using numbers as in 5 (d), rank the *relative* impact of your firm on the subject market. ______ ______ ______ ______ ______

f. The freight cost per unit of shipment to each buying location is ______ ______ ______ ______ ______

g.

6. The (general) price of the product considered in question 5 in a sale to a buyer located at your facility (whether or not any sales are made there) "would be" ______.
7. Your competitors are (check one):
   a. located near you, b. spread over the market area, c. located together at a distant point, d. increase with distances, e. decrease at more distant buying points, f. other (please specify) ______
8. *Assume* you have no competitors supplying the aforementioned 5 buying points. Would the demands for your product generally be a) greatest among buyers located close to you, b) greatest among buyers located at substantial distance from you, c) the same at all locations.

UNITED ENERGY RESOURCES
TEXAS A&M UNIVERSITY
VIRGINIA STATE UNIVERSITY

REFERENCES

Ackley, G., "Spatial Competition in a Discontinuous Market," this *Journal,* LVI (Feb. 1942), 212–30.
Ackoff, R. L., *Scientific Method* (New York: John Wiley & Sons, 1962).
Beckmann, M., *Location Theory* (New York: Harper Brothers, 1970).
Capozza, D., and R. Van Order, "Pricing Under Spatial Competition and Spatial Monopoly," *Econometrica,* XLV (Sept. 1977a), 1329–38.
——, and ——, "A Simple Model of Spatial Competition," *Southern Economic Journal,* XLIV (Oct. 1977b), 361–67.
——, and ——, "A Generalized Model of Spatial Competition," *American Economic Review,* LXVIII (Dec. 1978), 896–908.
Caws, P., "Definition and Measurement in Physics," in C. W. Churchman and P. Ra-

toosh, eds., *Measurement: Definitions and Theories* (New York: John Wiley & Sons, 1959).
Chow, G. C., "Tests of Equality Between Sets of Coefficients in Two Linear Regressions," *Econometrica*, XXVIII (July 1960), 591–605.
Conover, W. J., *Practical Nonparametric Statistics* (New York: John Wiley & Sons, 1971).
Dewey, D., "A Reappraisal of F.O.B. Pricing and Freight Absorption," *Southern Economic Journal*, XXI (July 1955), 45–54.
Eaton, B. C., and R. G. Lipsey, "The Introduction of Space into the Neoclassical Model of Value Theory," in M. J. Artis, and A. R. Nobay, *Studies in Modern Economic Analysis* (Oxford: Blackwells, 1977), 59–96.
Frisch, R., *Statistical Confluence Analyses By Means of Complete Regression Systems* (Oslo: University Economics Institute, 1934).
Greenhut, J., and M. L. Greenhut, "Spatial Price Discrimination, Competition and Locational Effects," *Economica*, XLII (Nov. 1975), 401–19.
——, and ——, "Nonlinearity of Delivered Price Schedules and Predatory Pricing," *Econometrica*, XLV (Nov. 1977), 1871–76.
Greenhut, M. L., M. J. Hwang, and H. Ohta, "Observations on the Shape and Relevance of the Spatial Demand Function," *Econometrica*, XLIII (July 1975), 669–82.
——, and H. Ohta, "Monopoly Output Under Alternative Spatial Pricing Techniques," *American Economic Review*, LXII (Sept. 1972), 705–13.
Phlips, L., "Spatial Pricing and Competition," Commission of the European Communities, *Studies Competition-Approximation of Legislation Series*–Brussels (1976).
——, "Intertemporal Price Discrimination and Sticky Prices," Presented at Summer Workshop, University of Warwick, 1977.
Robinson, J., *The Economics of Imperfect Competition* (New York: Macmillan, 1933).
Smithies, A. F., "Monopolistic Price Policy in a Spatial Market," *Econometrica*, IX (Jan. 1941), 63–73.
Toro-Vizcarrando, C., and T. D. Wallace, "A Test of the Mean Square Error Criterion For Restrictions In Linear Regression," *Journal of the American Statistical Association*, LXIII (June 1968), 558–72.
Watson, D. S., *Price Theory and Its Uses* (Boston: Houghton-Mifflin, 1968).

Economica, **48**, 79–86

Spatial Pricing in the United States, West Germany and Japan

By M. L. Greenhut

Texas A & M University

This paper investigates the spatial pricing policies of a sample of firms in the United States, West Germany and Japan. We begin in Section I by providing general results for the three countries. These suggest that f.o.b. pricing is the exception rather than the rule. Furthermore, there appear to be significant differences between the countries in the degree of spatial price discrimination.

The remainder of the paper examines whether the inter-country differences in spatial discrimination can be explained by a theory of spatial pricing. Section II uses the theory of spatial pricing proposed in Greenhut and Greenhut (1975) to derive an operational model. In Section III the parameters of this model are estimated from the individual country data and the results are discussed. Section IV presents the conclusions.

I. Price Findings for Sampled Firms

The data used in this study were obtained from a survey of firms in the three countries. In each country target regions were selected with (a) similar urban–rural proportions, as restricted by (b) existing acquaintanceships with professors in or near these urban–rural centres. Survey constraint (b) was imposed after a mailed questionnaire "pilot study" in the United States had indicated a likely need for follow-up mailings, phone calls and even interviews before a sufficient number of responses from a particular place (e.g., a particular state in the United States) could be expected.

After selecting our comparable survey areas, firms were picked at random from industrial lists of business establishments in each country, and questionnaires were mailed to them. The questionnaire is reproduced in the Appendix. The firms that returned questionnaires were compared to non-responding firms. No distinction in size of firm, industry type or location was apparent for any country or sub-region studied. Among the respondents, we dropped from the sample all firms that were not subject to a significant freight cost (defined to be a 5 per cent *minimum* "freight cost to delivered cost ratio" on sales to at least one distant market point). Our findings on pricing strategies are summarized in Table 1.

Firms in the United States tend to price discriminatorily. Of 174 sampled firms, less than one-third priced non-discriminatorily (f.o.b.). The spokesmen for the remaining firms (67 per cent) admitted that they did *not* add full freight cost to their mill price on all of their distant sales. These firms therefore priced discriminatorily. The tendency to price discriminatorily is even greater in West Germany and Japan, with the percentage of discriminating firms approximately 79 and 82 per cent respectively. It is obvious, therefore, that discriminatory

TABLE 1
NUMBERS OF FIRMS ADOPTING VARIOUS PRICING STRATEGIES

Country	Non-discriminatory f.o.b. mill pricing	Discriminatory: Uniform pricing only	Discriminatory: Other discriminatory pricing only	Discriminatory: Mixed pricing	Discriminatory: Total discriminating	Total
The U.S.A.	57(33)*	37(21)	28(16)	52(30)	117(67)	174
West Germany	7(21)	11(32)	5(15)	11(32)	27(79)	34
Japan	6(18)	9(27)	3(9)	15(46)	27(82)	33
Overall	70(29)	57(24)	36(15)	78(32)	171(71)	241

* Numbers in parentheses indicate the percentage of the country totals given in the last column.

pricing is not only possible in countries that have legislated against this practice, such as the United States, but is *the* prevalent pricing practice.

To investigate in more detail the possible differences between countries in the tendency of firms to price discriminatorily, a 3 × 2 contingency test was applied. The null hypothesis was that there are no inter-country differences in the proportion of discriminatory firms. The χ^2 value of 4·23 compares with a critical value of 4·60 for a 10 per cent significance level, and therefore provides some evidence of significant inter-country differences in price discrimination. Such differences may, of course, arise for a number of reasons. We shall later focus attention on the possibility that the firms in these countries may not view government restrictions on profit maximizing pricing in a uniform way.

II. OUR THEORY AND OPERATIONAL MODEL

The delivered prices charged at a set of buying points by competitive firms located at a given production centre were derived in Greenhut and Greenhut (1975). Its schedule can be written

$$(1) \qquad P = \frac{1}{c+x}(xb + c\bar{k}) + \frac{c}{c+x}\bar{T}$$

where P denotes the delivered price to a particular market point, c stands for the spatial competition factor (e.g. the number of sellers located together at the production centre who supply a particular distant market point), $\bar{k}$ is the average marginal cost of production of the selling firm, and $\bar{T}$ stands for the average distribution (transportation) cost of all firms supplying that market point; parameters x and b represent the concavity and price intercept of the demand curve, respectively.

The first term in equation (1) gives the mill price of the firms at the production centre, while $(c/(c+x))\bar{T}$ reflects the slope of the delivered price schedule (DPS) as the transport cost contribution changes with distance. The greater the number of suppliers (c) at the production centre, the lower is the mill price and the steeper is the slope of the DPS.

The existence of a rival production centre at a distance tends to reduce the average distribution cost ($\bar{T}$) of supplying each buying point located between the centres. It also increases the competition factor c and generates greater freight absorption at all intermediate buying points, compared with the single production centre case. These results can be generalized to cover sales to buyers not directly located between the production centres, and to multiple production centres located in a variety of spatial configurations.

Two of the several principles derived in Greenhut and Greenhut (1975) ought to be restated here.

(1) The greater the concentration of firms at a production centre, the lower is the mill price and the steeper is the discriminatory delivered price schedule. In fact, the DPS approaches the f.o.b. price schedule under conditions of extreme localization of industry.

(2) Competitive entry at a distance generates lower discriminatory delivered prices at all overlapping market points located between the production centres. A linear DPS may, in fact, give way to curvilinear schedules, or kinked linear schedules owing to spatial heterogeneities (e.g., in demand and competition).

Our operational model stems directly from the above theory, but requires broader terms than those presented in the earlier paper. In order to formulate an effective operational model that can explain industrial price policies empirically, the concepts that businessmen employ in explaining their firm's pricing policies in different markets must be used. For example, it was evident during the "pilot-study" phase of this investigation that company officials were reluctant to identify their competitors, and the location of rival plants, at specific market points. Instead they asserted simply that slightly different goods are produced "*around* here or there", warehoused "in this or that *area*", distributed by wholesalers located "near or far", and so on. We found it more practical and consistent to investigate the degree of competition (most intense, least intense, etc.) at a particular buying point, than to ask for the particular source of the competition. Even when we did ascertain the origin of a rival's product—chiefly during personal interviews—we often were not told the distribution channels, the exact freight cost, or the mill price (and production cost) at that origin point. Fortunately, such specific data are required only in the theory, and for the purposes of the survey we were able to accept less precise items of information.

An implicit form of our spacial-price theory is given by:

$$(2) \qquad G = f(c, d, t, o).$$

Freight absorption (G) is a function of the pattern of competition (c), the demand pattern (d), the cost of transport (t) and other factors (o). In our empirical studies we did not focus attention on single factor attributes, such as the number of competitors a firm confronts, the shape of the demand curve (x), average marginal costs ($\bar{k}$) or average transport costs ($\bar{T}$). Instead, we considered it necessary to subdivide our parameters into a system of 13 explanatory variables which would approximate the essential components of our theory. The selected regression model is given by

$$(3) \qquad G_i = \beta_0 + \beta_1 HO_i + \beta_2 TR_i + \beta_3 L_i + \beta_4 C_i + \beta_5 D_i + \beta_6 SFA_i + \varepsilon$$

where HO represents two dummy variables for product differentiation, TR a set of four transportation dummies, L measures the spatial location of competitors (two variables), C and D the degree to which competition and demand change with distance (two variables each), and SFA indicates the relative importance of freight cost. These variables are all defined in detail in the notes to Table 2. The subscript i refers to the ith firm. The freight absorption G_i was defined as

$$(4) \qquad G_i = 1 - \frac{1}{4} \sum_{j=2}^{5} \frac{P_{ij} P_{i1}}{t_{ij} - t_{i1}}$$

where P_{ij} and t_{ij} represent the delivered price and freight cost of the ith firm per unit sale in its jth market.

Certain variables in the model promote lower prices via greater freight absorption, and vice versa. For example, one dummy variable stands for increasing competition from rivals at more distant market points. When this occurs, the firm will charge lower prices at such distant points, *ceteris paribus*, in effect absorbing more freight cost; the coefficient on this variable should therefore be positive. Conversely, when demand is greater at distant market points, higher prices obtain, *ceteris paribus*; hence less freight cost would be absorbed and the corresponding coefficient in regression equation (3) should be negative.

III. Empirical Data Evaluated

Table 2 summarizes the regression results of our study of spatial pricing practices in the United States, West Germany and Japan. The overall findings dovetail closely with spatial price theory, despite the omission in our operational model of factors that may well influence the pricing policies of firms in free enterprise countries. Our data indicate that the location of competitors and the

Table 2

Summary of Regression Results†

						Variables‡
	(1) Product types			(2) Types of carriers used		
Countries	HO_1	HO_2	TR_1	TR_2	TR_3	T
USA	−0·322 (0·21)	−0·017 (0·015)	0·142 (0·10)	0·342 (0·132)	0·342 (0·26)	0·042 (0·03)
West Germany	−0·173 (0·16)	−0·361 (0·30)	0·334 (0·31)	0·013 (0·016)	−0·113* (0·06)	0·411* (0·24)
Japan	−0·110* (0·064)	−0·137 (0·088)	0·031 (0·036)	−0·058 (0·085)	0·472 (0·44)	0·423 (0·32)
Theoretical sign	−	−				+

† Regression coefficients and standard errors (in parenthesis) are recorded under each explanatory variable. *, **, *** denote significance at 10, 5 and 1 per cent levels, respectively.

‡ Variables (1)–(5) are dummy variables taking the values 0 or 1. They are defined as follows:

(1) $HO_1 = 1$ if the firm's product is substantially different from that of competitors; $HO_2 = 1$ if product is slightly different; $HO_1 = HO_2 = 0$ when the product is identical to that of competitors. Coefficients on both HO_1 and HO_2 are expected to be negative since a firm would absorb less freight cost if its product differs from rivals.

(2) The primary mode of transportation is indicated by $TR_1 = 1$ in the case of railways; $TR_2 = 1$ for roads and $TR_3 = 1$ for waterways. The excluded category is air carriers.

$T = 1$ if the firm owns its own carrier; its coefficient is expected to be positive because such firms have more opportunities for absorbing freight costs.

(3) $L_1 = 1$ if competitors are evenly dispersed over the market area; $L_2 = 1$ if competitors are sited together at a distant location; $L_1 = L_2 = 0$ then competitors and the subject firm are located at the same site.

degree of competition, as represented by variables L_1, L_2, CD and CI in Table 2, were *in general* the most important factors influencing spatial pricing policies. Each of these four variables were significantly different from zero *in each country*, highlighting the importance for pricing policies over economic space of the type of changes in competition that take place as sales distances increase. The spatial demand variables, DD and DI, are distinctly of secondary importance.

The consistent sign and significance of the locational patterns L_1 and L_2 support our theoretical prediction that the greater the concentration of firms at a production centre, the lower is the mill price and the steeper is the DPS. In contrast, dispersion of competition tends to flatten the DPS or cause it to assume a curvilinear form, rising at first before bending down.

Freight costs were relatively higher among the firms of West Germany and Japan than those of the United States. The spatial friction factor SFA was correspondingly found to be more significant in determining the pricing patterns of the firms in those countries.

Finally, an additional (Chow) test was run to determine whether there are any differences between the pricing practices of the sampled firms of West Germany, Japan and the United States. For this test a slightly different data set and model were used pursuant to which company officials were asked to assign ordinal values to particular spatial demand patterns, besides specifying changes in demand and competition as distances increased. They were also asked to provide the number of their competitors at different market points. (See, for example, items 5d–5f in the questionnaire in the Appendix.) Table 3 provides the results of

TABLE 2—*cont.*

(3) Competitor location patterns		(4) Pattern of competition		(5) Pattern of demand		(6) Freight costs	
L_1	L_2	CD	CI	DD	DI	SFA	
0·784**	0·649*	–0·037*	1·075**	0·735	–0·002	1·734	$R^2=0{\cdot}3297^*$
(0·37)	(0·38)	(0·02)	(0·51)	(0·68)	(0·002)	(1·31)	$F=2{\cdot}1434$
0·325***	0·142**	–0·134*	0·654**	0·041	–0·012	0·110*	$R^2=0{\cdot}2467^*$
(0·12)	(0·069)	(0·078)	(0·31)	(0·03)	(0·23)	(0·066)	$F=2.1426$
0·314*	0·440*	–0·354**	0·128*	0·034	–0·115	0·326*	$R^2=0{\cdot}3142^{**}$
(0·18)	(0·37)	(0·17)	(0·075)	(0·026)	(0·087)	(0·19)	$F=2.7834$

Coefficients on L_1 and L_2 are expected to be positive, since dispersion or distant location of competitors typically results in higher absorption of freight costs.

(4) $CD = 1$ if the competition decreases with distance; $CI = 1$ if it increases with distance; $CD = CI = 0$ represents unchanged intensity of competition over the market area. The coefficient on CD is expected to be negative (and that on CI positive) because absorption of freight cost would be lower if competition declines with distance.

(5) $DD = 1$ if the underlying *gross* demand for the product declines with distance; $DI = 1$ if demand increases; $DD = DI = 0$ if demand is uniform. DD should have a positive coefficient and DI a negative coefficient for reasons similar to those given for CD, CI.

SFA is a continuous variable measuring the firm's *average* spatial friction (i.e. the relative importance of freight cost) as defined by $SFA_i = \frac{1}{4}\sum_{j=2}^{5}\frac{D_{ij}}{P_j}$ where D_{ij} and P_j denote the unit freight cost and delivered price of firm i to the jth market.

TABLE 3*
CHOW TEST

	F statistic from Chow test	Level of significance (%)	Firms from same universe
USA v. W. Germany	9·62	0·5	No
USA v. Japan	2·819	1·0	No
WG v. Japan	1·2278	insignificant	Yes

* Neither the model underlying Table 2 nor the one that served as the basis for this table violated the classical linear regression model. For example, the problem of multicollinearity may appear to be prominent since, if competition increases as distance increases, one might expect respondents to claim that the underlying magnitude of demand would decrease. To evaluate this and other relationships, the incremental contribution of each predetermined variable was calculated and compared with the joint contributions of all variables simultaneously obtained. The differences between the incremental sums and the R^2 of all variables operating simultaneously were checked and the degree of multicollinearity found to be very slight.

the Chow test. The hypothesis tested was whether the firms in the sampled countries were drawn from the same universe, in which case their respective DPSs should be of the same type. The test indicated that the sampled American firms belong to a different universe than the firms of West Germany and Japan. The delivered prices of firms in West Germany and Japan did not always increase with distance; in fact, *sharply negative* changes in delivered price frequently characterized their sales over increasing distances along a given transport line. Thus a firm located in Karlsruhe, which may have priced in Bonn at a level 110 per cent that of its price in Karlsruhe, would quite conceivably price at, say, 90 per cent of its Karlsruhe price on sales in Münster, although transportation costs to Münster exceed those to Bonn. This type of pricing, easily explained in theory (Greenhut and Greenhut, 1977), was *never found* among the prices of the 174 sampled firms in the United States. Instead, the American firms *always* charged higher prices to more distant buyers, or *at a limit* followed uniform delivered prices over their market space. Quite conceivably it is the Robinson–Patman Act that causes the delivered price patterns of American firms to differ from those of firms in West Germany and Japan.[1] Nevertheless, discriminatory freight absorption is still characteristic of the pricing schedules of American firms, and in this respect the pricing policies of American firms are similar to those of firms in West Germany and Japan.

IV. CONCLUSION

In a recent paper, Eaton and Lipsey (1978) assume f.o.b. pricing in deriving the conclusion that a free enterprise space economy would generate positive profits in the long run. In a somewhat differently oriented paper on spatial economics, Beckmann (1976) concluded that f.o.b. pricing is socially preferable to discriminatory pricing in the long run with zero profits. However, his conclusion follows from the implicit assumption of fixed locations for firms in both the short *and* long run, and a market space divided equally between them. Phlips (1976), using an entirely different framework, stressed the likelihood that discriminatory, rather than f.o.b., pricing would be practised. Evidence cited by Norman (1981) also suggests that uniform pricing, an extreme form of spatial price discrimination, is widespread in Great Britain.

The survey data used in this paper indicate significantly greater use of discriminatory pricing policies, compared with f.o.b. pricing, in the countries studied. Our results suggest that theorems based on f.o.b. pricing may be comparatively unimportant, and that attention should be given to determining the impact of spatial price discrimination on microeconomic theory and, of course, location theory.

Our findings also show differences in the pricing practices of firms in different countries. Not only did we find that West German and Japanese firms discriminate in price more than American firms, but their discriminatory practices differ significantly from those of the American firms. The observed differences suggest that an important variable *may* be missing from our operational model, and this variable may well be governmental (statutory) interference. In particular, we have drawn attention to the possible influence of the Robinson–Patman Act in the United States.[2] Many Americans believe the Robinson–Patman Act makes *all* kinds of geographic price discrimination illegal, and this may lead to the Act being given undue emphasis by those responsible for the price schedules of their firms, thus accounting for the differential behaviour of American firms.

ACKNOWLEDGMENTS

The author wishes to thank his son John for useful suggestions and Professors S. Li and M. J. Hwang for help with both computations and model design. A deep debt is owed to Professors R. Funck, M. Streit, R. Thoss, and H. Seibert, who helped survey the firms in Germany; and to Professor H. Ohta and T. Yoruzo, who organized the survey of firms in Japan. Additional thanks are due to many others who assisted in the American survey, in particular W. Matthews, S. Holmes, G. Anders and J. Spivey; and to Professors R. Gilbert, R. Battalio, and H. Hwang for valuable suggestions. Funds that helped support this survey were provided by the National Science Foundation.

APPENDIX: QUESTIONNAIRE USED IN SURVEY

Firm Name Telephone Number

Official Supplying Data

1. Classify your activity by selecting a standard product or service below.
   The good manufactured is ; the service supplied is ; or the good distributed is
2. Is the item in question (check one):
   (a) substantially different, (b) slightly different, (c) identical to competitors products?
3. How do you typically transport: (a) by highway, (b) rail, (c) water, or (d) air? (check appropriate answer)
4. Do you typically use your own transport facility? (a) yes (b) no (check one)

5. Please describe below a typical shipment of your product (or service) from your facility in to five different buying locations:

	1	2	3	4	5
(a) Specify the buyer's location (e.g. Chicago, Ill.)					
(b) The delivered price at the buyer's location is					
(c) The number of competitors is					
(d) How would you rank your competition at these buying points? (1) the greatest your firm faces, (2) the next greatest, (3) etc. (Possibly you will assign the same number to several customer buying points.)					
(e) Approximate the percentage of your total sales that your company sells to each of the locations					
(f) Using numbers as in 5 (d), rank the *relative* impact of your firm on the subject market.					
(g) The freight cost per unit of shipment to each buying location is					

6. The (general) price of the product considered in question 5 in a sale to a buyer located at your facility (whether or not any sales are made there) "would be"

7. Your competitors are (check one):
(a) located near you, (b) spread over the market area, (c) located together at a distant point, (d) increase with distances, (e) decrease at more distant buying points, (f) other (please specify)

8. *Assume* you have no competitors supplying the aforementioned five buying points. Would the demands for your product generally be (a) greatest among buyers located close to you, (b) greatest among buyers located at substantial distance from you, (c) the same at all locations?

NOTES

[1] In one recent case under the Robinson–Patman statute, the Utah Pie Company was found to have charged a lower (delivered) price in a distant market than that charged in its home market. One spokesman interviewed by this author also admitted that his company had followed this kind of pricing policy, but upon the advice of lawyers eliminated the lower (delivered) price at distant market points in favour of a more moderate freight absorption practice.

[2] See also the discussion in Kaplan *et al.* (1958); Scherer (1970); and Greenhut (1974).

REFERENCES

BECKMANN, M. (1976). Spatial Price Policies Revisited. *Bell Journal of Economics*, **7**, 619–630.

EATON, B. C. and LIPSEY, R. G. (1978). Freedom of Entry and the Existence of Pure Profit. *The Economic Journal*, **88**, 455–469.

GREENHUT, J. G. and GREENHUT, M. L. (1975). Spatial Price Discrimination, Competition and Locational Effects. *Economica*, **42**, 401–419.

—— —— (1977). Nonlinearity of Delivered Price Schedules and Predatory Pricing. *Econometrica*, **45**, 1871–1876.

GREENHUT, M. L. (1974). *A Theory of the Firm in Economic Space* (2nd printing). Austin, Texas: Lone Star Press.

KAPLAN, A. G., DIRLAM, J. B. and LANZILOTTI, R. F. (1958). *Pricing in Big Business: A Case Approach*. Washington, D.C.: The Brookings Institute.

NORMAN, G. (1981). Uniform Pricing as an Optimal Spatial Pricing Policy. *Economica*, **48**, 87–91.

PHLIPS, L. (1976). Spatial Pricing and Competition. In *Studies in Competition*. Approximation of Legislation Series. Brussels: Commission of the European Communities.

SCHERER, F. M. (1970). *Industrial Market Structure and Economic Performance*. Chicago: Rand McNally.

DIFFERENCES IN SPATIAL PRICING IN THE UNITED STATES: A STATISTICAL ANALYSIS AND CASE STUDIES

M. L. Greenhut, M. Hwang, and S. Shwiff*

Abstract

This paper focuses attention on spatial pricing patterns of American firms. It identifies price strategies by statistical comparison of firms in Colorado with those located elsewhere in the United States. Competitive factors are found generally to dominate the pricing schedules of firms in other states, while the pricing schedules of Colorado firms are found to be influenced chiefly by demand patterns. Multi-product case examples are presented which spotlight pricing differences between firms located in a distributional-center type of state, such as Colorado, and those in other states. The cases also help explain why certain variables were uniquely important in Colorado.

I. Introduction

This paper will focus attention on the spatial pricing patterns of firms in the United States, stressing differences between firms sampled in the state of Colorado and those located elsewhere in the United States. Along with details provided by case examples it will be found that because Colorado is essentially a distributional center vis-a-vis states chiefly characterized as manufacturing centers, the spatial pricing pattern of Colorado firms differs significantly from that which generally prevails in the United States.

We shall sketch (only) in Section II of the paper the current theory of spatial pricing. Section III, in turn, outlines a related operational-statistical model. Details of the theory and the operational model will be left for other papers, as referenced below. We then set forth our Colorado data, comparing them with findings obtained for other American states. Section IV presents two case studies for the purpose of illustrating the special character of the Colorado data. Section V summarizes the paper's findings and proposes selected conclusions.

---

*Alumni Distinguished Professor, Texas A&M University; Associate Professor, West Virginia University; and Economist, Economic Affairs Department, Adolph Coors Company, respectively, USA. This paper is based on research funded by the National Science Foundation. We would like to thank A. Loviscek and J. Evans for computer-related assistance.

Date received: November 1983; Revised: April 1984.

II. General Theory of Spatial Pricing

Following along the lines of Dupuit (7), Pigou (24), and Robinson (26), spatial price theory (Hoover (18), Greenhut (13), Beckmann (1), Greenhut, Ohta (17), Greenhut and Greenhut (10), Greenhut, Hwang and Ohta (15), Capozza and Van Order (3, 4, 5, 6) Phlips (22, 23), Benson (2) and Norman (21)) has distinguished two main pricing variants; nondiscriminatory and discriminatory. Nondiscriminatory pricing in the spatial context is exemplified by f.o.b. mill pricing. This pricing variant has been stressed in the literature of location economics (von Thünen (18), Weber (29), Lösch (20), Isard (19), Smith (27), Richardson (25), and Eaton and Lipsey (8, 9)). It involves aggregating the individual demand curves that apply to each of a seller's market points. The levels of the resulting delivered price schedules are found to depend on the convexities of demand curves at all market points.

Discriminatory spatial pricing differs from f.o.b. mill pricing in that each market point is treated as a separate entity, with the profit maximizing calculus applied to each buying point rather than to aggregate demand. Global maximum profits thus obtain since individual marginal revenues are equated with the relevant marginal production cost (16). Viewing convexity of the curve from above, it is manifest that demand concavity of the form $p = b - ax^{1/2}$ at a particular market point or demand convexity of the form $p = b - ax^2$ will affect the level of price applicable at each particular market point. Differential intensities of competition at the individual market points have corresponding impacts in determining the particular price at the market point (10). The discriminatory delivered price schedule (i.e., the price including freight cost at the buyer's location) will therefore typically involve nonunit increases with unit increases in freight costs. (See Greenhut and Greenhut (11) for the exception.) The applicable delivered price schedule (DPS) may be positively sloped; it may be nonlinear with increases in distance (freight costs); or it may be linearly increasing at values greater than or less than the unit increase in freight costs; it may even involve negative dips (i.e., a lower delivered price at a distant market point compared with the price charged in the home market of the seller). A limitless variety of schedules actually obtain (10, 11, 14).

Let us stress finally that regardless of the demand conditions, the buyer distributions, and/or the levels of competition that exist over the landscape, it is simply the case that a seller who selects a unique mill price and adds full freight to each buying point is pricing f.o.b. mill. Under this form of pricing and assuming constant marginal cost, the entire schedule is raised or lowered depending strictly on the aggregate effect of the competitive conditions, the number of buyers (city sizes), and demand curve types that apply over the space. In contrast, since discriminatory pricing involves treating each market (point) separately, the sizes of the cities (e.g., number of buyers) along a transport line, or the sizes of the cities at any and all points in a plane market are non sequitur under constant marginal costs of production. Because net demand convexity at a point alone counts, it follows—to repeat—that a limitless variety of discriminatory schedules obtain. This is all we need appreciate for the purpose of ths paper. The facts that the elasticity(ies) of the individual market demand curves and the levels of competition in a market primarily determine the particular discriminatory prices charged at each point are covered in the literature, but basically beyond the needs of this paper.

DIFFERENCES IN SPATIAL PRICING IN THE UNITED STATES

III. The Operational Model and Statistical Findings

The model used in our survey of pricing patterns required broader terms than those specified in the theory. To view the requisite transformation, consider first the implicit form of the theory that we set forth in Section II of the paper:

(1) $F = f(C, D, S, O)$.

where the freight absorption F, that relates to a particular pricing policy is influenced by the competition factor, C, the demand factor, D, the spatial freight cost factor, S, and all other forces, O, that affect spatial price patterns. The regression equation corresponding to (1) which helps us evaluate the individual firm's pricing practice is then given by:

$$(2) \quad F^s_{ij} = \beta^s_0 + \beta^s_1 NC^s_{ij} + \beta^s_2 RC^s_{ij} + \beta^s_3 RI^s_{ij} + \beta^s_4 RD^s_{ij} + B^s_5 LC^s_{ij} + \beta^s_6 DP^s_{ij} + \beta^s_7 SF^s_{ij} + \varepsilon^s_{ij}.$$

where the superscript "s" stands for the sth state, and the subscript "ij" denotes the ith firm selling to the jth buyer in that state.

In the model given by (2), $F_{ij} = 1 - (P_{ij} - P_{i1})/D_{ij} - D_{i1})$ where F_{ij} stands for the rate of freight absorption on unit sales to the jth market by the firm, P_{ij} and P_{i1} are the delivered prices the subject firm respectively charges in the jth and 1st markets, while D_{ij}, D_{i1} are the freight costs on unit sales to the jth and 1st markets. This freight absorption rate in effect defines the underlying character of the firm's spatial pricing policy. Each respondent was asked to supply data for five separate market points.

The explanatory variable NC relates to the number of competitors the firm confronts at different market points. On the basis of our theory, prices would be lowered whenever the intensity of competition increases and sellers increase their absorption of freight costs. The NC coefficient should, accordingly, bear a positive sign in our multiple regression analysis.

The variable RC provides the rank (or extent) of the competition assigned by the seller to his different markets. The smaller the number, the more intense is the competition as the ranking system used in the questionnaire employed the numbers 1, 2, 3, 4, and 5 to indicate the greatest, next greatest, etc., level of competition the firm confronted in each of the five markets reported. Following this format, the coefficient for RC should be negative; this follows since when competition is severe at a given market point, a small numerical subtraction would yield the applicable rate of freight absorption for that market.

The variable RI provides the subjective ranking of the importance of the given market to the seller. The calculation and interpretation of this measure is similar to that of RC. Thus we expect a negative coefficient for this variable.

RD provides the subjective ranking of the dominance the firm is considered to possess over rivals in a given market. Because market dominance often results from a locational advantage and, in any case, should allow a low freight absorption rate, our model again utilizes smaller numbers for the greater impacts. Thus a positive coefficient for RD is to be expected.

The variable LC establishes the locational ordering of competitors.

Following the same number system (i.e., smaller numbers define greater intensities), we project a distribution in which the intensity of competition from rivals increases as distance increases. The effect is that the LC coefficient should always be negative since greater competition will be expected at points of increasing distance and hence greater freight absorption.

The variable DP is a dummy variable designed to depict a spatial demand pattern in which a greater reduction in applicable demands can be expected at more distant market points. The assignment process that provides the DP value is, therefore, similar to that of LC, and a negative coefficient is expected which would yield the appropriate freight absorption effect.

Finally, our model includes the variable SF; it stands for the spatial friction on the firm's sales at different market points. A positive coefficient should obtain because the greater is the cost of distance, the more leverage a firm will have in adjusting its price.

Pursuant to equation (2), a mail survey was conducted of firms selected randomly from Dun's Million Dollar Directory. Our overall sample involved two thousand companies in the United States. Via the mail survey, followed by telephone calls and some personal interviews, 310 completed observations were available for statistical analysis. We applied multiple regressions to the data in deriving the best linear approximation of delivered prices.

Overall Findings

Our data point to significant differences in the regression coefficients that distinguish the Colorado firms from those in other states. In particular, Table 1 compares the firms surveyed in the state of Colorado with those of the United States in general. The R^2 values are low, even considering the fact that R^2 values are usually low when cross-section data are used. Some of the parameters that were obtained were not of the expected sign; these occurrances may relate to a high degree of dependence between many of the independent variables. However, all significant values did possess the expected sign.

Two factors in our model, NC and RC, respectively provide objective and subjective measures of the intensity of competition that the firm faces. Our results indicte that firms throughout the United States generally respond quite sharply to changes in competition. The result of this, namely delivered prices which do not vary on a unit basis with unit increases in freight cost, is discriminatory pricing. In particular, the delivered price of the representative firm tends to be lowered (raised) whenever competition (NC and RC) is substantial (not substantial).

Our findings indicate that firms in Colorado emphasize different factors, namely the variables RI, RD, and DP. In further contrast, firms throughout the nation were more responsive (10% level) to the remaining variables, LC and SP, than Colorado firms.

The results spotlighted above suggest that the Colorado firms do contrast noticeably from those in the other states. Recall in this context that our theory predicted a dip-bump type of DPS schedule whenever spatial demands are heterogeneous. And we did find a responsiveness to local demand differences in the DPS of the firms in Colorado, particularly columns RI, RD, and DP. (Again see Table 1 which treats Colorado as an independent state distinct from the other states of the United States.) However, for reasons that will be evident from our case studies, this responsiveness tends to induce a somewhat different type of pricing practice than the competitive factors. It was this particular

TABLE 1

REGRESSION RESULTS: COLORADO AND ALL OTHER STATES#

States	N	Variables								
		Intercept	NC	RC	RI	RD	LC	DP	SF	R^2
Colorado	39	0.8476	-5.8232	3.9939	-4.7451**	2.0411**	1.1465	-2.2405**	0.0388	0.4782
		(0.73)	(-1.62)	(1.60)	(-1.95)	(1.60)	(0.64)	(-2.23)	(0.32)	
U.S.A.	271	0.6345*	2.5537***	-0.8233***	-2.2188*	0.9489	-0.5694*	-0.4643	0.0462*	0.3053
		(1.52)	(4.38)	(-2.34)	(-3.25)	(1.34)	(-1.62)	(-1.02)	(0.57)	

***Significant at 1%
**Significant at 5%
*Significant at 10%

#The figures in parentheses are t statistics.

contrast which, in fact, prompted the present writers to investigate further the differences and similarities in the price schedules of firms located in Colorado with those located elsewhere in the United States. These differences suggested possible advantage in conducting an analysis of covariance, which analysis not only enabled further testing but was directed towards the end of identifying more conclusively the forces that produced the significantly contrasting data. In this new analysis, Colorado firms were removed from the entire United States sample.

Covariance Analysis

The fundamental question is whether the regression coefficients for the firms in a given state are statistically different from those of firms in other states. If they do differ significantly from each other, the related need is to ascertain the variables which account for these differences. Of course, differences in uncontrolled variables, such as natural resources, tradition, state regulations, etc. tend to make some states and regions more efficient in producing and/or distributing certain products. Such heterogeneities would affect pricing schedules indirectly through resulting differences in competition, buyer locations, rival locations, and similar variables.

The main impact of uncontrolled variables should relate primarily to the β_0 (intercept) value of equation (2). We propose this impact because industrial differences, resource cost differences, and the like should reappear essentially in overall lower or higher price schedules for firms in a given state compared to firms in another. Quite differently, any one of the seven control variables should produce substantially changing freight absorption rates distinct from the upward lifting (downward) effect of the variables excluded from the model. Thus if, for example, NC increases significantly with distance and is a vital pricing determinant in a particular state or region, the derived β_1 value in equation (2) can be expected to be smaller than otherwise, thus yielding a flatter DPS slope. Our covariance analysis would test whether the difference in the intercepts and the slopes of the variables are indeed significant. If they are, the subject analysis should lead us to the variables which controlled (i.e., dominated) the firm's spatial price schedules. Suggestion as to "why" a significant difference occurs is a fundamental goal of the study.

Table 2 relates to our covariance analysis. It indicates that significant differences in overall homogeneity and slope apply to the multiple regression of the Colorado firms compared to the sampled firms located elsewhere in the United States. To fulfill the objectives noted above, the new regression given by equation (3) was used:

$$(3) \quad F = A_1 + A_2W_2 + B_1NC + B_2RC + B_3RI + B_4RD + B_5LC + B_6DP + B_7SF$$
$$+ C_1W_2NC + C_2W_2RC + C_3W_2RI + C_4W_2RD + C_5W_2LC + C_6W_2DP + C_7W_2SF,$$

where W_2 is a dummy variable equal to 1 for an observation in the first class (Colorado) and to 0 otherwise (states other than Colorado). In particular, the A_i's stand for the intercept differences, while the B_i's and C_i's stand for the differences in slope variables within the first class and between the classes, respectively.

TABLE 2

ANALYSIS OF COVARIANCE FOR DIFFERENCES BETWEEN COLORADO AND OTHER U.S.A. FIRMS

	d.f.	Calculated F	Tabulated $F_{0.01}$
Test for difference in overall homogeneity	8,302	4.12	2.45
Test for difference in intercept	1,302	0.01	6.60
Test for difference in slope	7,302	4.70	2.60

The resulting new regression for the Colorado firms and those in general in the United States is given by (4), where the figures in parentheses are the t statistics:

$$
\begin{aligned}
(4)\quad F = {} & 0.848 - 0.038\,W_2 - 5.823\,NC + 3.944\,RC - \underset{(2.00)}{4.745^{**}RI} \\
& + \underset{(2.90)}{2.041^{**}RD} + 1.146\,LC - \underset{(-2.40)}{2.241^{**}DP} + 0.039\,SF \\
& + \underset{(2.90)}{9.790^{***}W_2NC} - \underset{(-3.18)}{7.613^{***}W_2RC} + \underset{(1.30)}{2.536^{*}W_2RI}. \\
& - \underset{(-1.67)}{2.261^{*}W_2RD} - 2.130\,W_2LC + \underset{(2.16)}{2.104^{**}W_2DP} + 0.234\,W_2SF
\end{aligned}
$$

The results of (4) indicate that the slopes of RI, RD, and DP in Colorado are significantly different from zero at the 5% level. This finding is also completely consistent with the data given in Table 2. Moreover, there are significant differences in the slopes of variables for the Colorado firms compared to the firms in the other states. In particular, the slopes of the variables NC and RC are significantly different at the 1% level for the Colorado firms vis-a-vis those in the other sampled states, while DP is significant at the 5% level, and RI and RD at the 10% level. It is manifest that competitive factors are the most important factors contributing to the difference in the pricing schedules of firms in other states vis-a-vis those in Colorado.

Comparing equation (4) results with those of Table 2 indicates that competitive factors, NC and RC, generally affect pricing schedules of firms in other states, while the pricing schedules of Colorado firms are influenced chiefly by the demand pattern, DP, the firm's market share, RI (its rank of importance in a particular market), and the importance (dominance) of a market, RD. What this difference signifies in terms of pricing can be understood readily in conjunction with our case studies. But first, consider the following:

Besides identifying the variables which account for different pricing schedules, the question of why variables behave differently warrants consideration. In this regard, we propose that tradition and resource base play major roles in determining the types of products that are produced and distributed in states. In general, the state of Colorado is a leading distributional center of manufactured products, especially ski-related products. Brand name and the location of firms in "Colorado" become significant in the selling of their specialties. It could, therefore, be expected that a market's dominance, RD, and the demand pattern over distances, DP, would tend to be leading factors determining the pricing schedules of Colorado firms, perhaps more so than competition. To further understand our findings and also to identify the variables that were not specified in our model, we next present two multi-product firm case studies. We consider them to be representative of firms in Colorado as they focus attention on considerations which stand behind (i.e., explain) the variables that were found to be most important in our overall sample.

IV. Case Examples

Case One

The manufacturer-distributor firm we shall refer to as case one is representative of many manufacturing firms in Colorado. The subject firm is located in the Denver metro area. It produces several related consumer products and distributes them throughout the United States. In light of the reluctance on the part of the firm's spokesman to discuss particular aspects of his firm's operation, we can simply provide broad statements below about his firm's overall pricing pattern. Let us note first, however, that the firm in question is a rather large employer of workers. Let us also note the fact that Denver is the major distributional and financial center of Colorado, and that its wholesale and retail trades employ about 25% of the state work force while government employs 18.6% and manufacturing only 15%. Though a movement of firms to locations outside of the Denver SMSA has taken place in recent years, significant future economic growth is being projected for Colorado, and in particular for Denver. Realization of this projected growth will depend basically on water and energy supplies besides economically feasible sewage treatment facilities. Since the subject firm produces a number of diversified but related products, we concentrate first on two of its products, the one a component part of a heavy (durable) consumer good, the other a lightweight, home used product. (For illustrative purposes only, let us conceive of the second product as, say, a garden water sprinkler.)

Product One

The firm's spokesman indicated that brand name is critically important in sales of product one. Since the spokesman considers the firm to be dominant throughout its market space, it does not compete actively in price. Instead, it basically sells on an f.o.b. basis, while preferring to ship with freight prepaid. The firm's spokesman indicated that some attempts have been made to offer prepaid freight discounts to customers who order larger volumes of its products, thus constituting a form of spatial price discrimination. Nevertheless, to maintain and extend its market share, the firm relies primarily on the goodwill associated with its brand name. (See Table 3 below for illustrative characterization of the way the firm's spokesman described the competition faced by the firm and, in turn, its sale price-freight cost position.) Note in particular with respect to Table 1 (which records the Regression Results Among the States Surveyed) that the variables RD and RI were found to be significant in Colorado at the 5% level. One would expect that because the firm relies on brand name for maintaining its market shares, particularly in the western part of the United States, its delivered price schedule would clearly reflect freight cost difference. Moreover, we have already observed that RD and RI are of secondary importance among the firms in the United States, a result which contrasts sharply from that applicable to the subject firm. When RD and RI are important, it would follow from this firm's product one that only slight (to zero) freight absorption in pricing would be needed, i.e., f.o.b. pricing.

TABLE 3

	1	2	3	4	5
a. Specify the buyer's location - either by cities or distance (e.g. L.A. or 200 miles NE). If using distance, indicate direction.	L.A.	Salt Lake City	Boise	Portland	Seattle
b. The delivered price at buyers location is __ (Multiply or divide each item by any number you want provided you use the same number on each item.)	1.597	1.592	1.598	1.589	1.597
c. The number of competitors is___	3	3	3	3	3
d. How would you rate your competition at these buying points? (1) the greatest your firm faces, (2) the next greatest (3) etc. (Possibly you will assign the same number to several buying points.)	1	4	5	2	3
d. Approximate the percentage of your total sales that your company sells to each location	50%	20%	10%	10%	10%
f. Using numbers as in 5(d), rank the relative impact of your firm on the subject market.	1	1	1	2	2
g. The freight cost per unit of shipment to each buying location is ___ (Approximations are acceptable. Moreover, if you changed the real values in question 5(b) by some multiplier, please apply the same multiplier here.)	.027	.022	.028	.023	.029

Product Two

The market for the firm's second good, the light household product, is subject to considerably greater price competition throughout the firm's market space than is product one. Here the firm does not price f.o.b. mill, preferring instead a prepaid freight system including discounts for large volume-distance orders. The firm's spokesman indicated that on orders above a certain size, his company prepays most of the freight cost, thereby providing customers with substantial savings. The firm's market share is not sustained by brand name importance; so, the discriminatory price schedule it follows is considered to be necessary to the firm's being able to maintain and extend its market area to the far western part of the United States. Note the significant difference in the firm's pricing (row b) and freight cost (row g) at different points vis-a-vis its RD (row f) and RI (row e), all of which suggests that for this firm's product two, competitive impacts dominate (as holds more typically for firms located in other states).

TABLE 4

	1	2	3	4	5
a. Specify the buyer's location--either by cities or distance (e.g. L.A. or 200 miles NE). If using distance, indicate direction.	L.A.	Louisville, Ky.	Syracuse, N.Y.	Kansas City	Amarilo, TX
b. The delivered price at buyers location is __ (Multiply or divide each item by any number you want provided you use the same number on each item.)	9.97	9.95	9.75	9.73	9.43
c. The number of competitors is____	4	5	5	3	4
d. How would you rate your competition at these buying points? 1) the greatest your firm faces, 2) the next greatest 3) etc. (Possibly you will assign the same number to several buying points.)	1	3	2	5	4
e. Approximate the percentage of your total sales that your company sells to each location.	30%	20%	10%	30%	10%
f. Using numbers as in 5(d), rank the relative impact of your firm on the subject market.	4	1	3	1	2
g. The freight cost per unit of shipment to each buying location is __ (Approximations are acceptable. Moreover, if you changed the real values in question 5(b) by some multiplier, please apply the same multiplier here.)	1.21	.80	.99	.97	.67

The subject firm's pricing policies thus dovetail with the general findings of section III where the slopes of RI and RD were found to be significant at the 5% level for Colorado firms, and were clearly important for product one (not two) of case one. Comparing products one and two thus sheds some light on Colorado firms in general as well as the subject firm. Note further from Tables 3 and 4 that product two carries a much higher freight burden in a relative sense than product one—that is, as a percentage of delivered price. At the same instance, both products are subject to increasing competition at more distant market points. It is, therefore, not surprising at all that the firm's spokesman claims that a particularly aggressive pricing policy is required for product two in order to maintain sufficient sales of this product as distance increases.

Case Two

Another manufacturer-distributor firm located in Colorado reported diverse price-location forces that tend to be underemphasized in classical location economics. In particular, there exists in the subject industry an obvious willingness on the part of customers to visit the firm's offices in arranging for purchases of its goods. In other words, the buying scheme practiced in the industry affects the subject firm's sales-price patterns.

The firm in question manufactures some soft goods, while distributing many soft and hard goods, all of which are used chiefly by skiers in the United States. In light of its multiple product lines, even including suntan lotion, it is veritably impossible to focus attention on only one product of the firm in evaluating its pricing policies. Moreover, the firm's spokesman did not want to discuss all important aspects of the firm's overall operations. This induced (required) the present writers to evaluate the firm's policies and practices in a somewhat generalized form. Thus we consider below a composite good, one for each of the three categories of goods handled by the subject firm. In this context, we shall refer to one of its products as low-priced shoftware, the second as high-priced software, and the third as hardware (e.g., a specific part of the equipment used by a skier). Let it finally be noted that the subject firm is considered to be representative of a broad spectrum of Colorado's industries, at least in the sense that it is a relatively large firm which not only produces but also serves as the distributor of its own products to retailers.

Category One

The firm's spokesman stressed availability of its products, not price, as the vital factor determining sales throughout the United States. With particular regard to its low-priced software, the spokesman claimed that markets for its product exist everywhere in the country, even including sporting goods stores in such non-ski resort areas as Houston, Texas. The spokesman was, in fact, reluctant to claim that the Colorado market is more important than the firm's market in, say, Massachusetts, as centered in Boston. In fact, he decided to assign only a slightly higher (more important) rank to Colorado and moderately lower ranks to all of the other representative markets of his firm. Simply put, software items are priced either fairly or not. An f.o.b. price system, even in the presence of significant freight costs which run as high as 6% of delivered price in many markets, will therefore not eliminate (or even noticeably reduce) sales. This judgment applied to extreme competitive conditions, such as selling in markets where a specific rival(s) is incurring practically zero freight costs and hence underpricing the subject firm's good significantly. (See Table 5 below for an illustrative characterization of the way the firm's spokesman described the sale price-freight cost competition faced by the firm. Note further that in complying with non-disclosure practices, we are deliberately failing to indicate whether the prices and costs below are in dollars, pounds, marks, or even for a unit of the good, twenty units of the good, one hundred pounds of the good, etc.) Most significantly, as prices charged to consumers rise, the RD of the firm decreases. Moreover, the data of row e suggest that no market is more important than another and hence that RI is not a critical factor in pricing the firm's software products. This very condition, i.e., no particular market is critically important, may readily (and fully) account for nondiscriminatory f.o.b. pricing.

TABLE 5

	1	2	3	4	5
a. Specify the buyer's location--either by cities or distance (e.g. L.A. or 200 miles NE. If using distance, indicate direction.	Colorado Ski Resort	St. Louis	Northern Cal.	Phil.	Boston
b. The delivered price at buyer's location is__(Multiply or divide each item by any number you want provided you use the same number on each item.)	696	PLUS	FREIGHT		
c. The number of competitors is___	10	10	10	10	10
d. How would you rate your competition at these buying points? 1) the greatest your firm faces, 2) the next greatest, 3) etc. (Possibly you will assign the same number to several buying points.)	2	1	1	1	1
e. Approximate the percentage of your total sales that your company sells to each location.	10	10	10	10	10
f. Using numbers as in 5(d), rank the relative impact of your firm on the subject market.	1	2	2	3	3
g. The freight cost per unit of shipment to each buying location is__ (Approximations are acceptable. Moreover, if you changed the real values in question 5(b) by some multiplier, please apply the same multiplier here.)	0	24	28	36	40

The identically same overall conditions characterized the firm's high-priced softwares. Note that different market points were used in Table 6 compared with Table 5, this for the purpose of distinguishing statistically the firm's high-priced softwares from its low-priced softwares. Nevertheless, the present writers were made sharply cognizant of the fact that, at least in the mind of the firm's spokesman, price was unimportant compared to dependability of shipment. That is to say, availability of the particular items at the moment of consumer demand for the good was claimed to be the key determiner of sales. In contrast with its low-priced softwares, the representative high-priced software goods carried even higher freight burdens in the relative sense—as high as 13% of delivered price in the sales of the firm to many of its markets. In further contrasts with its line of low-priced software goods, competition was certainly greater at the most distant market points. Nevertheless, an f.o.b. price policy was followed, and differential price disadvantages claimed to be basically unimportant. As with its low price software, the RD factor could be a controlling factor behind the firm's pricing policy whereas the importance of a market was not a directly dominating price determinating force. (See Table 6, where the same dollar, pound etc. caveats applicable to Table 5 are relevant.)

TABLE 6

	1	2	3	4	5
a. Specify the buyer's location--either by cities or distance (e.g. LA or 200 miles NE). If using distance, indicate direction.	Colorado Ski Resort	Dallas	Sac.	N.Y.	Boston
b. The delivered price at buyer's location is__(Multiply or divide each item by any number you want provided you use the same number on each item.)	67 per	suit PLUS	FREIGHT		
c. The number of competitors is.___	8	8	8	8	8
d. How would you rate your competition at these buying points ? 1) the greatest your firm faces, 2) the next greatest, 3) etc. (Possibly you will assign the sane number to several buying points.)	2	2	2	1	1
e. Approx. the percentage of total sales that your company sells to each location.	10	10	10	10	10
f. Using your numbers as in 5(d), rank the relative impact of your firm on the subject market.	1	2	2	3	3
g. The freight cost per unit of shipment to each buying location is__ (Approx. are acceptable. Moreover, if you changed the real values in question 5(b) by some multiplier, please apply the same multiplier here.)	0	4	6	8	10

It is with respect to the firm's hardware that significant locational market disadvantages apply, albeit limited only to the more distant markets of the firm. The firm's spokesman nonetheless stressed the importance of competitive constraints, notwithstanding its use of a different distributing warehouse and location needed to cut freight costs as much as possible. One would indeed anticipate this last statement upon observing the almost 20% freight cost to delivered price in Boston. (See Table 7 where, again, the same caveats and conclusions as those applicable to Tables 5 and 6 are relevant.)

There are three significant aspects of the present case study which help manifest the difference between the industry types in Colorado vis-a-vis firms in other states in the United States. They are as follows: 1) The spokesman proposed that the firm's locational choice would have been basically the same if its only products were hardware rather than software. He repeatedly emphasized that wide ranges applied to all of the firm's sales, and that dependability of shipment and reliability of service were the dominant factors in selling. It was in this context that he praised over and over the performance (reliability) of the

United Parcel Service (UPS). 2) No consideration was extended to pricing discriminatorily as a means of promoting sales in any market. 3) The competitive price factors so clearly important in our section III findings for firms in other states was not important at all in the subject Colorado firm's pricing.

TABLE 7

	1	2	3	4	5
a. Specify the buyer's location--either by cities or distance (e.g. LA or 200 miles NE). If using distance, indicate a direction.	Denver	Minne.	Colorado Ski Resort	Sac.	Boston
b. The delivered price at buyer's location is__(Multiply or divide each item by any number you want provided you use the same number on each item.)	45 PLUS FREIGHT				
c. The number of competitors is__	6	6	6	6	6
d. How would you rate your competition at these buying points? 1) the greatest your firm faces, 2) the next greatest, 3) etc. (Possibly you will assign the same number to several buying points.)	1	1	2	1	1
e. Approx. the percent of total sales that your company sells to each location.					
f. Using your numbers as in 5(d), rank the relative impact of your firm on the subject market.	1	1	1	2	2
g. The freight cost per unit of shipment to each buying location is__ (Approx. are acceptable. Moreover, if you changed the real values in question 5(b) by some multiplier, please apply the same multiplier here.)	0	5	3	7	9

It is comparatively simple to deduce further from all of the above data that the firm's location was readily resolved in favor of deriving some goodwill sales advantages. In particular, the firm's spokesman did assert that prestige might be derived from his firm's location in Colorado compared with what might apply if the home site were, say, in Jackson, Mississippi. Whatever freight cost disadvantages prevailed were minimized, if not offset completely, by the fact that the nonhomogeneous goods in the subject industry are sharply differentiated and demands for them are rather inelastic. This demand condition signified that we have on hand a case study in which resources could be conceived to be ubiquitous, while freight costs can be considered to be basically unimportant notwithstanding their high dollar ratios to final delivered prices. Most important to our emphasis on pricing in free enterprise economies, as summarized in section 1 of this paper, is the fact that the firm's marketing network is a factor of great importance to the Colorado industry in question. The emphasized willingness of customers to visit the subject firm's offices in arranging purchases of goods helped reduce the need to discriminate in favor of more distant buyers, a condition which also applies to its hardware items. It warrants final note that the firm's spokesman did suggest that profits were inadequate on some of its manufactured ski equipment hardware.

V. Conclusions

Our section III findings provided the thesis that significant differences exist in the spatial pricing patterns of the firms sampled in the state of Colorado compared to those located elsewhere in the United States. It was further apparent that competitive factors generally affect pricing schedules in the United States, while the pricing schedules of Colorado firms are chiefly influenced by the demand pattern, the market's importance, and the market dominance of the firm. These forces reflect the oft-used characterization of Colorado as a marketing-distributional center, especially with respect to many far western markets.

Our case studies provided vistas extending beyond the statistical model as they sharply pointed out the importance of sales-marketing considerations in the location of firms in Colorado while also identifying variables that were not specifically included in our model. We found, for example, that tradition and brand name played a particularly important role in the products of one of our firms. And it was further manifest that f.o.b. pricing systems are followed much more frequently by Colorado firms than by firms in the other sampled states. This particular difference will also be seen to stem from the excluded variables in the model, e.g., manufacturers of ski equipment in Colorado and those in other categories have a site selection advantage which centers on the demand factors of location distinct from the cost factors of location that would likely be more important in the location of firms in other states. To some extent, the products and locational characeristics of the sampled Colorado firms (e.g., the importance of brand names) may not have been captured sufficiently by the included variables in our model. In fact, it is manifest that while the market dominance and importance factors promoted f.o.b. pricing by the Colorado firms, different reasons could have existed which would have accounted for their importance and which, in turn, would have been reflective of (promotive of) discriminatory pricing. A breakdown of each of the RD, RI factors into two separate subgroups may have carried advantages. What the addition of other variables would provide in terms of final results must be left to further studies. For the present, it suffices to suggest that f.o.b. pricing over long distances is more likely to be practiced when goods are sharply differentiated, when no particular market is critically important, when market dominance does not change radically over space, and when locational choices are sharply influenced by a desire for a specific geographic identification. When standard cost or market access advantages are prominent, discriminatory pricing appears to be the rule.

REFERENCES

1. Beckman, M. (1970). Location Theory (New York: Harper Brothers).
2. Benson, B. (1980). "Löschian Competition Under Alternative Demand Conditions," American Economic Review, 70, 1098-1105.
3. Capozza, D. and R. Van Order. (1976). "Pricing Under Spatial Competition and Spatial Monopoly," Econometrica, 45, 1329-1338.
4. Capozza, D. and R. Van Order. (1977). "A Simple Model of Spatial Competition," Southern Economic Review, 44, 361-367.

5. Capozza, D. and R. Van Order. (1978). "A Generalized Model of Spatial Competition," American Economic Review, 68, 896-908.
6. Capozza, D. and R. Van Order. (1980). "Unique Equilibria, Pure Profits, and Efficiency in Location Models," American Economic Review, 70, 1046-1053.
7. Dupuit, J. (1962). "On Tolls and Transport Charges," International Economic Papers, 7-31.
8. Eaton, B. and R. Lipsey. (1976). "The Non-Uniqueness of Equilibrium in the Loschian Model," Amerian Economic Review, 66, 77-93.
9. Eaton, B. and R. Lipsey. (1977). "The Introduction of Space into the Neoclassical Model of Value Theory," in Studies in Modern Economic analysis, M. J. Artris and A. R. Nobay, eds. (Oxford: Blackwells), 59-96.
10. Greenhut, J. and M. L. Greenhut. (1975). "Spatial Price Discrimination, Competition, and Locational Effects," Economica, 42, 401-419.
11. Greenhut, J. and M. L. Greenhut. (1977). "Nonlinearity of Delivered Price Schedules and Predatory Pricing," Econometrica, 45, 1871-1875.
12. Greenhut, J., M. L. Greenhut, and S. Y. Li. (1980). "Spatial Pricing Patterns in the United States," Quarterly Journal of Economics, 96, 320-350.
13. Greenhut, M. L. (1956). Plant Location in Theory and in Practice (Chapel Hill: University of North Carolina Press).
14. Greenhut, M. L. (1981). "Spatial Pricing in the U.S.A., West Germany, and Japan," Economica, 48, 79-86.
15. Greenhut, M. L., M. Hwang, and H. Ohta. (1975). "Observations on the Shape and Relevance of Spatial Demand Functions," Econometgrica, 43, 669-682.
16. Greenhut, M. L. and H. Ohta. (1972). "Monopoly Output Under Alternative Spatial Pricing Techniques," American Economic Review, 62, 705-713.
17. Greenhut, M. L. and H. Ohta. (1975). Spatial Price Theory and Market Areas (Durham: Duke University Press).
18. Hoover, E. M. (1946). Location and Economic Activity (New York: McGraw-Hill Book Co.).
19. Isard, W. (1956). Location and Space Economy (Cambridge, MA: MIT Press).
20. Lösch, A. (1944). Die Rawliche Ordnung der Wirtschaft (Jena: Gustav Fisher).
21. Norman, G. (1981). "Uniform Pricing as an Optimal Spatial Pricing Policy," Economica, 48, 87-91.
22. Phlips, L. (1976). "Spatial Pricing and Competition," Studies Competition—Approximation of Legislation Series (Brussels: Commission of the European Communities).
23. Phlips, L. (1980). "Intertemporal Price Discrimination and Sticky Prices," Quarterly Journal of Economics, 94, 525-542.
24. Pigou, A. C. (1932). The Economics of Welfare, 3rd ed. (London: Macmillan & Company).
25. Richardson, H. (1973). Regional Growth Theory (New York: John Wiley and Sons).
26. Robinson, J. (1934). The Economics of Imperfect Competition (London: Macmillan & Company).

DIFFERENCES IN SPATIAL PRICING IN THE UNITED STATES

27. Smith, D. M. (1971). Industrial Location: An Economic Geographical Analysis (New York: John Wiley and Sons).
28. Von Thünen, J. H. (1875). Der Isolierte Staat in Beziehung auf Landwirtschaftslehre und Nationalokonomie, 3rd ed. (Berlin: Schumacher Zarchlin).
29. Weber, A. (1909). "Reine Theorie des Standorts," Uber den Standort der Industrien, Part I (Turingen). This book has been translated by C. J. Friedrich as Alfred Weber's Theory of the Location of Industries (Chicago: University of Chicago Press, 1928).

M. L. GREENHUT, M. HWANG, AND S. SHWIFF

Firm Name ______________________________ Telephone No. __________
Official Supplying Data ____________________

1. Classify your main activity and indicate the product or service:
   good manufactured is __________ , service supplied is ____________
   good distributed is ____________.
2. Is the item in question (check one):
   a. substantially different, b. slightly different, c. identical to competitors products.
3. How do you typically transport: a. by highway, b. rail, c. water, or d. air. (Check appropriate answer)
4. Do you typically use your own transport facility? a. yes, b. no. (Check one)
5. Please describe below a typical shipment of your product (or service) from your facility in ____________ to five different buying locations:

	1	2	3	4	5
a. Specify the buyer's location (e.g. Chicago, Ill.	____	____	____	____	____
b. The delivered price at the buyer's location is	____	____	____	____	____
c. The number of competitors is	____	____	____	____	____
d. How would you rank your competition at these buying points? (1) the greatest your firm faces, (2) the next greatest, (3) etc. (Possibly you will assign the same number to several customer buying points.)	____	____	____	____	____
e. Using numbers as in 5(d), rank the importance of this location to your total sales.	____	____	____	____	____
f. Using numbers as in 5(d), rank the relative impact of your firm on the subject market.	____	____	____	____	____
g. The freight cost per unit of shipment to each location.	____	____	____	____	____

6. The (general) price of the product considered in question 5 in a sale to a buyer located at your facility (whether or not any sales are made there) "would be" ____________.
7. Your competitors are (check one):
   a. located near you, b. spread over the market area, c. located together at a distant point, d. other (please specify) ____________________.
8. Assume you have no competitors supplying the aforementioned 5 buying points. Would the demands of your product generall by: a) greatest among buyers located close to you, b) greatest among buyers located at substantial distance from you, c) the same at all locations.

Thank you.

[10]

Discriminatory and Nondiscriminatory Spatial Prices and Outputs under Varying Market Conditions

By

M. L. Greenhut and **H. Ohta**

Introduction

It can be shown that the spatial monopolist necessarily tends to discriminate in price because it is more profitable than simple f.o.b. mill pricing *regardless of the form of the assumed gross demand function*[1]. And it can also be shown that discriminatory pricing over an economic space yields greater monopoly output than does simple f.o.b. mill pricing, again *regardless of the form of the assumed gross demand function*[2]. This

Remark: Part of this paper was presented in lectures given by one of the authors at the University of Karlsruhe and acknowledgement to students and Professor Rolf Funck for helpful comments is in order. The authors also wish to acknowledge their appreciation to Professor R. B. Ekelund for his helpful comments. They also wish to thank the editors of the Duke University Press for permission to use some materials in their book (*Spatial Prices and Market Areas*, forthcoming 1975) as the basis for the more general formulation to be set forth in this paper. Support given by the National Science Foundation for research on this general subject demands final recognition and warrants an expression of thanks.

[1] This proposition requires the condition that demand vanishes at some critical *finite* level of price. Detailed discussion of this requirement will appear in a paper being written by the present authors under the title, "Generalization of the Classical Theory of Spatial Price Discrimination." The general proof provided in that paper justifies the more restricted proof provided herein of the subject proposition. This proposition, in turn, serves as component part of several related propositions set forth in the present paper.

[2] This proof involves demonstration of the continuity of the spatially derived nondiscriminatory marginal revenue (MR) function, and a proof that the discriminatory marginal revenue curve of the spatial monopolist always lies to the right of his simple (nondiscriminatory)

pricing system involves a generally lower price schedule. Possibly most important, discriminatory pricing may often be practiced by *competitive* firms in economic space. It is this last mentioned facet of spatial pricing which distinguishes spatial price discrimination theory most sharply from the counterpart classical view of price discrimination.

These several propositions suggest that the exhaustive categorization of demand possibilities used and evaluated in classical spaceless price discrimination theory had narrowing effects on spatial price discrimination theory. The resulting somnolent state reflected the classical argument that relative shapes (elasticities) of demand curves in separable markets determined the existence of price discrimination; moreover, it reflected the related claim that output effects also depended on relative demand curve shapes besides the level of the marginal cost curve and the discontinuity, if any, of the MR curve[1]. Thus in the writings of E. M. Hoover and A. Smithies[2], the relations between elasticity and price changes along the individual buyer's demand curves were conceived to be all important[3]. These writers focused attention on the question of the direction of the discrimination, viz. against distant or nearer buyers, while not stressing in any way the classical question of output or the possibility that spatial competitors might systematically employ discriminatory prices. It is, however, precisely with respect to output, competitive price discrimination, and related matters that spatial price discrimination theory becomes sharply distinctive. Its vital features, we propose, are: (1) monopolistic price discrimination is coterminous with profit maximization in a space economy even when gross demand curves (in the different markets) are identical, (2) output is *always* greater when the spatial seller discriminates in price than when he pursues straight f.o.b. mill pricing, (3) price

marginal revenue curve. The general proof provided in M. L. Greenhut, and H. Ohta, "Monopoly Output under Alternative Spatial Pricing Techniques", *The American Economic Review*, Vol. 62, Menasha, Wisc., 1972, pp. 705sqq., justifies the special proof provided herein. This proposition, in turn, serves as component part of several related propositions to be set forth in the present paper.

[1] Arthur C. Pigou, *The Economics of Welfare*, 3rd Ed., London, 1929. — Joan Robinson, *The Economics of Imperfect Competition*, London, 1933.

[2] E. M. Hoover, "Spatial Price Discrimination", *The Review of Economic Studies*, Vol. 4, London, 1936/37, pp. 182sqq. — Arthur Smithies, "Monopolistic Price Policy in a Spatial Market", *Econometrica*, Vol. 9, Menasha, Wisc., 1941, pp. 63sqq. — *Idem*, "Optimum Location in a Spatial Competition", *The Journal of Political Economy*, Vol. 49, Chicago, Ill., 1941, pp. 423sqq.

[3] For example, in Hoover's view if elasticity changes more than directly and proportional to a change in price, discrimination proceeds against nearer buyers; if elasticity varies directly and proportionately to a change in price, there is no discrimination; if elasticity varies directly with, but less than proportional to, the change in price, or if the elasticity is constant *or* varies inversely to the change in price, discrimination proceeds against distant buyers.

schedules are generally lower under spatial price discrimination than under straight f.o.b. mill pricing, and (4) competitors in economic space may often be expected to practice the same order of price discrimination as the spatial monopolist.

This paper will provide proof and illustrative exposition of these and related vital facets of spatial pricing under diverse demand and market conditions. It assumes a given distribution of buyers and evaluates the impacts of demand and supply functions. In particular, concave, linear, and convex demand functions will each be specified in order to determine the relationships existing between the given demand functions and the propositions set forth above. Then inquiry is made into the impacts of competition at distant market points in order to determine the generality of the thesis that discriminatory pricing is the common price pattern in economic space.

I. Assumptions

For simplicity only (and not actually restrictive of the general theses), assume that (A) each seller is located at the center of the line market, (B) each seller is spatially separated from his rivals[1], (C) buyers are distributed evenly along a line, (D) the buyers' gross demand functions are identical, (E) the freight cost per unit of output per unit of distance is constant, (F) marginal production costs are also constant, and (G) positive profits are attainable. The assumption of identical gross demand functions means that if it were not for varying distances from the seller, the demand of any buyer would be the same as that of any other buyer. In the language of space economic theory, buyers' demands at their own mill are identical[2]. It warrants further mention that these assumptions conform basically to those hypothesized by Hoover and Smithies[3].

The initial price model, which will shortly be set forth as Model I, involves price discrimination against buyers located nearer to the seller.

---

[1] Depending on how far the sellers are separated from one another, we will define the subject seller as either a spatial monopolist or spatial oligopolist (competitor).

[2] See M. L. Greenhut, *Microeconomics and the Space Economy, The Effectiveness of an Oligopolistic Market Economy*, Chicago, 1963, Chapter IV. Note that assumption (D), in effect, is not merely a simplifying but a necessary assumption designed to isolate the pure impact of economic space on profits, outputs, and prices.

[3] See Hoover, *op. cit.* — Smithies, "Monopolistic Price Policy in a Spatial Market", *op. cit.* — *Idem*, "Optimum Location in a Spatial Competition", *op. cit.* — In reference to assumption (E), let us note that Hoover assumed a constant marginal cost of production while Smithies did not. In justifying his practice, Smithies correctly pointed out that the pricing technique followed by the firm is independent of the form of the cost function. The simplest cost function *could* therefore be readily assumed, where marginal cost (MC) is conceived as zero. For our objectives, positive MC is assumed herein.

The second model (Model II) does not involve discrimination at all, and may be referred to as the nondiscriminatory f.o.b. mill (or net mill) price system. Our *emphasis on* a particular discriminatory system and the f.o.b. mill price system of the spatial monopolist (or of the competitive spatial oligopolist)[1] under conditions of high transportation costs does not exclude still other pricing techniques available to firms in economic space. For example, spatial firms may follow uniform delivered pricing policies over space, or equalizing f.o.b. mill price systems by zones, or base point pricing[2].

The assumption of oligopolistically competitive conditions in economic space signifies that some rival(s) might locate (or are located) at an economically proximate distance from the subject seller. This constraint means that an upper limit to the profit maximizing delivered price is imposed on the seller by his distant competitors. In turn, the seller's (profit maximizing) sales radius is circumscribed. Nonetheless, the main conclusions derived from the spatial monopoly model will be seen not really to be altered by conditions of spatial competition. Most of our immediate attention will, thus, be centered on the monopolist in economic space. The last section of this paper is reserved for the question of impacts of competition at a distance on the prices, profits, and outputs of the firm under conditions otherwise corresponding to those evaluated previously for the spatial monopolist.

II. Two Models of Spatial Pricing

The first spatial pricing system (Model I), given the assumptions set forth previously in this paper, consists of the following set of equations:

$$(2\text{—}1)\quad q_D = f\,(p_D) \qquad \forall D \ni D_o \geq D \geq 0\,,$$

$$(2\text{—}2)\quad F_D = F\,(q_D, D) \qquad \forall D \ni D_o \geq D \geq 0\,,$$

$$(2\text{—}3)\quad t_D = \frac{F_D}{q_D} \qquad \forall D \ni D_o \geq D \geq 0\,,$$

$$(2\text{—}4)\quad m_D = p_D - t_D \qquad \forall D \ni D_o \geq D \geq 0\,,$$

[1] See August Lösch, *Die räumliche Ordnung der Wirtschaft*, 2., neu durchgearb. Aufl., Jena, 1944. — Also see M. L. Greenhut, *Plant Location in Theory and in Practise, The Economics of Space*, Chapel Hill, N.C., 1956.

[2] The base point system, for example, is not mentioned specifically later on in the paper because: (a) the subject matter interest of this paper is confined to competitive pricing practices thus ruling out collusive pricing, and (b) the base point system is a special form of the second pricing technique to be set forth above.

$$(2\text{—}5)\quad C = cQ + C_o\,,$$

$$(2\text{—}6)\quad Q = 2\int_0^{D_o} q_D\, dD\,,$$

$$(2\text{—}7)\quad \Pi = 2\int_0^{D_o} m_D\, q_D\, dD - C > 0\,,$$

$$(2\text{—}8)\quad \frac{\partial \Pi}{\partial D_o} = 0\,,$$

$$(2\text{—}9)\quad \frac{\partial \Pi}{\partial q_D} = 0\,,\quad \text{or}\quad \frac{\partial \Pi}{\partial m_D} = 0 \quad \forall D \ni D_o \geq D \geq 0\,,$$

where p_D = the delivered price at a consuming point D miles away from the seller; q_D = the quantity of demand at the point D; F_D = the cost of shipping q_D to a point D distance from the seller; t_D = the freight rate of shipping q_D over the distance D; m_D = the mill price applicable to the point D; C = the total cost of production; c = constant marginal cost of production; C_o = fixed cost; Q = the total quantity sold of the commodity; Π = the profit; D = the distance from the seller to a given consuming point; and D_o stands for the market extremity.

Equation (2—1), under assumption (D), signifies that there exists an *identical* gross demand function *f* at any point D such that $D_o \geq D \geq 0$ on the line market. Equation (2—2), pursuant to assumption (E), specifies freight cost as a function of q_D and D. Equation (2—3) defines the "freight rate" as the freight cost per unit of quantity. This freight rate turns out to be equal to αD pursuant to assumption (E)[1]. Equation (2—4) indicates that the mill price which is applicable to any given consuming point is equal to the delivered price less the full freight cost in shipping a unit of the good to that point in the market. Equation (2—5) stands for the production cost function which is a linear function of Q pursuant to assumption (F). Equation (2—6), in accordance with assumptions (A) and (C), defines the aggregate (i. e., total) quantity of the commodity that is shipped over the entire (linear) market by the subject seller. Equation (2—7), in turn, defines profit as the difference between net revenue (i. e., revenue net of freight cost) and production cost. Equations (2—8) and (2—9) are the first order conditions for profit maximization. In particular, equation (2—8) signifies that the market must be adjusted to the size (D_o) which maximizes the seller's total profit. Equation (2—9), in turn,

[1] We define the freight rate t_D as F_D/q_D in equation (2—3), i.e. $t_D = F_D/q_D$. Combining this definition with assumption (E), which specifies that $t_D/D = \alpha$, yields: $t_D = F_D/q_D = \alpha D$.

determines the mill price applicable to each independent submarket, which price maximizes profits to each point in the space and, hence, total profits.

The second spatial pricing system (call it Model II) involves essentially the same equations as those of Model I. However, the fundamental equation (2—9) must be modified pursuant to Model II as follows:

(2—9)' $\frac{\partial \Pi}{\partial q_D} = 0$ or $\frac{\partial \Pi}{\partial m_D} = 0$, where *each is subject to*

(2—10) $m_D = m$.

In other words, a unique mill price is required by Model II.

It warrants emphasis that mill price could be different under Model I for all consuming points. In contrast, the seller who is following Model II maximizes his profit subject to the additional constraint (2—10). Multiple mill prices vis-à-vis uniqueness of mill price manifest the basic difference between spatial price discrimination and simple f.o.b. mill pricing.

III. Profit Maximizing Conditions Specified

The profit maximizing conditions of Model I may be reduced to more specific forms via the substitution in equations (2—8) and (2—9) of all relevant constraints (2—1) through (2—7). Thus equation (3—1) is derived from (2—5), (2—7), and (2—8)[1].

(3—1) $m_{D_0} = c$ or $q_{D_0} = 0$.

It signifies that the market boundary point D_0 must be at the point where the mill price applicable to that point has fallen to MC or demand vanishes.

[1] Substituting (2—7) into (2—8) yields:

$$\frac{\partial \Pi}{\partial D_0} = 2\frac{\partial}{\partial D_0}\int_0^{D_0} m_D\, q_D\, dD - \frac{\partial C}{\partial Q}\frac{\partial Q}{\partial D_0} = 0$$

$$\Rightarrow 2\frac{\partial}{\partial D_0}\int_0^{D_0} (m_D - c)\, q_D\, dD = 0 \quad \text{since } \frac{\partial C}{\partial Q} = c \text{ by (2—5)}$$

$$\Rightarrow 2\,(m_{D_0} - c)\, q_{D_0} = 0 \Rightarrow m_{D_0} = c \text{ or } q_{D_0} = 0.$$

In turn, equation (3—2) is derivable from equations (2—2) through (2—7) along with (2—9)[1].

$$(3\text{—}2)\quad \frac{\partial\,(p_D q_D)}{\partial p_D} = c + \alpha D \quad \forall D \ni D_o \geq D \geq 0\,.$$

It states that the marginal revenue earned at any point on the line market must be equated with the marginal cost of production and transportation to that point.

The profit maximizing conditions for Model II are specifiable in a similar way. Thus:

$$(3\text{—}3)\quad q_{D_o} = 0\,.$$

$$(3\text{—}4)\quad \frac{\partial m}{\partial Q}\,Q + m = c \text{ or } \frac{\partial}{\partial m}\left[2\,m \int_0^{D_o} f\,(m + \alpha D)\,dD\right] = 0.$$

Equation (3—3) is counterpart to (3—1). But note. the seller's mill price cannot fall to the level of marginal production cost for any buyer as it does in (3—1) because the assumptions of positive profits and in particular the uniqueness of price in Model II rule this out; thus equation (3—3) signifies that D_o must be so determined that demand vanishes at the extremity of the seller's market[2]. Equation (3—4), in turn, is another

---

[1] Equations (2—5), (2—7) and (2—9) yield:

$$\frac{\partial\,\Pi}{\partial\,q_D} = 2\,\frac{\partial}{\partial\,q_D}\int_0^{D_o}(m_D - c)\,q_D\,dD = 0$$

$$\Rightarrow 2\,\frac{\partial\,[(m_D - c)\,q_D]}{\partial\,q_D} = 0$$

$$\Rightarrow 2\,\frac{\partial\,[(p_D - \alpha D - c)\,q_D]}{\partial\,q_D} = 0 \quad \text{since } m_D = p_D - \alpha D$$

by (2—2) through (2—4)

$$\Rightarrow \frac{\partial\,(p_D\,q_D)}{\partial\,q_D} - \alpha D - c = 0 \quad \forall D \ni D_o \geq D \geq 0\,,$$

where $\partial(p_D\,q_D)/\partial q_D$ stands for marginal revenue earned at a point D miles away from the seller while D stands not only for the distance in miles but also by (2—2) for the marginal cost of transportation in dollar terms.

[2] $\frac{\partial\Pi}{\partial D_o} = 0 \Rightarrow 2\,(m_{D_o} - c)\,q_{D_o} = 0$ as before (p. 315, footnote 1). But Model II is subject to the constraint (2—10), i.e. $m_D = m$ for all D. Therefore $m_D = c \Leftrightarrow m = c$. However, $m = c$ in turn implies that total net revenue $(m - c)\,Q$ is also zero. Obviously, this does not lead to profit maximization. Instead, m_{D_o} must be strictly greater than marginal cost of production, and accordingly $2\,(m_{D_o} - c)\,q_{D_o} \Rightarrow q_{D_o} = 0$.

profit maximization condition which is counterpart to (3—2) and subject to the constraint (2—10). It shows marginal revenue equated to marginal production cost, and quantity supplied vanishing at the market periphery. Thus, m in (3—4) stands for the single (unique) mill price applicable to all points D such that $D_0 \geq D \geq 0$, while f stands for the function of p_D which in turn equals m + D by (2—2) through (2—4) subject to (2—10).

The delivered price of the firm is determined under Model II by adding to the uniquely derived profit maximizing mill price of the firm the freight cost applicable to the given point in the market. In the previous Model I, however, there is no *unique* mill price because the mill price depends on the point in the market area for which the delivered price applies. A set of mill prices obtains under Model I which may be viewed by subtracting from delivered prices the freight cost to the location for which the delivered price is derived.

IV. Demand Curves and Spatial Prices

In the subsequent analysis, the following three alternative specific gross demand curves applicable to any point D are considered:

(a) $p = -\sqrt{2bq} + \frac{3}{2}b$, a concave demand curve where $\frac{9}{8}b \geq q \geq 0$,

(b) $p = b - q$, a linear demand curve where $b \geq q \geq 0$,

(c) $p = \frac{1}{b}q^2 + \frac{3}{4}b$, a convex demand curve where $\frac{\sqrt{3}}{2}b \geq q \geq 0$,

where here and henceforth the subscript D is omitted from the variables. The condition that the three curves are tangent at the point $\left(\frac{1}{2}b, \frac{1}{2}b\right)$ leads to the numerical forms of (a), (b), and (c).

A more general form of the concave demand curve is as follows: $p = -\gamma\sqrt{q} + \delta$. However, in order that it be equivalent to the simplified linear curve given in (b) above, i. e., equivalent in other respects than shape, it *must* yield the same equilibrium price as the one which would hold for the linear curve when *spaceless* and costless equilibrium applies; specifically, it must be tangent to the linear curve at the point $\left(\frac{1}{2}b, \frac{1}{2}b\right)$ where the slope $\frac{dp}{dq}$ is -1. Thus, γ and δ are uniquely determined when the two conditions, viz. $p = \frac{b}{2}$ and $\frac{dp}{dq} = -1$ both at $q = \frac{b}{2}$, are satisfied. Correspondingly, the specific coefficients for the convex case are obtained via the general form $p = -\gamma q^2 + \delta$.

Figure 1 — *Three Alternative Demand Curves*

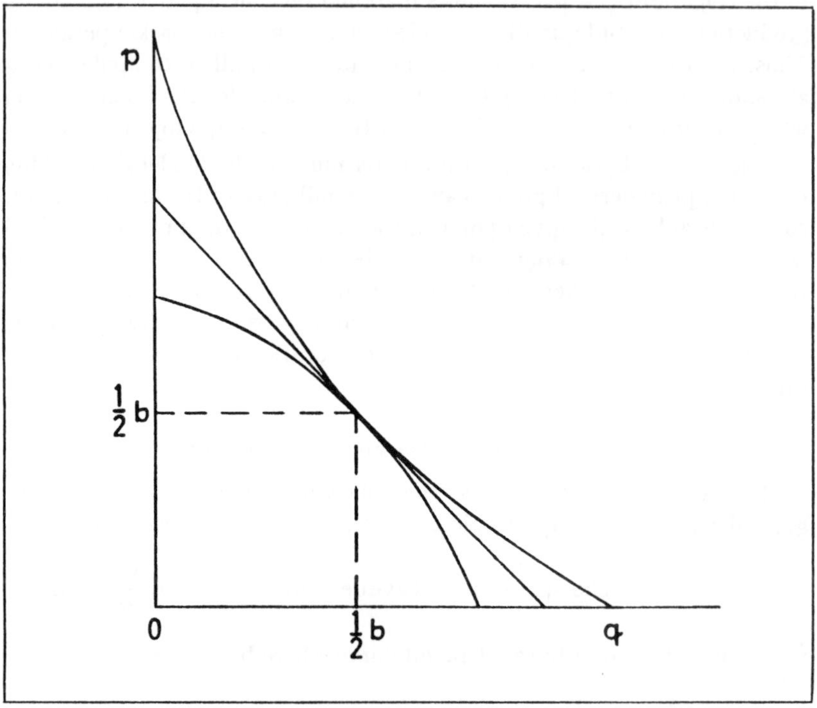

It is significant to note that all three functions have the desirable property of (monotonically) decreasing elasticity. Demand curves of constant elasticity (e. g., the rectangular hyperbola) or increasing elasticity (e.g., part of an ellipse) are ruled out as is also a decreasing elasticity curve whose change in elasticity is less than proportional to the change in price. The former entails negative freight absorption, the second either negative or excessive freight absorption, and the third negative freight absorption[1]. In the instances of negative freight absorption, discriminatory prices would proceed against distant buyers but would not be feasible in practice in light of resale possibilities[2]. In turn, excessive freight absorp-

[1] M. L. Greenhut, M. Hwang, and H. Ohta, "Price Discrimination by Regulated Motor Carriers: Comment", *The American Economic Review*, Vol. 64, 1974, pp. 780sqq.

[2] Nondiscriminatory f.o.b. mill pricing alone is feasible in the space economy when the demand curve is of the type to require negative freight absorption. See Hoover, *op. cit.* — Wassily Leontief, "The Theory of Limited and Unlimited Discrimination", *The Quarterly Journal of Economics*, Vol. 54, Cambridge, Mass., 1940, pp. 490sqq. — Greenhut, *Plant Location in Theory and Practise*, *op. cit.*,

tion violates stability conditions[1]. Thus all of these demand curve types — if they existed — are therefore irrelevant under the objectives of comparing stable price levels, profits, and outputs under ***discriminatory*** and *nondiscriminatory* pricing over economic space. Moreover, one would expect curves whose elasticities decrease more than proportional to a decrease in price to be the empirically most realistic curves besides having a fundamental theoretical basis, as evidenced at the limiting points of demand[2]. It is, therefore, proposed that the above three specifications are fully general representations of the economically relevant concave, linear, and convex demand curves, in so far as concerns the subject matter of this paper.

Our assumption of tangency at (1/2)b conforms to the spaceless monopolists's profit maximizing equilibrium price under zero variable costs of production. This assumption readily serves as a departure point to evaluate spatial demand impacts numerically. Of course, this could have been handled generally without tedious numerical specifications included, such as those contained in the equations, notes, and tables below. Figures 2 to 5 which depict graphically most of the fundamental relations derived herein could instead have been set forth by themselves to provide the "generalizing" view of the fundamental relationships established here. Advantages relating to numerical derivations and findings militated, however, against pictorial views alone; these data provide materials which researchers on the subject can use in going behind our results as well as for cross-checking purposes. Initially, then, we shall work from the numerical specifications of demand previously given to derive selected values and relationships that would apply to the different pricing systems described by our Models I and II. The figures themselves — let us however recall — provide the simpler view as well as fully general characterization of the economic relationships which this paper claims underscore pricing in the space economy.

The concave demand curve (a) may readily be employed under Model I in deriving profit maximizing values, such as the profit maximizing revenues $\hat{R}$ (where the symbol ^ is used to refer to such maximization). That is to say, evaluation of the concave demand curve under Model I

[1] See Greenhut, Hwang, and Ohta, *op. cit.*

[2] It is manifest that effective-real demand curves must be subject to the constraint $\frac{de}{dp}\frac{p}{e} > 1$, at least in the neighborhood of the price intercept. See *ibid.*

can yield the profit maximizing market size $\hat{D}_o$,[1] the maximum profit (inclusive of fixed cost) $\hat{R}^*$,[2] the profit maximizing output $\hat{Q}$,[3] and the profit maximizing price $\hat{p}$.[4]

In different order, we obtain for Model II the profit maximizing mill price ($\hat{m}$) and distance ($\hat{D}$) under concave demand[5], as well as the profit

---

[1] Revenues under the concave demand curve (a) are $R = 2\left(-\sqrt{2\,bq} + \frac{3}{2}\,b\right)q$. Then set $\frac{dR}{dq} = 2\,(c + \alpha D)$ to obtain:

$$(1a)\qquad q = \frac{1}{2b}\left(b - \frac{2}{3}\,(c + \alpha\,D)\right)^2.$$

Since point demand vanishes at the profit maximizing market extremity, i.e. at $D = D_0$:

$$(2a)\qquad \hat{D}_0 = \left(\frac{3}{2}\,b - c\right)/\alpha.$$

[2] The total maximum profit (or net revenue) can be obtained as follows:

$$(3a)\qquad \hat{R}^* = 2\int_0^{\hat{D}_0} (pq - Dq)\,dD = \frac{3\left(b - \frac{2}{3}\,c\right)^4}{16b\alpha}.$$

[3] Profit maximizing output $\hat{Q}$ is:

$$(4a)\qquad \hat{Q} = 2\int_0^{\hat{D}_0} q dD = \frac{\left(b - \frac{2}{3}\,c\right)^3}{2b\alpha}.$$

[4] Substituting (1a) into the demand function (a) provides the delivered price $\hat{p} = \frac{1}{2}\,b + \frac{2}{3}\,(c + \alpha D)$, with the constraint $\left(\frac{3}{2}\,b - c\right)/\,\alpha \geq D \geq 0$ given by equation (2a). This price result later is shown in Figure 2 as the price line $p_I^1p_I^1$. Profit maximizing mill prices then are determined, by way of definition, as $\hat{m} = \hat{p} - \alpha D = \frac{1}{2}\,b - \frac{1}{3}\,\alpha D + \frac{2}{3}\,c$.

[5] Note that $p = -\sqrt{2bq} + \frac{3}{2}\,b = m + \alpha D$. Thus:

$$(5a)\qquad q = \frac{1}{2b}\left\{\frac{3}{2}\,b - (m + \alpha D)\right\}^2.$$

The aggregate output Q (not $\hat{Q}$) produced by the seller for whom sales radius D_0 applies is:

$$(6a)\qquad Q = 2\int_0^{D_0} q dD = \frac{-1}{3b\alpha}\left(\frac{3}{2}\,b - m - \alpha D_0\right)^3 + \frac{1}{3b\alpha}\left(\frac{3}{2}\,b - m\right)^3, \quad \text{and}$$

$$(7a)\qquad R^* = (m - c)\,Q = \frac{(m - c)}{3b\alpha}\left[-\left(\frac{3}{2}\,b - m - \alpha D_0\right)^3 + \left(\frac{3}{2}\,b - m\right)^3\right].$$

Table 1 — *Spatial Prices, Distances, Profits, and Outputs*

Demand type	Model	$\hat{m}$	$\hat{D}_o$	$\hat{R}^*$	$\hat{Q}$	$\hat{p}$
Concave	I	$\frac{b}{2} - \frac{1}{3}D^* + c$	$\frac{3b - 2c}{2\alpha}$	$\frac{3}{b\alpha}\left(\frac{1}{2}\right)^4 \beta_1^4$	$\frac{1}{2b\alpha}\beta_1^3$	$\frac{b}{2} + \frac{2}{3}D^*$
	II	$\frac{3b + 6c}{8}$	$\frac{9b - 6c}{8\alpha}$	$\frac{1}{b\alpha}\left(\frac{3}{4}\right)^6 \beta_1^4$	$\frac{2}{b\alpha}\left(\frac{3}{4}\right)^5 \beta_1^3$	$\frac{3b + 6c}{8} + \alpha D$
Linear	I	$\frac{b}{2} - \frac{1}{2}D^* + c$	$\frac{b - c}{\alpha}$	$\frac{1}{6\alpha}\beta_2^3$	$\frac{1}{2\alpha}\beta_2^2$	$\frac{b}{2} + \frac{1}{2}D^*$
	II	$\frac{b + 2c}{3}$	$\frac{2b - 2c}{3\alpha}$	$\frac{4}{\alpha}\left(\frac{1}{3}\right)^3 \beta_2^3$	$\frac{4}{9\alpha}\beta_2^2$	$\frac{b + 2c}{3} + \alpha D$
Convex	I	$\frac{b}{2} - \frac{2}{3}D^* + c$	$\frac{3b - 4c}{4\alpha}$	$\frac{3\sqrt{b}}{20\alpha}\beta_3^{\frac{5}{2}}$	$\frac{\sqrt{b}}{2\alpha}\beta_3^{\frac{3}{2}}$	$\frac{b}{2} + \frac{1}{3}D^*$
	II	$\frac{3b + 6c}{10}$	$\frac{9b - 12c}{20\alpha}$	$\frac{2}{\alpha}\left(\frac{3}{10}\right)^3 \sqrt{5b}\,\beta_3^{\frac{5}{2}}$	$\frac{2}{\alpha}\left(\frac{3}{10}\right)^2 \sqrt{5b}\,\beta_3^{\frac{3}{2}}$	$\frac{3b + 6c}{10} + \alpha D$

$D^* = c + \alpha D, \quad \beta_1 = b - \frac{2}{3}c, \quad \beta_2 = (b - c), \quad \beta_3 = b - \frac{4}{3}c$

maximizing $\hat{Q}$ and the maximum profit $\hat{R}^*$.[1] Moreover, the set of delivered prices over the space, that is $\hat{m} + D$, may finally be derived[2].

All results, including those similarly obtainable for the other demand curves, are recorded in Table 1. But only a preliminary statement on the results recorded in the table is set forth below, as detailed discussion of their implications is reserved for the concluding sections of the paper. Consider here only the following:

The $\hat{m}$ for Model I (which applies to any of the demand curve types specified above) is a decreasing function of distance D. In other words, buyers nearer to the seller are required to pay higher mill prices. In this sense, the buyer more proximate to the seller than another buyer is discriminated against under the requirements of Model I. On the other hand, the profit maximizing mill price is, by definition of the f.o.b. mill price system, uniquely given under Model II.

For another comparison, the mill price or mill price schedule under Model I is mechanically derived from the profit maximizing delivered prices. The strategic variable for Model I is, in other words, the delivered price, while the key variable for Model II is the mill price.

V. Conclusions Applicable to Spatial Monopoly

Columns $\hat{m}$, D_0, and $\hat{p}$ in Table 1 indicate that the more distant buyers are charged comparatively lower prices under Model I. Specifically, price received at the seller's mill decreases with distance. Moreover, delivered prices as well are lower under Model I than they are under Model II at comparatively remote distances as shown in Figure 2. It follows,

---

In order to obtain the profit maximizing set $\{\hat{m}, \hat{D}_0\}$, we then take the partials of R with respect to m *and* D_0, and set each to zero. These equations contain two unknowns, namely m and D_0. Their solutions are $\hat{m} = 3\,(b + 2\,c)\,/\,8$, $\hat{D}_0 = (9\,b - 6\,c)\,/\,8\,\alpha$. Other solutions may be found as well, but they are not profit maximizing.

Another and in fact somewhat simpler method of solution requires taking equation (3—3) into consideration to obtain $D_0 = \frac{(3\,b/2) - m}{\alpha}$. Substituting this D_0 in (7a) and then differentiating the result with respect to m yields the same solution set $\{\hat{m}, \hat{D}_0\}$.

[1] Substituting $\{\hat{m}, \hat{D}\}$ into (6a) and (7a) yields $\hat{Q} = \frac{1}{6b\alpha}\left(\frac{9}{8}\,b - \frac{3}{4}\,c\right)^3$ and $\hat{R}^* = \frac{(3b - 2c)/8}{6b\alpha}\left(\frac{9}{8}\,b - \frac{3}{4}\,c\right)^3$.

[2] The set of profit maximizing delivered prices in terms of distance D for Model II is $\hat{p} = \hat{m} + \alpha D = \frac{3}{8}\,(b + 2c) = \alpha D$, subject to the constraint $(9b - 6c)\,/\,8\alpha > D > 0$.

therefore, that discriminatory pricing provides a greater (profit maximizing) sales distance for the seller than does straight f.o.b. mill pricing.

Colum $\hat{D}_0$ of Table 1 also reveals the dependence of sales distances on demand curve shapes. Thus, the linear demand curve, so typically stressed in the literature on spatial markets[1], is revealed to yield a smaller profit maximizing distance than the concave demand curve, but a greater trading distance than the convex demand curve[2].

We find from column $\hat{R}^*$ that the discriminatory pricing system is the more profitable regardless of whether demand is concave, linear or convex, and thus regardless of the elasticity involved. (Cf. Hoover-Smithies' opposing contention that the subject pricing is not always the actual price policy for a spatial monopolist.) Profits for the concave, linear, and convex demand alternatives are repeated in a slightly different (rounded) form in Table 2 for easier comparisons.

Table 2 — *Profits and Outputs Compared, Ratios Model I/Model II*[a]

	Concave demand	Linear demand	Convex demand
Profits	$\frac{3}{2.8} = 1.07142$	$\frac{3}{2.6} = 1.15384$	$\frac{3}{2.4} = 1.25000$
Outputs	$\frac{4^4}{3^5} = 1.05349$	$\frac{9}{8} = 1.12500$	$\frac{25}{9\sqrt{5}} = 1.24229$

[a] Table 2 shows that outputs produced under Model I are greater than those produced under Model II by 5.349%, 12.5% and 24.2% when demands are concave, linear, and convex, respectively.

Column $\hat{Q}$ indicates that output is greater under discriminatory pricing than it is under nondiscriminatory f.o.b. mill pricing. And, again, this result applies respectively to each of the demand curves considered above.

[1] For example, see Lösch, *op. cit.* — Smithies, "Monopolistic Price Policy in a Spatial Market", *op. cit.* — *Idem*, "Optimum Location in a Spatial Competition", *op. cit.* — Edwin Mills and Michael R. Lav, "A Model of Market Areas with Free Entry", *The Journal of Political Economy*, Vol. 72, 1964, pp. 278sqq.

[2] See Greenhut, *Plant Location in Theory and Practise*, *op. cit.*, pp. 304sqq., where, by another derivation, it is shown that for any given distance D, price is greater under concave demand than under linear demand than under convex demand. We find the same result via Figure 2 and Table 1, as well as the result that a concave demand curve of the type (a) in this paper will yield the greatest market area size with the correspondingly highest prices vis-à-vis the curves derived from functions (b) and (c) above.

Column $\hat{p}$ indicates for the demand curves drawn in Figure 1 that the rate of freight absorption under Model I, defined as $1 - \frac{dp}{d(\alpha D)}$, is $\frac{1}{3}$ in the concave case, $\frac{1}{2}$ in the linear case, and $\frac{2}{3}$ in the convex case. These freight absorption *relations* apply *in general* to concave, linear, and convex demands. It can also be shown that whenever these curves are of decreasing elasticity and are tangent at the spaceless profit maximizing

Figure 2 — *Spatial Price Schedule under Alternative Demands and Alternative Pricing Practices*[a]

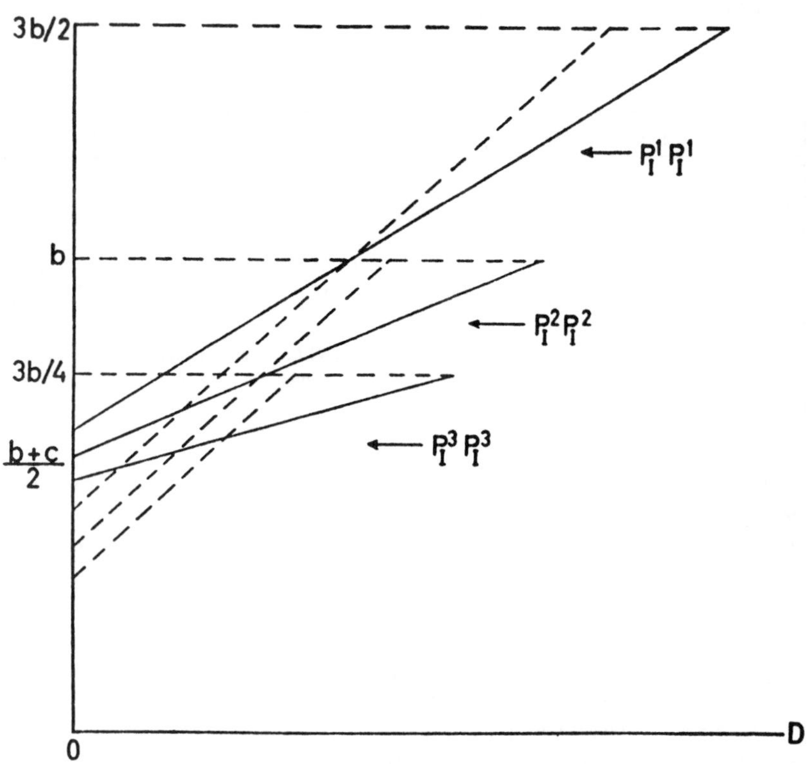

[a] The lines $P_I^1 P_I^1$, $P_I^2 P_I^2$ and $P_I^3 P_I^3$ represent the delivered prices derived from Model I under the concave, linear, and convex demand curves, respectively, as a function of distance D. Broken lines represent corresponding delivered prices for Model II, respectively, under concave, linear and convex curves.

price, but — unlike Figure 1 — are each constrained to the extent that the same maximum price value (i. e., price limit) applies to each, the absorption rate again is greatest for convex demand and least for concave demand, ceteris paribus[1]. In the same general connection, observe that the rate of freight absorption under Model II is nominally zero for all three cases since actual freight costs are being added to the given profit maximizing mill price. However, in deriving the mill price, prices smaller than the nonspatial price are obtained; specifically, the nonspatial prices $b/2 + 2c/3$, $(b + c)/2$, $b/2 + c/3$ are greater than the spatial prices $(3b+6c)/8$, $(b + 2c)/3$, $(3b + 6c)/10$. It follows, accordingly, that some freight is absorbed in the process of establishing the spatial price in all of the given demand situations. (See Figure 2.)

VI. Spatial Competition and Pricing Policies

The main conclusions formulated above remain unchanged if spatial competition occurs at a distance such that the demand for a seller's product is eliminated at what otherwise would be the subject seller's natural peripheral market points. For purposes of brevity and simplification, only the linear demand function will be considered in the present discussion.

Table 1, column $\hat{p}$, provides the delivered price schedule under Model I when there is no exogenously imposed restriction on the length of the seller's market. Let us present again the result for row 3, column $\hat{p}$ as:

$$(6\text{—}1)\quad p = \hat{p} = \frac{1}{2}(b + c) + \frac{1}{2}\alpha D, \quad \frac{b - c}{\alpha} \geq D \geq 0 .$$

[1] For a proof, let $p = f(q)$ stand for a demand function of the general form. Then profit maximization under $MC = c$ requires, at every D, the condition $MR = \frac{d}{dq}[p - \alpha D]\, q = f'(q)q + [f(q) - \alpha D] = c$. Differentiating this condition with respect to D yields:

$$f'' \frac{dq}{dp}\frac{dp}{dD} q + f' \frac{dq}{dp}\frac{dp}{dD} + f' \frac{dq}{dp}\frac{dp}{dD} - \alpha = 0$$

$$\therefore\ 1 - \frac{dp}{dD} = 1 - \frac{\alpha}{2 + \frac{f''}{f'} q};$$

clearly, the rate of freight absorption depends upon the convexity of the demand, i.e., f''. Since $q > 0$ and $f' < 0$, concave demand, i.e., $f'' > 0$, requires the absorption rate to be less than $\alpha/2$, linear demand requires it to be equal to $\alpha/2$, and convex demand requires it to be greater than $\alpha/2$.

But now apply a price ceiling to (6—1), namely:

$$(6\text{—}2)\ p = p_o,\ b \geq p_o \geq \frac{b + c}{2}$$

where p_o is the exogenously given maximum delivered price which the seller is able to quote[1]. His maximum sales distance is thus constrained by a price restriction[2]. Substitution of (6—2) into (6—1) yields:

$$(6\text{—}3)\ \hat{D}_o = \frac{2p_o - (b + c)}{\alpha}$$

A graphical solution for $\hat{D}_o$ of Model I follows from (6—3) which is given by the distance $\hat{D}_I$ in Figure 3. This distance is determined by the intersection of the two lines PP (reflecting equation (6—1)) and P_oP_o (reflecting equation (6—2)).

Now substitute $\hat{D}_o$ respectively in the integrated output and profit functions applicable to linear demand. Such substitution, when applied under (6—3), yields for Model I:

$$(6\text{—}4)\ Q_I = \int_0^{\hat{D}_o} q\, dD = \left(-(b - p_o)^2 + \frac{1}{4}(b - c)^2\right) / \alpha$$

$$(6\text{—}5)\ R_I^* = \int_0^{\hat{D}_o} (p - c - \alpha D)\, q\, dD$$

$$= \frac{1}{12\alpha}\{(b - c)^3 - 8(b - p_o)^3\}.$$

[1] When p_o is at its upper limit b, the system converges to that of spatial monopoly, and when p_o is at its lower limit, $(b + c) / 2$, the system converges to the spaceless one. This follows because the value $p_o = b$ establishes the ceiling b for the delivered price. Obviously if delivered price could rise to b, no exogenous constraint applies to the price or sales radius. When $p_o = (b + c) / 2$, i.e., when the delivered price ceiling is $(b + c) / 2$, the price limit equals the profit maximizing spaceless equilibrium price; this value indicates that no buyer exists who would pay a (delivered) price greater than the nonspatial price.

[2] Martin J. Beckmann (*Location Theory*, New York, 1968, p. 34) provides an alternative view of competition than that followed here. By diagram, he demonstrates varying market size possibilities if the firm undercuts the rival's price p_o or meets it. Such pricing, however, might open up a Pandora's box consisting in part of Robinson-Patman restrictions which stand against any contention of good faith pricing necessary for workable competition. Equation (6—2) is thus assumed herein partly to avoid discussion of the myriad claims, counterclaims, price possibilities, etc., that may exist; most vitally, it focuses attention strictly on the profitability of discriminatory pricing vis-à-vis f.o.b. mill pricing under the *equivalent conditions* that the market periphery is determined *at a point* (not zone) as the firm's delivered price reaches the value p_o.

Figure 3 — *Spatial Prices and Market Areas under Competition*

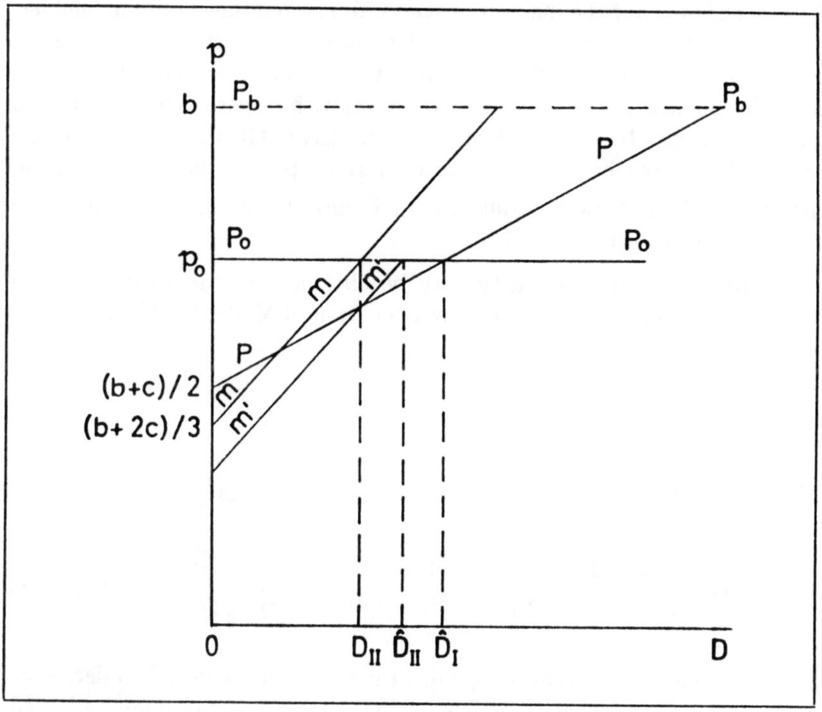

The derivation in Model II is a little more complicated. Recall the following:

$$(6\text{—}6)\ p = m + \alpha D\,.$$

Combining (6—6) with the same price constraint as (6—2) then yields:

$$(6\text{—}7)\ D_o = (p_o - m)/\alpha\,.$$

Equation (6—7) designates the sales radius in terms of the maximum delivered price, parametrically given as p_o and the as yet undetermined mill price m. Taking the partial derivative of the integrated revenue function with respect to mill price m and to market size D_o, with each subject to (6—7), and then setting the results to zero yields (6—8) and (6—9).

$$(6\text{—}8)\ \hat{m}_o = \frac{1}{3}\left(2b + c - \sqrt{(b - c)^2 + 3\,(b - p_o)^2}\right)$$

$$(6\text{—}9)\ \hat{D}_o = \frac{1}{3\alpha}\left(3p_o - 2b - c + \sqrt{(b - c)^2 + 3\,(b - p_o)^2}\right).$$

Solutions $\hat{m}_o$ and $\hat{D}_o$ can be presented graphically, as in Figure 3 above. Note that D_{II} is not the maximum sales radius when the maximum delivered price is given by the line P_oP_o, since m does not stay at $(b + 2c)/3$ when the size of the market available to a seller is reduced. Rather, m must decline because the derivative of (6—8) with respect to p_o (constrained as it is to values $b > p_o \geq (b + c)/2$ is positive. The delivered price line in Model II must be shifted downward given p_o less than p_b, i. e. from mm to m'm'. The sales radius $\hat{D}_{II}$ in Figure 3 applies, accordingly, to the price constraint P_oP_o.

Profit maximizing quantity may be obtained by substituting (6—8) and (6—9) into the integrated output function of Model II. Thus:

$$(6\text{—}10)\quad Q_{II} = \int_0^{\hat{D}_o} q \, dD = \left(b - \hat{m}_o - \frac{\alpha}{2}\hat{D}_o\right)\hat{D}_o$$

$$= \{(b - c)^2 - 3\,(b - p_o)^2 + (b - c)\sqrt{(b - c)^2 + 3\,(b - p_o)^2}\}/9\alpha$$

$$(6\text{—}11)\quad \frac{dQ_{II}}{dp_o} = \left\{2 - \frac{b - c}{\sqrt{(b - c)^2 + 3\,(b - p_o)^2}}\right\}\frac{b - p_o}{3\alpha} > 0 \quad \forall p_o < b.$$

Observe from (6—11) that as p_o falls, the total output of a firm decreases monotonically in accordance with the lowering of its maximum delivered prices. In turn, differentiating (6—4) with respect to p_o yields:

$$(6\text{—}12)\quad \frac{dQ_I}{dp_o} = 2\,(b - p_o)/\alpha > 0 \quad \forall p_o < b.$$

Thus Q_I is also a monotonically decreasing function with lower p_o over the domain $b > p_o \geq 0$. Moreover, pursuant to (6 — 4), $Q_I = (b - c)^2/4\alpha$ when $p_o = b$; but $Q_I = 0$ when $p_o = \frac{b + c}{2}$. From (6 — 11), $Q_{II} = 2\,(b - c)^2/9\alpha$ when $p_o = b$; but $Q_{II} = 0$ only when $p_o = 0$. Thus, $Q_I > Q_{II}$ when $p_o = b$; in contrast, $Q_I = 0$ when $p_o = \frac{b + c}{2}$ while $Q_{II} = 0$ only when $p_o = c$. A similar statement holds for R* by appropriate differentiations. The results are given in Figure 4, where again the circumflex is affixed to the Q's and R*'s in order to indicate profit maximizing values, and the bar is used to indicate the existence of competitive limits to these values.

Figure 4 — *Outputs and Profits under Different Levels of Competition*

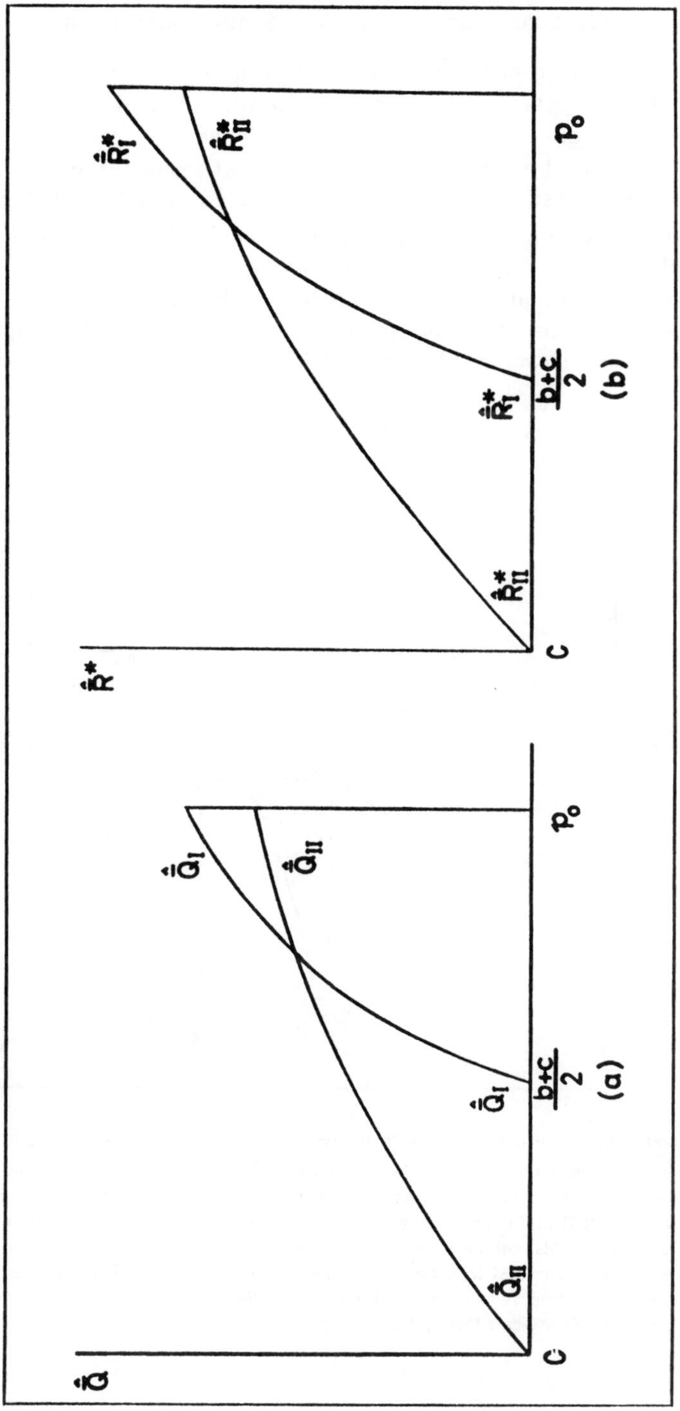

VII. Conclusions Applicable to Spatial Competition

Do the above results lead to the conclusion that a firm under spatial competition resorts — in general — to the nondiscriminatory f.o.b. pricing technique? To answer this question, define pure (windfall) profit Π as an excess of return R over fixed cost F. Next assume three alternative levels of fixed cost, as illustrated by F_1F_1, F_2F_2, and F_3F_3 in Figure 5, and include $\hat{R}_I^*$ and $\hat{R}_{II}^*$ of Figure 4(b). If the fixed cost reflective of the optimal firm size is as high as F_1F_1, Model I yields the long-run zero profit equilibrium at p_1.[1] At this point, Model II yields $\Pi < 0$. Thus, the firm adopts discriminatory pricing even under zero profit competitive equilibrium whenever fixed cost is higher than F_2F_2. If fixed cost is as

Figure 5 — *Price Policies in the Zero Profit State*

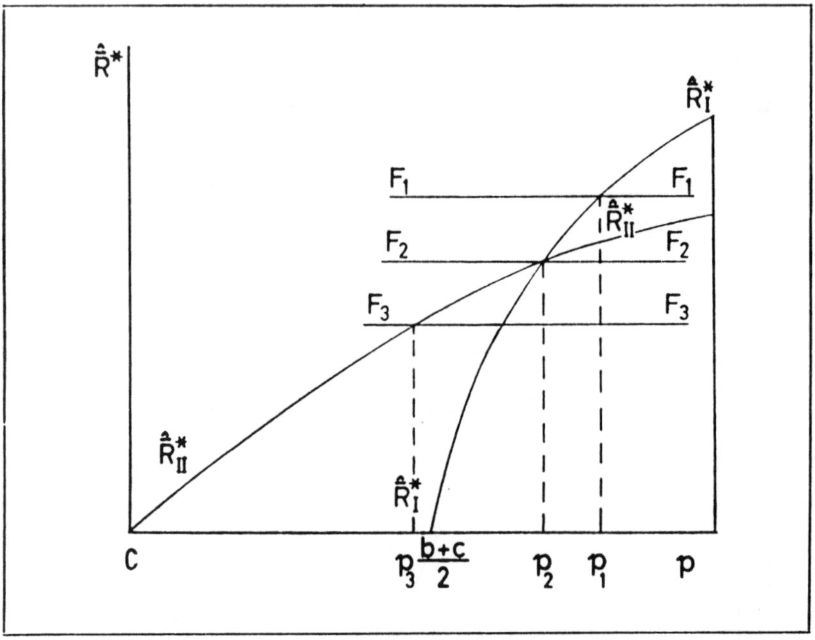

[1] Manifestly, the firm will maximize profits for any given price p_0 (in Figure 5) and accordingly will select the higher of the alternative $\hat{R}_I^*$ and $\hat{R}_{II}^*$ curves. The basic process exists regardless of the level of fixed cost in the short run. However, realize that the existence of short-run windfall profits or losses will give rise to entry or exit of firms until a price is established which yields both long-run zero profits and the optimal firm size, i.e., the *optimal* level of fixed cost associated with *the* short-run average cost curve which is tangent to the long-run average cost curve at its point of lowest cost. See M. L. Greenhut, *A Theory of the Firm in Economic Space*, 2nd Print., Austin, 1974.

high as F_2F_2, the zero profit equilibrium is obtained at p_2 with Model I and Model II being equally profitable. The firm is now indifferent between the two alternative pricing practices. If, finally, the fixed cost is lower than F_2F_2, e.g., as low as F_3F_3, Model II yields zero profit equilibrium at p_3 while Model I yields negative profit Π. The firm must switch its pricing practice from discriminatory pricing to f.o.b. mill pricing as the degree of competition increases, i.e., as the maximum delivered price falls to lower and lower values.

It has thus far been proven that the level of fixed cost plays a decisive role in determining whether or not the firm applies discriminatory or nondiscriminatory pricing under the zero profit competitive equilibrium. This conclusion is supported by the simplifying assumptions that both the freight rate and marginal cost of production are fixed. It is manifest, however, that these costs play a similar role as does fixed cost in the subject problem. In fact, the higher are these costs, the lower are the $\hat{R}_I^*\hat{R}_I^*$ and $\hat{R}_{II}^*\hat{R}_{II}^*$ curves; they both shift *downward*. In turn, the switching point moves *downward*. But then, given the fixed cost at the F_2F_2 level, the higher marginal cost and/or freight cost requires the firm to practice discrimination under the zero profit competitive equilibrium. It follows that F_2F_2 no longer defines the indifference level of costs between the alternative spatial pricing practices under the given conditions of competition. We may conclude that the relative importance of *costs in general*, i.e., freight as well as production costs, *determine the firm's pricing practices under spatial competition*. It follows that if as is claimed in M. L. Greenhut[1], the friction of distance and/or uncertainty are significant costs in a space economy, then even a weak form of competition would tend to wipe out economic surpluses before the switching point favoring nondiscriminatory pricing is reached. It is quite likely therefore that a firm will adopt discriminatory pricing which yields greater outputs than does f.o.b mill pricing over space even in the presence of spatial competition and the long-run prospect of zero profits. Empirical testing of these propositions should be of interest to many economists in several ways, particularly those concerned with antitrust laws such as the Robinson Patman Act.

* * *

[1] See Greenhut, *A Theory of the Firm in Economic Space*, *op. cit.*

[11]

Monopoly Output Under Alternative Spatial Pricing Techniques

By M. L. GREENHUT AND H. OHTA*

The objective of this paper is to compare the effect on output of spatial price discrimination with that of simple f.o.b. pricing. A possible conclusion would be that if discrimination does not increase output, such pricing is undesirable from the standpoint of social welfare even though it proves to be more profitable for the spatial monopolist. Current subject matter interest thus reflects the question whether the discriminatory delivered price *level* of the spatial monopolist is high or low relative to the set of delivered prices resulting from a policy of f.o.b. mill pricing.[1]

Our problem is, therefore, closely related to the discussion by A. C. Pigou-Joan Robinson and Edgar Edwards of outputs produced by a discriminatory and nondiscriminatory (simple) monopolist. Their formulations of the problem were, unfortunately, too general to provide clear answers to specific questions such as whether or not the existence of economic space helps yield greater (or lesser) outputs under discrimination than does simple monopoly pricing. We shall answer this and related questions precisely by presenting a proof that *monopoly* outputs are *always* greater under spatial price discrimination than they are under simple f.o.b. mill pricing. Throughout the paper we abstract from special forces, such as adverse income effects associated with discriminatory prices.

I. A Basic Difference in Nonspatial and Spatial Price Discrimination: Total Output

Classical (nonspatial) economics describes the discriminating monopolist as the supplier of greater *or* smaller outputs than the nondiscriminating monopolist, depending on the relative shapes of the demand curves. It can easily be shown, however, that whether greater outputs are produced under discriminatory monopoly also depends in part on the level and/or shape of the cost function. It is this additional property which is the relevant, in fact the basic, force behind the alternative views that apply to nonspatial price discrimination. The purpose of the present section is not to take issue with classical theory, but to reformulate it in a spatial framework from which comparisons may be drawn. Apart from discrimination by licensed practitioners of medicine, law, and dentistry, much of the price discrimination by firms encountered today occurs along geographical lines.

The Spaceless Framework

As a point of departure for our basic model assume, as did Pigou and Robinson, the existence of two markets, each of which possesses a linear demand curve. Let these curves be parallel and differ only in their price and quantity intercepts. Let Market I contain the stronger demand while Market II is characterized by the weaker. Assume that there is no cost of distance or, alternatively, that the economic space separating the markets from the seller is the same.

In Figure 1(a) and (b), the horizontal axes, respectively, measure the individual demand q_i and the aggregate demand Q of the two markets. The vertical axes measure the aver-

* Professor and lecturer at Texas A&M University and Aoyama Gakuin University, respectively. We wish to thank Robert Ekelund and W. D. Maxwell for helpful suggestions and criticisms. This paper is based on research funded by the National Science Foundation.

[1] In another paper, we are examining the impact of economic space on the pricing practices of the spatial monopolist. In contrast to prevailing spatial theory, the proposition is advanced that regardless of the shapes of the assumed (demand) curves, the spatial monopolist increases his profits by absorbing relatively larger quantities of freight on sales to buyers located at greater distances from his plant. The specification that demand vanishes at some high (finite) price along with a resale proviso will be shown to be sufficient to establish the full scope and generality of this proposition.

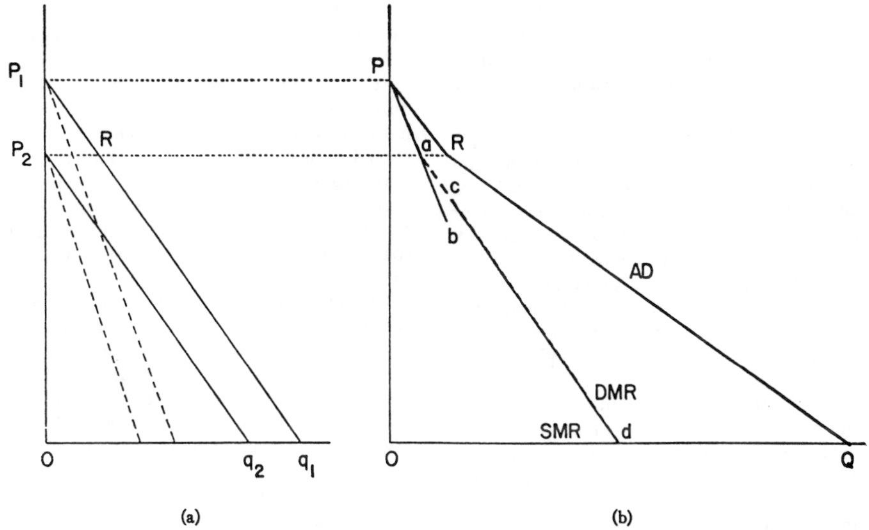

FIGURE 1

age and marginal revenue values for the simple and discriminatory monopolies. The lines p_1q_1 and p_2q_2 in Figure 1(a) stand, respectively, for the average revenue curves, in Market I and Market II. The line *pRQ* in Figure 1(b) is the horizontal sum of the two average revenue curves. This aggregate curve (*AD*) applies to a simple monopoly. Its marginal revenue curve, *SMR*, is the broken curve *pbcd*.[2] Correspondingly, the aggregate *demand* curve under discriminatory monopoly is also *AD*; but, an average *revenue* curve is conceptually imaginable which—in light of the different prices charged in the two markets—would yield for the discriminating monopolist a higher net price on sales to both markets at all given-identical total outputs compared to that derived by the simple monopolist. (We do not show this average revenue curve in Figure 1.) The *continuous curve pacd* is the discriminatory marginal revenue, *DMR*, curve. It is the horizontal sum of the two marginal revenue curves, and must be distinguished from the discontinuous *SMR* curve *pbcd*. The intersections of *DMR* and *SMR* with the marginal cost curve determine whether or not total output *Q* is greater under discriminatory monopoly than simple monopoly.

Case I. If *MC* cuts the *pa* portion of *DMR*, there will be no difference between the outputs produced by a discriminatory monopoly and a simple monopoly. In effect, only one market, namely Market I, is served *even if the monopolist otherwise would practice discrimination*. (See Robinson, p. 196.)

Case II. If *MC* cuts the *ab* portion of *SMR*, and also the *ac* portion of *DMR*, the intersection of *MC* with *DMR* lies to the right of the intersection of *MC* with *SMR*. Total output in this case is greater under discriminatory pricing than under simple monopoly pricing. (See Pigou, pp. 286, 809.) Market I alone is served by the simple monopoly whereas both markets are served by the discriminating seller. Correspondingly, the

[2] This diagram, in particular Figure 1(b), is based on Robinson's Figure 65A (p. 201). A diagram by Pigou (p. 809), designed for similar analytical purposes, is inferior to Robinson's in the sense that it requires a constant marginal cost (Pigou's supply price).

equilibrium price is necessarily higher in the case of simple monopoly pricing than p_2 while the price in Market II is lower than p_2 in the price discrimination case. (See Figure 1.)

Case III. If *MC* cuts the *cd* portion of *DMR* (which is overlapped by *SMR*), then total output is once again the same under the two different pricing systems. Unlike Case I or II, however, both markets are now served. Although total output remains unchanged, the output shipped to Market II increases by the precise amount by which demand is cut in Market I as a result of the change in the pricing technique from simple to discriminatory pricing.[3]

Of the three cases, Robinson apparently emphasized Case III. She identified it with the rather elementary case of linear demand.[4] Although Case I may be trivial, Case II will be shown to be highly relevant to a spatial analysis of discriminatory pricing.

The Spatial Framework

To appreciate the relationships relevant to the space economy, conceive of buyers being *evenly distributed* along a line or over a plain with each and every buyer having the same identical (gross) demand curve.[5] Then the net demand curve of a buyer (or a group of buyers) one mile away from the seller must be different (to the seller) than the demand curve of a buyer located at the seller's door. The net demand curve of a buyer two miles away, three miles away, etc. are, in turn, all different in the eyes of the seller.[6] A number of parallel linear functions can thus be used to portray the net demands confronting the seller. While a single seller cannot serve spatial markets in which the freight cost burden is prohibitive, it should be clear that more distant buyers (or markets) may be served by a discriminating monopolist compared to a simple f.o.b. pricing monopolist. Cases I and III above are, therefore, inapplicable, and Case II alone is relevant under spatial monopoly. But let us now probe into this matter more deeply.

Consider three different net demand curves representing markets located adjacent to, near to, and distant from the seller, respectively. Assume further that: 1) Every buyer's gross demand curve is linear and identical, of the form $p=b-3aq$, and that the aggregate gross demand curve is specifiable as $p=b-aQ$, where b and a are positive constants. 2) The freight rate (or cost of distance) is zero between the seller and the adjacent market, $(1/3)b$ over the distance from the seller to the near market, and $(2/3)b$ for the distance between the seller and the distant market. 3) Each market contains $\frac{1}{3}$ of the total number of buyers. Figure 2 may, then, be constructed as a simple extension of Figure 1.[7]

Observe that Case III, i.e., where *DMR* and *SMR* merge into the segment *cd* in Figure 1, is now relatively unimportant since the line *cd* has become relatively shorter in a threefold market division vis-à-vis the old twofold division of buyers. A new *df* portion of *DMR* has appeared which is ***not overlapped*** by *SMR*. One might well expect, accordingly, that outputs will often be different.

The following conclusions apply: If mar-

[3] See Pigou, p. 809; Robinson, p. 192. And see R. Battalio and Ekelund for a discussion of the importance of cost in output changes under price discrimination.

[4] Compare Robinson, p. 192. More generally, she observed that output is the same when the relative adjusted concavities of the two demand curves are the same.

[5] This spatial system conforms to the framework used by Edgar Hoover, Arthur Smithies, and Donald Dewey in which buyers are evenly distributed along a line or over a plain, individual gross demands are identical, and freight rates are significantly positive.

[6] In other words, the spatial gross demand function, i.e., the demand function at the customer's own mill, must be distinguished from its related net demand function, i.e., the demand visualized by the seller as applicable *at the seller's site*. The two are sharply distinct when freight costs are significant.

[7] Let Q stand for the aggregate net demand such that:

$$Q = \frac{b-p}{3a} \;\forall p \ni p_1 > p \geq p_2,$$

$$= \frac{b-p}{3a} + \frac{b-(b/3)-p}{3a} \;\forall p \ni p_2 > p \geq p_3,$$

$$= \frac{b-p}{3a} + \frac{b-(b/3)-p}{3a} + \frac{b-(2b/3)-p}{3a}$$

$$\forall p \ni p_3 > p \geq 0$$

This aggregation provides the kinked demand curve *pRSQ*. Similarly, the *DMR* and *SMR* curves are specifiable rigorously, as given later.

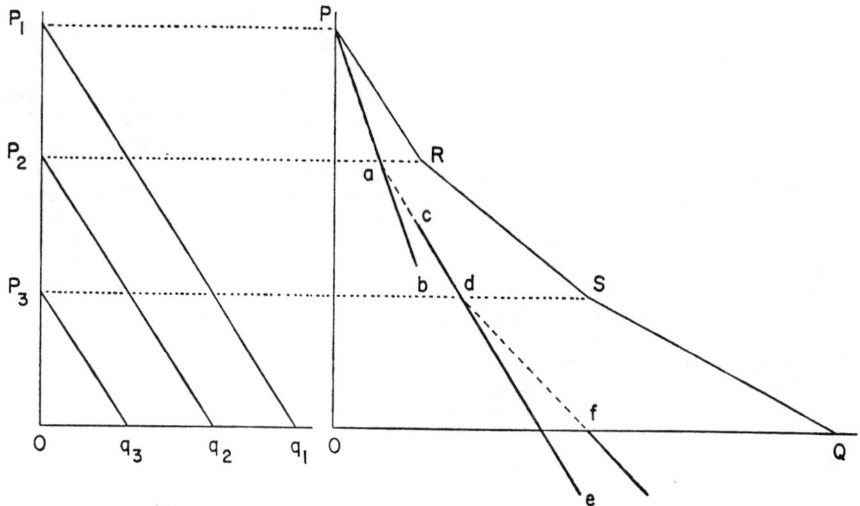

(a) (b)

FIGURE 2

ginal cost is so high that the *MC* curve cuts the *ac* portion of *DMR*, total output would clearly be greater under discrimination than it would be under simple monopoly. If the *MC* curve cuts the *cd* portion of *DMR* $=SMR$, the total outputs would be the same. If *MC* were still lower so that it cuts the *df* portion of *DMR*, total output once again would be greater under discriminatory pricing than simple monopoly pricing. Diverging total outputs become more and more likely under linear demand, the "finer" the division of markets in economic space.

II. Spatial Equilibrium Given The Linear Gross Demand Curve

Consider the "line" situation where n spatially separated markets of the same size are identifiable, and each buyer's gross demand curve is linear of the form $p=b-naq$. The freight rate per unit of distance may now be defined by the constant value b/n, where b stands for the price intercept of the gross demand curve of a buyer at a given site on the line market. Thus, for example, the buying market one distance unit from the seller involves a freight rate equal to b/n, the buying market two distance units from the seller involves a freight rate equal to $2b/n$, etc. The price intercepts ($p_1, p_2, \ldots, p_n$) of the net linear demand curves are, therefore, definable as $p_i=b-(i-1)b/n$, where $i=1, 2, \ldots, n$. (See Figure 3.) The aggregate demand function may then be established arithmetically by summing all of the net demand curves. We obtain (1), as derived below,[8] and (1′) similarly.[9]

[8] With respect to (1), consider the following:

$$Q=\frac{b-p}{na} \forall p \ni p_1 > p \geq p_2,$$

$$=\frac{b-p}{na}+\frac{b-(b/n)-p}{na}=\frac{2b-(b/n)-2p}{na}$$

$$\forall p \ni p_2 > p \geq p_3,$$

$$=\frac{2b-(b/n)-2p}{na}+\frac{b-(2b/n)-p}{na}$$

$$=\frac{3b-(3b/n)-3p}{na} \forall p \ni p_3 > p \geq p_4,$$

$$=\frac{3b-(3b/n)-3p}{na}+\frac{b-(3b/n)-p}{na}$$

$$(1)\quad Q = \frac{i[(b-p)-(i-1)b/2n]}{na}$$

$$\forall\, p \ni p_i > p \geq p_{i+1} \quad (i = 1, 2, \ldots, n),$$

and

$$(1')\quad \lim_{n\to\infty} Q = \frac{(b-p)^2}{2ab} \;\forall\, p \ni b \geq p \geq 0$$

The discriminatory marginal revenue, *DMR*, is obtainable via the horizontal summation of all net individual marginal revenue curves, with each horizontal intercept value being one-half that of the respective net demand curve. Dividing the right-hand side of (1) by two, therefore, yields *DMR* or, more rigorously, it yields the inverse function of aggregate marginal revenue under price discrimination. Thus:

$$(2)\quad Q = \frac{i[(b-p)-(i-1)b/2n]}{2na}$$

$$\forall\, p \ni p_i > p \geq p_{i+1} \quad (i = 1, 2, \ldots, n),$$

and

$$(2')\quad \lim_{n\to\infty} Q \;\frac{(b-p)^2}{4ab} \;\forall\, p \ni b \geq p \geq 0,$$

where p now stands for values to be read along the marginal revenue curve. This formula (2), or (2′), would provide the total output produced by the seller. Moreover, the formulas permit comparison of spatial output with the spaceless economy output. Thus, if marginal cost and marginal revenue were zero, p in (2) assumes the particular value $p = p_{n+1}$. Substituting $i = n$ and then $p = 0$ in (2) and (2′), respectively, yield:

$$(2^*)\qquad Q = \frac{(n+1)b}{4na};$$

and

$$(2^{*\prime})\qquad \lim_{n\to\infty} Q = \frac{b}{4a}$$

Comparison of (2*′) with (2*) at $p = 0$ indicates that when marginal production cost is zero, the spatial output $Q = b/4a$ is less than the output $Q = b/2a$ of the spaceless ($n = 1$) economy. In other words, if buyers are successively (evenly) distributed along a line, total output under discriminatory monopoly would, in the limit, be reduced to half that which would have been produced if all buyers had been concentrated at sites next to the seller.[10]

$$= \frac{4b-(6b/n)-4p}{na} \;\forall\, p \ni p_4 > p \geq p_5,$$

$$= \frac{i(b-p)-i(i-1)b/2n}{na} \;\forall\, p \ni p_i > p \geq p_{i+1},$$

where $p_i = b-(i-1)b/n$, $i = 1, 2, \ldots, n$, and n stands for the number of submarkets *visualized*, but not necessarily served by the seller.

[9] As n approaches a large number, any p in the domain $p_i > p \geq p_{i+1}$ can be approximated by:

$$p = (p_i + p_{i+1})/2$$
$$= [2-(2i-1)/n](b/2),$$

by substitution of price intercepts p_i;

$$\therefore\quad i = (1/2) + (b-p)n/b$$

In order to define Q in terms of p alone, substitute this value of i into the general formula for Q, which yields:

$$Q = \frac{b-p}{2na} - \frac{b[(b-p)(n/b)-(1/2)]}{4n^2a} + \frac{(b-p)^2}{ab} - \frac{(b-p)^2(n/b)-(b-p)/2}{2na},$$

$$\lim_{n\to\infty} Q = \frac{(b-p)^2}{2ab} \;\forall\, p \ni 0 \leq p \leq b$$

[10] The ratio r of spatial demand to spaceless demand applicable at any marginal cost = marginal revenue level is given by equation (2) divided by the counterpart spaceless marginal revenue equation $Q = (b-p)/2a$. Thus:

$$(a)\quad r = \left(\frac{i[b-p-(i-1)b/2n]}{2na}\right) \Big/ \left(\frac{b-p}{2a}\right)$$

$$= \frac{i[b-p-(i-1)b/2n]}{(b-p)n},$$

where i is an integer whose value depends on p such that $p_k > p \geq p_{k+1} \Rightarrow i = k$; e.g., if $p_3 > p \geq p_4$, then $i = 3$. This formula (a) reappears in much simpler form under certain conditions. To derive this simpler form, it helps to recall from the definition $p_i = b-(i-1)b/n$ that the price intercept of the strongest market is given by $p = b$; in turn, the price intercepts of the other spatial markets are fully specified by $k+1$, where $i = k = 1, 2, \ldots, n$.

(over)

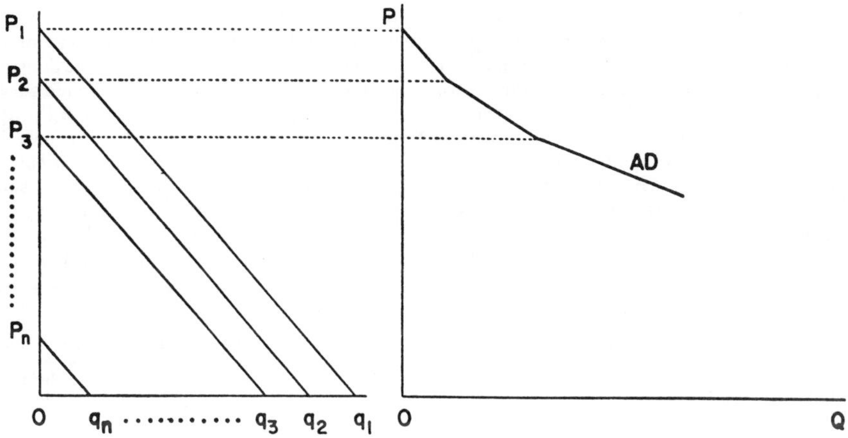

(a) (b)

FIGURE 3

Consider now the form of *SMR* for later comparison with *DMR*. Observe first that it is *not* a continuous function *nor* a one-to-one function. (See Figure 1 or 2.) In other words, even though p may be taken as a function of Q, the Q relating to *SMR* is not a function of p since more than one Q value relates to some of these p's. Since *SMR* is not a one-to-one function, no inverse function may be derived for it that would compare with (2). We may, nevertheless, rewrite (2) as (3) and subsequently specify a new domain for it:

$$(3)\quad p = b - \frac{(i-1)}{2}\frac{b}{n} - \frac{2na}{i}Q \qquad (i = 1, 2, \ldots, n),$$

where, to repeat, the domain must be redefined to establish a different function. We define this domain in (4), as derived in turn below:[11]

$$(4)\quad \frac{(i+1)ib}{2n^2a} > Q \geq \frac{(i-1)ib}{2n^2a} \qquad (i = 1, 2, \ldots, n)$$

If then MC is at the level p_{k+1}, both i and p in equation (a) have been provided; viz., $i=k$ and $p=p_{k+1}=b-kb/n$. Substituting these particular values of i and p in (a) yields the desired relation:

$$(b)\qquad r = \frac{k+1}{2n}, \qquad k = 1, 2, \ldots, n$$

Formula (b) is not defined when $k=0$, since this condition implies $p=b$ in (a). and that the denominator (as well as numerator) of formula (a) are zero. Most importantly, formula (b) demonstrates that the lower is $MC(=MR\equiv p)$, i.e., the larger is k, the higher is the ratio of spatial to spaceless demand. *Ceteris paribus*, when $MC=0$ the ratio 1/2 applies, which indicates that in the limit aggregate spatial demand is one-half that of spaceless demand.

[11] The domain Q for *SMR* may be partitioned for each point of Q at which a kink in the aggregate demand AD occurs. Following previous definitions, and assumptions of freight rates and market distances, the price intercepts $(p_1, p_2, \ldots, p_n)$ of the net linear demand curves occur at the values $p=p_i=b-(i-1)b/n$, $i=1, 2, \ldots, n$. Substituting for p in (1) then yields the critical values of Q at which kinks of AD occur, namely:

$$Q_i = \frac{i(i-1)b}{2n^2a}$$

and

$$Q_{i+1} = \frac{(i+1)ib}{2n^2a} \qquad (i = 1, 2, \ldots, n)$$

The relevant partitioned domain is defined above as (4).

Formulas (4) and (3) establish the domain and the corresponding range of the marginal revenue of the simple (nondiscriminatory) monopolist. From elementary economics, we know that the level of p in (3) is determined by the level of MC. Hence the total output produced under simple monopoly, given the MC, can be obtained by (3) provided that i is also given. And i (the number of markets served) turns out to be a function of p as n approaches a large number. By elementary substitution,[12] we obtain:

$$\text{(5)} \qquad \frac{i}{n} = \frac{2(b-p)}{3b}$$

Substituting (5) into (3) and taking the limit yields:

$$\text{(6)} \qquad \lim_{n\to\infty} Q = \frac{2(b-p)^2}{9ab}, \qquad \forall\, p \ni b \geq p \geq 0$$

The single formula (6) provides the total output produced under simple spatial monopoly as n approaches infinity.[13] We see that when the spatial market is "finely" divided, Q becomes a one-to-one function of p over the domain $b \geq p \geq 0$. This fine division also implies that the marginal revenue curve under simple monopoly, i.e., SMR, approaches a continuous curve, as shown in Figure 4. An alternative (direct) proof of this continuity relation simply requires substitution of the lower limit value (i.e., the smallest output value Q when $i=k$) and then the upper limit value (i.e., the largest output value Q when $i=k-1$) of (4) into (3). Doing so yields:

$$\text{(7)} \qquad p_i = b - \frac{(i-1)}{2}\frac{b}{n} - \frac{2na}{i}\,\frac{i(i-1)b}{2n^2a} = b - \frac{3ib - 3b}{2n},$$

and

$$\text{(7}'\text{)} \qquad p_i' = b - \frac{(i-2)b}{2n} - \frac{2na}{i-1}\,\frac{i(i-1)b}{2n^2a} = b - \frac{3ib - 2b}{2n},$$

where (7) gives the upper value for p at the kink in the aggregate demand curve and (7′) gives the lower value for p.[14] It follows that $p_i - p_i' = b/2n$, and:

$$\text{(8)} \qquad \lim_{n\to\infty} (p_i - p_i') = 0$$

Compare now the limiting SMR in (6) with the limiting DMR which was derived in (2′). Remarkably, the value Q in (2′) is

[12] Substitute the inverse of (3), i.e., (2), into (4). This process yields:

$$\text{(a}'\text{)} \qquad \frac{2n}{3b}(b-p) + 1 \geq i > \frac{2n}{3b}(b-p) - \frac{1}{3}$$

Because i is an integer and the interval of i is greater than unity, i.e., 4/3, inequality (a′) provides either one or two values for i depending on the value of p. Thus, i in general is not a function of p. This result stems, of course, from the fact that SMR is not a one-to-one function. Nevertheless, (a′) can be rewritten in the more revealing form (b′):

$$\text{(b}'\text{)} \qquad \frac{2}{3b}(b-p) + \frac{1}{n} \geq \frac{i}{n} > \frac{2}{3b}(b-p) - \frac{1}{3n}$$

This indicates that if n is a large number, i/n may be approximated by $2(b-p)/3b$, as in (5).

[13] It might also be noted that (6) conforms to the limiting aggregate demand function (1′), actually being its marginal curve. To see this, consider the inverse of (1′), i.e., (1″) below:

$$\text{(1}''\text{)} \qquad p = b - \sqrt{2abQ^*}, \quad \text{where } Q^* = \lim_{n\to\infty} Q$$

The total revenue and the marginal revenue are respectively given by:

$$\text{(a}''\text{)} \qquad pQ^* = bQ^* - (2abQ^*)^{1/2}Q^*,$$

$$\text{(b}''\text{)} \qquad \frac{d(pQ^*)}{dQ^*} \equiv p = b - \frac{3\sqrt{abQ^*}}{\sqrt{2}};$$

$$\therefore \text{(c}''\text{)} \qquad Q^* = \frac{2(b-p)^2}{9ab}$$

[14] For a specific example, consider the limiting value p in equation (3), given $i=3$. We obtain $p=b-b/n-(2/3)naQ=(n-1/n)b-(2/3)naQ$. Next, inserting the same $i=3$ in (4) yields $((4)3b/2n^2a)>Q\geq 3(2)b/2n^2a$. The upper value for p at the kink in the aggregate demand curve is then derived by substituting in $p=(n-1)/n)b-(2/3)naQ$ the lower limit value of Q when $i=3$, i.e., the smallest output of Q, as in (7). In turn, the lower value of p at the kink under simple monopoly is given by substituting into (3) the upper limit value of Q when $i=2$, i.e., the greatest output, as in (7′).

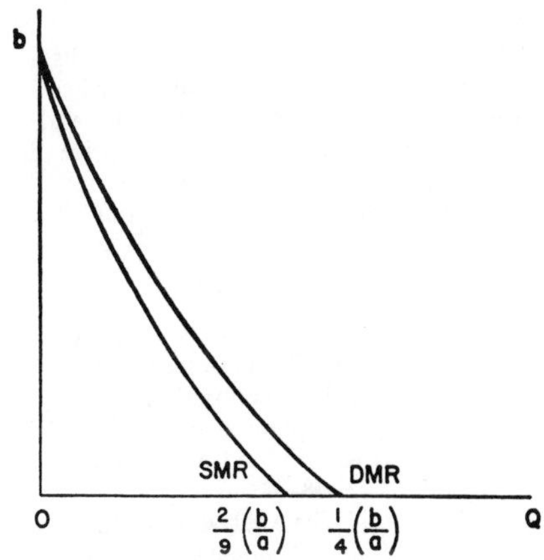

FIGURE 4

strictly greater than Q in (6) for all p such that $b > p \geq 0$, as is shown below:

$$(9) \quad \frac{(b-p)^2}{4ab} > \frac{2(b-p)^2}{9ab} \; \forall\, p \ni b > p \geq 0$$

This relation is sufficient to justify Figure 4. Besides continuity, we see in Figure 4 that the *DMR* curve always lies above the *SMR* curve, except at $p = b$. Manifestly, the quantity produced in the case of linear gross demand must always be greater under spatial monopoly price discrimination than under simple f.o.b. spatial monopoly pricing.

III. The Spatial Model Generalized for Non-Linear Demand

Our thesis that total output increases under spatial price discrimination holds true regardless of the shape and/or level of the *MC* curve. Moreover, it does not depend on the linear demand curve assumption, since non-linear curves may be approximated by linear lines over small intervals. To obtain aggregate demand, minuscule linear portions of any (concave or convex) demand curve may be added successively. The resulting *SMR* and *DMR* curves must then have fundamentally the same characteristics as those specified above at the conclusion of Section II of this paper. This basic idea supports our proposition that total output is greater under *spatial* discrimination than under simple spatial monopoly *regardless of the shape of the gross demand curve.*[15]

IV. Conclusions

Spatial price discrimination, we have therefore shown, yields larger outputs than does simple f.o.b. mill pricing, *regardless of the shape of the gross demand curve.* This conclusion justifies Pigou's anticipation that total output is likely to be greater under discriminatory monopoly than simple monopoly as the number of separate markets increases (see p. 287). But Pigou based his expectation on the claim that third degree discrimination blends into first degree discrimination as the number of separate markets increases, an identity requiring a perfectly inelastic demand curve in each submarket and, in turn, complete appropriation of consumer surplus.[16] Pigou's expectation of greater outputs was, therefore, circumscribed unnecessarily. From a somewhat different perspective, Robinson also stressed output effects.[17] She pointed, in general, to the in-

[15] Direct proof of this proposition will be provided to interested readers upon request of the authors.

[16] See Pigou, p. 287, where he states that third degree discrimination approximates first degree discrimination as the number of markets increases. To recall his formulations, the first degree involves the charging of a different price for each unit of the commodity sold such that the price for each unit exacted equals its demand price; that is to say, no consumer's surplus at all is left to any buyer. The second degree of discrimination is simply an incomplete form of the first degree; it involves a different price for a different set of units of the commodity with some consumer's surplus left over. The third degree would obtain if the monopolist were able to classify his customers by groups . . . and could charge a different price to the members of each group, as in Figure 1.

[17] Robinson argued contra Pigou that whether or not output is greater under discrimination than simple monopoly ". . . depends not upon the number of markets but upon the relative concavities of the separate demand curves" (p. 201). More specifically, she claimed that total output would be greater or less under monopoly price discrimination depending upon whether the more elastic of the demand curves in the separate markets is more or less concave than the less elastic demand curve; in turn, outputs would be the same if the demand curves are straight lines or if the relative adjusted

determinacy of total output quantities under simple monopoly and discriminatory pricing.[18] Our own basically general formulation applies to economic space, and relates to the inevitable separation of *DMR* and *SMR*.

It is useful at this point to recall a by-product of our analysis, namely that total demand is less when buyers are divisible into *n* different submarkets along a line than when they are all concentrated at the seller's location. An even more compelling view of the distinction between spatial and non-spatial output is indicated by the rule that the output of the former compared to the latter is less the higher is the level of marginal costs. It follows that if production costs and freight costs are significant, simple aggregation of gross demand curves must involve serious overestimation of effective demand. Identical gross demands over space are, in fact, significantly different net demands when the friction of distance is great.

The several conclusions drawn above stem from the assumptions that buyers are evenly distributed along a line or over a plain with each having identical tastes and hence identical gross demand curves. These assumptions are, however, neither intrinsic nor crucial to our basic conclusions. Just so long as successively shrinking net demand curves characterize the demands of more distant buyers, our conclusions hold regardless of other facets of buyer distribution and/or tastes.[19] In the space economy, price discrimination always yields greater output for the spatial monopolist than does simple f.o.b. pricing.

concavities are equal. Her argument holds only if *all markets* are served under simple monopoly as well as under discriminatory monopoly. And see Robinson, pp. 190–194. In other words, her argument is based on Case III in Section I.

[18] Also see F. M. Scherer where, pursuant to Pigou's formulation, he concludes that if demand functions are linear, "... output under discrimination will be identical to output under simple uniform-price monopoly ... ", and where pursuant to Robinson's analysis, he states "... it is impossible to determine whether on balance third degree discrimination increases output ..." (p. 254).

REFERENCES

R. Battalio and R. B. Ekelund, Jr., "Output Change Under Third Degree Discrimination," unpublished manuscript.

D. Dewey, "A Reappraisal of F.O.B. Pricing and Freight Absorption," *Southern Econ. J.*, July 1955, *22*, 48–54.

E. O. Edwards, "The Analysis of Output under Discrimination," *Econometrica*, Apr. 1950, *18*, 168–72.

M. L. Greenhut, *A Theory of the Firm in Economic Space*, New York 1970.

——— and H. Ohta, "The Classical Theory of Spatial Price Discrimination," unpublished manuscript.

E. M. Hoover, "Spatial Price Discrimination," *Rev. Econ. Stud.*, June 1937, *4*, 182–91.

A. C. Pigou, *The Economics of Welfare*, 3d ed., London 1929.

J. Robinson, *The Economics of Imperfect Competition*, London 1933.

F. M. Scherer, *Industrial Market Structure and Economic Performance*, Chicago 1970.

A. Smithies, "Monopolistic Price Policy in a Spatial Market," *Econometrica*, Jan. 1941, *9*, 63–73.

[19] What we have shown in the present paper is that the Case III requirement cannot apply if the monopolist faces innumerably many weaker and weaker markets along with a strongest market, the situation inherent to a space economy, *ceteris paribus*. See Greenhut, pp. 113–14.

[12]

Monopoly Output under Alternative Spatial Pricing Techniques: Reply

By M. L. Greenhut and H. Ohta*

Our 1972 paper originally proposed that discriminatory outputs are necessarily greater than nondiscriminatory outputs under conditions of spatial monopoly. This proposition was proved under a linear demand function and in a sense generalized in the same paper by intuitive speculation which indicated that the result would hold for non-linear demand cases as well. That speculation was confirmed later in our 1975 book, where we proved that it *holds for all non-linear demands of the particular form given by*

$$(1) \qquad p = a - bq^{\alpha} \quad a, b, \alpha > 0$$

The proof we entered on the basis of (1) does not, however, cover all *conceivable* demand forms. For this reason, our original proposition remains limited.

Song-ken Hsu contends more selectively that our 1972 argument was *misleading.* While we fully agree that any proposition can mislead, we do not accept his counterexample to our own proposition. The fact is that he inadvertently selected an example which does *not* disprove our claim. He assumed the demand form

$$(2) \qquad f(p) = \exp[-\beta p], \beta > 0$$

But a consumer preference pattern of the order of (2) would not provide any incentive at all for a firm to price discriminatorily over its spatial market area. Equation (2) demand is therefore irrelevant and inapplicable to our claim that discriminating pricing generates greater outputs than does f.o.b. pricing. To appreciate the irrelevance of (2), consider the marginal revenue *MR*, which is derivable from it, namely:

$$(2') \qquad p = f^{-1}(q) = -\frac{1}{\beta} ln\, q$$

$$pq = -\frac{q}{\beta} ln\, q$$

$$MR = p - \frac{1}{\beta}$$

The monopolist with no constraints on his spatial price policy equates each spatial submarket's marginal revenue, as given by (2'), with his marginal production (c) and transportation cost (t). This process establishes

$$(3) \qquad p - \frac{1}{\beta} = c + t \qquad t \geq 0$$

The profit-maximizing mill price (m) in any submarket is accordingly:

$$(4) \qquad m(t) \equiv p - t = c + \frac{1}{\beta}$$

which is the result that Hsu derived.[1]

But what indeed has been demonstrated? Nothing! Hsu has simply provided a demand form which does not generate price discrimination. His demand form yields only a unique f.o.b. price. And so his claim that output and other welfare effects of discriminatory pricing are identical to those of nondiscriminatory pricing is spurious. Phrased otherwise, a valid counterexample to our proposition must be based on a well-defined demand which

*Professor, Texas A&M University, and associate professor, Aoyama Gakuin University and University of Houston (adjunct), respectively.

[1]The c in (4) is not required to be a constant. Instead, it may be assumed to be a function of the firm's total output $Q = \int_0^{\infty} f(m + x)\, dx$, which in turn is a function of mill price m. It follows accordingly that the equilibrium level of c in (4) is simultaneously determined along with Q and m.

provides a firm with incentive to discriminate spatially in the price it charges. For reasons disclosed in our 1975 book (chs. 4, 5), *and not altered by Hsu*, we thus will continue to maintain our original proposition without modification, that is until a meaningful counterexample can be constructed. Hsu's present argument is interesting. But it only proposes a one-sided price practice, and accordingly neither limits our thesis nor in any way supports his extreme charge that it misleads.

REFERENCES

Melvin L. Greenhut and Hiroshi Ohta, "Monopoly Output under Alternative Spatial Pricing Techniques," *Amer. Econ. Rev.*, Sept 1972, *62*,705–13.

______ **and** ______, *Theory of Spatial Pricing and Market Areas*, Durham 1975.

S.-k. Hsu, "Monopoly Output under Alternative Spatial Pricing Techniques: Comment," *Amer. Econ. Rev.*, Sept. 1979, *69*, 678–79.

Output Effects of Spatial Price Discrimination Under Conditions of Monopoly and Competition

MELVIN L. GREENHUT
Texas A&M University
HIROSHI OHTA
Aoyama Gakuin University, University of Houston

I. Introduction

Pigou [12] contended that monopoly output would increase under price discrimination, but limited his theory to a special case in which his third degree discrimination blended into first degree discrimination. Robinson [13] pointed to the indeterminacy of output effects under simple monopoly and discriminatory pricing. She claimed that total output would be greater or less under monopoly price discrimination depending upon whether the more elastic of two demand curves in separate markets is more or less concave than the less elastic demand curve; in turn, outputs would be the same if the demand curves are straight lines or if the relative adjusted concavities are equal. Her argument holds only if *the same number of markets* are served under simple monopoly as under discriminatory monopoly, a requisite condition typically inapplicable to simple f.o.b. mill pricing vis a vis discriminatory pricing over space.

Greenhut and Ohta [5] effected a basic change in focus by casting the subject on the cornerstone of spatial differentiation of markets. Increased output was derived as the fundamental result of geographic price discrimination. Holahan [8] then applied the concept of consumers' surplus in place of output as a more general measure of welfare. He found that while price discrimination increases monopoly output and generates greater welfare than f.o.b. pricing, the price discrimination shown by Greenhut and Ohta [6] to be possible under conditions of spatial *competition* would provide smaller welfare

71

than would f.o.b. pricing. Beckmann [2] then appeared to prove that welfare is decreased (using now *his* broader concept of consumers' plus producers' surplus) while output remains invariant under discriminatory pricing compared to f.o.b. pricing. However his argument required the Pigou-Robinson condition of fixed market numbers. In one fell swoop, output in spatial price theory was returned to where Pigou and Robinson had left it in spaceless price theory.

This paper relaxes the traditional Pigou-Robinson view that only monopolists discriminate in price by indicating that when spatial competitors invade the market areas of other sellers they would generally discriminate in price, *ceteris paribus*. It futher demonstrates that the discriminatory output of the individual firm may be less than the nondiscriminatory output but that *industry* output and welfare will be greater under conditions of spatial competition. Its difference from Holahan rests on the use of Beckmann's welfare index which adds producers' surplus to consumers' surplus. Its difference from Beckmann is the most substantial of all, as explained later. In effect, this paper extends the models presented in [4] and partly generalized in [6], doing such under the objective of determining output effects of discrimination in total *and* for unit areas of space under contrasting models of spatial competition. In the process, it contends that the natural spatial separation of markets which results from costly distance casts an entirely different light on the subject than that of spaceless microeconomic theory.

II. Output Effects of Fixed Market Spaces

Assume that (1) homogeneous buyers are distributed evenly along a linear market; (2) freight rates are identical throughout the market per unit of distance from the sellers' plants; (3) sellers produce identical products and are also located along the line market, though spatially separated from each other at fixed distances; (4) rivals select as their own mill price the mill price of the subject firm; and (5) any change in mill price is followed immediately by rivals with the result that the market area of any two competing sellers is divided equally between them. This equal market area division thus holds regardless of the mill price variations competitive firms may contemplate or effect.

To illustrate the assumptions, suppose as in Figure 1 that two firms are located at the extreme points of the linear market AB. Suppose further that the mill price of the seller located at point A is m_0; then, the mill price of the seller at B would also be m_0. The delivered prices at 0 are therefore equal to the price intercept of the individual buyers' demand curves, as specified by equation (1) below.[1] If the seller at A lowers his mill price to m_1, the seller at B

1. Implicit to this assumption is the requirement that the slope of the delivered price line $m_0 0'$ equals the freight rate per unit quantity per unit distance.

will also lower his mill price to m_1. As a consequence, neither seller can sell beyond point 0. This boundary divides the market equally between the firms. If mill price were higher than m_1, the firms' market areas are naturally (not competitively) reduced to a size less than the area $A0$ (or $B0$).

In the present model of spatial competition, a linear individual (or submarket) demand curve (and correspondingly a well-defined nonlinear aggregate demand [4]) may be postulated as a simplifying device at any point i on the line market. Thus

$$p = b - anq_i, \qquad i = 1, 2, \ldots, n \tag{1}$$

where p stands for the delivered price (equal to mill price m plus freight), q_i for the ith submarket's demand, and n stands for the number of submarkets into which the entire market may be partitioned. The net demand functions at any spatial point are, in turn, specifiable as

$$m = b - anq_i - (i - 1)b/n, \tag{2}$$

or, equivalently

$$q_i = \left[(b - m)/a - (i - 1)b/an\right]/n \qquad i = 1, 2, \ldots, n \tag{2a}$$

It must be stressed that not all net demand curves implied above are relevant from the standpoint of competitive sellers. The net demand curves of the buyers located beyond the point 0 (in Figure 1) are irrelevant and inoperative from the standpoint of either the seller located at A or the one located at B. Subject to the constraint just noted, competitive aggregate demand Q is therefore obtainable via (2a) as

$$Q = \left\{\textstyle\sum_{i=1}^{k}\left[(b - m)/a - (i - 1)b/an\right]\right\}/n, \quad b - (k - 1)b/n > m \geqslant 0, \tag{3}$$

where k now stands for the number signifying that the kth submarket located at 0 in Figure 1 comprises part of the market space of the firm.[2] It follows, for example, that if the third submarket happens to be the market located at 0, equation (3) is specifiable as

$$Q = \left\{\textstyle\sum_{i=1}^{3}\left[(b - m)/a - (i - 1)b/an\right]\right\}/n \qquad m_o > m \geqslant 0, \tag{3a}$$

where $m_o = b - 2b/n$ is the price intercept of the smallest net demand curve, as depicted in Figure 2.

Equation (3) is convertible to integral form as n approaches ∞, which requires continuous distribution of buyers along the line market. Letting $Q^* = \lim_{n\to\infty} Q$, we obtain

$$Q^* = \left\{\textstyle\int_0^{x_o}\left[(b - m - x)/a\right]dx\right\}/b, \tag{3b}$$

2. The competitive demand function of the present model provides the domain $m_o > m \geqslant 0$, omitting the irrelevant domain given by $b > m \geqslant m_o$. Cf. [3] and [4].

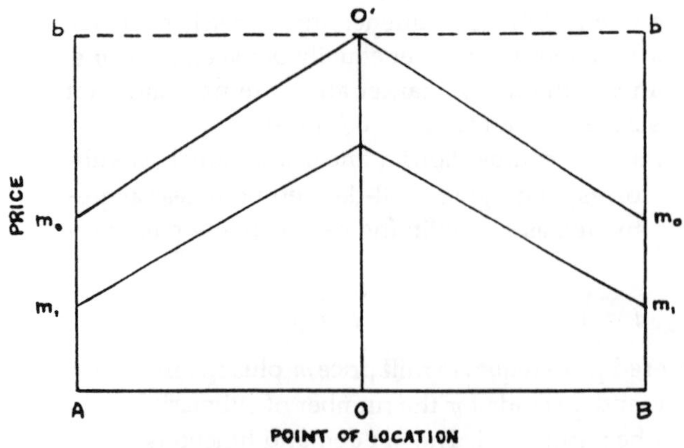

Figure 1. Market Area Being Fixed Under Spatial Competition

where $x_o = (k - 1)b/n$. Because $x_o + m_o = b$, we obtain

$$Q^* = \{\int_0^{b-m_o} [(b - m - x)/a]dx\}/b,$$
$$= [b^2 - m_o^2 - 2(b - m_o)m]/2ab, \qquad m_o > m \geqslant 0 \tag{3c}$$

This equation is the limiting formula for the *aggregate spatial* demand function under competition. The curve is linear over a specified (particular) domain because the individual gross demand curves are linear [4]. The simple marginal revenue curve, *SMR*, which corresponds to (3c) is given by

$$SMR = (b + m_o)/2 - [2ab/(b - m_o)]Q,$$
$$(b - m_o)(b + m_o)/2ab \geqslant Q > (b - m_o)^2/2ab \tag{4}$$

And the domain of *SMR* in (4) is given by the corresponding domain of (3c).[3]

To obtain the discriminatory marginal revenue under competition requires specification of the relevant individual marginal revenue functions. This specification is effected via (2a) as

$$MR_i = b - (i - 1)b/n - 2anq_i \qquad i = 1, 2, \ldots, k \tag{5}$$

where k, to recall, is an integer conditioned on the location of the kth buyer at the boundary point 0 depicted in Figure 1.[4] To derive *DMR*, or its inverse

3. The upper bound value of Q is obtainable by substituting the lower bound value of m in (3c), whereas the lower bound of Q is obtained by substituting the upper bound value of m, i.e., m_o, in (3c).

4. Since the mill price m_o and the freight rate applicable to the kth submarket, namely $(k - 1)b/n$, are assumed to add up to the price intercept b, it directly follows that $m_o + (k - 1)b/n = b$. Therefore, it also follows that $m_o = b - (k - 1)b/n$, so that a rise in k implies a fall in m_o and *vice versa*.

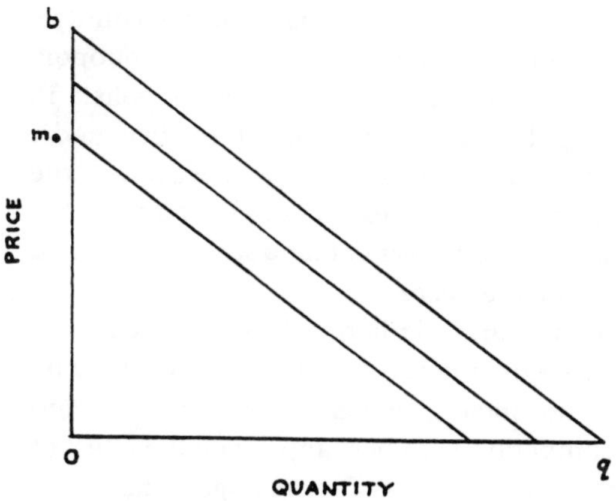

Figure 2. Relevant Net Demand Curves When $k = 3$

requires, in turn, horizontal summation of (5); i.e., the aggregation of the inverse of (5) with $MR_i = R$ for all $i = 1, 2, \ldots, k$. This step yields

$$Q = \{\textstyle\sum_{i=1}^{k} [b/2a - (i-1)b/2an - R/2a]\}/n, \qquad m_o > R \geqslant 0 \tag{6}$$

where R stands for the level of equalized marginal revenues.[5] The limiting formula for (6) is

$$\begin{aligned} Q^* &= \{\textstyle\int_0^{x_o} [(b - R - x)/2a]dx\}/b \\ &= (b - R)x_o/2ab - (x_o^2/4ab) \\ &= (b - R)(b - m_o)/2ab - (b - m_o)^2/4ab \qquad m_o > R \geqslant 0 \end{aligned} \tag{6a}$$

since, as before, $x_o + m_o = b$. Inverting (6a) provides DMR, which curve is identical to SMR of (4). In particular, the relation below holds:

$$\begin{aligned} &DMR = (b + m_o)/2 - [2ab/(b - m_o)]Q, \\ &(b - m_o)(b + m_o)/2ab \geqslant Q > (b - m_o)^2/2ab \end{aligned} \tag{6b}$$

and the following theorem applies:

Theorem I: If the type of spatial competition is such that each seller's market area is fixed irrespective of the firm's price policy, and if the individual buyers' gross demand curves are linear, the outputs produced under the alternative pricing techniques, viz. f.o.b. mill pricing and discriminatory pricing techniques, are the same.

5. The value of the upper bound of the domain of this function is given by the vertical intercept of the smallest MR curve, in turn given by substituting $i = k$ and $q = 0$ in (6). The lower bound of the domain, of course, is zero, since negative marginal revenue is economically irrelevant.

Theorem I might be considered as the competitive spatial output counterpart to the classical (nonspatial) Pigou-Robinson proposition on monopoly output [12], [13]. It is significant that what holds true for monopolists in classical spaceless economic theory applies to the *particular* competitive model thus far assumed in this paper.[6] The result does not apply, however, to the spatial monopoly case [5]. And as demonstrated next, it does not apply to the spatial competition models which involve nonlinear demand schedules and/or to zero profit equilibria with varying market sizes.

We have proposed that contrasts (and similarities) between classical results and our findings for the space economy are not completely covered by Theorem I since the theorem does not include the critically important zero profit equilibrium state of spatial competition. To best appreciate the effect of the zero profit state on discriminatory output, consider once again the representative seller described by Theorem I. This seller assumes his rival(s) will always follow his price policy such that the size of his market area is fixed regardless of whether he practices discriminatory or nondiscriminatory pricing. Such behavioral assumption (which is often called the Löschian type) can eventuate in either of the two alternative delivered price schedules depicted in Figure 3(a), where our representative seller is assumed to be located at A and his rival at B, and their alternative spatial price schedules are the discriminatory schedule P_DP_D and the f.o.b. schedule P_FP_F. Now, Theorem I indicates that these price schedules yield the same outputs. In contrast, the profits under discriminatory pricing are (by definition) required to be greater than those of the f.o.b. mill system. If we assume for the limiting case that $A0$ in Figure 3(a) provides zero profits under f.o.b. pricing, the related discriminatory seller's zero profit market size would be smaller than $A0$. As a consequence, a greater number of sellers can survive in the market under price discrimination than under f.o.b. pricing, the additional seller(s) being located at the then existing most profitable site(s), such as at 0 in Figure 3(a). The prices at and around the new site 0 are, of course, lower than the dotted portion of P_DP_D depicted in Figure 3(b).[7] Manifestly, the aggregate output that is obtainable in a zero profit discriminatory equilibrium state under the new

6. This result is strictly applicable to the special competitive case thus far considered, though the same output results would, of course, apply to the case of identical "adjusted concavities" á la Robinson of the individual spatial (net) demand curves. Mrs. Robinson's concavity criterion can be shown to fail in some cases [7] and hence is neither general nor precise. Her basic analysis points nevertheless to some particular combinations of concave and convex demand curves which would yield a neutral or negative output effect under conditions of discrimination. It should be manifest that the same conclusion would apply to such particular combination of a set of heterogeneous spatial (net) demand curves.

7. The new entrant(s) at sites such as 0 may or may not be similar in the technological sense to the old established firms at A and B, Figure 3(b). The only required condition is that the MC of the last entrant(s) be at the level which eliminates excess profits for all firms. Note further that the conception of a representative firm is nevertheless allowable even if firms are of unequal sizes over the economic landscape, as explained in [6, Appendix to Chapter 10].

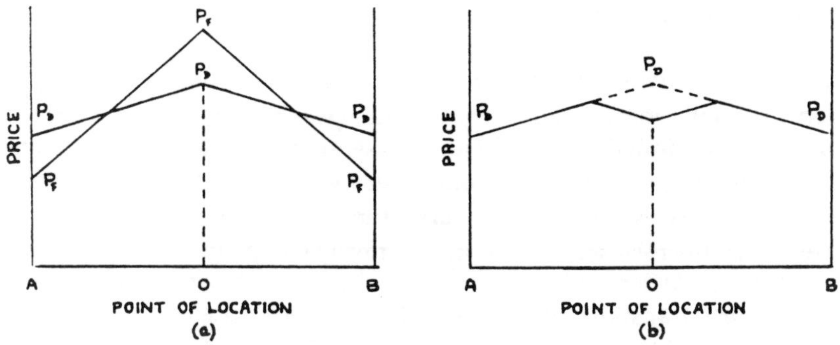

Figure 3. The Delivered Price Schedules Under Alternative Price Policies and Plant Locations

kinked delivered price schedule (which is partly lower than P_DP_D) must be greater than that resulting from the P_DP_D schedules. Via Theorem I, the output must also be greater than that resulting from P_fP_f. Theorem II is thus established:

Theorem II: If the individual buyers' gross demand curves are linear and if each seller's market area is to be limited parametrically to the size where no excess profit can prevail, the zero profit equilibrium yields a greater individual firm output under f.o.b. pricing but a larger industry-wide output under discriminatory selling.

Theorems I and II have been predicated on homogeneous linear gross demand curves. Manifestly, the over-riding importance of Theorem II compared to the trivial-special state assumed by Theorem I justifies our having used a linear demand function in developing these theorems rather than the more general demand function that was used elsewhere [6] in our analysis of monopoly outputs. That is to say, the greater entry-generating effect of spatial price discrimination with its resulting savings of transport costs and hence lower delivered price schedule signify that greater outputs will obtain as a general rule under competitive price discrimination over space than the output total stemming from f.o.b. mill pricing. Exceptions to this rule would require extreme Robinsonian combinations of *heterogeneous* demand concavities. And even then, we would propose that a Robinsonian exception which would involve sharply decreased outputs by the individual firm would tend to be offset by the output increasing effects of (1) the greater number of firms existent in a spatial zero-profit state under discriminatory selling, and (2) the significantly lower prices and negligible freight costs that new entrants would charge over the otherwise high price-demand vanishing sectors in the space economy. Our final thesis therefore contends that the basic spatial monopoly output conclusion [5,6] applies in the event of spatial competition as well.[8]

It warrants final mention that a kinked discriminatory price schedule over space, similar to our Figure 3(b) schedule, was proposed by Hoover [9]. In our case, the dotted portion of the kinky spatial price schedule at and around site 0 in Figure 3(b) stems from the entry of a rival at that point, while the kinks in Hoover's price schedule arise simply from each seller's anticipation (fear) that his rival sellers will price perfectly competitively. Hoover thus utilizes the $p = MC$ principle, where MC includes the marginal costs of production *and* transportation. The delivered price schedule of Hoover's competitor accordingly falls sharply after a certain market point is reached. This sharp decline involves an increasing rate of freight absorption. The demand-creating and hence output-increasing effect of discriminatory pricing compared to f.o.b. pricing are therefore also manifest under conditions of Hooverian spatial competition.

III. Output Effects of Variable Market Spaces

Our previous models and conclusions were formulated essentially on the assumption that (1) locations are fixed, and (2) any change in *mill* price by one seller will be followed immediately by his rival. Market areas, accordingly, were fixed and invariant, given of course the price policy followed by the representative firm. These assumptions are rigid and simplifying but conformable to the literature [1; 3; 11].[9]

The present authors have recently relaxed the above assumptions in an alternative model of spatial competition in which delivered price at market boundary points is parametrically fixed and less than that possible under spatial monopoly conditions [4]. Our specification has the effect of neither fixing firms' market areas nor the mill prices of rivals; instead, both market areas and mill prices are variable in the eyes of competitors and must be determined simultaneously for all firms.

Under a very different objective and design, it was shown in [6, Chapter 11] that when locations and mill prices are variable *and* fixed costs comparatively high, discriminatory pricing remains more profitable than f.o.b. mill pricing. However, it was also shown that when fixed cost is relatively small (i.e., with respect to the intercept price), discriminatory prices would be

8. Cf. W. Holahan [8] where basically the same conclusion was derived from a more restricted model which assumed constant marginal costs of production as well as linear demand. Our fundamental propositions require neither constant marginal cost nor linear demand, though Theorems I and II *are* based on linear demand for the purpose of serving as a comparative departure point from Joan Robinson's pioneering work on the subject.

9. Classical examples of alternative models where each seller considers (conjectures) the mill price(s) as well as location(s) of rival(s) to be fixed are Hotelling [10] and Smithies [14].

replaced in time by f.o.b. mill prices provided entry and exit are open. This particular model, which thus treats market boundary limits as variables, indicates accordingly that discriminatory pricing is not always the best price policy for spatial competitors. However, if industries in the present-day space economy are characterized by comparatively high (explicit and/or implicit) fixed costs (due to technological requirements and/or behavioral uncertainty arising from spatial separation of economic agents), the firms in this alternative model also tend to discriminate provided this type of pricing is not proscribed by law, custom, or mores. The profitability of discrimination under this alternative behavioral model, as in [4], can be shown to dovetail with an output-increasing effect.

To best appreciate this last proposition, consider the following system of equations under discriminatory pricing:

$$p = b - anq, \tag{7}$$

$$b - 2anq = \bar{k} + bi/n \qquad i = 1, 2, \ldots, (b - k)/(b/n) \tag{8}$$

$$p \leqslant p_o, \qquad b > p_o > (1/2)b \tag{9}$$

where p stands for the delivered price at any given distance i, q is the quantity demanded at that point (the subscript i being omitted here and henceforth), $\bar{k}$ is the marginal cost of production (henceforth assumed to be zero without loss of generality), bi/n is the freight rate applicable to distance i and p_o is the maximum delivered price which is parametrically given to the firm at its market boundary.

Equation (7) provides a linear demand curve at any given location i along a line market. Equation (8) gives the marginal condition for profit maximization, i.e., the marginal revenue obtained at any point of the market must be equated with the marginal costs of producing and transporting the good to the given market point. Equation (9) establishes the price ceiling constraint applicable at the firm's market boundary point, where $(1/2)b$ would be the profit-maximizing discriminatory price at the initial production center, as well as the (parametric) minimum delivered price chargeable at that point if a set of competitors had located immediately adjacent to that production center.

Total profits over the market area are therefore specifiable as

$$\begin{aligned} \Pi_D &= \textstyle\sum_i [p - (b/n)i]q - F \\ &= b^2/4a\left[\int_0^{x_o} (1 - x)^2 dx - F\right], \qquad x_o = (2p_o/b) - 1 \\ &= (b^2/12a)\left[1 - 8(1 - p_o/b)^3\right] - F, \end{aligned} \tag{10}$$

where F stands for fixed costs.

Correspondingly, following Holahan [8], the average quantity produced per area QA_D is readily specified as

$$QA_D = (b/2a)\{\textstyle\int_0^{x_o}(1 - x)dx\}/x_o, \qquad x_o = [(2p_o)/b] - 1$$
$$= (b/4a)[3 - (2p_o/b)] \tag{11}$$

It warrants stress that not only π_D but also QA_D are set forth in terms of the competitive maximum delivered price level p_o. This price, in turn, is uniquely determinable by equation (10) in a zero profit equilibrium state. Then, for example, if fixed cost equals $0.074b^2/a$, the maximum delivered price under a discriminatory pricing policy in the zero profit equilibrium can be computed readily via (10) as $P_{oD} = 0.75872b$, where the subscript D refers to discriminatory pricing and o to the competitive (zero profit) equilibrium. Substituting the present p_{oD} in the p_o's of equation (11) and in the subsequent equations ((12)–(14)) provides the competitive solutions set forth in the table below in conformance to the cost $F = 0.074b^2/a$. Alternative solution sets corresponding to alternative values of F are also provided in the table.

So much for discriminatory pricing. Similar computations for f.o.b. mill pricing can be readily effected. The fundamental problem for a firm pricing f.o.b. mill is to maximize profits subject to the condition that the same unique mill price applies to all buying points in the market area. Let m stand for this mill price; total profit can then be specified as

$$\pi_M = m\textstyle\int_0^{x_o}[(1 - m/b - x)/a]dx - F, \qquad x_o = (p_o - m)/b$$
$$= (mb/2a)[(1 - m/b)^2 - (1 - p_o/b)^2] - F, \qquad a \geqslant p_o \geqslant m \tag{12}$$

The first order condition for profit maximization yields

$$\partial\pi_M/\partial m = (p_o - p_o^2/2b - 2m + 3m^2/2b)/a = 0$$
$$\therefore \quad m = (2b - \sqrt{(3p_o^2 - 6p_ob + 4b^2)})/3, \qquad b \geqslant p_o \geqslant 0 \tag{13}$$

where we disregard the irrelevant one of the two solutions for m. In sharp contrast to the Löschian type of spatial competition in which rivals followed each other's price moves identically, it should be observed *and* stressed that the GO model of spatial competition [4] *lowers* mill price since differentiating m in (13) with respect to p_o provides

$$dm/dp_o = -(3p_o^2 - 6p_ob + 4b^2)^{-(1/2)}(p_o - b) > 0, \qquad b \geqslant p_o \geqslant 0 \tag{14}$$

As p_o decreases because of spatial competition, so does the mill price m.

The subject difference in conclusion gives rise to related changes in the previously given findings on profits, outputs, and price levels for the competitive price model vis a vis selected post-Löschian models. In particular, substituting the solution of m of equation (13) in equation (12) yields

$$\pi_M = (b/27a)(2b - \sqrt{(3p_o^2 - 6p_ob + 4b^2)})(-3p_o^2/b^2 + 6p_o/b$$
$$+ \sqrt{(3p_o^2/b^2 - 6p_o/b + 4)} - 2) - F \tag{15}$$

Correspondingly, the average quantity produced per area QA_M is also readily specified under mill pricing as

$$QA_M = \sum_i q/x_o = \left[\int_0^{x_o} b(1 - m/b - x)dx\right]/ax_o, \qquad x_o = (p_o - m)/b$$
$$= (4 - 3p_o/b + \sqrt{(3p_o^2/b^2 - 6p_o/b + 4)})b/6a \tag{16}$$

In the general case where discriminatory pricing is profitable (with exception given below), combining Holahan's model [8] with Beckmann's [2] measure of welfare establishes greater welfare under competitive price discrimination over space compared with f.o.b. pricing.

Equations (10), (11), (15), and (16) also place us in position where we can readily compare all implications of a zero profit equilibrium under discriminatory pricing vis a vis those applicable to f.o.b. mill pricing. Recall in this context that when fixed cost $F = 0.074b^2/a$, the maximum delivered price under discriminatory pricing is $p_{oD} = 0.075872b$ in the related zero profit equilibrium. Equation (15) indicates that the same fixed cost yields $p_{oM} = 0.9794b$ as the maximum delivered price under mill pricing when zero profit competition prevails. Thus $F = 0.074b/a$ establishes $p_{oD} < p_{oM}$, which relation implies greater profitability of discriminatory pricing compared to mill pricing. However, this particular situation does not *ipso facto* imply that firms *always* adopt discriminatory pricing. It also does not imply that firms always produce greater outputs under discriminatory pricing than under f.o.b. mill pricing. Alone implied is an unambiguous determination *and comparison* of alternative zero profit states given the level of fixed cost (as explained further below) which would *warrant* use of either the one or other pricing technique from the standpoint of society as well as that of the individual firm.

To understand the last statement, note initially that when $F = 0.074b^2/a$, $QA_D > QA_M$. This result implies greater industry output (or average output per area) under discriminatory pricing than mill pricing given fixed cost as high as (or higher than) $0.074b^2/a$. Industry output, however, can be seen to be smaller under the discriminatory price equilibrium than under the f.o.b. mill equilibrium when fixed cost is comparatively low. When, for example, fixed cost equals $0.066b^2/a$, p_{oD} remains lower than p_{oM} and discriminatory pricing continues to be more profitable than mill pricing. However, it follows under the same condition that $QA_D < QA_M$, and that industry output is greater under mill pricing than under discriminatory pricing. In other words, it is therefore possible over a small range of fixed costs for firms to practice discriminatory pricing notwithstanding a resulting smaller amount of output produced for society, as in column II of the table. Still lower levels of fixed costs would reveal both the profitability and desirability of mill pricing over discriminatory pricing. Manifestly, the advantage of the *GO* model [4] is its conformance to classical economic theory since entry at a distance decreases market size and, in turn, lowers mill price rather than increasing it as in the

Table I. Fixed Costs and Price, Output Effects

	I	II	III	IV	
F	0.074	0.066	0.058	0.050	b^2/a
P_{oD}	0.75872	0.70357	0.66366	0.63148	b
P_{oM}	0.97949	0.77578	0.67722	0.59631	b
QA_D	0.37063	0.39821	0.41816	0.43425	b/a
QA_M	0.34369	0.45756	0.51899	0.57187	b/a

Löschian model and related analysis [8]. At the same instance, we derive a competitive market exception to the rule that greater output would obtain under spatial price discrimination.

Let us further stress the finding that Robinsonian conclusions apply to the space economy only under three models: (1) Our own model of spatial competition with the restrictive condition of special (low) levels of fixed cost. (This condition, let us however note, fails to recognize the fundamental "cost" of behavioral uncertainty in the space economy.) (2) Beckmann's model [2], to be discussed in Section IV. Or (3) a model which contains extremely fortuitous combinations of differential buyer demand concavities as distances from the seller's plant site increase. Manifestly, the subject of price discrimination assumes an entirely different focus and set of results (including the concept of discrimination practiced by competitive firms) when the cost of distance is observed to be relevant in the sales of a product. To the extent that affiliated suburban department stores and other branch shops in outlying parts of a city post prices higher than those charged at their major (initial) stores in the central business district, but which prices are not greater by the cost of distance from the central place to the suburban district, we have on hand an example of the importance and general use of spatial price discrimination. In effect, such pricing thus prevails not only with respect of shipment of goods by rail or truck or plane, but as a result of the travel costs of consumers.

IV. Conclusion

How did Beckmann [2] obtain results sharply different from those recorded above in this paper? The answer is simple. He assumed collusion between two sellers in space in the form of the territorial (market area) pools that characterized American business practices in the nineteenth century before the Sherman Anti-trust Act. The upshot of his assumption of *fixed* market areas between duopolists (in the long run as well as in the short run) generated results counterpart to Pigou-Robinson. Our paper stresses competitive (unorganized) oligopoly in space, not the organized market type.

We further stress that different conclusions apply to different models of spatial competition. Under a Löschian type of spatial competition, on which most conventional spatial models are based, discriminatory pricing yields greater profits in the short run *and* a greater competitive industry output in the long run than f.o.b. mill pricing. In contrast, discriminatory pricing is not always the best policy for the firm from the standpoint of profits under the *GO* model of spatial competition. However, whenever the firm freely chooses its best pricing policy, it typically turns out to be the maximizing one in terms of *QA* also and welfare too.

Not only have we traced herein contradictory conclusions from alternative models of spatial competition, and from classical spaceless economic theory, but in Sections I and II we also implicitly derived the theorem which is presented below as our fundamental theorem, namely: *A free enterprise system typically provides greater welfare to society when firms are allowed to seek maximum profits*.

To phrase our fundamental theory differently, a laissez-faire approach in place of anti-trust restrictions on spatial pricing would allow firms to select the price policy that conforms best to the market conditions to which they are subject. *Ceteris paribus*, output would be maximized under the spatial price policy that happens to maximize the profits of the representative firm.

We contend finally that use of space*less* economic theory in formulating laws (such as the Robinson-Patman Act in the United States) which, in effect, classify spatial price discrimination as monopolistic practice simply reveals the irrelevance of a vast body of microeconomic theory. (Observe that the conclusion entered above holds *even if* extreme combinations and arrangements of nonlinear functions happen to apply to a given market and country. Such exception to our Theorem II, based as it would be on a most unlikely combination of concave demands over space, would itself be special and accordingly *not affect* in any way the conclusion cited above.) We trust that at least the need to reexamine classical theory has accordingly been sharply indicated by the fundamental theorem presented here.

References

1. Beckmann, M. *Location Theory*. New York: Random House, 1969.

2. ______, "Spatial Price Policies Revisited." *Bell Journal of Economics*, Autumn 1976, 619–30.

3. Gannon, C. A., "Fundamental Properties of Löschian Spatial Demand." *Environment and Planning*, 1971, Vol. 3, no. 3, 282–306.

4. Greenhut, M. L., M. Hwang, and H. Ohta, "Observations on the Shape and Relevance of the Spatial Demand Function." *Econometrica*, July 1975, 669–82.

5. Greenhut, M. L. and H. Ohta, "Monopoly Output Under Alternative Spatial Pricing Techniques." *American Economic Review*, September 1972, 705–13.

6. ______ and ______. *Theory of Spatial Prices and Market Areas*. Durham: Duke University Press, 1975.

7. ______ and ______, "Joan Robinson's Criterion for Deciding Whether Market Discrimination Reduces Output." *Economic Journal*, March 1976, 86, 96–97.

8. Holahan, W. L., "The Welfare Effects of Spatial Price Discrimination." *American Economic Review*, June 1975, 498–503.

9. Hoover, E. M., "Spatial Price Discrimination." *Review of Economic Studies*, June 1937, 182–91.

10. Hotelling, H., "Stability in Competition." *Economic Journal*, March 1929, 41–57.

11. Mills, E. S. and M. R. Lav, "A Model of Market Areas with Free Entry." *Journal of Political Economy*, June 1964, 278–88.

12. Pigou, A. C. *The Economics of Welfare*, 3rd ed. London: Macmillan and Company, 1929.

13. Robinson, J. *The Economics of Imperfect Competition*. London: Macmillan and Company, 1933.

14. Smithies, A., "Optimal Location in Spatial Competition." *Journal of Political Economy*, June 1941, 423–39.

[14]

IMPACTS OF DISTANCE ON MICROECONOMIC THEORY*

by M. L. GREENHUT†
Texas A & M University

Economic theory has traditionally included time in its interpretation of economic relationships. Costly distance, on the other hand, has not been included in the basic framework of economics, being fundamental to special studies only, such as the evaluation of interregional differences in production (Ohlin 1935) and theories of plant location (Lösch, 1944; Hoover, 1946). The failure to analyze the cost of distance within the framework of microeconomic theory signifies that policy makers and users of econometric models implicitly rely upon a sharply circumscribed microeconomic structure before offering their panaceas for economic problems.[1] But though it would be challenging as well as hopefully illuminating to demonstrate how inclusion of costly distance (i.e. economic space) affects one's view of, say, inflation, recession, stagflation, and the like, and hence one's policy set for macroeconomic problems, the design of the present paper is much more restricted. We seek instead chiefly to demonstrate how microeconomic theory is affected by the concept of costly distance.

It follows from the objective stated above that extensions of the question of impacts of costly distance to topics of particular interest to regional scientists, such as interregional programming, or to special topics of interest to economists, such as monetary *vs.* fiscal policy, must be left to other writings. To some extent, they have already been set forth elsewhere (Ohlin, 1935; Devletoglou, 1971; Eaton, Lipsey, 1977). These extensions simply reflect, or at best come close to, the

*Manuscript received 5. 11.75; final version received 13.12.77.

†The author wishes to acknowledge his thanks to R. Battalio, A. Chalk, D. Dewey, J. Greenhut, M. Hwang, H. Ohta, S. Y. Li, C. C. Mai, C. Maurice, J. Trimble and an anonymous referee of this journal for their valuable critiques and suggestions, and the National Science Foundation for helpful funding of his research on price discrimination over costly distance.

[1]It is well contended by Eaton and Lipsey (1977) that spatial concepts help resolve many of the basic philosophical shortcomings of spaceless economic theory. These writers provide specific examples of shortcomings of perfect competition theory, and in addition discuss other problems associated with the use of neoclassical theory that are resolved by use of the spatial framework of thought (See Greenhut, 1974, in particular Chapters 4, 12).

vast subject matter of interest in this paper. In somewhat corresponding pattern, our present emphasis is further restricted, being confined to only the broader significance of the impacts of costly distance on microeconomic theory. This paper thus provides only an overall view of a subject which itself goes beyond pure theory to include the practice of applying that theory to the economic problems of our time.

I

A prime effect of distance on microeconomic theory is to make many classical market types conceptually implausible. Consider in this regard Professor Chamberlin's monopolistically competitive market. A typical classroom example of that market type has been the "haircutting" industry. Since the individual barber, hence each shop, is slightly different than the next, and since each is small and, most vitally, unimportant among the large number of rival shops in the industry, the market is characterized as monopolistically competitive. The related theory proposes that the infinitesimally small, slightly differentiated barbershops which comprise the industry maximize profits by equating marginal revenues with marginal costs. For each shop a best price exists, which typically is the same as that prevailing elsewhere, particularly since each barber and each shop is fundamentally alike.

The reality of economic life is that geographic space is costly and can thus be conceived of as an economic space. In such space, the small barbershop proves to be an oligopolist, not a monopolistically competitive firm. It is only in the form of one shop being tied competitively to another which, in turn, is tied to another shop and still to others *as if by a chain* that the entire group of barbers comprise an industry.[2] In no case is the behaviour of each barber and each firm that of the microscopic-mechanical robot described in the literature. Rather, each seller is cognizant of his closest rivals, each is affected by the prices of said rivals, and from time to time each is aggressively concerned over how the rival (down the street) will react to his own actions. Costly distance limits consumers in choosing suppliers, and in the process establishes a network of spatial oligopolists.

Alas for simple theory, when owners of firms are of finite size and are potential adversaries of others, when their firms are neither infinitesimally small nor managed mechanically by robotical decision-makers,

[2]Chamberlin (1935) actually discussed briefly the chain oligopoly market attributable to space (see his Appendix C), but otherwise stressed monopolistic competition in his pathbreaking work.

when in fact an interdependency arises between the managers (owners) of firms, each of whom may act unpredictably and emotionally, behavioural uncertainty permeates the business scene (Hartwick, J. M., Hartwick, P. G., 1971). This uncertainty makes mockery of the elementary adjustments of supply to demand and the facile conclusions of classical competitive economic theory. Simply put, the world of economic space is underscored by oligopolistic markets (Lösch, 1944; Greenhut, 1956; Churchill, 1967), and oligopoly itself is marked by behavioural uncertainty.

The impact on microeconomic theory of the "space—oligopoly—uncertainty" relationship forms the fundamental cornerstone of spatial microeconomics. At the same instance, it marks the subject of special interest in this paper. Examined below are *two* special kinds of analytical differences (problems) *vis-à-vis* classical microeconomics which stem from the relation set described above. Then the following three sections of the paper deal with the overall consequences of the "space—oligopoly—uncertainty" effect on general microeconomics theory, with a final section pointing out some of the policy implications of adding space to time in economic theory.

II

(1) It is manifest that the concepts of maximum profit and economic man are altered in a theoretical framework predicated on behavioural uncertainty (Miller, Starr, 1960; Horowitz, 1970) compared to one which assumes certainty or even the operation of statistical probabilities, as in the Knightian world of risk (Knight, 1921). When in place of a sum certain, or a statistical mean, a decision maker confronts a whole spectrum of alternative payoffs, each of which in the Bayesian sense is equally as likely to occur as any other payoff, different decision makers (applying their own subjective probabilities) will tend to adopt different strategies. So-called economic men who opt always for the best return become a confusingly differentiated group of individuals, some of whom maximax, some of whom maximin, some of whom adopt criteria of pessimism or regret in resolving their decision problems, *ad infinitum*. The nice cosy world of identically acting and reacting mechanical robots is replaced by a network of decision makers among whom no two think, act, and look alike. A theoretical world of short-run chaos is evident, as can easily be described by reference to the matrix Table 1.

Imagine a firm may invest as alternative capital sums, a, b, . . . , f in a particular type of plant. Let the firm be subject to different kinds of price and locational competition from its rivals; e.g., rivals may collude with our firm in pricing, or they may price competitively, or hyper-competitively, etc.; moreover, they may disperse evenly over the market, localize together at a production point, etc. Uncertainty combinations consisting of the several independently different states of rivals' price and location policies run from 1,2, . . . , z. They are underscored by different payoff rates, X_{ij} ($i = 1,2, \ldots, z$; $j = a$,b, . . . ,f), each evaluated with respect to the particular investment that may be selected by the *representative firm*.

TABLE I

Uncertainty Combination	Investments a	b	. . . .	f
1	X_{1a}	X_{1b}	. . . .	X_{1f}
2	X_{2a}	X_{2b}	. . . .	X_{2f}
.	.	.		
.	.	.		
.	.	.		
z	X_{za}	X_{zb}	. . . .	X_{zf}

Machine breakdowns, plant accidents and other disturbances also affect operations, hence profits. But if they are determinable statistically (i.e. if a history of the frequencies of occurrence applies), we will call them risks rather than uncertainties since objective (statistical) probabilities apply to them (Knight, 1921). It follows that the oligopolistic firm is subject to risk as well as to behavioural uncertainty and that a set of projected rates of returns under conditions of risk (*distinct from behavioural uncertainties*) also apply to each alternative investment $a,b, \ldots, f$, given each behavioural uncertainty. Not only are the net payoff rates X_{ij} identifiable, as provided in Table 1, but standing behind each of the X_{ij} rates is a set of alternative rates which relate to each risk combination that exists in conjunction with a given uncertainty-investment state. Each of these alternative payoff rates is weighted by the probabilities associated with the given risk combination. Thus a joint probability function $p\,(x_1, x_2)$ actually characterizes decision making under behavioural uncertainty, where x_1 is the random variable for the z uncertainty combinations and x_2 is another random variable for, say, n risk combinations. The marginal probability function for the uncertainty combinations can thus be given as

$$p_1\,(x_1) = \sum_{x_2=1}^{n} p\,(x_1, x_2)\ .$$

We conceive herein of uncertainty combinations being independent of risks, i.e. $p(x_1, x_2) = p_1(x_1)\,p_2(x_2)$. Subjective probabilities apply to these uncertainty combinations because there is insufficient statistical basis for establishing objective likelihoods for them. If the decision maker rather than act as a Laplacian believes it is quite unlikely an uncertain event will occur, he would assign a probability close to zero. If he believes it is likely to occur, he assigns a probability close to one. It is the multiplication of each payoff in Table 1 by each marginal uncertainty probability that establishes a mean (expected) payoff for each investment (column). So, the maximum profit investment chosen by the economic man is thereby determined. It involves identical recognition and selection by all who accept the assigned probabilities, but possibly different choice by those who apply different subjective probabilities. Some decision makers may, in fact, simply select the investment offering the highest payoff rate in Table 1, or the maximum of the minimum payoff rates, etc. In any case, what is economic decision making reappears as a much more involved concept in spatial economic theory than in neoclassical economic theory (Greenhut, 1966).

(2) In the same way that Table 1 enables us to recognize the deep complexity of economic behaviour which underscores the space economy, it is also apparent that each firm is significantly important and hence that each is subject to a negatively sloping demand curve. Any customary, nicely formed horizontal average revenue (AR) function that is tangent to average cost (AC) in the long run, and hence equal to marginal cost (MC) becomes a remnant of the world of costless (or nonexistent) distance. Worse yet, in a sense, the average revenue curve of a seller under conditions of behavioural uncertainty is obscured, involving as it does a real (true) average revenue curve which omniscience alone could forecast; so, an imaginary average revenue curve is conjectured and viewed by the representative seller. It is fortunately the case for oligopoly theory that the concept of the long run implies that the conjectural errors made by managers of viable firms tend to be less damaging than those made in other firms, and in fact that the decision makers of viable firms are "right" more often than are others (Alchian, 1950). In light of this long-run outcome *and* the requirement of conserving space in this article, we need not pursue further the effects of behavioural uncertainty on the average revenue curve. Instead, we can leave this subject to other writings and centre attention here on the fundamental differences between the aggregate market demand curve that one derives in spaceless economics and the aggregate demand curve one obtains in spatial economics under other-

wise equal conditions. We shall initially assume for simplicity the most elementary individual demand curve possible, the negatively sloping linear demand curve.

The firm's market in a world of spatial separation of buyers is made up of a set of locationally different components. Any elementary (spaceless economy) assumption of individually homogeneous demand functions, such as $p = a - bnq$, where the n stands for number of consumers and the other symbols (parameters) have customary meaning, will yield the simple aggregate function $p = a - bQ$, where $Q = nq$. *In contrast* we shall demonstrate below that the sum of individual linear demand functions becomes a different aggregate in the world of economic space. That aggregate demand function will be observed to be a quadratic when buyers are distributed continuously along a line, and a cubic when they are dispersed continuously over a plain. To see this, note that if

$$p = a - bq, \qquad a, b > 0 \qquad \text{.........(1)}$$

$$q = \frac{1}{b}(a - p) \qquad \text{.........(2)}$$

or

$$q = \frac{1}{b}[a - (m + t'D)] , \qquad \text{.........(3)}$$

where delivered price p equals the firm's mill price m plus the constant freight rate t' times distance D. In the spaceless world of $t' = 0$, we would have

$$q = \frac{1}{b}(a - m) \qquad \text{.........(3')}$$

Spaceless aggregate demand (i.e. aggregate demand in a world of costless distance) is $Q = nq$. Thus

$$Q = \frac{n}{b}(a - m) \qquad \text{.........(3'')}$$

Assuming distance is costly and n buyers are distributed along a line, the maximum market radius D_0 is derived by setting $q = 0$ in 3). So we have

$$D_0 = \frac{a - m}{t'} \qquad \text{.........(4)}$$

The aggregate demand with density V at each spatial point in a continuous market case is

$$Q = V\int_0^{D_0} \frac{1}{b}[a - (m + t'D)]\, dD, \qquad 0 < D < \frac{a - m}{,} \qquad \text{.........(5)}$$

$$= \frac{V(a - m)^2}{2bt'} ,$$

where the value a provides the maximum economic distance (price intercept). In corresponding manner, if n submarkets are conceived to be distributed continuously over a plain, the circle with an economic radius a applies. The result is

$$Q = \frac{V}{b}\int_0^{2\pi}\int_0^{D_0}(a - m - t'D)DdDd\theta \qquad \text{.........(6)}$$

$$= V\,\frac{\pi(a - m)^3}{3bt'^2},$$

where evaluation of the first and second derivatives of Q with respect to m indicates that the domain of the economically relevant (i.e. positive quantity) portion of the cubic demand function includes only the range over which the demand curve is concave from above *as in the uniform line distribution given by* 5).

The effective aggregate of a set of linear demand curves of buyers distributed over a line or plain is, in each case, concave upward. In contrast with Lösch (1944); Stern (1972) and partial contrast with Gannon (1971), it was in fact shown by Greenhut, Hwang, Ohta, (1975) that *regardless of the convexity of the local (gross) demand curve*, the aggregate market demand function is concave from above. Consider the relation

$$Q = f(m + t'D), \quad \forall D \qquad \text{.........(7)}$$

where for simplicity we assume (and henceforth) that $V = 1$. The aggregate spatial demand is

$$Q = \int_0^{2\pi}\int_0^{D_0} f(m + t'D)\,DdDd\theta, \quad D_0 = \frac{a - m}{t'} \qquad \text{.........(8)}$$

where the parameter 'a' again stands for the price intercept. It can be shown by straightforward methods that d^2Q/dm^2 is positive. So the spatial demand curve is concave from above regardless of whether the local demand curve is smoothly convex, linear, or concave from above. Differences in market (aggregate) demand rest only on the basis that the individual convex demands aggregate to a concavity less pronounced than would the linear demand curves and, in turn, less than the concave demands.

The analysis noted above broadly applies to firms whose market boundaries (limits) are circumscribed by competitors. But results depend on the type of spatial competition that is conceived, with diverse competitive reactions and models having been proposed by Lösch (1944), Hotelling (1929), Smithies (1941), Hoover (1946), Isard (1956), Beckmann (1970), Gannon (1971), Capozza and Van Order (1977b) and others. In one model, the aggregate "competitively-reduced" demand curve is concave throughout; in other cases, a two-section curve results with the concavity of the lower section depending on the local (gross) demand function, and its position depending, in turn, on the writer's assumption of competitive reactions. Quite important to the analysis of impacts of costly distance on microeconomic theory is the fact that separation of buyers and sellers signifies possibility of market intrusion by distant rivals. The effect is that deriving the representative competitor's average revenue schedule does not simply involve subtracting a predesignated number of homogeneous demands from the market demand curve. Instead, the shape of the aggregate demand curve, the shape of the firm's average revenue schedule, the shape of the marginal revenue curve and in turn the output produced, *etc.*, involve complications which relate to significant functional variations as behavioural assumptions are changed. Not only do the results contradict neoclassical principles in many cases, but a related consequence is that the application of economic theory and interpretations of empirical data (e.g. Capozza and Attaran, 1976) are also different.[3] Indeed, as shown by Capozza and Van Order (1977), certain competitive conditions in the space economy would yield higher prices than the spatial monopoly price even in the zero profit equilibrium. It is manifest that spatial microeconomics involves more than simply an added dimension.

III

One particularly vital facet of the locational differentiation of buyers *and* the concomitant condition of market separation is that *price discrimination* becomes naturally feasible (Hoover, 1935-36; Greenhut, 1956; Beckmann, 1970; Greenhut, Ohta, 1972). It can, indeed, be shown that this type of pricing could be practised not only by monopolists, but also by locationally identical or locationally differentiated competitors in the space economy (Greenhut, J., Greenhut, M. L., 1975; Phlips, 1976). The whole subject complexifies well beyond that of the nice distanceless world of Pigou (1932) and Robinson (1934). It is thus the case that cost of distance not only entails oligopolistic markets and behavioural uncertainty, it not only changes the concepts of profit maximization and rational economic behaviour, it not only involves more complex demand functions and alters one's interpretation of economic data, but it changes the theoretical perspective of what may be monopolistic and *what may be competitive pricing.*

[3]Different elasticities obtain on the aggregate demand function depending on the behavioural reactions of the spatial competitors, which type of phenomenon tends to be ignored in spaceless economic theory. An effect is that data which are interpreted as reflecting collusive (organized) pricing under the perspective of spaceless economic theory would be interpreted as competitive (unorganized) pricing in spatial economics (Greenhut, Hwang, Ohta, 1975; Phlips, 1977).

Spatial price discrimination differs from nondiscriminatory pricing over space (typically referred to as f.o.b. pricing) by involving an equality *in each market* of the marginal revenue obtained in that market with the (aggregate output) *marginal cost* of the firm. Individual market profit maximization thus replaces the equality of aggregate (all markets) marginal revenue with the applicable marginal cost (Hoover, 1935-36; Greenhut, Ohta, 1972). Spatial price discrimination is, therefore, counterpart to spaceless price discrimination (Pigou, 1929; Robinson, 1934; Battalio, Ekelund, 1972) in the sense that discriminatory pricing is generally the price technique that globally maximizes profits. It differs in the sense that separable markets must be assumed to exist in classical spaceless economics whereas in spatial economics market separation results naturally as a direct consequence of varying distances to the buying locations. Of course, it also differs since freight cost becomes an integral part of the profit maximizing process. Still other contrasts apply as we shall see.

Consider in this context the monopolist who faces a general demand function of the form $p = a - bq^x$. If said monopolist is subject to costly distance, he would view the effective demand function at any consuming point as that given by

$$p = a - t - bq^x, \qquad \text{.........(9)}$$

where p, a, t, b, q are positive, and where for simplicity t (for $t'D$) stands for the freight *cost* to a buyer's location with the unit of distance implicitly involving one unit of transport cost. Let us further stress that for present purposes x is taken as positive.[4] The marginal revenue

[4]The demand given by (9) can be shown to be general for the space economy by requiring the exponent to fall between $-1 < x < \infty$. Values less than -1 are ruled out since they involve positively sloped marginal revenues. When the exponent is negative and greater than -1, the demand curve is sharply concave from above; when it is positive but less than unity, the curve is moderately concave; when unity, the demand curve is linear; when greater than unity, the related demand curve is convex. These different demands yield differently sloped delivered price schedules. However, let us further rule out those schedules which involve discrimination against distant buyers, as was justified for the space economy by Hoover (1935-36) in light of repackage-resale opportunities. This means our present focus requires the discarding of all negative exponent possibilities. In this connection, we further note that negative exponents require $b < 0$ and either that the sharply concave portions of the demand curve be elliptical in shape, or produce curves such as the rectangular hyperbola, which curves respectively involve unlikely demands that have increasing or constant elasticity throughout the range of the curve. One other important negative exponent curve must be ruled out for reasons of the direction of discrimination. This is the curve whose elasticity decreases less rapidly than price throughout the range of the function. To repeat in part, these types of demand curves need not be evaluated here, especially since it can be shown (Greenhut, Ohta, 1975, Chapter 5) that only the direction of the discrimination is altered, not the basic conclusions drawn above in the text. For our purposes then, equation (9) is fully general. And see Greenhut, J., Greenhut, M. L. (1975) for detailed analysis of spatial price formuli resulting therefrom.

on sales to the subject market is then

$$MR = a - t - b\,(x + 1)q^x. \qquad \text{.........(10)}$$

So, equilibrium supply at cost of distance t, given marginal cost k, can be derived as

$$q = \left[\frac{a - t - k}{b\,(x + 1)}\right]^{1/x}. \qquad \text{.........(11)}$$

Substituting (11) into (9) yields the discriminatory price received by the seller on sales to that location. Adding the freight cost t to that location establishes the delivered price

$$P_{Dt} = a - b\left[\frac{a - t - k}{b\,(x + 1)}\right] = \frac{1}{x + 1}\,(xa + k) + \frac{1}{x + 1}\,t. \qquad \text{.........(12)}$$

The market extends to the price intercept limit where $P_{Dt} = a$; hence the market periphery is set by the value $a - k$.

Under nondiscriminatory (f.o.b.) pricing, the function

$$q = \left[\frac{1}{b}\,(a - t - p)\right]^{1/x} \qquad \text{.........(13)}$$

must be aggregated from $t = 0$ to $t = a - p$. This yields

$$Q = \int_0^{a-p}\left[\frac{1}{b}(a - t - p)\right]^{1/x} dt \qquad \text{.........(14)}$$

$$= \left(\frac{1}{b}\right)^{1/x}\left(\frac{1}{x + 1}\right)(a - p)^{(x+1)/x},$$

which is the total demand at price p. Solving for p, converting to marginal revenue (MR), and then equating the aggregate MR with marginal cost k yields the profit-maximizing nondiscriminatory output (not the global profit maximizing output). The related price is found to be

$$p_f = \frac{1}{1 + 2x}\,[xa + (1 + x)\,k]. \qquad \text{.........(15)}$$

At the boundary of the firm's market area, t is added to mill price p_f and made equal to the price intercept a. The simple nondiscriminatory spatial monopolist's market runs accordingly to the limit $\frac{1 + x}{1 + 2x}\,(a - k)$, which for all economically relevant x values (i.e. those producing a stable market equilibrium) is less than the discriminatory market limit shown above as $a - k$. Since his markets are naturally separable, the spatial monopolist discriminates in price except for extremely specialized demand situations (Greenhut, J., Greenhut, M. L., 1977), which need not be evaluated in this paper. A further obvious caveat to our statement is that he discriminates unless proscribed by law, custom, or an attempt to maintain goodwill by charging full freight cost to each buyer, or the like.

There are two broad types of spatial *competition* which involve price discrimination and thus warrant analysis here: (1) the situation where all rivals are located at the same production centre, and (2) the case where some rivals are located at a distant production centre. Let us initially assume all producers are located at the same production point and adjust the Cournot (1927) type $MR = MC$ equation given by (16) to the spatial form (17). Thus

$$p\left(1 - \frac{1}{er}\right) = \phi'(q), \text{ and} \qquad \text{.........(16)}$$

$$p\left(1 - \frac{1}{er}\right) - T = \phi'(q), \qquad \text{.........(17)}$$

where for the problem at hand we replace t by the freight cost T, and where e stands for elasticity, r for the number of rival sellers competing in a given market, and $\phi'(q)$ for the average of the r firms' marginal cost values. Most vitally, the functions (16) and (17) can be shown to conform not only to Cournot's competitive equilibrium but to classical (standard) principles (Greenhut, J., Greenhut, M. L., 1975). Under the simplifying but not necessary assumption of homogeneous size firms and production functions[5], (17) can be quickly accepted as

$$p\left(1 - \frac{1}{er}\right) = \bar{k} + \bar{T}, \qquad \text{.........(18)}$$

where the average of all firms' marginal production and transport cost are designated by $\bar{k}$ and $\bar{T}$, with

$$\bar{k} = \frac{1}{r}\sum_{i=1}^{r} k_i, \; \bar{T} = \frac{1}{r}\sum_{i=1}^{r} T_i,$$

and where the subscript i relates to the i_{th} firm which, for example, sells to a market T_i dollars from its plant.[6] Now elasticity e for the function (9) can, *via definition*, be found to equal $\frac{1}{x}\left(\frac{p}{a-p}\right)$.

Substituting this value into marginal revenue and equating with marginal production plus transportation costs yields the competitive discriminatory delivered price

$$P_D = \frac{1}{r+x}(xa + r\bar{k}) + \frac{r}{r+x}\bar{T}, \qquad \text{.........(19)}$$

[5]For present purposes it is best to assume homogeneous production functions of degree one, so that $\Phi'(q)$ can be designated as k. However, it will be manifest that the basic conclusions stated below also apply to a heterogeneous space economy, as in Greenhut, J., Greenhut, M. L. (1975).

[6]The relevance of $\bar{k}$ and $\bar{T}$ is established in Greenhut, J., Greenhut, M. L. (1975) when sellers are located at either the same or at different sites under the same or different production cost functions. For the moment, we continue to conceive of all sellers being located at the same production center.

which equation establishes delivered price under conditions of spatial competition. This equation reveals the condition that discriminatory delivered price is a function of the number of rivals 'r', the power of the demand function 'x', the highest price 'a' that buyers would pay, the marginal cost '$\bar{k}$' (or, in words, the average of all firms' marginal cost), and uniquely to our interests $\overline{T}$, the *average transportation cost* of shipping the product from the r firms' location to a particular buying point. Clearly, if all firms are located together *and* $r \rightarrow \infty$, the discriminatory price descends to the competitive price $\bar{k}$ (as given by the initial term on the right-hand side of equation (19)); and the delivered price in turn involves addition of the entire freight cost. An infinite number of competitors located at a point in space, therefore, yields perfect competition in space (Greenhut, 1974, Chapter 4), and its related pricing pattern is f.o.b. pricing. (This result seemingly provides a justification for f.o.b. pricing.[7]) Greater levels of competition clearly involve increases in the slope of P_D from that of the monopoly level. Moreover, we also see from (19) that the degree of discrimination is, itself, a function of the values of 'x'.

Extending from (19), it is further apparent now that if half of the firms are located at each of *two* production centres situated at the extreme ends of a linear buying space, $\overline{T}$ is the same at all market points, and we (surprisingly) obtain uniform prices over space. Variations in numbers, locations, *etc.*, of firms can easily be made which produce broken (nonlinear) delivered price schedules (Greenhut, J., Greenhut, M. L., 1977). Further extension of the basic analytical framework to include heterogeneous demand, etc., is central to this facet of spatial economics. Manifestly an economist's evaluation of anti-trust laws hinges on his theoretical frame of reference, and this depends, in turn, on his inclusion or failure to include the cost of distance as a structural variable in his analytical framework of thought (Phlips, 1976, 1977). More pointedly, the fact that spatial competitors discriminate, and the fact that industrial location is affected by spatial price practices (and hence so too is location theory) attest to the distinctive impact of cost of distance on microeconomic theory.

Economists using classical theory often condemn price differentials *per se* without recognizing their competitive (as well as monopoly) origins. Equally vital, divergence arises in the output-welfare effects obtained in spatial microeconomics from those of classical Pigouvian-Robinson spaceless economics. This last fundamental difference can be demonstrated in two steps.

[7]Classical support for f.o.b. pricing, and its related condemnation of discrimination can be contested on certain welfare grounds, as is done later in this paper.

The initial step was taken in (Greenhut, Ohta, 1972, 1975). It was shown there under conditions of spatial monopoly that greater output prevails when firms discriminate in the space economy *vis à vis* the unchanged output that would apply in the spaceless economy. And see Stevens, Rydell (1966); Phlips (1976); Greenhut, J. (1977).

The second step *in turn* requires introduction of spatial competition to ascertain whether the same output effect of discrimination can be deduced. Affirmative findings were reported by Holahan (1975) based on the conventional Lösch behavioural assumption of fixed market spaces in the short run. An alternative price ceiling type of spatial competition, however, was found in (Greenhut, Ohta, 1975) to yield less definite conclusions. It was, in particular, proposed there that a relatively high fixed cost required discriminatory pricing for profit maximization, and that this pricing system provides greater output than does f.o.b. mill pricing. But relatively low fixed costs were shown to imply opposite results. In fact, for all fixed costs less than some threshold value, substantial entry is required for the zero profit state and f.o.b. pricing alone becomes feasible.

The above body of analysis is extendable to include welfare comparisons. For example, a consumers' and producers' surplus over space are respectively definable, and diverse welfare indices are available, including the oft-used addition of consumers' surplus to producers' surplus. Normalizing such index in terms of the average value *per area*, and then comparing the long-run results obtained for f.o.b. and discriminatory pricing in the cases where either price system may prevail, would reveal greater welfare typically existing under the price ceiling type of competition when firms price discriminatorily. Most vitally, these findings apply not only to spatial monopoly markets but also spatially competitive ones. They stand in significant contrast to the different results set forth by Beckmann (1976) where the strict assumption of fixed market areas (in effect, a territorial pool) is made as the consequence of assumed collusion between all sellers. But what derives in his analysis as advantages for f.o.b. pricing, and hence appears as the counterpart competitive pricing system to that of spaceless economics, reappears in vastly different light when the real-fundamental assumption of classical microeconomics is set forth in spatial economics, namely free entry and exit in the form of changing locations, market sizes, and numbers of firms.

Differences of the kind noted above focus sharp attention on the scope of spatial price theory and the vital need to formulate microeconomic theory on the basis of distance as well as time. What *are* properly designed antitrust policies, what *are* welfare effects, and what output and price effects *obtain* must be evaluated under specific as well as the more general conditions that provide character to the space economy. These spatial conditions, in turn, generate conclusions that contrast sharply from those of neoclassical economic theory, and in the process emphasize the need to add the distance parameter to the existing body of microeconomic thought (Eaton, Lipsey, 1977; Phlips, 1977).

It is further proposed in a more restricted context that distance casts a very different and special light on industrial pricing. Let us, in fact, note that initial empirical studies being conducted by this writer and colleagues under a National Science Foundation grant appear to indicate significant dominance of spatial price discrimination, *vis-à-vis* f.o.b. mill pricing in Germany and Japan, and *slightly less* prevalent (yet dominant) use in the U.S.A. among competitive firms subject to costly distance. The extent and importance of price discrimination appears not only to be more vital to the real spatial economy than that conceived in classical economics, but even to vary noticeably among the indicated free enterprise economies.

IV

Economic space requires negatively sloped AR functions. What happens, one might then ask, to specific principles in welfare economics, for example the triple relationship $AR = AC = MC$ which classical theorists use to herald (a) the technological efficiency of the free enterprise economy, (b) its maximizing of consumer wants, and (c) the production-steering dominance of the consumer? All of these appear in danger of falling by the wayside (Demsetz, 1959; Archibald, 1962, 1967; Barzel, 1970; Schmalensee, 1972). But note, if economic space also rules out monopolistic competition, even the excess capacity cum infinite solutions set of Chamberlinean economics (which Sherrard, 1951, and Stigler, 1954, would say is theoretically empty) does not apply. We are apparently worse off because of the *existence* of costly distance, left with a world of indeterminate oligopoly rather than the debated world of monopolistic competition.[8]

[8]Eaton and Lipsey (1976) essentially propose that economists must give up the idea of a unique market area equilibrium when dealing with the space economy. Even more generally, they argued in (1977) that the unique production efficiency of classical theory does not apply, which condition does not carry significant loss in their opinion. These same views were once subscribed to "in part" by the present writer (1956, in particular Chapters 11, 12). But use in effect of the same underlying analysis as that which Eaton and Lipsey (1977) applied to reject perfect competition led this writer to the conclusion that firms in spatial oligopoly would operate, in equilibrium, at the point of minimum average production cost (Greenhut, 1974).

The world of spatial oligopoly in the long run *is*, we contend, resolvable. However, our own argument is so complex requiring, as it does, detailed evaluation of the meaning of opportunity cost and related matters that we must simply refer the interested reader to Greenhut (1974, Chapters 5, 8). Suffice it to say for the present that though the distance factor establishes a world of oligopoly, excess capacity does not apply *à la* Chamberlin (1935); Barzel (1970); Archibald (1962); Schmalensee (1972), nor for that matter does productive inefficiency, Dewey (1958); Greenhut (1974, 1975); Ohta (1976, 1977).

V

The subject of welfare in the space economy unfortunately extends well beyond the classical welfare propositions cited above and the theoretical mapping possible therefrom. It is just *inadequate and insufficient* in spatial microeconomics to hold that each profit maximizing production centre produces the output which entails lowest technological average cost of production. Correspondingly, the condition that marginal revenue products of productive factors are in identical proportions to their prices is not sufficient to ensure the lowest possible cost of any output much less the lowest cost of all inputs. Rather, one must go beyond the average cost of production curve in demonstrating the lowest possible costs for the space economy, which condition itself involves questions of the location of industry and the trading areas over which firms sell.

Suppose firms are improperly located (e.g. all firms in a given industry are located in Detroit, Michigan, when in fact some should be located in Chicago, Illinois and others in Granite City, Illinois). The *de facto* production cost plus transportation cost would thus be higher than it could have been. Correspondingly, even though the firms are located properly, if they sell mistakenly to the wrong buyers, in effect increasing transport distances unnecessarily, total costs would not be the lowest possible. Analysis of the space economy not only requires determination of the input-output relations of the firm in stable equilibrium, but examination of its location and the size and shape of its market area. Any simple demonstration that the firm produces at its lowest average production cost level in the long run does not *ipso facto* make production plus transportation costs the lowest possible. Locational efficiency and sales territory efficiency must be determined.

After Hotelling (1929), including Lerner and Singer (1937), Copeland (1940), Smithies (1941), Lewis (1945), Lösch (1944), Greenhut (1956), Isard (1956), and Richardson (1973), the literature has stressed the likelihood of dispersion of industry resulting from the cost and demand conditions underscoring plant location. In particular, it can be shown that decreasing cost of production in the long run promotes dispersion of firms in an industry; so too does concave demand (Greenhut, 1956). And this curve, as already mentioned, was shown to result from individual demand curves which are homogeneous except for distances (e.g. locations in different parts of a city). Manifestly, assuming differences among buyers in income, wealth, or simply tastes at any market point has equivalent effect as the assumption of identical demands except for distance. An aggregate concave demand curve for a given market, among a set of markets each similarly constructed, thus obtains at each market point; and this type of curve can in fact be shown to promote an ideal long-run dispersion of industry.[9] The

[9]Consider the total revenue (TR) curves in the footnote sketch below, where the tangency point is conceived to obtain at a point of identical elasticity on each

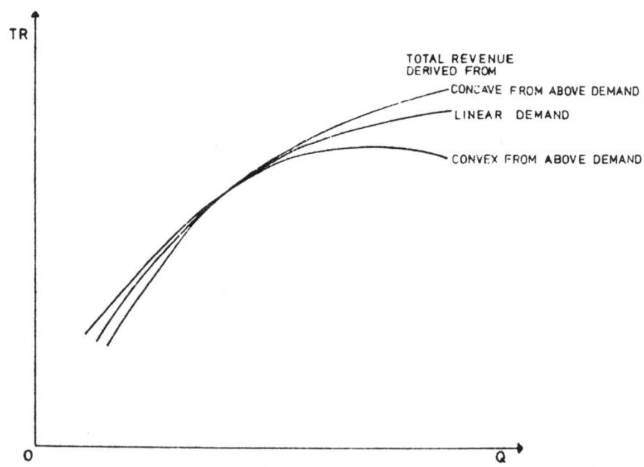

related demand function, to which point we also assume $MR = MC$. Then add a cost of distance to MC to form a higher MC curve, and observe (by visualizing the derivatives to the TR curves) that the elasticity at any output lying to the left of the tangency point in the sketch above would be greatest on the convex demand curve and least on the concave curve. *Ipso facto*, considering only the new MC curve (i.e., with cost of distance included), it follows that to the left of the tangency point where $MR = MC$ *for the* linear demand function, $MR < MC$ or $MR > MC$ respectively with respect to the concave and convex curves. So the profit maximizing spatial seller subject to concave demand would charge a higher price while the seller facing convex demand would charge a lower price than the seller confronted with a linear demand. If the same fixed limit price 'a' applies to all market points under each demand type, the seller subject to concave demand would tend to economize on distance. In effect, in contrast with the Hotelling solution of industrial localization (1929), sellers subject to concave demand thus disperse to quartile, sextile, octile, points, etc., along a line market *depending on the number of firms*. Clearly Hotelling's centre clustering solution applies, as it was specified, simply to spatial duopolists who are subject to infinitely inelastic demand.

costly distance factor of location was actually recognized rather generally in the literature to generate industrial scattering, e.g. Deschesnes (1945); Chamberlin (1953). This conclusion is further enhanced by considering maturing industries where the long-run influence is easily seen to promote recognition and selection of optimal locations (Hoover, 1946; Greenhut, 1956, 1974). These influences were even central to Richardson's (1973) theory of spatial development.

None of the above is designed to say that the classical cost analysis of Weber (1909), when dressed in modern garb to include production functions, as by Moses (1958), Sakashita (1968), Bradfield (1971), and Khalili, Mathur, Bodenhorn (1974), fails to provide reasons for some tendency to localize industry, as indeed is so often observed in practice. The fact is that conditions do prevail which support intra-industry localization (Gannon, 1973). However, the point warranting emphasis here is not only has it been demonstrated that an optimal spatial distribution tends to be brought about in the long run, as a natural-direct result of the forces identified as governing plant location, but even an historical mistake (e.g. developing an industry in the *wrong* city) is, in the fundamental sense, offset in time by newly developed infra structures (Greenhut, 1974). This does not mean, of course, that a free enterprise-space economy proffers *perfect* results. The very condition of bankruptcies manifests the second best quality of any system involving men. It simply means that short-run errors in location and investment tend to be eliminated in time, with the final distribution equilibrium over space proving to be of economic order.

Much the same result is evident in analyses of the market areas of firms (Predöhl, 1925; Lösch, 1944; Hoover, 1946). Though the Löschian findings were temporarily derailed by Mills and Lav (1964), and further examined by Eaton and Lipsey (1976), there is clear indication that not only does theory suggest firms will use the right channels (market space) for their products (Greenhut, 1956, 1974; Stern, 1972; Greenhut, Ohta, 1975), but empirical data strongly suggest existence of market sizes falling well below those that would yield inefficient use of space (Greenhut, Hwang, Ohta, 1976). Most vitally, however, even if such data demonstrated existence of a set of near circular market areas which do not cover the entire space, this particular outcome, in the absence of organized (collusive) oligopolistic practice, was shown simply to be the natural result of the cost-demand conditions that happen to prevail. The competitively based space economy is accordingly marked by sets of firms distributed efficiently in the long run which also use the space efficiently.

VI

The final point at issue is clearly this: what advantages stem from applying spatial concepts in addition to time in economic theory? Our answers are virtually limitless if individual topics are used to illustrate the resulting gains. We shall cite only a few of them below.

(1) Theoretical conception of oligopolists rather than of perfect competitors, simple monopolists, or monopolistic competitors generates a change in one's overall view of antitrust statutes. Even more pointedly, policy proposals dealing with industrial pricing change when spatial price analysis is applied (Phlips, 1976, 1977).

(2) One's approach to public utility regulation would clearly change, for in the classical world of microeconomics the trilogy $AR = AC = MC$ is eulogized and policy pronouncements take the form of choosing as the desired prescription either $AR = AC$ or the different price value where $AR = MC$ (Scherer, 1970). In the world of spatial economics, $AR = AC$ is coterminous with $AR > MC$ which, however, can be shown to involve $AR = MC'$, where this MC' includes variable cost ascriptions for uncertainty (Greenhut, 1974). Let it suffice under present objectives to say that the view becomes sharper and the dichotomy obliterated as one uses for his conceptual building blocks the larger size (oligopoly) firm rather than the perfect competitor (Phlips, 1976, Eaton, Lipsey, 1977). To say the least, the inductive leap from theory to practice is narrowed substantially.[10]

(3) One's view of the impact on prices of excise taxes, income taxes and the like changes as the structural parameters of the theorist centre upon sets of spatial oligopolists rather than the simple classical market forms (Greenhut, 1974).

(4) The significance of basing point pricing (and its locational effects), the true meaning of equalizing prices over space, and indeed of other kinds of geographic price discrimination all appear in sharper light by definition of the fact that the theoretical models are designed to examine these very questions. It has, in fact, been shown that varying degrees of spatial competition and different locational orderings generate different systems of spatial pricing. When looked at from viewpoints lacking the space economy perspective, some price

[10]See Scherer (1970, p. 522) for a fine discussion of conventional views and an expression of the related frustrations which lead to use of different standards in rate making. On the other hand, space economic theory suggests that emphasis on determining (and comparing) the industrial uncertainties applicable to regulated *vis à vis* nonregulated industries (e.g., via normalizing the variance(s) of profit(s) among the firms) would provide a basis for determining the zero profit mark-up price above classical average costs, as with $AR = MC'$.

practices *ipso facto* would likely appear to be ethically wrong. Small wonder that certain kinds of geographic price discrimination have been considered to be bad since the theorist himself lives in a mind's eye world of dimensionless space and has not taken the pains to analyze the economic-competition forces that require (or promote) different kinds of spatial pricing patterns (Greenhut, J., Greenhut, M. L., 1975, 1977).

(5) Finally, let us suggest that the subject of administered prices (Means, 1972; Singer, 1970; Weston, 1972) appears in different light (Greenhut, Hwang, Ohta, 1975; Phlips, 1977) as one views a system that is variable with respect to space as well as time. Indeed, macroeconomic theories of inflation and even impacts of labour unions on prices would be viewed differently as one changes his focus from the classical world of spaceless economics to the world of economic space.[11] The same result holds for such subjects as the vertical integration of firms affecting, as it does, economic policy with respect to a country's deregulation of petroleum prices. Clearly, there are many in the United States who fear that permanently higher prices will follow deregulation of natural gas besides believing higher prices would promote absorption of small dealers by the large refining companies. They claim that all of this is bad! But the entire subject appears in different light as one's theoretical framework changes (Greenhut, Ohta 1976).

Without emphasizing Galbraithean conclusions, not necessarily subscribed to by this writer, it suffices to say in conclusion that the science of economics has limited itself for too long a time to the cosy-simple world of zero frictions of distance. As even the pedestrian crossing a side-street in a small town has recognized, the world of shopping and simple living includes a cost to him in going from one place to another (Leigh, 1946; Isard, 1949; Stevens, Rydell, 1966; Devletoglou, 1971; Phlips, 1976; Eaton, Lipsey, 1977). Rational man economizes on cost, among which are the costs of living where he happens to live *vis-à-vis* the cost of living elsewhere *and* buying goods produced elsewhere. He must also evaluate the costs of working in enterprises located at different points in his preferred space before he can find his own optimal position.

[11]Eichner and Kregel proposed (1975, p. 1309) that the failure of the neoclassical model to take the inflationary process into account, when combined with the reluctance of economists to abandon the neoclassical model, has converted the "Golden Age into a limping one". Not only is theoretical error likely in econometric research dealing with microeconomic problems (Phlips, 1977), but the Keynesian-Monetarist frameworks of thought remain separate and distinct from a real-world supportive microeconomics.

REFERENCES

Alchian, A. (1950). "Uncertainty, Evolution, and Economic Theory", *Journal of Political Economy*, Vol. 58, No. 3, pp. 211-221.

Archibald, G. C. (1961). "Chamberlin versus Chicago", *Review of Economic Studies*, Vol. 29, No. 78, pp. 2-28.

——————— (1967). "Monopolistic Competition and Return to Scale", *Economic Journal*, Vol. LXXVII, No. 306, pp. 405-17.

Barzel, Y. (1970). "Excess Capacity in Monopolistic Competition", *Journal of Political Economy*, Vol. 78, No. 5, pp. 1142-49.

Battalio, R. and Ekeland, R. (1972). "Output Change Under Third Degree Discrimination", *Southern Economic Journal*, Vol. 39, No. 2, pp. 285-290.

Beckman, M. (1970). *Location Theory*, New York, Harper Brothers.

——————— (1976). "Spatial Price Policies Revisited", *Bell Journal of Economics* Vol. 7, No. 2, pp. 619-630.

Bradfield, M. (1971). "A Note on Location and the Theory of Production", *Journal of Regional Science*, Vol. 11, No. 2, pp. 263-266.

Capozza, D. and Attaran, K. A. (1976). "Pricing in Urban Areas Under Free Entry", *Journal of Regional Science*, Vol. 16, No. 2, pp. 167-182.

——————— and Van Order, R. (1977a) "Pricing Under Spatial Competition and Spatial Monopoly", *Econometrica*, Vol. 45, No. 6, pp. 1329-1338.

———————, ——————— (1977b). "A Simple Model of Spatial Competition", *Southern Economic Journal*, Vol. 44, No. 2, pp. 361-367.

Chamberlin, E. H. (1935). *Theory of Monopolistic Competition*, Cambridge, Mass., Harvard University Press.

——————— (1953). "The Product as an Economic Variable", *Quarterly Journal of Economics*, Vol. 67, No. 1, pp. 1-29.

Churchill, G. (1967). "Production Technology, Imperfect Competition, and the Theory of Location: A Theoretical Approach", *Southern Economic Journal*, Vol. 34, No. 1, pp. 86-100.

Copeland, M. A. (1940). "Competing Products and Monopolistic Competition", *Quarterly Journal of Economics*, Vol. 55, No. 1, pp. 1-35.

Cournot, A. (1927). *Researches into the Mathematical Principles of the Theory of Wealth*, New York, The Macmillan Company.

Dechesnes, L. (1945). *La Localisation des Diverses Productions*, Bruxelles, Les Editions Compatables, Commerciales et Financières.

Demsetz, H. (1959). "The Nature of Equilibrium in Monopolistic Competition", *Journal of Political Economy*, Vol. 67, No. 1, pp. 21-30.

Devletoglou, N. (1971). *Consumer Behaviour*. London, Harper & Row.

Dewey, D. (1958). "Imperfect Competition No Bar to Efficient Production", *Journal of Political Economy*, Vol. 66, No. 1, pp. 24-33.

Eaton, B. C. and Lipsey, R. G. (1976). "The Non-Uniqueness of Equilibrium in the Löschian Model", *American Economic Review*, Vol. 66, No. 1, pp. 77-93.

——————, —————— (1977). "The Introduction of Space into the Neoclassical Model of Value Theory" in M. J. Artis and A. R. Nobay (eds.), *Studies in Modern Economic Analysis*, Oxford, Blackwells, pp. 59-96.

Eichner, A. S. and Kregel, J. A. (1975). "An Essay on Post-Keynesian Theory: A New Paradigm in Economics", *Journal of Economic Literature*, Vol. XII, No. 4, pp. 1293-1314.

Gannon, C. A. (1971). "Fundamental Properties of Löschian Spatial Demand", *Environment and Planning*, Vol. 3, No. 3, pp. 283-306.

—————— (1973). "Central Concentration in Simple Spatial Duopoly: Some Behavioral and Functional Conditions", *Journal of Regional Science*, Vol. 13, No. 3, pp. 357-375.

Greenhut, J. (1977). "On The Economic Advantages of Spatially Discriminatory Prices Compared with F.O.B. Prices", *Southern Economic Journal*, Vol. 44, No. 1, pp. 161-166.

——————, Greenhut, M. L. (1975). "Spatial Price Discrimination, Competition, and Locational Effects", *Economica*, Vol. 42, No. 168, pp. 401-419.

——————, —————— (1977). "Nonlinearity of Delivered Price Schedules and Predatory Pricing", *Econometrica*, Vol. 45, No. 8, pp. 1871-1876.

Greenhut, M. L. (1956). *Plant Location in Theory and in Practice*. Chapel Hill, University of North Carolina Press.

Greenhut, M. L. (1966). "The Decision Process and Entrepreneurial Returns", *The Manchester School*, Vol. XXXIV, No. 3, pp. 247-267.

——————— (1974). *A Theory of the Firm in Economic Space* (2nd printing), Austin, Lone Star Publishing Co.

——————— (1975). "A Theoretical Mapping from Perfect Competition to Imperfect Competition", *Southern Economic Journal*, Vol. XLII, No. 2, pp. 177-192.

———————, Ohta, H. (1972). "Monopoly Output Under Alternative Spatial Pricing Techniques", *American Economic Review*, Vol. 62, No. 4, pp. 705-713.

———————, ——————— (1975). *Spatial Price Theory and Market Areas*, Durham, Duke University Press.

———————, ——————— (1976). "Related Market Conditions and Interindustrial Merger", *American Economic Review*, Vol. 66, No. 3, pp. 267-277.

Greenhut, M. L., Hwang, M., Ohta, H. (1975). "Observations on the Shape and Relevance of the Spatial Demand Curve", *Econometrica*, Vol. 43, No. 4, pp. 669-682.

———————, ———————, ———————

(1976). "An Empirical Evaluation of the Equilibrium Size and Shape of Market Areas", *International Economic Review*, Vol. 17, No. 1, pp. 172-190.

Hartwick, J. M., Hartwick, P. G. (1971). "Duopoly in Space", *Canadian Journal of Economics*, Vol. XVII, No. 4, pp. 485-506.

Holahan, W. L. (1975). "The Welfare Effects of Spatial Price Discrimination", *American Economic Review*, Vol. 65, No. 3, pp. 498-503.

Hoover, E. M. (1946). *Location and Economic Activity*, New York, McGraw Hill.

——————— (1936-37). "Spatial Price Discrimination", *Review of Economic Studies*, Vol. 4, pp. 182-191.

Horowitz, I. (1970). *Decision Making and the Theory of the Firm*, New York, Holt, Rinehart and Winston.

Hotelling, H. (1929). "Stability in Competition", *Economic Journal*, Vol. 39, No. 154, pp. 41-57.

Isard, W. (1956). *Location and Space Economy*, Cambridge, Mass., MIT Press.

Isard, W. (1949). "The General Theory of Location and Space Economy", *Quarterly Journal of Economics*, Vol. 63, No. 4, pp. 476-506.

Khalili, A., Mahtur, V. K. and Bodenhorn, D. (1974). "Location and the Theory of Production: A Generalization", *Journal of Economic Theory*, Vol. 9, No. 4, pp. 467-475.

Knight, F. (1921). *Risk, Uncertainty, and Profit*, Boston, Mass., Houghton Mifflin Company.

Leigh, A. H. (1946). "Von Thunen's Theory of Distribution and the Advent of Marginal Analysis", *Journal of Political Economy*, Vol. 54, No. 6, pp. 481-502.

Lerner, A. P. and Singer, H. W. (1937). "Some Notes on Duopoly and Spatial Competition", *Journal of Political Economy*, Vol. 45, No. 2, pp. 145-186.

Lewis, W. A. (1945). "Competition in Retail Trade", *Economica*, Vol. 12, No. 48, pp. 202-234.

Lösch, A. (1944). *Die raumliche Ordnung der Wirtschaft*, Jena, Gustav Fisher.

Means, G. C. (1972). "The Administered-Price Thesis Reconfirmed", *American Economic Review*, Vol. 62, No. 3, pp. 292-306.

Miller, D. W. and Starr, M. K. (1960). *Executive Decisions and Operations Research*, Englewood Cliffs, New Jersey, Prentice Hall, Inc.

Mills, E. and Lav, M. R. (1964). "A Model of Market Areas with Free Entry", *Journal of Political Economy*, Vol. 72, No. 3, 278-288.

Moses, L. N. (1958). "Location and the Theory of Production", *Quarterly Journal of Economics*, Vol. 72, No. 2, pp. 259-272.

Ohlin, B. (1935). *Interregional and International Trade*, Cambridge, Mass., Harvard University Press.

Ohta, H. (1976). "On Efficiency of Production Under Conditions of Imperfect Competition", *Southern Economic Journal*, Vol. 43, No. 2, pp. 1124-1135.

——————— (1977). "On the Excess Capacity Controversy", *Economic Inquiry*, Vol. 15, No. 1, pp. 153-165.

Phlips, L. (1976). "Spatial Pricing and Competition", Commission of the European Communities, *Studies Competition-Approximation of Legislation Series*.

——————— (1977). "Intertemporal Price Discrimination and Sticky Prices", presented at Summer Workshop, University of Warwick.

Pigou, A. C. (1932). *The Economics of Welfare* (3rd edition), London, Macmillan & Co.

Predöhl, A. (1925). "Das Standortsproblem in der Wirtschaftstheorie", *Welt Wirtschaftsliches Archiv*, Vol. 21, No. 1, pp. 295-321.

Richardson, H. (1973). *Regional Growth Theory*, New York, J. Wiley and Sons.

Robinson, J. (1934). *The Economics of Imperfect Competition*, London, Macmillan & Co.

Sakashita, N. (1967). "Production Function, Demand Function and Location Theory of the Firms", *Papers and Proceedings of the Regional Science Association*, Vol. 20, pp. 109-122.

Schmalensee, R. (1972). "A Note on Monopolistic Competition and Excess Capacity", *Journal of Political Economy*, Vol. 80, No. 3, pp. 586-591.

Scherer, F. N. (1970). *Industrial Market Structure and Economic Performance*, Chicago, Rand McNally & Co.

Sherrard, A. (1951). "Advertising, Product Variation, and the Limits of Economics", *Journal of Political Economy*, Vol. 59, No. 2, pp. 126-142.

Smithies, A. (1941). "Monopolistic Price Policy in a Spatial Market", *Econometrica*, Vol. 9, No. 1, pp. 63-73.

——————— (1941). "Optimum Location in Spatial Competition", *Journal of Political Economy*, Vol. 49, No. 3, pp. 423-439.

Stern, N. (1972). "The Optimal Size of Market Areas", *Journal of Economic Theory*, Vol. 4, No. 2, pp. 154-173.

Stevens, B. H. and Rydell, C. P. (1966). "Spatial Demand Theory and Monopoly Price Policy", *Papers and Proceedings of the Regional Science Association*, Vol. 17, pp. 195-204.

Stigler, G. (1945). *Five Lectures on Economic Problems*, London, Longmans, Green and Company, Ltd.

——————— and Kindahl, J. (1970). *The Behavior of Industrial Prices*, New York, Columbia University Press.

Weber, A. (1928). *Über den Standort der Industrien*, Part I, "Reine Theorie des Standorts", Tubingen, 1909. This book has been translated by C. J. Friedrich as *Alfred Weber's Theory of the Location of Industries*, Chicago, University of Chicago Press, 1928.

Weston, J. F. (1972). "Pricing Behavior of Large Firms", *Western Economic Journal*, Vol. 10, No. 1, pp. 1-18.

[15]

MR. DORWARD AND IMPACTS OF DISTANCE ON MICROECONOMIC THEORY*

by
M. L. GREENHUT
Texas A & M University

At times in reading Dorward's critiques I wondered if he was actually referring to me or to someone else. This is not to say that his basic *summary* of my space oligopoly theory was not precise enough; rather, it is to say that his critiques appeared to omit parts of the book in which that theory was developed as well as to ignore supporting articles to the subject paper which expanded upon important facets of that theory. This reply will not include detailed explanation (or re-explanation) of the theory, which type of reply could actually enable me to stress essential properties that were ignored by Dorward. I shall refer instead strictly to statements made by Dorward that specifically contradict (or is it downplay?) those I stressed in that theory.

I Slope of the Demand (*AR*) Curve Facing the Firm

Dorward asserts that the idea of a negatively sloping *AR* curve with increased elasticity of demand resulting from new entrants is incompatible with the "chaining" of oligopoly that I have posited for the space economy. He further states (p.251) that "a flattening of the *AR* curve must be primarily dependent on the occurrence of multiple (unlimited) locations at given production centres". All right, in (1970) I stressed that "... long-run oligopolistic *competition* is spurred initially by competitive impacts from firms located close to each other ..." (p. 61), and that this involves "... increased output and lower prices ... from the location of new firms at already established production points" (p. 61). I noted further that any new distant locating firm "may compete actively in price for markets extending from its site towards the older production point ..." (1970, p. 61). On the basis of my definition of a *feasible* distant location (1970, p. 115; originally 1956, p. 65), it was demonstrated that the extent of the spatial competition depends upon the distant firm's production-cost disadvantages compared to its freight-cost savings on sales to buyers located at distances from the old production

*Manuscript received 18.3.81; final version received 29.5.81.

centre in the direction of the new entrant. I further proposed in my space oligopoly explanation that while long-run *competition* may be spurred initially by production centre entrants, entrants located at a distance generate oligopolistic competitive impacts. In fact, virtually all of (1970, Chapter 6 and, in particular, pp. 108–120) dealt with this idea.[1]

Within the same space oligopoly thesis, I further indicated that "With additional new entry, the differentiations due to space, name, and possibly service and product diminish in character and importance. . . . With larger and larger numbers of firms located at all points in the market . . . it becomes increasingly difficult for buyers to distinguish between them. If it were not for the limits placed on numbers by indivisibilities and uncertainties, the market would convert into . . . the atomistic market type. . . . But the conditions of indivisibility and uncertainty do exist. They place natural limits on entry, with geographical indivisibilities combining with technological indivisibilities to restrict entry . . ." (1970, p. 158, and analysis pp. 159–205). Dorward's further comment that my statement on barriers to entry "weakens (my) assumption of free entry" (p. 246, fn. 2.) does not strike me as being valid in any way at all.

II Market Area Shapes, Number of Rivals, and Demand Elasticities

One of Dorward's strongest criticisms, but a quite incorrect one, has to do with what he implies is one of my assumptions in (1970, 1978). He argues that my representative firm will face a maximum of six rivals under conditions of spatial competition. Clearly prior remarks in Section 1 suggest that I never viewed a uniform distribution of firms over space. In fact in (1956, Chapters 11, 12), I demonstrated that even under Lösch's homogeneous plane assumption, a heterogeneous distribution of firms making profits eventuates in a space economy. Dorward nevertheless views six rivals as requisite in my theory and that the firm's market area alone changes because of further entry, actually shrinking as a result of entry. Dorward concludes from this that the elasticity of demand for the representative firm's product is *not* a function of the number of firms in the economy. I suggest instead that empirical studies would reinforce my claims of (a) limited entry, (b) a gradual shift of the demand facing the representative firms, (c) increased desire for a good as alternative sources of supply come into being, and hence (d) increased flattening *and* greater price elasticities along the industry demand curve and the firm's *AR* curve. In fact, in terms of industry demand, it is *the central*

[1]Since Dorward believes Cournot's model would help, I must note that I have used that model selectively in many writings, e.g., Chapter 6, 1970, though it is not intrinsic to spatial price theory.

theorem of spatial competition that *effective consumer demands increase naturally as transport costs fall because of the entry of firms over space.*

The most recent literature on spatially competitive f.o.b. pricing (starting with Greenhut, Hwang, Ohta, 1975; Capozza, Van Order, 1977, 1980; and Ohta, 1980) has centred attention on conjectural reactions of spatial oligopolists while utilizing what has been referred to as Löschian, Hotelling-Smithies, and Greenhut-Ohta models. The interaction between *demand curves*, price policies, plant location, and new entry that was first proposed in (1956) has been well extended to include comparisons of elasticities of spaceless and spatial demands *under diverse forms of competitive behavioural reactions*. Competitor reaction lags correspondent to consumer reaction lags may well apply (Scheidell, 1978). If I added to the above literature the writings on spatial price discrimination (as referenced in the 1978 paper; and since then the two very recent papers by Norman, 1981; that of Phlips, 1980; and my own of 1980, 1981), the full impacts of competition and competitive locations on the pricing pattern of the representative firm would be clearly revealed. Most fundamentally, the tie up between competitive entry and behavioural reactions that has been stressed by many has been viewed to depend on market size; thus it is a partial function of the number of firms throughout the economy. For example, Capozza and Van Order in (1978) observed that entry will cause price to fall *under certain behavioural conditions* as the firm's market space shrinks and the demand for its product becomes more elastic.[1] How Dorward could claim otherwise from my own writings is surprising, especially since he cites the Capozza-Van Order paper *and* they indicated that their paper stemmed from one of mine which dealt with the effects on product prices of alternative behavioural reactions. What could be lost sight of are the differences in short-run and long-run reactions.

III Imputation of uncertainty

Possibly the underlying confusion that exists in Dorward's mind concerning my imputation of an opportunity cost for behavioural uncertainty derives from the fact that he is "an industrial economist with a heavily applied orientation". This may well have created an epistemological bias in his evaluation of my theory. I suggest this in light of his apparently different view of the concept of "equilibrium" than that which I believe classicists possess. The subject concept is, of course, simply a logical tool that is employed to enable consideration of a very complex reality in simplified form. I agree,

[1]Actually price rises or falls (and demand becomes more or less elastic) depending upon the behavioural assumption that is made and the basic shape of the individual consumer demand curves (Greenhut, Hwang, Ohta, 1975; Capozza and Van Order, 1977, 1978; Benson, 1980, 1981; Ohta, 1980).

a unique position tends not to exist in the real world, at least in terms of a single price, a single size firm, etc. But explanation of the economic forces at work necessitates use of expository tools which bring us to a single value or point (such as the *unique* Chamberlinean tangency point I still claim is relevant). Actually, analysis of an equilibrium position should entail evaluation of disequilibria states (see virtually all of Chapter 8, 1970, especially pp. 345–353), which particular analysis focuses attention on the way opposing forces operate in tending to move the economic system in a given direction.

Dorward's concept of the long run seems to depend upon the specific criticism he is making. To consider further his discussion of uncertainty, note that he correctly implies all things change in the long run. This does not mean, however, that theory cannot stress underlying trends, even if the long run is never reached. The long run serves as a planning horizon for the firm, even though the firm always operates in the short run. Plant location may itself be a long-run decision, albeit once a location is chosen, the firm is again operating in the short run and possesses a new planning horizon which may well involve future relocation.

In discussing the concept of uncertainty as presented in (1970, 1978), Dorward presents an emphasis other than that which I believe is warranted. First, he ignores the fact that the return for uncertainty is a residual in my model, not a reward for a functional input. The effect in my theory is that the minimum point on the technological cost curve alone counts, not the minimum cost point on the adjusted curve. Secondly, he contends that (in my theory) entrepreneurs must "know" the level of uncertainty. My theory simply postulates that each entrepreneur estimates subjectively the level of uncertainty. If a guess turns out to be correct, the firm receives appropriate returns, and the entrepreneur is satisfied with his choice of activity; otherwise he is in over his head or intends to assume greater uncertainty. All one must do is rank alternative activities and determine the returns required from them. Thirdly, consider Dorward's comment about the existence of "different classes of potential entrants [that] face different levels of uncertainty depending on [differences in] their potential net advantages . . ." (bracketed inserts mine). Back in this journal in (1966), and also in the paper under criticism (1978), I proposed that an $\bar{X}$ payoff applies to each uncertainty state ($i = 1, \ldots, n$) with ". . . *no* accepted-by-all set of probabilities assignable to uncertainties". Differences obtain because of the contrasting perceptions of the managers of firms. In fact, behavioural uncertainty (as opposed to risk) derives from the very condition that even if there were a lengthy chain of history, the expected behaviour and required returns of businessmen would *not* be agreed upon. Accordingly, there is no single, identical, absolute return in the real world that is perceived of by all entrepreneurs in an industry. But note, my agreement and stress on intraindustry differences (to say nothing of interindustry differences) is limited to the short run, during which period economic rents (profits if you prefer) may even be counter to the principle of greater returns for greater uncertainty. In the long run, however, I contend that economic rents become *well ordered* as the viable members of an industry develop, in effect, a commonality of *spirit* and uniform approach to decision problems. This leads to identical *structures* of risk and uncertainty for a *properly defined industry* (1970, pp. 41, 198, 315). The definition of industry, in still other words, is critical, and it is for a *properly defined industry* that I proposed (and continue to propose) long-run intraindustry identities and long-run interindustry differences in the risk-uncertainty structures of surviving firms (and see Ohta, 1976).

The model finally contends that intraindustry *regional* cost differences may apply in the long run, albeit necessarily being compensated for by regional demand elasticity differences that must arise (1970, pp. 162, 170–186). This last thought explains, perhaps, the fundamental difference between Dorward's view and mine. Differential risks and uncertainties serve as a basis for distinguishing industries. They warrant different net returns, and in the process generate contrasting degrees of competition and entry. Behavioural reactions will vary, different short-run price effects will prevail, some perverse, some not, as in the literature on spatial prices. In the long run, however, an ordered state is brought about that is uniquely characterized, as in Dorward's Fig. 1. Until then, entry, exit, relocation, profit-losses apply as members of the industry move *towards* classical demand, supply results. If Dorward is saying the long run never exists nor eventuates except in the mind's-eye, then yes; if he is stating that short-run perversities *always* prevail, then alas little is left of economic theory, for our world is indeed characterized by spatial oligopoly and possibly contrasting kinds of behavioural reactions. I proposed and still propose that an orderly state does *underlie* the long-run path of free enterprise economies. Against that signpost, general macro and micro predictions *and* policies can be formed.

Final Note

The economic theory under discussion involved my combining specific fundamental postulates I considered requisite to my overall framework of thought with established concepts which did not violate these postulates. For example, as part of my proposed determinate oligopoly solution, I drew from spatial price theory the principle of increasing elasticity of demand resulting from the entry of firms at diverse points over the landscape, and I used axiomatically the classical economic concept of differential rents. In essence,

Dorward has attacked these building blocks while *not disproving the theorem I deduced from them.* At the most he appears to reject the method of employing *related concepts and theories* in formulating an economic model, while apparently preferring to start anew from empirical observations.

What is the proper methodology? I would contend that both are acceptable. However, to my way of thinking, it is often most precise to strive to decrease the level of abstraction in reformulating existing models. Such procedure enables one to approach a complex reality by moving systematically from one level of abstraction to another. By selecting the most relevant real-world attributes derived from existing models, we can link them together in new models. It is in this context that I ascribed the attribute of uncertainty onto the classical *LRAC* curve while using a Chamberlinean equilibrium focus to derive a vastly different result than that established by Chamberlin in his theory of monopolistic competition. The upshot, in my view, was (is) a transformation from the theory of pure competition. Dorward indicates his leaning against, but I believe too narrow a view of, this aspect of my work when (on p. 256) he closes by stating that "... *short cuts* to the construction of such an extended microeconomic theory by an *adaptation* of standard non-spatial models, such as that of Chamberlin, are unlikely ... etc." (italics mine). I would propose that adaptation is the key to a decreasing abstraction process, and that it is the most efficient method for pushing some frontiers of knowledge forward. In any case, the *solution* I proposed was itself left unchallenged in my opinion. I hope at some future time to be able to package it up more effectively than perhaps I did in the past. As Dorward would probably agree, the space dimension is intrinsic to effective economic inquiry.

References

Benson, B. (1980). "Löschian Competition Under Alternative Demand Conditions", *American Economic Review*, Vol. 70, No. 5, pp. 1098–1105.

———— (1981). "Spatial Microeconomics: Implications for the Use of Concentration Ratios to Represent Market Power", *Review of Regional Studies*, forthcoming.

Capozza, D. and Van Order, R. (1977). "Pricing Under Spatial Competition and Spatial Monopoly", *Econometrica*, Vol. 45, No. 6, pp. 1329–1338.

———— and ———— (1978). "A Generalized Model of Spatial Competition", *American Economic Review*, Vol. 68, No. 5, pp. 896–908.

———— and ———— (1980). "Unique Equilibria, Pure Profits, and Efficiency in Location Models", *American Economic Review*, Vol. 70, No. 5, pp. 1046–1053.

Dorward, N. (1981). "'Impacts of Distance on Microeconomic Theory': A Critique", *The Manchester School*, Vol. 49, No. 3, pp. 245–258.

Greenhut, J., Greenhut, M. L. and Li, S. (1980). "Spatial Pricing Patterns in the United States", *Quarterly Journal of Economics*, Vol. 94, No. 375, pp. 329–350.

Greenhut, M. L. (1956). *Plant Location in Theory and in Practice*, Chapel Hill, University of North Carolina Press.

———— (1966). "The Decision Process and Entrepreneurial Returns", *The Manchester School*, Vol. 34, No. 3, pp. 247–267.

———— (1970). *A Theory of the Firm in Economic Space* (2nd printing 1974), Austin, Texas, Lone Star Publishing Co.

———— (1978). "Impacts of Distance on Microeconomic Theory", *The Manchester School*, Vol. 46, No.1, pp. 17–40.

———— (1981). "Spatial Pricing in the U.S.A., West Germany, and Japan", *Economica*, Vol. 48, No. 189, pp. 79–86.

————, Hwang, M. and Ohta, H. (1975). "Observations on the Shape and Relevance of the Spatial Demand Function", *Econometrica*, Vol. 43, No. 4, pp. 669–682.

Lösch, A. (1944). *Die Räumliche Ordnung der Wirtschaft*, Jena, Gustav Fisher.

Norman, G. (1981). "Spatial Competition and Spatial Price Discrimination", *Review of Economic Studies*, Vol. 48, No. 151, pp. 97–112.

———— (1981). "Uniform Pricing as an Optimal Spatial Pricing Policy", *Economica*, Vol. 48, No. 189, pp. 87–91.

Ohta, H. (1976). "On Efficiency of Production Under Conditions of Imperfect Competition", *Southern Economic Journal*, Vol. 43, No. 2, pp. 1124–1135.

———— (1980). "Spatial Competition Concentration, and Welfare", *Regional Science and Urban Economics*, Vol. 10, No. 1, pp. 3–16.

Phlips, L. (1980). "Intertemporal Price Discrimination and Sticky Prices", *Quarterly Journal of Economics*, Vol. 94, No. 3, pp. 525–542.

Scheidell, J. (1978). *Advertising Prices and Consumer Reaction: A Dynamic Analysis*, Washington, D.C., American Enterprise Institute.

Reprinted from THE SOUTHERN ECONOMIC JOURNAL
Vol. XLII, No. 2, October 1975
Printed in U.S.A.

A THEORETICAL MAPPING FROM PERFECT COMPETITION TO IMPERFECT COMPETITION*

M. L. GREENHUT

Texas A & M University

This paper focuses attention on the similarities underscoring an unorganized imperfectly competitive market and the perfectly competitive market. Its resulting theory is believed to be an original interpretation of competitive equilibrium in that imperfect market.[1] Though our main conclusions are obtained by references to a competitive *spatial* market, the thesis presented herein applies in general to any unorganized imperfectly competitive market, spatial or spaceless. Because of this condition, such *spatial* particulars as the locational distribution of industry, the shapes of the market areas of firms, the impacts of distance on demand curves, and the like, need not be discussed here and hence are left to other writings [11; 14; 15]. Only the frame of reference in this paper is set along spatial lines, and this essentially for descriptive purposes alone. The upshot is that our real focus is on any unorganized imperfectly competitive market, as characterized and defined below in Section I.

I. IMPERFECT COMPETITION AND UNCERTAINTY

Economic space implies oligopoly, for even barbershops in an economy subject to costly distances illustrate existence of an oligopoly market not the monopolistically competitive market of Chamberlinean theory.[2] Our imperfectly competitive market

* This paper reflects a set of lectures and seminars presented at the Universities of Mannheim, Münster, and Karlsruhe in April 1972 and June–July 1973. Professors and students involved encouraged the formulation of this paper, but all errors are, of course, the author's alone. Acknowledgement of thanks for their many helpful comments is due Prof. Drs. M. Streit, R. Thoss, R. Funck; Dr. H. Hellmann, Mr. H. von den Hagen, Ms. D. Trost; and to former students, Professors M. Hwang and H. Ohta. Further debt is acknowledged to Professors A. Kerr and R. W. Pfouts for critiques and suggestions and to the National Science Foundation for research support which facilitated the writing of this paper.

[1] In some respects, the present paper will be seen to involve similar conclusions to those derived by H. Demsetz [4; 5; 6]. But the formulation herein and the foundation for our results (e.g., economic space and opportunity costs), in addition to our basic theorems, are sharply distinctive and different from those of Professor Demsetz.

[2] Perhaps the Chamberlin-Kaldor dispute on the semantics of imperfect competition/monopolistic competition should be mentioned here. Let it be proposed that the term monopolistic competition could readily appear to include an open entry but organized oligopoly, while the term imperfect competition could easily strike one as including the unorganized (competitive) oligopoly stressed in this paper. (See N. Kaldor [18, esp. 525ff.], Chamberlin [3], Hibdon [16], Robinson [23], and Ross [24].) Since the present paper, in fact, contends that each firm is relatively important in economic space, the incrementally small (i.e., the unimportant) differentiated competitor is a non-sequitur to our system of thought. Spatial firms, we shall argue, generally are oligopolists, organized or competitive. The term imperfect competition is therefore preferred to the term monopolistic competition, since it would appear to focus attention on competitive (unorganized) oligopoly markets more so than does the reference monopolistic competition.

thus consists only of markets characterized by interdependencies among rivals; moreover, our focus is restricted to firms which do not collude (or organize)—i.e., it is restricted to competitive duopolists or oligopolists. Central to the form of imperfect competition stressed in this paper is the existence of identifiable rivals, which relationship implies behavioral uncertainty. In fact, when we speak of uncertainty in the context of imperfect competition, we shall have in mind chiefly the behavioral uncertainty which characterizes relations between business men who compete with each other. It follows that unpredictable behavior stemming from individual and group reactions to political and social events is essentially a non sequitur to the interests of this paper. Such uncertainty has actually been generic to all existing *major frameworks of economic thought* and is therefore neither at issue nor in need of stress herein. Put more specifically, uncertainties related to natural resource differences, to politics, to environment, and the like, could prevail regardless of assumptions covering the interdependencies of rivals. Present emphasis centers upon the meaning and impact of oligopolistic (behavioral) uncertainty on business policies. This emphasis holds even though risk and other forms of uncertainty do interact with behavioral uncertainty. It is manifest that before we are in position to outline our theory, we must explain how behavioral uncertainty differs from risk.

Uncertainty generates alternative outcomes, a condition which applies to all types of uncertainty. In this regard it is similar to risk. However, behavioral uncertainty requires sharply distinguishable treatment from that usually accorded to risk. Risk states are marked by objective probabilities. For example, on the basis of historical evidence, a 20 percent probability may be ascribed on any given day to the possibility that no machine in a certain plant will break down while a 30 percent probability applies to one machine being under repair, *etc.* These probabilities are statistical probabilities, hence agreed upon by all observers. In contrast, there are no commonly accepted probabilities which may be assigned to the outcomes stemming from uncertainty. For example, the likelihoods assigned to the occurrence in oligopoly markets of the alternative possibilities of hypercompetitive pricing or collusive pricing would be strictly subjective; such weighting would apply even if the chain of history were lengthy since the expected behavior of business men (subject to antitrust constraints, etc.) would not be agreed upon by independent observers. In sum, uncertainty states contrast sharply from alternative risk states, as different decision-makers need not agree on the likelihood of occurrence of any one uncertainty state whereas they would agree on the objective (statistical) probabilities which underscore risk.

Two independent subsets of probabilities and in turn payoffs are identifiable since the risk states typically occur independently of uncertainty states; but whether or not always independent, risk states are nonetheless contained within any given uncertainty state. This condition may readily be viewed by noting that machines will break down regardless of how firms price their goods. A range of payoffs attributable to the number of machines under repair thus applies to any (and each) uncertainty state, as the condition of uncertainty determines the level of the payoffs while the prevailing risk state provides the particular plus or minus value around the mean payoff expected from that state of uncertainty. It is worthy of additional note that since any one risk will exist coterminously with any other (for example, one machine may be in repair at the same time that unduly high temperature outside a plant may require greater energy for use in cooling inside), the concept of risk state really signifies risk combination; similarly, the related probability becomes a compound probability. The very same principles apply to uncertainty, where hypercompetitive pricing may be associated with a decision to locate a branch plant in Atlanta rather than

Birmingham. But regardless of whether or not we think of compound or simple states of uncertainty, the weight (i.e., probability) assigned to the uncertainty state remains subjective; in contrast, objective probabilities apply to risk.

Consider, accordingly, a particular state of uncertainty, such as collusive pricing associated with a branch plant having been located in Atlanta. Given this particular combination (or state), there further exists under it a set of risk payoffs (A_1, A_2, $\cdots$, A_m) and associated risk probabilities (P_1, P_2, $\cdots$, P_m).[3] If the payoffs *are then weighted by their associated probabilities*, an expected payoff ($\bar{X}$) obtains. Manifestly an $\bar{X}$ payoff applies to each state $i = 1, \cdots, n$ of uncertainty, so that we really have $\bar{X}_i$ alternatives. As noted above, there is no "accepted-by-all" set of probabilities assignable to uncertainties since some decision-makers may regard one uncertainty state as being quite likely to occur while others may weight their conjectures heavily in expectation of the occurrence of a different state of the uncertainty. Hence there is no individually weighted set of $\bar{X}_i$ values which would necessarily be identical to the weights assigned each $\bar{X}_i$ value by another decision-maker.

Present day theorists, following in the tradition set forth by Knight [19], are readily attuned to the above classification, and in fact to the joint relationships which exist between states of risk and uncertainty. But the classically oriented economist bypassed these forces. He centered his attention on certainty, or in more recent years focused occasionally on risk while ignoring true uncertainties. At least he ignored those uncertainties predicated on the behavior of businessmen, accepting at the most the possibility that uncertainties of life and death of particular people, or changes in political institutions, could affect the business firm. But even here the proviso was implicitly added that all decision-makers *could* and *did* evaluate these forces identically.

When an unorganized imperfectly competitive market is considered, behavioral uncertainty applies. It does not matter whether this behavioral uncertainty is conceived of as operating in concert with other uncertainties or by itself. What alone matters is that a special industry differentiating return is required in compensation for the uncertainty of investment in the uncertain market. Though this differential is a complicating element in economic analysis, it provides at the same time the basis for an easy mapping from perfect competition to unorganized imperfect competition. To simplify our forthcoming discussion, and in deference to the interaction between behavioral uncertainty and other uncertainties, we shall henceforth use the term uncertainty *in the composite sense*, except when specification to the contrary is necessary; correspondingly, we will for simplicity in words drop the term unorganized in our references to imperfectly competitive markets, except when detailed specification offers advantage. Let it suffice accordingly to repeat that space implies oligopoly and oligopoly involves nonobjectively predictable interaction.[4] This relations set accepted, the next section of this paper is in position to contend that uncertainty is a supply-determining cost which rises monotonically as uncertainty increases. Section III will then impute this cost to the average cost curve which has been (classically) conceived of by economists for markets not characterized by uncertainty. The upshot of such imputation will finally be shown to involve only a single (unique) stable tangency solution of Chamberlinean order rather than the infinity of stable tangency solutions commonly believed in the history of economic thought to be possible.

[3] The notation followed here assumes that the risk probabilities are independent of the uncertainty state. A *mean* value of the payoffs conjectured for the alternative risk conditions can therefore be computed for a given state of uncertainty.

[4] That economic space culminates in oligopoly is suggested in [7], [17], [21], [26; 27], and stressed in [22], [11; 14], [9], [24].

II. A SKETCH OF OUR THEORY

It is basic to our theory that the greater the uncertainty the greater is the required longrun return [12]. This monotonicity does not violate the distinction between objective and subjective probabilities. Indeed, the fact that executives who are operating under uncertainty will differently resolve their shortrun decision problems does not alter longrun economic relations in any significant way [10]. Why? Because even though shortrun differences and guesswork based on hunch, optimism, fear, a maximin criterion, etc., are evident in decision-making under uncertainty, survivors must be those whose expectations and actions happened to be correct. This result relates to the "screening" effect of competitive entry and exit. If such screening effect did not exist, firms could indeed earn greater returns in the long run on investments involving smaller uncertainty.

The gist of our thesis is, therefore, that only shortrun enterpreneurial returns may run counter to the principle of greater returns for greater uncertainty; in the longrun, these returns become well-ordered as a natural consequence of the laws of competition and the rule of opportunity costs. This longrun ordering conforms to the belief that viable (surviving) members of *an industry* develop in time a commonality of spirit and a uniform approach to decision-making, even in the presence of uncertainty. This uniformity extends all the way to the point where the capitalization structures of the firms in an *industry* can be assumed to be the same. But what is meant by *industry*? What are identical capitalization structures? What is the nature of the return required for uncertainty, and on what basis is it ordered? Answers to these questions must be entered immediately.

Let *industry* be defined as the set of activities producing substantially *similar products* under sales conditions characterized by the identically same structure of risk and uncertainty. In this context, conceive of a set of expected (mean) payoffs for each uncertainty state u_i, where again $i = 1, \cdots, n$ stands for the alternative states provided by the applicable uncertainties. A range of alternative payoffs which relate to the alternative risk states underscores each expected $\bar{X}_i$. Considering the entire spectrum of industries in an economy, it further follows that longrun intraindustry differentials in the relevant $\bar{X}_i$ values would reflect differential profits for the different uncertainty combinations in each industry. These differential profits provide the basis for measuring uncertainty. For example, if the highest and lowest expected $\bar{X}_i$ returns are considered, alternative returns are at hand which may be referred to loosely as the measure of uncertainty of investment in the subject industry. This uncertainty may then be compared with the corresponding uncertainty range in other industries. In a more technical sense, the range of expected payoffs can serve as the measure of uncertainty provided that appropriate adjustments are made for amounts invested and other considerations are made [12]. In other words, a measure or index of uncertainty can be conceived which involves comparisons of all $\bar{X}_i$ returns within and between industries.

Present purposes do not require details as to how an uncertainty index may be derived. Rather, the essential ideas are that a range of payoffs characterizes economic activity in free enterprise systems and that for each industry in the economy a particular range of returns would help identify the uncertainty of the investment.[5] In corresponding pattern, under any uncertainty state $i = 1 \cdots n$ (for example the state of hypercompetitive pricing and branch plant location in Atlanta. . .), a range of payoffs

[5] It is part of this viewpoint that longrun survivors in the unorganized oligopolistic industry possess a commonness in approach and character and that identical profit rates eventuate for a given uncertainty. In other words, notwithstanding the guesswork which initially prevails, entrepreneurial survivors are those whose expectations and actions proved to be correct. Incidentally, this does not mean that survivors in any industry are always the most efficient entrepreneurs who once were part of the industry. Viability of economic performance relates to more than the initial set of skills [8].

x_k obtains for the particular uncertainty i due to the $k = 1 \cdots m$ alternative states of risk that exist. One might therefore compare the lowest *expected* return (i.e., the $\bar{X}_i$ resulting from the worst state of uncertainty) with the lowest possible x_k return applicable to that same uncertainty state. The $\bar{X}_i - x_{ik}$ range (as adjusted for investments and statistical criteria which, to repeat, need not be discussed here) would provide a measure of risk, where to repeat the i selected is the one applicable to the worst possible uncertainty state and where the particular k value similarly relates to that i besides involving the worst situation possible with respect to risk.

The basis for classifying industry, as defined at the outset to the present remarks, has thus been established. To repeat, we define an industry as a set of firms whose members produce substantially similar products under the identically same *structure* of risk and uncertainty. Manifestly, by similar risk and uncertainty structure, we mean the index (or measure) of risk and uncertainty must correspond among the firms producing highly comparable products.

Our focus on oligopoly—hence on relatively large size firms—behavioral uncertainty, and interdependencies requires not only that oligopolistic industry be defined but also that individual payoffs be compared. However, comparison of payoffs relates to and involves capitalization structures, though not necessarily the sizes of firms. A simple solution is available to us in this regard. Pursuant to the idea that viable firms will be those whose decision problems under uncertainty were resolved similarly, the capitalization structures of firms belonging to an industry can be conceived both in logic and for simplicity as the same in the longrun. This similarity applies in the sense that identical ratios of funded debt to equity capital will exist, as *to repeat* the common character of success among surviving firms in the presence of competitive entry and exit can be expected to produce such identity. Most importantly, note that the entry-exit-producing identity means that when we impute uncertainty as a cost of investment later on in the paper for any and all member firms of a particular industry, the applicable imputation rate can be ascribed *uniformly on the basis of the equity investment* made in the firm. Different financing techniques and contrivances of company officials can therefore be regarded as shortrun distinctions only in our theory; similarly, different sizes of firms can be mushroomed together in our focus on the representative firm alone, or on directly comparable (large and small) representative firms. Such focus can further be supported by the observation that any analysis of longrun equilibrias requires study of underlying economic returns alone, so capital structures may be considered the same.

The stage is thus set for the final questions posed above: what is the nature of the payment required for uncertainty, and what is its basis? The common (single) answer to these questions is rooted in the concept of *opportunity costs*. This means that a scissors relation underscores uncertainty since opportunity costs relate to both the income received in an alternative performance and the expenditure of funds or services which would yield that income. More generally, since it is manifest that certain job incomes require different applications of energy, we may think in the real terms of energy expenditures rather than specifying investment dollars or heat calories used up in providing services, etc. Before a best-lost alternative can be identified, the income and energy expenditure sides of all alternatives must, in other words, be evaluated. Moreover, in a world of uncertainty, ascriptions of lost opportunities to the selected activity require imputation of the cost of differential uncertainties, which imputations can be applied to both or to either the income or energy expended side of the selected activity.

To view the problem at hand, following [13], let superscript a in (1) below designate the factor's best alternative. Assume that if the factor of production was used in the alternative activity, its working lifetime would be M^a and its expected net revenues would be r^a. In earning this income, let energy units e^a normally be used up in each appropriate production (or calendar) period of time. To simplify, we assume that energy units are the same in each unit production period of time.) Let the net revenue and cost values be discounted by i_1 and i_2, where the discount parameters include a subjective addition for uncertainty. But in conceiving of this *subjective* discount, note that if the uncertainty of receiving the income produced in the alternative activity is great compared to that in the selected activity, i_1 will be great, while if the uncertainty effects on the factor's working lifetime in the alternative activity are great (i.e., the danger to the factor is great), i_2 will be small, *ceteris paribus*. After discounting, dividing, summing the quotients, and dividing by M^a, net revenues are obtained in the ratio form R^a.

$$R^a = (\sum_{j=1}^{M^a} \{[r_j^a/(1 + i_1)^j]/ [e_j^a/(1 + i_2)^j]\})/M^a. \quad (1)$$

Next, multiply R^a by the discounted average unit period energy expenditures applicable to the subject activity, as in (2). This multiplication yields r^s in (2), the linearized net revenue requirement in the subject activity, where superscript s refers to the subject activity while M^s and i_2' respectively stand for the working lifetime and the rate of discount on the energies expended in the chosen activity. Thus:

$$r^s = (R^a)\{[\sum_{j=1}^{M^s} e_j^s/(1 + i_2')^j]/M^s\}. \quad (2)$$

Note finally that e in (1) and (2) must be conceived of as both the energy expenditure the owner would like to have the factor expend in any unit period of time and the expenditure optimally ordered by the prevailing technology. Economic theory requires this conformability, for if it did not prevail the factor would be high in cost and exit from the industry in the longrun.

The revenue requirement r^s thus includes the return ordered for uncertainty in an oligopolistic economy. This requirement r^s is the factor's transformed opportunity cost, and it may or may not equal the factor's return for uncertainty in the activity. It further follows from this concept of opportunity costs that profit maximization approaches utility maximization, since leisure, danger, uncertainty, etc., serve as an intrinsic part in the discount process, hence in the evaluation of lost opportunities. Each decision-maker seeks, of course, not to maximize uncertainty but to cover the uncertainty he accepts. If focus on uncertainty alone is desired in (1) and (2), its impact can be isolated theoretically from all other income and energy components.[6]

The question dealing with uncertainty has thus been answered. Uncertainty is simply a determinant of supply which so *interacts with and relates to* other facets of lost opportunities as to be distinguishable only theoretically from them. Moreover, though lost opportunities (including the uncertainty component) can be treated exclusively in vari-

[6] When economic space is introduced, the cost of uncertainty must be covered in the longrun. There might be n combinations of uncertainty existing in a particular industry. The payoff for the uncertainty combinations may be estimated from the lost opportunity cost, as explained above. Of course, since there is no universally agreed upon probability which is assignable to each payoff, the reaction to uncertainty differs among individuals, as would be reflected in the discount rate of equations (1) and (2). In turn, the selection of uncertainty combinations and, therefore, the sought-after payoffs differ among firms in the shortrun. In the longrun, however, the firms whose managers chose correctly (i.e., those who viewed the uncertainty combinations with better *ex ante* anticipation than others) will have covered their lost opportunity cost; hence, their firms will have proven to be viable. Those who made the wrong short-run decisions (i.e., those who centered their attention on uncertainty combinations which did not occur with the frequency visualized by the decision-maker) will have failed to cover their lost opportunity cost; their firms will have exited (or otherwise be changed in) the market. In sum, entry and exit give rise to a longrun level of payoffs for the uncertainty applicable to an industry and help establish the longrun equilibrium output discussed later in this paper.

able input cost form (e.g., see [14, Appendix to Chapter 5]), a fixed cost (lost opportunity) approach is easier to apply. Section III will initially use this approach.

In so far as risk is concerned, all firms in a given industry face the same risk probabilities. It is only the conception of uncertainty likelihoods which differs in the shortrun. In the longrun, however, all viable firms must, in effect, be conceived to have forecasted similarly. Moreover, if we ascribe the opportunity cost of risk and uncertainty to the firm's classical average cost curve, and if we assume the special case where each firm is of the same size and otherwise homogeneous, the individual firms would have the same *AC* curve in the longrun. If individual differences in size are conceived, all minimum points of the AC curves will be on the same level, albeit the curves are not otherwise identical throughout. But all of this anticipates final relations in our theory. For the moment, let us specify what we must do next.

Section III, as implied above, will focus attention primarily on the opportunity cost of uncertainty. It will employ the fixed (lost opportunity) cost approach initially. In addition, it will conceive of returns received by entrepreneurs which stem in part from their service inputs and in part from the (risk and) uncertainty in their equity investment. It will be contended that the range of returns *attributable to uncertainty* converges under longrun competition to an *ex post* value which simply compensates the owners of surviving firms for their "uncertain" investment.

III. DETAILS OF OUR THEORY

The *AC* classical curve in Figure 1 is designed to serve as the classical average cost curve. It includes all explicit payments and all classical implicit rental costs, i.e., for capital, for entrepreneurial services, and for self-owned (and used) land. But let oligopolistic uncertainties exist. Then the lost opportunity return for uncertainty becomes a burden to the subject activity. This burden may be treated as an "added" fixed cost, which when ascribed to the *AC* classical curve in Figure 1 brings about the *AC* adjusted curve.[7] It follows that the minimum cost on the adjusted curve will occur at an input-output point greater than that applicable to classical costs. However, before proceeding further, a few additional words in explanation of opportunity costs and thus of the *AC* classical curve are required.

It is well established in economic theory that lost opportunities are part of the cost of any given economic activity. Intrinsic to this concept is the requirement noted in Section II that the entrepreneur and his self-owned land and capital be used optimally. This requirement stems from the definition of best alternative and the condition that *there exists* a chosen activity. If optimal use did not obtain, production would be characterized by use of variable inputs which are not matched by the required efficient amounts of entrepreneurial inputs, such as in services, land, and/or capital. The consequence of nonconformability would be high cost production. The entrepreneur, in effect, would either be imputing a relatively high charge for his services, if he is the productive factor out-of-line with the prevailing technology, or his land and/or capital must be overworked or underworked, as the case be. In time, competition would force him out of the market or else his firm would be absorbed by or managed by others.

Given nonconformance, it follows further that either the otherwise best alternative could not be the best possible opportunity, *or* else, as noted above, the subject activity

[7] The inclusion of a subjective adjustment in a free enterprise economy will later on be understood not to alter the underlying requirement of objective results in the marketplace. In this connection, it may suffice for the moment to recall our previous assertion that in the longrun all viable firms in a given industry are characterizable as having made equally correct decisions. This assertion, which will be verified analytically in Section IV of this paper, converts a subjectively based phenomenon to the level of objective fact.

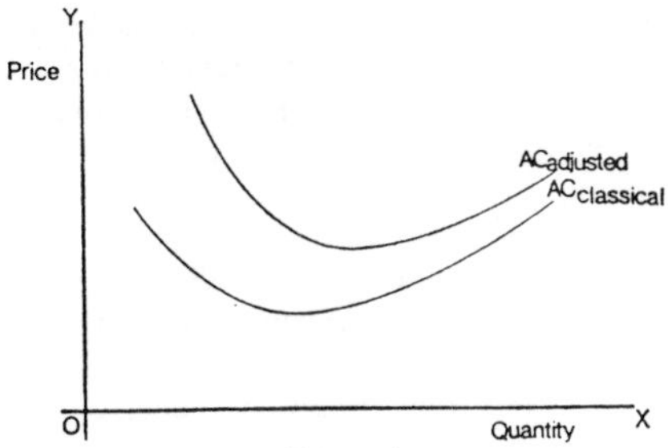

FIGURE 1

would not remain economically sound.[8] It is accordingly the case that the representative classical *AC* curve drawn in Figure 1 implicitly reflects optimality in entrepreneurial inputs in the best alternative *and* corresponding conformability of these inputs to the technology of the selected activity. It follows that any ascription for the lost-opportunity uncertainty component must also be intrinsically conformable to technological conditions. That is to say, any computation for uncertainty must be based on the longrun optimal cost investment in the selected and foresaken activity. No other referential point is possible.

To appreciate fully the requirement specified above, note that in a continuum of lost opportunities, any use of the *currently prevailing* rate of return in the best alternative *as the basis for determining the rate of return required in the chosen activity* must immediately and always yield zero profits or losses. The meaning of lost opportunities thus requires reference to the longrun competitive rate of return in the factor's best alternative, not the currently prevailing return. Most significantly, the investment at the optimal cost position on the *LRAC* curve of the firm involves more than just the requirement that opportunity costs be based on the absolutely lowest acceptable (longrun) returns; it extends to the principle that *under a longrun focus* owner-entrepreneurs must require the assurance that *given the worst expected condition*—i.e., the situation where competition has pressed the firm's price over time to the lowest likely set of net returns—the firm would still be competitive with respect to the other (viable) members of the industry. In other words, the lowest cost point on its classical *LRAC* curve (i.e., the certainty, or a risk only adjusted *LRAC* curve) must provide a viable competitive position; otherwise, the firm can never exist in the longrun under conditions of competitive entry and exit in the economy. This principle, which later on will be derived deductively, serves as a fundamental postulate (or axiom) in our system of thought, as it also did (albeit only implicitly) in the classical theory of perfect competition. It was surprisingly overlooked completely in the Chamberlinean theory of monopolistic competition, probably because writers immersed in classical microtheory typically had fudged over the required meaning of lost opportunity costs.

It warrants final mention that the longrun optimal cost requirement does not violate but rather conforms to the opportunity cost concept formulated in Section II as equations (1) and (2). The essential difference is that in equations (1) and (2) the opportunity cost of the human factor of production, i.e., of the owner-entrepreneur of a firm with a limited

[8] We might consider here in note the possibility of renting more land or capital if technological requirements exceed the quantity possessed by the entrepreneur or, given the same conditions, of having the entrepreneur apply more service inputs than he typically wants to provide. Under opposite circumstances, the possibility of renting out excess land or capital or providing some services elsewhere might be considered. With respect to the initial possibility set, it is suggested that an inadequate land or equity investment will cost the borrower a land or capital rental premium. In the same key, a normally inadequate work-time capacity would involve a premium for the extra effort required of the entrepreneur. These nonconformances may, therefore, be ruled out. In corresponding pattern, an extra cost will be likely to occur in disposing of any surplus land, capital, or service input units; thus the ownership of excessive land, capital, or service time must also be ruled out. It is, of course, true that if a high degree of intra and interindustry factor divisibility is assumed, excesses can be disposed of easily. However, complete factor divisibility would be unlikely *even if* production functions were linearly homogeneous.

lifetime, was considered. Now, our focus is on the longrun, and the viability of the firm over this period of time is being analyzed. It is as if the period of time considered in equations (1) and (2) involves r_j^a and e_j^e values for the period during which longrun entry and exit have been completed. To include uncertainty as a cost via equation (2) thus requires application of the opportunity cost rate and optimal investment total which would prevail after entry and exit of firms have occurred. But the present subject is more complicated than has thus far been suggested. Classical factor inputs are functional; the uncertainty component—on the entrepreneur's investment—is not. This distinction requires evaluation at this time.

Functional and Residual Returns

Service inputs, subject to any risk or uncertainty component which constrains men in their willingness to engage in an activity, clearly involve a functional performance. As a matter of definition which defers to classical practices, the land and capital inputs of the entrepreneur will be treated as functional inputs, subject in effect to the risk and uncertainty involved in their use. Let it be noted that the return for risk on capital will also be treated initially as a functional return, in a sense to reflect classical writings and essentially to isolate attention on the impact of behavioral uncertainty. Were it not for the evolution of economic thought which up to recent times had included only risk and not behavioral uncertainty as a basic property in microeconomic theory, the two could have easily been presented together in the initial formulation of our model. Indeed, the two will be joined in a modified version of the model presented later on in the paper. However, for the moment, the opportunity cost of risk in the subject industry (based on the range of returns described earlier in this paper) is considered to be part of the classical conception of average cost.

The classical *AC* curve of Figure 1 is thus presently defined to contain all explicit payments for land, labor, and capital, as well as the traditionally included implicit costs for land, labor, and capital. Payments required for investing under conditions of risk and for providing services subject to personal risks and uncertainties are therefore part of the classical *AC* curve. The overall conception of the model may be helped by realizing that all loan capital funds, as well as the entrepreneur's risk capital, can be conceived to reappear in the form of working and fixed capital. The sum of these capitals, in turn, will be referred to as the capital investment of the firm.[9] Most importantly, let it be stressed that only uncertainty on the capital investment is *excluded* at this time from the concept of classical costs.

The classical *AC* curve in Figure 1 thus relates (essentially) to functional performances. The *AC* adjusted cost curve differs from the classical *AC* curve to the extent that it includes *in addition to classical costs* the opportunity (fixed) cost for oligopolistic uncertainty. The part of the total income which is available in payment of the fixed cost (requirement) for uncertainty on the capital investment can be regarded as a residual return. This residual part of the total earned can *in the shortrun* be greater than, equal to, or less than the fixed cost requirement described above. We shall prove below, however, that only a tangency of the average revenue curve to the *AC* adjusted curve which occurs directly above the classical optimal average cost point can prevail in the longrun equilibrium. Let us reemphasize

[9] Observe the distinction that is being drawn between the risk and uncertainty portions of the entrepreneur's actual capital investment. That is to say, the entrepreneur's total capital investment is viewed in the form of working and fixed capital, including an intangible capital component reflecting the uncertainty of the investment. For the total capital, a total return is earned based on the productivity of the capital. This return includes a return required for risk on investment and a return required for uncertainty. Such conception enables the theorist to isolate uncertainty from risk, which practice is desirable given the fact that the literature of the past conceived exclusively of risk (and associated objective probabilities) in its theory of the competitive firm.

for a last time that our theory utilizes as its beginning point the amount of investment required for lowest cost production on the firm's *LRAC* curve *in both the lost opportunity and the selected activity*. This point of departure, or fundamental assumption if you prefer, has intuitive appeal. Nevertheless, we shall also establish its relevance in Section IV of the paper as a logical consequence of spatial economic interdependencies and competitive entry and exit. It will follow that the unique importance of the investment required for lowest possible production costs can accordingly be said to serve axiomatically in our framework of thought.

Tangency and Disequilibrium

Suppose a Chamberlinean tangency is assumed at *h* in Figure 2 for output *ob*. Apparently the firm is receiving its required return for uncertainty, with all other factor payments also being met. This Chamberlinean tangency is, however, not an equilibrium state in the imperfectly competitive market. An elemental but vital condition restricts the equilibrium tangency solution to a unique place on the *AC* adjusted curve, not any place, as explained below.

Consider the output *ob* and the related input quantity at this input-output point. The land and service energy applications are, in the aggregate, less at output *ob* than those ordered by optimality conditions in the best alternative. For example, at output *oe* total investment *oefj* is (must be) greater than the total investment *obgk* required in producing *ob*; if it were not, the firm would produce quantity *oe* at the minimum average cost *ef* and then store or discard quantity *eb*. To produce a smaller output than *oe* requires, in general, a smaller total cost (and investment) than that needed by *oe*; so, *obgk* must be less than *oefj*. *But* the fixed return for uncertainty *kghm* (= *jfdl*) that is transformed to the subject activity from the lost opportunity is based on the optimal cost investment *oefj*. For an investment less than *oefj*, a return for uncertainty less than *kghm* would appear to be sufficient. But note again, the uncertainty return allocable to uncertainty at output *ob* is indeed *kghm*. It is, therefore, manifest that a tangency at *h* marks a disequilibrium position which actually provides surplus returns and promotes entry. More generally, disequilibrium of some kind will be seen to apply to a tangency at a point such as *h* in Figure 2 on any other comparably adjusted *AC* curve of the same order as *AC* adjusted.

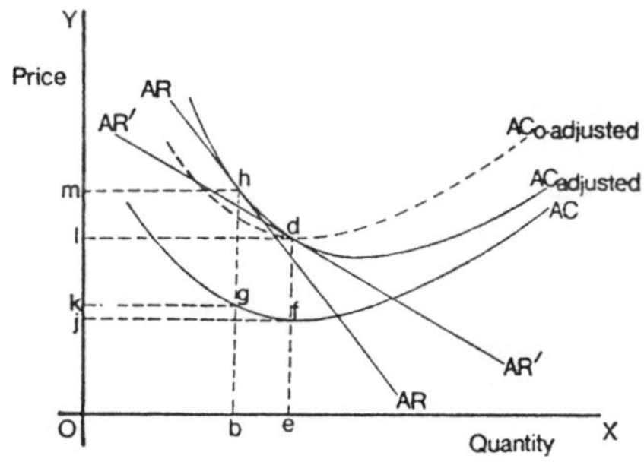

FIGURE 2

It may appear strange that tangency to the fixed cost adjusted *AC* curve at *h* induces entry. Even stranger is the implication that no other adjusted *AC* curve for the subject firm can be conceived (which would lie below *AC* adjusted at point *h*) to which point the tangency would be of equilibrium order. Related to this implication is the corollary that *no imputation rate* exists for less than optimum input which, in effect, would so compensate the manager(s) and other factors that neither entry, expansion, nor exit is induced. The analysis presented below explains in detail the uniqueness of the equilibrium-producing imputation rate.

Another Tangency and Disequilibrium

Let the *AR* curve tangent at *h* in Figure 2 be shifted (twisted, etc.) downward as a result of entry to what may appear as a stable equilibrium level where no further entry would occur. Conceive of the new *AR* curve (call it *AR**, but not drawn in Figure 2) as being tangent to some AC_0 "adjusted" curve. Let this AC_0 adjusted curve lie to the left of and be lower than the AC (fixed cost) adjusted curve of Figure 2 over outputs smaller than the optimal output *oe*. The AC_0 curve, therefore, has slightly flatter slopes over the output ranges noted above since the logic supporting it requires variable cost imputations throughout, and these imputations must sum to a value less than the fixed cost imputation assumed in Figure 2 for all outputs $0 \leq \chi < Oe$. (Note that beyond *Oe*, the conception of variable imputations would require AC_0 to rise above AC adjusted.) The actual marginal revenue (MR) viewable at the tangency of AR^* and AC_0 must, in turn, be greater than the accountant's marginal cost (MC). This is so because the tangency in question (for example, a tangency to AC_0 at output *ob*) involves equality between MR and the marginal cost value (MC_0) not MC. And MC_0 is of course $> MC$ since AC_0 implicitly includes an increasing *variable cost ascription to total cost*.[10] What one might contend *could appear* as a possible equilibrium point *to the entrepreneur* (and let us henceforth often call him the manager) actually involves an insufficient output to the engineers and the accountants of the firm, since $MR > MC$.[11] (We would suggest in fact that most owners are also opting for increased output so that they may attain their lost opportunity target.) It is only at a tangency to the fixed cost adjusted AC curve that $MR = MC$; but then other firms are induced to enter if the related output is in the environs of *ob*. It can, indeed, now be shown that the only stable-equilibrium point (insofar as concerns owners, potential owners, managers, engineers, and accountants) obtains at output *oe*.

Tangency and Equilibrium

Suppose new entry takes place after a tangency has existed at *h* in Figure 2. The AR curve thus falls below AC adjusted. Let the new return for uncertainty be perfectly commensurate with the investment *obgk*, by which we mean the rate of return corresponds to the rate optimally mapped from the best alternative, namely R^a of equation (1). But if this *were* the case, entrepreneurial factor inputs (capital, land, and/or services) would not be commensurate with the amounts ordered by the optimal alternative and planned for the selected activity; moreover, for reasons explained above, the engineering-accounting advice would be to expand since $MR > MC$. The factors, and more generally the firm, would sooner or later drop out of the market and be replaced by factors and a firm(s) of different size in a different location(s) whose members were possessed of different lost alternatives. Possibly a smaller size enterprise, such as a firm with single plant or smaller number of branch plants than the one assumed by *oe* in Figure 2 would enter the market. And for this firm, an output such as *ob could* mark its classical optimality. It may alternatively have been

[10] Note that the *limiting AC_0 curve* is the particular curve which *mirrors the classical AC curve*. This particular limiting form arises when the opportunity cost for uncertainty is ascribed as a variable cost which increases linearly with greater inputs. Such imputation (and related curve) would be governed by exactly the same law of variable proportions as that which gives shape to the classical AC curve. But this curve, or any other AC_0 curve which includes a partial variable cost imputation for uncertainty, would possess an MC_0 curve that is $> MC$. Thus, regardless of the assumptions underscoring the imputation, the change in total cost as inputs increase is greater by the value of whatever variable cost imputation is ascribed for uncertainty than is the change in total cost as output increases when no varying charge for uncertainty is included. In other words, MC_0, as defined, must always be greater than classical MC.

Note finally that the limiting form proposed above for the AC_0 curve and the alternative limiting form previously proposed for the adjusted AC curve—namely when the fixed cost ascription is made to the classical AC curve—signify that the MC curve which belongs to an AC adjusted curve must always be $\geq$ the classical accountant's or engineer's MC curve at competitive outputs $<$ *oe*. The equality sign holds, of course, only when the fixed cost adjusted AC curve is considered.

[11] Manifestly, the *ceteris paribus* impact of entry is for product (location) differentiation to decrease as substitutability increases; hence, the leftward-downward AR^* curve cannot be steeper than the original curve and, in turn, MR must be greater than MC at such output as *ob*.

the case that tangency at point *h* prevailed initially; then some entry, exit, and, in general, relocation of firms take place which in the net sense shifts the *AR* curve to *AR'*. Only at a tangency point related to the minimum classical cost point would stable equilibrium be reached. This result applies because it is only at such point that classical costs are completely covered while at the same time other income remains to compensate the entrepreneur in full for the prevailing level of oligopolistic uncertainty in the subject activity.[12]

It may appear to be a remarkable result that the shape (and slope) of the *AR* curve could (and would) change by exactly the right amount to produce a tangency to the *AC* adjusted curve at the point which happens to involve the particular input-output quantity at which classical optimality in cost obtains. But this requirement and result is no more surprising than (nor different from) the classical trilogy $AR = AC = MC$. It takes place in the imperfectly competitive economy for exactly the same reason that it would occur in a perfectly competitive world; namely, an excess (or deficit) otherwise exists in returns stemming from the prevailing demand conditions and competition *in the industry* compared to what the opportunity cost (parameter), *based as it is on returns throughout the economy*, would require for risk (and uncertainty). The size and sites of plants and firms are alterable in the oligopolistic economy over time. Economic surpluses or deficiencies produce—via competitive entry, relocation, and exit—the forces which change the number of firms, the extent of competition over a given market area, and hence the height and slope of the *AR* curve.[13]

[12] H. Demsetz [4; 5] reaches a similar conclusion by conceiving of variations in selling inputs which enable alternative quantities of the good to be sold at respectively optimal prices. Because he assumes that there are alternative selling input levels and that the selling cost function conforms to classical principles of diminishing returns, he obtains a bell-shaped average revenue curve. He refers to this curve as *MAR* (where *M* stands for *mutatis mutandis*). When the *MAR* curve is tangent to the classical (inverted bell-shaped) average cost curve at the minimum point of the *AC* curve, a nonexcess capacity longrun equilibrium exists. By taking the selling cost applicable to this long run position as a fixed cost and by adding it to the classical average cost curve, he obtains a figure in his later article [6] similar to our Figure 2. Significantly, however he recognizes that after sufficient entry or exit had taken place, the *MAR* curve may be tangent to the *AC* curve at other positions than the least cost combination point. If the tangency takes place before or after the lowest cost point of *AC*, rationalization of size by firms would often occur. Unfortunately from the standpoint of uniqueness of result, there is no assurance that rationalization of size by firms must occur. As Professor Demsetz points out with respect to an initial tangency of Chamberlinean kind, one firm with multiple plants may not replace two firms with a resulting decrease in cost "if the differentiated products are not identically produced" [4, 28]. Moreover, if the effect of entry is such as initially to elicit tangency between *MAR* and *AC* over the decreasing returns to scale portion of *AC*, rationalization to optimal size occurs only if "no diseconomies of firm size (in contrast to plant size)" exist [4, 29]. Finally, he notes that the *MAR* curve may not be bell-shaped, but rather might be linear of negative slope. A myriad of possibilities thus exists, and his attempt to prove that monopolistically (or imperfectly) competitive markets are theoretical mappings from pure competition is reduced to the thought that anything might exist, including no excess capacity.

The present paper has proceeded differently, claiming that the one *is in fact a strictly one to one and onto mapping from the other*. Moreover, rather than utilize a strange *MAR* curve (which is, in fact, an irrelevant dynamically formulated *AR* curve), the momentary-relevant static *AR* curve is used with the opportunity cost of behavioral uncertainty being revealed as the force promoting a stable efficient equilibrium. The conditions of competitive free entry and exit alone are required in imperfectly competitive markets. Critiques of Demsetz' theory by Archibald [1], Barzel [2], and Schmalensee [25], unlike that proposed here, are in terms of Demsetz' selling cost. They tend to stress classical negativity of the *AR* curve and, in effect, to ignore Demsetz' *MAR* curve; in the process, they derive Chamberlinean results, in contrast to the unique equilibrium claimed herein.

[13] In an economy where firms may have different numbers of plants and hence different levels of lowest *LRAC* curves [14; 10], the exit of some firms may lead to entry of a larger number of *smaller* firms. The new combination of smaller size firms signifies a larger number of alternative sources of the good, decreasing product differentiation, and a greater total output. This set of changes would produce leftward-shifted and flattened *AR* curves coterminous with the leftward-shifted *AC* curves of the new firms. Correspondingly, other sets of changes could be elicited, depending on the economic situation which prevails. What is uniformly the case with respect to changes is that the opportunity cost parameter for returns under uncer-

Indeed, it will shortly be demonstrated that the industry can be (and will be in selected situations) marked by all sizes of firms (large and small) such that, in effect, a fully continuous output total applies rather than discrete jumps in output resulting from a discrete number of homogeneous firms. In this forthcoming demonstration, we shall also stress the idea that imputations for lost opportunities can be added in a step-by-step manner to the lowest level (of the explicit cost only) average cost curve. In the process, the generality of our theory will be manifest.[14]

IV. A GENERAL THEOREM

In contrast to preceding analysis, though yielding the same conclusion, let us henceforth conceive of a classical *AC* curve which does *not* include any payment or imputation for the services of hired managers. (Thus the classical *AC* curve that is henceforth depicted does not include the actual salaries paid nor the implicit payments which would apply in the longrun.) More generally, all imputations for entrepreneur's land, capital investment, and services are excluded from the classical *AC* curves now being described. These exclusions make generalization of the theory possible, such that the theory can be seen to relate either to markets where the cost of distance is unimportant (and uncertainty possibly nonexistent), or, of course, to markets where the cost of distance is actually significant. The following theorem can (and will) then be established: ***Different size firms of different efficiencies may be viable in the longrun, but only at their own functional optimal cost positions.***

To understand the theorem, define *the most efficient* firm, i.e., the optimal-optimorum firm, as that firm which conforms perfectly to the prevailing state of arts and produces its optimal output at the same or lower classical average cost than can any other firm. A direct consequence of this definition of efficiency is that the classical average cost of the optimal-optimorum firm is lower *over all outputs* before imputations are effected than the lowest classical average cost of all nonoptimal-optimorum firms. But though the optimal-optimorum firm can produce any output at lowest classical average cost, our theorem nevertheless requires that in order for this firm to prove to be viable, it must produce at its own optimal cost output in the longrun. This output is necessary because even if it is now assumed that managers do not require full opportunity costs from the activity in question, so that, in effect, their services are imagined to be perfectly divisible, and all they require (as was assumed previously in the paper) is the same *rate* of return (equation (1) Section II) on their input applications as that which they required at their optimal cost input point, the firm becomes high in cost over all of its nonoptimal input-output points. In other words, even applying only the same opportunity cost *rate* (rather than a premium rate) for any nonoptimal output raises its adjusted *AC* level *for that output* above the level of any other firm which happens to produce this output at its own lowest classical average cost.

The result stated above can be understood by focusing attention on the most efficient

tainty is determined by the general equilibrium parameters of the economy at large. The specific returns in any industry (i.e., the *AR* curve) may be relatively favorable or unfavorable at any point in time.

[14] Though our system of thought centered attention on the longrun optimal cost investment, and thus in turn on the size of firm that would exist in the longrun, static shortrun *pictures* could have been conceived of by the reader throughout most of the analysis given above. The only difference in requirement would have been that while equations (1) and (2) of Section II would still establish the lost opportunity rate of return, the lowest cost point on a *given* classical shortrun *AC* curve rather than the optimal cost investment on the classical *LRAC* curve would have provided the investment total to which the opportunity cost rate would be applied at that given moment of time. Diagrammatic conceptions of tangencies, such as at point *h* in Figure 2, for all shortrun firms would, in turn, then appear essentially the same as when the longrun optimal cost investment is used, except that the set of optimal size shortrun investments planned by owner-entrepreneurs would have to be conceived of as asymptotically approaching *from moment to moment* the optimal size investment of the longrun.

firm's optimal cost output and conceiving of another firm of the same capacity which produces the same product at a slightly lesser efficiency (i.e., at a slightly higher classical average cost). After the imputations for owner-managers are made, such (second-best) firm's adjusted *AC* curve at that output must be on the same level as the optimal-optimorum firm if it is to be viable. But then conceive of another firm which is so staffed and organized that its optimal output is slightly smaller than that of the second-best firm just considered. Let the same opportunity *rate* of return apply to the services of its owner-manager(s) as that applicable to the second-best firm; total required return for this third-best firm is, accordingly, still less than for the second-best firm. After all imputations, its altered *AC* curve is on the same level at its optimal cost output *as* that of the second-best firm *and* the optimal-optimorum firm at their optimal cost outputs. Let us next assume that the demand allocable to the optimal-optimorum firm warrants for it only that output which happens to be optimal for the third-best firm. The optimal-optimorum size firm cannot survive because after imputing its lost opportunity cost rate at the subject output (i.e., ascribing T_1 in Figure 3 at output *ob* to the *cl LRAC* (curve), its relevant *AC* adjusted curve at that output is revealed to be higher than that of the third-best firm.[15] The theorem is, therefore, established. Competi-

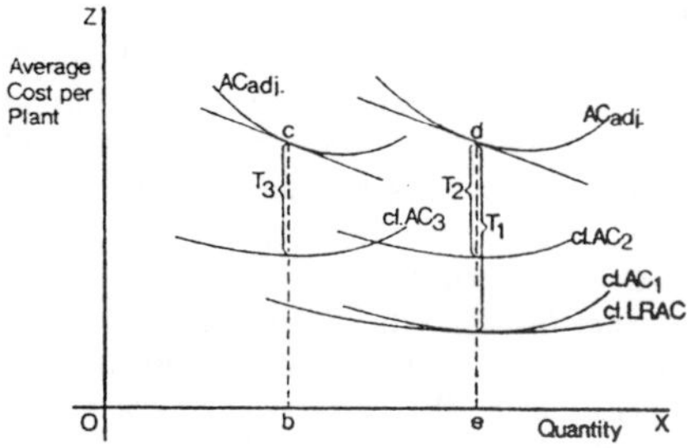

FIGURE 3

tively viable firms are those for which the allocable demand enables production at the firms' optimal cost positions.

To view this vital theorem in a slightly different way, observe that after imputations (such as the optimal cost rate R^a of equation (1) or, in fact, a higher rate than R^a) are effected for services at some smaller than optimal output point, the adjusted cost of the optimal-optimorum firm (or one of similar capacity) would be greater at such non-optimal cost (smaller) output than that of a smaller size firm which would produce that given output optimally. If the demand allocable to all firms is assumed to be the same and unchangable, and of smaller magnitude than that given by the curve tangent to *AC adj* at *d*, related (large) size firms must eventually leave the market. They will exit in favor of a set of smaller firms which, in the equilibrium described by Figure 2, would produce the subject output optimally; alternatively, the manager(s) of these (larger) firms will leave the industry in the longrun, being replaced by men of lesser ability who effect a smaller capacity for the subject firm.

It is thus proposed that a longrun equilibrium in imperfectly competitive markets may be conceived. These markets may be marked by the presence of a few optimal-optimorum size firms whose managers have the same capacity for work, employ the same technology, are of the same size, and produce the same output as that of rival managers. At that moment in time, nonoptimal-optimorum

[15] Figure 3 depicts shortrun plant sizes for Firms 1, 2, and 3, and the classical *LRAC* curve for Firm 1. Recall in this regard that a fully variable input treatment of the lost opportunity costs of uncertainty would yield lowest adjusted costs for Firms 1 and 2 at the classical lowest cost output *oe* and for Firm 3 at *ob*. (Cf. AC_0 of Figure 2 at point *d* with *AC* adjusted at that point.) Figure 3 thus depicts the longrun equilibrium position where firms which are of similar as well as different capacities are each using their optimal shortrun (equal longrun) plant sizes in producing their optimal cost outputs. In other words, including all classical *LRAC* curves and all variable and fixed cost adjusted *LRAC* curves in Figure 3 would involve corresponding points of lowest classical and variable adjusted *LRAC* curves at outputs *oe* and *ob* respectively.

firms may also comprise the market. They may be smaller in size or even of the same size as the optimal-optimorum firm, as in Figure 3. In fact, only a quasi-efficient result may obtain in the sense that there may exist in a particular market only firms which are not characterizable as the optimal-optimorum firm(s).[16] In either event, since the managers of these firms are slightly less efficient men, they produce the good at a slightly higher average cost (before the imputations for services are made) than the cost of the optimal-optimorum firm. The common reference point for all surviving firms is their individual production at their own classical optimum cost points.

V. CONCLUSIONS AND GENERALIZATIONS

This paper contends that space implies oligopoly and that oligopoly involves behavioral uncertainty. This uncertainty is a supply-determining cost which rises monotonically as the uncertainty increases. In the *ex post* sense, the cost of uncertainty converges to a fixed value. Imputing this cost to the classical average cost curve brings about an adjusted average cost curve. It is only at the tangency point to the adjusted average cost curve which lies directly above the classical optimal average cost point that windfall profits or losses are eliminated and stability exists. Corresponding efficiency can be shown for locational distributions and the market areas of firms. But—as was stated at the outset of the paper—this facet of the space economy must be deferred to other writings [14, Chapter 13].

The above statements relate essentially to Sections I, II, and III of the paper. They would have applied to Section IV as well *if* the difference in the average cost curves had been predicated only on the cost of uncertainty on the capital investment. The fact of the matter is that *all* imputations were left out of the conception of the classical AC curve in Section IV. This practice was followed in order to stress the idea that imputations for lost opportunities can be added in a step-by-step manner to the lowest level (of the explicit cost only) average cost curve. Then, just so long as some residual return is required, an adjusted average cost curve lying above a classical average cost curve can be conceptualized, as in Figures 1–3. The residual return attributable to the factor (or force) which accounts for the adjusted cost curve is conditioned by the twin requirements that all factor inputs must conform to the technology of the selected industry as well as to the best alternative. This means, in turn, that only the optimal output point on the classical AC curve reflects the input quantities required for longrun viability. This input-output level alone marks the basis for successful longrun *competition* in imperfectly competitive markets.

List of Symbols

A = A payoff for risk
u_i = A payoff for uncertainty
P_i = A probability applicable to a risk payoff
X_i = An expected payoff for risk given an uncertainty i
R^a = Opportunity cost income rate in alternative activity
M^a = Working lifetime in alternative activity
r^a = Net revenues in alternative activity
e^a = Energy expenditures in alternative activity
i = Discount factor
M^s = Expected lifetime in subject activity
r^s = Linearized net revenue requirement in subject activity
e^s = Energy expenditure in subject activity.

[16] See [8] for an application of probability theory with conclusions corresponding to those given here.

REFERENCES

1. ARCHIBALD, G. C., "Chamberlin versus Chicago." *Review of Economic Studies*, October 1961, 2–28.
2. BARZEL, Y., "Excess Capacity in Monopolistic Competition." *Journal of Political Economy*, September–October 1970, 1142–1149.
3. CHAMBERLIN, E. M. *Theory of Monopolistic Com-*

petition. Cambridge: Harvard University Press, 1935.

4. DEMSETZ, H., "The Nature of Equilibrium in Monopolistic Competition." *Journal of Political Economy*, February 1959, 21–30.
5. ———, "The Welfare and Empirical Implications of Monopolistic Competition." *Economic Journal*, September 1964, 623–641.
6. ———, "Do Competition and Monopolistic Competition Differ?" *Journal of Political Economy*, January–February 1968, 146–148.
7. DEWEY, D., "Imperfect Competition No Bar to Efficient Production." *Journal of Political Economy*, February 1958, 24–33.
8. FARRELL, M. J., "Some Elementary Selection Processes in Economics." *Review of Economic Studies*, July 1970, 305–319.
9. FRIEDMANN, J. and W. ALONSO. *Regional Development and Planning*. Cambridge: MIT Press, 1964.
10. FURUBOTN, E., "Long-Run Analysis and the Form of the Production Function." *Economia Internazionale*, February 1970, 3–35.
11. GREENHUT, MELVIN. *Plant Location in Theory and in Practice*. Chapel Hill: University of North Carolina Press, 1956.
12. ———, "The Decision Process and Entrepreneurial Returns." *Manchester School*, September 1966, 247–267.
13. ———, "The Spatial and Nonspatial Firm." *Weltwirtschaftliches Archiv*, September 1970, 87–113.
14. ———. *A Theory of Firm in Economic Space*, 2nd printing. Austin: Lone Star Publishing Company, 1974.
15. ———, M. HWANG, and H. OHTA, "Observations on the Shape and Relevance of the Spatial Demand Function." *Econometrica*, June 1975.
16. HIBDON, JAMES. *Price and Welfare Theory*. New York: McGraw-Hill, 1969.
17. HOOVER, E. M. *Location and Economic Activity*. New York: McGraw-Hill, 1946.
18. KALDOR, N., "Professor Chamberlin on Monopolistic and Imperfect Competition." *Quarterly Journal of Economics*, May 1938, 513–529.
19. KNIGHT, FRANK. *Risk, Uncertainty, and Profit*. Boston: Houghton Mifflin Company, 1921.
20. LEWIS, W. A., "Competition in Retail Trade." *Economica*, August 1945, 202–234.
21. LÖSCH, AUGUST. *Die räumliche Ordnung der Wirtschaft*. Jena, Germany: Gustav Fischer, 1944.
22. MACHLUP, FRITZ. *The Economics of Sellers' Competition*. Baltimore: The Johns Hopkins Press, 1952.
23. ROBINSON, JOAN. *The Economics of Imperfect Competition*. London: Macmillan, 1934.
24. ROSS, WILLIAM. *Business in a Free Society*. Columbus: Charles E. Merrill Books, 1966.
25. SCHMALENSEE, R., "A Note on Monopolistic Competition and Excess Capacity." *Journal of Political Economy*, May–June 1972, 586–591.
26. STEVENS, BENJAMIN, "Linear Programming and Location Rent." *Journal of Regional Science*, Winter 1961, 15–26.
27. ———, "Location Theory and Programming Models: The von Thünen Case." *Regional Research Institute Discussion Paper Series*, November 1967,
28. VON NEUMANN, J. and O. MORGANSTERN. *The Theory of Games and Economic Behavior*. Princeton: Princeton University Press, 1947.

[17]

Mr. Gripsrud and a Theory of Oligopoly

By

M. L. Greenhut

I. Introduction

In view of limited space, I will confine myself essentially to answering just the specific arguments raised by Mr. Gripsrud rather than providing the more general formulations which could be set forth. However, before we can proceed with direct answers, it is essential that we establish the epistemological basis for the theory in question; i. e., what does the theory signify in the purely theoretical sense distinct from the particular policies one can derive from it? We shall use Mr. Gripsrud's own generally fine summary of the theory as our departure point, albeit with one basic change in overall view.

II. The Requisite Perspective

Mr. Gripsrud is correct when he states that I consider my theory to be isomorphic to and interchangeable with the theory of pure competition. But what an isomorphic system is and what interchangeability signifies in economics must be explained, especially since we shall see that interchangeability applies only in a limited special sense.

By isomorphic systems — in the context of my theory — we mean that the long-run position of the spatially competitive oligopolist is directly counterpart to that of the purely competitive seller as technological efficiency is shown to eventuate while factors cover their opportunity costs and consumer wants are maximized. The essential relationships reflect identical goals and means to reach them and the result is corresponding functional factor returns in the two systems, *ceteris paribus*. The "basic" difference is that factor scarcity in my theory is increased by whatever uncertainty applies to the factor; hence the factor's marginal revenue product is, in turn, increased. A factor return "a" in one system converts, therefore, to a related return, call it "k" in the other system.

From a strictly scientific rather than metaphysical standpoint, the most important difference in factor returns is that due to the owner of the firm on his capital investments, for it is this factor which seemingly generates different production signals; however, though the behavioral uncertainty prevalent in oligopoly markets requires different entrepreneurial returns in the subject economic systems, and relates in turn to differently sloped average revenue schedules, these differences stand essentially alone. Final results are fundamentally the same. One might anticipate, accordingly, that the advantage of conceptualizing a negatively sloping average revenue schedule would be vital for short-run problems since the basic long-run economic results are isomorphic. This is indeed the contention we shall enter here. But first let us move the background picture towards completion.

Our theory proposes specifically that each factor still exists albeit different returns and scarcities may apply; most vital, *profit or loss promotes entry and exit, ceteris paribus, to the limit where factors earn their opportunity costs, consumer wants are fulfilled, and efficiency prevails.* Nevertheless, as we indicated above, many basic differences prevail with respect to short-run problems notwithstanding the long-run isomorphism designated here. Lest misinterpretation arises, however, as to what our long-run identity signifies, we must note what is *not* implied by our *economic* isomorphism, after which we can quickly spell out what it *does* imply. In the process, the meaning of interchangeability will be established as well as the basis provided for evaluating Mr. Gripsrud's critiques.

Our isomorphic relation does *not* imply that if functional factors are also subject to uncertainty, the final long-run equilibrium in the spatial economy differs from the purely competitive economy only by way of price levels. Industry outputs will also generally be different. What alone must *appear* the same in the economist's view (apart from entrepreneurial goals) is production at the least-cost combination *and* the maximizing of consumer wants under the prevailing technology and cultural (institutional) values. It is *in this sense* that the one system is isomorphic to the others and that the theory of the spatial firm can be considered as a fully general theory[1]. Mr. Gripsrud's initial critique, we shall see, fails to

[1] In the theory under consideration, we can go from the one to the other system easily and quickly. Since the special case of pure competition was never before viewed to contain oligopolistic equilibrium (or say spatial properties) and itself can be derived from our model of competitive *spatial* oligopolists (as Mr. Gripsrud suggests over his pages 509 sqq.), we propose the theory of the spatial firm as the general theory.

recognize this type of correspondence; his other critiques fail to recognize that policies and paradigms may differ as one centers attention on, say, the right side rather than the left.

III. Critique 1

Mr. Gripsrud suggests that though my concept of uncertainty is acceptable to some extent, it fails because it is institutionally based rather than natural as is land rent. More pointedly, he contends that any return for uncertainty on the owner's capital investment is economically different from the classical-functional, noninstitutional origins of the differential rent payments due to land, skills, etc. But his argument is spurious. The payment for behavioral uncertainty is itself inextricably mixed with any payment for uncertainty as a physical (natural) phenomenon; indeed, the same relations hold true for any differential payment, such as for land fertilities. Even more importantly, there is no economic difference between a factor of production requiring a return commensurate with its (his) marginal revenue product *in payment for* its (his) scarce fertility (skill) and the capital factor requiring (and warranting) a return for its scarcity attributable to institutional forces. The economic results are the same whether or not scarcity is of institutional or natural origin, as the greater the shortage or relative advantage of a factor, the greater is its marginal revenue product[1]. What counts in any economic system is the interaction between performances, institutional and natural, as expressed in the valuation of factors resulting from demands set by consumers and government, *ad infinitum*[2]. It is this mix which distinguishes the social from the physical sciences.

[1] Mr. Gripsrud suggests that uncertainty depends on the organization of industry and accordingly that as industry structure changes, so does uncertainty. He proposes that uncertainty is, therefore, not analogous to differential land rent and cannot be treated the same way. The fact that the level of uncertainty varies with entry or exit of firms does not, however, present any problems. Differential land rents also vary with entry or exit, such that in a classical short-run situation we can conceive of differential land rent increasing while profits decrease as more producers of a given crop enter the field.

[2] True distinction is that basic inputs warrant compensation for a functional performance while uncertainty on the owner's investment generates residual payment; the distinction between natural uncertainty and institutional uncertainty is meaningless in *the context of our theory* which stresses their inextricable mix. But even the functional-residual difference that I contend *does apply* to owner's capital in our framework of thought is *non sequitur* in the context of Mr. Gripsrud's comments. This follows because the classification only serves as a theoretical distinction for *viewing* the returns to the factors of production. *It does not alter the point of minimum cost* on the classical (technological) average cost curve, *and hence it does not affect the equilibrium input-output* point in the market.

IV. Critique 2

Mr. Gripsrud further objects to the theory on the grounds that the cost functions are, may I say, idealistic. One gains the impression from his paper that in his view the classical cost curves exist only in the mind's-eye of the economist distinct from the cost functions and heterogeneous size plants that actually prevail in our world. Of course, Mr. Gripsrud is actually objecting to all microeconomic theory not just mine. But even so, I am not sure he is correct. My answers below relate, however, only to my own theory, though I must refer him for complete answer to the book he referenced rather than to my article, since upwards to 20 pages were devoted to the subject cost functions in that book[1].

For present purposes, conceive of multi-plant firms, such as the BASF complex in Germany. Also conceive of the contrasting sizes of firms that exist in any country, such as the generally unknown small Granite City Steel Company in the United States compared with the well-known giant-size U. S. Steel Company. In any multi-plant, multi-office world where different size firms exist, we can conceive in the long run of a continuous cost function in which economies and diseconomies *do prevail.* Moreover, in such world (and theoretic conception), each firm need not have plants of homogeneous size; instead, they would orient the size of each plant to the market space served by that plant. The result in the space economy is that both a short- and long-run set of average costs can be conceived which, *in the limit,* conforms to the classical conceptions of costs.

V. Critiques 3 and 4

Mr. Gripsrud also objects (3) to the average revenue schedule that I used. He proposes instead that interdependencies exist in the utilities derived from products sold by oligopolists. More generally, he proposes (4) that in the complex world of the business community, decisions are not simply made as one would have them made in the context of economic theory. He implies that the economic problems of our time cannot be readily resolved by the classical theory of the firm, as set forth in the conception of pure competition.

I could hardly agree with Mr. Gripsrud more. But he takes my assertion that my theory of a competitive oligopoly is isomorphic to the theory of pure competition out of context. What is most relevant to the subject at hand is that businessmen are *not mechanical robots* reacting perfectly to predictions of *long-run* states; rather they are men operating in a world of uncertainty many of whom *tend to prefer leaving or raising prices* in

[1] M. L. Greenhut, *A Theory of the Firm in Economic Space*, 2nd Print., Austin, 1974, pp. 178 sqq.

the presence of inadequate sales rather than lowering them, at least in the very short run. Moreover, in no way at all does the theory of the spatial firm preclude recognition of short-run inflexibilities; by being based on oligopoly theory and hence behavioral uncertainty, it contains different paradigms than those of classical economics. Most important of all, any focus on oligopoly markets would prompt the scholar to view businessmen as activists not robots in economic affairs. The theorist might, for example, explain inflation differently than would an economist who thinks in terms of the purely competitive market alone. The former might conceive of businessmen who tend to view demand as inelastic above prevailing prices during inflationary periods. Certainly many firms price in this backlight successfully during such periods with the effect of generating a belief of perspicacity among the managers of viable firms. This attitude appears to prevail rather than the counter-view that even though high prices succeeded, lower prices might have done even better at that time, depending of course on the elasticities at the subject prices on what would then have been a *rightward-shifted demand curve*. So a theorist focusing on oligopoly markets could conclude that attempts to control inflation must recognize the attitude of the managers of big firms and their tendency to raise prices even when credits is tight.

My theory, as Mr. Gripsrud noted, is dedicated essentially to long-run phenomena. It is this sense alone that I proposed an economy which produces certain results, ceteris paribus, and for which the basic conclusions under competitive oligopoly correspond to those of pure competition. In the short run, as indicated above, one would have to evaluate problems quite differently. But let me explain this critical thought in somewhat further detail.

Several pages in the subject book were devoted to emphasizing how different my economic policies would be compared to economists whose orientation lies along the lines of the theory of pure competition. I pointed to such differences notwithstanding the isomorphisms of the long-run structures of the two frameworks of thought, since predictions of short-run effects by the respective theories need not, of course, be identical. My theory of wages *and* of the impact of labor unions would be quite different from that of the followers of pure competition. My policies concerning excise taxes and income taxes would also contrast sharply from theirs. As Mr. Gripsrud observes, my approach to antitrust statutes would be of substantially different order[1]. And as suggested above, my approach to inflation would also be different from that of economists who conceive only of pure competition.

[1] For details, see my "An Economic Theory for Use in Antitrust Cases", *University of Houston Law Review*, January 1970, pp. 318 sqq.

VI. Other Critiques

Mr. Gripsrud suggested that my theory of competitive oligopoly was a limited view of imperfect competition since monopolistic competition was unfortunately left out. However, in no economy where the cost of distance is significant can there be monopolistic competition of the order conceived of by Chamberlin. Even in the "hair-cutting" industry, the simple act of crossing streets to obtain a hair cut from an alternative shop involves a cost. Though there may be *many many* barbershops in, say, Hamburg, only a few alternative sources of supply are open to a given consumer. Each barber is, in turn, an oligopolist tied interdependently *as if by a chain* to others located nearest to him. Chamberlin recognized this relation in Appendix C of his book but ignored it in the body of his great work.

Another critique warrants mention here. Mr. Gripsrud asserted that the theory of the spatial firm contained only the price dimension. He based this assertion strictly on the subject article. But this is not true even with respect to the article as the number of variables in our proposed analytical framework depends on the subject matter of basic interest to its user. Other variables, such as different kinds of spatial pricing, various levels of competition, and so forth can be included, to say nothing of the spatial heterogeneities of resources, product types, locations, demand curves, etc. one can assume. In fact, in a forthcoming book with H. Ohta[1], special attention will be focused on the relationships between discriminatory pricing over space and nondiscriminatory (i. e., f. o. b. mill) spatial pricing, and in turn the resulting outputs as well as the impacts of these pricing types on market sizes and shapes; in fact, all of this will be evaluated under assumptions of *different* demand curve types, *different* levels of competition, *etc.*

Finally, Mr. Gripsrud's equations (1) and (2) imply my having claimed that the *utilities* received by all people in the space economy are greater than or equal to those obtained in the spaceless (purely competitive) world. But I am not claiming this at all. My claims are simply that (1) costly distance (i. e., economic space) rules out perfectly or purely competitive markets as well as monopolistically competitive markets, and that (2) under conditions of competitive oligopoly (not organized oligopoly or monopoly), long-run relationships prevail which correspond to those of purely competitive markets. The mere definition of distance as a cost would tend (I suggest) to reduce utilities ceteris paribus compared to what would hold if distance was, in effect, a free good.

---

[1] M. L. Greenhut and H. Ohta, *Spatial Prices and Market Areas*, Durham, 1975, forthcoming.

VII. Conclusions

May I sum up my reply to Mr. Gripsrud by noting: (1) I do not believe his critique of my position on differential payments for uncertainty is properly founded. But I readily recognize that a reading of only a single paper and/or even isolated parts of a book could easily cause the concern he had in this regard. I rather imagine, in fact, that had I been him, I too might have had the same concern. (2) As for his critique of my cost curve, here again I can only suggest my belief that what I set forth is appropriate. At the best, I would refer him to the original text for a more complete answer; at the least, the suggestions given above in this reply will hopefully resolve the matter under discussion. (3) As for his objection to my average revenue schedule, I can only propose that in theory we sometimes utilize conceptions which abstract sharply from the true world around us. But this does not make the theory wrong! (4) Possibly his most important critique really goes beyond the paper in question and was answered in the book. I would suggest, accordingly, that he misread my thesis that an unorganized (competitive) oligopoly market *is* isomorphic to the purely competitive market. What he is suggesting as helpful tools for analysis would be those that I *could* accept for *short-run matters* without loss of position. In other words, nothing in my theory of the spatial firm precludes his quest for new paradigms to shed light on selected problems uppermost in his mind. I too would join in this search, as I believe I have too often witnessed the error-prone use of market place theory as the guideline for short-run policies in a world of spatial interdependencies[1]. Indeed, Mr. Gripsrud, in no way at all do I wish to be identified with the practitioners of the purely competitive market place; rather, I would feel much more comfortable in your company provided you accept my thesis that until an entirely new and better theory is conceived which uncovers long-run tendencies in free enterprise systems, my theory of spatial oligopoly is clearly better than the theory of pure competition. To say the least, it reduces the possibility of errors in short-run policies[2].

---

[1] Example of a horror stemming therefrom is the Robinson-Patman Act in the United States.

[2] Greenhut, *A Theory of the Firm in Economic Space, op. cit.*, pp. 55—58; 353—369.

The Manchester School Vol LVII No. 3 September 1989
0025–2034 $2.50 248–261

A THEORY OF OLIGOPOLISTIC COMPETITION*

by
M. L. GREENHUT
Texas A&M University
and
W. J. LANE†
University of New Orleans

I INTRODUCTION

The view of economic markets referred to as "contestability" indicates that free entry (properly defined) is sufficient to result in optimal prices—i.e., Ramsey prices. (See Baumol, 1982; Baumol, Panzer and Willig, 1982; Baumol, Bailey and Willig, 1977; and Panzer and Willig, 1977.) This result holds even in a market where substantial economies of scale would dictate the existence of only one firm in long-run equilibrium. Hence, "contestability" has extended the efficient pricing result of perfect competition's "invisible hand" to oligopoly (and monopoly) markets. We show that in a competitive oligopoly market—i.e., with free entry—yet another welfare result can be added to the list derived by Baumol *et al.*: production will occur at minimum average cost.

"Contestability" indicates that an oligopolistic industry would choose the least cost method of producing any specific output level; we show that individual firms will produce at the output level which minimizes average cost. In the sense of production efficiency our analysis is in the same spirit as contestability. However, there are some major differences. First, the entry we envision is of a more traditional form, rather than the special "hit and run" type that they assume. Second, our result occurs because of changes in both the firm's cost relations and the demand function facing the firm, rather than from changes in the cost relation alone.

Our proposition stands in stark contrast to the view of oligopoly markets taken by many economists. Indeed, one group takes the extreme position that *all* oligopoly firms are equivalent in their price and output effects to a (non-contestable) monopoly. Professor J. K. Galbraith succinctly summarized this view when he stated that "numerous key industries are now dominated by a handful of huge firms, and modern microeconomics makes no

* Manuscript received 16.2.87; final version received 18.4.88.
† We would like to thank Charles Smithson, Bruce Benson, Chao-cheng Mai, Jack Meyer, Ming Hwang, Hiroshi Ohta, Jack Scheidell, Charles Stewart, Louis Phlips and Neil Dorward for their helpful suggestions and critiques. In particular, Professor Dorward's published challenges on Greenhut's writings along this line, as well as his subsequent critiques, advisories and suggestions for improving this paper can only be regarded as professionalism at its best.

real distinction between the monopoly of one firm and the tacit agreement of oligopoly of the few" (1981). A less extreme view, shared by many economists, is that oligopoly markets exhibit at least some elements of market power. For example, the non-cooperative Cournot/Nash oligopoly model with entry predicts that production will not take place at the point at which average cost is at its minimum, even though economic profits will be zero in the long run.

However, a developing literature takes a vastly different view of oligopoly behaviour. (See, for example, Benson, 1980a,b; Ohta, 1977; Demsetz, 1959, 1967, 1968, 1972.) M. L. Greenhut's spatial price theory (1956, 1974), in conjunction with the extensions and critiques of others (Ohta, 1976; Dorward, 1981a,b), also represents a departure from the traditional position.

The present paper will generalize Greenhut's spatial theory and demonstrate the existence of a technologically and allocatively efficient oligopoly economy.[1] Our analysis and final conclusion require one basic condition—free entry and exit. Two competing oligopoly firms can be enough to provide efficient market results.

We will show that the traditional oligopoly models have overlooked several important factors. First, they have ignored the fact that risk averse decision makers will have to be compensated for bearing the risk inherent in oligopoly situations. The average cost curves in existing models do not account for this cost and this understates the true costs facing entrepreneurs in oligopolistic markets. Second, the type of behaviour assumed in existing models produces short-run equilibria which are not long-run equilibria unless all firms are identical. We remedy these omissions by explicitly incorporating oligopolistic uncertainty into the costs of doing business and by positing a long-run equilibrium that is consistent with free entry and unequal-sized firms.

II Oligopolistic Behavioural Uncertainty

A distinction between risk and uncertainty was first made by Knight (1921). Since then some have sought to simplify this distinction to that covering situations (i.e., alternative states) for which the probabilistic outcomes are objectively determinable (risk) and those for which only subjectively determined probabilities can be assigned (uncertainty).

Whether or not this distinction coincides perfectly with that of Knight, it is the latter concept, assigning subjective probabilities to resolve states of uncertainty, that forms the subject matter of this paper. Certainly all firms face risks and uncertainties of various sorts in their day-to-day decision making. Their willingness to bear uncertainties is incorporated into the rate of

[1]This paper does not deal specifically with spatial oligopoly (locational) equilibrium. For a discussion of this topic, see Beckmann (1968); Eaton and Lipsey (1976, 1977); Capozza and Van Order (1980); Norman (1981); Greenhut (1956, 1978); and Greenhut and Hwang (1979).

return required by each industry. However, the characteristic that distinguishes oligopoly from other market structures is interdependence among firms. This creates a unique type of behavioural uncertainty among sellers who must concern themselves with rival firms' actions and reactions. We centre attention, therefore, on the role of the entrepreneur in subjectively ascertaining and dealing with the oligopolistic uncertainties to which his firm is subject. Both the explicit incorporation of oligopolistic uncertainty into the firm's decision-making apparatus and the subjective role of the entrepreneur in this decision differentiate our model of oligopoly from most other such models.

Oligopolistic uncertainty exists because the essence of an oligopoly market is interdependence—each firm's actions affect the profitability of all other firms. Since no one firm can perfectly anticipate either the actions of its rivals or how its rivals will react to its own actions, uncertainty is inherent in this market structure. Note further that oligopolistic uncertainty is fundamentally different from the uncertainty that exists in the other market structures. In the other market structures—e.g., competition—the uncertainty that exists is the result of the unpredictable behaviour of consumer demand. Oligopolists face this risk but also face the uncertainty that results from the unpredictable behaviour of rivals. This rivalry places the firm into a "game" situation where the firm's actions will evoke unpredictable responses from rivals. Non-oligopolistic firms also face risks and uncertainties, but oligopolists face all these *plus* the unpredictabilities of rivalrous behaviour. We will be using the terms behavioural uncertainty and oligopolistic uncertainty interchangeably below to describe the situation that arises in oligopolistically competitive markets.

Any theory of oligopoly, by definition, considers the interdependence that relates to this uncertainty, but until now no model has explicitly incorporated the costs of bearing it. A multitude of other oligopoly models posit possible ways that firms may incorporate interaction into their decision making and the very number of such models reflects the uncertainty that economists have as to how firms interact. In this paper, we explicitly recognize and account for the oligopolistic (behavioural) uncertainty which exists in markets with few firms—an uncertainty that is over and above any other risk or uncertainty that may arise in competitive markets. We also model how risk averse firms will demand a rate of return over and above that of perfect competitors in order to induce a willingness to bear this uncertainty. Actually, it is uncertainty, not risk, that firms are averse to in this case, but we will substitute the more common, though inaccurate, nomenclature.

Our emphasis is thus on uncertainty rather than risk; the behavioural action in question is not objectively measurable. Nevertheless, entrepreneurs will make a subjective estimate of the expected rate of return that each will require before entering the market. This required rate of return on investment is then an opportunity cost corresponding to "normal" profit. It will be incorporated into the firm's cost curves as discussed below. Although the rate of return in question is arrived at subjectively, we will show that, in the long-run equilibrium, all oligopolists in a given activity share a common assessment of the opportunity cost of behavioural uncertainty, and thus will demand a common rate of return for bearing this uncertainty. This commonality exists only in the assessment of the amount of uncertainty and not in beliefs about behaviour itself. This uncertainty does not go away in the long run since firms still face the possibility that rivals will react unpredictably and therefore still face market uncertainty.

Furthermore, the return necessary to compensate entrepreneurs for bearing oligopolistic uncertainty will differ from the return earned by functional inputs. In classical theory, returns on the proprietor's land, labour and capital stock are recognized as opportunity costs that must be added to the explicit cost of the firm. These imputed costs relate to functional performances on the part of the relevant factors of production. Our point is that, in addition to these functional returns, there exists an uncertainty return. Since behavioural uncertainty characterizes an oligopolistic industry, entrepreneurs in that industry will demand a minimum expected return before they will be willing to commit their personal talents and financial resources to that market. This return will be based on their subjective assessment of the uncertainties involved and on their subjective level of risk (uncertainty) aversion. And, as with the minimum profit necessary to keep the entrepreneur's services, the imputed costs for oligopolistic uncertainty is a residual return. Hence, the cost of competitive oligopolistic uncertainty is independent of the level of output produced, i.e., the cost of this oligopolistic uncertainty is a fixed cost. It will be a function of the size of investment made and not of the output decision that occurs after the investment is in place.

III The Impact of Competitive Oligopolistic Uncertainty on Cost

So far, we have demonstrated that the classical average cost curve is insufficient for an oligopolistic market. To those explicit and implicit costs reflected in the classical cost curve, the cost of competitive oligopolistic uncertainty must be added. Let us now demonstrate how this will affect the nature of the equilibria that obtains.

The traditional result that all oligopoly markets—even oligopoly markets characterized by competitive entry and exit—are inherently inefficient is predicated on the existence of what we refer to as a Chamberlin (1946) equilibrium. Such an equilibrium is illustrated in Fig. 1. In this figure, the average cost curve, AC_c, is the neoclassical—Marshallian—average cost curve. That is, the average cost curve includes all of the classical imputations; so, differentials for skill, land fertility, etc., are ascribed to the *AC* curves of the inframarginal firms.

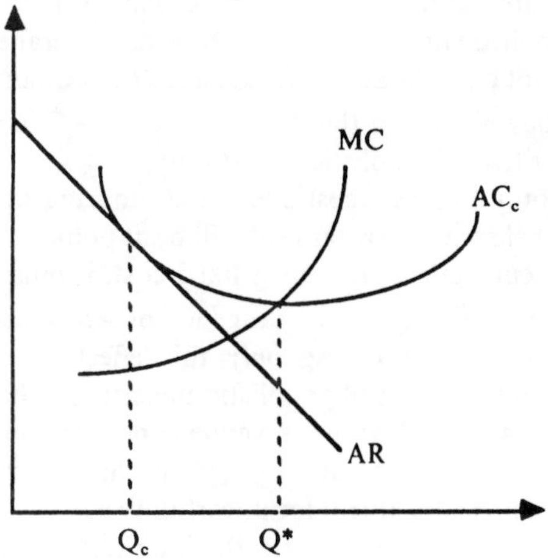

FIG. 1

Given free entry and exit in this market, the average revenue will be shifted so as to establish a tangency equilibrium with the Marshallian AC curve. In Fig. 1, this tangency occurs at an output level we have denoted as Q_c. And since this tangency will necessarily occur at an output level less than that associated with minimum average cost ($Q_c < Q^*$ in Fig. 1), inefficiency is implied.

The inclusion of the cost of uncertainty shifts the classical cost curves upward. We have illustrated this effect in Fig. 2 as the shift from AC_c to $\overline{AC}$.

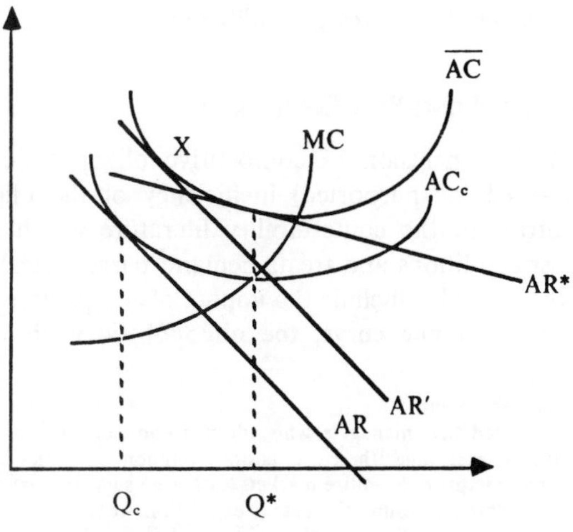

FIG. 2

With competitive free entry and exit, there will be a long-run tangency between the oligopolistic firm's average revenue and average cost curves. But this tangency will not occur at an output such as Q_c, as Chamberlin supposed. Rather, the tangency will be on the $\overline{AC}$ curve, since $\overline{AC}$ includes the cost of bearing the competitive oligopolistic uncertainty.

Considering only this new cost effect and ignoring the adjustments to revenue discussed below, the new tangent will be at point X in Fig. 2. Because the shift in the revenue curves reflects a fixed cost, it must be true that for every Q, $\partial\overline{AC}/\partial Q < \partial AC_c/\partial Q$, so the tangency of AR' must be at a greater output than Q_c. Thus, considering *only* this effect, it is clear that the traditional model, by ignoring oligopolistic uncertainty, has overstated the inefficiency. We will show below that revenue considerations can remove the remaining inefficiency and raise output to Q^*, but first we must show that all firms will have the same adjustment for uncertainty costs.

This is equivalent to saying that, in the long run, all entrepreneurs in a given market will demand the same rate of return for bearing uncertainty. There may be short-run differences in the reactions of managers to each other and the way these reactions are perceived; so, there may be differences in the way short-run decisions are made.[2] But, in the long run, the viable firms will be managed by decision makers with a common view of the uncertainty in their industry. If there were differences in required rates of return, due to differing risk assessments or levels of risk aversion, then managers demanding too high a premium (those whose opportunity costs were too high) would be driven from the market and replaced with lower cost producers in the same way that firms with higher production costs are driven out by the competitive process. This results in a commonality of perspective among all firms remaining in the market in the long run and therefore $\overline{AC}$ curves that are the same distance above the AC_c curves in equilibrium.[3]

IV Free Entry and Long-Run Equilibrium

We have shown that inclusion of competitive oligopolistic uncertainty reduces the perceived (or purported) inefficiency of the oligopoly firm. However, in contrast to the contestability literature which concentrates exclusively on cost conditions and treats demand parametrically, our story does not end here. If we also include the impact of competitive entry on the oligopolist's average revenue curve, the oligopolistic inefficiency will be

[2]Dorward (1981) stressed this point.

[3]Porter (1979) has suggested that managers who adopt a common view of the uncertainty prevailing in the market (and therefore adopt common strategies and conjectural variations) may not comprise the entire market. Rather he suggests that a given industry may be divided into strategic groups. For ease of exposition, we refer to the commonality of perspective of all managers in the market, but the analysis would also apply to strategic groups within an industry rather than the industry as a whole.

eliminated and the oligopolist will produce the level of output that corresponds to the minimum point on the neoclassical average cost curve.

Consider a competitive oligopoly industry producing homogeneous goods, with each firm subject to a common, identifiable level of oligopolistic uncertainty.[4] According to neoclassical theory, the minimums of average cost for all firms in the industry will be at the same level after all Marshallian rents are imputed; so, we treat $AC_{c,\min}$ as reflecting the minimum of the neoclassical average cost curves for *all* firms in the industry.[5]

In this short-run context, the entry of new firms causes a parallel, inward shift of all firms' average revenue functions, reducing profits to zero as illustrated by point X in Fig. 2. If, however, the market is made up of different-sized firms, an inconsistency exists. Since the demand curves are parallel (and thereby have the same slope) and since there can exist only one price for the homogeneous product, the fact that the different-sized firms produce different quantities implies that firms will face different elasticities of demand at the equilibrium. Since marginal revenue is related to elasticity η by the formula

$$MR = P\left(1 - \frac{1}{\eta}\right)$$

and since $MR = MC$ at the profit maximizing output, it must be the case that if firms are not all the same size, they will have different marginal costs in the traditional equilibrium. If they really perceive themselves to be facing parallel demand curves, then larger firms will have lower marginal costs than smaller firms. This result occurs in spite of the fact that, after imputation for scarce factors, all firms will have the same minimum average cost. This issue does not arise in most discussions of Cournot equilibria because it is assumed (implicitly) that all firms are of the same size and have identical cost functions.

This zero-profit equilibrium, or any other with the property that firms have differing elasticities, is not satisfactory since it implies that firms will have differing marginal costs. Though each firm has $MR = MC$, the MRs are functions of the conjectural variations which in turn are based on perceptions of the behaviour of other firms which, finally, is related to their costs. Our presumption is that low marginal cost firms will alter their conjectural variations when they realize that their assumptions about how their competitors will behave may have been wrong. In particular, the low cost firms are in a much better position to expand output than firms with higher MCs

[4] The concept of a "common uncertainty" corresponds to the concept of "adjusted risk classes" in the current finance literature.

[5] It warrants emphasis that the imputation of Marshallian rents to a low-cost firm does not depend on markets being perfectly competitive. All that is required is that there be at least one other potential user of the productive assets of the firm willing to bid the price on these assets up to the point where the total return equals that of the marginal firm(s) in the subject market. This establishes the true opportunity cost of the assets—including the rents relevant in calculating the firm's minimum average cost (*cf.* Chamberlin, 1946, p. 22).

and incorporating this into conjectural variations will increase the elasticity of the perceived AR curve, which increases MR, which leads to increased output.

As is the case with all static models, we do not model the dynamic adjustment process; we can only characterize what properties an equilibrium must have and check to see whether any given situation satisfies these conditions. We have shown that the traditional oligopoly models do not satisfy these conditions and will now demonstrate a model that does. In our model, each firm recognizes that its share of the market output will be determined by its costs relative to those of its rivals, i.e., efficiency considerations dictate how market demand will be allocated among firms.

In the long run, the decision maker recognizes the inconsistency and non-optimality of the short-run conjectural variations and adjusts to behavioural assumptions that are consistent with the underlying cost conditions in the market. One set of long-run conjectural variations which is consistent with the equalization of marginal costs across firms is that firm i's share (α_i) of industry output is determined by the output Q_i^* at which the firm minimizes its neoclassical average cost.[6] That is, firm i's share will be $\alpha_i = Q_i^*/Q^*$ where $Q^* = \Sigma Q_i^*$. In the neighbourhood of this cost minimizing output, average revenue will be allocated proportionately among the firms. Hence, firm i's output will be $Q_i = \alpha_i Q$; and, if the market demand is $P = P(Q)$, firm i will view its individual demand curve as $P = P(Q_i/\alpha_i)$. Thus, a *pro rata* allocation of market demand results. Note again that this represents perceptions in the long-run equilibrium and is not a description of behaviour at every point in time. Note further that a key feature of this long-run demand configuration is that, at any given price, every firm will have the same elasticity of demand and will operate at the same average and marginal cost. This equilibrium is illustrated by the tangency of AR^* and $\overline{AC}$ in Fig. 2.

To see how this approach leads to an equilibrium in which costs are minimized, consider a simple, two-firm oligopoly market as illustrated in Fig. 3. Denote the Marshallian average cost function for firm 1 as $AC_1(Q_1)$ and for firm 2 as $AC_2(Q_2)$. Define the respective outputs at which these two neoclassical average cost functions are minimized as Q_1^* and Q_2^*, where $Q_1^* < Q_2^*$. As noted above, neoclassical theory guarantees that

$$AC_{1,\min} = AC_1(Q_1^*) = AC_2(Q_2^*) = AC_{2,\min} \tag{1}$$

[6] In a spatial context, Ohta (1976) has shown how the combination of (i) entry of firms producing perfect substitutes (causing parallel shifts of the demand curve) and (ii) entry of spatially separated firms (causing the demand curve to rotate) can lead to a tangency between average revenue and average cost at almost any point on the average cost curve. However, changes in both the slope and location of the average cost curve could also occur as a result of physical product differentiation or advertising, rather than spatial separation; so, Ohta's mechanism is more general than the spatial model in which it was developed and provides an alternative mechanism for deriving the results of this paper.

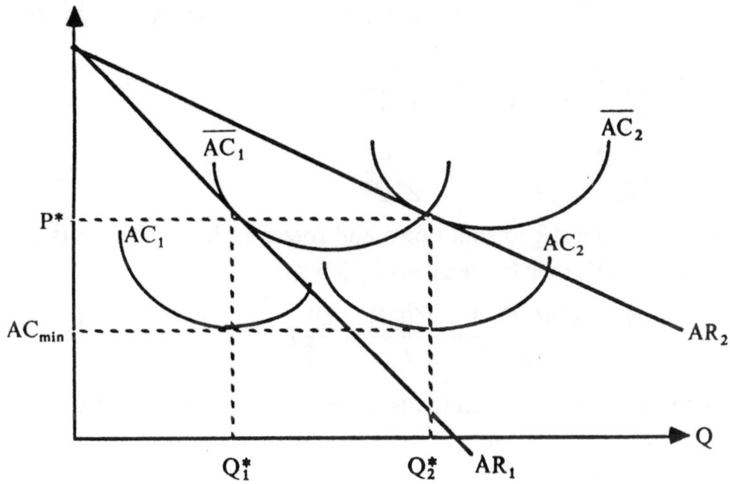

FIG. 3

The cost of behavioural uncertainty is imputed according to the firm's capacity as measured by the output, Q_i^*, at which the Marshallian average cost curve is at its minimum. Denote the fixed cost of oligopolistic uncertainty for an investment consistent with this output as R. The fixed cost of behavioural uncertainty, when computed as a rate of return, depends on the level of investment, i.e., the firm size. We use the size at which Marshallian average costs are minimized as our basis for imputation since it is the simplest and most commonly accepted approach. Also, we argue below that it is the correct approach.[7] Then, for all firms to face the same minimum adjusted average cost when there are different-sized firms in the market, the fixed cost of oligopolistic uncertainty for the investment that will yield an output of Q_2^* must be $(Q_2^*/Q_1^*)R$. Therefore, the adjusted average cost curves—including the imputation for the cost of behavioural uncertainty—for the two firms are

$$\overline{AC}_1 = AC_1(Q_1) + \frac{R}{Q_1} \tag{2a}$$

$$\overline{AC}_2 = AC_2(Q_2) + \left(\frac{Q_2^*}{Q_1^*}\right) \cdot \left(\frac{R}{Q_2}\right) \tag{2b}$$

[7]Imputations of the fixed costs according to other definitions of firm size would imply differing levels of investment and thus differing rates of return for bearing oligopolistic uncertainty among firms in the same market. We argue above that this cannot be the case when competitive entry is possible.

Since $dAC_1(Q_1^*)/dQ_1 = dAC_2(Q_2^*)/dQ_2 = 0$, the slope of $\overline{AC}_i$ at Q_i^* is given by

$$\left.\frac{d(\overline{AC}_1)}{dQ_1}\right|_{Q_1 = Q_1^*} = -\frac{R}{(Q_1^*)^2} \tag{3a}$$

$$\left.\frac{d(\overline{AC}_2)}{dQ_2}\right|_{Q_2 = Q_1^*} = -\frac{R}{Q_1^* Q_2^*} \tag{3b}$$

If entry causes the AR to shift down and rotate such that AR_1 is tangent to $\overline{AC}_1$ at output Q_1^*, then (since $\alpha_1 = Q_1^*/Q^*$)

$$\frac{dAR_1}{dQ_1} = \frac{dP(Q_1^*/\alpha_1)}{dQ_1} = \frac{P'(Q^*)}{\alpha_1} = \frac{Q^*}{Q_1^*}P'(Q^*) \tag{4}$$

Setting the slope of AR_1 equal to the slope of $\overline{AC}_1$ at Q_1^* we obtain

$$\frac{Q^*}{Q_1^*}P'(Q^*) = \frac{-R}{(Q_1^*)^2}$$

or

$$Q^* Q_1^* P'(Q^*) = -R \tag{5}$$

We can rearrange equation (5) to yield

$$\frac{Q^*}{Q_2^*}P'(Q^*) = \frac{-R}{Q_1^* Q_2^*} \tag{6}$$

In equation (6) the right-hand side is the slope of $\overline{AC}_2(Q_2^*)$ and the left-hand side is the slope of $AR_2(Q_2^*)$. Thus, in equilibrium, if firm 1 is operating at the neoclassical minimum cost point, firm 2 will also be producing that output for which its neoclassical average cost is minimized.

In summary, after all classical differentials are ascribed, the average cost of all firms will be equal, including firms that are more efficient or less efficient, and including firms that are large, medium, or small.[8] Because this occurs at the minimum of the average cost curve, and because firms all charge the same price, we can also be sure that the marginal costs, marginal revenues and elasticities are also equal for all firms. This is then truly a long-run equilibrium from which no firm has an incentive to depart.

In the preceding, we have identified three conditions leading to this long-run equilibrium: (1) market demand (average revenue) is allocated pro-

[8]Different-sized firms can exist in our theory, both in the short and long run. Then, if any excess profit exists above the return to all factors (including compensation for uncertainty), the excess must be temporary. This result holds notwithstanding contentions by Eaton and Lipsey (1978, 1979) and Capozza and Van Order (1980) that the space economy yields extra profits. Their theories are essentially predicated on the premise of spatial indivisibilities and one-size efficient firms. In this paper, the possibility of entry by small firms guarantees that if excessive profit exists, some small firm(s) can enter to capture those profits, with other size adjustments taking place as the industry approaches the long-run equilibrium.

portionately according to the firms' minimum (neoclassical) average cost output, (2) the fixed cost of oligopolistic uncertainty is imputed at the minimum point of neoclassical average cost and (3) firms of differing sizes may enter and exit freely. From these conditions it follows that, if one firm is operating at that output at which (neoclassical) average cost is at its minimum, all other firms are also operating at their efficient outputs. Graphically, this means that the situation depicted by Q^* in Fig. 2 is indeed an equilibrium in an oligopolistic market. The equilibrium we have obtained mathematically and illustrated graphically satisfies all of the conditions required for the existence of a long-run equilibrium:

(1) All marginal equalities must be satisfied.
(2) All firms must produce using least-cost combinations of inputs.
(3) The cost of competitive oligopolistic uncertainty must be covered.
(4) All firms must share a common view of alternative activities.
(5) A uniform price must be charged for a homogeneous product.
(6) The relation between returns and the uncertainty must be monotonically increasing.

Our conclusion rests heavily on the condition that the cost of competitive oligopolistic uncertainty be imputed at the output corresponding to the minimum point on the (neoclassical) average cost curve. Were it the case that the cost of this uncertainty was imputed other than that given in equations (2a) and (2b), all of the conditions necessary for the existence of an equilibrium would not be satisfied. For example, if the adjusted average cost curves were obtained as

$$A\hat{C}_1 = AC_1(Q_1) + \frac{R}{Q_1} \tag{7a}$$

$$A\hat{C}_2 = AC_2(Q_2) + \theta\left(\frac{R}{Q_2}\right) \tag{7b}$$

where $\theta \neq Q_2^*/Q_1^*$, any resulting tangencies would yield different prices for the two firms—i.e., different profit maximizing prices would exist for the homogeneous product. This clearly would not result in an equilibrium since condition (5) above would be violated.

We can further demonstrate that the efficient output (i.e., Q^* in Fig. 3) must be the equilibrium by determining whether any other tangency can satisfy the conditions for an equilibrium. Using Fig. 2 again, consider—as did Dorward (1981)—the tangency of average revenue curve AR' with the $\overline{AC}$ curve at point X. At X, there exists a cost incentive for the firm to produce a greater output, if it can also create additional demand for its good (Ohta, 1976, 1977). So, there is an incentive for the owners of the firm to buy out the rival(s) (or for spatial firm owners to relocate the firm's plant(s)), if that action would shift its AR curve rightward relative to the point of its tangency at X.

Moreover, if the firm produced at point X, it would not be producing in the most efficient way to meet that demand. The consequence is that an entrant with lower average cost at that output level would be able to enter and supplant this firm, or at least cause the demand to be reallocated. The firm in Fig. 2 can survive at a lower price than the price associated with X if it can sell more output. It is precisely the assumption of entry by different-sized firms that upsets the possibility of X being an equilibrium. This entry condition, along with the long-run conjectural variations described above, cause the average revenue curve in Fig. 2 to rotate from AR' to AR^* in the long run. Thus, the tangency of AR^* to $\overline{AC}$ at output Q^* is the only equilibrium output level. This is the only tangency that satisfies all of the conditions required for a long-run equilibrium.

V Conclusions

This model of oligopolistic competition produces a long-run equilibrium that is determinate in terms of market price and quantity, but not in the configuration of firms. While the number and size of firms in the market is not unique, we do know that each firm will produce the level of output which minimizes its Marshallian average costs and that each firm will charge the price which provides the competitive rate of return on investment, including compensation for bearing the related oligopolistic uncertainty. Price is determined by the tangency of average revenue and adjusted average cost, where the adjustment is based on the amount of oligopolistic uncertainty inherent in a particular market.

In this model, endogenous free competitive entry and exit of firms of various sizes lead, as would be expected, to the zero profit result. This will imply a unique price, output, and cost, but the equilibrium will not be unique—many different configurations of numbers and sizes of firms may work. This is in agreement with the empirical literature that finds the long-run average cost curve to be dish-shaped, i.e., flat-bottomed, and, since this is a model of the market and not the firm, we do not model how each individual firm determines its size. Instead, it is the adjustments in the market behaviour of all firms in the long run which distinguish our model from others: given (1) the incorporation of the cost of bearing oligopolistic uncertainty into the cost function and (2) the incorporation of cost differences into the conjectural variations that determine the revenue function, decision makers will adopt a long-run perspective concerning the portion of industry demand allocable to each firm. Specifically, this requires that one firm's share of industry demand be determined by its cost of production relative to other firms.

The reassessment of conjectural variations and the resultant competition for market share combined with free entry leads to the result that competitive oligopolists will be production efficient. The theory presented in this paper indicates that short-run distortions due to miscalculations in how rivals will respond and to temporary cost advantages are eliminated over time, with the final distributional equilibrium proving to be economically ordered. An oligopolistic market characterized by competitive entry and exit will be an efficient allocator of resources in the long run. Hence, the concerns of Galbraith and others about the efficiency of oligopolistic markets are valid only when non-competitive, collusive actions prevail or when barriers to entry and exit exist.

References

Baumol, W. J. (1982). "Contestable Markets: An Uprising in the Theory of Industry Structure", *American Economic Review*, Vol. 72, No. 1, pp. 1–15.

Baumol, W. J., Bailey, E. E. and Willig, R. D. (1977). "Weak Invisible Hand Theorems on the Sustainability of Multiproduct Natural Monopoly", *American Economic Review*, Vol. 67, No. 3, pp. 350–365.

Baumol, W. J., Panzar, J. C. and Willig, R. D. (1982). *Contestable Markets and the Theory of Industry Structure*, San Diego, Ca., Harcourt, Brace and Jovanovich.

Beckmann, M. (1968). *Location Theory*, New York, Random House.

Benson, B. (1980a). "Spatial Competition: Implications for Market Area Delineation in Antimerger Cases", *Antitrust Bulletin*, Vol. 25, No. 4, pp. 729–749.

Benson, B. (1980b). "An Examination of U.S. v. Philadelphia National Bank in the Context of Spatial Microeconomics", *Industrial Organization Review*, Vol. 8, No. 1, pp. 27–65.

Capozza, D. and Van Order, R. (1980). "Unique Equilibria, Pure Profits, and Efficiency in Location Models", *American Economic Review*, Vol. 70, No. 5, pp. 1046–1053.

Chamberlin, E. H. (1946). *The Theory of Monopolistic Competition* (5th Edition), Cambridge, Mass., Harvard University Press.

Demsetz, H. (1959). "The Nature of Equilibrium in Monopolistic Competition", *Journal of Political Economy*, Vol. 67, No. 1, pp. 21–30.

Demsetz, H. (1967). "Monopolistic Competition: A Reply", *Economic Journal*, Vol. 77, No. 306, pp. 412–420.

Demsetz, H. (1968). "Do Competition and Monopolistic Competition Differ?", *Journal of Political Economy*, Vol. 76, No. 1, pp. 146–148.

Demsetz, H. (1972). "The Inconsistencies in Monopolistic Competition: A Reply", *Journal of Political Economy*, Vol. 80, No. 3, pp. 592–597.

Dorward, N. (1981). "'Impacts of Distance on Microeconomic Theory': A Critique", *The Manchester School*, Vol. 49, No. 3, pp. 245–258.

Eaton, B. C. and Lipsey, R. G. (1976). "The Non-Uniqueness of Equilibrium in the Loschian Model", *American Economic Review*, Vol. 66, No. 1, pp. 77–93.

Eaton, B. C. and Lipsey, R. G. (1977). "The Introduction of Space into the Neoclassical Model of Value Theory" in M. J. Artis and A. R. Nobay (eds.), *Studies in Modern Economic Analysis*, Oxford, Blackwells, pp. 59–96.

Eaton, B. C. and Lipsey, R. G. (1978). "Freedom of Entry and the Existence of Pure Profits", *Economic Journal*, Vol. 88, No. 35, pp. 455–469.

Eaton, B. C. and Lipsey, R. G. (1979). "The Meaning of Market Pre-Emption: the Persistence of Excess Capacity & Monopoly in Growing Spatial Markets", *Economica*, Vol. 46, No. 182, pp. 149–158.

Galbraith, J. K. (1981). "From Marx to Friedman, Agreement on Monopolies", *Houston Chronicle*, August 18, 1981, Section 1, p. 13.

Greenhut, M. L. (1956). *Plant Location in Theory and in Practice*, Chapel Hill, N.C., University of North Carolina Press.

Greenhut, M. L. (1974). *A Theory of the Firm in Economic Space* (2nd printing), Austin, Texas, Lone Star Publishing Co.

Greenhut, M. L. (1978). "Impacts of Distance on Microeconomic Theory", *The Manchester School*, Vol. 46, No. 1, pp. 17–40.

Greenhut, M. L. and Hwang, M. (1979). "Estimates of Fixed Cost and the Size of Market Areas in the United States", *Environment and Planning*, Vol. 11, No. 9, pp. 993–1009.

Knight, F. H. (1921). *Risk, Uncertainty, and Profit*, Boston, Mass., Houghton-Mifflin.

Norman, G. (1981). "Spatial Competition and Spatial Price Discrimination", *Review of Economic Studies*, Vol. 48, No. 191, pp. 97–111.

Ohta, H. (1976). "On Efficiency of Production Under Conditions of Imperfect Competition", *Southern Economic Journal*, Vol. 43, No. 2, pp. 1124–1135.

Ohta, H. (1977). "On the Excess Capacity Controversy", *Economic Inquiry*, Vol. 15, No. 2, pp. 153–165.

Panzar, J. C. and Willig, R. D. (1977). "Free Entry and the Sustainability of Natural Monopoly", *Bell Journal of Economics*, Vol. 8, No. 1, pp. 1–22.

Porter, M. E. (1979). "The Structure Within Industries and Companies' Performance", *Review of Economics and Statistics*, Vol. 61, No. 2, pp. 214–227.

[19]

Appendix A

There are many facets to the theory in Chapter 19 that warrant further specification for interested readers. Initially, note that in our basic presentation we described the entrepreneurial function as consisting of two sides: services and investment. The service facet does *not* include promotional services. They are conceived of as a sunk cost to the business, not entrepreneurial at all. Our focus on oligopolies further suggests that emphasis in this appendix on large corporations is desirable; the fact that such emphasis carries the advantage of also including small single proprietorships in our thought framework suffices to justify the following analysis of entrepreneurship in a large corporate firm.

The entrepreneurial function

Under the aforementioned conceptual basis, entrepreneurial services in our framework are the managerial services that typically are paid for in the form of salaries and bonuses. Notwithstanding the explicit payments, our theory assumes only an implicit cost for all top-echelon manager services reflective of lost-opportunity costs. In effect, the salaries and bonuses paid to the firm's managers are conceived over time to dovetail with the implicit costs charged to the firm, in which costs we include the differential rent payments for the greater skills of a firm's managers than those of managers of other firms.

Our conception of the firm further requires that the investment funds of stockholders approach – in the long run – the capacities (capabilities) of the firm's managers. This condition means that though the stockholders and managers in the real world of corporate-form organizations may be two different sets of people, our representative firm is based on a conformability between the optimal cost investment and managerial capacities. This conception is counterpart to the single-proprietorship firm that is made up of an entrepreneur whose investment funds match his physical (mental) abilities (capacity). The same consequence also applies as the lowest-explicit-cost production point plus all differential rents (e.g., for skill) enable the firm to be competitive. Then, given sufficient "stick-to-itiveness" in overcoming short-run disappointments, the firm survives in the long run. It further follows that our counterpart view for the large firm requires varying short-run sizes as managers and investors (including the amount of equity investments) change over time, stabilizing ultimately for the surviving firms at a certain size; that size, in turn, is based essentially on the type of people attracted to the firm as its managers. Across industry lines and within each industry, we therefore have a full set of different-size firms, each characterized by managers who conform to the underlying technology (state of the art) that generates the most efficient production possible for that firm.

Our view of the firm and industry can be depicted quite simply. Conceive of an industry in which the costs and outputs of all *potentially viable firms* appear flat-lined. Of course, there exist outputs and costs beyond

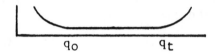

Figure 19A.1. Cost curve.

the efficient range (i.e., firms that are too small and too large), because only the flat-line section in Figure 19A.1 offers a chance for survival in the long run. As in Chapter 19, *which firms survive* depends on short-run events. In other words, we can have many firms of size q_0 or a few firms of size q_t, or a set of in-between sizes. Firms smaller or larger than q_0 or q_t, respectively, will disappear over time. Our theory thus specifies that long-run survivors in the industry are efficient, but not necessarily managed by the most capable men, who may, of course, be in other industries; all that is required is that the viable firms look like the representative firm described and depicted in Chapter 19, whose AC, including differential rents, places it somewhere between (and including) the q_0 and q_t sizes.

It should also be noted that the industrial divisibility conceived of under our theory (i.e., optimum-cost firm sizes anywhere between q_0 and q_t in the sketch) involves some number of firms, determined in part by short-run luck and ultimately by long-run demand. The alternative sizes of individual firms further explain the differences between our theory and those of Eaton and Lipsey or Capozza and Van Order. Profits in our theory are squeezed to the (normal) level commensurate with the behavioral uncertainty underscoring divisible investments (within the q_0–q_t range) in the industry.

Imputing the cost of behavioral uncertainty as a variable not fixed cost

Let us define

$$r = Rs = R\mathrm{AC}_0 q_0 \qquad \text{(A19.1)}$$

where, here, R stands for the lost-opportunity rate of return (i.e., r_0 in the basic Chapter 19 presentation), and s is the optimal cost investment on AC_c; hence, $r = R\mathrm{AC}_0 q_0$. Next, conceive of a variable cost imputation, in fact two alternative forms of it, as either

$$r' = Rs' = R\mathrm{AC}_a q_a \qquad \text{(A19.2)}$$

where subscript a relates to the actual output, or

$$r' = Rs' = R\mathrm{AC}_0 q_a \qquad \text{(A19.3)}$$

Refer to (A19.2) as the ψ variable cost adjustment and (A19.3) as the ϕ variable cost adjustment. Next define

$$C=f_1(Q) \tag{A19.2a}$$

where $f_1(Q)$ is a cubic function that generates a monotonically increasing cost as total output Q increases. Then,

$$C^*=f_1(Q)+u \tag{A19.2b}$$

where $u=u(Q)=f_2(Q)$, and where $f_2(Q)=\psi f_1(Q)$. Thus,

$$C^*=f_1(Q)+\psi f_1(Q)$$

so that

$$\mathrm{MC}^*=\frac{dC^*}{dQ}=f_{1Q}+f_{2Q}=(1+\psi)f_{1Q} \tag{A19.2c}$$

and

$$\mathrm{AC}^*+\frac{C^*}{Q}=\frac{f_1(Q)}{Q}+\frac{f_2(Q)}{Q}=\frac{(1+\psi)f_1(Q)}{Q} \tag{A19.2d}$$

Alternatively, from (A19.3) we have

$$C=f(Q) \tag{A19.3a}$$

Then,

$$C^*=f(Q)+u \tag{A19.3b}$$

where $u=u(Q)$ now equals ϕQ. Therefore, $C^*=f(Q)+\phi Q$, so that

$$\mathrm{MC}^*=\frac{dC^*}{dQ}=fQ+\phi \tag{A19.3c}$$

and

$$\mathrm{AC}^*=\frac{C^*}{Q}=\frac{f(Q)}{Q}+\frac{\phi Q}{Q}=\frac{f(Q)}{Q}+\phi \tag{A19.3d}$$

It is manifest that the (A19.2) conception of r' entails

$$r'=\psi f_1(Q)=\psi \mathrm{AC}_a q_a \tag{A19.2'}$$

Therefore,

$$\psi=R \tag{A19.2''}$$

(rate of return on some actual dollar investment). The (A19.3) conception of r' in turn establishes

$$r'=\phi Q=R\mathrm{AC}_0 q_a \tag{A19.3'}$$

which means

$$\phi = RAC_0 \qquad \text{(A19.3'')}$$

(the dollar requirement due to the percentage R on the AC_0 amount). Of course, $AC_a > AC_0$ for all $a \neq 0$.

Note that the tangency to the fixed-cost (r) adjusted curve induces entry at points short of the technological optimal cost output; this result occurs because of the windfall profits that exist over such points. Now we find, via our variable-cost (r') conception, a disparity between MR and MC for all AR tangencies to the r' adjusted AC curve due to equating MR with MC*. Note that this disparity applies when uncertainty is imputed by the entrepreneur-investor as a variable input in perfect conformance to technology (the ψ adjustment) or when it is imputed per unit of output (the ϕ adjustment). In each case, new entry into the market by erstwhile accountants, engineers, and economists is encouraged by the apparent failure of the entrepreneur to produce where MR equals the MC that appears on the firm's books.

We favor the fixed-cost r approach. But more important, the final results of the variable-cost r' approach match the fixed-cost approach. To see this, recognize that imputing a cost for the behavioral uncertainty that underlies investments in oligopoly markets can be effected only by the investor. No accountant, engineer, economist, or any other individual knows another person's lost-opportunity costs, including the way the person conceives of investment returns. It is only in the mind's eye of the individual investor that an adjustment to marginal cost exists, and this adjustment obtains if and only if we want to imagine the investor changing the firm's income requirement in conformance to the actual investment. Thus, if we let MC change as inputs or outputs change, we have lost the basic property of the firm, namely, that all individuals require a return for their services and investments based on their conceptions of their lost opportunities. In turn, we have lost the idea that when selecting a given activity, the individual has in mind a total work and investment performance [symbolized by s in (A19.1)] and a lost-opportunity rate of return [symbolized by R in (A19.1)]. The product r of Rs, in other words, is our target. It is the belief that one will gain r returns, which justifies selecting a given employment or, as is of sole interest here, a given investment.

It follows from the foregoing that if we conceive of variable-cost adjustments for uncertainty based on inputs and technology (the ψ adjustment) or based directly on output quantities (the ϕ adjustment), an artificial adjustment is also needed for marginal revenues. This adjustment is also strictly in the mind's eye of the entrepreneur, who, simply put, aspires to the return r, not r'. So we define the several adjustments required under variable imputations in the particular activity as

$$\psi' = \frac{r}{q_a} = \frac{RAC_0 q_0}{q_a} = (RAC_0) \quad (RAC_0 > 1) \tag{A19.4}$$

for all tangencies where $q_0 > q_a$. And we define proxy-related ψ^* for the ψ involved in (A19.2) as

$$\psi^* = \frac{r'}{q_a} = \frac{RAC_a q_a}{q_a} = RAC_a \tag{A19.5}$$

And for (A19.3) we then have

$$\phi^* = \frac{r'}{q_a} = \frac{RAC_0 q_a}{q_a} = RAC_0 = \phi \tag{A19.6}$$

Note that the numerator in the third term of (A19.4) is greater than in (A19.5). Thus, $\psi' > \psi^* > \phi^*$. So, besides the hired expert's disequilibrium view of MR > MC at any tangency to an r' adjusted curve, the entrepreneur is also in disequilibrium as he conceives of an adjusted MR greater than MC. Moreover, for all output points beyond the technological optimal cost point where AR may equal the r' adjusted value, we have

$$\psi' = (RAC_0) \quad (RAC_0 < 1)$$

$$\psi^* = RAC_a$$

$$\phi^* = RAC_0$$

Hence, $\psi' < \phi^* < \psi^*$. Of course, where $q_a = q_0$ in the third terms of (A19.4), (A19.5), and (A19.6), $\psi' = \psi^* = \phi^*$. The long-run equilibrium marked by the Chapter 19 tangency of AR to the r adjusted curve at the optimal technological cost output is therefore directly counterpart to what variable cost imputations would generate.

To sum up our findings: Tangency of AR to the r adjusted curve at what would be a typical Chamberlin excess-capacity point involves profits and potential entry. Tangency to the lower adjusted average-cost curves, the ψ and ϕ adjusted AC curves, involves disequilibrium, because (in his mind's eye) the entrepreneur has not fulfilled his objective $r = Rs$; moreover, the hired experts of the firm are favorably inclined to quit the firm and enter the market with their own enterprise, because, by their books, the entrepreneur is producing at an MR > MC point. It further follows that any tangency to some AC adjusted curve falling (by some process) between the r adjusted and the r' adjusted curves of (A19.2) and (A19.3), and which is short of the technological optimal cost point, still makes the entrepreneur appear not to be maximizing. Moreover, though the entrepreneur himself may be approaching the return r for a smaller investment than the s investment he had intended, we can expect either entry by others and/or the entrepreneur's desire to expand by investing more.

Simply put, either the industry is profitable or it is not yielding enough to the firm's entrepreneur-managers and to the stockholders on the equity investments that the firm has accumulated with the objectives of conforming to its management's capacities.

Final statement

One might ask, What are the effects of different proportions of funded debt to equity investment on our theory? Our answer to this question can be quite terse. We define an industry narrowly as involving (1) a product that is a member of an identifiable group of products, (2) identical risk-uncertainty structures among firms, and (3) financial structures that are also identical among all member firms (i.e., identical funded debt/equity ratios based on that which *over time* has appeared to be the successful financial balance). This definition applies strictly to our long-run conception, which in turn only signifies the position toward which the industry moves before a new exogenous shock sets it off on another new long-run trend. More broadly, we can view as members of the (almost) same industry all firms (1) whose products are among those of an identifiable group of products, (2) provided that among its producing firms, identical (or sufficiently similar) underlying uncertainty structures prevail. Pursuant to this designation, financial contrivances are then considered to alter the levels of uncertainty and required return on the equity investment in the particular firm. But, most important, the monotonicity of yields per dollar investment based on uncertainty levels remains the basic requisite.

Econometrica, Vol. 43, No. 4 (July, 1975)

OBSERVATIONS ON THE SHAPE AND RELEVANCE OF THE SPATIAL DEMAND FUNCTION

BY M. L. GREENHUT, M. HWANG, AND H. OHTA[1]

The purpose of this paper is to set forth a general theorem on the shape of the free spatial market demand curve and on the shape of the spatial competitive market demand curve. It is demonstrated that the free spatial demand curve is necessarily convex to the origin *regardless of the shape of the individual demands which comprise it*. But the shape of the spatial competitive market demand curve is shown to depend upon the behavioral assumptions used in the competitive model. Three basically different competitive models are presented with contrasting results. Elasticity and price effects under each type of competition are determined and evaluated as is the effect of spatial competition on prices. Different interpretations of price data tend to result from conceptions of aggregate spatial demand curves vis a vis the classical spaceless demand curve.

1. INTRODUCTION

A. LÖSCH [**8**, pp. 106–108] anticipated that the shape of the free spatial (regional) demand curve would be concave to the origin when the individual (local) demands were convex to the origin. K. G. Denike and J. B. Parr [**2**, pp. 50–51] argued against Lösch that if the individual (local) demand curves are convex, the (aggregate) spatial demand curve is also convex. Their argument is partially correct. They erred, however, in believing that the concavity (convexity) of the spatial demand depends strictly upon the concavity (convexity) of the individual demand. C. A. Gannon [**3**, pp. 295–299] correctly pointed out the flaw in Denike and Parr's paper and claimed generality for his own work.

Gannon's analysis appeared to provide a general treatment of spatial demand. Unfortunately, Gannon also failed to establish a definitive general theorem. The purpose of this paper is to set forth such a theorem. In particular, Section 2 of this paper will prove that the free spatial demand curve is necessarily convex—given the same general set of assumptions used by the writers mentioned above—*regardless of the shape of the individual demand*. In the event of competition, spatial demand will be shown to depend on the expected reaction of rivals to price cuts. Under one type of behavioral assumption (Section 3), spatial demand will be seen to depend directly on the individual (local) demands, being concave (convex) when the individual demand is concave (convex). Alternative behavioral assumptions lead to different conclusions (Section 4). The impacts of spatial competition on mill prices are, therefore, demonstrated to be specifiable only after the behavior patterns of competitors to rival firm's price policies are given. How evaluation of empirical data is affected by one's conception of spatial demand, and in fact the relevance of the spatial market demand curve vis a vis the market demand conceptualized in traditional spaceless microeconomic theory will be discussed in our concluding Section 5.

[1] This paper is based on research funded by the National Science Foundation. The authors wish to thank R. Battalio and an anonymous referee for helpful critiques and suggestions.

2. CONVEXITY OF THE FREE SPATIAL DEMAND CURVE UNDER CONDITIONS OF SPATIAL MONOPOLY

Our assumptions are as follows:

(i) A monopolist is located at a point on an unbounded plain where buyers are evenly and continuously distributed.

(ii) The demand densities for the product at all points on the plain are the same, and the demand curves are negatively sloped over the relevant domains.

(iii) The freight rate is proportional to distance.

(iv) The monopolist does not discriminate in price but instead charges a given f.o.b. mill price to all buyers.

The above assumptions clearly support a specification of the demand density q as a function of the delivered price p which, in turn, is a function of the mill price m and distance D from the seller's site. Thus:

$$q = f(m + kD), \qquad f_m = f'\frac{\partial p}{\partial m} = f' < 0, \tag{2.1}$$

where k is a constant standing for the freight rate per unit of distance, f_m stands for the partial derivative of f with respect to m, and f' stands for the first (total) derivative of f with respect to p. Aggregate spatial demand Q is then given by either (2.2) or (2.2)′:

$$Q = 2\pi \int_0^{D_0} Df\,(m + kD)\,dD, \tag{2.2}$$

$$Q = \int_0^{2\pi}\int_0^{D_0} Df\,(m + kD)\,dD\,d\theta, \tag{2.2$'$}$$

where D_0 is indirectly defined by:

$$f(m + kD_0) = 0, \qquad \text{i.e., } m + kD_0 = f^{-1}(0). \tag{2.3}$$

The two specifications of spatial demand are perfectly equivalent and henceforth only (2.2)′ will be used.

It is manifest that Q in (2.2)′ is a function of m and D_0. The first derivative of (2.2)′ with respect to m is, therefore, given by

$$\begin{aligned} \frac{dQ}{dm} &= \frac{\partial Q}{\partial m} + \frac{\partial Q}{\partial D_0}\frac{dD_0}{dm} \\ &= \int_0^{2\pi}\int_0^{D_0} Df_m(m + kD)\,dD\,d\theta + \int_0^{2\pi} D_0 f(m + kD_0)\frac{dD_0}{dm}\,d\theta \\ &= \int_0^{2\pi}\int_0^{D_0} Df_m(m + kD)\,dD\,d\theta < 0, \end{aligned} \tag{2.4}$$

since $f(m + kD_0) = 0$ via (2.3) and $f_m < 0$.[2] The second derivative in turn is:

$$(2.5) \quad \frac{d^2Q}{dm^2} = \int_0^{2\pi}\int_0^{D_0} Df_{mm}(m + kD)\,dD\,d\theta + \int_0^{2\pi} D_0 f_m(m + kD_0)\frac{dD_0}{dm}\,d\theta$$

$$= \int_0^{2\pi}\int_0^{D_0} Df_{mm}(m + kD)\,dD\,d\theta - \frac{1}{k}\int_0^{2\pi} D_0 f_m(m + kD_0)\,d\theta,$$

$$\text{via} \quad \frac{dD_0}{dm} = -\frac{1}{k} \quad \text{from (2.3).}$$

The sign of the second derivative appears at first glance to be indefinite. Such claim by [**3**, p. 297] was said to stem from the condition that the first term could be either negative, zero, or positive, while the second term on the right-hand side of (2.5) is nonnegative. However, the sign *is* determinate, since using integration by parts on the first term reduces equation (2.5) to:

$$(2.5)' \quad \frac{d^2Q}{dm^2} = \int_0^{2\pi}\left[\frac{1}{k}Df_m(m + kD) - \frac{1}{k^2}f(m + kD)\right]_0^{D_0} d\theta$$

$$-\frac{1}{k}\int_0^{2\pi} D_0 f_m(m + kD_0)\,d\theta$$

$$= \frac{1}{k^2}\int_0^{2\pi}[-f(m + kD_0) + f(m)]\,d\theta$$

$$= \frac{1}{k^2}\int_0^{2\pi} f(m)\,d\theta > 0, \qquad \forall m < f^{-1}(0).$$

Thus, the free spatial demand function is necessarily convex to the origin.[3] The subject convexity does not require Denike and Parr's condition that $f_{mm} > 0$;[4] it also does not require Gannon's condition that $|f_m(m + kD_0)|$ be large relative to f_{mm} and that $k(= |dm/dD_0|)$ be small relative to f_{mm}.[5]

[2] Cf. Denike and Parr [**2**, p. 50]. Their result is the same, but their formulation is unnecessarily complicated.

[3] It can be shown, and was in fact pointed out by a referee, that the subject result is invariant with respect to an alternative assumption of consumers distribution over space, i.e., an assumption that the density of demand declines with distance according to α/D, where α is a parameter.

[4] In [**2**, p. 51], it is claimed that $(d^2Q/dm^2) \gtreqless 0$ iff $f_{mm} \gtreqless 0$. These relations are incorrect and stem directly from an error in formulation. Specifically, the authors induced from the valid statements $f(m + kD_0) = 0$ that $f_m(m + kD_0) = 0$; however, the latter statement is invalid. The condition $f(m + kD_0) = 0$ does not imply $f_m(m + kD_0) = 0$ since (i) if $f_{mm} \leqslant 0$, the derivative of a *well defined demand curve* which is linear or concave to the origin cannot be zero at the price intercept, and (ii) via (2.5)′ we find that the nonzero right hand term in (2.5) must yield $(d^2Q/dm^2) > 0$. The result of $f_{mm} > 0$ is clearly the same.

[5] See [3, Corollary 8].

3. THE SHAPE OF THE SPATIAL DEMAND CURVE UNDER LÖSCHIAN COMPETITION

Suppose a seller is confronted by competition in n directions and that his buyers are evenly distributed over this space.[6] The spatial demand may then be defined as follows:

$$(3.1)\qquad Q = n\int_0^{D_0} f(m+kD)\,dD, \qquad f^{-1}(0) > m \geq m^*,$$

$$\text{with} \quad D_0 = \frac{f^{-1}(0) - m}{k}, \quad \text{and}$$

$$= n\int_0^{D_0^*} f(m+kD)\,dD, \qquad m^* > m \geq 0,$$

$$\text{with} \quad D_0^* = \frac{f^{-1}(0) - m^*}{k},$$

where m^* stands for a *least upper bound* for mill price that eventuates under certain degrees of competition, and in turn determines the competitively curtailed market size D_0^* of the firm. Ceteris paribus, reduction of mill price from $f^{-1}(0)$ to lower levels such as m^* will increase the firm's market area; at the same time, the firm's quantity produced will increase on two counts: price and market size. However, further reductions in m may well elicit reaction(s) from the rival firm(s).[7] The market size would be limited in such event and, in fact, can be regarded as of fixed size D_0^*, i.e., as not extendable to greater distances.

The first derivative of Q with respect to m is accordingly:

$$(3.2)\qquad \frac{dQ}{dm} = -\frac{n}{k}f(m), \qquad f^{-1}(0) > m \geq m^*,$$

$$= \frac{n}{k}[f(m - m^* + f^{-1}(0)) - f(m)], \qquad m^* > m \geq 0.$$

Observing that $f(m - m^* + f^{-1}(0)) = f(f^{-1}(0)) = 0$ when $m = m^*$, and recalling the continuity of f, it is manifest that dQ/dm is everywhere continuous. Moreover, equation (3.2) demonstrates that the slope of the competitive spatial demand, i.e., $|dQ/dm| \forall m < m^*$, is strictly flatter than that of the free spatial demand since $f(m) > f(m - m^* + f^{-1}(0)) > 0 \forall m < m^*$.[8] A flatter $|dQ/dm|$ implies a steeper

[6] To be rigorous, the distribution of buyers is mathematically different from that assumed in the preceding section of this paper. However, no practical difference in results exists between the two specifications. The new specification is used because it is much easier to employ than the other in case of spatial competition.

[7] This, of course, is not the case in an alternative model of competition, e.g., H. Hotelling [7], where the rival's mill price is assumed to be fixed. In a model of the Hotelling order, extension of market area beyond D_0^* is possible; thus the related competitive spatial demand is both greater and more price elastic than that conceived above. This relation will be proved in Section 4 of the paper.

[8] $f(m) > f(m - m^* + f^{-1}(0))$ since $m - m^* + f^{-1}(0) > m \forall m^* < f^{-1}(0)$. In turn, $f(m - m^* + f^{-1}(0)) > 0$ since $m - m^* + f^{-1}(0) < f^{-1}(0) \forall m < m^*$. It then follows that $(n/k)[f(m)] > (n/k)[f(m) - f(m - m^* + f^{-1}(0))]$, i.e., the slope of the free spatial demand is greater than the slope of the competitive spatial demand.

$|dm/dQ|$ and hence a steeper transposed Marshallian demand. One might, nevertheless, anticipate that competitive spatial demand would be more price elastic than is free spatial demand.[9] However, it is in fact and in general *less* elastic than the latter under the particular oligopolistic behavioral assumption intrinsic to the present model. Indeed, this statement is supported by a class of individual demand curves of comparatively general form, such as:

$$(3.3) \qquad p = b - aq^{\alpha}, \qquad a, b, \alpha > 0,$$

where b is the price intercept and hence equivalent to $f^{-1}(0)$ in the text above. For the purposes of spatial price theory, (3.3) is, in fact, completely general.[10]

In proof of the proposition, consider the ratio $R = e_c/e_f$, where e_c and e_f respectively stand for the elasticity of competitive spatial demand and free spatial demand. Pursuant to (3.1), (3.2), and the assumed individual demand (3.3), these elasticities are specifiable as:

$$(3.4) \qquad e_c = -\left(\frac{dQ}{dm}\frac{m}{Q}\right)_c = -\frac{n}{k}\left[\left(\frac{m^* - m}{a}\right)^{1/\alpha} - \left(\frac{b-m}{a}\right)^{1/\alpha}\right] \times \frac{m}{n\int_0^{D_0^*}\left(\frac{b-m-kD}{a}\right)^{1/\alpha} dD}$$

$$(3.5) \qquad e_f = -\left(\frac{dQ}{dm}\frac{m}{Q}\right)_f = \frac{n}{k}\left(\frac{b-m}{a}\right)^{1/\alpha}\frac{m}{n\int_0^{D_0}\left(\frac{b-m-kD}{a}\right)^{1/\alpha} dD}.$$

Thus from $R = e_c/e_f$, we obtain:

$$(3.6) \qquad R = \frac{1-\gamma}{1-\delta}, \qquad \text{where} \qquad \gamma = \left(\frac{m^* - m}{b-m}\right)^{1/\alpha} \qquad \text{and} \qquad \delta = \left(\frac{m^* - m}{b-m}\right)^{(1+\alpha)/\alpha}$$

[9] The subject anticipation is based on the fact that the free spatial demand Q is greater than the competitive spatial demand Q for any given mill price. Cf. [**3**, Theorem 5].

[10] Spatial pricing may, of course, be of discriminatory or nondiscriminatory order. But the natural separation of markets which makes price discrimination possible tends to preclude discrimination against distant buyers, since nearer buyers favored by the discrimination could repackage and resell the product for profit. Moreover, discrimination against distant buyers can be shown to arise from demand curves of constant or increasing elasticity or a demand curve of decreasing elasticity whose changes in price exceed the changes in elasticity; i.e., $0 < (de\ dp)(p/e) < 1$. Such demand curves are not only extremely restrictive and special with respect to their properties but involve negative freight absorption (and in one special case excessive freight absorption) which tend not to be found in practice. In contrast, the set of demand curves given in (3.3) not only would support price discrimination against nearer buyers, but these curves contain structural perquisites which are neither restrictive nor unlikely to be found in practice. For purposes of spatial price theory (including discriminatory as well as nondiscriminatory pricing), the set given by (3.3) serves accordingly *in general*.

Since $b > m^* > m$ under competition, the ratio $(m^* - m)/(b - m)$ is less than unity and hence $\gamma < 1$, $\delta < 1$ and $\gamma > \delta$. The numerator of the ratio R is necessarily less than its denominator, i.e., $R < 1$. Competitive spatial demand is, therefore, necessarily less elastic than is free spatial demand for individual demands of type (3.3) as given above. The conditions of decreasing elasticity with price and an R ratio in (3.6) of less than unity signify that competitive mill price may be greater than monopoly mill price when a firm's market area is fixed in size because of competition at a distance. This higher price occurs unless marginal production costs fall rapidly as the quantity of output is decreased.

The second derivative of Q with respect to m is as follows:

$$(3.7)\qquad \frac{d^2Q}{dm^2} = -\frac{n}{k}f_m(m), \qquad f^{-1}(0) > m \geqslant m^*,$$

$$= \frac{n}{k}[f_y(y) - f_m(m)], \qquad m^* > m \geqslant 0,$$

where $y = m - m^* + f^{-1}(0)$. Thus, spatial demand is necessarily convex to the origin for all m such that $f^{-1}(0) > m \geqslant m^*$. In sharp contrast, spatial demand for all m reflecting $m < m^*$ is either convex or concave depending upon either $|f_y| < |f_m|$ or $|f_y| > |f_m|$. In reference to the condition $y > m$ (see note 8 supra), it follows that $|f_y| \gtreqless |f_m|$ if $f_{mm} \lesseqgtr 0$. The competitive spatial demand is convex (concave) iff the individual demand f is convex (concave).[11] It, therefore, follows that the shapes of competitively reduced spatial demand curves are the same as the individual demand curves from which they are derived.

To sum up, our theorem states that *the spatial demand curve is always convex for noncompetitive prices m such that* $f^{-1}(0) > m \geqslant m^*$. But *it is either concave, linear, or convex for competitive prices m* $< m^*$, *depending directly upon the shape of the individual* (*local*) *demand.* It may thus be noted that three alternative forms of spatial demand curves under competition can be conceived. These forms are illustrated in Figure 1. Panel (a) depicts the spatial demand derived from convex

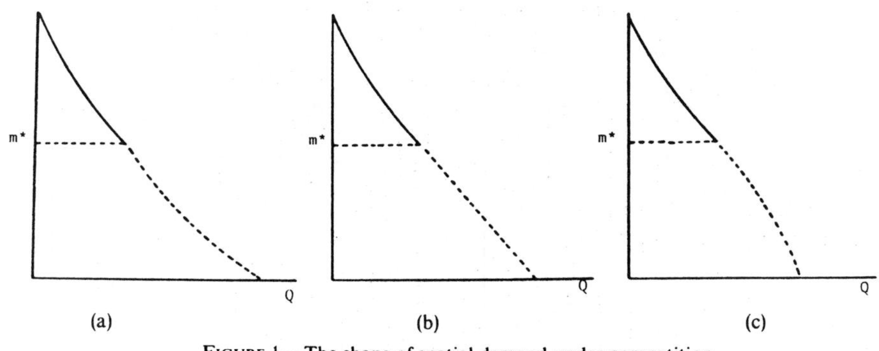

FIGURE 1.—The shape of spatial demand under competition.

[11] Cf. [3, Corollary 4].

individual demand curves. Panel (b) in turn assumes linear individual demands. Panel (c) requires concave individual demand curves. They involve an inflexion point at $m = m^*$.

4. SPATIAL DEMAND UNDER TWO ALTERNATIVE MODELS OF SPATIAL COMPETITION

The competitive spatial demand curves derived in Section 3 stemmed directly from a particular behavioral assumption that was implicit in the analysis presented there. This assumption requires evaluation at the present time. In particular, the impacts of alternative behavioral assumptions on the spatial firm's market demand curve must be determined. For easier references, the model presented in Section 3 can be called the Lösch model while the two alternative models of the present section can be called the Hotelling-Smithies (HS) model and the Greenhut-Ohta (GO) model.

The Lösch Model in Review With Emphasis on Implicit Assumptions

The firm in this model is not subject to competition whenever its mill price is greater than the critical level m^*. Indeed, there is no effective competition in the space economy in the present instance because the firm's natural market boundary has been reached at points so distant from competitor sites that their delivered prices would lie above the price intercept limit of buyers located at these boundary points. This situation can be viewed readily in Figure 2. Thus, for example, if the mill price of the firm located at point 0 in Figure 2(a) is as high as m_2, the delivered price schedule over space may be represented by the line m_2m_2, the slope of which is determined by the freight rate k. Delivered price reaches its maximum $f^{-1}(0)$ at distance D_{02}, which distance marks the firm's natural market limit. A lowering of mill price from m_2 to m^* (or a raise from m_2 to m_1) causes the delivered price schedule to shift down (up) to the line $m^*m^*(m_1m_1)$. This change increases (reduces) the firm's market limit from D_{02} to D_0^* (or from D_{02} to D_{01}). In either event, the firm's market area is so small over this range of prices that a rival(s) located at 0′ would not react to the subject firm's change in price.

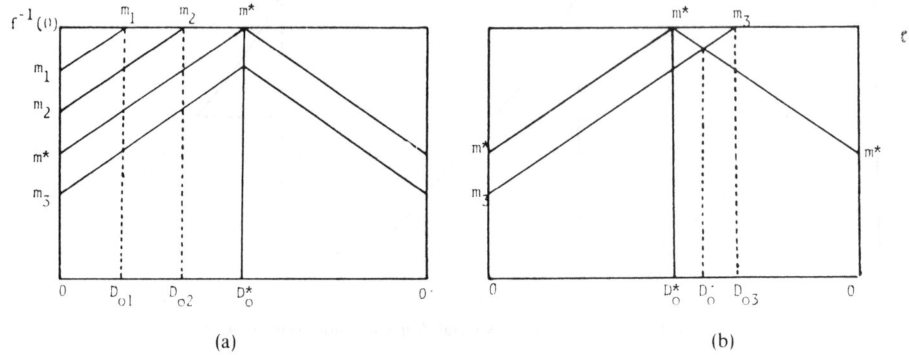

FIGURE 2.—Alternative models of rival reactions.

It is unfortunately the case from the standpoint of the firm located at 0 that its market area cannot be enlarged simply by a lowering of its mill price below the critical level m^*. Any reduction in mill price, say from m^* to m_3, could be expected to induce immediate and identical change in price by the rival located at 0'. In the process, the market boundary point would be left unchanged at D_0^*. The critical mill price m^* is the highest price possible for a firm subject to the particular degree and type of spatial competition implicit to Figure 2(a), i.e., to *space fixing* competition at boundary point D_0^*. The model of spatial competition set forth in Section 3 thus involves parametric treatment of the firm's market area D_0^*, while the related m^* provides the highest price possible for the firm given nondiscriminatory pricing and sales to that boundary point. Most significantly, the spatial demand function specified in (3.1), which we can refer to as the Löschian demand function, is less elastic under conditions of spatial competition than is the free spatial demand curve. It follows ceteris paribus that the equilibrium mill price will be higher under spatial competition than under spatial monopoly, a most surprising (and empirically unlikely?) conclusion.

The HS Model

In his famous model of spatial duopoly, Hotelling [7] assumed that each firm considers its rival's mill price to be fixed. Suppose this assumption is used, but instead of his related assumption of perfectly inelastic buyer demands, let us combine it with Smithies' elastic demand assumption [**10**]. A vastly different spatial demand function than that of (3.1) arises as a consequence of this combination. To appreciate this result, let the firm at site 0 (henceforth Firm A) regard its rival's mill price as fixed at the level m^*. (See Figure 2(b).) Firm A then visualizes the fixed delivered price schedule m^*m^* of its rival. This firm can enlarge its own market area from the zero distance to D_0^* by lowering its own mill price from $f^{-1}(0)$ down to m^*. Over this range of prices, firm A can be described as having disregarded both the rival firm's location at 0' and the rival firm's price schedule m^*m^*.

The HS demand function overlaps the free spatial demand over the domain m, where $f^{-1}(0) \geqslant m > m^*$. In sharp contrast to the Lösch model, as Firm A lowers its mill price below m^*, say from m^* to m_3, it continues to enlarge its market area, in Figure 2(b) from D_0^* to D'_0. The increase in size of market is, however, only one-half that which a spatial monopolist would have acquired given the price change to m_3, i.e., the HS firm's market is increased in size by $(D_{03} - D_0^*)/2$. It goes without saying that this limit to market growth stems in part from the rival firm's price schedule m^*m^*, and the intersection between it and the subject firm's price schedule m_3m_3 at D'_0. Full specification of the spatial demand function under HS competition is provided by:

$$Q = n\int_0^{D_0} f(m + kD)\,dD, \qquad f^{-1}(0) > m \geqslant m^*, \qquad \text{with} \tag{4.1}$$

$$D_0 = \frac{f^{-1}(0) - m}{k}$$

$$= n\int_0^{D_0'} f(m + kD)\,dD, \qquad m^* > m \geqslant 0, \qquad \text{with}$$

$$D_0' = \frac{2f^{-1}(0) - m^* - m}{2k},$$

$$(4.2)\qquad \frac{dQ}{dm} = -\frac{n}{k}f(m), \qquad f^{-1}(0) > m \geqslant m^*,$$

$$= -\frac{n}{k}\left[f(m) - \frac{1}{2}f\left(f^{-1}(0) - \frac{m^* - m}{2}\right)\right], \qquad m^* > m \geqslant 0,$$

and

$$(4.3)\qquad \frac{d^2Q}{dm^2} = -\frac{n}{k}f'(m), \qquad f^{-1}(0) > m \geqslant m^*,$$

$$= -\frac{n}{k}\left[f'(m) - \frac{1}{4}f'\left(f^{-1}(0) - \frac{m^* - m}{2}\right)\right], \qquad m^* > m \geqslant 0.$$

Expression (4.1) indicates that the HS demand curve lies above the Löschian demand but falls below the free spatial demand for any mill price m such that $m^* > m \geqslant 0$. The exact shape of the HS demand is given by (4.3). If local gross demands are either linear or convex to the origin, the HS demand is convex to the origin.[12] If local gross demands are concave, the shape of the HS demand is indeterminate, albeit the requisite condition for convexity or concavity is nevertheless unambiguously specifiable.[13]

The elasticity of the free spatial demand curve may be compared with the HS and Löschian demand curves. In particular, the free spatial demand curve is more elastic than the HS demand curve over corresponding prices when local demand is of the general form $p = b - aq^\alpha$, where $a, b, \alpha > 0$; and, it is still more elastic than the Löschian demand curve.[14] Two important implications of the elasticity

[12] If local gross demands are linear, then $f'(m) = f'((m + kD_0^* + f^{-1}(0))/2)$ so that $f'(m) - \frac{1}{4}f'((m + kD_0^* + f^{-1}(0))/2) < 0$. If they are convex to the origin, then $|f'(m)| > |f'((m + kD_0^* + f^{-1}(0))/2)|$ since $(m + kD_0^* + f^{-1}(0))/2 = m + (kD_0^* + f^{-1}(0) - m)/2 > m$ so that again $f'(m) - \frac{1}{4}f'((m + kD_0^* + f^{-1}(0))/2) < 0$ Equation (4.3) therefore guarantees the condition $d^2Q/dm^2 > 0$ for each of these cases.

[13] It is concave for any mill price such that $|4f'(m)| < |f'((m + kD_0^* + f^{-1}(0))/2)|$. It is not concave otherwise. See also note 12.

[14] Pursuant to (4.1), (4.2), and assuming individual demands of the form $p = b - aq^\alpha$, demand elasticity under HS competition is as follows:

$$\text{(i)}\qquad e_c' = \frac{m(1+\alpha)\{(b-m)^{1/\alpha} - (1/2)(m^* - m)^{1/\alpha}\}}{\alpha\{(b-m)^{(\alpha+1)/\alpha} - [(m^* - m)/2]^{(\alpha+1)/\alpha}\}}.$$

The elasticities of Löschian and free spatial demand are correspondingly and respectively specifiable via (3.4) and (3.5) as follows:

$$(3.4)'\qquad e_c = \frac{m(1+\alpha)\{(b-m)^{1/\alpha} - (m^* - m)^{1/\alpha}\}}{\alpha\{(b-m)^{(\alpha+1)/\alpha} - (m^* - m)^{(\alpha+1)/\alpha}\}},$$

$$(3.5)'\qquad e_f = \frac{(1+\alpha)m}{\alpha(b-m)}.$$

Simple but somewhat tedious algebraic manipulations of equations (i), (3.4)′, and (3.5)′ produce the relations $e_f > e_c' > e_c$.

relationships are as follows: (i) HS competition tends to yield a lower mill price in the space economy than does Löschian competition; (ii) each of the subject forms of competition tends to produce higher mill prices than the price charged by the profit maximizing spatial monopolist. But this last result is unfortunate since an increase in competition should not be expected to increase the firm's mill price. The need for a third (alternative) model of spatial competition is therefore indicated.

The GO Model

This model was originally designed for the purpose of comparing market sizes and shapes under competitive pricing [**6**]. It assumes that the firm regards neither its own market area nor its rival's mill price as fixed, treating them instead as variables. Only the firm's delivered price at its market boundary is taken as a datum. Phrased alternatively, a price ceiling at the firm's boundary points is parametrically given under the GO model of spatial competition, and the resulting spatial demand is accordingly specifiable as follows:

$$(4.4) \qquad Q = n\int_0^{D_0''} f(m + kD)\,dD, \qquad D_0'' = \frac{p_0 - m}{k},$$

where D_0'' stands for the distance from the firm's mill to the market boundary and p_0 represents the parametrically given delivered price ceiling, which is assumed to be less than the price intercept $f^{-1}(0)$.[15]

First and second order differentiation of (4.4) with respect to m respectively yield:

$$(4.5) \qquad \frac{dQ}{dm} = \frac{\partial Q}{\partial D_0''}\frac{dD_0''}{dm} + \frac{\partial Q}{\partial m}$$

$$= -\frac{n}{k}f(p_0) + n\int_0^{D_0''} f_m(m + kD)\,dD, \qquad D_0'' = \frac{p_0 - m}{k},$$

$$= -\frac{n}{k}\,f(m) < 0;$$

$$(4.6) \qquad \frac{d^2Q}{dm^2} = -\frac{n}{k}\,f_m(m) > 0.$$

The shape of the GO demand function is thus strictly convex to the origin in conformance with free spatial demand, and thus somewhat different from the HS and competitive Löschian demands. Since the slope of the GO demand function is exactly the same as that of the free spatial demand (cf. (4.5) with (2.2)), it can be conceived of as a simple *horizontal leftward shift* of the latter curve. (See Figure 3.) It follows that the GO demand is *necessarily* more elastic than the free spatial demand for any relevant mill price. This conclusion holds in general and does not

[15] If $p_0 = f^{-1}(0)$, the competitive spatial demand function would converge to that of the free spatial demand function.

require a particular gross demand function, such as that given by (3.3). The critical distinguishing feature of the GO demand function compared with the Lösch and HS demand functions lies in the fact that the elasticity of the former is not only greater at comparable prices than that of the alternative competitive models, but is also more elastic than that of the free spatial demand. A remarkable implication of this result is that the GO type of spatial competition tends to *lower* mill price whereas the Lösch-HS models tend to *raise* it.

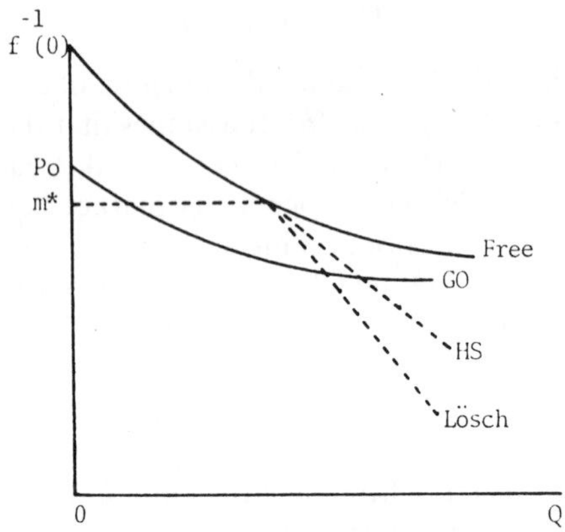

FIGURE 3.—Alternative spatial demand function.

5. CONCLUSIONS

A provisional statement is required before evaluating the scope and need for the analysis given above. In this context, observe again the restriction that our derivations of the spatial demand curve presupposed f.o.b. mill pricing. But this pricing system cannot typically be expected to prevail in the space economy because spatial discrimination can always be shown to be both more profitable and to yield greater outputs than f.o.b. mill pricing in all monopoly and in many competitive situations.[16] This limiting thought suggests that the relevance of comparing spatial and nonspatial gross demand curves must, in turn, be confined to applications which are in the same key. But on to the scope and need for theorems on spatial demand curves.

Consider the theory of cost-push price inflation, or the multiple theses dealing with concentrated markets and industrial pricing; in fact, consider the broader subject of general microeconomic theory. Regardless of which focus is kept in mind, a commonality of framework prevails in the sense that typically each subject in the past has been formulated without conceptual inclusion of economic space. The related analysis has centered, in turn, on competitive vis a vis simple monopoly

[16] For a discussion of monopoly outputs under alternative spatial pricing techniques, see M. L. Greenhut and H. Ohta [5].

or organized oligopoly pricing. But in the classical competitive model, any aggregation of identical individual market demands provides an industrial market demand curve which is identical in shape (and form) to the individual demands. *Interpretation of empirical findings, in turn, would tend to reflect this identity.* On the other hand, aggregation of identical gross individual demand curves by a spatial monopolist or by a cartel selling over an economic space produces a convex to origin demand curve.[17] Special price effects, therefore, arise because of space compared with the counterpart prices that would obtain under conceptions of zero cost of distance.[18] *Interpretations of empirical findings, in turn, would tend to change.*

It is significant to note in contrast to the monopoly or slight competition cases that if spatial markets are assumed to be restricted in size, in the sense that other firms locate at a distance from a specified seller (or set of sellers) and limit the market of pre-established firms to D_0^*, as in the Lösch model, the shape of the aggregate demand curve reflects the individual demand curves. If, on the other hand, the rival firm's spatial price schedule is assumed to be given to a particular firm, as in the HS model, the spatial demand curve becomes typically convex to the demand curve.[17] Special price effects, therefore, arise because of space compared

[17] Consider, as an example, a spaceless demand curve:

$$Q = \frac{1}{a}(b - p), \tag{i}$$

where Q is the spaceless aggregate demand of n buyers, b is the price intercept, a is the slope of the demand curve, and p stands for price. Individual buyer demand is therefore $q = (1/an)(b - p)$, and the profit maximizing price and output are respectively $p = b/2$ and $Q = b/2a$.

To compare the spaceless world with a spatial world, the same total number of buyers is required for the space economy as in (i), i.e., a particular density distribution must be assumed such that aggregate spatial demand is as follows:

$$Q = \frac{1}{a\pi b^2}\int_0^{2\pi}\int_0^{D_0}(b - m - kD)D\,dD\,d\theta, \tag{ii}$$

where D_0 again is the maximum straight-line market distance, and $\pi b^2 = n$. Let k be unity so that $D_0 = b - m$. Equation (ii) can easily be converted to:

$$Q = \frac{(b - m)^3}{3ab^2}, \tag{ii)$'$}$$

and the profit maximizing mill price and related output level determined to be $m = b/4$ and $Q = 9b/64a$. Significantly, the price and output level in a spatial monopoly world is lower than in the monopolized market in which cost of distance is zero, ceteris paribus. Moreover, the elasticity at common prices on the two curves is different, being more elastic at corresponding prices greater than zero on the spatial monopoly curve than on the spaceless monopoly demand curve. A tendency to lower prices rather than raise them thus underscores pricing by a market widening spatial monopolist, ceteris paribus. This condition, in turn, dramatizes whatever historical evidence may be set forth [e.g. **9**] supporting fixed-administered prices by a cartel or set of oligopolists located at a single production center whose *total* sales are increasing. On the other hand, if the industry can be shown to be characterized by the existence of rival production centers whose market areas tend to overlap, support for contrasting interpretation would obtain [e.g., see **11**]. (It warrants mention as an aside that the elasticity differences given in this note to illustrate how spatial economic theory affects interpretations of statistical data were based on linear demand curves, but nevertheless apply in general [**5**]; exceptions relate to the cases of identical spaceless demand curves whose domains involve either (i) constant elasticity, (ii) increasing elasticity, or (iii) an elasticity which decreases less than the related decrease in price. Such demand curves nevertheless support the basic argument being presented in the text above.)

[18] See [**4**, Appendix to Chapter 6] where it is shown that mill price decreases when a seller extends his market area over costly distances.

origin. It could be concave only if the individual demands are very concave. In the GO model, on the other hand, the spatial demand is necessarily convex to the origin.

Related to alternative shapes of the spatial demand functions are diverse elasticity and price possibilities: (i) The Lösch-HS types of spatial competition *lower* the demand elasticities and accordingly tend to *raise* the equilibrium mill prices. In sharp contrast, (ii) the GO type of competition *raises* the demand elasticity and accordingly tends to lower the equilibrium mill price. In the broadest sense, the elasticity at any price on the *competitive* spatial demand curves may be greater, less, or the same as that of the *free* spatial demand curves, depending upon the particular model assumed to be relevant. One would expect it to be less given the Lösch-HS models;[19] in turn, one would tend to argue that what might appear to be an administered price unresponsive to competition is, in fact, a competitively determined price whose character is attributable to the elasticity lowering effects of spatial competition.[20] Adherence to the GO model would imply that increases in spatial competition should lower mill prices quoted by the firm; hence the GO model supports an administered price thesis if in reality prices stayed the same or were raised in the presence of increased competition, ceteris paribus. In any and all events, empiricism predicated on theories designed for a spaceless world may well be lacking or insufficient in the world of economic space.[21] Suffice it to say for our purposes that spatial price theory often points towards different conclusions than classical price theory. It is for this reason that the reality and properties of spatial demand curves require study by economists interested in econometric models designed to predict and explain prices in free enterprise economies.

Texas A. and M. University,
West Virginia University,
and
Aoyama Gakuin University.

Manuscript received January, 1973; last revision received June, 1974.

[19] As indicated in (3.6), $e_c < e_f$ and if the m^* stemming from competition is greater than the monopoly price m, the competitive price will be greater than the monopoly price provided marginal costs are relatively stable, i.e., not increasing too rapidly with output. Moreover, as competition increases from level c_0 to c_1, distance D_0^* decreases and m^* therefore rises. The Löschian demand curve breaks off upward and to the left of the original Löschian demand curve. Pursuant to (3.6), it further follows that $e_{c_1} < e_{c_0}$ and that price will rise, provided again marginal costs continue to be relatively stable over the relevant range of output. Lösch's space model would therefore suggest that findings of a low monopoly price may not be the result of monopolistic enlightenment or beneficence. In the language of a U.S. Supreme Court decision, the Lösch conception suggests that the low pricing "trust" is not necessarily a good "trust."

[20] For example, see disagreements and interpretations by [**9**, **11**, **12**] and in this general context, see [**1**].

[21] G. C. Means [**9**] shows that in 10 specific business cycle contractions and 56 specific expansions the administered-price thesis is supported in 85 per cent of the cases, as the subject prices showed either no tendency to change or else contra-cyclical behavior. But Means' findings could be interpreted differently as was suggested in note 17. For example, if the markets in recent periods of time can be shown to have involved fixed distances in all old and newly established market directions, it may not have been organized (i.e., administered) oligopolistic price fixing which produced the fixity of price or contra-cyclical behavior, but possibly a *lagged* yet direct-cyclical effect of competitive impacts traceable to recently established production centers.

REFERENCES

[1] Arrow, K. J., D. Block, and L. Hurwicz: "On the Stability of the Competitive Equilibrium, II," *Econometrica*, 26 (1959), 82–109.

[2] Denike, K. G., and J. B. Parr: "Production in Space, Spatial Competition, and Restricted Entry," *Journal of Regional Science*, 10 (1970), 49–63.

[3] Gannon, C. A.: "Fundamental Properties of Löschian Spatial Demand," *Environment and Planning*, 3 (1971), 283–306.

[4] Greenhut, M. L.: *A Theory of the Firm in Economic Space*. Second printing, Austin: Lonestar Publishing Co., 1974.

[5] Greenhut, M. L., and H. Ohta: "Monopoly Output under Alternative Spatial Pricing Techniques," *American Economic Review*, 62 (1972), 705–713.

[6] ———: "Spatial Configurations and Competitive Equilibrium," *Welt Wirtschaftliches Archiv*, 109 (1973), 87–104.

[7] Hotelling, H.: "Stability in Competition," *Economic Journal*, 39 (1929), 41–57.

[8] Lösch, A.: *The Economics of Location*. New Haven: Yale University Press, 1954.

[9] Means, G. C.: "The Administered Price Thesis Reconfirmed," *American Economic Review*, 62 (1972), 292–306.

[10] Smithies, A.: "Optimal Location in Spatial Competition," *Journal of Political Economy*, 49 (1941), 423–439.

[11] Stigler, G., and J. Kindahl: *The Behavior of Industrial Prices*. New York: Columbia University Press, 1970.

[12] Weston, J. Fred: "Pricing Behavior of Large Firms," *Western Economic Journal*, 10 (1972), 1–18.

[21]

On Demand Curves and Spatial Pricing

M L GREENHUT
Texas A and M University

1 Introduction

The paper begins with a brief examination of two general but sharply alternative demand forms, each of which commands several properties wanted by economists, such as increasing quantities demanded at lower price, continuity, and negative-sloped marginal-revenue functions. The two demand forms are

$$p = \beta - \frac{\alpha}{x} q^x , \qquad \alpha, \beta > 0 , \tag{1}$$

$$p = \beta - \frac{\alpha}{x} q^x , \qquad \alpha > 0 , \quad \beta \gtreqless 0 , \quad -1 < x < 0 , \tag{2}$$

where p is price and q is demand.

Form (1) is defined as less convex than the negative exponential given by Stevens and Rydell (1966), or its alternative log form, derived as Ic by Greenhut and Greenhut (1977). (The properties of the demand form referred to as the negative exponential are described later.)

Now, the less convex subset (1) includes the linear demand. Little need be said about it. On the other hand, the more convex demand curve requires details which will also establish the methodology that the reader can use to go beyond the conclusions that shall be specified for subset (1). In particular, from equation (2) we have

$$\gamma q^x = \beta - p , \tag{3}$$

where $\gamma = \alpha/x$. Via the differentiation process, we obtain

$$e = -\frac{p}{q}\frac{\mathrm{d}q}{\mathrm{d}p} = \frac{p}{x(\beta - p)} > 0 . \tag{4}$$

Manifestly, $e > 0$ when $x < 0$ and $\beta \gtreqless 0$, provided $\beta < p$, for which case (that is, $x < 0$) we also require β to be less than marginal cost k in order to limit sales in any market.

Marginal revenue (R_{M}) is, therefore,

$$R_{\mathrm{M}} = (1 + x)p - \beta x = p + (p - \beta)x > 0 , \tag{5}$$

and

$$\frac{\mathrm{d}R_{\mathrm{M}}}{\mathrm{d}q} = (1 + x)\frac{\mathrm{d}p}{\mathrm{d}q} < 0 , \tag{6}$$

$$\frac{\mathrm{d}e}{\mathrm{d}p} = \frac{\beta x}{[x(\beta - p)]^2} \lesseqgtr 0 \quad \text{if} \quad \beta \gtreqless 0 . \tag{7}$$

Given $\beta > 0$, $\mathrm{d}e/\mathrm{d}p$ is negative, and the demand curve can be characterized as of increasing elasticity. If $\beta = 0$, $\mathrm{d}e/\mathrm{d}p$ is 0, and the demand curve has constant elasticity throughout. If $\beta < 0$, $\mathrm{d}e/\mathrm{d}p$ is positive, and the demand curve is of decreasing elasticity, where the proportional changes in p are greater than those in e throughout the curve (see Greenhut and Ohta, 1975).

2 More and less convex demands

The more convex demand-curve subset provides several interesting propositions, one of which is to deny Robinson's claim that "adjusted concavity", defined as $eq^2\,(\mathrm{d}^2p/\mathrm{d}q^2)$, establishes the result that a more elastic demand curve cannot be "consistently less concave" (Robinson, 1929, note 1, pages 198, 200). Using, for example, the form $p = \gamma q^{-1/e_1}$ for market 1, and $p = \gamma q^{-1/e_2}$ for market 2, with $\gamma > 0$, $e_1 > e_2 > 1$, yields a more elastic demand curve in market 1 that remains consistently less concave than the less elastic curve. The reason is that adjusted concavity is less in market 1, that is

$$\left(1 + \frac{1}{e_1}\right)p > \left(1 + \frac{1}{e_2}\right)p\,.$$

The upshot is that regardless of costs a monopolist subject to these demands in two separate markets would, under Robinson's criterion, sell a smaller discriminatory output than nondiscriminatory output. This result would hold only if the discriminatory marginal revenue curve lies consistently below the nondiscriminatory curve, call it the simple marginal revenue curve; but, as shown by Robinson, *this is impossible* since total revenue under price discrimination cannot be less than under nondiscriminatory pricing. Robinson's criterion thus leads to the contradiction of X and not X at the same instant. We must, accordingly, probe further towards determining whether different outputs apply to more convex or to less convex demand curves, and then ascertaining which demand-curve subset, (1) or (2), is the likely one to occur in the real world.

3 Output effects of discriminatory and free on board pricing

In a paper devoted to the subject of the output effects of the demand curves (1) and (2), Lee (1986) demonstrates the following.

The output differences between discriminatory and free on board (fob) pricing stem from two conditions: first, discriminatory pricing allows the monopolist operating under a less convex demand curve to have a greater market area; second, different mill prices at all locations (market) generate different outputs compared with those under fob pricing, unless the demand curve is completely inelastic. This second effect is approximated by Robinson's (1929) adjusted concavity principle.

The first condition is inapplicable under a more convex demand curve because of the unique characteristic of the demand curve. That is, under the more convex demand curve, the market is infinite in size both for the fob pricing firm and for the discriminatory pricing firm. This follows because the net demand curve has no price intercept (that is, the curve never touches the vertical axis) regardless of the market distance between the seller and the buyer. However, this unique characteristic of spatial demand curves would also bring about different aggregate marginal revenue curves for the fob firm and the discriminatory pricing monopolist. Hence, outputs would be different depending upon pricing policy. More fundamentally, we should conceive of a finite price limit which would limit the market area of the monopolist. However, to generalize in order to compare competitive with monopoly outputs, let me simply begin my analysis by *assuming* the same finite market space under both pricing systems, such as a national boundary line might impose on a firm subject to a more convex demand curve. This conception serves as the departure point for the evaluations that follow.

3.1 *The analysis*

Consider the demand form

$$q = \left[-\frac{1}{2b}(a - m - tr) \right]^{-2}, \tag{8}$$

where m is the mill price, t is the freight rate, r is the distance from the seller's location to the site of a particular buyer, and the a, b parameters are positive numbers. Total aggregate demand under fob mill pricing over the market length L is

$$Q_{\text{fob}} = \frac{4b^2}{t}\left(\frac{1}{a - m - tL} - \frac{1}{a - m} \right), \tag{9}$$

and profit under constant marginal cost c is

$$\Pi = (m - c)Q_{\text{fob}}, \tag{10}$$

The optimal fob mill price is then

$$m_{\text{fob}} = c + [(c - a)tL + (c - a)^2]^{1/2}. \tag{11}$$

Substituting equation (11) into equation (9) establishes the fob mill firm's profit-maximizing output:

$$Q_{\text{fob}} = \frac{4b^2}{t} \frac{tL}{\{a - c - [(c - a)tL + (c - a)^2]^{1/2} - tL\}\{a - c - [(c - a)tL + (c - a)^2]^{1/2}\}}. \tag{12}$$

Determining the discriminatory mill price m_D requires two basic steps:

$$\Pi_{max} = (m - c)q$$
$$= (-2b)^2(m - c)(a - m - tr)^{-2}, \tag{13}$$

and

$$\frac{\partial \Pi}{\partial m} = (-2b)^2(a - m - tr)^{-2}[1 + 2(m - c)(a - m - tr)^{-1}] = 0 .$$

Hence,

$$m_D = 2c + tr - a , \tag{14}$$

since $a - m - tr \neq 0$. Total discriminatory output is then

$$Q_D = \int_0^L \left[-\frac{1}{2b}(a - m_D - tr) \right]^{-2} dr$$
$$= -\frac{b^2}{t}(a - c - tr)^{-1} \Big|_0^L$$
$$= \frac{b^2}{t}\left(\frac{1}{a - c - tL} - \frac{1}{a - c} \right) . \tag{15}$$

Output comparisons of equations (12) and (15) establish

$$Q_{fob} = \frac{4b^2}{t} \frac{tL}{\{X - [(-Y)(-X)]^{1/2}\}\{Y - [(-Y)(-X)]^{1/2}\}}, \tag{16}$$

and

$$Q_D = \frac{b^2}{t}\left(\frac{1}{X} - \frac{1}{Y} \right) = \frac{b^2}{t}\frac{tL}{XY}, \tag{17}$$

where $X = a - c - tL$, and $Y = a - c$. It follows that

$$\frac{Q_D}{Q_{fob}} = \frac{1}{4}\left[2 - \frac{X + Y}{(XY)^{1/2}} \right] . \tag{18}$$

Hence, $Q_D/Q_{fob} > 1$ if $(X + Y)/(XY)^{1/2} < -2$. That is, $Q_D > Q_{fob}$ if $X + Y + 2(XY)^{1/2} < 0$.

By substitution, we obtain

$$X + Y + 2(XY)^{1/2} = -[(c + tL - a)^{1/2} - (c - a)^{1/2}]^2 < 0 . \tag{19}$$

Therefore, $Q_D > Q_{fob}$.

The result obtained by Greenhut and Ohta (1972), henceforth GO, thus applies under the more convex demand curves as well as for the less convex demands. But note the following differences.

3.2 *Conclusions to be drawn*

In contrast to the GO result (1972), where the greater output involved a larger market area under spatial price discrimination than under fob pricing, the results for the extremely convex demand curve (2) apply even more forcefully. Recall that the present finding, $Q_D > Q_{fob}$, was based on the same market size L under either pricing system. Hence, this finding contrasts sharply to Beckmann's (1976), who, working with linear demand and a fixed (same size) market, obtained $Q_D = Q_{fob}$[1]. Since profits are greater under discriminatory pricing, I propose for set (2) [as holds for *the linear demand case* (Greenhut, 1978)] that if $\Pi_{fob} = 0$ when $L_{fob} = L_D$, more firms will enter the market under discriminatory pricing. This entry will produce a still lower set of prices and smaller distances for the discriminatory sellers—and, hence, a greatly expanded total output. This is the same basic long-run entry result established by GO (1975), albeit now it results even more distinctively. In the present case, demands of the more convex order provide greater output for a firm selling over an identical market length as a fob firm[2]. In addition, we now have a greater number of firms and, hence, a much greater total output in a zero profit equilibrium.

4 The relevance of the demand-curve subsets

We are at the point where the relevance of each demand-curve subset warrants discussion. In this context, the present section is subdivided into two parts, the first covering aspects of discriminatory pricing, the second providing applications of the pricing results that relate to demand-curve types (1) and (2).

4.1 *Discriminatory pricing differences under demands (1) and (2)*

Hoover (1937) observed for the increasing elasticity, constant elasticity, and decreasing elasticity cases of subset (2) that the subject elasticity conditions induce the firm to discriminate against distant buyers. He noted that this is unlikely to occur in practice because of resale opportunities. [Also see Greenhut (1956) for a geometrical demonstration of changes in elasticity with distance under subset (2) demand curves.] The less convex demand induces discrimination against nearer buyers, tending to extend the market space of the firm in the process. In fact, the prevalence of discriminatory pricing in free enterprise countries (see Greenhut, 1981) as well as the theoretical cornerstones for it under conditions of spatial *competition* (Greenhut and Greenhut, 1975) suggest

(1)As noted in the introduction, the linear demand is a member of the less convex demand-curve subset. Assuming it, Beckmann derived identical outputs and eventually concluded that social welfare is enhanced under fob pricing.

(2)We can appreciate the difference in results intuitively by recognizing that the more convex demands (2) lead to discrimination against distant buyers. This set enables significant sales to be made to proximate buyers, whereas at the great distances, where price is higher for the discriminatory seller vis-à-vis the fob seller, sales do *not* fall off significantly (see section 4 for details). Thus, the result that $Q_D > Q_{fob}$ under demand set (2) and $L_D = L_{fob}$, but $Q_D = Q_{fob}$ under demand set (1) given $L_D = L_{fob}$, is easily understood.

the likelihood of (in fact, prevalence of) subset (1) under-scoring the free enterprise economies of the world. Moreover, the full set of discriminatory pricing discussed by Phlips (1983), including amusement park pricing, checkbook pricing, bundled goods pricing, freight rate and utility power pricing, etc, also suggest the prevalence of the less convex demand form. But more on this later. For the moment, it suffices to note that subset (1) would generate discriminatory pricing in favor of distant buyers and subset (2) favors nearer buyers. What about fob pricing?

Regardless of demand-curve type, the fob mill price is invariant with respect to the locations of buyers. Also, the delivered price at any buyer's location is greater than the mill price by the amount of freight cost to the buyer's site. What the more convex demand curve connotes vis-à-vis the less convex demand curve is simply that each extension of the market area brings into the seller's total market a buyer (or set of buyers) whose demands are less elastic at any given price than are the demands of more proximate buyers. This condition is opposite to that of less convex demands, where, for example, the (net effective) linear demand of the more distant buyer—being shifted downward compared with that of the more proximate buyer by the amount of freight cost applicable per unit of product delivered to that site—is more elastic at any given price. Under subset (2), aggregate market demand elasticity is, therefore, less for any given area than under subset (1), and the mill price is accordingly higher under subset (2) than subset (1), ceteris paribus.

4.2 *Applying the analysis by example*

As noted at the outset to this section, besides evaluating fob and discriminatory price differences for demands (1) and (2) in section 4, I will also apply the results. Essentially, that assertion meant that in this subsection the different effects of competition and demands (1) and (2) on fob prices will be discussed. Discriminatory pricing is ignored here by recalling that the impact of demands (2), rather than demands (1), is simply to steepen the firm's delivered-price schedule, shifting, as it were, the price discrimination to favor proximate buyers instead of distant buyers. If competition then occurs at a distance, the representative firm's market space is decreased. But, since each submarket is treated separately, apart from losing more distant buyers to distant rivals, the firm's other market prices stay the same[(3)]. Accordingly, attention here can be confined to competitive impacts on fob prices.

[(3)]There are conjectural variation impacts, particularly in cases of uniform pricing *and* the pricing of goods in order to discourage *potential* entry. For the purposes of this paper, such cases can be ignored [see Greenhut et al (1986, chapters 7, 12, and 13) for exceptions and details].

It has been noted by many observers that an increase in the number of doctors of medicine (MDs) raises the price (fees) they charge. It has been proposed (Greenhut et al. 1985) that this, and related, phenomena are readily explained by a tie-up between less convex demand curves *and* Löschian (price matching) competition, whereas other forms of conjectural variations would establish classical supply-price effects regardless of demand-curve types. For present purposes, it suffices to note that the significantly unique tie-up between less convex demand curves and Löschian competition was also found by Benson (1986) to apply to the pricing of breakfast cereals. What I want to do here is probe behind these findings. Specifically, I want to imagine below what the more convex demand-curve type *in effect* would involve regarding frequency of one's use of *and* the fees charged by MDs, dentists, lawyers, accountants, etc.

Take the less convex set first. This means that the cost of distance (d) or time (t) will cause a consumer to buy only a relatively small quantity of the good or service over any period of time, and that a subsequent reduction in price will elicit a relatively greater increase in the quantity purchased than for the case where no d, t costs were involved. In turn, the unique negative exponential demand curve would require the relative change in acquisitions resulting from changes in price to be the same whether or not there were costs of distance or time applicable to the subject good or service. Finally, the more convex subset signifies that a reduction in price would elicit a smaller increase in the quantity wanted when d, t costs were important vis-à-vis the case where d, t costs do not apply. In detail, consider the following hypothetical possibilities.

Let demand subset (1) apply. Suppose an older person would visit his/ her MD three times a year if waiting time and distance travelled to the MD were costless. But then assume that time and commuting costs (arduous trip) are significant and that the customer thus confines his/her use of the MD to one visit a year. Next assume that a lowering of fees in the costless time or spaceless case prompts four trips per year, whereas a corresponding reduction of fees in the real world might induce three trips per year (for example, the lower fees enable the customer to drink a lot of booze during the trip making it less arduous than otherwise). Note further that e is greater (actually increased) in the time and/or commuting cost case. Indeed, we might propose that the customer switches from using a less to more specialized MD as a consequence of the lowering of fees when time and/or distance is costly. The converse holds for an increase in fees. In particular, in the classical (no distance or time cost) world, two visits may replace three when fees are raised, whereas when d, t costs are important, one visit every two years (along with using a quack) may replace the practice of one visit every year [see table 1, demand (1)].

The negative exponential demand would signify that when fees go down the customer in the classical world would visit the MD four times in place of three; and one and a third times in place of one when *d, t* costs are significant. (Note the proportional change in visits is the same in either world.) In turn, an increase in fees would decrease the number of visits respectively to 2 and 0.66 (see table 1). Observe, as explained elsewhere (Greenhut et al, 1986), that in the case of negative exponential demand the downward shifted demand curve (because of *d, t* costs) retains the same elasticity at any given price as the original demand curve.

For the more convex set it is best to imagine a poor hypochondriac who increases his/her visits from 3 to 4 and from 1 to 1.10, respectively, as fees are lowered slightly in the classical *and* the costly *d, t* worlds. This consumer can be conceived in the *d, t* world to require regular examination, even if by a witch doctor, but not to be induced noticeably by the lowering of fees to be examined more often. In turn, an increase in fees which decreases classical world visits noticeably has scarcely any behavior effect on the individual when distance and time are costly; the number of visits in that world falls only to 0.99, a quack being good enough for most purposes, but not in any way being a more or less perfect substitute (see table 1).

What does competitive entry mean? It means lower waiting time and/or lower commuting costs. Suppose further we assume each MD believes that other MDs will react identically to the subject MD's changed actions, that is, raise or lower fees equivalently. Call this the Löschian (L) behavioral conjecture. Alternatively, let each MD ignore the rival's change. Call this the Greenhut-Ohta (GO) behavior. As shown elsewhere (Greenhut et al, 1985), L behavior and entry under

Table 1. Annual visits to the MD.

Demand	World	Given original fees	Given lowered fees	Given raised fees
(1)	classical world[a]	3	4	2
	world of *d, t* costs	1	3	0.50
Negative exponential	classical world[a]	3	4	2
	world of *d, t* costs	1	1.33	0.66
(2)	classical world[a]	3	4	2
	world of *d, t* costs	1	1.10	0.99

[a]The purpose of the table is to compare the impacts of *d, t* costs under different demand curves. I use the same classical world numbers for each demand curve as the departure point. Note further that demand (1) is illustrated with numbers that reflect a concave demand rather than the linear or convex demand members of that set.

demand (1) raises the fees of MDs, whereas under demand (2) it lowers the fees. GO behavior and demand (1) or demand (2) lowers the fees. The reader can interpret these findings in the context of table 1, for which an exogenous change in fees was assumed. Manifestly, since output effects in response to prices are in the same direction under fob pricing as under discriminatory pricing, regardless of demands (1) and (2), but the price-relative output effects vary considerably, the question of the relevance of demands (1) and (2) is important. It is to the matter of relevance that I turn in the following section of this article. Simply put, how likely is it that we would experience demand (1) in practice rather than demand (2)?

5 Characteristics of demand-curve subsets

5.1 *Characteristics of the negative exponential demand curve*

Suppose the dq/q relation for all constant dp changes is itself a constant over the whole demand curve [call it the basic (demand) curve]. Then from $e = -(pdq)/(qdp)$, we recognize that a *greater elasticity* exists on the basic demand curve *at all higher prices*, given invariable dp increments *and* the condition that the decreased dq value associated with the smaller q yields a constant dq/q ratio at each higher price.

Suppose next we shift that basic curve downward. This would establish elasticity values for the shifted curve that are identical to those on the basic demand curve, for any given (same) price on each curve. Via the proof given elsewhere (Greenhut et al, 1986), we can further deduce the facts (a) that the dq/q ratio is a constant throughout the range of constant dp changes on the negative exponential demand curve, and (b) that *the elasticity of demand increases along that curve as price goes up.*

5.2 *Characteristics of the increasing elasticity demand curve*

Consider next a significantly different demand curve, one whose elasticity decreases at higher prices (that is, a curve customarily referred to as a demand curve of increasing elasticity, the definition—increasing elasticity—given with respect to a lowering of price). Such a curve requires a substantial decrease in the dq part (for example, approaching 0) of the dq/q relation (ratio) at higher prices in order for lower elasticity to be obtained as price goes up. Moreover, we know (Greenhut et al, 1986) that the elasticity is less on the downward shifted curve at any comparable price. It warrants repeated emphasis that the numerical decrease in the dq value has to be substantial since the q value is also less. (The dq number is falling to lower values than the decreased q.) In other words, extreme convexity throughout applies to this curve. It is manifest that downward shifted curves are characterized by increasingly inelastic values at a given price vis-à-vis the basic curve. Moreover, at all higher prices on the downward shifted curve, elasticity is *sharply* less than it is on the basic curve, again at all corresponding prices. The shifted curve is of even greater increasing elasticity (by definition) than the basic curve.

5.3 *Characteristics of the constant elasticity demand curve*
Consider next a demand curve whose elasticity is constant over all prices. Then at higher prices, for a given d*p*, we must have, via $e = -(p\mathrm{d}q)/(q\mathrm{d}p)$, a decreased d*q*/*q* ratio in perfect offset to the greater *p*/d*p* value. Again, since the *q* values are smaller, the decreased numerical value of d*q* over all higher prices must be significant, but not as low as that required for the curve of increasing elasticity. (To repeat, the decrease in d*q*/*q* on the constant elasticity demand curve must only offset the increase in *p*/d*p*.) It follows that the elasticity is less on the downward shifted curve than it is on the basic curve at any comparable price. This results because the constant elasticity of the basic curve entailed lower d*q*/*q* ratios *at higher prices* and, hence, a lower d*q*/*q* on the shifted curve than on the basic curve at the same (given) price. Moreover, note that, unlike the basic curve, the downward shifted curve is a curve of increasing elasticity rather than constant elasticity.

5.4 *Characteristics of a decreasing elasticity demand curve that is more convex than the negative exponential*
Consider finally a demand curve whose elasticity increases *somewhat* at higher prices (that is, it decreases somewhat at lower prices) rather than being of the types 5.2, 5.3 described above. The present curve is, therefore, comparable with the negative exponential demand curve to the extent that its elasticity is greater at higher prices. However, since the d*q*/*q* ratio is constant along the negative exponential, we know that the increase in *elasticity* at higher prices on the present curve is relatively less than the relative increase in the *p*/d*q* ratio. (This follows since the elasticity along the negative exponential curve rises at higher prices in perfect conformance to the rise in *p*/d*p*.) Thus, the d*q*/*q* ratio is smaller at higher prices, but its lower value is more than offset (that is, it is comparatively less) than the rise in the *p*/d*p* value. In still other words, d*q* decreases more on the subject basic curve at higher prices than it does on the negative exponential curve. However, the d*q*/*q* ratio at higher prices is not nearly as numerically small as on the constant elasticity and especially the increasing elasticity demand curves. But, as with these curves (that is, the constant and increasingly elastic demand curves), the elasticity is less at any comparable price on the downward shifted curve vis-à-vis the basic curve, because the d*q*/*q* ratio is less than that on the basic curve at the given price. Moreover, because the d*q*/*q* value is less at higher prices on the basic curve, even though relatively smaller than the increase in price (since elasticity must increase at higher prices on that curve), it further follows that again the demand is more inelastic at any given price on the downward shifted curve vis-à-vis the basic curve.

5.5 *Summary—subset (2)*

To sum up the present findings on the more convex demands, note that, for the decreasingly elastic curve, the decrease in elasticity on the downward shifted curve is less at comparable prices than when the basic curve is of constant elasticity; and, it is much less than when the basic curve is of increasing elasticity.

5.6 *Relevance of demands (1) and (2)*

Observe finally that for each of the demands described in the sections following the discussion of the negative exponential demand curve, the elasticity is less on the shifted curve than on the basic curve at any given price. The fundamental property required for this effect is a *substantial* lowering of the numerical value of dq, and hence a *decline* in the number dq/q, no matter how high the price. This is *a most unlikely phenomenon at higher and still higher prices* since the consumer is required to want the good or service no matter what the price[4]. Alternatively, a *substantial increase* in quantity is required no matter how low the price and how large the original quantity. The requirements are too stringent in general for this demand curve to typify the economy.

6 Conclusion

In this paper I have proposed that demands (1) warrant theoretical emphasis. Hence, these demands typically should be used to interpret empirical findings, such as for amusement park pricing, utility pricing, the fees of MDs, the prices of cereals, ad infinitum. Heterogeneous demands (over time and space), and such functions as $p = \beta/(q + \alpha)$, could warrant consideration and analysis in the many contrasting situations we are likely to find in the real world. Demand subset (2) is rather extreme given the analysis in this paper.

References

Beckmann M J, 1976, "Spatial price policies revisited" *Bell Journal of Economics* 7 619-630

Benson B, 1986, "Increasing product variety and rising prices" manuscript under review; details available from the author, Department of Economics, Florida State University, Tallahassee, FL 32306

Greenhut J, Greenhut M L, 1975, "Spatial price discrimination, competition, and locational effects" *Economica* **42** 401-419

Greenhut J, Greenhut M L, 1977, "Nonlinearity of delivered price schedule and predatory pricing" *Econometrica* **45** 1871-1876

[4]Interestingly, if one wants to contend that demands for medical services may be of this shape, then market entry must lower fees regardless of conjectural variations, or else some other factor dominates pricing in that industry. A cancer or accident victim with governmental subsidy may have demands (2). But the empirical findings regarding fees are for general services not those centered on life-and-death situations.

Greenhut M L, 1956, *Plant Location in Theory and in Practice* (University of North Carolina Press, Chapel Hill, NC) 4th printing, 1982 (Greenwood Press, Westport, CT)

Greenhut M L, 1978, "Impacts of distance on microeconomic theory" *The Manchester School* **46** 17–40

Greenhut M L, 1981, "Spatial pricing in the USA, West Germany, and Japan" *Economica* **48** 79–86

Greenhut M L, Hung C S, Norman G, Smithson C, 1985, "An anomaly in the service industry: the effect of entry on fees" *The Economic Journal* **95** 169–177

Greenhut M L, Norman G, Hung C S, 1986 *Imperfect Competition: A Spatial Approach* (Cambridge University Press, Cambridge)

Greenhut M L, Ohta H, 1972, "Monopoly output under alternative spatial pricing techniques" *The American Economic Review* **62** 705–713

Greenhut M L, Ohta H, 1975 *Theory of Spatial Prices and Market Areas* (Duke University Press, Durham, NC)

Hoover E M, 1937, "Spatial price discrimination" *Review of Economic Studies* **4** 182–191

Lee C S, 1986, "Output effects of price discrimination" manuscript under review; details available from the author, 60-5 Shinheung-Dong, Gun San, Junbuk, South Korea

Phlips L, 1983, *The Economics of Price Discrimination* (Cambridge University Press, Cambridge)

Robinson J, 1929 *The Economics of Imperfect Competition* 2nd edition (St Martin's Press, New York)

Stevens B H, Rydell C P, 1966, "Spatial demand theory and monopoly price policy" *Papers of the Regional Science Association* **17** 195–204

PART III

APPLICATIONS OF SPATIAL MICROECONOMICS

Theoretical Error, Economic Space, Price Theory and Data

John Greenhut
M. L. Greenhut
Hiroshi Ohta*

I

The late Professor Morgenstern stressed two types of error in the use of economic data in applied economics [17]. The first one, more easily recognized than the second, was called measurement error. This error relates to mistakes made in recording data, in which category he included typing errors, errors arising from the use of machines, errors related to misinterpreting questionnaires, and even errors attributable to the deliberate withholding of information which omission is distortive. The claim by Professor Morgenstern that the average measurement error in physics is about 10% should arouse particular concern among economists as to the accuracy of the data which supposedly represent economic phenomena.

The second type Professor Morgenstern referred to is observational error. These include errors which arise when economists use or generate data that do not relate precisely to the concepts comprising their theory. For example, the government statistic GNP is not identical with the Keynesian Y. In Professor Morgenstern's words on economic data: " . . . they often measure, describe, or simply record something that is not exactly the phenomenon in which the economist would be interested" [17, p. 14].

Interprepation of economic data is subject to an error in addition to those of measurement and observation. This error relates to economic theory, and we shall call it theoretical error. Theoretical error may be defined to exist when data which appear to support one theory would also support an opposite theory derivable under a sharply different framework of thought. Theoretical error thus constitutes more than just statistical bias.[1] It includes specification errors due to (a) the nature of econometrics, or shall we say the art of econometricians who formulate economic theory to fit the data (e.g., utilizing lags, as noted below), and (b) those attributable to analytical contrivances designed to make the data fit a theory (e.g., selecting functional forms that appear to work). Its spectrum goes beyond these errors to include simple definitional error as well as misinterpretations of data resulting from an imprecise theory; in related manner, it embraces the failure to recognize the full implications of the data, which failure relates in turn to *limited theoretical frameworks of thought*.

Theoretical error becomes especially evident when a researcher is obsessed with a theory and fails to recognize its sensitivity to the basic postulates that form it. For example, if a researcher is mesmerized by an overly restricted theory, the questions he asks may fail to uncover the data that would formally reject it, as perhaps in the Monetarist-Keynesian dispute. Moreover data which fail to disconfirm a theory actually may support a sharply different theory, possibly one unknown at the time. Theoretical error not only produces a bias in statistical estimates corresponding to that which stems from errors of observation and measurement, but in substance involves the generation of data sharply circumscribed by the theoretical perspective of the researcher.

A rather pointed example of what we have in mind relates to statistical tests of the administered inflation thesis. This thesis was derived initially from statistical findings by Means [15] who claimed that oligopolists in concentrated industries lagged behind other sellers in changing prices over the cycle. His data (taken as if a proven fact of concentrated markets) was then *interpreted* (explained) by Galbraith [7] and Ackley [1] who individually set forth comparable theories to account for the data. They proposed, in effect, that oligopolists hesitate to raise prices in fear of promoting either the entry of new firms and/or higher wage demands by labor unions. They contended that prices are raised later on in the cycle. *But* no precise time sequence for changes in prices was provided in their theories.

Theoretical Error, Economic Space, Price Theory and Data

Among the tests designed to substantiate the Galbraith-Ackley administered inflation theory was one by Weiss [27, 28]. He concluded that over the 1940–1969 period, an administered inflation occurred only once, between the years 1953 and 1959, whereas concentration had a neutral effect during the period 1959–1963. Dalton [5], using the same data sources and overall time period employed by Weiss, found a positive effect for 1958–1963. Yet Dalton also viewed his findings to be supportive of the administered inflation theory since concentration should have a positive effect during the catch-up years following inflation. Confusion, in other words, prevailed as to which were the catch-up years, the 1955–1958 period as Weiss proposed, or the 1958–1963 years as Dalton proposed (which, by the way, were lag years according to Weiss). This dichotomy was not resolved by the subject writers *nor clarified in the theory*.

As Lustgarten [13] so aptly put the point " . . . interpretation of these authors illustrates the ambiguity of the administered price theory. Both 'positive' and 'no effect' . . . were regarded as consistent with the administered price inflation phenomenon for 1958–1963, while both "positive" and "negative" effects were considered as consistent for 1967–1969." His own findings, via a different model and data resembling Phlips [21], failed to support (or as in the case of Phlips—contradicted) the theory in question.

The nature of the problem may be revealed even more fundamentally by our reference to a prior writing of two of the present authors (along with M. Hwang [10]). It was demonstrated there (pp. 679, 680) that Means' starting point dovetails implicitly with a spatial economic framework of thought which requires collusive division of market spaces between firms. In other words, data which under Means' theoretical framework indicate competitive pricing would require industrial cartels under a spatial framework of thought which recognizes differences in location among the firms. in the industry. Use of an overly restrictive theory may thus yield critical misinterpretations of econometric statistics. But consider further the following:

We are not contending that spatial concepts are necessary or indispensable.

That question belongs to papers of different design than the present one. Rather, we are focusing attention strictly in the need to employ precise, complete, and relevant theories in econometric research. At the same instance, we recognize that econometricians often regard specification error as indicating theoretical error. Our definitional difference is designed to stress the fact that given data may support opposite market conditions (e.g., cartel not competitive conditions). Thus we leave for the term specification error the idea of statistical bias as well as the mathematical devices designed to rectify such bias. Theoretical error is defined to exist, to repeat, when data appear to support one theory but would also support an opposite theory that is derivable from a sharply different framework of thought.

More fundamentally than references to the administered inflation thesis and to interpretative differences stemming from, say, the inclusion vis-a-vis non-inclusion of firm's locations is the oft-indicated need in economics to define a market *and* region before obtaining and applying data. Simply put, when an economy is viewed from the perspective of space, not only does an oligopolistic market system apply to each buying point in space [9, 11], but the degree of concentration depends on the designated area within which competition is to be evaluated. Concentration of firms over a given small market space may be great whereas on an aggregate industry basis—which ignores economic space—the industry may be designated as a nonconcentrated one. Precise specification of market areas, and hence indication of which *are* the competitive firms, must be based on a *very precise theory* of relevant market spaces and regions. Quite significantly, such theoretical specifications have yet to be formulated (and agreed upon) by economists. (Note in this regard that factor analysis and other so called regional science attempts to designate economic regions, etc. have not been agreed upon as satisfactory by any means at this time.) In sum, we contend that sufficient theory—along with equally precise data reflecting such theory —are prerequisites to statistical disconfirmation (or verification, if you will) of economic theory. Our brief reference to the administered price inflation thesis suggests that spatial concepts are not only prerequisite to using and interpreting data but have themselves not yet been set forth in the literature.

Theoretical Error, Economic Space, Price Theory and Data

This paper, pursuant to the above contention, will seek to demonstrate in some detail how spurious economic theories can be, and then later on to suggest what can be done about them in order to make statistical tests feasible even before more specific theory and concepts have been formulated. Initially, we attempt to develop the meaning of theoretical error more fully with the aid of a simple model. A major emphasis will be to demonstrate via spatial price theory how given data may support opposite conclusions which stem directly from contrasting theoretical frameworks. The related prevalence of theoretical error among economists who try to apply economic theory, for example to such matters as anti trust violations, will then be discussed. Finally, we will suggest how economic methodology may be altered in order to minimize the extent to which apparently supportive economic data help obscure the existence of theoretical error.

II

It is likely that most government lawmakers and regulators have never studied spatial price theory. At best we can only hope they have been enlightened by some knowledge of the spaceless theory of perfect competition. But then there would be at least two principles that most government officials probably believe characterize the free enterprise system: (1) an increase in competition is likely to lower prices and (2) a decline in demand promotes lower prices, unless the long-run industry supply price is negatively sloped.

Application of these principles is widespread. With regards to the first principle, the idea has been fostered in the United States that breaking up the major oil companies would increase competition and cause prices to fall. Principle (2) has been applied in the following manner: if demand falls and prices do not, then prices are administered by the firm; consequently the firm in question does not respond to the forces of a free market.

These interpretations of the free market mechanism—or deviations from it—characterize much of the regulation of our free enterprise system. But since they are based on a restricted and unrealistic theory of atomistic firms and markets, one wonders if perhaps theoretical error is not distorting the picture of and remedy for the "evils of big business." A more general and realistic theory would recognize the spatial (time) structure over which markets extend. It is instructive, therefore, to ascertain whether or not the above principles do apply to *spatial* pricing in a free market.

We do not have to look far to recognize that *they do not*! Economists armed with the so-called Löschian theory of spatial competition have long accepted the result that increased entry generates a higher (*not lower*) mill price than had previously existed [3, 9, 12, 16]. This result, which is contrary to principle (1), was shown in [10] to depend on the particular behavioral assumptions that are used; e.g., (a) at the outset of any given time period the locations of firms are already set, and (b) the competing firms assume their rivals will adopt the same mill price as their own so that they in effect consider their respective market areas as fixed. The opposite result was shown in [10] to stem from the conception of a different type of spatial competition which involves parametric treatment of the price ceiling imposed on the firm's delivered price schedule over space.

One might anticipate in light of the above that the price lowering effects of greater levels of competition relate *exclusively* to the type of spatial competition assumed. But this too is not the case! Contradictory results from the same model of spatial competition can, in fact, be derived by assuming different types (forms) of consumer demand. The Löschian model of competition can, in fact, be shown to generate *lower* mill prices when the individual buyers are assumed to be distributed uniformly along a transport route and in addition their demand curves are of a different form than that typically conceived of in the literature. Manifestly, there exists a multiplicity of theoretical possibilities available to explain a given set of observations of prices over geographic space.

The multiplicity of theoretical possibilities available to explain price levels over an economic space vis-a-vis the classical price effects viewed under the perspective of a spaceless world can be spotlighted easily. We conceive below of buyers being uniformly distributed along a line market and take as the spatial demand density function

II—(1) $q = f(p)$

In II—(1), q and p stand respectively for the demand density and delivered price applicable at some point on the line market. The delivered price under f.o.b. mill pricing is then given by

II—(2) $p = m+tD,$

where m stands for the mill price, t for the freight rate per unit of distance, and tD for the freight cost applicable to a market D distance from the seller.

The spatial aggregate demand function under the Löschian type of space fixing competition is then specifiable via II—(1) and II—(2) as

II—(3) $$Q = 2\int_0^{D_0} f(m+tD)dD,$$

where D_0 is the market distance limit set by Löschian competition while the multiplier 2 indicates our simplifying assumption that each (representative) firm is confronting 2 rivals located in two (opposite) directions from it. The elasticity of the spatial aggregate demand subject to Löschian competition is then definable via II—(3) as

II—(4) $$e_L = -\frac{m}{Q}\frac{dQ}{dm} = \frac{-m\int_0^{D_0} f_m(m+tD)dD}{\int_0^{D_0} f(m+tD)dD}$$

This elasticity e_L clearly approaches the elasticity e of the individual point demand derivable from II—(1) when the space is costless, i.e., when $t=0$. Thus:

II—(5) $$\lim_{t\to 0} e_L = -\frac{mf'(m)}{f(m)} = e, \qquad m = p$$

Otherwise, e_L is not necessarily equal to the elasticity of the individual point demand, instead being specifiable as:

II—(6) $$e_p = -\frac{mf'(m+tD)}{f(m+tD)}, \qquad \forall\ tD \geq 0$$

Now, according to the Stevens-Rydell definition of demand convexity, $f(p)$ in II—(1) is more (or less) convex than a *negative exponential* whenever $-f'/f$ decreases (or increases) as p increases [25, pp. 196–198]. See Ohta [19, 20] for a more general definition of demand convexity. It follows that the spatial demand becomes more elastic compared to the spaceless local demand *iff* the assumed demand function f is less convex than a *negative exponential*, i.e.:

$$\text{II—(7)} \qquad -\frac{f'(m+tD)}{f(m+tD)} > -\frac{f'(m)}{f(m)}, \qquad \forall\ tD>0$$

$$-\frac{f'(m+tD)m}{f(m+tD)} = e_p > -\frac{f'(m)m}{f(m)} = e, \ \forall\ m>0 \text{ and } tD>0$$

More generally, the spatial point demand becomes more and more elastic as tD increases. It therefore follows that the spatial aggregate demand becomes more and more elastic as the firm's market area D_0 increases under the present condition of specific demand convexity.[2] Conversely, if D_0 is reduced in accordance with the Löschian type of spatial competition, the elasticity of spatial aggregate demand e_L must increase if only the demand curve f is more convex than a *negative exponential*, or equivalently if it is *relatively more convex* [19, 20]. If on the other hand the demand curve f is less convex than a *negative exponential*, or *relatively less convex* [19, 20], e_L must decrease as Löschian competition reduces D_0. It follows that if particular marginal costs of production remain fairly stable, Löschian entry necessarily brings about higher or lower mill prices depending on the relative convexity of the assumed demand density function.

What may be called the paradox of spatial competition—i.e., a rise in mill price due to competition—is readily derivable from the particular type of competitive behavior prevailing in the space economy *and* the consumers' demand curve forms. Moreover, this paradox of spatial competition is, in fact, in a Siamese twin relationship to what Stevens and Rydell called the " paradox of spatial monopoly ".[3] Contrasting results therefore relate not only to the different types of competition that may apply between production centers, but to the different demand conditions that exist. It is therefore impossible to determine *a priori* whether f.o.b. mill prices would fall or rise due to changes in competition.

The complexity of economic relationships is well known. We see in the present case (as summarized in Table I) that the effect of increased competition on prices depends on the way rivals view their market spaces, and the form of the demand curves that happen to prevail. If in his conception of market conditions, the theorist uses Lösch's framework but rejects the idea of mill price rising as competition increases, he must reject demand curves of the form II—(7). But, then, three alternative theories briefly discussed here are available to explain the observation of falling mill prices under conditions of greater entry: (a) Löschian competition based on demand curves more convex than the negative exponential; (b) a price ceiling theory of competition based on demand curves less convex than the negative exponential; (c) a price ceiling theory of competition based on demand curves more convex than the negative exponential.[4] In no way at all, however, may observations of price changes and the number of (and location of) competitors establish which of the three variants referred to herein is the best (and let us say *the* explanatory) theory. In fact, we do not even *dis*prove the Löschian market area view of spatial competition simply because a given empirical observation of falling mill prices would appear to contradict the theoretical implication of rising mill pices.

Table I Impact of Competition on the F.O.B. Mill Price
Under Alternative Market Conditions

Demand Types / Competition Types	More Convex Than Negative Exponential	Less Convex Than Negative Exponential
Löschian	down	up
Price Ceiling	down	down

Viewed from the other side, we can propose that few, if any, attempts have been made to explain rising prices in terms of an *increase* in spatial *competition*, because competition is typically believed to *lower* prices, not to raise them. The differences in theoretical framework and economic policy reflective of a space vis-a-vis spaceless economy clearly warrant further study.

The observations set forth above reveal the limited scope of principle (2) and all seemingly supportive data which appear to conform to the classical relationships between demand and price. In fact, they acquire special significance in light of our earlier discussion of the administered price thesis. That thesis, let us recall, was claimed by many to be supported by much empirical data, while not limited by observations that many prices go up during periods of weak demand since administered pricing, average cost over the cycle pricing, and the like could be used to account for significant numbers of exceptions. The present paper contends, however, that the "inverse" pricing which does exist is "perverse" *only in the context of the theory of perfect competition.* Opposite price results to those long-heralded in classical economics are perfectly natural responses in competitive Löschian oligopoly markets under conditions of demands less convex than the negative exponential. Please note, we also *do contend* that spatial markets of this order have more likely basis as real-world competitive structures than the classical spaceless model of economic theory [9]. Businessmen need not possess ulterior motives for sacrificing profits (such as limiting wage demands) in adjusting their prices inversely to shifts in demand [see 13, 18, 22]; they need only be profit maximizers in a Löschian world of competitive spatial oligoplists subject to demands which are less convex than the negative exponential.

We also propose that "average cost" pricing attributable to governmental regulations indicates that "inverse" pricing is completely distinct from administered pricing. But we shall not dwell on the theory of average cost pricing since it is oft-described in standard texts of economic principles. Let it suffice to note that regulated public utilities, e.g., natural gas pipelines, receive a return based largely on their fixed costs (or rate base). This rate base is influenced, however, by the quantity supplied. So a fall in demand which reduces the quantity sold raises the price charged per unit (while the total return remains virtually the same). As a consequence, inverse pricing would typify regulated industries subject to high fixed costs. In corresponding form, unregulated industries subject to large fixed costs may find it comparatively easy to accept governmental price guidelines when their average fixed costs are low (e.g., during expansionary periods), while altering the pressure of declining profit margins by raising prices during periods of recession.

The gist of these "revelations" is that the principles of perfect competition which legislators and regulators apparently follow *do not apply unqualifiedly* to a realistic model of the economy, e.g., the spatial model including governmental interferences. The observations, definitions, interpretations, and tests formed within the framework of perfect competition are, we contend, likely to be saturated with theoretical error. And government policy may, in many cases, be completely opposite to what would be the appropriate policy [22]. Small wonder that inflation and unemployment recently soared at the same time that governments were attempting to control *or* is it fine-tune their economies. Small wonder Nordhaus [18, p. 64] asserts that "economists have shown little inventiveness in designing durable antidotes to inflation other than recessions."

III

The existence (if not prevalence) of theoretical error has profound implications on economic methodology. The most widely accepted methodological position among modern economists is "logical positivism." This methodology was clearly stated by Bridgman [4] and various "operational philosophers," for example, Rapoport [24]. It has been advanced in a sense by Samuelson [25], and less restrictedly by Friedman [6] and Machlup [14].

The position of logical positivism is essentially that the basic assumptions of theory are not subject to independent verification. Only deduced hypotheses are testable. And if an hypothesis is testable, then at least indirectly so too is the set of assumptions underlying the theory. If the conclusions (or theorems) of a model are found to be in sufficiently close correspondence with reality, then the basic assumptions of the model can be considered acceptable.

The existence of theoretical error puts a damper, however, on the prospects that economic theory can really be tested. In the backlight of the Austrian School, it may well be that observations can only provide the data which should be explained by a theory. Most assuredly, the present paper has shown that conjecturing in terms of a particular theory can often induce the economist to interpret data as if his theory is verified. Too frequently, he is biased in favor of the theory supposedly being tested.

Economic methodology takes on a new focus in the above light. It is simply ***not enough*** to utilize the assumptions of a theory if its conclusions appear "successful", for our judgement of the success of a theory tends to be warped by the theory itself.[5] We contend that economists ***must*** evaluate directly the assumptions of a theory ***when*** an alternative set of radically different assumptions can lead to the same conclusions. This methodology may be called "economic pragmatism". It does not offer the prospect of easy measurement and testing. But at least we will not be led by our methodology to confirm glibly what raw intuition and suppositionsly tested (testable) theory might have led us to expect. It would, we propose, enable us to minimize—if not avoid—theoretical error. Moreover, we must go one step beyond, as noted below.

Recall from our introduction the claim that economists need a complete, a precise and relevant (nonempty) theory to serve as the basis for an operational model which, in turn, could generate and *then* aid in interpreting derived data. With particular respect to administered prices, Nordhaus [18] observed in the same vein that the pervasiveness of sticky prices "across time and space" is not only a recognized fact but a "phenomenon in search of a theory." Phlips [23] pointed out in this key that the rationalizations set forth by economists to explain sticky prices involved accepting non-optimizing behavior as a fact of the business world *or* else adopting the industrial organization *folklore* which Means had fostered when he linked rigid prices to market concentration. Phlips went on to observe that the substantial amount of empirical evidence subsequently put forward to explain sticky prices has been typically conflicting and inconclusive, which condition he said "should cause no surprise, as formalized theoretical results necessary for the concentration of meaningful empirical tests, were essentially lacking." [23, pp. 525, 526]. To Phlips, the theoretical assumptions which were used as the basis for empirical work were not part of a derived *meaningful theory*. The further result was that industrial price data have more recently been explained on such contrasting levels as monetarism or a revival of the Wilson-Andrews [29] claim that prices are set on the basis of cost normalized over the business cycle. Phlips' own acceptance of the latter assumption was derived in [23] via applying the variational calculus *to* the spatial price theory formula set forth in [8], though in his system—as noted earlier—time interest cost on the storage of goods is substituted for transport cost.[6]

Phlips' application of the variational calculus to the theory intrinsic to equation (16b) illustrates the use of a complete, *precise* theory. We propose it as an example of what could be a complete, precise theory since it allows inclusion of (possibly all) relevant alternative demand types besides different degrees of competition arising from alternative rival locations or changing periods of time; any and all of these can serve as the arguments against which the data may be obtained and evaluated. Most significantly, the relevance of particular demands, types of competition, and inventory policy can presumably be ascertained by direct examination. Then sticky price data can be evaluated in the context of determined variations in demand, competition, and inventory policy occurring over space and time.

But how would one know when a theory such as that reflected by equation II—(4) is the correct, complete, precisely specified theory? More generally put, when does one have a complete precisely specified (empirically testable) theory rather than, say, a supposititiously testable theory? Manifestly, preference for one theory over another can lead to dispute and challenge. One thing alone is certain: simply using data directly in search of a theory, or derivatives thereof to support some theory, which is the methodology (approach) that seems to be used more and more in recent years by the members of our profession, is self-defeating. It is this methodology that magnifies theoretical error. Indeed, the econometricians' approach was originally tied to developing as meaningful and complete a theory as possible, before anything else. Only later on would statistical test of other properties of the theory be made and this at the relevant time and place.[7] Though we next argue by analogy, we do indeed strongly propose that discarding the theoretical basis for generating economic data corresponds to a failure to select the assumptions carefully in formulating an economic theory. The razor, in still other words, is double edged. Meticulous selection of assumptions in constructing economic theory is vitally necessary before a specific hypothesis can be framed against which other statistical tests are designed. Failure to establish the postulational (cause-effect) roots of a theory is analogous to (a) obtaining data without the insights of a complete theory and then (b) interpreting that same data as if they constituted a theory in their own right. This procedural *faux pas* generates theoretical error, and in substance is similar to placing the proverbial cart before the horse.

[Notes]

* The authors are respectively Chief Economist, Cooper Industries, Inc., Alumni Distinguished Professor of Economics, Texas A & M University, and Professor of Economics, Aoyama Gakuin University. They recognize their debt to R. Basmann, R. Battalio, and especially to the late O. Morgenstern for critiques and suggestions.

1) Indeed, attempts to rectify the statistical bias, e.g., via the instrumental variable technique, generate interpretative differences with respect to regression results.

2) Consider the following demand specifications:

$$q_x = f(m+x),\ x \geq 0$$

Where x may be interpreted as the freight cost per unit quantity applicable to distance D, i.e., $x = tD$, in the present context. If elasticity of demand e_x in terms of mill price increases as x increases, then it implies:

(i) $e_0 \leq e_x$ or more generally

$e_x = e_{x+h}$, $\forall x$ and $h \geq 0$

where $e_x = -\dfrac{dq_x}{dm} \dfrac{m}{f(m+x)}$, $\forall x \geq 0$.

Now, the sum of less elastic demand and more elastic demand, e.g., $q_0 + q_x$, is:

(ii) $q_0 + q_x = f(m) + f(m+x)$

The elasticity of this aggregate demand is then:

(iii) $e_\Sigma = w_0 e_0 + w_x e_x$,

where $w_0 = \dfrac{f(m)}{f(m)+f(m+x)}$, $w_x = \dfrac{f(m+x)}{f(m)+f(m+x)}$

It readily follows from (i) and (iii) that

(iv) $e < e_0 e_\Sigma < e_x$

For proof, let $e_x = e_0 + \alpha$, where $\alpha \geq 0$ since $e_x \geq e_0$. Then:

(v) $e_\Sigma = w_0 e_0 + w_x(e_0 + \alpha)$

$= (w_0 + w_x)e_0 + w_x \alpha$

$= e_0 + w_x \alpha \geq e_0$

since $(w_0 + w_x) = 1$ and $w_x > 0$. In turn, let $e_0 = e_x - \beta$, where $\beta \geq 0$ since $e_x \geq e_0$. Then:

Theoretical Error, Economic Space, Price Theory and Data

(vi) $e_\Sigma = w_0(e_x - \beta) + w_x e_x$
$= (w_0 + w_x)e_x - w_0\beta$
$= e_x - w_0\beta \leq e_x$

where (v) and (vi) establish (iv) as claimed.

3) See [26, 199] where the authors correctly point out that when the spatial demand density function is less convex than the *negative exponential*, " the same friction of space that grants a monopoly to a producer " increases elasticity of demand thus reducing his " monopoly power ". More entry and less spatial friction under the same condition of demand convexity should therefore increase the firm's monopoly power—*raising competitive mill prices.*

4) If the market area is set by a price ceiling type of competition (i.e., where $m+tD_0=p_0$, with p_0 representing the parametrically given delivered price ceiling and hence $D_0=(p_0-m)/t$), the aggregate spatial demand is specifiable as:

(i) $$Q = \int_0^{\frac{p_0-m}{t}} f(m+tD)dD$$

Elasticity of demand in this case e* is then given by:

(ii) $$e^* = \frac{f(m)m}{tQ}$$

Thus as p_0 decreases, Q decreases and $f(m)$ stays constant regardless of the form of the function f. Greater competition therefore necessarily brings about higher elasticity e^* and correspondingly lower mill price *ceteris paribus* under this particular type of spatial competition where a parametric price ceiling applies.

5) It has been said that the huge deficit in the USA for fiscal 1983 and 1984 will crowd out the private sector and keep interest rates high. Statistically the deficit can be projected to lead to a relatively smaller growth in M_2 vis a vis M_1, *ceteris paribus*. If the first derivative of the M_2, M_1 rates fails to predict the change in the interest rates, the second derivative may work. If so, have we really verified the presumption that a deficit crowds out the private sector? How about the Keynesian argument that GNP and savings will rise?

6) Since space microeconomic theory rejects completely the supposed significance of market concentration [10], and as Phlips observes [23, p. 537], actually demonstrates instead that cost increases are less fully transmitted into prices by the more concentrated industries, the complete dependence of statistical interpretation on the theory itself is manifest. Rather generously, Phlips notes that his own prior regression analysis of concentration effects [23, note 7] was predicated on the simple classical theoretical framework, and in his word " admittedly " in error. The relevance of intertemporal price discrimination, he goes on to demonstrate, lies along the same theoretical lines as discrimination between spatial markets. It provides, at the same instance, a more complete and precise theoretical basis for statistical applications than otherwise has marked our discipline.

7) Manifestly in formulating a theory, selected assumptions may themselves stem from observational premises. (And see [2].)

References

[1] G. Ackley, "Administered Prices and the Inflationary Process," *American Economic Review*, May 1959, 49, 419–461.

[2] R. Basmann, *Economic Theories and Their Technological Applications: I. The Role of Observational Concept*, unpublished manuscript.

[3] M. Beckmann, *Location Theory*, New York, 1968.

[4] P. W. Bridgman, *The Logic of Modern Physics* (New York: The Macmillan Co., 1927).

[5] James A. Dalton, "Administered Inflation and Business Pricing: Another Look, *Review of Economics and Statistics*, Nov. 1973, 40, 516–519.

[6] M. Friedman, " The Methodology of Positive Economics," *Essays in Positive Economics* (Chicago: University of Chicago Press, 1953), 3–43.

[7] J. K. Galbraith, " Market Structure and Stabilization Policy," *Journal of Political Statistics*, May 1957, 39, 124–133.

[8] J. Greenhut and M. L. Greenhut, " Spatial Price Discrimination, Competition, and Locational Effects," *Economica*, Nov. 1975, 401–419.

[9] M. L. Greenhut, *A Theory of the Firm in Economic Space*, 2nd printing (Austin: Lone Star Publishing Co., 1974).

[10] ____, M. Hwang, and H. Ohta, " Observations on the Shape and Relevance of the Spatial Demand Function," *Econometrica*, July 1975, 669–693.

[11] M. L. Greenhut and H. Ohta, *Theory of Spatial Pricing and Market Areas* (Durham: Duke University Press, 1975).

[12] A. Lösch, *The Economics of Location*, New Haven, 1954.

[13] S. Lustgarten, "Administered Inflation: A Reappraisal," *Economic Inquiry*, June 1977, 191–206.

[14] F. Machlup, *The Basing Point System* (Philadelphia: Blakiston, 1949).

[15] G. Means, *Administrative Inflation and Public Policy*, Washington, D.C. Anderson Kramer Associates, 1959.

[16] E. Mills and M. Lav, "A Model of Market Areas with Free Entry," *Journal of Political Economy*, June 1964, 72, 278–88.

[17] O. Morgenstern, *On the Accuracy of Economic Observations* (Princeton: Princeton University Press, 1965).

[18] W. D. Nordhaus, " Inflation Theory and Policy," *Papers and Proceedings of the American Economic Assoc.*, May 1976, 59–64.

[19] H. Ohta, " Spatial Competition, Concentration and Welfare," *Regional Science and Urban Economics*, 1980, 10, 3–16.

[20] ____, " The Price Effects of Spatial Competition," *Review of Economic Studies*, 1981, 48, 317–325.

[21] L. Phlips, " Business Pricing Policies and Inflation—Some Evidence from E.E.C.," *Journal of Industrial Economics*, Nov. 1969, 18, 1–14.

[22] ____, "Spatial Pricing and Competition," Commission of the European Communities, *Approximation of Legislation Series*, Brussels 1976.

[23] ____, "Intertemporal Price Discrimination and Sticky Prices," *Quarterly Journal of Economics*, May 1980, 94, 525–42.

[24] A. Rapoport, *Operational Philosophy* (New York: Harpers, 1954).

[25] P. A. Samuelson, *Foundations of Economic Analysis* (Cambridge, Mass.: Harvard University Press, 1947).

[26] B. H. Stevens and C. P. Rydell, "Spatial Demand Theory and Monopoly Price Policy," *Papers, The Regional Science Association*, 1966, 17, 195–204.

[27] L. W. Weiss, "Business Pricing Policies and Inflation Reconsidered," *Journal of Political Economy*, April 1966, 74, 177–178.

[28] ____, "The Role of Concentration in Recent Inflationary Price Movements: A Statistical Analysis," *Antitrust Law and Economic Review*, Spring, 1974, 4, 109–121.

[29] T. Wilson and P.W.S. Andrews, *Oxford Studies in the Price Mechanism* (Oxford: Clarendon Press 1951).

Ann Reg Sci (1992) 26:257–267

The Annals of
Regional Science

Alternative uses of spatial microeconomics

John G. Greenhut[1] and Melvin L. Greenhut[2*]

[1]Arizona State University West, Phoenix, AZ 85069-7100, USA
[2]Texas A & M University, College Station, TX 77843-4228, USA

Abstract. This paper contends that classical spaceless price theory is excessively limited. In contrast, the spatial model provides a robustly general framework such that it even sheds light on the beta statistic in portfolio theory and the capital asset pricing model (CAPM), which led to 1990 Nobels for Markowitz and Sharpe. The paper further demonstrates that the spatial dimension advances other facets of economics, including product differentiation theory, waiting time and advertising impacts on prices, etc. Indeed, the subject of international dumping of goods is shown to have ties to spatial microeconomics besides imperfect competition theory. This paper's objective is therefore to demonstrate some of the inclusiveness of spatial microeconomics.

This paper is to some extent a reorientation of a paper (Greenhut and Greenhut 1991) presented at the WEA International 1991 Conference. Rather surprisingly, it may seem, is the fact that the convention paper was part of the Finance Section meetings of the conference; that is, it was a paper strictly on finance. But what does finance theory (or practice) have to do with regional science? Even more significantly, what does it have to do with this journal's issue *in honor of (and to the memory of) Claude Ponsard?*

Our answer to the above questions is simply that the subjects are interwoven, as the present reorientation of the WEA paper will demonstrate in part. To be sure, the paper that follows discards most of the materials included in the convention paper, where emphasis was on the effects of different *types* of inflation on stock prices. In their place, this paper establishes the regional scientist's interest in the way firms price over an economic landscape. The main purpose of this

* Respectively, Associate Professor of Finance and Business Economics, Arizona State University West; Abell Professor of Liberal Arts and Distinguished Professor of Economics, Texas A&M University and Adjunct Distinguished Professor, University of Oklahoma.
Correspondence to: J.G. Greenhut

paper is therefore to go off in a different direction, and well beyond the convention paper by demonstrating here that the concept of beta in portfolio theory and the capital asset pricing model (CAPM) model, which led to 1990 Nobels for Markowitz and Sharpe, is in fact a theoretical bedfellow of the world of spatial price theory. Beyond this, the present paper will further demonstrate that not only does CAPM have ties to, let us now say, plant location theory, or the impacts of costly distances, but so too do many other subjects, as will shortly be noted. We are accordingly proposing that this paper's objective is to demonstrate some of the inclusiveness of spatial microeconomics, as we in effect are also contending that classical spaceless price theory is extremely limited. It is in this context that this paper adds in our opinion to the memory of the multiple writings of Claude Ponsard.

Section I of the paper proposes that the capital asset pricing model (CAPM) of finance theory can be advanced by an industrial organization (structures) framework. Section II then converts our industrial structures model to a spatial price theory model, in effect enhancing CAPM by the information that can be gained from spatial microeconomics. These initial discussions establish the foundation for Sect. III's demonstration that the landscape (or say the economic distance parameter) can also serve as proxy for the advertising and storage of goods (e.g. Phlips 1983a, b; Smith 1989), as proxy for product differentiation by a firm and firms, including the interdependence of product types and spatial pricing alternatives (e.g., de Palma et al. 1986), as proxy for address models (e.g., Lowell 1970), as proxy for waiting time impacts on prices (e.g., DeVany 1976; Saving 1982), and also as proxy for international trade (e.g., Vernon 1979). Most importantly, this paper proposes that the economic landscape is fundamental to advanced microeconomic theory (as in Phlips and Thisse 1982). But first a few introductory remarks about CAPM are relevant for the specialists in regional science who may not be familiar with this facet of finance theory.

Finance theory's CAPM

This paper focuses initial attention on the beta statistic, a parameter which relates the volatility of a company's stock return against that of all stocks in the market. Considerable research has attempted to uncover empirically the accounting factors which determine individual company beta values, but the statistical results have been conflicting and generally inconclusive. Correspondingly in a sense, theoretical derivations of the determinants of beta have been limited largely to the income volatility that stems from the firm's leverage of fixed assets and debt.[1] No economic theory concerning the determinants of volatility at the gross profits level has been proposed nor has any been advanced which adequately identifies beta differences *among industries*; for instance, some industries such as gold mining and petroleum have extremely volatile earnings and stock prices, yet possess

[1] For interested readers, a survey of research on the association between accounting variables and beta can be found in Foster (1986) and Beaver (1989).

some of the lowest betas that can be found.[2] This paper will contend that the spatial price theory which is so often used by regional scientists and economists implicitly explains the impact of industrial characteristics on betas.[3]

I. CAPM and industrial structures[4]

Consider the profit maximizing requirement of marginal revenue $p(1-1/e_i)$ equal to the ith firm's marginal cost (MC_i) in an $i = 1, \ldots, n$ firm homogeneous good industry. This relation can be easily converted to an industrial structures perspective. Specifically, if we define g_i as the relative change in the quantity produced in the industry (dQ/Q) to that of the individual firm $d(q_i/q_i)$ *and* multiply g_i by e_i, we obtain the industry's elasticity E; i.e., $e_i g_i = E$. Substituting E/g_i for e_i in the firm's $MR = MC$ equation, and then aggregating over the i firms in the industry, with $\sum g_i/n = G$ and $\sum MC_i/n = MC$, yields $P[1-G/E] = MC$.

We designate G as the industry's competitive Gravity index. It follows then from the inverse of $[1-G/E]$ that $P = MF \cdot MC$, where the markup factor, MF, equals $[E/(E-G)]$. The rate of change in price P is approximated by the sum of the percentage increases (decreases) in MF and MC. Increases in the percentage change in price therefore do not depend on concentration ratios, but rather on changes in the G index and/or elasticity. With respect to elasticity E, we obtain the critical relation:

$$\frac{d(MF)/MF}{dE} = \frac{-G}{E \cdot (E-G)} < 0 . \tag{1}$$

A decline in elasticity produces an inflationary impact on price through the markup factor; and, significantly, this impact is most pronounced in markets with low E and/or high G values. *Ceteris paribus*, high beta values stemming from large earnings volatility would obtain in low elasticity, high competitive-gravity industries.

---

2 Rosenberg and Guy (1976a) provided an overall framework for understanding the differences among industry betas by formulating beta as a function of relative responses of a business to major factors that affect the overall economy. Perhaps due to difficulty in operationalizing this framework, Rosenberg and Guy (1976b) only offered an empirical estimate of the degree to which different industry betas were not explained by accounting fundamentals. For example, the beta for gold stocks was found to be only 0.36 on average compared to an estimated 1.187 based on accounting variables such as debt leverage. The authors did not offer theoretical explanation as to why industry betas differ, but could only state the importance of including these measured differences in industry betas in projecting the beta of an individual company. The arbitrage pricing theory, originating with Ross (1976), provides an alternative empirical methodology for linking stock returns to economic factors. The more specific research presented in Greenhut and Greenhut (1991), which we are outlining here only briefly given the purposes of this paper, is oriented towards enhancing the operationality of these finance theory frameworks. This is done in the backlight of the spatial pricing practices of industries which are of central interests to economists and regional scientists.

3 An appendix to this paper provides further background on portfolio theory, the capital asset pricing model, and beta for interested readers.

4 As mentioned previously, this section only sketches some of the material presented in the convention paper. For full details, contact either author.

The industry's G index can be seen to vary naturally from 0 to 1, according to three classifications. (a) The zero value applies, for example, when the representative firm is so small that a change in its quantity has no observable impact on the total quantity produced in the industry. Let us refer to this "perfectly competitive" industry as Industry 1. (b) If the other firm(s) ignored a given firm's change in quantity, with the effect of some discernible change taking place in the industry's total output, the gravity index would range between zero and one. Let us refer to the product in question as the output of Industry 2. (c) The limit value for G is unity. This obtains when all firms in an industry seek to maintain their relative shares. Phrased otherwise, if the relative change in the industry's total output is in proportion to that of the individual representative firm, G equals 1. Of course, not only may all firms endeavor to maintain their individual market shares in conformance to either a cartel structure or the practice of conscious parallelism of action, but this industry, call it Industry 3, may also depict a simple monopolist.

II. From industrial structures to delivered prices

Directly identifying quantity-price conjectural variations is virtually impossible in the real business world. In effect, the conjectural variations approach is just an abstract analytical device for use in the ivory tower. However, ascertaining the way that firms price over their market spaces is not a difficult empirical study at all.[5] Observations along this line would reveal the relevant industrial structure for a firm, and in turn enable a much more penetrating application of the CAPM approach to stock prices. The spatial price policies of firms are, we now propose, intrinsic to the earnings volatilities of firms, and hence the beta values of finance theory. Accordingly, we shall examine price patterns instead of quantity conjectures, doing this by reversing our references to the industries described earlier, beginning initially now with Industry 3.

Industry 3 depicts firms whose dq_i/q_i remains in constant proportion to dQ/Q. These firms would pursue a delivered price system, *DPS*, over an economic landscape which is of such form that if one firm raises (lowers) its delivered price schedule (DPS), the other(s) in conformable reaction would match that change. Industry 2, on the other hand, then consists of establishments whose managers ignore a DPS change by the representative firm. Finally, Industry 1 relates to the situation where the rival firm(s) reacts oppositely to a change in the representative firm's DPS, lowering its price if the rival raises its price and vice versa.[6] The respective spatial price systems described here are referred to in spatial microeconomics as Löschian (Industry 3) pricing, Hotelling (Industry 2) pricing, and Greenhut-Ohta (Industry 1) pricing.[7] Note further that Industry 3 can be

---

5 See Greenhut et al. (1980).

6 See Hamilton et al. (1989), where in effect Cournot is our Industry 2. This Cournot case approaches a Bertrand Industry 1 instance when spatial transport costs are very low for the Bertrand firms *and* the firms in the Cournot model approach a very large number.

7 See Phlips and Thisse (1982), Part I Hotelling and Lösch Approach, pp 11–130, and Part II The Greenhut-Ohta Approach, pp 131–194.

characterized as having a homogeneous market structure (i.e., its member firms act identically to each other); Industry 2 can be called a Cournot Industry (i.e., its firms ignore each other); while Industry 1 depicts a heterogeneous structure (i.e., its member firms act oppositely to each other).

Under Industry 3 (Löschian spatial pricing), any decrease (increase) in price by the firm(s) at one production center is matched by the firm(s) at a distant-but rival production center. Under Industry 2's approach, often also referred to as the Hotelling-Smithies approach, a change at one center in the basic mill price, and thus in the delivered prices therefrom, fails to elicit a response from the rival center. Under Industry 1 pricing, a reduction (increase) in mill price at one point promotes an increase (reduction) in mill price at the distant center.[8]

Profits are basically greatest under Industry 3 pricing, then comes Industry 2, with Industry 1 yielding the lowest profits. Volatility of earnings stem, in turn, from industry type and the factors evaluated previously in this paper, e.g., basic demand elasticities. The overall result is that theories of finance and portfolio management, as in CAPM (or the arbitrage pricing theory, APT) tie up directly with industrial organization theory and the microeconomics of space. In fact, going beyond this paradigm, we would suggest that evaluations of CAPM, and in particular the macroeconomic impacts of inflation, indicate minimal earnings volatility in the case of a market structure characterized by Industry 1 pricing. This is so because demand elasticity is greatest in that case with G approaching zero.

More inclusively than stated above, any increase in elasticity because of entry reduces the rate of change of the markup $\{[d(MF)/MF]/dE<0\}$, while the opposite of course results when firms exit the industry. In the initial event, the increase in price in Industry 1 does not keep pace with the rate of increase in cost, whereas in the latter event it is exaggerated. We recognize further that a decrease in elasticity due to inflation triggers a higher multiple. And given the last mentioned instance, a homogeneous structure, or say Industry 3 competition, would generate the greatest multiple of all.

III. Product differentiation, waiting time and other extensions

A critically important facet of models of stock market prices is that the major stock exchanges center on oligopoly firms and regulated monopolies; ipso facto, theories concerning prices over an economic landscape are theories of oligopolistic enterprises, some in collusion with others, some under substantial regulation and control by government, and some in a form of spatial competition with each other, such as the types of competition described above in this paper. The economic landscape generates a world of oligopolistic industries. These, to repeat, are also the industries whose stocks are bought and sold in the market. More than that they are the industries on which microeconomic theory must be constructed.

---

8 See Greenhut et al. (1987), particularly Chapts. 2 and 3.

"Space" and "distance" and the world of oligopolies provide results which are not only important to such fields as finance theory (or vice versa if you prefer), but in effect are also intrinsic to a variety of economic phenomena. As noted in our introduction, a vital tie-up is that which relates to product differentiation. Indeed, the individual product variants of firms can be viewed as if each is located along a spectrum of consumer desires, where each variant has a well-defined "market area". The spatial framework of thought naturally uncovers the effects of new product variants as well as enabling comparisons of product varieties under a number of different market structures (Lowell 1970; Lancaster 1979; Salop 1979; Scherer 1979; Vernon 1979; Novsheck 1980; Salant 1980; Phlips and Thisse 1982; Anderson 1986; Neven 1986; de Palma et al. 1988).

As another example, it is well recognized that demands for many products and services are limited not only by the price of the good or the fee that is charged but also by other costs of acquisition, such as waiting time or storage costs (DeVany 1976; DeVany and Saving 1977; Phlips and Thisse 1981; Saving 1982; Smith 1989). This is particularly true in evaluating service activities, including privat medical-care alternatives; simply put, the spatial analogy sheds new light on the positive relation between fees and the number of medical practitioners (M. L. Greenhut et al. 1985 a).

Spatial analysis of market entry (Benson 1985) can lead to consideration of the regulation of airlines (Greenhut et al. 1991), and in turn the address models (Archibald et al. 1986). These lead back to the impacts of mergers and antitrust regulation, all made more tractable and realistic once the imperfectly competitive environment of firms is taken into account (Benson and Greenhut 1989). Similarly, the efficiency and welfare implications of such economic practices as the bundling of goods (so-called tying contracts), bank charges on checking accounts, wage discrimination by sex and education, quantity discounts, and the nonlinear price schedules charged by telephone companies, are amenable to spatial analysis (Phlips 1983 a, b).

We also contend that the spatial framework sheds light on a number of important international trade issues. A tariff barrier, for one example, has many of the properties of a transport cost, from which it can be shown that an ad valorem tax has different impacts than a specific tax (Greenhut and Norman 1986). International-trade theorists are in fact becoming particularly concerned with two phenomena that do not fit easily into "traditional" spaceless economic theory: the emergence of the multi-national enterprise and the increasing proportion of trade flows that is accounted for by intra-industry trade (Vernon 1979; Buckley and Casson 1987; Dunning 1987). In addition, many trade theorists are concerned with the dumping issue (Brander and Krugman 1983; Greenhut et al. 1985 b). Spatial microeconomic analysis provides insights into why companies and industries change their orientation from a chiefly export-based operation to one which strictly emphasizes local markets, and most generally one that deals in both markets, with intra-industry trade going each way (Norman and Dunning 1984).

Beyond the above noted particular subject applications, it was previously suggested that the spatial dimension should underlie all of microeconomic theory besides that of time. In particular, it is well established in spatial price theory that the mere facts of costs of distance and a limited number of sites available at any point in space signify the prevalence of a comparatively small number of firms in any market. Thus an action-reaction interdependence prevails between the firms of an industry, and between production centers (Greenhut and Greenhut 1975). A Löschian landscape, for example, can be imagined, with oligopolistic firms occupying central stage. It has long been a joke that every economist has his or her own theory of oligopoly. The inference exists that there is no deterministic oligopoly outcome, and hence as is argued so often by members of the Chicago School, microeconomics should, and must be rooted in the purely competitive framework. The present authors believe otherwise.

Consider in this regard the Greenhut et al. (1987, Chapter 19) solution. They recognized the existence of behavioral uncertainty in oligopolistic industries as a unique uncertainty, one that is intrinsic to a market characterized by sellers who identify their rivals and who act as well as react according to their conjectures about the rivals' behavior. They argued that this uncertainty is a cost, just as is risk. Unlike risk, however, and in accordance with standard literature in operations research and economics, they regarded it as a subjective cost, not as the objective (statistical) cost which underlies the different returns one can expect to receive under risk. It follows that the variance of net receipts, positive and/or negative, to which oligopolists are subject demands a residual payment which – in the long run – must cover the degree of behavioral uncertainty that underlies a given industry. It is a small, yet formidable step to recognize that this residual income adds on to the standard average cost that viable firms must and will recover in the long run.

In their theory, the behavioral uncertainty cost generates a new average total cost curve, call it ATC_u. Most dramatically, the subject authors demonstrated that in a competitive free entry/exit oligopoly market a tangency between the oligopolist's negatively sloping average revenue curve and the ATC_u eventuates, doing this at a point directly above the minimum long-run technological average cost point of classical economic theory. The conclusion is that the oligopoly firms which dot an economic landscape must cover their explicit and all implicit costs (including the cost of behavioral uncertainty) in the long run; then, if competition prevails between these firms, they will cover these costs exactly via the free entry and exit of firms which eliminates the short-run surpluses and losses that exist. It should be manifest that this theory, which in turn can be shown to stem from present day location theory, not only identifies the firms whose ownership shares can be bought and sold in the market, but whose short-run income variances establish unique firm risks which portfolio managers (and the CAPM model) seek to diversify away.

Pursuant to the above, the paper further contends that emphasis on oligopoly market relations, i.e., in effect emphasis on the costs of space (distance), is fundamental to the very core of economic theory. And we deliberately did stipulate economic theory, not just microeconomics; this was done in belief that, to the extent that macroeconomic policy prescriptions are plotted against the backdrop of the *perfectly flexible* price-output, entry-exit world of pure competition, economic policy practitioners must (and will continue) to err quite substantively.

It suffices under this paper's objective and page limitations that we have merely sketched the generality of the spatial framework. (Additional and more detailed discussion of this issue can be found in Greenhut et al. 1987.) We lament that its generality has yet to be recognized throughout the profession. Most importantly, however, let us note again in this last regard that given the cost of distance, the world of industry is one of oligopoly. Failure to evaluate and understand the oligopoly market implies theoretical emphasis on pure competition and/or on monopolistic competition and/or on simple monopoly, each of which will often be an unproductive exercise, especially if applied directly to the world of business. Such misplaced emphasis completely ignores the sequential world of location and price equilibrium under cooperative and noncooperative games between decision makers who readily identify their rivals (as in Thisse and Vives 1988). The world of economic space can alone provide empirical evidence. It must also be used in the theoretical work of economists.

IV. Final remarks

"Quantity conjectures" are often derogated as being derived from extreme abstraction. In contrast, the way that firms in an industry *price* over space can be determined directly. That focus therefore provides a precise view of industrial structures without need for extreme abstraction. Indeed, the firm's pricing not only provides a gravity index but along with demand elasticity, product type, and the state of the macroeconomy, also point to beta relationships. These several relationships can, in turn, provide a rich perspective of past and future stock prices.

Given improved predictability of future betas compared with that possible on the strict basis of historical values *or* on the basis of historical values adjusted by special subjectively included considerations, it would follow that portfolios can be evaluated more precisely. Then the set of portfolios designed for different risk aversion levels could be made increasingly continuous and hence appropriate for more investors. Standing behind applications of betas would be an oligopoly theory which per se deals only with empirically observable events. One would hope that as this correlation is considered, the other many extensions of spatial price theory, which include analytical analogues and insights into product differentiation theory, advertising policies, inventory storage etc., will also be recognized. The composite would be a microeconomic theory based not just on time but on space and, accordingly, a theory which can furthermore provide a realistic-substantial foundation for evaluating the economic policies of governments.

Appendix

The basis for the capital asset pricing model (CAPM) was formed by the portfolio theory developed by Harry Markowitz, whose work along with others mentioned below can be reviewed more completely in texts on financial management or investments, such as Hirt and Block (1990, Chapter 20). For present purposes it suffices to say that Markowitz demonstrated how an investor can reduce the variance of the returns on his investments through portfolio diversification. As a consequence, the investment decision for a particular asset hinges not only on its contribution to the overall return, but also on the asset's impact on total portfolio variance. Markowitz derived the variance of the portfolio to consist of the variances of the individual investments and the covariances between all of the assets in the portfolio, according to:

$$\mathrm{VAR}(R_p) = \frac{1}{N^2} \cdot \left[\sum_i \mathrm{VAR}(R_i) + \sum_i \sum_{j \neq i} \mathrm{COV}(R_i, R_j) \right] , \tag{A1}$$

where R_p and R_i respectively represent the expected return for the investment portfolio and the individual assets $i = 1, \ldots, N$. Practical application of the theory, therefore, unfortunately involves the determination of $N \cdot (N+1)/2$ variances and covariances for an N asset portfolio. For a portfolio comprising 100 stocks, 5,050 variances and covariances would have to be determined.

To remedy this computational problem, Markowitz proposed relating the future returns of an asset to the *average* expected return on all assets combined, rather than each separately. That relationship is provided by beta, which is the slope coefficient calculated as $\mathrm{COV}(R_i, R_m)/\mathrm{VAR}(R_m)$ in the simple linear regression between the asset's return and that of the overall market:

$$R_i = \alpha_i + \beta_i \cdot R_m + \varepsilon_i \tag{A2}$$

where R_m is the expected return for the total market. The portfolio variance then can be shown to derive as:

$$\mathrm{VAR}(R_p) = \mathrm{VAR}(R_m) \cdot \frac{1}{N} \sum_i \beta_i + \frac{1}{N^2} \sum_i \mathrm{VAR}(\varepsilon_i) \tag{A3}$$

which requires a relatively low $2 \cdot N+1$ values: N individual betas plus N individual residuals (volatility not related to the market) plus 1 total market variance. The task of calculating portfolio variance of 100 stocks thus reduces to 201 unknowns.

The refinement using beta meant significant savings in implementing portfolio theory. More importantly, perhaps, it opened up a new point of view for financial theorists. William Sharpe, John Litner, Jan Mossin, and Jack Treynor are regarded as the chief architects of CAPM, which sets forth the price of an asset in terms of its expected, or required, return as:

$$R_i = R_f + \beta_i \cdot [R_m - R_f] , \tag{A4}$$

where R_f is the expected return on a risk-free security, commonly considered to be US Treasury Bills. This equilibrium is formed by arbitrage opportunities that would exist between investing in the individual asset or a portfolio that consists of $(1-\beta_i)$ percentage of funds invested in Treasury Bills and the remaining β_i percentage of funds in a market basket such as the S&P 500. Associated with this equation are the Markowitz portfolio concepts that: (1) investors will not require a return based upon the full range of uncertainty (i.e., total variance) of returns on an asset, but only on the component that stems from the overall market volatility (which accordingly cannot be diversified away), and (2) CAPM achieves minimal portfolio risk/variance for a given expected return, or alternatively maximum return for a given level of risk. Quite clearly, what led to 1990 Nobels for Markowitz and Sharpe relates directly to a subject which spatial price and regional science theorists have been investigating since World War II; namely, the different residual returns for different behavioral uncertainties that each competitive oligopoly firm must cover.

References

Anderson SP (1986) Equilibrium existence in the circle model of product differentiation. In: Norman G (ed) Spatial pricing and differentiated markets. Pion Press, London, pp 19–29

Archibald GC, Eaton BC, Lipsey RG (1986) Address models of value theory. In: Stiglitz JD, Mathewson GF (eds) New developments in the analysis of market structures. MIT Press, Cambridge, MA, pp 3–47

Beaver WH (1989) Financial reporting: an accounting revolution. Prentice Hall, Englewood Cliffs, NJ

Benson B (1985) Increasing product variety and rising prices. Montana State Unversity Working Paper

Benson B, Greenhut ML (1989) American antitrust laws in theory and in practice. Gower, London

Brander J, Krugman P (1983) A reciprocal dumping model of international trade. J Ind Econ 15:313–321

Buckley PJ, Casson M (1987) The future of the multinational enterprise. Macmillan, London

de Palma A, Labbé M, Thisse JF (1986) On the existence of price equilibria under mill and uniform delivered price policies. In: Norman G (ed) Spatial pricing and differentiated markets. Pion Press, London, pp 30–42

DeVany AS (1976) Uncertainty, waiting time and capacity utilization: a stochastic theory of product quality. J Polit Econ 87:523–541

DeVany AS, Saving TR (1977) Product quality, uncertainty and regulation: the trucking industry. Am Econ Rev 67:587–594

Dunning JH (1987) Trade locations of economic activity, and the multinational enterprise: a search for an eclectic approach. In: Ohlin B, Hesselborn PO, Wijkman PM (eds) The international allocation of economic activity. Macmillan, London, pp 395–418

Foster G (1986) Financial statement analysis, 2nd edn. Prentice Hall, Englewood Cliffs, NJ

Greenhut JG, Greenhut ML (1975) Spatial price discrimination, competition, and locational effects. Economica 42:401–419

Greenhut JG, Greenhut ML (1991) Inflationary impacts on stock prices. Presented at the WEA International's 66th Annual Conference

Greenhut JG, Greenhut ML, Li S (1980) Spatial pricing patterns in the United States. Q J Econ 44:329–350

Greenhut JG, Norman G, Greenhut ML (1991) Economic and financial aspects of airline deregulation. Int J Transport Econ 18:3–30

Greenhut ML, Norman G (1986) Spatial pricing with a general cost function: the effects of taxes on imports. Int Econ Rev 27:761–776

Greenhut ML, Norman G, Hung CS (1987) The economics of imperfect competition. Cambridge University Press, London

Greenhut ML, Hung C, Norman G, Smithson C (1985a) An anomaly in the service industry: the effect of entry on fees. Econ J 95:169–177

Greenhut ML, Ohta H, Sailors J (1985b) Reverse dumping: a form of spatial price discrimination. J Ind Econ 34:167–181

Hamilton J, Thisse J, Weskamp A (1989) Bertrand vs. Cournot pricing in a model of location choice. Reg Sci Urban Econ 19:87–102

Hirt GA, Block SB (1990) Fundamentals of investment management. Irwin, Homewood, IL

Lancaster K (1979) Variety, equity, and efficiency. Columbia University Press, New York
Lowell MC (1970) Product differentiation and market structure. West Econ J 8:120–143
Neven D (1986) Address models of differentiation. In: Norman G (ed) Spatial pricing and differentiated markets. Pion Press, London
Norman G, Dunning JH (1984) Intra-industry foreign direct investment: its rationale and trade effects. Weltwirt Arch 120:522–540
Novsheck W (1980) Equilibrium in simple spatial (or differentiated product) models. J Econ Theory 22:313–326
Phlips L (1983 a) Applied consumption analysis. North Holland, Amsterdam
Phlips L (1983 b) The economics of price discrimination. Cambridge University Press, London
Phlips L, Thisse JP (1981) Pricing, distribution and the supply of storage. Eur Econ Rev 15:225–243
Phlips L, Thisse JP (eds) (1982) Symposium on spatial competition and the theory of differentiated markets. J Ind Econ 31:1–194
Rosenberg B, Guy J (1976 a) Beta and investment fundamentals, part I. Financ Anal J 32 (3):60–72
Rosenberg B, Guy J (1976 b) Beta and investment fundamentals, part II. Financ Anal J 32 (4):62–70
Ross SA (1976) The arbitrage theory of capital asset pricing. J Econ Theory 13:341–360
Salant DJ (1980) Quality, location choice, and imperfect competition. Doctoral Dissertation, University of Rochester
Salop SC (1979) Monopolistic competition with outside goods. Bell J Econ 10:141–156
Saving TB (1982) Market organization and product quality. South Econ J 48:855–867
Scherer FM (1979) The welfare effects of product variety. J Ind Econ 1:113–134
Smith D (1989) A generalized spatial pricing model. Doctoral Dissertation, Texas A&M University
Thisse JP, Vives X (1988) On the strategic choice of spatial price policy. Am Econ Rev 78:122–137
Vernon R (1979) The product cycle hypothesis in a new international environment. Oxf Bull Econ Statist 41:255–267

Review of Industrial Organization 7: 361–373, 1991

Industrial Structures Components of Finance Theory's CAPM

JOHN G. GREENHUT*
Arizona State University West, Phoenix, AZ 85069-7100, U.S.A.

and

MELVIN L. GREENHUT*
Texas A&M University, College Station, TX 77843-4228, U.S.A.

Abstract. A microeconomic pricing model is developed which explains the effects of industrial structures on profit margin and equity beta values. The model is placed into special use by illustrating what may appear to be contradictions in the stock prices and betas of specific companies, differences which are explained however by the theory that supports our model. The industrial organization theory established in the paper would therefore extend Finance Theory's Capital Asset Pricing Model. Many testable propositions which could disconfirm or fail to disconfirm certain facets of, if not the paper's basic theory, are set forth descriptively.

Key words. CAPM, beta, competition, industrial structure, cycles.

A microeconomics pricing model is developed herein which explains the effects of industrial structures on profit margins. The subject model points to certain forces that have either been overlooked or insufficiently identified in the literature, but which help account for differences in stock price valuations. In particular, the structure of an industry – but *not* in terms of number of firms – is intrinsic to stock price values. To support our thesis, the model is placed into special use by illustrating what may appear to be contradictions in the stock prices and equity betas of specific companies, differences which are explained however by the theory that supports our model. The paper then presents a set of testable propositions (alas not easily testable ones) which *could* disconfirm certain facets of, if not the basic theory that is set forth below. If on the other hand, the fundamental tests which can be conducted do not disconfirm our theory, then the lack of attention given by finance theory to microeconomic principles in general and, in particular, to industrial organization theory is established. We initially review very briefly the CAPM theory and the associated significance of the beta coefficient.

1. The Capital Asset Pricing Model

The 1990 Nobel Laureates in economics and their followers utilized the beta coefficient and the portfolio theory of Harry Markowitz in developing the Capital

Asset Pricing Model (CAPM). CAPM established the required rate of return on an asset as a function of beta, where beta is the slope coefficient in the simple linear regression which relates the rates of return on a particular security to the overall market. Since the regression estimate of beta is calculated as the correlation coefficient times the ratio of standard deviations, beta indicates only the portion of an asset's volatility that attributes to, or is explained by the market as a whole. It is accordingly said to measure only the 'market risk' not the 'total risk' which would also include the deviations that stem from unique, company-specific factors. Portfolio theory maintains that since unique risks can be eliminated through diversification, asset values are based simply on the compensation required for market risk.

A beta greater than, equal to, or less than one indicates that the market risk of an individual asset, and hence its required return, is greater than, equal to, or less than that of all assets. CAPM sets forth this relationship mathematically as $R_i = R_F + b_i(R_M - R_F)$, where R_i is the required return on security i, R_F is a risk free rate of return (e.g., on U.S. T-Bills), b_i is the beta coefficient, and R_M is the market index return (e.g., of the S&P 500). This linear relationship is derived as a result of arbitrage possibilities involving the purchase of the individual asset or a portfolio consisting of T-Bills and a diversified stock index. For present purposes, it suffices to note that a risk premium given by $R_M - R_F$ is added to the T-bill rate in providing the required return for all stocks in general. The beta of a specific security shows the multiple of the market risk premium that is required for the individual asset.

Empirical tests of CAPM generally support the linear relationship between the returns on individual stocks and the overall market.[1] However, CAPM has been shown to underestimate the actual returns on low beta stocks while overestimating those on high beta stocks. The most widely heralded problem with the theory centers on the instability of beta.[2] To implement CAPM, investors must project the beta of the subject stock. To be sure, historical betas can serve as a guide to the future and specific mechanical adjustments can be employed to account for instability tendencies, but judgmental considerations based on the theoretical underpinnings of beta also are necessary. It is toward this end that the present paper centers attention on the effect of industrial structure on the volatility of corporate earnings.

2. An Industrial Organization Pricing Model

Neoclassical microeconomics centers on the profit maximizing firm whose manager equates MR with MC; i.e., $p(1 - 1/e_i) = MC_i$ for the firm $i = 1, \ldots, n$ in a homogeneous product industry, and where $e_i = -(\mathrm{d}q_i/q_i)/(\mathrm{d}p/p)$. Let us propose a variable g_i, which serves as the firm's competitive gravity, and define it as the ratio of the percentage change in total industry output ($\mathrm{d}Q/Q$) to the percentage change in the firm's output ($\mathrm{d}q_i/q_i$); i.e., $g_i = (\mathrm{d}Q/Q)/(\mathrm{d}q_i/q_i)$. The industry demand elasticity relates to the elasticity at the company level according to $E = e_i g_i$,[3] Substituting E/g_i for e_i in the firm's $MR = MC$ equation *and then aggregating for all n firms* establishes the industry's equilibrium $P(1 - G/E) = MC$, where $G = \Sigma g_i/n$ and $MC = \Sigma MC_i/n$.

It is obvious that because g_i is the competitive index for the firm, G is the industry gravity index. As we shall shortly see, G is bounded naturally from 0 to 1. The industry equilibrium condition can be stated in terms of price as $P = MC \cdot [E/(E - G)] = MC \cdot MF$, where MF designates the industry's price markup factor over the industry's average marginal cost, with $MF = [E/(E - G)]$.

Manifestly, $MF = 1$ when $G = 0$ regardless of the industry's elasticity. When $0 < G \leqslant 1$, the industry's price is greater than MC, with the elasticity of demand for the product determining the magnitude of the markup. When $E \rightarrow \infty$, MF falls toward the unit value, the same as when $G = 0$.

As shown and discussed in greater detail by Perry (1982) and Greenhut and Greenhut (1991), three widely contrasting forms of competitive relations prevail. Each can be represented by the G index, as follows:

Industry (1)

Full gravity, which applies to an industry wherein the firms seek to maintain their market shares. This industry can arise by prearrangement or as the result of all firms responding coincidentally to economic events. Market shares remain constant in industries where the percentage change in output by an individual firm is matched in total by the other firms in the industry; in that case, $g_i = 1$ and $G = 1$.

Industry (2)

Independent gravity, which describes a Cournot industry within which other firms do not react to a change in any individual company's supply, i.e., the output of all other firms in the industry remains fixed. A change by the ith firm thus involves $dq_j = 0$ for all $j \neq i$, and this yields $dQ = dq_i$ and $g_i = q_i/Q$. The gravity index under Cournot competition is simply equal to the firm's market share, a share falling of course between 0 and 1. Under the model, the greater the number of firms, the smaller is any single company's share *and* the closer is g_i to 0. The industry's index is $G = (\Sigma q_i/Q)/n = 1/n$, which equals 1 when $n = 1$ and 0 when $n \rightarrow \infty$.

Industry (3)

Zero gravity applies to an industry within which the aggregate quantity is fixed. This constant requires the firms in the industry to act oppositely to each other as, for example, in the Greenhut-Ohta opposite conjectural behavior pattern.[4] Under zero gravity, $dQ = 0$ and in turn $g_i = 0$ and $G = 0$.

The three contrasts in competitive behavior described above constitute the most common conjectural variation responses proposed for oligopolistic industries.[5]

Although the G index captures diverse industrial relations by spanning the range from 0 to 1, with the gravitational 'pull' rising as the level of homogeneity in the industry increases, we need center our present attention only on the extremes represented above by Industries (1) and (3).

From the equilibrium relation $P(1 - G/E) = MC$, it is clear that for industry (1) with $G = 1$, $P(1 - 1/E) = MC$; and when $G = 0$ for industry (3), $P = K$. These relations respectively provide the classical profit maximizing conditions for a monopolized and a perfectly competitive market. Simply put, our gravity index captures price relationships which cover the spectrum from monopoly to perfectly competitive pricing. Most significantly, the monopolistic and perfectly competitive results do not depend in this formulation on the number of firms; rather, they stem directly from the *homogeneity of behavior* characterizing a particular industry. It follows that a totally homogeneous, full gravity industry, i.e., where all firms move together and thereby maintain constant market shares, prices the same as would a monopolist.[6] Since a monopoly firm possesses a constant 100% market share, it is actually just a subset of the industry characterized as (1).

At the other extreme is a perfectly heterogeneous industry. In such industry, a change in supply by an individual firm is offset by the opposite actions taken by competitors (i.e., the industry quantity remains constant). In these industries, there is no markup of price above the average marginal cost level.[7] The theory of perfect competition assumes that each firm is so small that a change in output by a single seller does not alter the aggregate supply; hence, perfect competition is a subset member of industry (3). Likewise, another subset member of industry (3) exists when a many-firm (homogeneous good) oligopoly utilizes Bertrand pricing over the economic landscape.

3. Industrial Structures Impact on Betas

Our gravity concept generates significant conclusions concerning the potential earnings volatility of industries characterized by alternative competitive structures. Since price is the product of $MC \cdot MF$, the rate of inflation in an industry can be approximated by the sum of the percentage change in the markup factor plus the percentage rise in average marginal costs.[8] Thus from $P = MC \cdot MF = MC \cdot [E/(E - G)]$, we generate $\%\Delta P = \%\Delta MC + \%\Delta[E/(E - G)]$, $\lim \Delta \to 0$. The ability to maintain or increase profits by raising price appreciably does not derive from the *type* of competitive structure or demand elasticity per se; rather, it is attributable to the *change* in each. If demand elasticity and competitive behavior are unchanged, the inflation rate reduces to the rate of increase in marginal costs. *The profit margin of price over marginal cost remains the same*, regardless of the industry's competitive structure, whether highly concentrated or not (or, shall we say, whether the industry is fundamentally monopolistic or perfectly competitive in the sense of containing numerous small firms). *No change*

in the percentage markup of price over marginal cost takes place when competitive responses and demand elasticity remain unchanged.

Variations in demand elasticity and competitive behavior can take place and, of course, do occur. They raise or lower the price/cost margin by affecting the markup factor, and thereby appreciably impact the bottom line on the P&L statement. Though differences in the rate of increase in marginal costs can account for differentials in inflation rates among industries, the source of volatility in earnings of concern herein is the variability of the markup factor. Since demand curves can take innumerable shapes, so that changes in price involve different increases or decreases in elasticity, this paper focuses attention on *changes in elasticity as the likely dominant source of earnings volatility*. This likelihood is particularly the case during periods of accelerating inflation when distortions in market demands tend to occur.

To assess the interdependent impact of changes in elasticity on corporate earnings, we need simply to evaluate the percentage change in the markup factor that relates to a change in elasticity. This is given by the differential $d[(MF)/MF]/dE = [-G/(E-G)^2]/[E/(E-G)] = -G/[E \cdot (E-G)]$, which obviously is less than 0. We therefore observe an inverse relationship applying to margin impacts and changes in elasticity. Specifically, an increase in elasticity reduces the rate of change in an industry's markup factor; the result is that the price increase in the industry does not keep pace with the rate of increase in costs. In contrast, a decline in elasticity triggers a higher price/cost multiple, and thus a rate of increase in output prices in excess of the rate of increase in costs. Only with constant elasticity will industry price changes remain in step with changes in costs.[9]

These relations set the stage for the derivation of our final and most important theoretical principle concerning earnings volatility. Note that the impact of a change in elasticity on the percentage markup is ***minimal when demand is extremely elastic and/or the competitive index is numerically small.***[10] Alternatively, the impacts are ***magnified in markets subject to relatively inelastic demand and/or a very homogeneous competitive structure***. The vital structural relation governing earnings volatility is that for a given change in elasticity, *ceteris paribus*, earnings would vary most in industries characterized by inelastic demands and homogeneous competition.

Now, of course, beta values do not derive merely from earnings volatility, but also from the timing and direction of the profits swing relative to that of other companies in the stock portfolio. It is vital, then, to consider earnings volatility from a macroeconomic standpoint. If high volatility for an industry runs counter to an economy-wide trend (e.g., the markup factor for an industry increases abruptly at times of generally tightening margins), the beta for that industry would be significantly low. Volatility in the same direction as the overall trend will, on the other hand, generate high beta stocks. We will return to this issue later, but for now let us probe further into the industrial characteristics that would explain differences in earnings volatility.

Industries whose products are similar and standardized, and whose economies of scale promote industry domination by a few firms, can be expected more so than others to develop price leadership (e.g., a basing point type of price system) and market share preservation patterns.[11] Example industries include steel, cement, plywood, mining, energy, automotive, and stock brokerage. In opposite pattern, industries producing substantially differentiated goods, such as restaurants (including fast food), clothing, entertainment, and home furnishings, are likely to be characterized by heterogeneous behavior and pricing. The market implications of firms stressing and creating substantive differences in their products and services is to reduce the variability of margins for the overall industry.[12]

We submit that industrial products can be classified broadly in the homogeneous, low elasticity group, while consumer goods will generally fit the heterogeneous, high elasticity class.[13] To the extent that product differentiation is more prevalent at the consumer level, while standardized reliability has greater importance at the industrial goods level, it follows that one would expect a more stable relationship to exist among the firms producing industrial goods and services. In fact, a leader firm will often surface, and typically dominate for a rather long period of time.

In between the two extremes of standardized verses substantially differentiated goods lies the slightly differentiated group whose member firms are likely to follow the Cournot form of competition. This industry type is the one where greater entry would bring about comparatively small stock market price changes. Thus we propose the hypothesis of moderate stock market price gyrations for these industries. In fact, the price swings will be reduced in magnitude towards that of the heterogeneous industry, the greater is the number of slightly differentiated firms in the industry, *ceteris paribus*. Conversely, if behavioral and related product-service uncertainties (e.g., heavy tort liabilities) sharply restrict entry, the underlying price swings in these industries will promote greater stock market price gyrations than otherwise, approaching those of the firms in the homogeneous industries.

It should be manifest that separation of all industries into three degrees of similarity or difference, each related to entrepreneur-predicted conjectural variations, must be tempered in individual industry cases. One must also incorporate – as we deliberately specified in the preceding paragraph – such particular-special characteristics as tort liability and overall entry/exit conditions. Adding to and subtracting from the three classes whatever special individual industry characteristics prevail will provide, in our opinion, a meaningful set of yardsticks that can be used in any index forecasting of market values.

4. An Illustration Which Helps Establish This Paper's Industrial Organization Extension of CAPM

Homestake Mining (HM), a gold mining company, and Adolph Coors (AC), a brewing company, provide illustrative examples. For reasons to be provided later,

HM reflects Industry 1 and AC Industry 3. According to Value Line, the equity betas for the two companies are currently 0.55 and 0.90 respectively. Both companies are financed largely by equity, so the higher beta for Coors is not explained by differences in financial leverage. Yet, of the two companies, HM's profits are far more volatile and unquestionably more difficult to predict. The coefficient of variation (CV) in the operating margin of AC over the past five years was only 0.14 compared to 0.40 for HM.

If cycles and volatility in earnings could be predicted accurately, stock prices would discount all upcoming cycles and need not themselves be highly cyclical. We take it as axiomatic that such forecasting accuracy does not prevail. Where earnings are volatile, one would also expect large swings in stock valuations. Such was indeed the case for HM over the past half decade. The CV in the total return on common stock in HM was 30.3, while AC's stockholders incurred milder swings with a 5.3 CV. Yet the beta is lower for Homestake.

RECONCILIATION

This paper's model is rooted in three major industrial market structures: (1) Homogeneity in products and reactions characterize Industry 1 (e.g., a price leader type of industry exists, or an older firm with well-established goodwill tends to prompt parallel action by rivals without violating any antitrust law, etc.). A greater earnings volatility is likely to exist in this industry. Moreover, we can expect particularly high markups for its firms when the demands for their products are inelastic. (2) If managers react moderately to changes in the prices of rivals, almost along the lines of "what they do doesn't affect me too much", we have on hand Industry 2. It can be shown that the competitive index here would range from zero to unity. (3) At the other extreme to Industry 1 is the Industry 3 market in which firms act oppositely to each other. In effect, managers of companies in Industry 3 decide that "whatever the rival does, an opposite policy is best for them". Price changes by firms in this market relate in general *only* to changes in the value of money, as the profit margins over variable costs should be relatively stable.

With respect to HM and AC, we recognize that the volatility in their earnings and stock returns were related in virtually opposite sequence to their betas, Coor's beta being relatively high notwithstanding its lower earnings volatility. Why is that the case? Certainly this dichotomy must be resolved! We believe it can be resolved, as proposed below:

Standard CAPM, when *adjusted by the theory* presented in this paper, very readily explains why a low beta would arise for HM even though its earnings and stock returns are highly volatile. First of all, the profit margins for mining companies (Industry 1) would be subject to particularly severe swings due to the high degree of structural *homogeneity* in the industry and its relatively *unstable* (changing) *elasticity*. The responsiveness of buyers to a change in gold prices is strongly affected by economic conditions. In a period of declining inflation rates, the basic demand for gold *as a hedge against inflation* tends to disappear. The effect is that gold prices fall precipitously under what in time becomes less and less inelastic demand during periods of disinflation. In contrast, gold prices increase substantially during times of high inflation. But this change in the price of gold has very little negative effect on the quantity demanded. One might even propose that sometimes the demand for gold may actually be increased by rising gold prices, as this commodity becomes a top quality investment during inflationary periods. The consequence is that general changes in economic activity eventually have particularly sharp *and* direct impacts on the earnings of mining companies. It has such effects by sharply reducing sales revenues during downturns in inflation while also squeezing profit margins; during times of accelerating inflation, earnings rise sharply due to the decreased elasticity and the homogeneous competitive structure of the industry. (Note that revenue and earnings from the sale of beer will remain largely unaffected by the business cycle.)

Having explained the greater volatility for HM than AC, we now propose that it is in part this high degree of volatility resulting from business cycle swings which ultimately works to the advantage of HM in exhibiting a relatively low beta for that company. Its elasticity swings are partially contrary to those of the more typical companies whose demands become increasingly elastic with inflation, and inelastic during deflation. Alternatively stated, HM's earnings cycle turns *after* that of the economy; it is only, for example, *after* the economy has clearly experienced recession (which finally reduces inflation) that the demand elasticity for gold would increase and profit margins would decline. In the spirit of CAPM methodology, the variation in HM would be seen as a unique company-specific risk, i.e., not directly related to the market in general. The contra-cyclical nature of its variations produces a low beta and, correspondingly, a reduction in the total risk of portfolios that include HM common.

To sum up this example: Coors is in a heterogeneous, differentiated products industry that is subject to a generally elastic demand. Changes in elasticity for its products can be expected to correspond in timing to that of the overall economy. The result is that although the CV of Coors is low, its volatility is close to that of the entire market. HM in Industry 1, on the other hand, is subject to rapidly changing elasticity over the cycle and homogeneous industry volatility; however, its earnings volatility has been partially countercyclical, yielding a comparatively low beta.

Understanding the reason behind this mining company's low beta is paramount for stock price forecasting. Rather than merely extrapolating the historical low beta to the future, the stock analyst must question whether future economic conditions will give rise to the countercyclicality that has existed over the past two decades in gold prices. In the past, cost pressures late in the business cycle have pushed inflation (and gold prices) upward at the same time that economic growth has been slowed, or even turned negative. But will this hold in the future? In the event that the initial stage of an upcoming recession primarily reflects demand weakness rather than declining productivity, inflation can be expected to subside more rapidly at the onset of recession than it has in the recent past. The volatility in HM would then correspond to the overall market's weakness, and what is now viewed in the CAPM thought process as unique risk would 'magically' become market risk. HM's beta would soar. This paper, accordingly, proposes that competitive indices and demand elasticity should be considered in the application of CAPM. The combination points critically, in turn, to diverse hypotheses which warrant empirical study.

5. Testable Hypotheses

The HM, AC case example provides one application of the concepts presented previously in the paper. More generally, and hence most importantly, it highlights the paper's objective. This objective was to provide the foundation for a more complete *understanding* of the relations between competitive reactions and the volatility of earnings as they impact corporate betas. Such foundation establishes several hypotheses which not only can be tested but which also suggest empirical studies that are predicated directly on economic theory.

Observe in this last connection that our prior discussions focused on the earnings volatility of companies in three different types of industries. We emphasized different demand elasticities, different earnings, *and* different beta impacts, which composites are also basic parts of industrial organization theory or, from a broader standpoint, accepted micro-macro economic theory. Correspondingly, several paradigms were identified as direct parts of the subject of corporate betas *and* the CAPM approach to stock market values. A contrast with bond prices could also be effected. However, alone vital given the objectives of this paper is the existence of a set of testable hypotheses which specialists in finance and econometric theory can examine and resolve. Viewing betas in the perspective of industrial organization theory, and then testing different betas and portfolios, can lead to better predictions of future market values in an uncertain world.[14] We shall conserve space by dividing the types of tests we conceive of into two groups, the initial Group A being of more elementary order, and Group B proposing analysis that will require years of research.

Testable Hypothesis (*TH-1*). It is said that the ability to maintain – if not to widen – profit margins is presumed to correlate with a high concentration ratio (as given for example by the Herfindahl–Hirschman index). Our model rejects this idea and instead proposes that a concentration index is *per se* irrelevant, the crucial element to profit margin volatility being the *change* in elasticity. Of course, measuring elasticity, much less changes in elasticity for any economic good is an intricate, extremely difficult investigation. A starting point is well provided for in Philips (1983).

Testable Hypothesis (*TH-2*). Differences in the rate of increase in marginal costs can account for differences in inflation rates among industries. But the primary source of volatility in margins is the variability of the markup factor, itself dependent on the market structure and changes in elasticity as they were identified previously in this paper. More formidable would be an empirical study which compares market structures and beta values across industry lines.

Testable Hypothesis (*TH-3*). We proposed that the effect of a change in elasticity on the percentage markup is minimal when demand is extremely elastic and/or the competitive index is quite low.[15] The opposite holds when demands are very inelastic and/or a very homogeneous competitive structure prevails. Correlating demand elasticities with competitive structures could be added to the research suggested under TH-2.

Testable Hypothesis (*TH-4*). This paper pointed to an inverse relationship between price level impacts and changes in elasticity, where an increase in elasticity lowers the markup factor, while a decrease raises it. Correlating price level changes with changes in elasticity (positive, zero, or negative) would provide significant insights into beta values and stock prices.

The five testable hypotheses which follow involve extensions of testable hypotheses 1–4 that would probe more directly into competitive indices and beta values.

Group B Testable Hypothesis (*TH-5*). Stock market price swings *ceteris paribus* can be projected to be the least for the firms in industries producing multi-differentiated goods, and which therefore tend to approach complete heterogeneity. These industries are also likely to be characterized by Greenhut–Ohta pricing over the economic landscape, where the firms' managers stress product differences, yet tend to price lower as competition increases. Changes in input prices would then have a substantially moderated impact on final good prices. Evaluation of this relationship *across industry lines*, especially industries characterized by substantial heterogeneity, would test our industrial organization thesis.

Testable Hypothesis (*TH-6*). Consider goods subject to price leadership patterns, such as the delivered price system which held in steel, cement, linseed oil, and plywood. A study of industries of this kind would be opposite in form to that recorded above under TH-5.

Testable Hypothesis (*TH-7*). Industries following Cournot type of competition would tend to have comparatively moderate stock market price swings. This should be particularly the case the greater the number of firms in the industry. This research project corresponds, of course, to those proposed under TH-5 and TH-6.

Testable Hypothesis (*TH-8*). Should we not infer from our case example *and* competitive gravity index theory that (a) homogeneous structures generate greater volatility of earnings, from which (b) if the volatility is countercyclical to that of the market, and (c) the demands for the products involved tend to become less elastic during the extreme swings in the overall economy's cycle, then it follows that the firms' beta values should be the lowest possible? Should we not also infer the opposite? Specifically the firms which are members of (a′) heterogeneous industry structures, (b′) whose swings correspond to the market, and (c′) whose demands are consistently elastic over the business cycle should have unit beta values, i.e., betas which conform closely to the overall market? What patterns typically do in fact prevail for homogeneous and heterogeneous competitive industry structures? If distinctive patterns *do exist*, study of a firm's earnings volatility and lead-lag positions must also uncover the forces behind them, which finding would, of course, provide greater understanding of companies, their industries, *and* stock market prices. These studies would extend naturally to evaluations of fixed cost/variable cost and equity/debt ratio impacts, and the like. They would accomplish this in the context of industry types that also tend to generate different kinds of managers and competitive quantity or price reactions, probably in reflection of the underlying levels of uncertainty which characterizes the industry.

Testable Hypothesis (*TH-9*). If behavioral and related product service uncertainties prevail (e.g., heavy tort liabilities) which sharply restrict entry, the underlying volatility in these industries will be marked by substantial stock market price gyrations. In the process of studying this issue, insights would obtain not only into stock prices and the volatility of earnings, but as suggested above, insight also into the type of managers who serve as a source (or basis) for a conscious (unconscious) parallelism of action in particular industries.

Summary Group B's Testable Hypotheses 5–8. It warrants special note here that the lowest corporate beta's are being proposed by these writers under the conditions assigned for homogeneous structures under TH-8. Very high beta values are, however, suggested by Testable Hypothesis 6 for homogeneous structures, provided there is no lead-lag conditions, as in TH-8. In contrast to the homogeneous structures, a beta value approaching unity is suggested for the heterogeneous industry type also characterized by TH-5. This corporate beta would be somewhat similar to that of the Cournot industry type that was suggested under TH-7, as well as for the heterogeneous structure proposed, *ceteris paribus*, under TH-5. Finally all of the aforementioned suggestions are subject to the fundamental *ceteris paribus* provision which would be violated by the conditions given under TH-9.

6. Conclusion

A brief, concluding note is warranted. Empirical studies based on theory are fundamentally important. Data in their own stead are really empty statistics, as the original members of the Cowles Commission, and for example Oskar Morgenstern (1965) had observed. This paper has provided what in effect is an industrial organization theory that extends finance theory. Its several propositions can be tested, hopefully to the advantage of portfolio managers as well as those who specialize strictly in finance and general economic theory. Let it be noted finally that in effect our industrial organization extension suggests that a researcher under CAPM could quickly view any industry's pricing patterns over space. That would suggest the competitive structure of the industry. If, for example, a homogeneous structure is likely to exist, this hypothesis can be tested. Assuming it is not disconfirmed, one can anticipate a substantial use of the bond market in these industries rather than strict (or substantial) use of equity capital. New interpretation of beta impacts would also result.

Notes

* Associate Professor, Finance and Business Economics, Arizona State University West; Distinguished Professor, Department of Economics, Texas A&M University. The authors wish to thank the two anonymous referees for their helpful comments.

[1] Summaries of major empirical tests of CAPM can be found in textbooks on portfolio management (e.g., Elton and Gruber, 1987). Critique of CAPM tests can be found in Roll (1977).

[2] Numerous articles have investigated the problem of beta instability over time. In this context, see Blume (1971) and Alexander and Benson (1982).

[3] Note that $e_i g_i = [(\mathrm{d}q_i/q_i)/(\mathrm{d}p/p)] \cdot [(\mathrm{d}Q/Q)/(\mathrm{d}q_i/q_i)]$, and therefore $= E$.

[4] Referred to as such and described in Capozza and Van Order (1978).

[5] See, for example, Perry (1982) where his conjectural variation specifications of $m = 1$, 0, and -1 correspond respectively to the industries we refer to as (1), (2), and (3).

[6] Needham (1975) took a similar approach in defining the individual firm's elasticity as a function of the elasticity of the market demand curve. He also recognized that monopoly results obtain when "each firm in the group assumes that its rivals will imitate its price and output policies" (p. 244), which is our totally homogeneous case.

[7] In the words of Fama and Laffer (1972): "a change in output by firm i is anticipated to be precisely offset by changes on the part of other firms. In this case, even though the number of firms is finite, the industry is perfectly competitive . . ." (p. 670), our perfectly heterogeneous case.

[8] $\mathrm{d}(P)/P = \mathrm{d}(MF \cdot MC)/(MF \cdot MC) = [MF \cdot \mathrm{d}(MC) + MC \cdot \mathrm{d}(MF)]/(MF \cdot MC) = \mathrm{d}(MC)/MC + \mathrm{d}(MF)/MF$.

[9] Demand of constant elasticity, although providing helpful simplification when it comes to empirical studies, is a narrow and unlikely demand specification for depicting real world relationships (Benson and Greenhut, 1989, p. 58).

[10] $G/[E \cdot (E - G)] = 0$ when $E = \infty$ or $G = 0$.

[11] See Benson and Greenhut (1989, Chapter 3).

[12] Of course, the situation where one firm's product falls in disfavor relative to the preferred differentiated good will result in unique volatility for those firms. Their betas will be unaffected by this unique risk.

[13] For an extensive examination of elasticity of consumer goods, see Philips (1983).

[14] As Varian (1990, p. 314) points out, "Maximizing *Stock Market Value* still has meaning" in the

world of uncertainty, from which it follows that such maximization remains the goal of management given "a well defined objective function . . . in nearly all economic environments".

[15] Recall Note 10.

References

Alexander, G. J. and Benson, P. G. (1982) 'More on Beta as a Random Coefficient', *Journal of Financial and Quantitative Analysis* **17**, 27–36.

Benson, B. and Greenhut, M. L. (1989) *American Antitrust Laws in Theory and in Practice*, Gower Publishing, London.

Blume, M.E. (1971) 'On the Assessment of Risk', *Journal of Finance* **26**, 1–10.

Capozza, D. and van Order, R. (1978) 'A Generalized Model of Spatial Competition', *American Economic Review* **68**, 898–908.

Elton, E. and Gruber, M. (1987) *Modern Portfolio Theory and Investment Analysis*, 3rd ed., John Wiley, New York.

Fama, E. F. and Laffer, A. B. (1972) 'The Number of Firm's and Competition', *American Economic Review* **68**, 670–678.

Greenhut, J. and Greenhut, M.L. (1991) 'A Theory of Inflationary Impacts on Stock Prices', WEA International's 66th Annual Conference.

Morgenstern, O. (1965) *On the Accuracy of Economic Observations*, Princeton University Press, Princeton.

Needham, D. (1975) 'Market Structure and the Firm's R and D Behavior', *Journal of Industrial Economics* **23**, 241–255.

Perry, M. (1982) 'Oligopoly and Consistent Conjectural Variation', *The Bell Journal of Economics* **13**, 197–205.

Roll, R. (1977) 'A Critique of the Asset Pricing Theory's Tests: Part I: On Past and Potential Testability of the Theory', *Journal of Financial Economics* **4**, 129–176.

Interest Groups and the Antitrust Paradox

Bruce L. Benson, M. L. Greenhut, and Randall G. Holcombe

Economists have generally assumed that the intention of the antitrust laws is to increase economic efficiency. Many observers, however, have noted that the antitrust laws are applied inconsistently and often do not use economic analysis to promote economic efficiency. Judge Robert Bork (1979) referred to this failure of the antitrust laws to promote economic efficiency as the "antitrust paradox," and Peter Asch (1970) called it the "antitrust dilemma." The special interest theory of regulation developed by Stigler (1971) and others assists in understanding the antitrust paradox, because pursuant to it one must not expect antitrust to be applied to benefit the general public.[1]

The special interest view of economic regulation has found its way into evaluations of the antitrust laws.[2] For example, Judge Richard Posner (1969, p. 87) claimed that Federal Trade Commission (FTC) investigations are seldom in the public interest and are undertaken "at the behest of corporations, trade associations, and trade unions whose motivation is at best to shift the costs of their private litigation

---

Cato Journal, Vol. 6, No. 3 (Winter 1987).

Bruce L. Benson is Associate Professor of Economics at Florida State University, M. L. Greenhut is Alumni Distinguished Professor of Economics at Texas A&M University, and Randall G. Holcombe is Professor of Economics at Auburn University.

[1]Stigler (1985) does not see the special interest theory as completely convincing in the case of antitrust. Some extensions of the special interest theory of government are found in Posner (1974), Peltzman (1976), McCormick and Tollison (1981), Becker (1983), and Holcombe (1985). Some of the many empirical examinations of the theory include Abrams and Settle (1978), Jarrell (1978), Kau and Rubin (1978), McCormick and Tollison (1981), Smith (1982), and Ross (1984). A parallel development to the literature on interest group regulation is the rapidly growing literature on rent seeking. See Tollison (1982) and Benson (1984) for a discussion of the relationship between the two developments and reviews of the relevant literature.

[2]See, for example, Posner (1969), Faith et al. (1982), Weingast and Moran (1983), Benson (1983b), Benson and Greenhut (1986), and High (1984–85).

to the taxpayer and at worst to harass competitors." The special interest theory of regulation goes a long way toward explaining the antitrust paradox, but there are important differences between antitrust and most other regulatory constraints on business. Moreover, there are many facets of antitrust that are not readily explained by that theory.

Several aspects of antitrust law differentiate it from the types of regulation that are normally considered within the special interest framework. Regulation is normally concerned with one or a few industries, but the antitrust laws are considerably broader in scope. In addition, the courts play a much more visible role in antitrust than they do in regulation. One can legitimately question how laws as broad in scope as the antitrust laws can be the product of special interests. One can further question how special interests could hope to benefit from court decisions that normally are considered to be outside the influence of narrow special interests.[3] These basic issues are evaluated throughout the paper.

Our thesis is that the antitrust laws are a result of a special interest struggle between small and large economic entities seeking changes in the general economic environment rather than the specific favors usually associated with special interest legislation. We explain why a rather general approach was sought for antitrust laws, not the typical goal of many narrowly focused special interests. We also explain Judge Bork's antitrust paradox, both in origin and application, and account for enforcement by both courts and governmental bureaus of the property rights assigned under the antitrust laws.

The Antitrust Process

There are three main participants in the antitrust process: special interests; legislators; and the commissioners, bureaucrats, and judges who interpret and enforce the statutes. These groups are not mutually exclusive. In particular, bureaucrats and commissioners may also act as interest groups and possess considerable political power that often is used to further their own interests. Stigler (1971) observed that the object of special interest groups is the transfer of wealth, but this is rarely accomplished by a simple transfer of funds from the public treasury, especially in the antitrust arena. Rather, as Benson (1984) noted, wealth transfers are provided through governmental assignments of or transfers of property rights.

[3]Posner (1972), Rubin (1977), Priest (1977), and Holcombe (1983, chap. 9) all suggest a type of invisible hand mechanism leading the courts to reach efficient decisions.

The process of assigning or transferring property rights can be divided into two distinct stages: first, the assignment of property rights; second, the enforcement of the resulting property rights assignment. The first stage is a legislative function; for the assignment to be worth anything, an enforcement mechanism must also be established. These two stages can be thought of as a single object demanded by interest groups because different enforcement levels are possible given any assignment of rights. Thus, one goal of interest groups is to obtain and defend favorable property rights.

When examining antitrust issues there is particular reason for distinguishing between the assignment and the enforcement of rights, because legislators assign antitrust rights but do not enforce them, even though in theory they could. Legislators delegate the enforcement function to agencies (commissions) and to the courts, and the legislature's delegates wield considerable power and independence.[4]

The Basic Model

Legislators favor special interest groups but never to the extent that the favored group would prefer. They favor the group up to the point where the marginal political benefit received in exchange for the favor equals the marginal cost in terms of lost support from other groups (Peltzman 1976, p. 217). Of course, the favored group would most prefer to receive greater benefits, that is, up to the point where the marginal benefit is zero. Stigler (1971, p. 4), Posner (1974, p. 350), Peltzman (1976), and Becker (1983) concluded that the political exchange in the United States results in an efficient transfer of wealth from a political perspective. There should be no excessive waste or unnecessary inefficiencies caused by such exchange. As Tullock (1965), Eckert (1973), Hilton (1972), Benson (1983b), and Benson and Greenhut (1986) observed, however, the bureaucrats and commissioners to whom the antitrust enforcement power is delegated do not have incentives to behave efficiently. Why the delegation? The answer is because the legislature has a time constraint, and time spent enforcing the rights it has granted reduces the new rights assignments that the legislature can make (Benson 1983b). In addition, the legislature requires the agreement of a large number of people for it to take

[4]In many cases, enforcement agencies have the ability to assign rights, bypassing the legislature. This opens the possibility that an agency might favor an interest group the legislature does not wish to support and tend to corrupt public officials (see Benson and Baden 1985). One would expect that any deviation between legislatively supported interest groups and agency-supported interest groups to be a short-run phenomenon, however, because ultimately the legislature can control the agency through its budget.

action, so it will be an inefficient organization for accomplishing the enforcement of rights (Erlich and Posner 1974). For these reasons, the legislature delegates the enforcement of the rights it assigns.

The favored interest groups will also want the enforcement function delegated. The theory of bureaucracy suggests that a bureau will produce more output than would be most preferred by the legislature (Tullock 1965; Niskanen 1968, 1971, 1975); and when enforcement of a rights assignment is the output, the result will be over-enforcement (Benson and Greenhut 1986). Because the favored interest will prefer a rights assignment larger than the legislature will grant, over-enforcement by the enforcing agency will benefit the special interest. This explanation applies not only to all types of regulation but to antitrust as well. Special interests will prefer that the enforcement of rights be delegated because the rights will be over-enforced, increasing the special interest's benefits. As Niskanen (1975) observed, agency managers' incentives are closely linked to the size of the agency's budget; and although his model was applied generally to bureaucracy, it fits antitrust as well.[5]

The antitrust model examined in this paper is a straightforward use of Niskanen's bureaucracy model applied to the regulatory environment characterized by Peltzman and others. In general, special interests approach the legislature with demands for favorable property rights assignments. And rights are assigned in a way that establishes a majority for the legislator. After assignment, enforcement is delegated to an agency that over-enforces. If one then considers the agency to be an interest group, one can even support the Stigler-Peltzman predictions of political efficiency. The initial assignment was made due to a political exchange with an interest group; but once the enforcement mechanism is in place, the enforcer becomes another interest group, thus increasing the demand for enforcement. The supposed conflict between the Stigler-Peltzman interest group approach and the Niskanen bureaucracy approach raised by Weingast and Moran (1983) may not exist at all if bureaucrats play an interest group role.

Several vital aspects of the antitrust laws warrant specification at this point. First, the laws are economy-wide rather than focused on just one or a few industries. Second, the laws are couched in very vague language, so that what constitutes a violation is largely a matter of interpretation. Third, the laws involve a commission. Fourth, they involve the courts. The importance of these features distinguishes

[5]Niskanen's early model (1968, 1971) has been subjected to a number of criticisms, several of which were dealt with by Niskanen (1975). See also Benson (1981, 1983a).

our antitrust model from the bureaucracy model and from Stigler's model of special interest legislation.

In essence, the antitrust laws represent a transfer of rights from large economic entities to small ones, the response of the legislator having been tuned to the times. This is why the laws are economy-wide in scope, rather than being centered on a few industries.

The advantage of having a vague statute is that it could be enforced, not only against those viewed as a present threat to small entities but also against any future threats. In addition, the special interest vagueness allows paradigms to be applied, such as the incipiency doctrine, in which substance can completely disregard the realities of existing competition and economic theory (Greenhut and Ohta 1979; Greenhut et al. 1985). It also explains away (and contradicts) the idea that the antitrust statutes were designed to improve the country's markets and to yield more efficient economic relationships.

What about antitrust enforcement being effected by commissions and courts? Are not appointed commissions less aggressive than the classical bureaucracy model would suggest? Hilton (1972), Eckert (1973), and others have proposed different outputs by commission regulators than by civil service regulators. Essentially, Hilton considered commissioners to be maximizing support, in effect seeking future employment.[6] But maximizing support is certainly consistent with favoring powerful political interest groups. Eckert viewed their salaries as being fixed and not tied to budget size; thus, he characterized commissioners as effort minimizers. It may appear to follow, then, that commissions have no real impact, as Stigler and Friedland (1965) suggested with respect to electric utilities. But commissions enforcing rights that are in the best interest of the regulated industry, as Stigler (1971) suggested is likely, could easily appear to be doing nothing if by doing "something" observers mean "restricting the industry." Furthermore, non-salary perquisites of the office are tied to the size of a commission's operator and level of enforcement. Thus, while the incentives for excessive enforcement may be relatively weak for a commissioner, they still exist, and the general conclusions of Niskanen's view of enforcers hold.

The courts also offer a basic difference vis-à-vis civil servants in the bureaucracy model. One difference is they are less subject to capture than are bureaus. A second difference is that they will be the final authority, because vague legislation fails to identify specific actions that violate the assigned rights. It is our objective to apply

[6]See also Mitnick and Weiss (1974), Russell and Shelton (1974), and Joskow (1974) for arguments similar to Hilton's.

the bureaucracy model to a set of laws, the antitrust laws, that are economy-wide in scope, vague, and enforced by commissioners and the courts.

Completing the Theory: Ambiguity and the Courts

The Sherman Act was basically inspired by and lobbied for by interest groups made up of small economic entities, particularly from the agricultural sector. Rather than a specific act aimed against, say, machinery companies, the general law could also protect small farmers from large banks or other present or future entities that might threaten them.[7] This same principle applies today with regard to civil rights legislation. Rather than specific laws, a general law to protect civil rights can be enforced by the courts against any present or future violators. The point is that if the special interest group has a large enough constituency and a distinct identity (for example, small economic entity, minority race), a general regulation enforced by the courts can provide more benefits to the interest group than a specific regulation.

While it is true that a series of specific regulations could accomplish the same thing, this would require the special interest to continue returning to the legislature for additional legislation whenever it appeared that a transfer of rights would be beneficial. A general transfer of rights from large economic entities to small ones will continue to benefit the small entities in specific instances that the small entities could not foresee. Because the characteristics of the recipient of the transfer are relatively well defined, this type of transfer will provide more benefits than would a specific regulation. With a general transfer of this type, however, it is not always clear when the law has been violated, so the courts enter as an interpreter of the intent that underlies the law. As long as the courts interpret the intent as being the protection of small economic entities from large ones, the small entities that compose the special interest will benefit from the transfer.

The ambiguity of a general transfer of this type also benefits the recipient, because one can never be certain when the line has been crossed that constitutes a violation. In the case of antitrust, this could cause large economic entities to wield their power carefully, lest they be accused of a violation. Again, this is to the benefit of the small economic units that made up the special interest.

[7]Note, however, that the Interstate Commerce Commission (ICC) act was passed at about the same time to regulate rail rates, in part because of pressure from farmers (and, of course, from the railroads themselves).

Another factor is that the courts are likely to be less influenced by special interests than by a governmental agency. In many circumstances a special interest would prefer enforcement by an agency as a means of increasing the effective transfer of rights, but this may not always be so. When rights are transferred from large economic entities to small ones, there is always the threat that once an enforcing agency is established, the large entities will use their economic power to influence the agency, resulting in a transfer of rights back to them.[8] When rights are being transferred from large entities to small ones, there is good reason for the special interest to prefer the enforcement of rights to take place through the courts. A court enforcer may prevent the large economic entities from capturing the enforcing agency.

In summary, antitrust laws tend to transfer rights from large entities to small ones. There are two reasons for special interests to prefer court enforcement. First, the general transfer can apply to cases not specifically mentioned in the law; court interpretation is required to identify these particular cases. Second, court enforcement will prevent the large economic entities from whom rights were transferred from capturing the enforcing agency to reverse the transfer.

Interest Groups and Antitrust

The demand for antitrust legislation began building during the 1870s and 1880s (Areeda 1974, p. 44). It involved the formation of many organizations "with revealing names like the National Anti-Monopoly Cheap Freight Railway League" (Neale 1970, p. 12). The primary source of pressure was from farm groups that faced what they perceived to be excessively high rail rates as well as high prices of farm equipment and other manufactured goods. They believed that the high prices were caused by monopoly power exercised in the market and by import tariffs. There was also a general belief among farmers that eastern financiers controlled the credit market and charged them unfairly high interest rates. "Dissatisfaction with manufacturers of farm machinery and other goods, railroads, and eastern financiers became the cry against monopoly" (Areeda 1974, p. 43), and because "the farmers were better endowed with political influence than economic strength, . . . organizations like the National Grange and the National Farmers Alliance insistently demanded

[8]This can be observed today in the Department of Energy. Originally established to control large oil companies, much of its early effects amounted to a transfer from large oil companies to small ones and to the general public. The department's recent programs, however, primarily benefit large energy producers.

some control of the railways and of monopolies in general" (Neale 1970, p. 12). Neale concluded that "the paramount aim of politicians" in passing the Sherman Act was to meet this demand for action by such organizations.[9]

The business interests that farmers opposed were not without political power themselves, and Congress did not choose full-scale regulation or nationalization of these enterprises due to the political pressure from business (Areeda 1974, p. 44). Thus, the Sherman Act represents congressional attempts to balance the interests of various interest groups, as described by Peltzman (1976). Interest group pressure rather than a desire for economic efficiency led to the passage of the Sherman Act, and Neale (1970, p. 473) noted that the courts have consistently refused to consider economic efficiency issues in judging whether an antitrust violation has taken place, although many Department of Justice and Federal Trade Commission economists stress such issues in their analyses.

The passage of the Sherman Act fits well into the model of special interest legislation. It was clearly understood at the time that farmers demanded some antitrust action and that the passage of the Sherman Act was a response to that demand (see Gordon 1963). It was never intended to produce efficiency; even the name gives away the fact that the law was intended as a transfer of property rights away from trusts. What else could antitrust mean?

The form of the Sherman Act can also be understood within the context of the model. The act was passed to benefit the farmers as a special interest group, but the businesses the act opposed also had considerable political power. In balancing the interests of both groups, Congress could hardly legislate away the businesses. Viewed in this light, the vague nature of the statute and the delegation of its enforcement to the Department of Justice and to the courts make good sense from the standpoint of the farmers for whom the act was passed. Because the act generally declares combinations, contracts, or conspiracies in restraint of trade to be illegal, it is simply a vague piece of legislation that endorsed the common law and was designed to protect small economic entities from being harmed by large ones. Because the farmers were small entities and the railroads, banks, and manufacturers were large entities, the act appears to be a one-way transfer of property rights to the farmers (and any other small businesses that might feel harmed).

[9]Baxter (1979) and Katzman (1980) have argued that there is no strong evidence that one group is being favored by the antitrust laws; but Williamson (1979), commenting on Baxter's argument, found room for disagreement.

The structure of the act benefited the farmers in several ways. First, because the act did not name offenders ahead of time (it was not aimed at railroads or banks specifically but at anyone acting to restrain trade), action could be taken not only against present offenders but also against future ones. Because individual farmers could always foresee being economically small entities in relation to the other businesses with whom they dealt, the umbrella of the act protected farmers from a wide variety of economic threats.

Second, because of the act's vagueness, it enabled small economic entities to bring complaints under the act in a wide variety of circumstances. That vagueness would also ensure that there was always the possibility of a violation, having the corollary effect of making larger businesses behave cautiously even before any enforcement proceedings began, simply because of the threat of action.

Third, because victims could bring complaints, the Sherman Act could be over-enforced, even though an agency does not have the direct power of enforcement.[10] As a result, the act ended up providing more benefits to the special interests that the act favored than Congress had originally intended. The act was an example of special interest legislation and was recognized as such at the time of its passage.

The next major development in antitrust was the passage of the Federal Trade Commission Act and the Clayton Act in 1914. The establishment of the FTC was the result of many sources of political pressure, including the big businesses that found themselves constrained by the vagueness of the Sherman Act. There was considerable pressure from business organizations for more clearly articulated standards, and some observers have concluded that the establishment of the FTC was a victory for those businesses that wanted to ensure their political power and protect themselves from competition (Areeda 1974, pp. 47–48; Kolko 1963). In this view, the FTC was created to advise businessmen, to approve of their collusive organizations, and to create order in markets. As in the model above, large businesses could not effectively capture the courts, but the FTC gave them an agency through which they could use their economic power and influence.

Clearly, the FTC is not solely a pro-business agency, but was developed through compromise. The *Ralph Nader Study Group*

[10]Neale (1970, pp. 374, 385) noted that both the Federal Trade Commission and the Department of Justice rely almost exclusively on complaints to determine when the antitrust laws should be enforced, and that complaints predictably come from those who believe they are being injured.

Report on Antitrust recognized that "in 1914 both sides—those advocating a kind of business advisor and those seeking more energetic trustbusting—compromised to produce the Federal Trade Commission" (Green et al. 1972). And Areeda (1974, p. 48) noted that "similar differences of opinion were reflected in the Clayton Act, passed in the same year. . . . These differences were compromised in the ultimate enactment." As Peltzman's theory of regulation would predict, the favored group will not receive the maximum possible benefit. The FTC and Clayton acts, however, can clearly be seen as a transfer of rights to big business in response to the larger-than-intended transfer away from big business that had been the result of the Sherman Act.

It is interesting that the 1914 rights transfer was reversed somewhat as the FTC and the courts began to rule against incipient violations. In *Triangle Conduit and Cable Company v. FTC* (168 F.2d 175, 7th Cir. [1948]), for example, the court held that manufacturers utilizing a basing-point pricing system in order to stabilize competition among themselves were in violation of the Sherman Act. In itself, this decision seems unremarkable.[11] But the court proposed that unilateral adoption of a basing-point pricing scheme by an individual firm could also be prohibited, as long as other firms might adopt similar schemes. Even if unilateral at the start, the court saw this as the first step toward a conspiracy (see Greenhut [1970] 1974, chaps. 7, 14). In *Fashion Originators Guild v. FTC* (381 U.S. 357, 367 [1965]), the Supreme Court held that it was an object "of the Federal Trade Commission Act to reach not merely in their fruition but also in their incipiency," and in *E. B. Muller and Co. v. FTC* (142 F.2d 511, 517 6th Cir. [1944]) the Sixth Circuit Court ruled that "the purpose of the Federal Trade Commission Act is to prevent potential injury by stopping unfair methods of competition in their incipiency." Clearly in antitrust cases this represents a transfer of rights from large economic entities to small ones. The party bringing the complaint has to show neither actual nor present harms; it must only show that some harm can be predicted as a result of the offending policy.[12]

Exemptions and Interest Groups

Perhaps the strongest evidence of the influence of interest groups on antitrust legislation lies in their success in gaining immunity to

[11]See Greenhut ([1956] 1983) for a concurrence with the decision.

[12]The incipiency doctrine reflects the public's distrust of oligopolies as well as the general failure (including that of economists) to distinguish between organized (collusive) and competitive oligopolies, the market prices and factor incomes of which are

the antitrust laws (Adams 1965). Agricultural interests comprised the major pressure group pushing for the early antitrust laws, so it is not surprising that agricultural organizations were able to obtain specific exemptions from coverage under the antitrust laws. Section 6 of the Clayton Act partially exempts agricultural organizations, allowing farmers to form cooperative associations without violating the law. The Capper-Volstead Act of 1922 extends the Clayton Act to exempt capital stock agricultural cooperatives that were not exempted under the Clayton Act.

The courts have interpreted the Clayton Act as allowing farm organizations to "set association policy, fix prices at which their cooperative will sell their produce, and otherwise carry on like a business corporation without thereby violating the antitrust laws."[13] Thus, agricultural interest groups—who were instrumental in having the antitrust laws passed as a transfer of property rights to them—also had the political power to see that the laws were not applied to them, even when their actions represented combinations or contracts in a restraint of trade that clearly would have been considered a violation if committed by another business entity. A similar exemption was given to fishermen's organizations in the Fisheries Cooperative Marketing Act of 1934. In some cases, the courts ruled in favor of the special interests; in others the interests were able to get additional acts passed that specifically exempted them.

In 1908, the Supreme Court ruled in *Lowe v. Lawlor* (208 U.S. 274) that a nationwide boycott organized by a union to persuade wholesalers and retailers not to buy a particular firm's product was an interference with the interstate shipment of goods and, therefore, a restraint of trade. The Court awarded treble damages and ordered the union and individual union members to pay shares of the award. Following the decision, labor union officials "immediately commenced pressure for exemption of labor from the antitrust laws." The drive resulted in the Clayton Act's declaration that labor organizations are exempt from the antitrust laws (Northrup and Bloom 1965, p. 313). Section 6 of the act reads: "[N]othing contained in the antitrust laws shall be construed to forbid the existence and operation of labor . . . organizations, instituted for the purposes of mutual help,

---

of opposite order (Greenhut [1970] 1974). This doctrine and its increasing use, reflected even in Judge Learned Hand's *Alcoa* decision, are based on the failure to recognize that conscious parallelism of action by oligopolists can derive from competitive behavior and in turn generate market-efficient results. The vested interests of those who identify with the small entities must condemn any form of Loschian conjectural variations behavior (Greenhut et al. 1975) and thus relegate the antitrust laws to a set of restrictions with no roots at all in any quest for economic efficiency.

[13]Maryland and Virginia Milk Producers v. United States, 362 U.S. 458, 466 (1970).

and not having capital stock or conducted for profits, or to forbid or restrain individual members of such organizations from lawfully carrying out the legitimate objects thereof, be held or construed to be illegal combinations or conspiracies in restraint of trade under the antitrust laws." Section 20 of the act prevents the use of federal injunctions against strikes, boycotts, picketing, and similar activities "in any case between an employer and employees, or between persons employed and persons seeking employment, involving or growing out of, a dispute concerning terms or conditions of employment."

Despite the Clayton Act's exemption of labor from the antitrust laws, the Supreme Court ruled in 1921 in *Duplex Printing Company v. Deering* (254 U.S. 433) that labor unions could be held accountable under the antitrust laws for some of their actions. In this case, a union that was trying to organize the Duplex plant had succeeded in getting members of other unions to refuse to handle the firm's products. The Court held that Section 20 protected a union only when its members were employed by the company they were acting against. The American Federation of Labor turned to Congress; after continual pressure, the Norris-La Guardia Act was passed in 1932, which deprived the federal courts of antitrust jurisdiction in almost all labor disputes.

The labor case parallels the agricultural case. Though labor interests were not actively seeking passage of the antitrust laws, this powerful lobbying group nevertheless managed to remain exempt from the laws' influence. If the courts did not rule in favor of a special interest, then the special interest was able to turn to Congress to have exemptions to the antitrust laws legislated for it.

Other exemptions could be mentioned. For example, if regulated industries are the beneficiaries of regulation, as Stigler (1971) argued, then the regulated firms should be able to protect their benefits from potential challenges through the antitrust laws. As Areeda (1974, pp. 105–14) and Adams (1965, pp. 277–84) noted, regulated industries are largely exempt from the antitrust laws. Similarly, the Miller-Tydings Act (1937) and the McGuire-Keough Act (1952) were results of a movement among small retailers that had successfully obtained passage of "fair trade" laws in 45 states prior to 1937. This legislation exempted firms from antitrust laws in states with legalized minimum resale prices. The "fair trade" laws, which are widely viewed as protecting small shopkeepers from the more efficient larger retail chains (in a clearly collusive manner in restraint of trade), caused Neale (1970, p. 276) to note that "many political groups which would yield to none in zeal for trust busting are to be found in the van of the so-called fair trade movement. . . ." The Robinson-Patman Act preventing price discrimination is yet another example of an antitrust law designed to protect a special interest, that interest once again being small retailers who could not buy in large enough quantities to receive quantity discounts often given to chains.[14] The exemptions to the antitrust laws are all easily recognized as the result of special interest pressure on the legislature.

The Antitrust Laws over Time

Neale (1970, p. 11) observed that "there is evidence that the aims and scope of antitrust policy have changed a good deal since the passage of the Sherman Act, and may easily change some more in the future." Following the interest group theory of regulation, this is precisely what one would expect if the relative strengths of interest groups change over time (Benson 1984; Weingast and Moran 1983). For example, Clarkson and Muris (1982) noted that prior to 1969 the bulk of the FTC antitrust enforcement was aimed at discouraging price competition under Robinson-Patman when it threatened the well-being of small firms. After significant criticism, the FTC in 1969 suddenly closed about 600 of its investigations, reorganized the commission's work to deemphasize Robinson-Patman, and began several large-scale industry investigations. Similarly, the settling of the AT&T case and the closing of the IBM case within months of each other can be seen as a response to a change in the political climate during the Reagan era.

Posner's (1969, p. 83) study of the FTC emphasizes that a congressman must support the demands of interest groups in his district, noting that "the welfare of his constituents may depend disproportionately on a few key industries. The promotion of the industries becomes one of his most important duties as a representative of the district." One might well expect cases to be biased in favor of the firms in the districts of legislators serving on committees that have oversight over the FTC; this is exactly what Faith et al. (1982) found. Weingast and Moran (1983, p. 775) reached a similar conclusion with regard to oversight committees, noting that "markedly different preferences on the committee lead to major shifts in agency policy." Because oversight committees are merely a reflection of interest group demands, Weingast and Moran and Faith et al. conclude that the FTC's output is best explained by the interest group theory.

[14]See Ross (1984) for a discussion of the interest groups who were influential in obtaining passage of the Robinson-Patman Act and for empirical estimates of the benefits obtained and the costs incurred by various groups as a result of the enforcement of the act.

This discussion places a different light on the general vagueness of the antitrust laws. Earlier, the vagueness of the laws was seen as a means to transfer rights to one well-defined group (for example, small economic entities) from other unspecified groups. Small farmers could obtain transfers from railroads, banks, manufacturers, and any other future economic threats without the threats being spelled out in the law. But the laws' vagueness also benefits the legislature; due to its oversight capacity, the legislature will be able to influence the type of enforcement in response to the changing power and demands of interest groups, all without writing a new law.

In light of the fairly obvious political nature of the passage and enforcement of antitrust laws, we might wonder why such widespread acceptance of the efficiency-enhancing goals of antitrust appears to characterize the economics profession. This view appears to be an after-the-fact rationalization, however, because economists were not advocates for or even concerned with passage of the earliest statutes. As Scherer (1970, p. 424) reported:

> About the only group in America other than big businessmen outspokenly unconcerned about the trust problem were the professional economists. Many were captivated by Darwin's theory of biological selection. They saw the growth of big business as a natural evolutionary response consistent with economies of scale, or when economics were patently absent from mergers, as a step necessary to eliminate cut-throat competition. But in that unenlightened era, the views of unenlightened economists concerning big business had little influence on public policy.

Clearly, Scherer holds with the efficiency-enhancing perception of antitrust, and he reflects the view that came to dominate the profession early in the 20th century.

Summary and Conclusion

This paper has fit the antitrust laws into the special interest theory of regulation, stressing the influence of special interests on antitrust. The paper also spotlighted the significant differences between antitrust and other forms of regulation, emphasizing the vagueness of the antitrust statutes, their broad focus, and the fact that the laws are generally subject to interpretation and enforcement by the FTC and the courts rather than by a narrowly focused agency. It is clear that the effects of antitrust diverge from those of other forms of regulation. For example, the interaction of vagueness and use of the courts sometimes requires legislators to pass new statutes in order to protect the favored special interest. On the other hand, to the extent that the

FTC serves as the final authority, the legislators' interest in reelection is being protected by insulating the legislature from direct responsibility for specific actions. Most generally, we propose that antitrust in the United States centers on special interest effects and the legislators' quests for reelection. The real antitrust paradox is to have expected legislatures to be concerned with the general welfare.

References

Abrams, Burton A., and Settle, Russell F. "The Economic Theory of Regulation and Public Financing of Presidential Elections." *Journal of Political Economy* 86 (April 1978): 245–57.

Adams, Walter. "Exemptions from Antitrust: Their Extent and Rationale." In *Perspective on Antitrust Policy*, pp. 273–311. Edited by Almarin Phillips. Princeton, N.J.: Princeton University Press, 1965.

Areeda, Phillip. *Antitrust Analysis*. Boston: Little, Brown and Co., 1974.

Asch, Peter. *Economic Theory and the Antitrust Dilemma*. New York: John Wiley and Sons, 1970.

Baxter, William F. "The Political Economy of Antitrust." In *The Political Economy of Antitrust: Principal Paper by William Baxter*, pp. 3–50. Edited by Robert O. Tollison. Lexington, Mass.: Lexington Books, 1979.

Becker, Gary S. "A Theory of Competition among Pressure Groups for Political Influence." *Quarterly Journal of Economics* 98 (August 1983): 371–400.

Benson, Bruce L. "Why Are Congressional Committees Dominated by 'High Demand' Legislators?" *Southern Economic Journal* 48 (July 1981): 68–77.

Benson, Bruce L. "High Demand Legislative Committees and Bureaucratic Output." *Public Finance Quarterly* 11 (July 1983a): 259–81.

Benson, Bruce L. "The Economic Theory of Regulation as an Explanation of Politics Toward Bank Mergers and Holding Company Acquisitions." *Antitrust Bulletin* 28 (Winter 1983b): 839–62.

Benson, Bruce L. "Rent Seeking from a Property Rights Perspective." *Southern Economic Journal* 51 (October 1984): 388–400.

Benson, Bruce L., and Baden, John. "The Political Economy of Government Corruption: The Logic of Underground Government." *Journal of Legal Studies* 14 (June 1985): 391–410.

Benson, Bruce L., and Greenhut, M. L. "Special Interest, Bureaucrats, and Antitrust: An Explanation of the Antitrust Paradox." In *Antitrust and Regulation*, pp. 53–90. Edited by Ronald E. Grieson. Lexington, Mass.: Lexington Books, 1986.

Bork, Robert H. *The Antitrust Paradox: A Policy at War with Itself*. New York: Basic Books, 1978.

Clarkson, Kenneth, and Muris, Timothy J. "Letting Competition Serve Consumers." In *Instead of Regulation: Alternatives to Federal Regulatory Agencies*, pp. 135–68. Edited by Robert W. Poole. Lexington, Mass.: Lexington Books, 1982.

Eckert, Ross. "On the Incentives of Regulators: The Case of Taxicabs." *Public Choice* 14 (Spring 1973): 83–99.

Erlich, Isaac, and Posner, Richard. "An Economic Analysis of Legal Rule-Making." *Journal of Legal Studies* 3 (January 1974): 257–86.

Faith, Roger L.; Leavens, Donald R.; and Tollison, Robert D. "Antitrust Pork Barrel." *Journal of Law and Economics* 25 (October 1982): 329–42.

Gordon, Sanford D., "Attitudes Towards Trusts Prior to the Sherman Act." *Southern Economic Journal* 30 (October 1963): 156–67.

Green, Mark J.; Moore, Beverly C.; and Wasserstein, Bruce. *The Closed Enterprise System: Ralph Nader's Study Group Report on Antitrust Enforcement*. New York: Grossman Publishers, 1972.

Greenhut, M. L. *Plant Location in Theory and Practice* [1956]. Westport, Conn.: Greenwood Publishing Co., 1983.

Greenhut, M. L. *A Theory of the Firm in Economic Space* [1970]. Austin, Texas: Lone Star Publishers, 1974.

Greenhut, M. L., and Ohta, H. "Vertical Integration of Successive Oligopolists." *American Economic Review* 69 (March 1979): 137–41.

Greenhut, M. L.; Hwang, C. S.; Norman, G.; and Smithson, C. "An Anomaly in the Service Industry: The Effect of Entry on Fees." *The Economic Journal* 95 (March 1985): 169–77.

Greenhut, M. L.; Hwang, C. S.; and Ohta, H. "Observations on the Shape and Relevance of the Spatial Demand Function." *Econometrica* 63 (July 1975): 669–82.

High, Jack. "Bork's Paradox: Static versus Dynamic Efficiency in Antitrust Analysis." *Contemporary Policy Issues* 3 (Winter 1984–85): 21–34.

Hilton, George. "The Basic Behavior of Regulatory Commissions." *American Economic Review* 62 (May 1972): 47–54.

Holcombe, Randall G. *Public Finance and the Political Process*. Carbondale: Southern Illinois University Press, 1983.

Holcombe, Randall G. *An Economic Analysis of Democracy*. Carbondale: Southern Illinois University Press, 1985.

Jarrell, G. "The Demand for State Regulation of the Electric Utility Industry." *Journal of Law and Economics* 21 (October 1978): 269–95.

Joskow, P. "Inflation and Environmental Concern: Structure Change in the Process of Public Utility Price Regulation." *Journal of Law and Economics* 17 (October 1974): 291–327.

Kau, James B., and Rubin, Paul H. "Voting on Minimum Wages: A Time Series Analysis." *Journal of Political Economy* 82 (April 1978): 337–42.

Katzman, Robert A. *Regulatory Bureaucracy: The Federal Trade Commission and Antitrust Policy*. Cambridge, Mass.: MIT Press, 1980.

Kolko, Gabriel. *The Triumph of Conservatism: A Re-Interpretation of American History, 1900–1916*. New York: Free Press, 1963.

McCormick, Robert E., and Tollison, Robert D. *Politicians, Legislation, and the Economy: An Inquiry into the Interest Group Theory of Government*. Boston: Martinus Nijhoff Publishing, 1981.

Mitnick, B., and Weiss, C. "The Siting Impasse and a Rational Choice Model of Regulatory Behavior: An Agency for Power Plant Siting." *Journal of Environmental Economics and Management* 1 (August 1974): 150–71.

Neale, A. D. *The Antitrust Laws of the U.S.A.* Cambridge: Cambridge University Press, 1970.

INTEREST GROUPS

Niskanen, William A. "The Peculiar Economics of Bureaucracy." *American Economic Review* 58 (May 1968): 293–305.

Niskanen, William A. *Bureaucracy and Representative Government.* Chicago: Aldine-Atherton, 1971.

Niskanen, William A. "Bureaucrats and Politicians." *Journal of Law and Economics* 18 (December 1975): 617–43.

Northrup, Herbert R., and Bloom, Gordon F. "Labor Unions and Antitrust Laws: Past, Present, and Proposals." In *Perspectives in Antitrust Policy,* pp. 312–54. Edited by Almarin Phillips. Princeton: Princeton University Press, 1965.

Peltzman, Sam. "Toward a More General Theory of Regulation." *Journal of Law and Economics* 19 (August 1976): 211–40.

Posner, Richard. "The Federal Trade Commission." *University of Chicago Law Review* 37 (1969): 47–89.

Posner, Richard. *Economic Analysis of Law.* Boston: Little, Brown, 1972.

Posner, Richard. "Theories of Economic Regulation." *Bell Journal of Economics and Management Science* 5 (Autumn 1974): 335–58.

Priest, George L. "The Common Law Process and the Selection of Efficient Rules." *Journal of Legal Studies* 6 (January 1977): 65–82.

Ross, Thomas W. "Winners and Losers under the Robinson-Patman Act." *Journal of Law and Economics* 27 (October 1984): 243–71.

Rubin, Paul H. "Why Is the Common Law Efficient?" *Journal of Legal Studies* 6 (January 1977): 51–63.

Russell, Milton, and Shelton, Robert. "A Model of Regulatory Agency Behavior." *Public Choice* 20 (Winter 1974): 47–62.

Scherer, F. M. *Industrial Market Structure and Economic Performance.* Chicago: Rand McNally, 1970.

Smith, Janet K. "Production of Licensing Legislation: An Economic Analysis of Interstate Differences." *Journal of Legal Studies* 11 (January 1982): 117–37.

Stigler, George J. "The Theory of Economic Regulation." *Bell Journal of Economics and Management Science* 2 (Spring 1971): 3–21.

Stigler, George J. "The Origin of the Sherman Act." *Journal of Legal Studies* 14 (January 1985): 1–12.

Stigler, George J., and Friedland, Claire. "What Can Regulators Regulate? The Case of Electricity." *Journal of Law and Economics* 5 (October 1965): 1–16.

Tollison, Robert D. "Rent Seeking: A Survey." *Kyklos* (1982): 575–602.

Tullock, Gordon. *The Politics of Bureaucracy.* Washington, D.C.: Public Affairs Press, 1965.

Weingast, Barry R., and Moran, Mark J. "Bureaucratic Discretion or Congressional Control? Regulatory Policymaking by the Federal Trade Commission." *Journal of Political Economy* 91 (October 1983): 765–800.

Williamson, Oliver. "Commentary." In *The Political Economy of Antitrust: Principal Paper by William Baxter,* pp. 77–93. Edited by Robert D. Tollison. Lexington, Mass.: Lexington Books, 1979.

Econometrica, Vol. 45, No. 8 (November, 1977)

NONLINEARITY OF DELIVERED PRICE SCHEDULES AND PREDATORY PRICING

BY JOHN GREENHUT AND M. L. GREENHUT

The sets of local demand functions which would generate either linear or nonlinear schedules in a heterogeneous as well as homogeneous space economy are determined by iterative applications of the separation of variables technique for solving differential equations. Nonlinear delivered price schedules which reflect profit maximization objectives are thereby identifiable. In turn, these schedules can be distinguished from those which involve strictly predatory price behavior.

A. MARSHALL [3] observed that "The first place among unfair methods of competition, which are denounced by the Anti-Trust Laws, is held by price discrimination; the chief variety . . . is . . . local price cutting." G. Ackley [**1**] in a similar context noted that f.o.b. pricing "has received the special blessing of certain economists and Government officials," and is probably considered by most economists as the desired (truly competitive) spatial pricing technique. Apparently the belief is widely shared that a large seller cannot readily undercut the price of a smaller competitor if he is constrained to straight-lined f.o.b. pricing. It is in this same backlight that Wilcox and Shepherd [**4**] observed that the early concern under Section 2 of the Clayton Act in the United States was to protect local firms from "predatory" price cutting by larger firms. They go on to note that geographic price cutting by large firms is now virtually illegal per se in the United States, even if the large firm controls only a small share of the market.

This brief paper will demonstrate that the local demand functions which generate linear delivered price schedules by spatial sellers are members of a well-defined but *narrow* class. Hence, deviations from linearity may well be representative of ordinary profit maximization, not predatory price cutting.

The general profit maximizing condition for a seller supplying a market situated n distance units from his plant is given by

$$(1)\qquad p\left(1-\frac{1}{e}\right)-nt=k,$$

where k is the marginal cost (parametrically identical over all values of n), t is the transportation rate, and e is the elasticity of demand. Let $q=f(p)$ so that $e=-f'(p)(p/f(p))$. For notational simplicity we also let f henceforth stand for $f(p)$, f' for $f'(p)$, etc. Elasticity may then be written as $e=-pf'/f$, which in turn allows (1) to be expressed as

$$(2)\qquad p+\frac{f}{f'}-nt=k,$$

when all buyers possess the same local demand $q=f(p)$.

The relationship between delivered price and the unit cost of transportation

$T(=nt)$ may be derived from (2) via the derivative

$$\frac{dp}{dT}=\frac{d(-f/f')}{dp}\cdot\frac{dp}{dT}+1=-\frac{(f')^2-ff''}{(f')^2}\frac{dp}{dT}+1. \tag{3}$$

Solving for dp/dT provides the slope of the delivered price schedule (henceforth often referred to as DPS), as given by

$$\frac{dp}{dT}=\frac{(f')^2}{2(f')^2-ff''}. \tag{4}$$

A derivation set forth in the Appendix yields the functions f which result in a constant value of dp/dT over all values of T in a homogeneous space. In order to fulfill this objective, we simply require $d^2p/dT^2=0$ (so that dp/dT is constant $\forall T$). Then by iterative applications of the separation of variables technique for solving differential equations, we obtain the desired functions. (See Appendix for details.)

Demand curves which provide constant dp/dT values for all T are found to be of the several subtypes given by

(Ia) $p=a-bq, \quad a, b>0,$

(Ib) $p=\frac{c}{b}-\frac{1}{b(1-a)}q^{1-a}, \quad a, b>0, \quad a\neq 1, \quad c>0$ when $a<1,$

(Ic) $p=\frac{c}{b}-\frac{1}{b}\ln q, \quad b>0$ and c generally $>0,$

(Id) $p=\frac{c}{b}-\frac{1}{b(1+a)}q^{1+a}, \quad a, b, c>0.$

Subtypes (Ia), (Ib), and (Id) may be grouped together in the form of

(II) $p=\beta-\frac{\alpha}{x}q^x,$

where $\alpha>0$, $x\neq 0$, and $\beta>0$ when $x>0$. (Manifestly, if $x<0$, no restrictions are placed on β.) When all buyers distributed over a given market area are assumed to possess the same demand curve, discriminatory pricing would appear in the form of a linear DPS *if and only if* demand is given by (II) or (Ic). (Specifically, since elasticity equals $p/x(\beta-p)$ and bp respectively for (II) and (Ic), the DPS derived for (II) is $P_{D_T}=(\beta x+k+T)/(x+1)$ and $P_{D_T}=(1/b)+k+T$ for (Ic). The DPS slopes are, in turn, $1/(x+1)$ and 1.) No other demands than (II) or (Ic) would provide a constant slope of the DPS in a homogeneous space (i.e., where buyers at every market point have the identically same gross demand curve.) Any demand curve which over certain prices is convex from above but over other prices concave from above, or a demand of some other order such as $p=\beta/(\alpha+q)$, where $\alpha, \beta>0$, would elicit a nonlinear delivered price schedule. Thus nonlinear pricing could often reflect the profit-maximizing reaction of a seller to a particular set of demand curves over his space.

May a linear schedule obtain in a heterogeneous space? The example below based on equation (II) demands reveals that it may. Note initially that since delivered price under (II) is not directly a function of α, we need not concern ourselves with variations in α. The slope of the delivered price schedule is thus completely provided by

$$\text{(III)} \qquad \frac{dP_{D_T}}{dT} = \frac{\partial P_{D_T}}{\partial x}\frac{dx}{dT} + \frac{\partial P_{D_T}}{\partial \beta}\frac{d\beta}{dT} + \frac{\partial P_{D_T}}{\partial T} = \frac{\beta - k - T}{(x+1)^2}\frac{dx}{dT} + \frac{1}{x+1}\frac{d\beta}{dT} + \frac{1}{x+1}.$$

Obviously, linear DPS is not ruled out by spatial heterogeneity. Uniform pricing or even a negatively sloped DPS may, in fact, be the profit-maximizing delivered price schedule in a heterogeneous space, though the a priori likelihood of dx and/or $d\beta$ fulfilling the linearity requirements in (III) can be conjectured to be virtually zero in practice.

Let us note finally that while this paper focuses attention on the DPS from the standpoint of demand alone, competition is also a factor affecting the slope of the DPS. But we need not conceive here of gross demand and then subtract competitive impacts at each market point therefrom, as was necessary in John Greenhut and M. L. Greenhut [**2**]. Rather, net demand is alone relevant in the context of the present inquiry. And here for linearity of the DPS, we recognize simply that whatever the gross demand may be and the competitive impact thereon, in order for a linear DPS to obtain, net demand must be of the order given by (Ic), (II), or the types which uniquely combine to make dP_{D_T}/dT equal to a constant. Everything else, *ceteris paribus*, generates nonlinear delivered price schedules among profit-maximizing firms and helps distinguish such schedules from those of predatory order.

United Energy Resources, Inc.
and
Texas A & M University

Manuscript received September, 1976; *revision received December*, 1976.

APPENDIX

The second order derivative d^2p/dT^2 is derivable from (4) in the text as

$$\text{(5)} \qquad \frac{d^2p}{dT^2} = \frac{[2(f')^2 - ff''](2f'f'') - (f')^2[4f'f'' - ff''' - f'f'']}{[2(f')^2 - ff'']^2}\left[\frac{(f')^2}{2(f')^2 - ff''}\right]$$
$$= \frac{(f')^3[(f')^2f'' - 2f(f'')^2 + ff'f''']}{[2(f')^2 - ff'']^3}.$$

Since the delivered price schedule is linear when $d^2p/dT^2 = 0$, we may observe that linearity implies $f' = 0$ and/or $(f')^2f'' - 2f(f'')^2 + ff'f''' = 0$. The initial condition requires an infinite slope of the inverse demand function, i.e., the demand *curve* is a vertical line. This case may, of course, be ruled out on practical grounds. The alternative condition is more difficult to interpret. Write it as

$$\text{(6)} \qquad f''' = \frac{2f(f'')^2 - (f')^2f''}{ff'}.$$

But $f''' = df''/dp$, $f'' = df'/dp$, and $f' = df/dp$, so that (6) reduces to the equivalent equation

$$(7)\qquad \frac{df''}{f''} = \left(\frac{2ff'' - (f')^2}{ff'}\right) dp = \left(2\frac{f''}{f'} - \frac{f'}{f}\right) dp = 2\frac{df'}{f'} - \frac{df}{f},$$

provided $f'' \neq 0$. If $f'' = 0$, the demand is linear, and we further find that $f''' = 0$ at the same instance that $(f')^2 f'' - 2f(f'')^2 + ff'f''' = 0$. Thus when all buyers in the same space possess the same linear demand, the delivered price schedule is linear.

Equation (7) is also contained in a set of nonlinear demands when f'' is either greater than or less than zero. In the initial situation where $f'' > 0$, we recognize that $f' < 0$ and $f > 0$. Therefore, expressing (7) as

$$(8)\qquad \frac{df''}{f''} = 2\frac{d(-f')}{-f'} - \frac{df}{f},$$

and integrating establishes

$$(9)\qquad \ln f'' = 2\ln(-f') - \ln f + \ln a = \ln \frac{af'^2}{f},$$

where a is a positive constant. Equation (9) is identical to

$$(10)\qquad f'' = \frac{af'^2}{f},$$

which specifies the demand concavity satisfying equation (6). In turn, (10) must be solved for the slope f', from which we can obtain the demand function f. The steps involved follow virtually the same pattern as (7)–(10). We obtain

$$(11)\qquad \frac{df'}{dp} = \frac{af'}{f}\frac{df}{dp},$$

$$(12)\qquad \frac{d(-f')}{-f'} = a\frac{df}{f},$$

$$(13)\qquad \ln(-f') = a\ln f + \ln b = \ln(bf^a)$$

and

$$(14)\qquad f' = -bf^a,$$

where $b > 0$. Continuing in the same manner as above, we are now able to derive the demand functions with $f'' > 0$ when f', f'', and f''' respectively satisfy equations (14), (10), and (6). From (14) we have

$$(15)\qquad f^{-a}\,df = -b\,dp,$$

$$(16)\qquad \frac{f^{1-a}}{1-a} = -bp + c, \qquad \text{if } a \neq 1,$$

and

$$(17)\qquad \ln f = -bp + c, \qquad \text{if } a = 1.$$

Since $q = f(p)$, (16) and (17) are respectively

$$(18)\qquad p = \frac{c}{b} - \frac{1}{b(1-a)}q^{1-a}, \qquad \text{if } a \neq 1 \text{ (and recall } a > 0),$$

$$(19)\qquad p = \frac{c}{b} - \frac{1}{b}\ln q, \qquad \text{if } a = 1.$$

Equations (18) and (19) specify concave demand curves from above ($f'' > 0$) which generate linear delivered price schedules. But our analytical framework is not quite complete; the alternative possibility $f'' < 0$ remains, for which equation we write (6) as

$$(20)\qquad \frac{d(-f'')}{-f''} = 2\frac{d(-f')}{-f'} - \frac{df}{f}.$$

Equation (20) is of course the counterpart to equation (7) and may be solved by the same technique as that used to obtain f from (7). Only one demand curve satisfies (20), namely

$$p = \frac{c}{b} - \frac{1}{b(1+a)} q^{1+a}. \tag{21}$$

The equation specifies the form that a convex demand curve *from above* must assume in order for delivered prices to rise linearly with distance.

REFERENCES

[1] ACKLEY, G.: "Price Policies," in National Resources Planning Board, *Industrial Location and Natural Resources.* Washington: U.S. Government Printing Office, 1943.

[2] GREENHUT, JOHN, AND M. L. GREENHUT: "Spatial Price Discrimination, Competition and Locational Effects," *Economica*, 42 (1975), 401–19.

[3] MARSHALL, A.: *Industry and Trade.* London: The Macmillan Co., 1919.

[4] WILCOX, C., AND W. G. SHEPHERD: *Public Policies toward Business*, 5th ed. Homewood, Illinois: Richard D. Irwin, 1975.

THE JOURNAL OF INDUSTRIAL ECONOMICS 0022-1821 $2.00
Volume XXXIV December 1985 No. 2

REVERSE DUMPING: A FORM OF SPATIAL PRICE DISCRIMINATION

M. L. GREENHUT, H. OHTA AND JOEL SAILORS*

This paper generalizes Joan Robinson's analysis of dumping under a spatial price theory framework. The dumping of goods is shown to be a natural form of spatial pricing rather than necessarily an act of predatory design. Viewed as such, dumping neither requires predatory motives nor competition in markets where the goods are to be dumped. A simple spatial monopoly model is used to derive the firm's optimal price policy on sales to nearby and to distant customers under different demand and cost conditions. The paper then resolves the question of "reverse" dumping which may or may not benefit the nearby "home country" customers.

A RECENT development in the theory of spatial price discrimination has led to some important findings, as aptly summarized by Dorward [1982]. Of particular note is the role of spatial competition in promoting rather than preventing price discrimination, as was demonstrated by Hoover's pioneering contribution [1937] and more recently by Norman [1981a], [1981b]. Moreover, spatial price discrimination has been shown to generate greater industry output than the non-discriminatory form (f.o.b. mill pricing). This output effect has been shown to occur even under the conditions where classical economics provide different results (Greenhut and Ohta [1975]). In fact, this output effect has been revealed to apply not only to a spatial monopolist but to spatial competitors. See Greenhut and Ohta [1972], [1975], Holahan [1975], Norman [1981a], Phlips [1976], etc.

Not every member of society benefits from spatial price discrimination since—as in the case of so-called dumping in international trade—customers located at substantial distances from the seller typically benefit from the discrimination while customers located nearest the seller are charged higher prices than otherwise. Rigorous analysis of the effects of distance on prices will be seen to provide new vistas for the international trade view of dumping. Thus, for example, a recent paper by Brander and Krugman [1983] on reciprocal dumping theory can be seen as a straightforward application, a sub-theory, in effect, of the Cournot-type model of spatial competition presented by Greenhut and Ohta [1975, Chapter 8, Appendix I].

* The authors are respectively Alumni Distinguished Professor, Texas A & M University; Professor, Aoyama Gakuin University and University of Houston (adjunct); and Professor, University of Houston. They acknowledge their debt to the National Science Foundation for the grant that helped support research related to this paper; and to Janet Kohlhase, University of Houston, and an anonymous referee for their valuable comments.

Let it suffice to observe for introductory purposes that all of the several types of discrimination stressed by economists, including those occurring between nations or of the spaceless economics form, can be evaluated in the context of spatial price theory. Alternative trade forms include charging lower prices (absolutely or just comparatively) to foreign buyers as well as charging comparatively *higher* prices to distant *foreign* buyers compared to *domestic* customers (that is, dumping in reverse). For reasons noted later, the present paper will *stress* the situations where spatial price discrimination offers relatively greater benefits to nearby customers contrary to the one-sided claims of the "home country" advocates who contend that foreign governments stand behind the international dumping of goods.

Dumping and reverse dumping *in international markets* are customarily evaluated directly on the basis of classical price discrimination theory where the usual assumption is that the home country's demand is less elastic than is the world's demand (the small nation assumption). This condition leads to a lower price in the export market than that charged in the domestic market, or what is called dumping. However, in the case of a *large* foreign economy, the basic demand conditions may well be such that the home demand is more elastic than the world demand. In such a case, reverse dumping would take place according to classical economics.

Price discrimination of the classical order requires a significant barrier between two markets, so that arbitrage between them does not negate the intended price discrimination. Also, the theory requires non-identical individual and/or non-identical market demand schedules so that price discrimination can be based on their differing elasticities. This latter assumption leads to the further condition that there exists some degree of monopoly. This condition avoids the identical, infinitely elastic average revenue schedules applicable under perfect competition. Still another classical case warrants mention, namely where prices differ in two markets, yet where the industry is competitive and/or the elasticities of demand are identical; we have in mind the situations where price differentials stem from cost differentials which lead, for example, to "cost justified" quantity discounts. This case is controversial as to whether it should be truly labeled as one involving discriminatory pricing (Hirshleifer [1976]). We shall see below that spatial price theory (which most generally evaluates international trade practices) does not require the restrictive assumptions of classical economics.

Section I of this paper reviews some established principles of spatial price theory. In particular, a couple of key concepts, namely discriminatory marginal revenue *DMR* and nondiscriminatory simple marginal revenue *SMR*, are tersely reviewed. These two concepts are then utilized in section II to generalize Mrs. Robinson's two market analysis of dumping. In our model the number of markets served by the spatial monopolist is itself a variable which depends upon the firm's pricing policy. Nevertheless, basically the same results as Mrs. Robinson's are shown to be obtainable from our model of spatial monopoly. The cost-of-production factors, in particular the existence of scale economies, are shown to be a common determinant of dumping. Section III then extends classical dumping theory to different frontiers beyond those of costless and costly distance. The demand factors, such as consumer thresholds, are shown to be another important determinant of the local consumer welfare as the monopolist firm practices discriminatory pricing. Section IV next relaxes the simplifying assumption of section III. Section V concludes the paper.

I. SOME ESTABLISHED PRINCIPLES OF SPATIAL PRICE THEORY

As demonstrated by Greenhut and Ohta [1972], [1975], the spatial monopolist's discriminatory marginal revenue (DMR), net of freight costs, tends to be greater than the nondiscriminatory simple marginal revenue (SMR) when homogeneous buyers are distributed uniformly along a transport route. To briefly review the vital relationship of $DMR > SMR$, consider the local demand density function of the form f:

(1) $$q_D = f(p_D), \qquad D \geqslant 0,$$

where p_D stands for the price charged to consumers located D distance units from the firm, and q_D is the corresponding demand density at market point D. This equation can be transformed to the firm's net revenue function, i.e., net of freight costs, in obtaining:

(1)′ $$m_D = f^{-1}(q_D) - tD$$

where t stands for a positive freight rate and m_D the mill price (or net revenue derivable from sales at market point D).

The SMR is the marginal curve to the aggregate demand

$$Q \equiv \int_0^{D_0} f(m+tD)\,dD, \qquad D_0 = (f^{-1}(0) - m)/t;$$

it derives from (1) in terms of a unique mill price, $m_D = m$, parametrically given to all market points D. Thus, given t, the aggregate demand is seen to be a unique function of mill price m: $Q = F(m)$. The related marginal revenue is correspondingly derived as $SMR = F^{-1} + (dF^{-1}/dQ)Q$. In contrast to this, the DMR is the horizontal aggregate of the marginal curves to (1)′ for all relevant D's. It can then easily be shown that an algebraic form of f, defined below, yields the result $DMR > SMR$ [1975, Chapter 4].[1]

(2) $$p_D = a - bq_D^{\alpha}, \qquad a, b, \alpha > 0$$

Since the profit maximizing calculus under the alternative pricing tech-

[1] The form of the demand represented by equation (2) belongs to the class of demands which are "relatively less convex" (Ohta [1980], [1981]). The "positive" output effects of spatial price discrimination does not, however, require or depend on this limited class of basic demands. The same $DMR > SMR$ result can be derivable also from the opposite class of basic demands, namely those which are "relatively more convex" (Ohta [1984, mimeo]).

niques equating these alternative MR's with the common marginal cost curve, the critical relation $DMR > SMR$ establishes an equilibrium output which is necessarily greater under discriminatory pricing than it is under f.o.b. pricing (that is, the invariable mill price system). This result obtains regardless of the form of the production cost function. Moreover, the conclusion remains basically invariant under conditions of spatial competition.

Contrary results conformable to Pigou–Robinson's findings (that is, $SMR \equiv DMR$) have been set forth by Beckmann [1976]. But they apply strictly to his assumptions of linear demand *and* fixed market spaces for each competing seller regardless of the pricing policy followed. The classical Pigou–Robinson and the Beckmann spatial results thus do not relate readily to situations in which the firm's market radius varies with its price. In particular, any pricing policy which yields higher profit induces greater entry, in the process generating smaller individual market areas in the zero profit equilibrium. Somewhat asymmetric results, accordingly, follow in that *in the long run* the individual firm's output is smaller, but the industry output is greater under spatially discriminatory prices than under nondiscriminatory f.o.b. mill pricing (Holahan [1975]).

Discriminatory pricing over distance signifies that a veritably limitless number of delivered price schedules apply over economic landscapes, each relating to the demand and competitive conditions that prevail at the different market points (Greenhut and Greenhut [1975], [1977], Greenhut [1981] and Phlips [1976]). Typically, mill prices were proposed to be higher for nearby customers and lower for distant buyers than those projected if the firm priced nondiscriminatorily rather than discriminatorily. This expectation signified greater benefits for nearby customers when the seller prices f.o.b. mill than when the seller discriminated spatially in his prices.

An important caveat applies to the last proposition which could easily be overlooked. Unlike the *general* proposition covering the output effect of spatial price discrimination, the demand curve must be of a well-defined form and the marginal cost of production must either be constant or increasing in order for spatial price discrimination to favor the distant (foreign) buyers. The constraint on marginal cost differs sharply from that of Mrs. Robinson in her finding that *home-country buyers may even benefit* from dumping, that is, when marginal production costs slope monotonically downward with output [1933]. Moreover, the correspondence between that particular Robinson result and one derivable from spatial price theory will later be seen to stem from a sharply contrasting assumption involving costly distance.

II. CORRESPONDENCES BETWEEN CLASSICAL DUMPING THEORY AND SPATIAL PRICE THEORY

Let us use Figure 1 to identify what happens to local prices and the firm's output when a spatial monopolist changes the firm's price policy from the

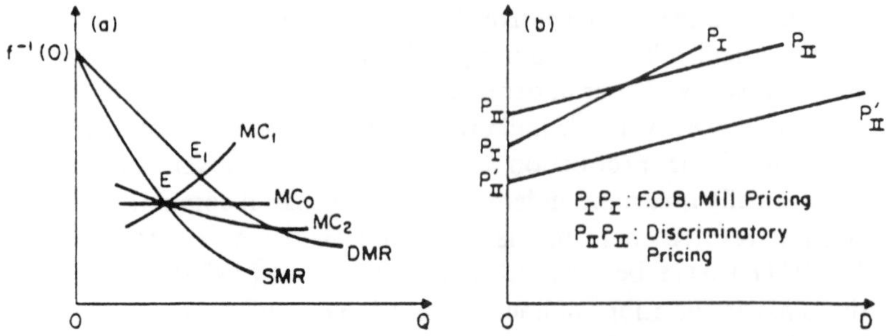

Figure 1
Alternative Cost Conditions and Spatial Price Schedules

nondiscriminatory f.o.b. mill form (referred to as Policy I) to the discriminatory form (Policy II). Figure 1(a) provides the marginal revenue curves, DMR and SMR, of the spatial monopolist and three alternative marginal cost curves: MC_0, MC_1 and MC_2. The initial nondiscriminatory price equilibrium at E shifts to either E_0, E_1 or E_2 when the firm changes its price policy to the discriminatory one; thus discriminatory output is unambiguously greater than simple monopoly output *regardless of how MC changes with output.* It is noteworthy that the increase in output is greater the smaller is the increase in (or the greater the decrease in) MC. Moreover, the equilibrium MC under discriminatory pricing is higher (lower) than the nondiscriminatory counterpart MC if and only if the MC slopes upward (downward).

It is important to recognize that the comparisons just noted are based on the common departure point E which itself may be given arbitrarily along SMR. Related to this point is a unique optimal f.o.b. mill price, which in turn determines a unique delivered price schedule under Policy I. (See the $P_I P_I$ schedule in Figure 1(b), where the horizontal scale measures the distance D while the vertical axis provides the delivered price.) Unlike the unique f.o.b. spatial price schedule $P_I P_I$ in Figure 1(b), the discriminatory price schedule $P_{II} P_{II}$ applicable to Policy II cannot be uniquely given because it depends on the alternative MC equilibria associated with E_0, E_1 and E_2.

Under the basic demand given by equation (2) *and* constant MC, it has been further established that $P_{II} > P_I$ at the zero distance cost point, while $P_{II} P_{II}$ is flatter than $P_I P_I$. Manifestly, the discriminatory price schedule is higher under increasing MC. We have established the following proposition:

Proposition 1. Given the demand equation (2), *a price policy change from f.o.b. to discriminatory pricing generates a welfare loss for the home country (more proximate) customers, which loss is greater under increasing marginal costs than constant marginal costs.*

Does Proposition 1 support the conventional notion that dumping *always* takes place at the expense of the home-country (nearby) customers? Our answer is no, *under equation* (2) *demands*. Consider in this regard the effect of a downward-sloping marginal cost curve, such as MC_2 of Figure 1(a). Note that the intersection of MC_2 with DMR involves a much lower equilibrium MC value and thus a much greater output than that applicable to the horizontal MC_0. It is therefore possible that the $P_{II}P_{II}$ schedule shifts downward all the way to the $P'_{II}P'_{II}$ schedule of Figure 1(b). This significantly lower schedule, to repeat, reflects the sharply lower equilibrium MC value applicable under discriminatory pricing, thereby establishing Proposition 2 predicated on the basic demand (2):

Proposition 2. Given the demand equation (2), *it is possible for all customers to benefit from spatial price discrimination (compared to f.o.b. mill pricing) when substantial economies of scale prevail.*

A case example of Proposition 2 exists when $\alpha = 1$ and the MC under the simple f.o.b. monopoly pricing is greater than $a/4$ while the equilibrium MC under the discriminating monopoly approaches zero. Our Proposition 2 is particularly remarkable in the Robinsonian sense since even home-country (nearby) customers would benefit from the discriminatory price system. This kind of pricing creates greater industry-wide output thereby benefiting all customers in the economy, *ceteris paribus*. The delivered price schedule $P'_{II}P'_{II}$ is simply lower than the f.o.b. $P_I P_I$ schedule throughout the space involved. This special "spatial price theory" case converts Professor Robinson's two country example of advantaged home country buyers to the more general situation which includes a full set of market points.

In summary to this point in the paper: Mrs. Robinson's "spaceless" theory of dumping has been generalized to include impacts of price discrimination on buyers who are distributed uniformly along a transport route. At the same instance, the theory of dumping has been altered to include the theory of spatial price discrimination under conditions where even nearer buyers benefit somewhat because of the resulting lower prices in the home market. Symmetric conclusions to those of Mrs. Robinson were obtained by assuming alternative marginal cost conditions. However, the concept of dumping requires further generalizing, as in the section that follows. We will observe there the case where the home-country (nearby) customers benefit directly *and* completely from the discrimination, *regardless of the shape of the marginal cost curve*. In the strict confines of spatial microeconomics alone, this case is similar to the situation where distant buyers are charged a phantom freight, that is, where a phantom freight is *in effect* added to the actual freight costs involved.

III. EXTENDING THE CLASSICAL THEORY OF DUMPING TO DIFFERENT FRONTIERS

Demand curves not included in the specification of (2), such as demand curves lacking finite price intercept values, can be said to be empirically irrelevant to the space economy. Irrelevance applies because the firm's market area becomes infinite if positive demand still obtains at the distant points where delivered prices are unimaginably high. Of course, a finite price intercept can be imposed on demand curves of types other than (2), which constraint would simply involve the concept of consumer thresholds as proposed by Devletoglou [1971]. The *a priori* basis for rejecting other demand functions would thus be eliminated, and need therefore arises to evaluate these demands in the context of the international–interregional dumping of goods.

Consider the *specific* demand curve:

$$(3) \qquad q = \alpha/p^2, \qquad \beta \geqslant p \geqslant 0$$
$$= 0, \qquad p > \beta$$

where the demand elasticity is assumed, for the time being, to be equal to 2.

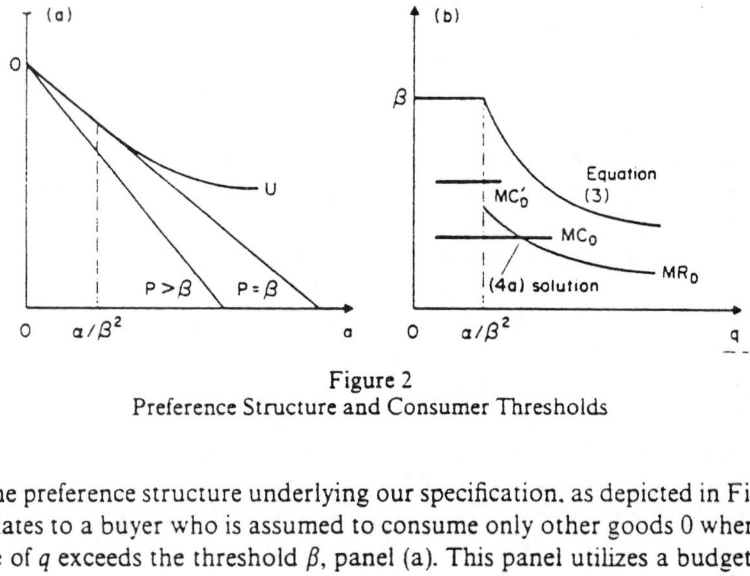

Figure 2
Preference Structure and Consumer Thresholds

The preference structure underlying our specification, as depicted in Figure 2, relates to a buyer who is assumed to consume only other goods 0 when the price of q exceeds the threshold β, panel (a). This panel utilizes a budget line $p = \beta$ which is merged with an indifference curve U over $q \leqslant \alpha/\beta^2$. The budget line $p > \beta$ indicates that demand for q vanishes completely at prices exceeding β, even if the demands at prices yielding positive q's happen to be of constant elasticity, as illustrated by Figure 2(b).

To develop the requisite background principles further, let us evaluate the implications of the price intercept of the (otherwise) hyperbolic demand curve given by (3). Towards this end, recall that third degree discriminatory pricing involves profit maximization in *each* and all of the relevant separate (spatially separated) markets. Thus for any given market point D we must have:

$$(4) \qquad MR_D \geqslant MC_D, \qquad D_{OII} \geqslant D \geqslant 0$$

where MR_D stands for the marginal revenue obtained on sales to a market point D distance units from the firm, MC_D provides the marginal production cost MC plus marginal cost of transporting the good to market point D, and the distance D_{0II} designates the boundary limit to the seller's market area under discriminatory price policy II.[2] To better appreciate the meaning of (4) assume a constant marginal production cost k, and also an invariable freight rate t. Condition (4) combined with (3) may then be decomposed advantageously into two parts, an equality and inequality, as specified by:[3,4]

$$\text{(4a)} \qquad \tfrac{1}{2}\sqrt{\alpha/q} = k+tD, \qquad \text{for } q > \alpha/\beta^2$$
$$\therefore q^* = \alpha/4(k+tD)^2, \qquad D^* \geqslant D \geqslant 0, \qquad D^* = (\beta/2-k)/t,$$

$$\text{(4b)} \qquad \beta > k+tD, \qquad \text{for } q \leqslant \alpha/\beta^2$$
$$\therefore q^* = \alpha/\beta^2, \qquad D_{0II} \geqslant D \geqslant D^*, \qquad \dot{D}_{0II} = (\beta-k)/t,$$

where q^* stands for optimal sales quantity to market point D. The left-hand-side of (4a) represents the marginal revenue from market point D and is directly obtainable from equation (3). This same marginal revenue curve applies to every market point D and is depicted by MR_D in Figure 2(b). Because of the assumed threshold β, this MR_D is valid, and can be equated with MC_D $(=k+tD)$ *only* for $q > \alpha/\beta^2$. However, as MC_D goes up with D to, say, MC_D' in Figure 2(b), equation (4a) no longer applies because of the discontinuity at $q = \alpha/\beta^2$. However, insofar as the firm can sell this quantity at the price β, this value also constitutes the marginal revenue MR_D of the firm. The firm is better off selling quantity α/β^2 just as long as the additional revenue β exceeds the additional costs, such as MC_D'. Inequality (4b) depicts such relations.

Substituting (4a) and (4b) into (3) provides the spatial discriminatory price schedule in terms of the distance variable D. This substitution establishes:

$$\text{(5)} \qquad P_{II} = 2k+2tD, \qquad D^* \geqslant D \geqslant 0$$
$$= \beta, \qquad D_{0II} \geqslant D \geqslant D^*$$

which yields Proposition 3 for the case of homogeneous consumers distributed uniformly over.

[2] Recognize with respect to (4) that the conventional $MR = MC$ condition is neither a necessary nor sufficient condition for profit maximization. The first order condition is not sufficient unless combined with the second in yielding maximum profits. It is not necessary since in cases such as the one represented by (3), $MR = MC$ is not an attainable condition, for example, when MC is as high as MC_D' in Figure 2(b) above. The maximum quantity which still yields an $MR > MC$ is the profit-maximizing quantity in this event. Quantities exceeding this particular solution involve $MR < MC$, and thus provide nonprofit-maximizing positions.

[3] The D^* is the critical distance that makes the firm's marginal costs MC_D barely equal to the maximum marginal revenue MR_D under (4a), that is, $MR_D^* = \beta/2$.

[4] The D_{0II} is the distance limit that makes MC_D as high as the threshold price level β. Clearly, no sales can willingly be made beyond this market point.

Proposition 3. Given demand of the form (3), the spatial monopolist will practice reverse dumping in the form of (5) unless legally or otherwise restricted, in effect creating phantom freight charges for distant consumers.

Following Hoover [1937] and Smithies [1941], the implications of (5) would be rejected on grounds of potential resale by nearer buyers to more distant ones. The constrained optimal solution for P_{II} could, in turn, be derived according to the method proposed by Greenhut and Ohta [1975, Chapter 5]. Dewey [1955], on the grounds of monopolistic power over buyers, and Olson [1972], on the grounds of extra cost of repackaging, accepted the possibility (feasibility) of phantom freight extras being added to delivered prices in demand situations characterized by equation (3). And though such pricing is tantamount to applying phantom freight charges which would most likely be illegal in the United States *if* the practice was coterminous with a systematically followed base point price schedule, there is accumulated evidence that sporadic forms of this type of pricing is practiced in the USA (Greenhut, Greenhut and Li [1980]), much more generally in W. Germany and Japan (Greenhut [1981]), and apparently elsewhere in Europe as well (Phlips [1976]). Notwithstanding the *a priori* arguments of Hoover and Smithies, the basis for evaluating the various implications of equation (3) is therefore provided. It follows that the discriminatory spatial price practice resulting from equation (3) demands must be compared with the f.o.b. price schedule that would exist under that particular type of demand function. Let us accordingly determine next the f.o.b. price structure that would stem from equation (3) demands.

Let m stand for the f.o.b. mill price. Then via (3) the quantity demanded at distance D is specifiable as:

(3)′
$$q = \alpha/p^2$$
$$= \alpha/(m+tD)^2, \qquad D_{0I} \geqslant D \geqslant 0$$

where D_{0I} refers to the limit distance under f.o.b. mill pricing, that is, $D_{0I} = (\beta - m)/t$. The aggregate demand Q over an assumed line market, where $q(p)$ is uniformly distributed, is then:

(6)
$$Q = 2\int_0^{D_{0I}} \alpha/(m+tD)^2\, dD$$
$$= 2\alpha(\beta - m)/tm\beta, \qquad D_{0I} = (\beta - m)/t$$

For any given mill price m, profit is defined by:

(7)
$$\pi = (m-k)Q = 2\alpha(\beta - m)(m-k)/tm\beta$$

Differentiating (7) with respect to m and setting the result equal to zero provides the unique profit-maximizing mill price; that is:

(8) $$d\pi/dm = 2\alpha[(k-m)+(\beta-m)]tm\beta - 2\alpha t\beta(\beta-m)(m-k)/(tm\beta)^2 = 0$$

$$m = \sqrt{k\beta}$$

The optimal spatial price schedule under f.o.b. mill pricing is therefore:

(9) $$P_I = \sqrt{k\beta} + tD, \qquad (\beta - \sqrt{k\beta})/t \geqslant D \geqslant 0$$

The essential feature of this equation may be stated in the form of Proposition 4 below.

Proposition 4. Given the demand (3)′, the profit maximizing f.o.b. mill price m is higher (lower) the higher (lower) is the price ceiling β vis-à-vis the marginal cost.

Now the discriminatory and f.o.b. pricing techniques stemming from equation (3) demands can be compared by evaluating equations (5) and (9). For $D = 0$, $P_{II} \lesseqgtr P_I$, depending on whether $\beta \lesseqgtr 4k$. That is to say, if the price ceiling β is greater than $4k$, or more generally when consumer thresholds are relatively high, the prices charged to nearby customers are lower under discriminatory pricing than they are under f.o.b. mill pricing, and *vice versa*.

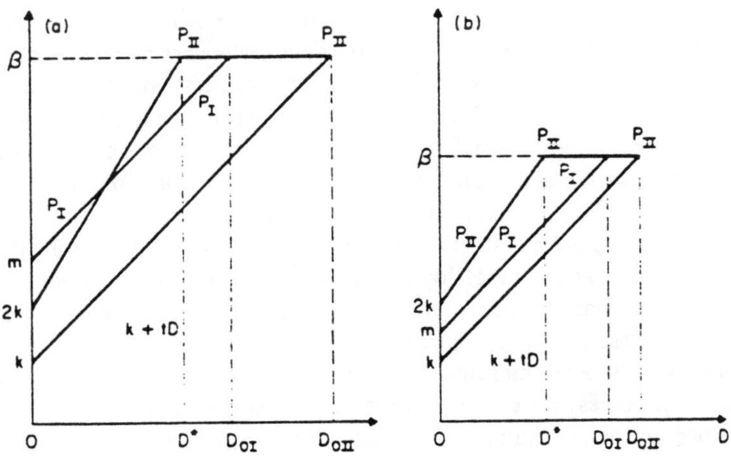

Figure 3
Consumer Threshold Levels and Spatial Price Schedules

Figure 3(a) depicts the two alternative spatial price schedules for $\beta > 4k$. These prices may be compared with those shown in Figure 3(b) for $\beta < 4k$. Note that the welfare implications for the nearby-distant sets of buyers are simply reversed as different levels of β are assumed. In particular, panel (a) of

Figure 3 indicates that a relatively high β combined with discriminatory pricing benefits buyers located proximate to the seller's plant while in panel (b) a relatively low β can be seen to benefit the same nearby buyers if f.o.b. mill pricing is practiced. A reversing of effects therefore applies to panels (a) and (b), given high and low β's respectively.

A caveat is in order at this point because in addition to benefiting nearby buyers, discriminatory prices can also provide advantages to *very distant* buyers (that is, those located between D_{0I} *and* D_{0II}); it does this since the latter groups of buyers would have been unable to purchase the good at all under the profit-maximizing f.o.b. mill price schedule but can purchase some of it at prices equal to or slightly below β, in the process creating a consumers' surplus.

Additional observations are warranted. The entire price schedule P_I can be recognized to shift upward (downward) in (9) as β is parametrically changed upward (downward). On the other hand, the price schedule P_{II} of (5) remains basically invariant to changes in β as only the size of the firm's market area can be altered.

To summarize briefly to this point: Diverse forms of dumping are possible under selected demands, such as those represented by homogeneous, constant demand elasticity conditions. (1) If the level of consumer thresholds (sensitivity for the commodity) is relatively high compared with marginal cost, the form of dumping which benefits nearby customers (and some very distant buyers) is most profitable for the seller, *ceteris paribus*. (2) If the threshold price is relatively low, dumping *in favor of nearby buyers* nevertheless results in a *loss to them*, in fact to *all* of the nearby consumers who could have been supplied under f.o.b. mill pricing. (For example, compare the two alternative delivered price schedules in Figure 3(b) over the market domain OD_{0II}.) (3) Regardless of the threshold price, the very distant consumers who would not purchase any units under f.o.b. mill pricing will benefit from discriminatory prices, as this price system alone enables them to purchase some positive quantity of the good. It follows that when dumping is viewed in the perspective of spatial price theory, more complicated asymmetric results obtain than those which derive from the classical view of prices.

It warrants special mention that dumping in favor of home (nearby) customers involves more complicated relationships than is evident by the typical protectionist argument one bears. This does not necessarily mean that predatory international dumping fails to exist. Rather, it simply suggests that profit-maximizing firms may price variously over space, and *home country advocates can frequently find examples of whatever they wish to claim is improper in the importing of goods from foreign countries.*

A related point is this: what appears to be *improper* may *not* be attributable to the predatory motives typically ascribed to the foreign seller. Rather, it can be that so-called discriminatory dumping in favor of distant buyers is strictly the result of profit maximizing pricing which, under different demand conditions, would have generated the opposite forms of pricing. Before laws are passed establishing "reference prices" which implicitly condemn foreign sellers, economists should probe deeply behind all facets of spatial pricing and the particular industry under examination. Indeed, not only have we previously noted the prevalence of discriminatory prices uncovered in the United States, W. Germany, and Japan, but diverse forms thereof reflecting heterogeneous demand and competitive conditions over the firms' market areas have been identified (Greenhut and Greenhut [1975], [1977]).

IV. A GENERALIZATION

Consider a demand curve defined generally as:

(10) $q = \alpha/p^x, \quad \beta \geqslant p \geqslant 0, \quad x > 1$

$= 0$, elsewhere—as previously specified.

The spatial price schedule under discriminatory pricing (Policy II) would then be provided by:

(11) $p_{II} = [x/(x-1)](k + tD), \quad (x-1)\beta/xt - k/t \geqslant D \geqslant 0$

$= \beta, \quad (\beta - k)/t \geqslant D > (x-1)\beta/xt - k/t$

The spatial price schedule under mill pricing (Policy I) can, in turn, be shown as:

(12) $P_I = m^* + tD, \quad (\beta - m)/t \geqslant D \geqslant 0,$

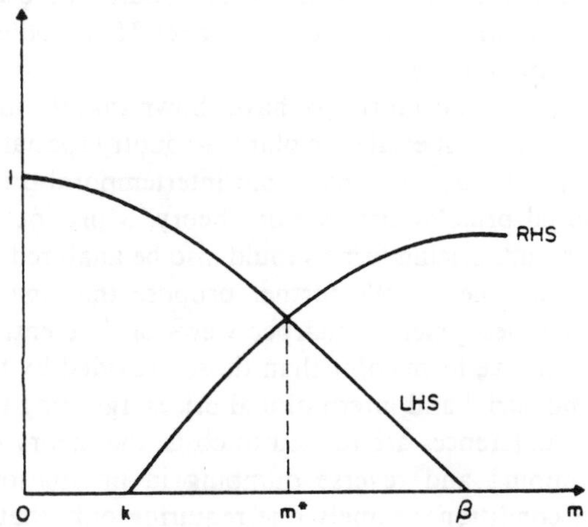

Figure 4
Marginal Cost, Threshold Levels and Equilibrium Mill Price

where m^* is the solution for m of the following equation:

$$(13) \qquad m^x-(2-x)\beta^{x-1}m-k(x-1)\beta^{x-1}=0, \qquad x>1$$

Existence of a solution falling between k and β is guaranteed since the present equation can be rearranged as:

$$(13)' \qquad 1-(m/\beta)^{x-1}=(1-k/m)(x-1)$$

In fact, the graphs of the LHS and RHS of this equation are unambiguously specifiable, with m^* determined at the intersection of the two curves in Figure 4. It can, furthermore, readily be seen that the equilibrium mill price m^* will be higher or lower depending on whether β (or k) is higher or lower. In contrast, via (11) we recognize that the delivered price is invariant under discriminatory pricing, being independent of β. The same general relations as those given in section III that were illustrated by Figure 3 therefore apply.

V. CONCLUSION

Many industrialists and advocates of "home country" products contend that the international dumping of goods is not only prevalent but an undesirable practice for two reasons: (1) it damages the home country by reducing the welfare of residents of the country; and (2) the industries in the nation which imports dumped goods can be damaged irreparably by the loss of domestic buyers. Of course, this second argument ignores the gains from comparative advantage. Moreover, the present paper has shown that the first argument is unacceptable since free trade would allow domestic (local) firms to maximize profits *market by market* and thereby to generate lower product prices under certain well-defined demand and cost conditions. *Quite significantly, this argument does not depend on (nor require) Mrs. Robinson's specification of decreasing marginal costs.*

Perhaps most importantly, we have shown that the international dumping of goods is simply a special case of intra-country spatial price discrimination, just as Phlips [1980] has shown that intertemporal price theory is a special case of spatial price discrimination theory. More inclusively, international sales of f.o.b. mill pricing firms should also be analyzed under the framework of spatial price theory. We further propose that spatial price theory and empirical realities generate sharper views of differential pricing (dumping) besides alternative forms of it than those provided by the classical spaceless theory of industrial and international prices. Ignoring the controversial case where price differences are related to costs, the theory of spatial pricing can explain dumping and reverse dumping in international trade under the simplest of conditions, namely one requiring only that buyers are spatially separated from a seller. Most vitally, insights into the dumping and reverse dumping process do not require the very restrictive, special assumptions that comprise the classical theory of price discrimination, such as the monopoly and non-identical demands assumptions. It follows that the most general exposition of price discrimination in international trade is the one based on the theory of spatial pricing.

ACCEPTED JUNE 1985

M. L. GREENHUT,
Department of Economics,
Texas A & M University,
College Station, Texas 77843,
USA.

H. OHTA,
SIPEB,
Aoyama Gakuin University,
Tokyo,
Japan.

J. SAILORS,
Department of Economics,
The University of Houston,
Houston, Texas 77004,
USA.

REFERENCES

BECKMANN, J., 1976, 'Spatial Price Policies Revisited', *Bell Journal of Economics*, 7 (Autumn), pp. 619–630.

BRANDER, J. and KRUGMAN, P., 1983, 'A "Reciprocal Dumping" Model of International Trade', *Journal of International Economics*, 15, pp. 313–321.

DEVLETOGLOU, N. E., 1971, *Consumer Behavior* (Harper and Row, London).

DEWEY, D., 1955, 'A Reappraisal of F.O.B. Pricing and Freight Absorption', *Southern Economic Journal*, 22 (July), pp. 48–54.

DORWARD, N., 1982, 'Recent Developments in the Analysis of Spatial Competition and Their Implications for Industrial Economics', *The Journal of Industrial Economics*, 31 (September–December), pp. 133–151.

GREENHUT, J. and GREENHUT, M. L., 1975, 'Spatial Price Discrimination, Competition and Locational Effects', *Economica*, 42, 4 (November), pp. 401–419.

GREENHUT, J. and GREENHUT, M. L., 1977, 'Nonlinearity of Delivered Price Schedules and Predatory Pricing', *Econometrica*, 45, 8 (November), pp. 1871–1875.

GREENHUT, J., GREENHUT, M. L. and LI, S., 1980, 'Spatial Pricing Patterns in the United States', *Quarterly Journal of Economics*, 94, 2 (March), pp. 329–350.

GREENHUT, M. L. and OHTA, H., 1972, 'Monopoly Output Under Alternative Spatial Pricing Techniques', *American Economic Review*, 62, 4 (September), pp. 705–713.

GREENHUT, M. L. and OHTA, H., 1975, *Theory of Spatial Pricing and Market Areas* (Duke University Press, Durham, NC).

GREENHUT, M. L., 1981, 'Spatial Pricing in U.S.A., West Germany and Japan', *Economica*, 48 (February), pp. 79–86.

HIRSHLEIFER, J., 1976, *Price Theory and Applications* (Prentice-Hall, Englewood Cliffs, NC).

HOLAHAN, W. L., 1975, 'The Welfare Effects of Spatial Price Discrimination', *American Economic Review*, 65, 3 (June), pp. 498–503.

HOOVER, E. M., 1937, 'Spatial Price Discrimination', *Review of Economic Studies*, 4 (June), pp. 182–191.

NORMAN, G., 1981, 'Spatial Competition and Spatial Price Discrimination', *Review of Economic Studies*, 48, 1 (January), pp. 97–111.

NORMAN, G., 1981, 'Uniform Pricing as an Optimal Spatial Pricing Policy', *Economica*, 48, 1 (February), pp. 87–91.

OHTA, H., 1980, 'Spatial Competition, Concentration and Welfare', *Regional Science and Urban Economics*, 10, 1 (February), pp. 3–16.

OHTA, H., 1981, 'The Price Effects of Spatial Competition', *Review of Economic Studies*, 48, 2 (April), pp. 317–325.

OHTA, H., 1984, 'The Output Effects of Spatial Price Discrimination Revisited' (mimeo).

OLSON, J. E., 1972, 'Price Discrimination by Regulated Motor Carriers', *American Economic Review*, 62, 3 (June), pp. 395–402.

PHLIPS, L., 1976, 'Spatial Pricing and Competition', in *Studies in Competition*, Approximation of Legislation Series (Commission of the European Communities, Brussels).

PHLIPS, L., 1980, 'Intertemporal Price Discrimination and Sticky Prices', *Quarterly Journal of Economics*, 3 (May), pp. 525–542.

ROBINSON, J., 1933, *The Economics of Imperfect Competition* (Macmillan, London).

SMITHIES, A., 1941, 'Monopolistic Price Policy in a Spatial Market', *Econometrica*, 9, 1 (January), pp. 63–73.

INTERNATIONAL ECONOMIC REVIEW
Vol. 27, No. 3, October, 1986

SPATIAL PRICING WITH A GENERAL COST FUNCTION; THE EFFECTS OF TAXES ON IMPORTS*

By M. L. Greenhut and George Norman

1. INTRODUCTION

One of the authors of this paper referred some years ago, in a somewhat different context, to a mislaid maxim in the "hope that the maxim in question will not be permanently mislaid" [Greenhut and Ohta (1976) p. 267]. Much the same hope can be expressed with respect to one of our objectives in this paper. It is a familiar principle in microeconomics that specific (or unit) taxes act somewhat differently from *ad valorem* taxes — although we would suggest that the full extent of this difference has not been investigated. There is also the suggestion in international trade theory that tariff barriers, and by implication local sales taxes, operate very much like transport costs and so can be analyzed like transport costs; in particular, just as we might expect spatial price discrimination through freight absorption, so we can expect spatial price discrimination through tariff (or sales tax) absorption.

What is not made clear is that there is a potential conflict between these two accepted wisdoms, determined by whether the tariff or sales tax is specific or *ad valorem*. We examine this conflict in some detail in this paper. We shall show that just as the profit maximizing producer can be expected to absorb some proportion of transport costs, so we can also expect him to absorb some proportion of the tariffs (or taxes) to which his goods are subject. But, the precise nature of tariff absorption depends crucially on the particular tariff barriers that exist. Only specific tariffs impact the same way as do transport costs. *Ad valorem* tariffs will be shown to have a very different effect; they will appear, at least in part, as a change in convexity of the individual demand function.

A related objective of the paper, and one with which we shall deal first in the analysis, is to show how an optimal spatial pricing rule can be derived when marginal production costs take a general form. The analysis of spatial competition and of spatial price discrimination has relied quite heavily on the assumption of constant marginal production costs. It follows naturally from this assumption that the price/quantity decisions applicable to a market at location i are independent of the price/quantity decisions at location j. The optimal discrimination pricing policy over a series of distinct markets under conditions of constant marginal production costs would be the one that maximizes profit at each market point.

What happens when this assumption is relaxed? Consider the simple example

* Manuscript received March, 1985; revised January, 1986.

illustrated in Figure 1 below in which marginal production costs (MC) are assumed to be monotonic increasing. If attention is confined solely to Market A (Figure 1(a)), profit is maximized in the usual manner with price P_A and quantity Q_A. Now add a second market B (Figure 1(b)) in which demand is to be satisfied by a shipment from A subject to per unit transport cost t_{AB}. Since production in market A is already Q_A, the marginal cost of supplying market B with an additional quantity q is given by

(1) $$MC_B = MC(Q_A+q) + t_{AB}.$$

In other words, it is derived by adding transport cost to that portion of the marginal cost curve in Figure 1(a) to the right of C. With this marginal cost curve, the profit maximizing supply to market B is Q_B at the price P_B.

But now consider market A. Total output has been increased to Q_A+Q_B; thus marginal cost in market A has been increased and exceeds the marginal revenue in A by the amount CD. If market B is to be supplied, it will be necessary to reduce output in market A from that which would have applied in isolation. Put another way, with variable marginal production costs, the profit maximizing price/quantity decision in any one market is no longer independent of the price/quantity decisions in other markets.

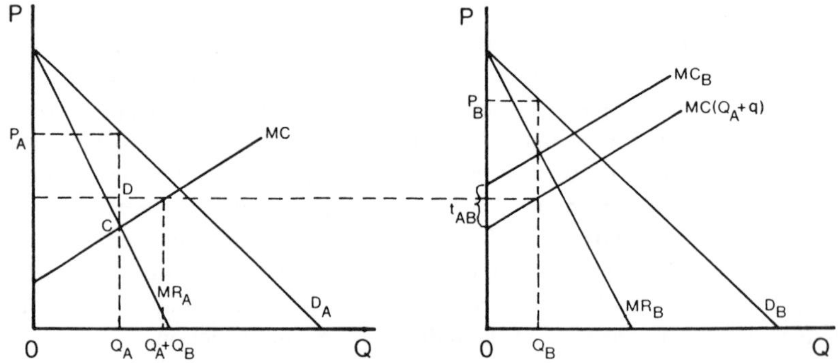

FIGURE 1

Solution of this problem is handled most effectively by the application of optimal control theory.[1] We show that the resulting optimal pricing rule has much in common with that which applies under the constant cost assumption. But surprisingly, perhaps, we show that while the mill price is affected by the shape of the cost function, the degree of spatial price discrimination is not, where by degree of spatial price discrimination we mean the proportion of transport costs absorbed in the mill price by the producer.

[1] It is, of course, possible to generate a solution by means of more straightforward techniques. The advantage of a control theory approach is that it gives us general results that apply in a variety of cases. In addition, this approach highlights the many close parallels between time and space — see also Phlips [1976, 1982] and Fratrik [1981].

One final point should be made in this introduction. We confine our attention in this paper to theoretical issues. It is quite clear, however,that our analysis is of practical and empirical relevance to the impact of commercial policies. One general example drawn from recent work on intra-industry trade may suffice to indicate the general direction that empirical extension of our analysis might take. It is to be expected from our analysis that exporters will absorb some proportion of tariff duties, the proportion being determined by specific market conditions. This will be evidenced as variation in the (tariff-free) declared price of exports, and calls into question the usefulness of the Hufbauer index as a proxy for product differentiation. We also show, in Section 4(d), that tariffs (or sales taxes) affect both domestic and import prices. It is, therefore, perhaps not surprising that the commercial policy implications of intraindustry trade are not at all clear cut — see Bradley and Norman [1985] and Kierzkowski [1984].

2. SPATIAL PRICING WITH NON-LINEAR MARGINAL COSTS

Our analysis is based on a model that is common to much of the analysis of spatial pricing [see, for example, Greenhut, Hwang and Ohta (1975), Holahan (1975) and Ohta (1980)], and which model underlies the example discussed above (Figure 1). We assume a (local) monopolist selling over a market area $[0, R]$, where R may or may not be specified *a priori*. The objective of the firm is to choose a delivered price schedule (or trajectory) $p(r)$ to maximize aggregate profit. Consumers are assumed to be identical and to be evenly and continuously distributed over the market area.[2] Demand at location r is given by the demand function[3]

(2) $$q(r) = q(p(r));\ q' < 0.$$

Transport cost per unit transported to r is $t(r)$ and total production cost $c(Q(R))$ is a function of aggregate output sold in the market area. The production cost function is assumed not to exhibit constant marginal cost.

The objective function in the control theoretic framework is total profit, the control variable is the delivered price schedule $p(r)$, the state variable is the total output $Q(r)$ sold over the market interval $[0, r]$. Total output in this interval is, then, given by

(3) $$Q(r) = \int_0^r q(p(\rho)d\rho$$

from which we derive the differential equation

(4) $$\frac{dQ(r)}{dr} \equiv \dot{Q}(r) = q(p(r))$$

[2] The continuity assumption is made for mathematical convenience. It does not affect the economic interpretation of our results.

[3] If consumer density is D, individual demand is $q(r)/D$.

relating state and control variables. (Note that we define $\dot{f}$ for any variable f as df/dr.)

Assume for the moment that the market radius is given. The optimal pricing problem is then

(5) $$\underset{p(r)}{\text{Maximize}}\ \pi = \int_0^R q(p(r))\{p(r)-t(r)\}dr - C(Q(R))$$

subject to

(6) $$\dot{Q}(r) = q(p(r))$$

Introducing the auxiliary variable $\lambda(r)$, we obtain the Hamiltonian

(7) $$H[Q(r), p(r), r, \lambda(r)] = q(p(r))[p(r)-t(r)] + \lambda(r)q(p(r))$$

and can specify the necessary conditions for profit maximization.[4] These involve equation (6) plus

(i) $$\dot{\lambda} = -\partial H/\partial Q(r)$$

(ii) $$\lambda(R) = \left.\frac{\partial(-C(Q(R))}{\partial Q(r)}\right|_{r=R}$$

(iii) H maximized with respect to $p(r) \Rightarrow \partial H/\partial p(r) = 0$

Consider condition (iii). Differentiating equation (7) with respect to price $p(r)$ gives

(8) $$q(p(r)) + q'(p(r))[p(r)-t(r)+\lambda(r)] = 0$$

Rearranging this equation gives

(8′) $$p(r)\left[1-\frac{1}{\varepsilon(r)}\right] = t(r) - \lambda(r)$$

where $\varepsilon(r)$ is the elasticity of demand at market location r and price $p(r)$.

It will be noted that the left side of (8′) is marginal revenue derived from the sales made to any market point r, while the right side "looks like" marginal cost, given that an appropriate definition of the auxiliary variable $\lambda(r)$ can be derived.

Consider conditions (i) and (ii). Since the state variable $Q(r)$ does not appear in the Hamiltonian, it follows that

(9) $$\dot{\lambda}(r) = -\partial H/\partial Q(r) = 0 \quad \text{for all } r.$$

Hence the auxiliary variable $\lambda(r)$ is a constant. From condition (ii) we obtain

(10) $$\lambda(R) = \left.\frac{\partial(-C(Q(R))}{\partial(Q(r))}\right|_{r=R} = -C'(Q(R))$$

[4] One problem that arises in specifying the maximising condition is that the state variable does not appear in the Hamiltonian. See Barnett [1975] for a discussion of the appropriate maximizing condition for a problem of this type.

where $C'(Q(R)) = \partial C(Q)/\partial Q(R) =$ marginal production cost at output $Q(R)$. Hence

$$\lambda(r) = -C'(Q(R)) \quad \text{for all} \quad r \in [0, R]. \tag{11}$$

Substituting into (8′) then gives the optimal price equation:

$$p(r)\left[1 - \frac{1}{\varepsilon(r)}\right] = t(r) + C'(Q(R)). \tag{12}$$

There is a direct analogy between equation (12) and the optimal spatial pricing equation that applies under a "constant marginal production cost" assumption. Under constant marginal cost, the profit maximizing delivered price schedule is such that marginal revenue equals marginal cost (of production plus transportation) at each selling location. In the non-constant case discussed here, the profit maximizing pricing policy is again that marginal revenue should equal marginal cost of production plus transportation at each selling location: but now the appropriate marginal production cost is that applicable to total output.

We can apply the above analysis to the example provided in the introduction to this paper. The discussion underlying equation (12) requires of the profit maximizing pricing strategy that marginal revenue equals marginal cost in each market, where in market B marginal cost includes transport costs, and where for both markets marginal production cost is $MC(Q_A + Q_B)$. In order to illustrate the profit maximizing price/quantity decision, we use a geometric device first suggested by Horst [1973].

Figure 2(a) illustrates market conditions in Market A assumed to be the sole producing point, and Figure 2(b), the market conditions in B. In isolation, output in A would be Q'_A and price P'_A. Now consider an increase in output to Q. Marginal cost increases to M, and output for market A would be reduced to Q_A. We can also construct what Horst termed a "marginal cost of exporting" schedule, where exports emanate from market A and are sent to market B. At marginal cost M, for example, $Q_AQ = Q_B$ would be exported to market B. Experimenting with different marginal costs allows us to construct the marginal cost of exporting schedule MC_X. Now add transport costs from A to B to generate the marginal cost (of exporting and transporting) to market B, $MC_X + t_{AB}$. Profit is maximized in market B by equating marginal revenue MR_B with marginal cost $MC_X + t_{AB}$. This gives total output Q in Figure 2, with Q_A supplied to market A and $Q_AQ = Q_B$ supplied to market B. Price in A is P_A and it is P_B in B. As is manifest, price in market A has risen and quantity fallen from that which applied in isolation. If, in contrast, marginal cost were decreasing, the addition of market B would have led to a reduction in price in market A and an increase in quantity supplied to that market.

One final point is worth observing in closing this section. We have already noted that equation (12) is appealingly similar to the profit maximizing equation that applies under constant marginal costs. It follows from equation (12) that the marginal production cost function will indeed affect the profit maximizing mill price (P_A in our example); however, the slope of the delivered price schedule

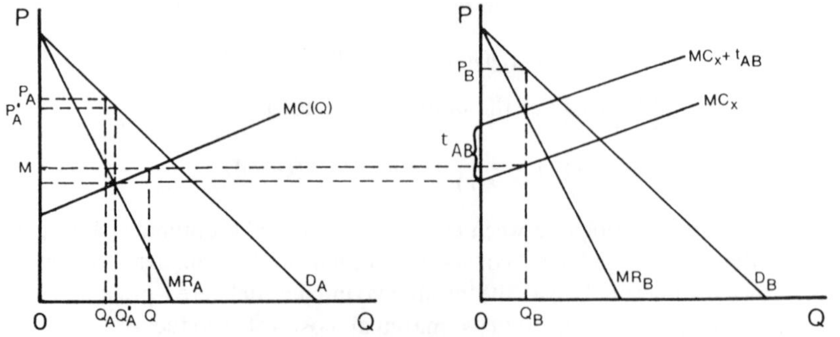

FIGURE 2
PROFIT MAXIMISATION WITH INCREASING MATGINAL COST

and hence the degree of spatial price discrimination[5] is totally determined by the individual demand functions $q(p(r))$. In other words, the degree of spatial price discrimination is independent of the precise form of the marginal production cost function.[6]

3. DETERMINATION OF THE MARKET BOUNDARY

The necessary conditions (i)–(iii) and equation (6) fully define the solution to the optimal control problem when the market boundary (time or radius) is specified *a priori*. However, a further condition is necessary when the market boundary is to be determined as part of the solution. Given the structure of our problem this condition is

(iv) $H[Q(R^*), p(R^*), R^*, \lambda(R^*)] = q(p(R^*)[p(R^*) - t(R^*)] + \lambda(R^*)q(p(R^*)) = 0$

where R^* is the profit-maximizing market boundary. Substituting from (11) gives

$$q(p(R^*))[p(R^*) - t(R^*) - C'(Q(R^*))] = 0 \tag{13}$$

Equation (13) will be satisfied by a finite value of R^* only if the demand function is such that there is a well-defined maximum price that consumers are willing to pay for the product: simply put, only if the demand function has an intersection with the price axis. Assume that this maximum price is $\hat{p}$. Then (13) indicates that the profit maximizing market radius R^* is such that:

[5] If the slope of the delivered price schedule is S, the degree of spatial price discrimination (equivalent to the proportion of freight costs absorbed by the producer) is $PD = 1 - S$.

[6] One may wonder whether similar problems arise when the producer is constrained, or decides to adopt an f.o.b. mill or uniform price. It is, in fact, very easy to show that optimal control theoretic techniques are not necessary in such situations, even if marginal production cost is non-constant. The principles applied in standard theory in determining the optimal f.o.b. mill price carry through directly to the variable marginal cost case.

(14) $$q(p(R^*)) = 0;\ p(R^*) = \hat{p}$$

It should be noted in passing that equation (14) also implies that price equals marginal cost (of production and transportation) at R^*, since if $q(R^*)=0$ then $\varepsilon(R^*)=\infty$ and, from (12), $p(R^*)=t(R^*)+C'(Q(R^*))$. In other words, the bracketed term in equation (13) is also satisfied as an equality.

It should be emphasised further that the mill price, $p(0)$, is not independent of the market radius, a property that is in sharp contrast to the constant marginal cost case. This should be clear from our discussion of Figure 2, but can easily be proved. Just introduce a third, more distant, market to Figure 2. It will be easily recognized that price in market A (the mill price in our example) will further increase above P_A; of course, also note that price in market B will exhibit a similar increase.

4. OPTIMAL PRICING BEHAVIOR WITH DIFFERENT TARIFF BARRIERS

We noted in the introduction to the paper that it has often been suggested that tariff barriers act in a manner similar to transport costs. We can use the results of Section 3 to indicate the extent to which this is true.[7] Moreover, these results enable us to investigate within a partial equilibrium framework the price/quantity effects of different tariff policies.

4.1. *Specific tariffs.* Two main types of tariff are the *ad valorem* tariff, which is levied as a percentage of the declared value of the goods imported, and the specific tariff which is levied as a given sum per unit of the goods imported. We shall concentrate in this section on specific tariffs since, as will be seen below, they act in a very direct way "like" transport costs.

Assume that each selling point r is a different country, that location 0 is the source of a particular commodity,[8] and that the specific tariff applied in r is $\tau(r)$ per unit.

Net receipts derived from each location r are then

(15) $$NR(r) = q(p(r))[p(r) - t(r) - \tau(r)]$$

and total profit with a specific tariff is given by

(16) $$\Pi_S = \int_0^R q(p(r))[p(r) - t(r) - \tau(r)]dr - C(Q(R)).$$

Comparison with equation (5) above indicates that the two objective functions are identical with the transformation

[7] The discussion in this section owes much to the analysis of Horst (1971, 1973). Horst was concerned with the impact of tariff barriers on location choice whereas we are more interested in the price implications of alternative tariff barriers.

[8] For the reader who finds this assumption difficult to accept it may prove simpler to envisage a finite number of countries (S, say) where each country S covers the "small" interval $[\hat{r}_S, \hat{r}_S + \Delta]$, $(S=1,\ldots,S)$ with $q(r)\neq 0$ for $r\varepsilon[\hat{r}_S, \hat{r}_S+\Delta]$ $(S=1,\ldots,S)$, and $q(r)=0$ elsewhere.

$$T(r) = t(r) + \tau(r)\,. \tag{17}$$

In other words, specific tariffs do indeed act identically to transport costs, and the analysis of Section 2 carries through completely. More directly, assume that tastes and income are roughly identical across countries, such that the individual demand functions are identical across countries (an assumption that is more or less reasonable if we confine attention to, for example, the Western industrialized countries.) Then the proportion of a specific tariff actually charged to consumers in a particular country will be determined by the "shape" of the individual demand functions. For example, if individual demand is linear, 50% of any specific tariff will be charged to consumers.

Now consider the effects on home and foreign markets of a change in tariff rates. To keep the analysis simple we confine attention, as in effect was done in Figure 2, to a two-country model, now U.S. and Foreign where U.S. is assumed to be the exporting country. Assume that production in U.S. is characterised by increasing marginal production costs. Further assume that initial transport costs to and specific tariffs in Foreign amount to $T(r)$. Consider an increase in specific tariffs such that $T(r)$ increases to $T'(r)$. The effects of this change are illustrated in Figure 3.

At the initial tariff level, price/quantity in U.S. and Foreign are respectively (P_{US}, Q_{US}) and (P_F, Q_F) where, corresponding to Figure 2, $Q_F = Q - Q_{US}$ and $P_F = P_{US} + (1/2)T(r)$ via the assumed linear demand functions. The curve MC_X is just that defined in Figure 2: the marginal production cost of the good to be exported from U.S. to Foreign.

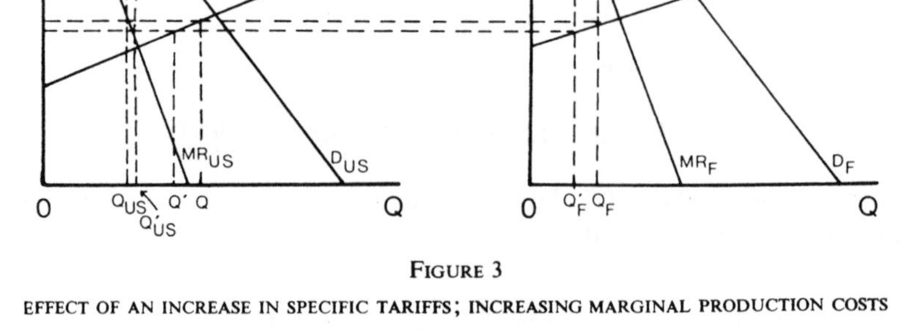

FIGURE 3

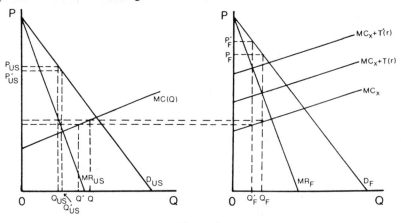

EFFECT OF AN INCREASE IN SPECIFIC TARIFFS; INCREASING MARGINAL PRODUCTION COSTS

As can be seen, when tariffs are increased price rises and quantity falls in Foreign to (P'_F, Q'_F), as is to be expected, while in U.S. there is an increase in local production and a consequent decrease in price. Total output, however, is reduced.

Now consider the outcome if marginal production costs are decreasing. This is illustrated in Figure 4. An increase in specific tariff again leads to an increase in price and decrease in quantity for imports to Foreign. For the U.S., however, we see that price increases to P'_{US} and quantity falls to Q'_{US} as a result of the increased tariff in Foreign, because the producers in the U.S. are now less able to exploit economies of scale in production.

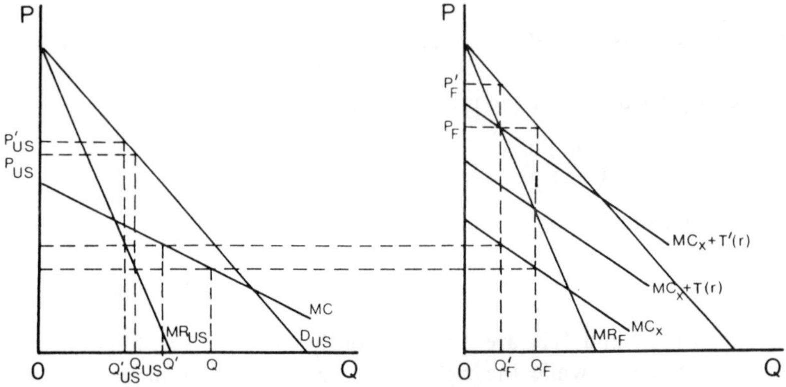

FIGURE 4

EFFECT OF AN INCREASE IN SPECIFIC TARIFFS: DECREASING MARGINAL PRODUCTION COSTS

In other words, the effects on U.S. of an increase in specific tariff barriers in Foreign depend crucially on the production conditions in U.S. (It should further be clear that if marginal production costs are constant, price/quantity decisions in U.S. are unaffected by changes in tariffs in Foreign.)

4.2. *Ad Valorem Tariffs.* Matters are not quite as straightforward if import markets apply ad valorem tariffs since — as was indicated above — these relate to the declared value of imports rather than to the quantity imported. In order to analyse the effects of an ad valorem tariff, assume that the declared value of the product exported to location r is $p_d(r)$ and that the ad valorem tariff rate is $\tau(r)$. Then price in location r is

$$p(r) = p_d(r)(1+\tau(r)) \tag{18}$$

and the tax payable by the exporter is

$$\text{Tax} = \tau(r)p_d(r)q(p(r)) = \frac{\tau(r)}{1+\tau(r)}\, p(r)q(p(r)). \tag{19}$$

Net revenue from location r is therefore

$$\begin{aligned} NR(r) &= q(p(r))[p(r)-t(r)] - \frac{\tau(r)}{1+\tau(r)}\, p(r)q(p(r)) \\ &= q(p(r))\left[\frac{p(r)}{1+\tau(r)} - t(r)\right] \end{aligned} \tag{20}$$

and total profits with *ad valorem* tariffs are given by

$$\Pi_A = \int_0^R q(p(r))\left[\frac{p(r)}{1+\tau(r)} - t(r)\right]dr - C(Q(R)). \tag{21}$$

As can be seen, an *ad valorem* tariff does not impact identically as a transport cost, but there is a sharp connection between the two. Given the objective function (21), the Hamiltonian for our optimal control problem is

$$H_A[Q(r), p(r), r, \lambda(r)] = q(p(r)\left[\frac{p(r)}{1+\tau(r)} - t(r)\right] + \lambda(r)q(p(r)). \tag{22}$$

The necessary condition for the profit maximizing price is

$$\frac{p(r)}{1+\tau(r)}\left[1 - \frac{1}{\varepsilon(r)}\right] = t(r) + C'(Q(R)) \tag{23}$$

or on reorganization

$$p(r)\left[1 - \frac{1}{\varepsilon(r)}\right] = (1+\tau(r))(t(r) + C'(Q(r)). \tag{23'}$$

Equations (23′) and (12) are quite obviously similar. The left side of (23′) is marginal revenue, while the right side is marginal cost of production and transportation increased by the amount of the *ad valorem* tariff rate. Profit is maximised by equating marginal revenue with this adjusted marginal cost.

The effect of an *ad valorem* tax is illustrated in Figure 5. Given (23′), the effect of an *ad valorem* tariff is to shift and rotate the $MC_X + t$ curve as shown. The qualitative comparative consequences of an increase in *ad valorem* tariffs are the same as for specific tariffs although, not surprisingly, the *ad valorem* tariff can be expected to have different quantitative results compared to those of a specific tariff.

We noted above, however, that our main concern is with the pricing implications of different types of tariff barriers, and it is in this respect that specific tariffs and *ad valorem* tariffs can be sharply contrasted. It is, of course, the case that the producer will absorb some proportion of *ad valorem* tariffs, just as he can be expected to absorb part of any specific tariff. To see why this is so, rewrite equation (23′) (using equation (18)), as

$$p_d(r)\left[1 - \frac{1}{\varepsilon(p(r))}\right] = t(r) + C'(Q(R)) \tag{23''}$$

where elasticity of demand is measured at the delivered price. Now assume an increase in the *ad valorem* tariff rate. The delivered price will increase given the declared value of imports $p_d(r)$. Assuming that the individual demand function is well-behaved, in that elasticity is an increasing function of delivered price,[9] the term in brackets on the left side of (23″) will increase, necessitating a reduction

[9] Note that by convention we measure elasticity as a positive number. The demand function will be well behaved so long as it is less convex than a rectangular hyperbola.

in the declared value of imports in order to maintain the equality in (23″). In other words, not all of an increase in the *ad valorem* tariff rate will be passed on to consumers as an increase in price. Some will be absorbed by the exporter and be exhibited as a reduction in the declared value of imports.

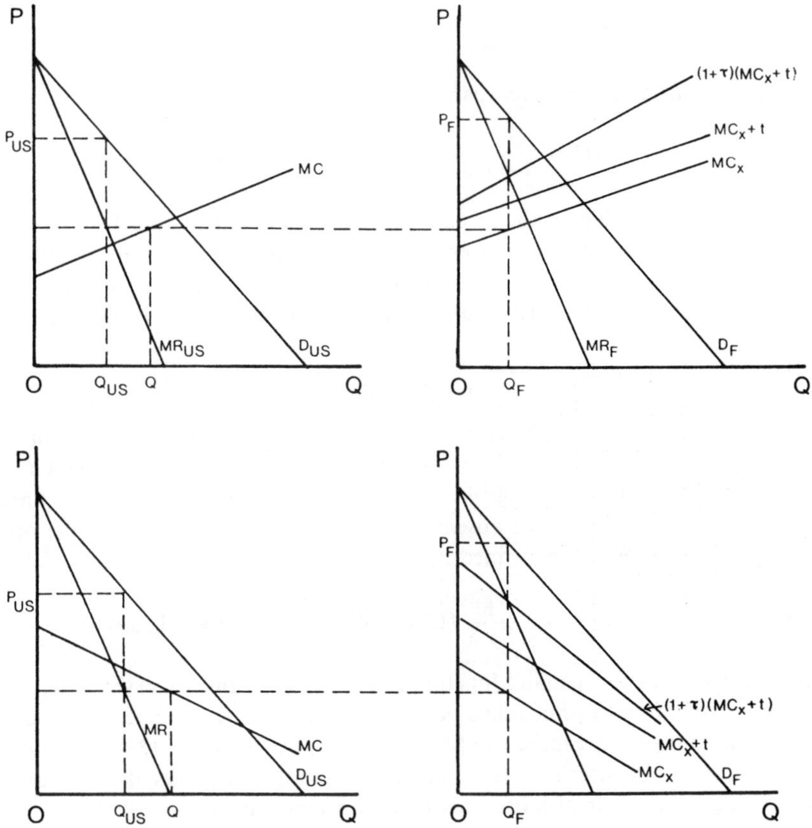

FIGURE 5
EFFECTS OF AN AD VALOREM TARIFF

4.3. *The Ad Valorem Tariff and Spatial Price Discrimination.* We are now in position to consider the effect of an *ad valorem* tariff on the degree of spatial price discrimination. To do so, we simplify matters by confining attention to a class of demand functions used extensively in the analysis of spatial pricing,[10]

[10] See Greenhut, Greenhut, and Kelly [1977] for a discussion of this class of demand functions. With respect to footnote 9, these functions are well-behaved as long as $x > -1$. Note further that when $-1 < x < 0$ the parameter a defines the minimum price that consumers are willing to pay. For a determinate solution to exist with $-1 < x < 0$ it is, therefore necessary that a lies below marginal cost for some range of marginal cost.

namely

$$p = a - \frac{bq^x}{x} \qquad (x > -1;\ x \neq 0:\ a,\ b > 0) \tag{24}$$

and assume a constant tariff rate $\tau(r) = \tau Vr$.

Elasticity of demand for this class of demand functions is

$$\varepsilon = \frac{p}{x(a-p)} \tag{25}$$

Substituting into (23′) and reorganizing gives

$$p(r) = \frac{ax}{1+x} + \frac{1+\tau}{1+x}(C'(Q(R)) + t(r)). \tag{26}$$

As can be seen, the higher the *ad valorem* tariff, the smaller is the degree of spatial price discrimination that will be employed by the producer if $x > 0$. Note further that the producer will discriminate against distant markets for $-1 < x < 0$: recall from footnote 5 that the degree of spatial price discrimination is given by

$$PD = 1 - \frac{1+\tau}{1+x} = \frac{x-\tau}{1+x}. \tag{27}$$

A sharp contrast should be drawn between equation (26) and the equation which would apply in the absence of any tariff barriers. It is well known [see Greenhut and Greenhut (1975)] that given (a) individual demand functions defined by equation (24), and (b) in the absence of tariffs (or local sales taxes), the optimal delivered price schedule is defined by

$$p_D(r) = \frac{ax}{1+x} + \frac{1}{1+x}(C'(Q(R)) + t(r)) \qquad (x > -1;\ x \neq 0). \tag{28}$$

The more convex the demand function (the lower the value of x) the greater is the slope of the delivered price schedule and the smaller is the degree of spatial price discrimination — see Figure 6. More specifically, equation (28) indicates that the producer will discriminate in favor of distant consumers if $x > 0$, and will discriminate in favour of more proximate consumers if $-1 < x < 0$.[11]

Now compare equations (26) and (28). The *ad valorem* tariff, unlike the specific tariff, acts in large part as if a change in convexity of demand has taken place. Thus if the underlying demand function is only weakly convex ($x > 0$ but $x < \tau$), the *ad valorem* tariff can act to reverse the direction of price discrimination.

This outcome has a number of important implications. Our analysis has been couched mainly in terms of the price effects of tariffs. It applies equally, however, to local sales taxes, such as those imposed in the United States or to the value

[11] The degenerate case of $x = 0$ gives the negative exponential demand function and f.o.b. (non-discriminatory) pricing.

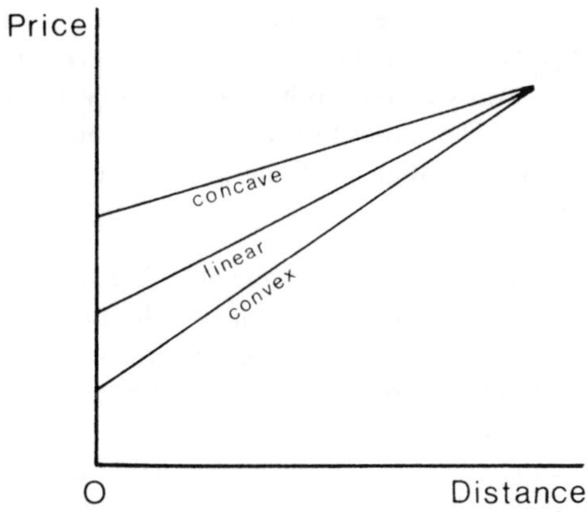

FIGURE 6

EFFECT OF CONVEXITY ON DELIVERED PRICES

added taxes that, for example, are imposed by the various member states of the European Economic Community. Our fundamental pricing equation (28) indicates that external incidence of f.o.b. pricing, which is taken by the regulatory authorities to be non-discriminatory, may well disguise a situation in which there is extensive spatial price discrimination.[12]

In addition, empirical work such as that by Hwang [1979] uses equation (28) as a basis for estimating the form of the demand function and, in particular, for estimating the convexity/concavity parameter x. These estimates need to be reevaluated in light of the discussion above. More fundamentally, our analysis lends further support to the assertion by Phlips [1980] and others that adequate empirical analysis of pricing policies requires a richer theoretical background, particularly of discriminatory pricing, than has been available.

Why should *ad valorem* tariffs or taxes raise such issues, particularly since first thoughts would suggest that demand (taste) is a datum and any tax imposed by government is merely an added cost? The answer lies in the fundamental distinction drawn in spatial price theory between the delivered price and the net price received by the producer. These two sets of prices are related in a well-defined way, determined by cost conditions and the shape of the individual demand functions. Any tax which so impacts marginal cost as to alter its slope then appears as a demand curve twisting effect, in the present case a twist towards greater convexity. The *ad valorem* tax has this effect because its higher rates with higher prices signify a marginal cost equality with a much greater marginal revenue, and this constitutes a mapping to (or transform to) the lower elasticity associated with a more convex demand function. Assuming further that a low

[12] Phlips [1983] observes that so-called normal cost pricing, (which we propose would probably strike regulators as desirable competitive pricing) is —at its roots— discriminatory pricing.

finite price limit applies in a given country where the demand happens to be relatively convex suggests the possibility that the *ad valorem* tax would cause the exporter to restrict the firm's market to his own country and to others which do not impose such a tax. The imposition of the tax, combined with (26), could yield a delivered price greater than the finite price limit in the country of significantly convex demands.

4.4. *Competitive Pricing: a brief digression.* We have assumed throughout our analysis that the producer is a monopolist. The pricing equations we have derived (particularly equation (26)) are so closely-related to the no-tariff spatial pricing equations, however, that our analysis can be extended with little alteration to a competitive environment.

In particular, we can relax the somewhat restrictive assumption that there is no market overlap between competitive producers located at different points in the market area. Consider, for example, the case analysed by Greenhut and Greenhut [1975] and illustrated in Figure 7.

Assume that there are m_1 sellers at location 1 and m_2 sellers at location 2, all producing a homogeneous product and all selling at all points on the line market between locations 1 and 2. Greenhut and Greenhut then show that the optimal spatial pricing equation with demand functions of the form given by equation (24) is

$$(29) \qquad p_D(r) = \frac{ax}{m+x} + \frac{1}{m+x}\{m\bar{k}+m_1T+m_2(d_2-T)\}$$

where T and d_2 are as defined in Figure 7, $m=m_1+m_2$ and $\bar{k}$ is the average of individual marginal production costs.

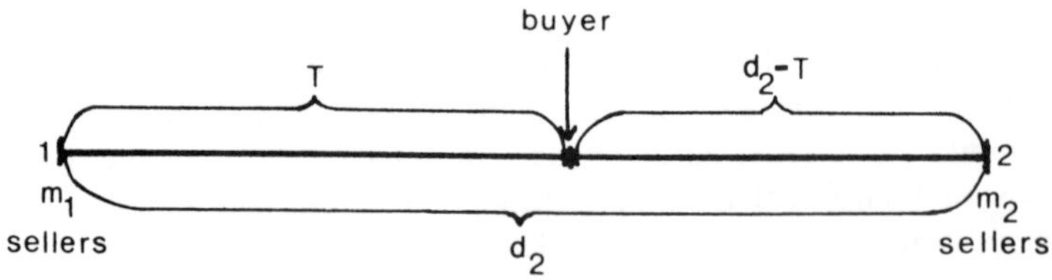

FIGURE 7
TWO PRODUCTION SITES ON THE BUYERS' LINE

The analogy with equation (28) is direct. It follows that the introduction of a specific tax will appear simply as an increase in transport costs (T). An *ad valorem* tax, on the other hand, requires that we replace the term $1/(m+x)$ by the term $(1+\tau)/(m+x)$. In other words, no matter whether we consider a monopolistic or competitive environment *ad valorem* tariffs appear in effect as a change in convexity of demand.

The relevance of this model to the analysis of intra-industry trade is worth emphasizing. By definition, there is two-way transportation (trade) between markets "near to" location 1 and markets "near to location 2: the Greenhut and

Greenhut model applies equally to point markets as to spatially extensive markets. Thus equation (29) is the relevant pricing equation in the context of intra-industry trade in identical products and allows investigation of the welfare implications of tariff barriers in such a context: see Brander [1981] for a related analysis.

5. CONCLUSIONS

If we relax the assumption that marginal production costs are constant then the producer who wishes to adopt a spatially discriminatory pricing scheme will find that he can no longer apply a simple "marginal cost equals marginal revenue at each selling location" rule. The basic point is that with variable marginal costs, price/quantity decisions at any location r are intimately related to the price/quantity decisions at all other selling locations. Optimal pricing requires a global view rather than a market by market approach.

The techniques of optimal control theory have been developed to cope with just such problems. When applied to spatial problems, the profit maximizing conditions for an optimal price policy with variable marginal costs reestablish the "marginal cost equals marginal revenue at each location" rule. However, now the appropriate marginal production cost is that applying to total output over the entire market area. In addition, the degree of spatial price discrimination is determined totally by the individual demand functions; it is independent of the form of the marginal cost function.

This analysis has a number of potential applications. In particular, it can be applied to the partial equilibrium analysis of the effects on an exporting country of tariffs imposed on imports. Specific tariffs applied to quantity exported act identically to transport costs. The exporter who is free to do so will, therefore, absorb tariff costs just as he would absorb freight costs, the proportion of the tariff absorbed being determined by the shape (convexity) of the individual demand functions.

Ad valorem tariffs apply to value exported, and do not act identically to transport costs. Again, however, the basic spatial pricing approach can be applied and the optimal pricing rule has much in common with that which would apply under specific tariffs. One thing which does emerge is that the degree of spatial price discrimination is affected by the *ad valorem* tariff rate. Such tariffs are treated in large part as if demand convexity had increased.

Most significantly, perhaps, this paper has demonstrated how underlying conditions that would make the dumping of goods abroad a natural result of consumer-business demands for goods can be converted into a reverse dumping situation via the imposition of an *ad valorem* tax. For nations obsessed with the goal of protecting home markets (e.g., vs. Japanese inroads) imposing an *ad valorem* tax rather than a specific tax can do the job. Of course, from a "puristic" standpoint, a related matter should be determined, namely whether the "comparative or possibly even absolute price advantage, as it were" in prices charged foreign buyers was due to subsidy or the like in the exporting country *or* was the natural result of less convex demands and/or as spatial price theory also emphasizes [e.g., Greenhut and Greenhut (1975)] greater competition in a more distant market than the local market.

Texas A & M University, U.S.A., and
University of Leicester, United Kingdom, respectively.

REFERENCES

BARNETT, S., *Introduction to Mathematical Control Theory* (Oxford: Clarendon Press, 1975).

BRADLEY, I. AND G. NORMAN, "Welfare Effects of Trade Restrictions on Intra-industry Trade under Monopolistic Competition," Discussion Paper No. 42, University of Leicester (May, 1985).

BRANDER, J., "Intra-industry Trade in Identical Commodities," *Journalof International Economics*, 11 (February, 1981), 1–14.

FRATRIK, M., *Spatial Discriminatory Pricing with a General Cost Function*, dissertation Texas A & M University (May, 1981).

GREENHUT, J. AND M. L. GREENHUT, "Spatial Price Discrimination, Competition and Locational Effects," *Economica*, 42 (November, 1975), 401–419.

———, ——— AND W. KELLY, "A Spatial Theoretical Perspective for Bank Merger Regulations," Proceedings on Bank Structures and Competition, *Federal Reserve Bank of Chicago* (April, 1977), 210–254.

GREENHUT, M. L., M. HWANG, AND H. OHTA, "Observations on the Shape and Relevance of the Spatial Demand Curve," *Econometrica*, 43 (July, 1975), 669–682.

——— and H. OHTA, "Related Market Conditions and Interindustrial Mergers," *American Economic Review*, 66 (June, 1976), 267–277.

HADLEY, G. AND M. C. KEMP, *Variational Methods in Economics* (Amsterdam: North-Holland, 1971).

HOLAHAN, W. L., "The Welfare Effects of Spatial Competition," *American Economic Review*, 65 (June, 1975), 498–503.

HORST, T., "The Theory of the Multinational Firm: Optimal Behaviour under Different Tariff and Tax Rules," *Journal of Political Economy*, 79 (September/October, 1971), 1059–1072.

———, "The Simple Analytics of Multinational Firm Behaviour" in M. B. Connolly, and A. K. Swoboda, eds., *International Trade and Money* (London: Allen and Unwin, 1973), 72–84.

HWANG, M., "A Model of Spatial Price Discrimination for the Price Schedule of Coal," *Journal of Regional Science*, 19 (May, 1979), 231–244.

KIERZKOWSKI, H., ed., *Monopolistic Competition and International Trade* (Oxford: Oxford University Press, 1984).

OHTA, H., "The Price Effects of Spatial Competition," *Review of Economic Studies*, 68 (April, 1981), 317–325.

PHLIPS, L., "Spatial Pricing and Competition," in *Studies Competition — Approximation of Legislation Series* (Brussels: Commission of the European Communities, 1976).

———, "Intertemporal Price Discrimination and Sticky Prices," *Quarterly Journal of Economics*, 94 (May, 1980), 525–542.

———, *The Economics of Price Discrimination* (Cambridge: Cambridge University Press, 1983).

TAKAYAMA, A., *Mathematical Economics* (Hinsdale: Dryden, 1974).

[29]

Economic Theories and Economic Policies

M.L. Greenhut

PREAMBLE

The present article, in its puristic simplicity, is merely designed to be practical, that is in so far as concerns the mid 1980s. It accepts as a datum the economic situation currently held in the United States. Also accepted is the fact that politicians have consistently misapplied ivory tower dreams (including Keynesian economics) and that this is our fundamental economic problem today, not ill conceived or irrelevant economics. What this article is designed to do is "to accept" the prevailing political culture and practices, and then to propose doing something better with the use of economic theory than is presently the case. This something better requires this article to set forth initially the economic theories that are prevalent today. In the process, it will be seen that deficits per se are in no way at all the fundamental economic problem in the nation today.

The Question

Consider an economy in a recession, such as 1981 and 1982. What prevailing macroeconomic theory and policy would best apply to that recession and recovery from it? Perhaps Keynesian economic policy would apply best to 1982 and 1983, and probably also to 1984. But Monetarism would be likely to best apply for 1985. This dichotomy of theoretical application, as well as, what is meant by Supply-Side economics and the limits which apply to each theory will be discussed.[1]

SOME COMPARISONS AND APPLICATIONS

Supply and Demand for Money, Prices and Output: Keynesians vs. Monetarists

Keynesians and Monetarists disagree as to how prices and output are affected by the supply of and the demand for money. The Keynesians believe that the

Review of Regional Economics and Business October 1984

money supply acts on the economy through its effect on interest rates, and that expansion of the money supply lowers interest rates and thereby induces business firms to borrow for the purpose of investing in new production capacity and expanded output. Monetarists, on the other hand, believe that the effect is more direct. In their view, an increase in the supply of money results in larger money balances than people wish to hold. The consequence of this extra money is simply that people (households and firms—all holders of money) will spend their surplus money, in the process increasing the demand for goods and services. The extra spending, as a result of the increased money supply, typically causes prices to inflate.

Each of the alternative effects described above does take place in the real world. The contrast between any two schools of economic thought generally lies in the stress they place on different variables. According to either the Keynesians or the Monetarists, the projected outcome of an increased money supply is an increased output of goods and services provided the increase in money supply occurs in the presence of under-utilized resources; however, even then, Monetarists would project price increases to the extent that the increase in the money supply was expected. If the increased money supply takes place under conditions of full employment of labor and capital or under supply-side limitations due to high taxes and substantial governmental interferences, inflation results under either theory, other things equal. What, then, is the real difference between them if the final effects of the theories are the same? Surprisingly, the answer is that a substantial difference arises in their policy proposals. [29]

POLICY DIFFERENCES

Keynesians believe that the level of investment is the unstable element causing economic fluctuations. The interest rate is treated as a major determinant of investment. Accordingly, they center attention on interest rate policy for stabilization, while also stressing fiscal policy—namely government spending and taxation. Monetarists see a more direct employment impact from the money supply, and hence regard the money supply rather than the interest rate as the main determinant of economic fluctuations. Therefore, the attention of the Federal Reserve System (henceforth the Fed) is focused on the money supply rather than on the interest rate.

The monetarist influence in the country was manifest on October 6, 1979 when the Fed decided to shift its policy target from a low interest rate to a restrained money supply. Such restrained money supply was predicted to slow the rate of inflation.

Monetarists advocate only a steady small increase in the money supply to match whatever increased output would result in the country from increased productivity. Therefore the government would not enter the economic area actively, just passively. It is the government which destabilizes the economy by interfering with the free market.[2] Keynesians, on the other hand, believe that private investment is the unstable factor in the economy, and that government must offset its volatility by manipulating the interest rate and by fiscal policy (e.g., government spending (G) greater than taxes (T)).

Monetarists advocate a government hands-off policy, even during a recession, contending that unemployment would be less in the long run if government would get out of the economic arena. Government's role should simply be to provide the right supply of money. Keynesians contend that government can intervene effectively in the economic arena, and in the process would limit the number of unemployed to an effective minimum.

THE MOST BASIC POINT OF DISAGREEMENT

Monetarists contend that fiscal policy (including type and total of government spending vis a vis type and total of tax receipts) is of little importance compared to monetary policy. For example, let the government pursue a deficit spending policy, but also let the Treasury Department obtain its funds by selling its bonds to individuals. The result of all this is that some people substitute treasury bonds for cash, which cash is returned to other members of the public as a consequence of the greater spending than tax receipts by the government. The total amount of cash held by the public (i.e., checkbook (demand) deposits) being the same means that no additional funds are available for acquiring the output of industry. According to many Monetarists, no expansion of the economy will follow from recession unless the supply of money itself was increased. The quantity of money (not fiscal policy) is the Monetarist's key to the cyclical ups and downs of the free enterprise system.

Keynesians object to the above scenario by contending that the incomes of many individuals have gone up because of the federal government's deficit.[3] The argument is that those who exchanged cash (and checkbook deposits) for treasury bonds have gained a preferred asset (the bonds); meanwhile, the recipients of their cash (checkbook deposits) have received an income for the new services or goods they have now provided to the government. Though the total amount of money in existence is the same as before, people feel wealthier, particularly those who gained an income. In fact, in the process of gaining that income, the nation's output (GNP) went up. Though the money total is the same, the initial recipients of the government spending will respend a substantial part of the total received; in the process, this also generates new income for others. But how can this take place if the money supply has not changed? Keynesians would answer that question by simply claiming that the turnover of money (its velocity) will have increased (as in effect occurs when greater credit is extended by merchants, credit card issuers, etc.).

Though Monetarists would concede some of the effects cited above by Keynesians, they would also assert in reply to it that sooner or later the total money supply (the currency and checkbook deposits in existence) must determine overall spending. This constraining total will bring the nation back to the level that its institutional-cultural base alone can provide. In still other words, if x dollars of money typically generate y dollars of output and a price level p, the sam x dollars will ultimately (say within a year or two or three) promote only y dollars of output at price level p. In contrast, Keynesians would assert that the existence of the deficit fiscal policy, the change in the asset holdings and incomes of people, signify per se a change in the economy's institutional-cultural base. Therefore a different output (say y') and perhaps a different price level (say p') will relate in time to the old money supply x.

From the Monetarists to the Supply Siders

Monetarists contend that there are inflationary tendencies intrinsic to our government's policies. By deficit spending the American public was mistakenly led to believe in the past that a new government spending program was costless. The taxpayer (who, of course, is not a professionally trained economist) only noticed that there was not a requirement to pay new taxes directly in order for the new spending program. Therefore the taxpayer did not challenge the lawmaker as he would if he were taxed directly as a result of a new government spending program. (Few taxpayers of the past realized that they were paying the cost of many new programs in

the form of higher consumer good prices. How many actually understood that inflation is fundamentally due to government economic policies?) Too many laws are quickly passed under deficit policies without weighing their pros and cons the way individuals do when spending their own money. The associated costs do not have [30]
to be explicitly considered, much less provided for in the legislation. Worse yet, by deficit spending (that is spending more than one receives as income), the government typically borrows from commercial banks and the Federal Reserve Banks so the money supply rises unduly!

Now, additional money at a time of full or near full employment signifies a relatively greater increase in money than increased output of final goods. This is simply inflationary. Moreover, the sale of additional quantities of government bonds raises the rate of interest. As already suggested earlier, private investment in new plant and equipment falls off as interest rates rise.[4] Indeed, as inflation progresses, illusory profits arise reflecting the under-depreciation of buildings and equipment and the valuation of inventory at low acquisition costs rather than much higher replacement costs. Uncertainty increases. As company officials become more and more uncertain about past and future policies, they tend to invest less than they would have done otherwise. The rate of increase in output declines, as in supply-side theory.

GOVERNMENT ATTEMPTS IN RECENT YEARS TO REDUCE UNEMPLOYMENT PROMOTED INFLATION

So when government spends more in order to reduce unemployment, inflation takes place. Consider also the following scenario: Suppose as in the recent past that government regulatory agencies—such as OSHA (Occupation, Safety, Health Administration), EPA (Environmental Protection Agency), CPSC (Consumer Product Safety Commission), CAB (Civil Aeronautics Board), and others—intensify their rules, and that new programs such as CETA (Comprehensive Employment Training Act) are proposed and set into effect by Congress. A result is increased paperwork and uncertainty. Interest rates go up because of deficit spending. People put more and more of their savings into precious gems, real estate development schemes, and the like. Thus the supply of loanable funds decreases, and interest rates continue the trend upwards. Business uncertainty continues to increase.

As inflation increases, illusory business profits are taxed, minimum wages go up as well as other business costs, prices rise again, and consumers go on non-buying "strikes." Investment falls. The process cumulates and becomes disastrous.

The Shifting Trade-Off Curve

Monetarists propose that not only are deficits inflationary, but increase unemployment notwithstanding the old idea that the nation can trade-off a little inflation in exchange for reduced unemployment. To appreciate this view, let us start with an inflation. Recall that there is an increasing tax-take on illusory accounting profits. This reduces business replacement of capital and investment in new technologies. Meanwhile, the consumer's loss to inflation continues to generate more and more uncertainty on his part. Any fears by labor and business of wage and price controls tend to induce a quick anticipatory upward push in wages and prices.

More and more women enter the work force to supplement their husband's decreasing real income. Monetarists point out that young people, some former housewives, and the less skilled workers who are hurt by Congress' raising of minimum wages beyond levels that firms would pay remain unemployed; in fact, more become unemployed. Suddenly it is clear that a large amount of government spending which, in the past, associated a 6 percent unemployment rate with less than 2 percent inflation, becomes associated with a 5 percent inflation rate, then say an 8 percent rate, then double digit rates. As more and more government spending takes place to reduce an unemployment rate considered to be too high, deficits increase, prices rise again, and unemployment continues its upward trend.

The steadily larger deficits of the late 70s increased inflation along with unemployment, a combined state called stagflation. Each increase in governmental activity was associated with increased unemployment compensation benefits. Worker disillusionment with personal income increased, so search time for new jobs also increased. The concept of full employment changed from one that accepted 3 percent of the workforce as unemployed to 4 percent to 5 percent to 6 percent. (Economists disagree today on what in fact is full employment in the United States.) At this point Monetarism merges with supply-side economics, but their basic analytical frameworks differ.

Supply-Side and Keynesian Economics

In our regard, supply-side economics is simply Keynesian economics from a different viewpoint. This so-called new economics places special emphasis on an income determinant—supply—that was fundamentally conceived of by Keynes as a dependent variable; it is not so regarded by Supply Siders. To understand the importance of this, it can be stressed that the economy viewed by Keynes was one which considered government as acceptable a demander of goods and services as are businesses and individuals. Supply-side fiscalists say that this is really not so! According to this view government spending leads to an increased bureaucracy, more regulations and controls over people, wasteful projects, greater taxes, ad nauseum. The effect is that as income (output) rises over the years because of increased government spending, the private sector tends to become less productive. The impact of this is that while nominal income may rise, say by $90 billion, because of a spending increase by government, real output (goods and services) may rise by only $75 billion in value, even though some labor and other resources remain unemployed. The $15 billion difference between dollar incomes received and real output produced, in other [31]
words, reflects a rise in money prices (inflation) alone.

The argument of the Supply Siders is as follows: As government increases its share of the economy, it raises taxes. Higher tax rates in turn dampen the stimulus of additional government expenditures. High marginal tax rates discourage work and investment, i.e., they dampen supply responses to increased public spending. Such a dampening output effect implies faster turnover of money and a progressive tendency toward inflation at higher and higher levels of unused resources, stagflation. The tendency as government grows is for it to divert resources from the private sector to less productive uses; this accentuates inflation at rising levels of unemployment.

The Basic Disagreement Between Supply-Side Economics and Keynesian Economics

What do higher marginal tax rates mean? They signify that any increase in money income will yield the household a smaller net amount than previously. If one's marginal tax rate is 40 percent, and the state of residence adds a 10 percent tax, the individual's net is at best $1 for an extra $2 earned. If the individual is a lower income earner, the income tax rates are less but a social security tax of, say, 6 percent applies to all of the individual's earned income. The overall effect is to lessen one's incentive to work harder.

In comparable manner, high tax rates induce individuals to seek tax havens. People invest differently than they may have preferred and spend more time in paperwork trying to cope with IRS requirements and to minimize the cost of IRS audits. Tax accountants and lawyers are hired. This promotes increased supplies of these people instead of encouraging them to work in other activities, which other work might provide true gratifications instead of the satisfaction one derives at trying to make sure Uncle does not knock on the door contending violations and demanding fiscal and other retributions.

High tax rates even induce individuals to seek other gratifications from work (e.g., a plushy office). This tends to subsidize business waste rather than economizing. Some people begin to do their own home repairs instead of working overtime for greater possible income and hiring someone else to do the home repairs. Simply put, the productivity of the work force tends to go downhill under the weight of high income taxes.

Possibly the most harmful impact of all according to supply-side economics lies in the discouraging effect of our nation's tax laws on risk-taking investment and saving. Japan does not tax capital gains and excludes from its income tax approximately the first $60,000 of interest earning deposits of the taxpayer—in effect taxing only the dividends received by people. The preponderant number of taxpayers in Japan thus pay a tax chiefly on currently earned income. This is one reason why the savings rate in Japan is so much greater than ours. Savings lead to risk-taking investments which, in turn, promote production of new capital goods and through them accelerating growth of output. In contrast, in the presence of high tax rates and inflation, one borrows money for consumption purposes, dissaving as it were.

Supply Siders further contend that because of the effects described above, the increases in output recently experienced in the United States have not been equivalent to the nominal income gains of people. Alternatively phrased, people in general are producing less for each extra dollar received compared to the way they did in the past. So inflation takes place even in periods of less than full employment. Moreover, the welfare state policies of the federal government, which find expression in the form of income support policies, including unemployment compensation, tend to encourage idleness. Along with food stamps, medicaid, and other programs (all of them meritorious to some extent), they induce many to postpone their return to active job searching while spending money faster. The upshot is the coexistence of inflation with substantial unemployment.[5]

WHY DID KEYNES IGNORE THE AGGREGATE DEMAND/AGGREGATE SUPPLY INDEPENDENCE?

It would be natural for the reader to wonder why Keynes assumed for periods of less-than-full employment that an increase in aggregate demand (AD) would generate a corresponding (perfectly matching) increase in the aggregate supply (AS) so that the price level would be basically unchanged? Why is it that now an increase in government spending (hence AD) under conditions of less-than-full employment generates inflation? Is the Keynesian theory simply wrong? The answer is probably already evident to you. Keynes was writing at a time when government represented a microscopic part of the economy; regulations were relatively few, income tax laws were comparatively simple, and marginal tax rates low. Given a catalyst, such as a substantial increase in government spending, Keynes anticipated that incentives to save and invest would be substantial, and private investment combined with "truly needed" government creation of goods and services would increase output (AS) in perfect correspondence to increasing demand (AD). For reasons already noted, the substantial growth in government paperwork, in income taxes, etc. has eroded the dependency of supply on demand.

The Basic Disagreement Between Supply-Side Economics and Monetarism

As is evident from the above, Supply Siders are essentially Keynesians. Hence, they regard the money supply as affecting the overall economy via the interest rate. In their conception, velocity changes as fiscal policy effects run through the economy. However, they conform to [32]
Monetarists in contradiction to Keynesians by recognizing that excessive use of fiscal policy will signify that deficits ultimately may not increase output at all, and that unemployment and inflation may occur together. This differs from Monetarism in that this stagflation need not involve a greater money supply. But note, the Monetarists ultimately join them since too much

government also typically means greater money quantities and hence inflation (with or without unemployment).

SUPPLY-SIDE ECONOMIC POLICY

Unlike the government spending demand-side Keynesians and the laissez faire (constant money supply increase) policy of the Monetarists, Supply Siders claim that a need exists to prop up business investment (Keynes' I function). The idea is stressed that a rise in total demand due to an increase in I will carry income at the (same) existing price level. Supply Siders would expect the Fed to be obliged simply to match the increased real output with a proportional expansion of money, ala the Monetarists.

Among measures to stimulate business investment, Supply Siders include: (1) a reduction in marginal tax rates, and (2) shifting the bias in the tax system away from consumption and borrowing towards saving and investment. The encouragement of IRAs, reduction in capital gains taxation, more liberal depreciation allowances are steps in that direction. Some Supply Siders recommend a shift in emphasis from the taxation of income to the taxation of consumption, via national sales and excise taxes, or a value-added tax. Tax deductions for interest payments on consumer borrowing remain a significant antisavings, proconsumption bias, which helps keep interest rates high. Another measure would be (3) to stop the inflation-creep of personal income tax brackets by indexation, which will be done starting in 1985.

Supply Siders, no less than Demand Siders, will differ on the details of the recommended policies but not on the priority of investment nor on the need to improve the responsiveness of supply. This view is that government regulation is too often obstructive rather than constructive; that it is excessive and unnecessarily costly in compliance; and that the share of natural resources diverted from the private sector to governments is too large to permit satisfactory growth in productivity or sustained high levels of unemployment.

Special Statement

Supply-side economics is based on the idea that demand does not necessarily elicit supply. Briefly put, it asserts that alternative types of demand will elicit differential outputs of goods and services. Thus a rise in AD may or may not be associated with an equivalent increase in real GNP even if it takes place at a time of unemployment. Supply Siders stress that the Keynesian model must be expanded to include variable supply responses to changes in demand. They agree with Monetarists that the money supply should be increased at a constant rate with increased output. All of the above reveals the intitial theme: which theory is correct, how bad are the current deficits?

WHICH THEORY IS CORRECT?

Probably each theory is correct—depending upon the prevailing point in history being discussed and the period of time over which the individual is concerned. Simple Keynesian demand-side theory may apply for a few years at any given point in time. Basic Monetarist economics may statistically (albeit statically) explain why the economy's condition in a given year is traceable directly to the money policy that began several years earlier. Advanced Supply-Side economics does not simply say the government tends to tax too much, but rather combines Keynesian economics with Monetarism, as proposed above: its system of thought accordingly represents a synthesis of the other two theories.

It follows from the above that the deficit fiscal policy of Keynesians, which prevailed over the most recent two decades (the 1960s and 1970s), led to stagflation in recent years, in much the pattern described by the Monetarists. The panecea is a decrease in deficits via decreased government spending. Certainly this is not the point in history to raise taxes, for—in accordance with the Keynesian framework—a tax increase would reduce savings by approximately the amount that the taxes are raised, which conclusion stems, in turn, from the contracting economy that basic Keynesian theory would contend must result. To repeat, this conclusion has been fully accepted. This leaves but one matter that has not been evaluated above, namely why are well-known economists, such as Mr. Feldstein wrong when they claim that interest rates in 1982, 83, ..., are too high, that such high rates will strangle the recovery, and hence that taxes must be raised? For answer to this question, consider the following:

Interest rates remained high throughout 1983 chiefly because investors were anticipating future inflation (via the great deficits taking place, and in conformance with predictions); moreover, an uncertainty premium applied. What higher taxes would bring—in the view of those who advocate such—would be less government borrowing and hopefully both a lower inflation expectation and lower uncertainty premium to be added to interest rates. The projected, overall lower rates of interest could encourage investment in offset to the contractionary effect of higher taxes. This is the expectation that those who seek higher taxes have in mind. In particular, it is feared that if federal government deficits continue, the Monetarist prediction of great inflation will result, and with it destructive effects on the economy. [33]

This study's view recognizes their argument, but stresses the fact that higher taxes generate supply-side problems which carry harmful (in fact worse) results to the economy. The only certain policy to follow in 1984 is for the public to require Congress to reduce government expenditures. Surely there exist wasteful expenditures and strictly lobby interest determined programs which real statesmen in Washington can eliminate. Surely the poor and the hungry need not (and would not) be victimized by eliminating wasteful expenditures. Surely pure Keynesians, pure Monetarists, pure Supply Siders and the ones who accept the synthesis proposed above must agree that the program of eliminating wasteful expenditures is the only immediate program that could be followed with certain improvement resulting in the economy at large. What, however, can be expected if the federal deficit continues to be high as 1985 approaches, as of course is likely to be the case? What is the impact of a substantial federal deficit during full employment?

The Facts of the Federal Deficit and Crowding Out

To answer the above, recognize that under conditions of excess demands for goods over a limited output, consumers will always win out over business firm intentions to invest in goods because inventories will be depleted; hence the net increase in investment by firms will be less than intended. The consumers' spending when excess demands exist crowds out private sector investments. In corresponding form, the government also wins out whenever it adds a demand for goods in excess of existing output. That is to say, the government will always obtain the output it seeks even in the presence of an excess demand for a limited output. This is accomplished because business inventories are reduced or less plant and equipment investment takes place than business firms intended; indeed, government may also attain its end partly as a consequence of less consumption than was planned. The government expenditure crowds out the private sector output.

To the extent the consumer loses out in the quest for goods because of the government demand, individual savings and loanable funds would immediately rise in partial offset to the deficit. To the more likely extent that government procures what businesses would have retained from the nation's output of that period (i.e. the inventories, plant and equipment firms intended and would otherwise have acquired out of the GNP produced in that period), there is one sector (the government) replacing another (the business sector) in the acquisition of the output produced in that period of time. It is particularly important to note that pursuant to national income accounting techniques (and the Keynesian theoretical counterpart), any difference (i.e. reduction) in actual business investment compared to planned business investment due to a government expenditure will not, in itself, change what is broadly referred to here as the business savings in the country. Rather total business savings are unchanged. These savings consist of business depreciation funds, the firms' net profit minus their dividend payments, and in addition the indirect and direct business taxes collected. All of these remain fundamentally the same given the total output produced by the firms at full employment. The essential difference, to repeat, of governments' excess demands is that firms hold smaller amounts of inventories and capital stock but more loanable funds than they would have otherwise. In sum, during the subject time period, the government acquires output in place of business firms and consumers. Most importantly, how the government spending is financed is non sequitur to the crowding out; the basic effect in every case is that government acquires some output that would have been obtained by firms and, to a probably small extent, some output that consumers would have acquired.

Deficit financing means that when other sectors are not forced by taxation to reduce acquisitions, a substantially greater total demand for goods and services will exist then otherwise, according to Keynesians. Moreover, if the financing of the deficit by the U.S. Treasury is obtained through bond acquisitions by the Federal Reserve Banks, a large increase in the supply of money results. (Note that checkbook deposits of individuals increase when the Treasury writes checks against the Federal Reserve Banks.) Thus when the Fed buys Treasury Bonds, the debt is monetized. Monetarists too would then propose directly rising price effects, and most Supply Siders who would accept the inflation result via the Keynesian framework will be joined by others who do so under monetarist inflation prescriptions. A deficit during full employment leads to inflation under each school of thought.

How bad then is the debt? But here let's think of either federal or private debt. Clearly it is not bad when future real incomes (i.e. outputs) are increased and hence available to pay off the debt. However, sooner or later any rise in debt at a time of full employment only pushes prices upwards ceteris paribus, and to the extent that the federal government debt is financed by Federal Reserve Bank creation of money, it is more inflationary than private debt. It follows that by 1985, 1986, if the economy is in (or close to) a state of full employment, renewed inflationary price increases can be expected, including in interests rate. With this, there will be greater business uncertainty and a repeat of 1978-1982, unless Congress reduces federal expenditures; alternatively, tax increases in 1985, 1986 can solve the budget deficit problem and reduce liquidity, but if excessive it would also provoke (possibly deeper) recession and low productivity, in effect as in 1980 and 1982.

Following the scenario set forth above, Supply Siders stress that taxes in place of the deficit would generally be a very poor solution to the deficit problem. It would be the worst possible solution during periods of less than full employment. To recall, the government will win out to some extent over consumers in the quest for [34]
current output; if it does this by taxing the consumer, savings do not go up as previously indicated; only taxes went up. Suppose government wins out over business investment and the public is also taxed. Actually weaker consumer demand must take place and a contraction may arise vis a vis that which would exist if the public were not taxed. Tax increases, in other words, must be fine-tuned, and then only at the point where a boom will otherwise ensue; at such time, large government spending either means inflation induced recession via deficits or recession via high taxes. The basic crowding out is the government expenditure. The danger of the deficits is chiefly at and near the full employment level, particularly when monetized by the Fed. The single, real solution for the deficit at points of full employment, when it is most dangerous, is to be in position to reduce unnecessary, wasteful government expenditures. Nothing less will be a sure winner for the public and the economy.

NOTES

[1]For present purposes, the rational expectations school of thought shall be included with that of the Monetarists.

[2]Monetarists further propose that when people correctly anticipate inflation, they adjust accordingly. The result is that money is ultimately neutral in effect as the underlying real economic forces finally prevail. It is the unanticipated government change in money supply, hence in private levels, that generate the booms and busts.

[3]Again, recognize that the deficit spending signifies greater cash (checkbook demand deposits) held by the net recipients of the government's expenditure-tax program, which amount of cash (checkbook demand deposits) was obtained from those members of the public who financed the deficit (i.e., bought the new bonds issued by the U.S. Treasury).

[4]Interest rates would rise even if the money supply is expanded in the vain hope of keeping them down. This is actually the result because inflation due to a relatively increased supply of money causes lenders to require higher interest returns; this follows because each dollar of interest at higher price levels (higher CPI) is of lower value than it used to be.

[5]For present purposes, let it suffice to say that Monetarists would generally agree with the arguments recorded above against Keynesian demand-side theory. Later on, further comparisons and contrasts between these three schools of thought will be provided.

M.L. Greenhut is an Alumni Distinguished Professor of Economics at Texas A&M University. *The author wishes to thank Charles Stewart and the editors of the University Press of America for permitting partial reuse of certain ideas included in my book with C. Stewart* **From Basic Economics to Supply Side Economics** *(Lanham, Maryland 1983). The author also wishes to thank Professors Gerald Dwyer and Jim Hibdon for their helpful critiques and suggestions.* [35]

AN ECONOMIC THEORY FOR USE IN ANTITRUST CASES

M. L. GREENHUT *

The complexity of antitrust cases is created by the fact that not only are legal questions involved, but economic ones as well. Often, the courts have struggled with such concepts as intent, percent of market control, and market structure in an attempt to resolve antitrust cases.

Dr. Greenhut argues that using such criteria ignores the fact that antitrust laws are essentially economic laws, and that they are best interpreted through economic theory alone. Using the basic setting of an unorganized oligopoly, he proposes that free market entry and exit should be a controlling factor in deciding antitrust cases. If free entry or exit is impaired, there should be an antitrust violation. Any market act or practice by a firm which would effectively limit the alternative sources in the market would be restraining. Thus, collusion between firms should be equally reprehensible as a restraint on entry.

I. INTRODUCTION

It has been a source of personal amazement how economists, steeped as they claim to be in a science of positivism, are able to advocate an "intent" or "market structure" test for resolving antitrust cases. For under the doctrine of positivism, the function of the scientist in economics is not to tell people what they should do, but to describe and explain the experiences of men and to evaluate the events of the time on the bases of selected criteria. As formulated in the area of "positive antitrust economics," one might well anticipate that the *market performance* of a firm would be the variable cited by economists as the proper basis for policy. Instead, American economists often claim that either the intent of the defendant or the market structure of the industry will best serve as the crucial factor of consideration.[1]

It is the thesis of this article that the adjudication of an asserted antitrust violation should not be based upon the intent of a corporate official. Rather, it is urged that statutes designed to accomplish economic effects can and should be evaluated with respect to their economic content. It follows, then, that violations

* Distinguished Professor of Economics, Texas A&M University. The author wishes to thank the editors of Appleton Century-Crofts for permitting him to use a few pages from chapter 15 of his new book, A THEORY OF THE FIRM IN ECONOMIC SPACE [hereinafter cited as GREENHUT 1970].

1. *See* Kahn, *Standards for Antitrust Policy*, 67 HARV. L. REV. 28 (1953). Professor Kahn does not endorse either the intent or market structure test. But he refers throughout his article to statements by jurists and economists which emphasize the one test or the other; on his own part, he appears to favor intent, especially in cases falling under Section 2 of the Sherman Act. "The inescapable conclusion is that, from a practical standpoint, the criterion of intent alone 'fills the bill' for a sensible antitrust policy in such cases." *Id.* at 52.

by firms of these statutes should be based upon *economic* effects.[2] This should hold true notwithstanding the fact that the same may be evaluated and applied against the backlight of noneconomic forces as well. The objective herein is to present a yardstick for lawyers to use in determining antitrust violations against the measuring rod of economic science alone. Moreover, the policy set (or yardstick) proposed herein should be readily understandable and applicable in the courts.

Not only should intent be irrelevant in cases involving an economic offense against the public, but also the market structure of an industry. That is, attempts to measure departures from atomistic (small firm) competition are poorly founded. Market structure tests speak in terms of *degrees* of monopoly or size. But measurements of the degree of monopoly, such as the one which compares the differential between the selling price and the variable costs of additional production (the comparison of price with marginal costs) are highly arbitrary. And similarly, the estimate of the degree of monopoly which is predicated on the proportion of the total sales in the industry made by the largest two, three, or four firms, as selected by the examining authority, is equally arbitrary. Measurements such as these reflect engineering and related differences between industries more than they relate to what is an acceptable or unacceptable concentration of economic activity.

Besides involving arbitrary measurements, it is significant that the market structure test actually places the expert in the position of determining right and wrong on the basis of the postulates which form a scientific model. In economic theory, ideal results are deduced from the assumption of an infinite number of microscopic size firms, for given specified additional conditions in the model of pure competition, such firms would produce efficiently and optimize consumer satisfaction in the process. But the proper yardstick for evaluating a claimed antitrust violation cannot relate to the postulations in an economic model any more than may the assumptions in a theory of the physical universe serve as the basis among physicists for their prescriptions of how best to conquer space. Assumptions as to the kind, size, and number of firms should be left as they are, simply as the basic beginning points in constructing a theory. Assumptions should not be confused with the consequents of a theory, and they cannot be applied as if they themselves provide the goal to be attained.

By the consequences of economic theory one gains the requisite material for defining and measuring the economically effective and ineffective, or the economic good or bad, in antitrust cases. One becomes completely unconcerned with intent, size of firms, number of firms, tilt of demand curves (average revenue), and the like. Only the results in the market should serve as the proper *economic* benchmark for evaluating the *economic* activity of a firm under an antitrust attack.

The attempt herein is to describe a theory which will provide a ready basis for recognizing whether the impact upon the economy of the firm's activity is or is not, and will or will not, be as favorable as possible, given the company practices under

2. It deserves mentioning, though it will be stressed in the text, that only the economics of statutes supposedly designed to effect selected economic ends are being considered. The ethical or social aspects of the laws to be referred to herein are not considered. It is assumed that Congress concerned itself with this when it enacted the various antitrust laws. For excerpts of various antitrust statutes, see Fig. 1, at 334, 335.

question. This theory will be presented in section II; how this theory may be applied will be illustrated in section III. But first, a caveat must be entered. This article is designed primarily for those who practice law. It must, accordingly, bypass matters at issue among economists. However, for those sophisticated in economic theory, it should be mentioned that the goal of profit maximization among firms, a long-accepted axiom among economists, is assumed. Further, a kinked average revenue curve is employed here to describe a competitive oligopoly, even though in other writings the author has used a fully continuous differentiable demand function. Finally, an oligopoly transform of the purely competitive model is employed, because it fits the world most readily seen by those outside of the economics profession and yields applications which oftentimes are easier to grasp and invoke than those viewed under the extremely abstract model of pure competition.[3]

For those economists who are fully acquainted with the details of the model to be sketched herein, but who believe the purely competitive model is far more reaching in its explanation of economic life in free enterprise systems, it should be realized that the results derived herein are identical to those of that model. The model presented herein centers on the question whether market entry is free, and if so, whether collusion or competition follows. Though it is cast on the basis of an oligopoly model, the guidelines derived are also central to the pure competition model that so long has been intrinsic to microeconomic science. What the transformed model does is to help avoid the inductive leap one must take from the abstractions of pure competition to the surrounding world. Indeed, it is this inductive leap which causes so many to fall back on intent or market structure tests rather than use the guidelines advocated herein.

II. The Proposed Theory

Consider a space economy[4] in which people and resources are discontinuously scattered, in which plant size[5] indivisibilities prevail, in which collusion between firms is not permitted, but in which there are risks and uncertainties attributable to such forces as consumer capriciousness, changing technology, and competitive business policies. In this economy, firms are able to identify their rivals. A competition develops between them whereby only a few sellers compete for a given market, even though there may be many sellers in the industry scattered throughout the nation. This market type is, therefore, one wherein sellers are tied to other sellers as if by a chain.[6] The result is an oligopoly[7] rather than what is called pure competition.[8] It is an oligopoly market because each firm or plant

3. For the professional economist who is unfamiliar with the transform used here, *i.e.*, the normative oligopoly model, see the Technical Appendix.

4. *I.e.*, an economic landscape.

5. This includes research, machines, financial strength, etc.

6. *See* E. CHAMBERLIN, THE THEORY OF MONOPOLISTIC COMPETITION (5th ed. 1946).

7. Oligopoly is a market in which sellers set their prices after considering the probable policy reaction of rivals.

8. Pure competition is an economic state whereby each firm is so small and unimportant that it has no noticeable impact on the policies of the other firms.

operating over an economic landscape and selling to a given market tends to be comparatively large and important, not atomistic as in classical, or pure competition, economics.

The theory of pure competition is predicated upon different assumptions than is oligopoly theory. This is apparent when one considers the *spatial* dispersion of, and limited access between, sellers and buyers, which may be postulated only in a theory of oligopoly. In contrast, basic to the pure competition model are selling units which are atomistic relative to existing demands, and buyer location at a point. Moreover, perfect knowledge, fully flexible prices, and ready access between sellers and buyers are typically postulated in that model. In oligopoly, each seller is accepted to be relatively significant in size. Also, the typical oligopoly model assumes the existence of imperfections in knowledge, price movements, and access between traders.

However, despite the differences in assumptions, the consequences of the theories have certain basic similarities. In either theory, a purely monopolistic or organized control of prices yields arbitrary prices compared to the results that would stem from active competition in price. In each market type a more efficient resource allocation results from free market entry and free market exit. And while the image of the firm in pure competition is less realistic than the image in a space oligopoly theory, even the oligopoly conception of the firm is a construct remotely removed from any real world enterprise.

The striking similarity between pure competition and a normative oligopoly theory is most readily evidenced by depicting the impact of new industry on the space oligopoly market. Through this entry the economy achieves a close approximation to real efficiency. And when the results are observed, one can readily see how the space oligopoly market conception establishes a ready basis for an economic policy that should be applied in the courts for statutes of economic design.

The process evolves as follows. Consider first a new product, a given market area somewhere in an economic space, and an original seller. Then assume a new competitor or two. Accept a kinked average revenue curve as a rough reflection of the type of price competition that is engaged in by these firms.[9] Then observe that as new market areas develop and new firms with new plants begin to dot the economic landscape, the kinked average revenue (or demand) curve visualized by the original duopolists or by the few original oligopolists shifts to the left for each seller.[10] If the firms in the industry are quite alike except for the locations of their plants, each seller will recognize substantially the same average revenue (or demand) function. The picture of *any one* firm is, therefore, generally represented in either Figures 3, 4, 5, or 6.

Suppose now that new firms enter a market characterizable as an open entry cartel. In other words, a trade association or some stronger institution exists under which selected practices of firms are influenced or controlled. As a result of the

9. See Fig. 2, at 335.
10. See Fig. 3, at 336.

new entries, the cartel directors would visualize a leftward shifting of the average revenue function along the horizontal axis for each of the original firms.[11] In contrast, if the oligopoly market is unorganized, or no cartel structure exists, each of the original sellers would conceive of a leftward *and downward* shift of the curve along both axes as new firms enter.[12] The effect of open entry on an organized oligopoly market is, in the broad sense, to cause prices to be maintained, while the tendency under unorganized oligopoly is for price to fall.[13]

New *unorganized* oligopolistic rivals have the effect of causing a general shrinkage in the magnitude of the demand curve conceived by a given seller.[14] If both the few old and the new unorganized rivals increase the total supply, all firms soon find that their sales are rather inadequate. Accordingly, a reduction in price *tends* to occur throughout the market.[15] Industrial homogeneity thus increases with new entry; for the differentiations between firms, which exist because of location and other matters, decrease as increases occur in the number of alternatives open to the consumer.

New entry in unorganized oligopoly raises the demand elasticities over the lower portions of the oligopolist's demand curve. That is to say, the expected relative responsiveness of the consumer to a change in the price of a good increases with entry. This result is traceable to the fact that the greater the number of rivals, the relatively smaller must be the reaction by other firms to the price change of a given seller; for manifestly, the price cutter must be less important than he was before the entry occurred.[16] It may even be suggested that a small range of price freedom arises for any seller when given sufficient entry of firms over the landscape. Sufficient entry has the effect of converting the original kinked demand curve into a three section curve.[17]

In Figure 6 there is a highly elastic portion[18] of the average revenue curve above the price P_1. This so-called highly elastic portion of the curve is represented by the top section of the curve. Over this range of prices, the contact, service, name, and product advantages which a concern may have over other concerns, insofar as certain buyers are concerned, are rather slight. The concern therefore obtains smaller sales at higher selling prices, provided rivals' prices are left unchanged and hence relatively low. In other words, if the firm depicted in Figure 6 prices at values greater than P_1, it experiences drastically reduced sales when rival firms fail to increase their prices in conformance to the high price of the subject firm. In the absence of *organized* oligopoly,[19] unchanged prices by other, rather

11. See Fig. 4, at 336.
12. See Fig. 5, at 337.
13. Compare sales at P′ on D′d′ in Fig. 5 with sales at P′ on DD′ in Fig. 4.
14. It is important to recall that new unorganized oligopolistic rivals may not revise prices upward with increases in price by a given seller, but would tend to lower prices in reaction to reduction in the price of another.
15. *E.g.*, from P′ or P″ on Dd to P^2 on D′d in Fig. 5.
16. Again, compare Fig. 4 with Fig. 5; where only the horizontal extent of the curve is lessened in Fig. 4; both the vertical and horizontal extent of the curve are lessened in Fig. 5.
17. See Fig. 6, at 337.
18. By highly elastic it is meant a relatively great quantity response to a change in price.
19. Organized oligopoly includes price leadership, cartel organization, and some trade association situations.

than price increases following price increases by others, may often be expected.

The third or lowest section of the curve is the inelastic portion. It includes the portion of the curve lying below price P_2. The setting of prices along this part of the average revenue function provokes sharp reaction from some rivals, and hence leads to only small increases in the sales of the firm under focus.

Between the upper and lower portions of the curve, which are identical in nature to the kinked Dd curves of Figures 3 and 5, there is a moderately sloping portion. This part of the demand curve falls between P_1 and P_2 and resembles the average revenue function that economists typically draw to illustrate the monopolist's (or the monopolistic competitor's) conception of the demand for his product. Over this range of the average revenue curve, the oligopolist stands alone. Any adjustment he makes in his price does not compel reaction among rivals. Any downward revisions do not occasion price wars, nor do upward changes price him noticeably out of phase with others in the market. In effect, his price changes have a more or less insignificant impact over this second portion of the curve, for over these values *his buyers* stay with him, while those buyers who prefer the products of his rivals remain largely uninfluenced by him. It might even be suggested that the firm has lost its identity over this range of prices, becoming in a sense "infinitesimal" in much the same way as the monopolistic competitor of Chamberlinean theory, or "alone" like the monopolist of classical theory. It will be observed, therefore, that over the highly elastic (first) or inelastic (third) portions of the curve, a different effect exists than over section two. The seller either prices himself largely out of the market[20] or intrudes on his rivals so as to cause them to react against him with price reductions of their own.[21]

Final results may be observed. First, the differentiations due to space, name, and possibly service and product diminish in character and importance as new firms enter the market. That is to say, the overall increase in the number of sellers throughout the market causes the demand curve that is viewed by a given seller to become more and more continuous and *generally flatter* in shape. With still larger numbers of firms located at all points in the market and over all areas, it becomes increasingly difficult for buyers to distinguish between each seller, and thus the three section curve of Figure 6 takes on the appearance of the second portion of the curve. If it were not for the limits placed on numbers by indivisibilities and uncertainties, the market would be converted into a many seller market in which each firm would become so infinitesimal and so much like its rivals, that downward changes in price would stimulate large increases in sales. This would eventuate since the sales of a new firm would not involve noticeable impact on the sales of the others in the industry. In time, the size of each firm would approach that of the atomistic, and the service, product, and spatial distinctions which would remain when many alternative sellers existed would be extremely slight. If entry is carried far enough, differentiations between firms must ultimately disappear; for there

20. This occurs when he raises his price somewhere over the first portion of the curve.
21. This occurs when he reduces his price somewhere into the third portion of the curve.

would be as many firms at one point in economic space (and throughout the landscape) as that visualized in the classic theory of pure competition.

It is important to note that indivisibilities and uncertainties underscore the capitalistic, free enterprise system. These two forces place natural limits on entry. Among these indivisibilities are mountain barriers, the nonubiquitous nature of water systems, the conditions of large concentrations of population, of sandy-desert areas, of limited numbers of grade A, B, and C sites, of limits to police and fire protection, and the control of municipalities. Technological indivisibilities in the form of plant and equipment, advertising, research, and organization control also exist. These indivisibilities combine to restrict entry. Moreover, they arouse uncertainties. And the uncertainties which develop become magnified by the intense competition that stems from the condition of readily identifiable rivals in the market.

The existing indivisibilities and uncertainties reach forward and backward, prompting price wars and price truces, advertising truces, branch plant competition, research competition, ad infinitum. Technological efficiency by the original members of an industry and by selected later entrants results from, and in turn promotes, new research and new product lines. This generates emphasis on the production and sales side of business activity, and creates in the process a noticeable gain through multiple products and related product mix.

All of these conditions are magnified over time. The brand new enterprises of later years tend to be replacements, not additions. The number of firms is limited, and the so-called Chamberlinean tangency solution (where economic profits disappear) is revealed to be inconsistent with the forces of indivisibility and uncertainty. The market adjusts itself to a return called *profits,* and this return becomes a part of the *natural limitations* on entry that prevail in the forms of indivisibility and uncertainty.

It is a basic premise in pure competition economics that the entry of efficient firms and the exit of inefficient firms leads ultimately to a market pattern in which technological efficiency is gained. Likewise, a substantially similar efficiency results in a space oligopoly model when entry and exit are maintained in the economy. For present purposes, it should be sufficient to accept as obvious the idea that if the entry of new firms is encouraged, these new enterprises may replace *some* of the old firms, while all surviving units will tend to rationalize their plants and company size toward the ideal optimum size. This rationalization toward optimum size occurs under unorganized oligopoly. It does not occur under organized oligopoly, since under this monopoly form pressures to minimize cost do not prevail.[22]

It is also a basic result from pure competition economics that not only should technological efficiency result, but resources should be allocated in perfect

---

22. For further explanation on the rationalization toward optimum size, *see* the Technical Appendix and note 23, *infra.*

compliance with consumer demands.[23] The similarity in result of the allocation of resources in accordance with consumer wants is traceable in a space oligopoly economy to the tendency for a hierarchical set of profit rates to arise for plants and firms from market area to market area. This set of profits, one may readily see, is based on the prevailing hierarchical pattern of indivisibilities and uncertainties in an unorganized oligopolistic economy. That is, a natural order of returns and resource allocation must prevail in an unorganized oligopolistic economy, just as it must in the unorganized, purely competitive economy of classical theory.

To conclude the theory portion of this article, the well-known theorem that monopoly leads to higher prices and to a poor allocation of resources should be recalled. Indeed, this claim may be established readily by recalling the previous statements about organized oligopoly. Viewing price P' along DD and DD' in Figure 4, and comparing it with price P'' and then P^2 on Dd and Dd' in Figure 5, one finds that whether it is a pure monopoly or an organized oligopoly, the price result tends immediately to be quite different than that of unorganized oligopoly. Manifestly, prices and profits remain above the levels set naturally by the forces of indivisibility and uncertainty when the oligopoly is organized.

In the extremely rare case of a pure monopoly, or the case where the public desires a pure monopoly to avoid cluttering up a landscape, regulation by a public body is needed. More germaine to the focus here, though, is the question of spatial oligopoly. One may then readily ask: (1) What is the basic antitrust policy standard to which the discussed economic theory points, and (2) how may it be applied? These two queries will be answered throughout the entire section that follows, though at this point the basic standard to which the theory of spatial (unorganized) oligopolistic competition points will be proposed: *the economy must guard against collusion (organized oligopoly) while favoring the free entry of firms throughout the market.*

III. The Standard and Some Illustrative Applications

Effective economic regulation of business has certain basic referential points. They are as follows: Encourage free entry, tolerate natural restraints, permit institutional restraints only where clearly necessary to arouse other desirable actions, and attack with force all other restrictions on competition of institutional origin. Against this screen, specific fact situations may be measured. Wherever the

23. For further explanation on the efficient allocation of resources according to consumer demands, see the Technical Appendix. For a detailed analysis and proof of the similarity in resource allocation according to consumer demands between oligopoly and pure competition, see M. Greenhut, Microeconomics and the Space Economy 193-221 (1963). For a good view of the fundamental properties of the normative oligopoly model, see Gurzynsky, *A Theory of Spatial Realities*, 34 South African J. Econ. 68-81 (1966). Note that the similarity in results referred to relate to purely theoretical findings. That many empirical studies suggest only an imperceptible loss exists because of the allocative inefficiency of monopoly is another matter of no concern, though to some extent it supports the claim that deviations from pure competition are not undesirable *per se*.

acts of an enterprise artificially limit the development of alternative sources of supply, the acts are those of monopolizing, and are accordingly bad. This highly elementary standard for social policy arises clearly from the proposed theory, and the following discussion will show that (1) no other standards are necessary, and (2) vital cases can be measured consistently on this basis. Select portions of the various antitrust acts will be examined, and they are set out in a separate chart for ease of comparison. Cases decided under these acts will be discussed in relation to the proposed theory.[24]

A. *The Sherman Antitrust Act – Section 2*[25]

One can select the *United States Steel Company* case of 1920,[26] the *Alcoa* case of 1945,[27] the *Columbia Steel* case of 1948,[28] the *United Shoe Machinery* case of 1953,[29] and the *DuPont* cellophane case of 1953[30] to serve as the basis for examining the meaning of Section 2 of the Sherman Act. This section holds that monopoly or the act of monopolizing is illegal. Under it, the courts have faced the question whether size itself is an offense. Lengthy discourses have inquired into the intent of the large size firm, the extent to which it dominated the industry, the meaning of the term industry, the ascertainment of commodities competing with the subject company's product, and the appraisal of all practices pursued by the firm over the years in question. What a task for a team of lawyers, especially since economists could not, and cannot, answer many of the questions about industry and products asked by the courts.

Under the proposed theory, it would not be the degree of market control, the definition of a product or an industry, the question of intent, or related matters that would govern, but the issue of practices. And by practices it is not meant

---

24. Economists and other readers outside of the legal profession who require somewhat greater recall of the cases described in the following footnotes may well fulfill their objective by selective readings in C. WILCOX, PUBLIC POLICY TOWARD BUSINESS 67-198 (1955).

25. See Fig. 1, I, at 333.

26. United States v. United States Steel Corp., 251 U.S. 417 (1920). Bad practices, such as dinners in which prices and related matters were discussed, were discontinued before the action was brought. The issue was thus whether size alone violated Section 2 of the Sherman Act. The Court held it did not. *Id.* at 444-46.

27. United States v. Aluminum Co. of America, 148 F.2d 416 (2d Cir. 1945). There were no bad practices worthy of note, but the company expanded to meet each new opportunity. It was held that such expansion, though natural and proper on the part of the directors, was bad because the company was so large. Vital to this decision was the measurement of market control by the firm. *Id.* at 430-31.

28. United States vs. Columbia Steel Co., 334 U.S. 495 (1948). Existing capacity in the West Coast areas was purchased by a subsidiary of United States Steel. This enabled the company to have a fair part of the West Coast market, as it did elsewhere in the country. The Court held that approximately 25 percent control of the market was reasonable, and expansion to this size was legitimate. *Id.* at 527-29.

29. United States vs. United Shoe Machinery Corp., 110 F. Supp. 295 (D. Mass. 1953). Practices in leasing equipment favored those who used United Shoe Machinery rather than rivals. The court held that practices which could be pursued by small firms without being condemned were bad when done by large firms. *Id.* at 343-45.

30. United States v. E. I. du Pont de Nemours & Co., 118 F. Supp. 41 (D. Del. 1953). DuPont produced approximately 80 percent of the total output of cellophane in the country. The Sylvania Company produced the rest. Cellophane was found to be used largely in food packaging and constituted as much as 46 percent of the transparent films used to package fresh produce. The court held that cellophane therefore competed with many other products. *Id.* at 197-206.

simply predatory acts and side-room bargains; rather, it is meant practices which restrain entry and which are otherwise not approved.[31]

It becomes irrelevant that, before a suit was instituted, United States Steel discontinued its pools and trade meetings, that Columbia Steel would control less than 50 percent of West Coast capacity, and that cellophane is in competition with other flexible wrapping materials. Relevant would be whether entry is restrained through man-made institutions without any clear offsetting advantage. The standards of Learned Hand in the *Alcoa* case come close to those that are integral parts of economic theory, but only close.[32] An industrial giant must have the right to enter new markets, even to anticipate new markets, for otherwise the giant loses its incentive to innovate and progress. By compulsory licensing and other arrangements, entry may be kept open. Of course, if the industry proves to be such that a firm reaps substantial economies of size, which when compared to the magnitude of demand permits only its continued existence, the natural monopoly market prevails and a special kind of regulation is accordingly in order. In the general instance, however, demand is not so limited relative to economies of size, and other firms therefore can be induced to enter by required patent licensing, imparting technical know-how, and the like.

For example, under the proposed theory, giant firms would be limited in their actions only by not having the right to buy up existing capacity *if* this limits significant entry by others *(Columbia Steel)*, or to use the technique of leasing with the effect of inhibiting entry into particular markets *(United Shoe)*, or to engage in cross-licensing agreements which are not open to other enterprises on proportionately equivalent terms *(DuPont* and *Sylvania)*. And by industrial giant it is meant not only the national concern, but any enterprise which by its practices effectively limits the number of alternative sources available to buyers in its market area. A rule of reason may be viewed;[33] however, what is reasonable under this

31. A more complicated search into such things as harmful effects is not fundamentally necessary to the free entry standard. Under the proposed standard it suffices simply to demonstrate that entry is restrained without *clear* offsetting advantages to the public, such as society claims for patents and patent pools. However, on harmful effects, see Oppenheim, *Federal Antitrust Legislation: Guideposts to a Revised National Antitrust Policy*, 50 MICH. L. REV. 1139 (1952).

32. *See* note 27, *supra*. Mere size, without practices which forcefully restrain, does not violate the proposed standards. *But see* Rostow, *The New Sherman Act: A Positive Instrument of Progress*, 14 U. CHI. L. REV. 567 (1947) for a full preference for the *Alcoa* view via the theory of pure competition.

33. Notice that a rule of reason stipulation is a natural part of the proposed standard, though in a slightly different way. Under the standard, one would inquire into the reasonableness of the defendant's acts only insofar as the gains by society (e.g., lower costs, innovations as under patent policy and patent laws) unmistakably outweight the restraints on entry that are embodied in the practice. What is reasonable about the practices must be judged in the light of society's view of the restraint. For example, though the restraint on free entry may be reasonable insofar as the competitive firms are concerned, it must be reasonable from the standpoint of providing clear benefits to society; and this will typically mean reasonable from the standpoint that entry into the market remains possible and likely. The proposed standards limit the possible range of the rule of reason.

See Wilcox, *The Verdict on Antitrust and Its Significance*, 46 AM. ECON. REV. 490-95 (1956). He notes that the Business Advisory Council (in its report on effective competition, submitted to the Secretary of Commerce late in 1952) favored an extension of the rule of reason approach whereas the report of Attorney General's National Committee did not urge any extension of the rule of reason. Under existing interpretation, the controversy is widespread; under the proposed theory, the controversy is unnecessary.

standard would be judged in the light of whether or not entry into the market remained possible and likely, or could be made possible and likely.

B. *The Sherman Antitrust Act – Section 1* [34]

Collusion between firms, such as price leadership,[35] price fixing,[36] trade associations which designate what members are to do,[37] rebates,[38] and intended parallelism of action[39] would be illegal per se; for Section 1 of the Sherman Act asserts that contracts, combinations or conspiracies in restraint of trade are illegal. In turn, artificial price hikes and monopolistic restraints would also violate the proposed standard. These restraints would have the effect of cartelizing an industry, so that even if open entry existed, society would not gain; only a horizontal movement of the average revenue curve would result from new entry, and not a change in ordinate values as well.[40] Conscious parallelism of action in the form of a systematically followed price practice over space would similarly be condemned. Manifestly, in a space economy, what is competitive oligopolistic pricing compared to organized oligopoly pricing is more easily determined than in a world of zero freight costs.

C. *The Clayton Antitrust Act – Sections 7 and 8*[41]

Sections 7 and 8 of the Clayton Act forbid intercorporate stockholding and interlocking directorates where the effect is to substantially lessen competition or to violate some other antitrust provision. When these sections have been scrutinized, the courts have considered problems in the context of the extent of market control possessed by a firm. But whether the market for Duco should include or exclude nonautomotive uses, or whether 23 percent ownership of another company is sufficient to establish dominance, and hence lessen competition,[42] should not be controlling. The proposed standard is concerned simply with the question whether market entry is still sufficiently open after the occurrence of the practice in question. If market entry is open, and collusion between firms on the same level is not permitted, then the market practice of the firm in question should not be halted.

---

34. See Fig. 1, II, at 333.
35. See American Tobacco Co. v. United States, 328 U.S. 781 (1946).
36. *See* United States v. Socony-Vacuum Oil Co., 310 U.S. 150 (1940); United States v. Trenton Potteries, 273 U.S. 392 (1927).
37. *See* United States v. Sugar Institute, 15 F. Supp. 817 (S.D.N.Y. 1934), *modified,* 297 U.S. 553 (1936).
38. Standard Oil Co. of N.J. v. United States, 221 U.S. 1 (1911).
39. Interstate Circuit v. United States, 306 U.S. 208 (1939).
40. See Figs. 4, 5, at 336, 337.
41. See Fig. 1, III, at 333.
42. United States v. E. I. du Pont de Nemours & Co., 353 U.S. 586 (1957). DuPont interests held 23 percent of the voting stock of General Motors. Only in the sales of Duco lacquers was there a clear chance that the influence of stock ownership might have governed General Motor's buying policy. The Court held that 23 percent ownership, against the background of overwhelming sales of Duco lacquers to General Motors, involved a substantial lessening of competition within the meaning of Section 7 of the Clayton Act. *Id.* at 595-96.

D. *The Celler Act*[43]

The Celler Act extends the provision of Section 7 of the Clayton Act to cover not only the acquisition of stock, but the use of stock to effect a merger. Therefore, it is felt that the act may be evaluated and applied in a manner similar to that proposed for Sections 7 and 8 of the Clayton Act. Thus, the purchase by one company of the assets of another should be objectionable whenever the existence of one firm in the place of two has the effect of restraining new entry in the market area in question.[44] Indeed, the act of purchasing existing facilities should be treated more harshly than other expansions. Thus, cost advantages gained from the merger should not outweigh the development of restraints against entry. The large firm that desires to expand further should be so permitted, but oftentimes not through the means of acquiring existing facilities.[45] The avenues open to new entrants should be kept as free as possible.

E. *Trade Marks and Trade Names – A New Act to Replace the Lanham Act*[46]

New entry tends to lead to efficient economic enterprise in place of inefficient plants and firms. But new enterprises are often confronted by an awesome array of existing marks and names.[47] This barrier is so formidable that oligopolistic markets tend to be more open to existing enterprises that are willing to expand to new product lines, than to completely new establishments. Limitations of this kind are not desirable. New firms must be encouraged to enter and to compete if a free enterprise economy is to prove efficient. One way of accomplishing this is to permit prospective rivals to copy rather closely the existing marks and names of established firms, provided that sufficient safeguards are established to protect the original firms from an encroachment on their reputation through the production of inferior goods.[48] By permitting close copy of marks and names, a change in the standards of advertising would arise. Formulas and expressions coined by advertising agencies would not tend to be as effective as in the past. Close copy of mark and name would require convincing consumers that their ability to distinguish between one brand and another is of vital advantage. And this conviction would involve informative advertising, not so-called persuasive advertising. The result would be easier entry into markets proffessing sufficient products.

F. *The Miller-Tydings*[49] *and Robinson-Patman Acts*[50]

Without going extensively into the Miller-Tydings and Robinson-Patman Acts,

43. See Fig. 1, IV, at 333.

44. See *In re* Pillsbury Mills, 50 F.T.C. 555 (1953). It might be noted that the ban on mergers is again becoming a major legal issue. *See* Newsweek, Nov. 3, 1969, at 78. This antimerger policy is readily evident against industries subject to some restrictions in their competition. *See* Dewey, *Mergers and Contents: Some Reservations about Policy*, 51 AM. ECON. REV. 255-62 (1961).

45. This was permitted in United States v. Columbia Steel Co., 334 U.S. 495 (1948). *See* note 28, *supra*.

46. See Fig. 1, V, at 334.

47. *See* Greenhut, *Free Entry and the Trade Mark-Trade Name Protection*, 24 S. ECON. J. 170-81 (1957).

48. *Id.*

49. See Fig. 1, VI, at 334.

50. See Fig. 1, VII, at 334.

it should be sufficient to note that traditional objections to the fair-trade Miller-Tydings Act would stand. With respect to Robinson-Patman, the proposed "more realistic" normative theory would regard the larger enterprise in a somewhat more kindly way than is the approach under present law. Specifically, injury to competition rather than injury to a competitor is clearly the desired standard. The concern is not with each individual firm, but with the overall system: the proposed space oligopoly theory does not extol the virtues of the small firm per se. Thus, the FTC power to limit quantity discounts should be eliminated. However, the making of symmetrical rules governing brokerage and other services, and the conception of ways to estimate manufacturing cost differentials would still be desirable. However, this last matter is not connected in any close way to the thesis of this article, and it must be reemphasized that atomistic competition, in itself, is not an end supported by the proposed theory.

G. *Patents and Vertical Integration under the Proposed Antitrust Standard*

Under the free entry (no collusion) norm, such antitrust problems as patent licensing and vertical integration fall readily in place. After a certain number of years, there should be compulsory licensing of new firms, though it is recognized that this is an area where social choice may prefer institutional restraints on entry in the belief that the innovations gained through such a policy would offset the limits to entry that would arise. But from the economic standpoint, licenses tendered to one firm should be tendered to both existing and future firms, though this practice itself points to the need for a further requirement. Proportionately equivalent terms, if restrictive as to price, output, and sales radius (market area), would have the effect of organizing the oligopoly. Therefore, restrictions under patents should be limited. It is suggested that the *Line Materials* case[51] comes closer to this idea than does the *General Electric* case of 1926.[52]

As firms build up and down in a vertically integrated form, the entry and competition of others tends to be restrained. Such considerations as total size, national dominance, 40, 62, or 83 percent market control, intent, and related matters should not be controlling. Rather, it should be impact on entry in the *affected market area* alone that must be controlling. This means that if the second stage is monopolized, entry will be restrained in the first stage.[53] But if the second stage offers alternative sources of demand, alternative sources of supply should therefore be possible.[54]

---

51. United States vs. Line Material Co., 333 U.S. 287 (1948). A price fixing arrangement between "cross-licensees" was held bad. *Id.* at 314-15.

52. United States v. General Electric Co., 272 U.S. 476 (1926). The Court held a patentee can fix prices to be charged by a licensee. *Id.* at 488.

53. See United States v. Yellow Cab, 332 U.S. 218 (1947). Clearly, if the buyer of a product is a monopolist, and this buying company is owned by a manufacturer, the manufacturer in question excludes other producers from the sales area in question. But note the precise analysis of this case by G. Stocking & M. Watkins, Monopoly and Free Enterprise 296-99 (1951), where it is pointed out that if the local monopoly itself is regulated, then the local authorities should not permit any abuse by the vertical integration.

One may generalize as follows: If from one community to another there exist different users of the output of the earlier stages, such as that in the trading area normally required for the erection of the earlier stage plant there are alternative buyers independent of the vertically integrated unit, entry per se will not have been restrained in violation of the law.

54. See generalization in note 53, *supra*.

IV. Conclusions

Any single standard for decision making cannot be applicable without reference to all possible fact situations that may arise. It is sufficient to note that the stresses and strains of a time period may be such as to require a modified use of a standard. Moral standards, ethics, customs, and social values of people change. The courts, in interpreting these impressions, may modify a standard so severely that it looks quite different from its original form.[55] Thus, it is recognized that even if business structures and policies are evaluated uniformly under the policy of keeping entry "as open as is possible under the existing forces of indivisibility and uncertainty," contrasting applications may nevertheless be obtained because yardsticks tend to be used in different frames of reference.

Economists, lawyers, and judges merely flirt with applications that are both logical and unvarying. Particularly in the social sciences are decisions likely to be far from impeccable under almost any criteria for judgment. It is in light of these conditions, or at least in the light of this writer's belief that such conditions exist, that the proposed theory is urged. It is not claimed that all fact situations are readily and simply adjudicatory on the designated basis. It is suggested only that all situations can be, and should be, judged in as simple and yet far reaching a context as possible. It is thus asserted that the free entry-no collusion requirement meets this test.[56]

As a result of the foregoing analyses, one comes to the following conclusions. Under pure competition theory, one would tend to extol the small firm and hence create such acts as Robinson-Patman. Moreover, injury to any competitor as well as to competition would be considered a bad practice. Correspondingly, protection would extend to all small firms by limits on lawful price differentials.

A strict application of pure competition economics to the antitrust field is disturbing when what appears to be the theory's preference for small firms is applied under the Sherman Act, and then related to the 20th century American business scene. Especially is this true if the person who applies the law happens to be a lawyer or judge. How small is small? Does the economist really want atomistic units? Clearly, the difficulties involved in applying the deductions of abstract economic theory are manifold, and this condition has led to varying and different standards from case to case, and judge to judge.

Thus one finds that size by itself has been held to be inoffensive. But on the other hand, one finds that such a view contradicts the assumptions of pure competition, so that a person steeped in this philosophic background may object to size alone. One court may inquire into intent, so that if a company is large, its

55. See Appalachian Coals v. United States, 288 U.S. 344 (1933). Though price fixing between firms has been customarily condemned, this policy was discarded during the depression years and in this case.

56. The standard does not require legitimate inference drawn only by economists, as was proposed by Mason several years ago. *See* Mason, *Market Power and Business Conduct: Some Comments*, 46 Am. Econ. Rev. 471-84 (1956). The lawyer and judge are equally qualified to apply the proposed standard, while alternatively "some kind of an expert" is needed to determine whether 70 percent control of a market is monopolistic or whether cellophane is part of a broader product.

practices combined with bad intent will constitute a violation of the Sherman Act. But, unfortunately, another court might find something reasonable in the intent despite the fact that the size of the firm is large. This court might reason that the economist does not really believe in nor want an economy of atomistically sized enterprises. What the economist believes, the court might feel, is that competition should be fair, workable, and *reasonable.* And indeed, for the judge who takes this liberty with the theory of pure competition, it is but a small step to maintaining that "reasonable" means reasonable behavior with respect to competitors; and this might be held even though society might regard the behavior as unreasonable to consumers. Manifestly, the courts have long accepted the responsibility of protecting business property rights. When this is accomplished and competition appears to be reasonable and considerate, the public, it can be said, will have to benefit sooner or later.

Thus, what happens under pure competition theory is a large amount of contradictory applications by different judges and courts, largely because economics itself seems to be too abstract and inapplicable without the "logical adjustment" that can be made by a court. As a consequence, experts at law are forced to examine questions that the economist cannot answer for himself: questions such as whether 23 percent, 60 percent, or 80 percent control is a monopoly, or whether the maintenance of small competitors is the supreme goal, or whether intent and reasonableness are proper and integral parts of effective entrepreneurship.

It is felt that the proposed theory and standards can be an easy and meaningful tool for jurists to use to measure antitrust violations. Price fixing and collusion in general, it should be recalled, lead to an ineffective economy, while a reasonable approximation to the effectiveness of pure competition can be expected if entry into the market and exit from it is kept open. It was proposed, therefore, that except from the standpoint of special society approval,[57] market entry must be kept open. Moreover, reasonable intent should be ignored. Also, size should be considered irrelevant; efficient firms should be permitted to reap the benefits of their efficiency without price limits being imposed by trade commissions. *Free entry and no collusion permitted,* it is asserted, are standards comparatively easy to recognize. Of course, the determination of when these standards are being violated must be, and will always remain, a matter of evidence.

---

57. *E.g.* patent laws. See note 32, *supra.*

FIGURES 1 THRU 6

I. The Sherman Act, section 2, provides: "Every person who shall monopolize, or attempt to monopolize, or combine or conspire with any other person or persons, to monopolize any part of the trade or commerce among the several States, or with foreign nations, shall be deemed guilty of a misdemeanor . . . ." 15 U.S.C. § 2 (1964).

II. The Sherman Act, section 1, provides: "Every contract, combination in the form of a trust or otherwise, or conspiracy, in restraint of trade or commerce among the several States, or with foreign nations, is hereby declared to be illegal. . . . Every person who shall make any contract or engage in any such combination or conspiracy . . . shall be deemed guilty of a misdemeanor . . . ." 15 U.S.C. § 1 (1964).

III. The Clayton Act, section 7, prohibited any corporation engaged in commerce from acquiring the shares of a competing corporation, or purchasing the stock of two or more corporations where the effect was to lessen competition. Clayton Act § 7, ch. 25, § 7, 38 Stat. 631 (1914), *as amended* 15 U.S.C. § 18 (1964).

The Clayton Act, section 8, prohibited interlocking directorates between corporations engaged in commerce, where one of them had a capital and surplus of more than $1 million, and where "the elimination of competition . . . between them would constitute a violation of any of the provisions of the antitrust laws." 15 U.S.C. § 18 (1964).

IV. The Celler Antimerger Act amended section 7 of the Clayton Act so that acquisitions of stock or assets are made illegal "where in any line of commerce in any section of the country, the effect . . . may be substantially to lessen competition, or tend to create a monopoly." 15 U.S.C. § 18 (1964).

V. The Lanham Act provided for the entry, on a Principal Register at the Patent Office, of trade-marks in the form of words or symbols which were used to distinguish the goods of a single seller, service marks in the form of devices used to identify a seller of services, certification marks covering the goods or services of several sellers, and collective marks used in sales made by the members of an association, such as a cooperative. It also provided for the entry, on a Supplemental Register, of names descriptive of goods and places; such marks were not accorded exclusive rights in the United States, but could be used in obtaining rights abroad. 15 U.S.C. §§ 1051-1127 (1964).

VI. The Miller-Tydings Act amended the Sherman Act to exempt from the federal antitrust laws interstate contracts fixing resale prices within those States where intrastate contracts had been legalized. 15 U.S.C. § 1 (1964).

VII. The Robinson-Patman Act made it illegal:
To discriminate among purchasers to an extent that cannot be justified by a difference in cost or as an attempt made, in good faith, to meet the price of a competitor. 15 U.S.C. § 13(a) (1964).
To pay a brokers commission if an independent broker is not employed. 15 U.S.C. § 13(c) (1964).
To provide supplementary services to a buyer or to make allowance for services rendered by a buyer unless such concessions are equally available to all buyers. 15 U.S.C. § 13(d),(e) (1964).
To knowingly induce or receive an illegal discrimination in price. 15 U.S.C. § 13(f) (1964).
To give larger discounts than those given others buying the same goods in the same quantity, or to charge lower prices in one locality than in another. 15 U.S.C. § 13(a) (1964).

Figure 1

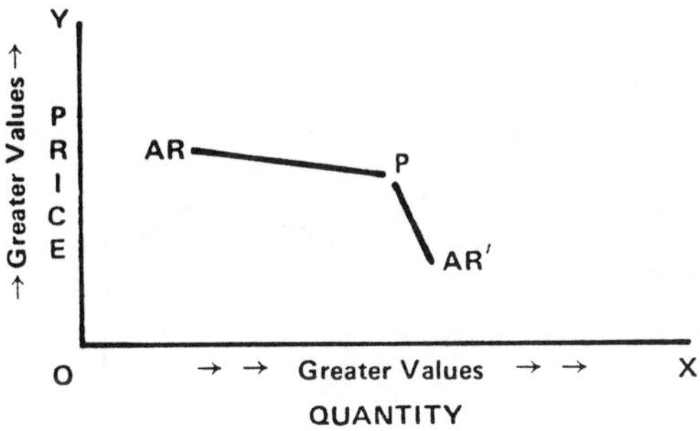

Figure 2

By the kinked average revenue curve is meant a demand curve of broken shape for a particular good. This broken curve runs from a point designated by AR to a point before the letter P, and then from a point below the letter P to the symbols AR′. The curve measures price along the vertical scale and quantity along the horizontal scale. One may readily see that as price is lowered from AR towards P, a relatively large change in quantity demanded takes place in the eyes of the owners of the firm. And as price is lowered below P towards AR′, a relatively small increase in quantity demanded is expected. Another way of viewing the curve is to say that above P the quantity sold falls off rapidly, say, because buyers shift to the products of rivals. If the price is lowered below P, sales scarcely increase. Significantly, the steep slope of the curve below P reflects the idea that if the seller cuts his price below P, his rivals believe they must also lower *their own prices;* if they do as expected only a small gain in sales for the price cutting firm results.

To sum up, a firm which visualizes a kinked average revenue curve finds no advantage in raising its price above P, because such policy tends to price the firm out of the market. (Note the fall in quantity demanded, or sales, above P.) In turn, price reductions often degenerate into price wars. Thus, according to this conception, collusion or tacit price leadership is a necessary prelude to willingness to change prices upward or downward in a systematic response to changes in overall consumer demand for the product in question. In effect, a kink is formed at the prevailing, hence stable, price P.

Duopolists (two sellers in a market) or oligopolists (three or typically just a few sellers in a market) tend to maintain a given price. They change their price only when convinced that their rivals will follow suit in a non hyper-competitive fashion, or when convinced that overall demand itself has changed so greatly that the old price is completely out-of-line with present realities. See E. MACHLUP, THE ECONOMICS OF SELLER'S COMPETITION 115-57 (1952) for support of the kinked AR curve in a space economy.

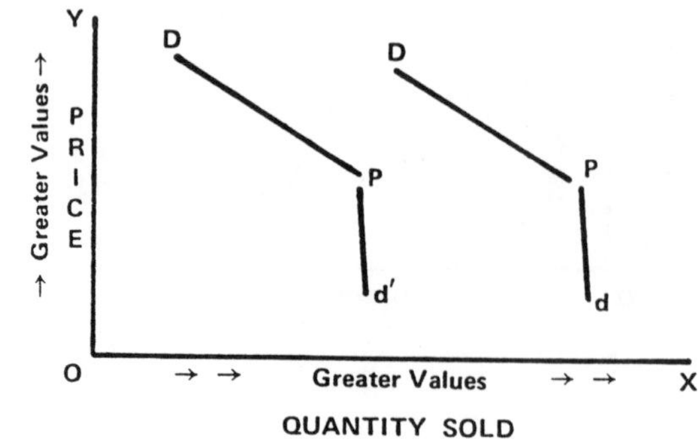

Figure 3

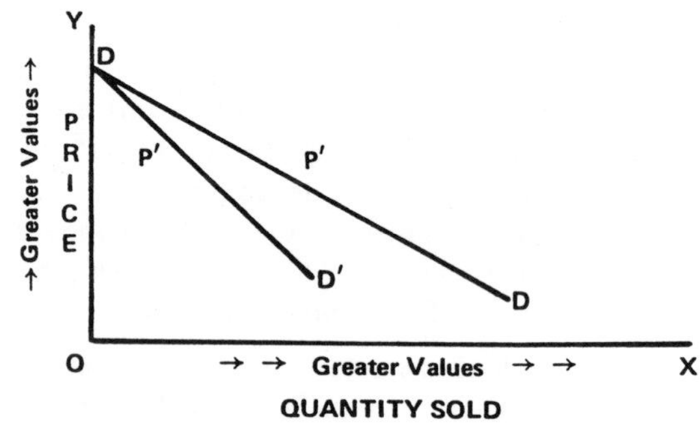

Figure 4

Control by a cartel (an organized central group which polices the practices of the firms in the industry) leads to the visualization of a typical demand curve such as DD, not a kinked one such as Dd in Figure 3. The effect of new firms in an open entry cartel is to reduce the sales for any one firm at any given price. The curve DD′ depicts the effect of this entry. Note again the leftward shifting occurs only along the horizontal scale, not the vertical scale as well.

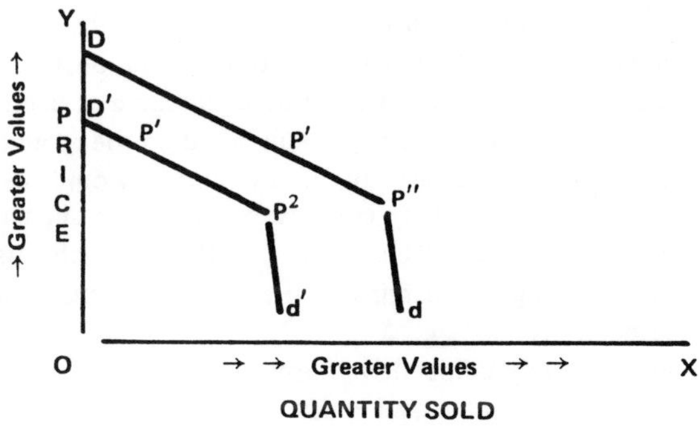

Figure 5

Added competition for any given unorganized oligopolist means that what might have been a relatively high price, yet one which permitted some significant quantity of sales (price P′ along Dd), might now represent a price too much higher than that charged by previous and new rivals. After entry, this price would yield an inadequate quantity sold (P′ along D′d′). The fact that the price P′ was out of line is accentuated when the new entry occurs, and the demand curve for the given seller shrinks. Unlike Figure 4, the D′d′ curve is not only leftward along the horizontal scale, but lower than the Dd curve.

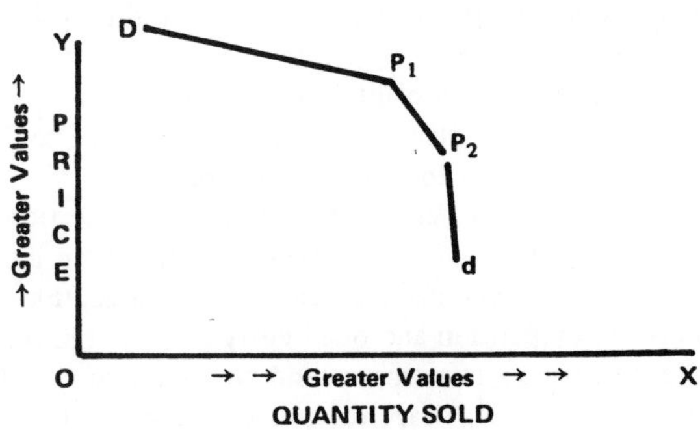

Figure 6

A TECHNICAL APPENDIX

It has been the thesis of this article that an unorganized space economy subject to free entry and exit conditions approaches in the long run the desirable properties of the purely competitive economy. This assertion will be buttressed in this brief appendix. Throughout this appendix, a basic demand curve of decreasing elasticity at lower prices is assumed. This curve may be justified on the grounds that its main alternatives, a constant or increasingly elastic curve, would be unlikely and exceptional. Significantly, the primary conclusions would be unchanged under any of these demands. The references "MC," "AC," "MR," and "AR" used throughout the appendix, stand for long-run marginal and average cost, marginal revenue, and average revenue respectively.

First consider the purely competitive norm of AR = MC. Then note that in the space economy, average revenue curves must tilt so that any efficient equilibrium must require that AR, MC be comparable from firm to firm. This can readily be shown. Let profits be arranged in an hierarchical order reflective of indivisibilities and uncertainties. This hierarchical arrangement is predicated upon exactly the same foci as are the classical theory's rents, which are payable for different risks and skills.[58] Next, temporarily assume that each firm produces at or near its optimum cost position. AR will exceed MC, which in turn approaches equality with AC. The excess of AR over MC and AC is predicated on the profit differential that one may attribute to the varying degrees of indivisibility and uncertainty that exist among industries. Indeed, if one regards indivisibility and uncertainty as a limiting factor of production (as a cost), AR > MC becomes AR = MC.

The same relationship may be explored somewhat differently. Assume the average cost level for a *given industry* is lower in one market area than another and that at first the same linear market demand curve prevails in each. Greater profits will clearly prevail in the low cost area. Thus, with open entry, relatively substantial competition will develop in the low cost area, and this will cause the average revenue curve for each plant to shift significantly to the left. A comparison between the average revenue curve of the plant in the low cost area with the counterpart average revenue curve of the plant in the high cost area would reveal a lower elasticity at any given output for the low cost area plant.[59]

If this hypothetical ended here, divergent AR > AC ratios would prevail at the given output in the two markets. However, profits in an industry tend to be equated from plant to plant, and market area to market area; this obtains from long established results of competition and open entry as viewed in economic theory. It follows that the returns on investment tend to be proportionate. Therefore, in equilibrium, the shapes of the average revenue curves in the two areas are altered, with the elasticity at the defined output in the low cost area tending to be the same, not less, as in the high cost area given the demand conditions cited above.

As between different industries any ratio divergence of AR with MC must then

58. For details on this matter, *see* Greenhut, *Decision Process and Entreprenurial Returns*, 25 THE MANCHESTER SCHOOL 247-67 (1966).

59. As the reference base, assume the ideal (least cost) output in each market.

reflect the difference in indivisibility and uncertainty. Therefore, what appears as a divergence when we speak of AR > MC actually amounts to a set of corresponding proportions.

If substantial and varying inequalities prevailed, some firms would not only be producing inefficiently, but the ratio of AR to MC would vary though differential indivisibilities and uncertainties are added to costs. However, a salutory effect exists from open entry. What competition means, as was noted in the body of the article, is a shrinking average revenue curve along the X and Y axes. The elasticity along the compressed curve is therefore greater at any given price. More generally, the development of substitutable goods (product wise or location wise) raises the elasticity of demand at any given price; in time, substitutable goods will cause the whole shape of the curve to be altered. The slope of the related MR curve accordingly becomes gentler, and with the limits to entry set by the requirement of profits related in hierarchical form to indivisibility and uncertainty,[60] there is a great likelihood that MR will equal MC at points close to where MC = AC.

Observe, however, one more force. If production appears to be stabilized at a point beyond the classical optimum cost position,[61] the stability can be shown to be illusory, as the market price will not be sufficiently greater than MC to support this production.[62] One may acquire intuitive understanding of this condition by realizing that it is a definition, and only a definition, which enables the economist to say AR > MC = MR by the relevant amount of indivisibility and uncertainty. Thus, if plants greater than optimum size happen to be experiencing profits equal to indivisibility and uncertainty, and indivisibility and uncertainty are defined as a variable cost, AR (and, of course, MR) would be revealed to be less than the adjusted MC which would include this cost. But, if AR < the adjusted MC (the cost visualized by the entrepreneur), production would be cut and output decreased.[63] Ultimately, then, the classical norms must be reached.

On the other hand, suppose that production is taking place at less than the classical optimum cost position, and that it appears to be in equilibrium because AR > AC precisely to the extent of the prevailing indivisibility and uncertainty rate in the industry. But here AR > MC by more than this rate, and it can be shown that the particular firm in question is not operating with its most effective short-run plant.[64] In effect, by rationalizing its operations, or being replaced by new firms, the position is approached where both AR > MC and AR > AC by the same amounts. By a change in definition, one approaches

60. This is true just as there exists a hierarchy of different rents for different risks and skills.

61. This stability seemingly would be marked by MR = MC and an AR which is greater than AC by the amount of the indivisibility and uncertainty that prevail in the market.

62. Details of this theory will be recorded in GREENHUT 1970, *supra**, and in Greenhut, *The Theory of the Spatial and Nonspatial Firm*, WELT WIRTSCHAFTLICHES ARCHIV (1970).

63. If adjustment is made to MC for indivisibility and uncertainty, a corresponding artificial adjustment must be made to MR. Adjusted MR < adjusted MC at points after the classical optimum cost position. *See* GREENHUT 1970, *supra**.

64. At outputs less than the classical optimum cost position, adjusted MR is revealed to be greater than adjusted MC. *See* GREENHUT 1970, *supra**.

AR = MC (adjusted) = AC (adjusted) only at the output which also yields classical optimal costs.[65]

In sum, the equilibrium conditions and positions of firms in a space economy are the transform of those in a purely competitive world. The differences that are identifiable center around: (1) The discontinuities which mark the average revenue curves, a condition primarily important in short-run analysis, (2) the indivisibilities in space and production, a condition which causes one to use the word "approach" rather than dogmatically speak of continuous functions and complete identities, and (3) the acceptance of multi-plant or large plant oligopolists as an inevitable part of the economic system. Most importantly, one finds the spatial oligopoly economy to be the counterpart to that of pure competition, and thus glean from it the twin standards of maintaining open entry and avoiding collusion in the market.

65. Adjusted MR is also revealed to be of the same value. *See* GREENHUT 1970, *supra**.

[31]

Related Market Conditions and Interindustrial Mergers

By M. L. Greenhut and H. Ohta*

William Baumol and David Bradford once introduced a paper in this *Review* by suggesting that its subtitle could be: *The Purloined Proposition or The Mystery of the Mislaid Maxim.* They proposed that the results contained in their paper had already appeared often in the literature, but that these results would still surprise many readers who tend to consider them at variance with ideas they had long accepted. The same caveat applies in many ways to the present paper. However, the literature which contends (as we do below) that important benefits stem from vertical integration has been predicated essentially on analysis of bilateral monopoly. It was, perhaps, this condition that prompted Fritz Machlup and Martha Taber to conclude their review of the literature by, in effect, rejecting the *Maxim* in question. Possibly this *Maxim*, even as repeated by S. Y. Wu, has been and continues to be *Mislaid* because proofs have been sketchy, chiefly diagrammatic, and the subject joined with that of bilateral monopoly. The upshot has been that a vital part of the *Maxim* has been lost, namely that the benefits stemming from vertical merger of successive monopolies dovetail with the effects of having perfect competition on the higher stage of production rather than monopoly. This particular identification, perhaps even more so than the generality of our proofs, nurtures our hope that the *Maxim* in question will not be permanently mislaid. We consider this *Maxim*, as set forth below, to be especially vital in this period of energy shortage and attacks on big business.

Our paper considers two types of related firms: producers of goods who have no monopsony power over input suppliers, and a monopolist input supplier.[1] The two theorems which will be deduced here are (I) *the price charged by the monopolistic supplier of an input is not affected by the market structure in the market for the final good, be it perfectly competitive, monopolistic, etc.*, and (II) *merger or collusion between the input supplier and the final good producer brings about lower prices, greater output and sales, and greater profits to the merged or colluding firms—a welfare gain.*[2]

In Section I we present our theorems for

* Professor, Texas A&M University, and associate professor, Aoyama Gakuin University, respectively. We wish to thank Ming-jeng Hwang for critiques and suggestions and Martin Bronfenbrenner who pointed out the intimate relation of the present work to that of Augustin Cournot. This paper is based in part on research funded by the National Science Foundation.

[1] Our analysis relates to all connected stages of production, e.g., raw materials to intermediate products to final products, consignor to consignee, inputs of labor in producing goods, etc. Simplicity in reference is gained, however, by conceiving generally in this paper of two particular connected stages of production: A) production of final goods, and B) production of the raw materials used as inputs in producing the final goods.

[2] In a sense, this second theorem is related to Cournot's theorem on production with joint inputs. However, some significant differences in analytical framework exist between the two. To begin with Cournot assumes that n kinds of raw materials, e.g. copper and zinc, are *jointly* used to produce a commodity, e.g. brass. His problem was to analyze the impact on price and quantity produced of a *horizontal* merger or collusion between the producers of the raw materials when the final commodity is sold under conditions of perfect competition. In contrast, our model will include among others the case where all producers are monopolistic, and our problem is to investigate the impact of *vertical* collusion between firms in different stages of production and/or distribution.

the two polar cases—perfect competition and monopoly—in the final good market structure. Section II extends our theorems to a Cournot-oligopoly final good market structure. Section III establishes the basic welfare results for varying as well as constant marginal cost situations and demonstrates the generality of our results by illustrating their applicability to such inputs as transportation services. Section IV concludes the paper with a discussion of some antitrust implications of the theory.

I

Consider a final good market demand function f of the form:

$$(1)\quad p = f(q),\quad f' = \frac{df(q)}{dq} < 0,\quad f(0) < \infty$$

where q stands for the quantity demanded at whatever price p is charged in that market. The correspondent to $f(q)$ may then be defined as:[3]

$$(2)\quad g(q) = f(q) + f'q, \qquad f' = \frac{df(q)}{dq}$$

$$= f(q)\left(1 - \frac{1}{e_f}\right), \qquad e_f = -\frac{dq}{df(q)}\frac{f(q)}{q}$$

The graphs of $f(q)$, $g(q)$, and $h(q)$, i.e., the correspondent to $g(q)$, are drawn respectively in Figure 1a, which assumes *for simplicity* a linear demand. Our analysis, however, is not restricted to this linearity assumption, as will shortly be demonstrated.

Three situations warrant analysis initially, namely (i) where perfect competition prevails in the final good (commodity) market and the input supplier is a simple monopolist; (ii) simple monopoly prevails in each market; and (iii) the monopolists in the two related industries collude. Later, in Section II, we shall examine as well the market where the final good is sold under imperfectly competitive conditions.

CASE (i): Consider first the case where the producer of the final good, firm A, is a perfect competitor. His profit maximizing calculus requires

$$(3)\qquad p = MC = c + r$$

where c relates to the original factor inputs used by firm A (say, labor) and r to the quantity of raw materials purchased from the input supplier, firm B, per unit of output q. Without loss of generality, c and r are assumed to be constant for the time being, an assumption relaxed later in Section II of the paper. Firm A's cost r constitutes firm B's revenue. Combining (1) with (3) provides the revenue function of B per unit output q on sales to A, i.e.:

$$(4)\qquad r = f(q) - c$$

Defined as such, (4) represents the average revenue of firm B in terms of q, *not* the average revenue (or price) it receives *per unit of raw materials* sold to firm A (and to other atomistic firms in the final good industry).[4] The marginal revenue for firm B, MR_B, is then:

$$(5)\qquad MR_B = g(q) - c$$

$$= f(q)\left(1 - \frac{1}{e_f}\right) - c$$

[3] The correspondent $g(q)$ is, in effect, the marginal revenue function of the final good producer if and only if monopoly prevails in that market. However, if perfect competition prevails in that market, the correspondent $g(q)$ constitutes the marginal revenue function for the monopolistic input supplier, indirectly and in part, but of course not for the competitive producer of the final good (see equation (3)). Incidentally, the concept of *correspondent* used herein should not be confused with Joan Robinson's correspondent which relates to a tangent to an average revenue function.

[4] Let the input material supplied by firm B be represented by M and the price of M by p_M. Then the average revenue of a unit of M can be specified as $p_M = (f(q) - c)q/M$. The average revenue per unit of q, specified in the text, is then readily derived as $r = (p_M M)/q = f(q) - c$. Note further that a constant r requires constant proportions between M and q for any p_M parametrically given to firm A; as noted above in the text, this fixed relation will be relaxed later in the paper.

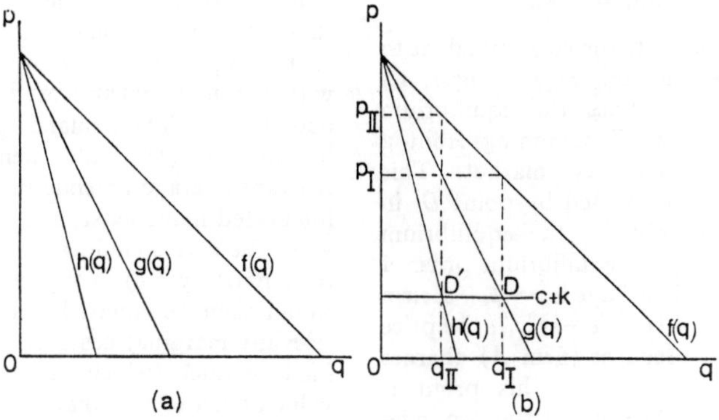

FIGURE 1

where the marginal revenue relates to an extra unit of output q, not input.

Profit maximization by firm B requires equating MR_B with its marginal cost of production k, also assumed to be constant for the moment. Thus:

$$(6) \qquad f(q)\left(1 - \frac{1}{e_f}\right) - c = k$$

or

$$g(q) = c + k$$

Associated with this equilibrium is output $q=q_I$ depicted in Figure 1b, which is produced under conditions of perfect competition in the commodity market and monopoly in the raw material market.[5] Correspondingly, the price of the final good is $p=p_I$ in Figure 1b, the average revenue per unit of q earned by firm B is $r=p_I-c$, so the input supplier's profit on his production for firm A is $\pi_B=[p_I-(c+k)]q_I$, while firm A is covering costs with $\pi_A=0$. Total profits in Case (i) are $\pi=\pi_B+\pi_A=[p_I-(c+k)]q_I$, an area easily observed in Figure 1b.

A mathematical summary of the preceding analysis helps shed light on certain important relationships. In particular, note that Case (i) consists of three fundamental equations, (1), (3), and (6), in three unknowns, p, q, and r. Equation (1), recall, represents the commodity market demand function, equation (3) the equilibrium condition for the competitive producers in that market, and equation (6) the equilibrium condition in the market of the monopolistic supplier of input materials. These equations may be solved simultaneously for p, q, and r at the equilibrium point D, as depicted in Figure 1b.

CASE (ii): Consider now a *monopolist* final good producer who is subject to the demand function given as (1). His profit maximizing calculus, i.e. $MR_A=MC_A$, provides:

$$(7) \qquad g(q) = c + r$$

which is the counterpart equilibrium condition to (3). Equation (7), however, also establishes the average revenue function of the monopolistic input supplier firm B in the form:

$$(8) \qquad r = g(q) - c$$

Firm B's profit maximizing condition $MR_B = MC_B$ may, in turn, be obtained from (8) as:

$$(9) \quad g(q)\left(1 - \frac{1}{e_g}\right) - c = k, \quad e_g = -\frac{dq}{dg}\,\frac{g(q)}{q}$$

[5] The amount $q=q_I$ is the aggregate supply by the n competitive producers of the final product.

or $$h(q) = c + k$$

where $h(q)$ represents the correspondent to $g(q)$.[6] (And see the curve $h(q)$ in Figure 1.)

Equation (9) defines the equilibrium condition for firm B stemming from a monopolized commodity market. This equilibrium is represented by point D' in Figure 1b. Accordingly, the equilibrium output is $q=q_{II}$, the equilibrium price of the raw material package is $r=p_I-c$, firm B's profit is $\pi_B=[p_I-(c+k)]q_{II}$, the price the final good producer (firm A) charges his buyers is $p=p_{II}$, and his profit is $\pi_A=(p_{II}-p_I)q_{II}$. The sum of the two independent monopolists' profits amounts to $\pi=\pi_B+\pi_A=[p_{II}-(c+k)]q_{II}$.

Figure 1b shows that output produced under the conditions of Case (i) is greater than that of Case (ii), i.e., $q_I>q_{II}$, and profits are also greater in Case (i) than Case (ii). Moreover, Figure 1b implies that the equilibrium input price is the same, i.e., $r=p_I-c$ in each case. *The input price charged by the monopolistic supplier is, therefore, invariant to the final good market structure*, be it either monopolistic or perfectly competitive. Moreover, it will be shown that the same conclusion holds also for imperfectly competitive final good markets. Section II will formally establish these relationships.

Though the equation system for Case (ii) has the same three unknowns, p, q, and r, it contrasts sharply from that of Case (i) by consisting of equations (1), (7), and (9) rather than (1), (3), and (6). As before, equation (1) sets forth the demand function, and equations (7) and (9) serve as counterparts to (3) and (6), respectively providing the average revenue and profit maximizing conditions for the input supplier, firm B.

CASE (iii): The greater profits available under Case (i) conditions compared to those of Case (ii) would induce the monopolistic supplier of inputs, firm B, to collude with the monopolistic producer of products, firm A. The demand function given by equation (1) would then become the relevant average revenue function for the integrated monopolist, and hence (2) provides the corresponding marginal revenue (alternatively $g(q)$ in Figure 1). This MR would then be equated directly with the relevant marginal costs of producing the final product (which are related to the value-added of the final good and that of its input), i.e., $c+k$. Equilibrium price and output therefore apparently dovetail with that of Case (i); i.e., $q=q_I$ in Figure 1. The pooled profits π for the integrated monopolist are, in turn, $\pi=\pi_B+\pi_A=[p_I-(c+k)]q_I$, with the profit resulting from collusion being the same as in Case (i).[7] Since profit in Case (i) exceeds that of Case (ii), it follows that profit in Case (iii) is also greater than that of Case (ii). Collusion pays from the standpoint of firms operating in related markets. Collusion also offers advantages to society since the final commodity price is lower and the output produced greater than otherwise. But the relations sketched above are based on the linear demand assumption; need exists for formal proof of these relations to include the more general case of non-linear demand.

A proof is available which requires two basic constraints on f in addition to the requirements that f', g', $h'<0$ and $f(0)>0$: namely, 1) the demand function f is limited to yield a correspondent g such that the horizontal lengths of the two curves are in fixed proportion, as is the case when f is of the algebraic form given later in footnote

[6] Equation (9) reveals the equality between the correspondent $h(q)$ minus the marginal cost of producing

[7] It should be stressed that the entire profit $\pi=[p_I-(c+k)]q_I$ is received by the monopolistic input supplier in Case (i) whereas the distribution of total profits in Case (iii) must be negotiated by the colluding firms, the lower limit for firm B being set by

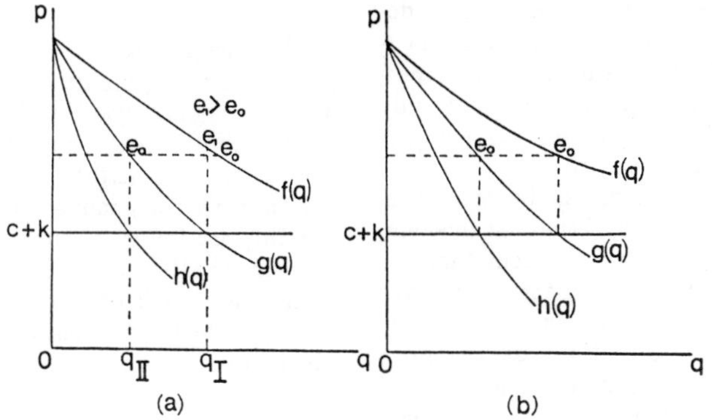

FIGURE 2

10; and 2) the elasticity of demand decreases with price, i.e., $de_f/dp>0$.[8]

To see the implication of proviso 1), consider arbitrarily two quantities q_I and q_{II} such that $f(q_I)=g(q_{II})$. It readily follows under proviso 1) that $e_f(q_I)=e_g(q_{II})$.[9] Combined with proviso 2), the present condition can be extended to the relations:

$$(10) \qquad e_f(q_I) \gtreqless e_g(q_{II})$$

if and only if $f(q_I) \gtreqless g(q_{II})$

We are, accordingly, now in position to prove the generality of our first theorem. To recall, Theorem I holds that the two alternative equilibrium conditions (6) and (9), i.e., $g(q_I)=c+k$ and $h(q_{II})=c+k$, generally imply $f(q_I)=g(q_{II})$, under well-defined demand functions given by the conditions specified above. Consider in this context the null hypothesis that $h(q_{II})=g(q_I)$ implies $f(q_I)\gtrless g(q_{II})$; via (10), this relation in turn implies $e_f\gtrless e_g$, as illustrated in Figure 2a. But this condition is impossible since combining (6) and (9) establishes:

$$(11) \quad f(q)\left(1-\frac{1}{e_f}\right)=g(q)\left(1-\frac{1}{e_g}\right), \qquad e_f, e_g > 1$$

$$\therefore \; e_f(q) \lesseqgtr e_g(q)$$

if and only if $f(q) \gtreqless g(q)$

In particular, note that $f(q)\gtrless g(q)$ implies $e_f \lessgtr e_g$, which contradicts the elasticity requirement derived from the null hypothesis and must therefore be rejected. The relations $g(q)=h(q)=c+k$ necessarily imply the remaining condition $f(q)=g(q)$, which condition alone consistently yields $e_f=e_g$ in (10) and (11). *Except for* the equality parts of the relations in (10) and (11), which alone are consistent, these equations reveal contradictory conditions derived from the equilibrium conditions

[8] Neither of these specifications is required when f is assumed to be of the specific algebraic form given in fn. 10. It warrants mention, however, in connection with the second constraint, that demand curves of constant or increasing elasticity are typically ruled out in the space economy since they generate the unlikely practice of discriminating against distant buyers, and this opens up the possibility of repackaging and resale by nearer buyers. For example, see Edgar Hoover, Arthur Smithies, and Greenhut, M. J. Hwang and Ohta. From the standpoint of spatial economics, therefore, the subject constraint is quite meaningful. Nevertheless, in fn. 10 below we shall include instances of increasing and constant elasticity that yield the same results.

[9] For proof consider the condition of $f(q_I)=g(q_{II})$. Then:

$$\frac{df}{dq_I}\frac{q_I}{f}=\frac{dg}{dq_{II}}\frac{q_{II}}{g}\frac{dq_{II}}{dq_I}\frac{q_I}{q_{II}}$$

$$\therefore\; e_f(q_I)=e_g(q_{II}) \quad \text{if } \frac{dq_{II}}{dq_I}\frac{q_I}{q_{II}}=1 \text{ or } \frac{q_I}{q_{II}}=\text{constant}$$

$g(q)=h(q)=c+k$. Under the defined demand function f subject to the aforementioned constraints, the equilibrium conditions $g(q_I)=h(q_{II})=c+k$ yield not only $f(q_I)=g(q_{II})$ but also implies $e_g(q_I)=e_f(q_{II})$, as illustrated in Figure 2b.[10]

The second theorem can be readily established with the aid of the first theorem. Observe from the first theorem that the value of the equilibrium marginal revenue $g(q_{II})$ of the monopolist firm A is the same under Case (ii) conditions as the price $f(q_I)$ set by the colluding monopolists of Case (iii). Since the price $f(q_{II})$ is in general higher than the corresponding marginal revenue $g(q_{II})$, it follows that $f(q_{II})>f(q_I)=g(q_{II})$. This relation establishes formally the proposition that Case (iii) and Case (i) as well provide a lower equilibrium price than does Case (ii). Since f is assumed to be a monotonically decreasing function of q, it further follows that $q_I>q_{II}$; i.e., the output produced under Cases (i) or (iii) is greater than that under Case (ii).

[10] A proof which utilizes the algebraic function $f(q)=a-bq^\alpha$ with varying combinations of the parameters a, b, and α is set forth below. Significantly, the combinations allowed include $a, b, \alpha>0$; $a, b<0$, $-1<\alpha<0$ (decreasing elasticity situations); and, in addition, $a=0$, $b<0$, $-1<\alpha<0$ as well as $a>0$, $b<0$, $-1<\alpha<0$, combinations which respectively establish economically stable equilibrium situations under conditions of constant and increasing demand elasticities as price decreases. Pursuant to the constraints set forth above on the function $f(q)=a-bq^\alpha$, the correspondents $g(q)$ and $h(q)$ are given by:

$$\text{(a)} \qquad g(q) = a - b(\alpha+1)q^\alpha$$

$$\text{(b)} \qquad h(q) = a - b(\alpha+1)^2 q^\alpha$$

Let $g(q_I)=h(q_{II})=c+k$ to obtain the specific values q_I and q_{II}:

$$\text{(c)} \qquad q_I = \left(\frac{a-c-k}{b(\alpha+1)}\right)^{1/\alpha}$$

$$\text{(d)} \qquad q_{II} = \left(\frac{a-c-k}{b(\alpha+1)^2}\right)^{1/\alpha}$$

Substituting q_I of (c) in q of the demand function $f(q)$ and q_{II} of (d) in q of the correspondent $g(q)$ yields:

$$\text{(e)} \qquad f(q_I) = a - \frac{a-c-k}{\alpha+1} = g(q_{II})$$

II

The thesis presented in Section I applied to a perfectly competitive or perfectly monopolized final good market. However, what about relationships where the final good market is neither perfectly competitive nor perfectly monopolized? To evaluate this possibility, assume an oligopolistically competitive market of the Cournot type where each firm considers its rival's supply to be fixed. Profit maximization for the representative firm requires:

$$\text{(12)} \qquad \frac{\partial(pq_i)}{\partial q_i} = f(q) + f'\frac{\partial q}{\partial q_i}q_i = f(q) + f'(q)q_i = c_i + r_i \qquad i = 1, 2, \ldots, m$$

where q_i stands for the ith firm's supply, c_i for the ith firm's marginal production cost in using original input factors, and r_i for the marginal cost of using the raw material input; alternatively, r_i provides (in terms of q) the price charged the ith firm by the monopolistic input supplier. Note that the unit value applies to $\partial q/\partial q_i$ in (12) because market demand equals the aggregate supply of the m oligopolistic firms, i.e.,

$$\text{(13)} \qquad q = \sum^m q_i$$

and any change in q_i is assumed under Cournot's framework not to elicit a change in supply by rival firms. Summing both sides of (12) over all i, dividing by m, and utilizing (13) establishes:

$$\text{(14)} \qquad f(q) + \frac{f'(q)}{m}q = c + r$$

where $c = \frac{1}{m}\sum c_i \qquad r = \frac{1}{m}\sum r_i$

For the purpose of this paper, c_i and r_i must be assumed to be the same as they would be under conditions of perfect competition or monopoly, i.e., the same as c

and r previously. Equation (14) may then be rewritten as:

$$(14') \qquad r = f(q) + \frac{f'(q)q}{m} - c$$
$$= f(q)\left(1 - \frac{1}{me_f}\right) - c$$

Equation (14') represents the monopolistic input supplier's average revenue function in terms of q under the specified Cournot conditions. When $m=1$, (14') is equivalent to (8), the case of monopoly in the final good market. As m increases, i.e., as more and more firms enter the final good market, the adjusted elasticity of demand $e_f^* = me_f$ increases by the multiplier m. And when m approaches ∞, (14') approaches (4) in reflection of perfect competition.[11]

To obtain the equilibrium price r per unit of raw material input for all in-between market conditions (i.e., where m is a finite number greater than one), some concrete form of the demand function f must be assumed, such as the $f(q) = a - bq^{\alpha}$ evaluated previously in footnote 10. That function represents a general form as it generates not only convex, linear, or concave demands, but curves of either constant, decreasing, or increasing elasticities of demand depending on the alternative combinations of parameters a, b, and α that are applied. (See fn. 10.) Equation (14') can then be particularized to:

$$(14'') \qquad r = (a - c) - \left(\frac{m + \alpha}{m}\right) bq^{\alpha}$$

The profit maximizing condition for the monopolist firm B is:

$$(15) \qquad (a - c) - \left(\frac{m + \alpha}{m}\right) b(\alpha + 1)q^{\alpha} = k$$

where the left-hand side of (15) represents the raw material supplier's marginal revenue while the right-hand side, i.e., k, stands for his marginal cost of producing the raw materials. Substituting in (14'') the equilibrium q obtainable from (15) yields:

$$(16) \qquad r = \frac{\alpha(a - c) + k}{\alpha + 1}$$

Remarkably enough, r does not depend on the number of producers in the final good market; viz., the raw materials price r charged the final good producer by the monopolistic input supplier is the same for any final good market type, whether it be simple monopoly (when $m=1$), duopoly ($m=2$), etc.[12] An invariance theorem on raw material inputs prevails regardless of selling conditions in the final good market under the specified Cournot behavioral assumption and the technical assumption on the form of the demand function.

A two-fold question remains with respect to oligopolistic competition in the final good market: 1) would horizontal merger between final good producers lower the market price of their good; and 2) would vertical merger between final good producers and the monopolistic supplier of raw materials lower the price of the final good? Answer to question 1) simply requires conceiving of a constant raw material price r (in addition to c). Differentiating (14) or (14') with respect to the number of competitive producers of the final good, yields—in conformance with (16)—the equation:

$$(17) \qquad \frac{dp}{dm} = \frac{-(r + c)\left(e_f + m\dfrac{de_f}{dp}\dfrac{dp}{dm}\right)}{(me_f - 1)^2}$$

This equation demonstrates that under the

[11] See John Greenhut and M. L. Greenhut for a development along this line which isolates the impacts on delivered price schedules of the location of rivals and the intensity of their competition at alternative points.

[12] Manifestly we are not in a bilateral monopoly situation since our final good producer is not a monopsonist but simply an oligopolist or, as in Section I of the paper, a monopolist or perfect competitor.

normality assumption of decreasing elasticity with price, the equilibrium price p must fall as the number of firms increases. It follows, accordingly, that horizontal merger, i.e., a decrease in m, raises the equilibrium commodity price p.

An asymmetric result obtains with respect to the vertical rationalization proposed under question 2). More specifically, profit maximization for any and all independent final goods producers is given by (12). But if these oligopolists, or just some of them, merge with the monopolistic supplier of the needed raw materials, the new profit maximization requires:

$$(18) \qquad f(q) + f'(q)q_i = c_i + k_i, \quad i = 1, 2, \ldots, j \leq m$$

where (18) assumes that $(m-j)$ firms do *not* merge with the monopolistic supplier of raw materials, and hence equation (12) applies to these $(m-j)$ firms. Of course, the marginal cost k_i of producing the raw material is lower than the comparable marginal cost (price) r_i in (12). Summing (18) and (12) over their relevant ranges then gives:

$$(19) \quad mf(q) + f'(q)q = \sum_{i=1}^{m} c_i + \sum_{i=1}^{j} k_i + \sum_{i=j+1}^{m} r_i$$

$$\text{where} \qquad q = \sum_{i=1}^{j} q_i + \sum_{i=j+1}^{m} q_i$$

Dividing both sides of (19) by m establishes:

$$(19') \quad f(q)\left(1 - \frac{1}{me_f}\right) = c + \frac{j}{m}k + \frac{m-j}{m}r = c + r - (r-k)j/m < c + r$$

provided that $r > k$, i.e., the average price charged per package of raw materials by the monopolist supplier is greater than the average marginal cost of supplying that package. Thus the *average* marginal costs, viz.,

$$\left(\sum^{m} c_i + \sum k_i + \sum^{m} r_{j+i}\right) \Big/ m$$

decrease as more and more firms collude (merge) with the firm that supplies the raw materials. Given the market demand function $f(q)$ and the fixed total number m of firms producing the final good, the same adjusted MR curve $f(q)[1-1/me_f]$ that was derived from the original $MR = f(q) \cdot (1-1/e_f)$ obtains. Thus equilibrium price $f(q)$ *falls* as average MC falls. Vertical merger lowers commodity price and increases the quantity demanded and the output produced.

III

We have thus far assumed fixed proportions of inputs to output. The basic welfare results scored above remain unaffected, however, by variation in marginal costs. In demonstrating this condition, two concepts of variable marginal costs are required, as we shall extend our previous analysis to include spatial price relations.

Consider a monopolistic producer who ships his commodity to spatially separated market points. Let the demand function (1) apply now to any one local market point. If a transportation service is provided by a monopolistic carrier, the carrier's average revenue function would be given by (8), where r would represent the freight rate applicable to the market point under consideration. The equilibrium condition for an independent monopoly situation between the carrier and shipper of goods is then given by (9), where c now represents the marginal cost of production while k provides the marginal cost of transportation. Note that k and c are specified differently in:

$$(20) \qquad k = \phi(q)$$

$$(21) \qquad c = \psi(Q), \qquad Q = \sum q$$

where the summation applies to all relevant market points. Thus k is a direct function of q, but c is not so related since a change in the particular supply q_1 may be carried out by an offsetting change in the supply q_2; the consequence would be that the total output produced Q and the related cost c are unchanged. For this reason, marginal production cost c does not vary with a change in supply q to a particular market point. We assume, however, that c does increase if (and only if) *aggregate* q (i.e., Q) increases.

The relation between c and k with respect to a change in q is illustrated in Figure 3. Marginal cost k of shipping goods is assumed in the figure to be a decreasing function of q; i.e., economies derive from using larger input quantities, with the effect $c+k$ decreases as q increases.[13] Suppose equilibrium prevails initially at D in a particular market, and that the input supplier (carrier) and his customer are independent monopolists. The question of impacts of collusion may, accordingly, be raised again.

Any change in equilibrium from, say, D to D' implies an increase in a particular market's supply as price is lowered. Collusion must, however, change the equilibrium price-quantity set *for all submarkets*. The consequence is that total output and cost of production increase (compare c with c' in Figure 3); correspondingly, the MC curve shifts from $c+k$ to $c'+k$, with final equilibrium taking place at point D''. This new position guarantees a greater output than that obtainable when the monopolists are independent. But the question arises as to whether or not an increase in c which results from collusion might occasionally be so great as to generate a smaller equilibrium output. To resolve this particular question, note initially that c rises only if *equilibrium* output increases; in other words, marginal production cost c increases only if the *equilibrium* output produced under Case (iii) conditions increases. If the equilibrium output does not increase, neither does the related marginal production cost. It further follows that the rightward placement of $g(q)$ compared to $h(q)$ cannot be offset by a change in c to c', and accordingly output must increase. This requirement fully establishes the generality of our proposition that output is greater and price lower for Case (iii) than Case (ii).

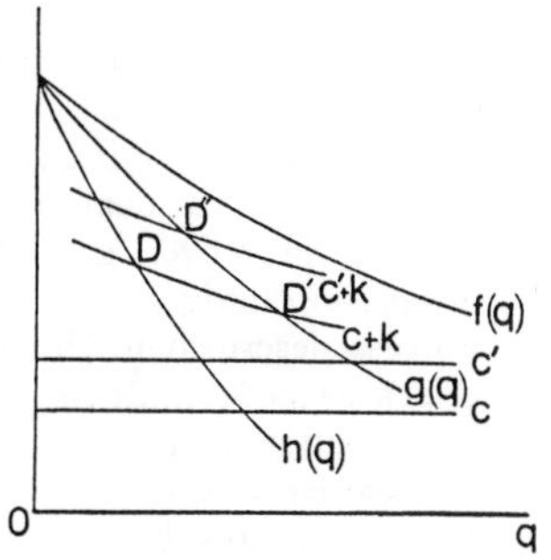

FIGURE 3

[13] Decreasing marginal cost k is not a required assumption for our proof.

IV

The comparative profitability of merged firms with that of individual monopolists is thus completely given by the demand condition $f(q)$. Maximum profits obtain if and only if marginal revenue $g(q)$ is equated with the lowest obtainable marginal cost, i.e., $c+k$ distinct from $c+r$. Any deviation from this equilibrium, such as in Case (ii), necessarily implies a decrease in profits.

The results obtained above apply to any particular market in which sales are made. Aggregate outputs and profits increase and prices are lower when vertical merger or some other rationalization process takes place between an input supplier and the user(s) of his product whenever the successive stages of production involve independent monopolistic powers. The surprising implication of these relationships is that excess capacity may be eliminated to a considerable extent by rationalization in related industries. Moreover, greater efficiency in production derives from the integration process described in this paper under imperfect market conditions.

The last contention is a sweeping one which is underscored by the fact that production generally requires the input of raw materials, intermediate goods, and services. Given a demand function for a good, one may deduce a derived demand function for, let us say, the intermediate good or service, such as transportation. This function would yield, in turn, another derived demand function, for example, for the tires used by the carrier, and so forth. Successively shrinking *correspondents* to derived demand functions thus obtain, as the smallest correspondent is equated with the relevant marginal cost to provide the equilibrium applicable under the case of independent monopolistic firms. This smallest correspondent obviously shrinks toward the origin as more and more related industries are subjected to independent monopoly powers. And the converse principle holds, as the smallest *correspondent* would be twisted upward by integration of firms in related industries. Equilibrium output increases as a result, except for the unlikely *and unstable* cost situation of rapidly decreasing MC in the region of the equality of marginal values that prevailed before the integration of firms.

In a related context to this paper, Donald Dewey contended that rationalization of firms increases efficiency in imperfectly competitive markets. This effect was said to arise since the merged firms can utilize one plant more efficiently in producing a small high-cost output than can two firms which would otherwise produce at very inefficient small output points. Only over a narrow range of outputs, where each plant must be utilized, would the costs of the unified firm necessarily involve the sum of the costs of *each* of the individual firms. In fact, Dewey argued that *even in such case* the unified firm would operate the single firm's plant(s) more efficiently at greater profit than that which would eventuate under a Cournot competitive equilibrium. The Dewey merger model unfortunately involves smaller output than the competitive model, and in this respect can be criticized by welfare theorists.

Our paper, similar to Dewey's, has *also* advocated merger as a source of increased efficiency in imperfectly competitive markets. But even closer to Wu's, it proposes vertical rationalization only for firms in related industries. We contend that merger of firms in related industries generates a greater output than the sum of the individual outputs of nonintegrated firms. In effect, this present paper has, therefore, illustrated *and* proved two theorems which were *implicitly* assumed by the present authors and Hwang in this *Review* on the type of (and direction of) discrimination practiced by motor carriers. That paper, in particular, anticipated the advantages to carriers and shippers of vertical integration in noting that freight rates were unaffected by the market structure in the shipper's industry (compare Josephine Olson). The roots of the present paper based as they are on successive stages of production thus include the distribution process as well as the production process. Indeed, one can readily conceive of freight rates covering certain specified places that converge in time under Commission regulations to the derived r_i values that were described above. By permitting shippers of goods the ownership of their own carriers (or permitting them vertical integration with existing contract or common carriers), cost k_i replaces r_i and in the process generates greater outputs and lower prices.

Other policy implications of our theorems should be manifest. For example, objections being expressed against the possible "take-over" of the retailing function by the larger oil companies under deregulation of "old oil prices" appear ill-founded as greater output and lower prices should result from that integration. Excluded from our analysis of related markets is only the possibility of bilateral monopoly, since our higher stage producer is not conceived to have monopsony buying power over the lower stage producer. All other related market situations fall within our analysis. Possibly most important of all are the antitrust implications of our findings which, to say the least, will prove shocking to many.[14] At the same moment, these implications will clearly warrant study.

[14] Consider a standard case before our courts involving vertical merger, such as United States v. Yellow Cab. Concern in that case was with a monopolistic buying firm (e.g. Yellow Cab or our firm A) which would exclude other input suppliers from certain markets if it merged vertically with a particular supplier of the needed input. In opposite situations, elimination of competition on the final good market level might appear questionable to many. However, strict interpretation of our theorems must yield an interesting difference in conclusions. A less rigid interpretation from a long-run perspective can be found in Greenhut, p. 366.

REFERENCES

W. J. Baumol and D. F. Bradford, "Optimal Departures From Marginal Cost Pricing," *Amer. Econ. Rev.*, June 1970, *60*, 265–83.

A. Cournot, *Mathematical Principles of the Theory of Wealth*, translated by N. T. Bacon, New York 1927.

D. Dewey, *The Theory of Imperfect Competition: A Radical Reconstruction*, New York 1969.

J. Greenhut and M. L. Greenhut, "Spatial Price Discrimination, Competition, Locational Effects," *Economica*, Nov. 1975, *42*, 401–19.

M. L. Greenhut, *A Theory of the Firm in Economic Space*, Austin 1974.

———, M. J. Hwang, and H. Ohta, "Price Discrimination by Regulated Motor Carriers: Comment," *Amer. Econ. Rev.*, Sept. 1974, *64*, 780–84.

E. M. Hoover, "Spatial Price Discrimination," *Rev. Econ. Stud.*, June 1937, *4*, 182–91.

F. Machlup and M. Taber, "Bilateral Monopoly, Successive Monopoly, and Vertical Integration," *Economica*, May 1960, *27*, 101–19.

J. Olson, "Price Discrimination by Regulated Motor Carriers," *Amer. Econ. Rev.*, June 1972, *62*, 395–402.

J. Robinson, *The Economics of Imperfect Competition*, London 1933.

A. Smithies, "Monopolistic Price Policy in a Spatial Market," *Econometrica*, Jan. 1941, *9*, 63–73.

S. Y. Wu, "The Effects of Vertical Integration On Price and Output," *West. Econ. J.*, May 1964, *2*, 117–33.

United States v. Yellow Cab, 332 US 218, 1947.

Related Market Conditions and Interindustrial Mergers: Reply

By M. L. Greenhut and H. Ohta*

Martin Perry happily accepted our results but reworked them in a way he considered more efficient. We appreciate his proving the results given in our paper, but do not agree that his technique (based on our paper) is the better one. Before buttressing this claim, let us observe that if he did not believe rigor is needed to establish the subject Mislaid Maxim, he should not have taken the time to recast our model in what he considers a more efficient form. Apparently he really believes the Mislaid Maxim does require the most penetrating analysis possible.

Let us save space by considering his Sections I and II together. We agree $g' < 0$ is sufficient for our Theorem II.[1] We do *not agree*, however, that Theorem I is unimportant, and hence that simply specifying $g' < 0$ is alone required. More specifically, Perry's statement that Theorem I is special implies its unimportance. But how many readers of the original paper or of these notes alone would agree with him that demonstrating the *invariance of a monopolist's* input supply price with respect to the market structure in the next stage, whether the final product sells at the perfectly competitive or a simple monopoly price, is per se unimportant? Rather in our view, this theorem is interesting, not intuitively obvious, and for reasons to be given below, very important.

Perry's next critique that the relations $fg^{-1} \gtrless gh^{-1}$ may hold is surprising in light of his emphasis on rigor "cum" simplicity, though let us say at the outset that the possibility of these relations was certainly not ignored when we specified the general form of f that establishes the equality.[2] Most fundamentally, Perry cannot simply assert, *as he did*, the importance of the unequal relations and hang us to the cross because we stressed $f[g^{-1}(c + k)] = g[h^{-1} \cdot (c + k)]$. Not only did he fail to demonstrate the superior relevance (and *robust* qualities) of the form he proposed, but even more surprisingly he completely misinterpreted the form he rejected, as is manifest by his contention that it provides either linear or constantly elastic demand curves when, in fact, we also demonstrated its relevance to concave and convex demand curves.

His next objection referring to decreasing returns violates an assumption we used in the part of the paper he is critiquing. Not only does he take us out of context by the subject remark, but he ignores the fact that later on in the paper we did change our assumption, in effect indicating the generality or, should we say, inclusiveness of our Theorem II *beyond its relation* to Theorem I. In sum, Perry's Sections I and II establish *on the basis of our model*, albeit in his restricted way, the Mislaid Maxim, Theorem II. We trust that further consideration of it, and also Theorem I, will take place in the years to come.

Perry's only (possible) real critique—other than for his references to what we should or should not have included in our paper—could therefore be contained in his Section III. But here *again* he took us out of context, actually in a more objectionable way than he did in the statement referred to

*Professor of economics, Texas A&M University, and associate professor of economics, Aoyama Gakuin University and University of Houston (adjunct), respectively.

[1]It is certainly the case that our second theorem alone can be deduced from a much less restrictive set of assumptions than that required to deduce both theorems simultaneously. Not only may the form of the demand function be relaxed, but the form of the *MC* curve can also be relaxed if Theorem II alone were deduced, as we ourselves demonstrated in Section III.

[2]Incidentally, fg^{-1} and gh^{-1} are misleading notations. They could mean $f \times g^{-1}$ and $g \times h^{-1}$, respectively, which are not what Perry means; what he really wants are $f(g^{-1}(c + k)) \gtrless g(h^{-1}(c + k))$.

in the paragraph above. Our evaluation of price effects of merger by a monopolist supplier of final market oligopolists was simply that alone. *Whether or not the firm would merge with just one or two or many downstream firms is basically non sequitur.* But to go with Perry's objective rather than ours, recall his argument that the upstream monopolist in our model allows the downstream stage "to compete away the monopoly profits" after the vertical integration has taken place. This argument is simply invalid. The correct proposition is that the downstream firms merging with the upstream monopolists would compete profits away *from all of the firms that may still remain independent.* What if no independent firms remain, one might ask as does Perry? He raises this query, in effect, as an extreme case since complete vertical integration subject to Cournot horizontal competition may not prove to be profitable to every participant (i.e., it may be profitable to some but not to all participants insofar as industry profits happen to be decreased under the circumstances). This particular possibility does not generate any problem, of course, for—if it happened to be the case—vertical integration would simply proceed in part, as the last firms willing to integrate would not receive an attractive contract offer from the upstream monopolist. Complete vertical integration under these circumstances would require horizontal merger as well for profit incentives. *In any case*, output is increased after vertical integration, be it complete or incomplete, and the conclusion we set forth in our paper remains invariant. Note further that Perry's argument that *industry profits* may be reduced after vertical integration has proceeded to its limit fails to distinguish individual firm incentives from industry profits, and only individual firm incentives count.[3]

May we conclude our reaction to Perry's observations by noting that our demonstration and findings dovetailed fully with the *subject matter we proposed* we would consider. His own analyses *in support of our findings* and his extensions in terms of his more restricted subject matter are reassuring.

The paper by John Haring and David Kaserman (henceforth H-K) argues in perhaps a more confined way than Perry that our assumptions are restrictive and the *Maxim unimportant.* A quick perusal of their critique compared with Perry's might suggest that their claim could be meritorious. For the reasons recorded below, we appreciate their observations, albeit as with Perry *rejecting all of them completely.* Consider the following:

We *did claim* that the Mislaid Maxim is "especially vital in this period of energy shortage and attacks on big business," *and we repeat that claim here.* Haring-Kaserman objected to it by contending that we used overly restrictive assumptions. They cited several economists who worked with models involving variable proportions rather than fixed proportions. Apparently in the H-K view, if the number of economists who use a different assumption than ours happens to be large, our assumption must be the restricted one.[4] We shall answer this particular charge by simply noting that diverse petroleum company representatives have advised us that the quantity of refined products per barrel of crude is essentially invariant to the alternative production processes that may be employed. Fixed proportions thus apply, at least in this part of the energy industry. Moreover, it is clear that besides the refining of crude, the ship-

[3]It is only along the lines of individual incentives for vertical integration that our Cournot assumption could (or should) be questioned. Indeed, if it were not for fear of antitrust prosecution, firm(s) which may collude vertically with input supplier(s) could readily identify the reaction functions of noncolluded firms and lead them accordingly. Then a Stackelberg leader-follower type of behavioral reaction would be required to replace our Cournot reaction. Our welfare conclusion on vertical integration could, in turn, be shown to remain unchanged again, which demonstration would be based on the more realistic condition of imperfect competition in all stages of production. A generalized analysis of vertical integration along this line must be reserved, however, to other writings.

[4]It has been argued by Robert Basmann that there is no sense in which assumptions are too restrictive or unrealistic; but let us accept H-K's words without methodological quibble.

ment of oil from the well to the refinery and the shipment again from the refinery to the dealer (each involving successive stages of production) is in fixed proportions. How much empirical relevance must one demonstrate before the related maxims can be considered important, and the underlying assumptions not considered narrow or restrictive?

The subject writers objected to our failure to include analyses of monopsony and bilateral monopoly in our paper. However, why should a downstream firm necessarily be a monopsonist? And frankly, in the world of spatial oligopoly and oligopsony, with overlapping market and supply areas, monopsony or bilateral monopoly would appear to be very unlikely market types. Let H-K deal with the narrow or restrictive markets, if in fact they really are interested in such markets.

Haring-Kaserman finally argue that they refuted our Theorem I by considering increasing marginal cost. They did this by substituting increasing marginal cost in place of the constant marginal cost that we assumed in Sections I and II of our paper. But which here is the more restrictive? Rather often we theoreticians are advised that real world firms produce at constant marginal costs over a wide range of output.[5] If, ***nevertheless***, we do accept ***their*** increasing or decreasing marginal cost assumption, our Theorem I would indeed be affected, ***and we never claimed it would not be!***[6] But we did not, of course, consider generality of assumptions for the sake of generality to be warranted in our paper, especially since, to repeat, constant *MC* and fixed input proportions appear to be ***the relevant conditions in the energy and distributive industries to which we directed our analysis***, and hence Theorem I *as stated* applied.[7]

Our position allows only one possible point of agreement between Perry, H-K, and us. And happily we *do agree*, although it is really with only an implicit idea of theirs: we agree the relevance of economic theory and the maxims which stem therefrom would be advanced if economic theory is so cast that it would shed light on important economic situations.

[5]Constant marginal cost applies to petroleum refineries up to around 90 percent of capacity.

[6]Theorem I is readily modifiable to include upward or downward sloping *MC* curves. Either our own Figure 1 or H-K's Figure 1 clearly implies that if the *MC* curve slopes upward (or downward), the input price applicable to the downstream industry would be higher (or lower) under competitive conditions than under conditions of monopoly. In no way is the insight or predictive power of our model restricted to a constant *MC* assumption; only Theorem I *as stated* requires constant *MC*.

[7]Incidentally, the impact of nonconstant marginal cost is not unfavorable to the Mislaid Maxim Theorem II.

REFERENCES

R. L. Basmann, "Modern Logic and the Suppositious Weakness of the Empirical Foundations of Economic Science," *Z. Volkswirt. und Stat.*, Heft 2 1975, *2*, 153–76.

M. L. Greenhut and H. Ohta, "Related Market Conditions and Interindustrial Mergers," *Amer. Econ. Rev.*, June 1976, *66*, 267–77.

J. R. Haring and D. L. Kaserman, "Related Market Conditions and Interindustrial Mergers: Comment," *Amer. Econ. Rev.*, Mar. 1978, *68*, 225–27.

M. K. Perry, "Related Market Conditions and Interindustrial Mergers: Comment," *Amer. Econ. Rev.*, Mar. 1978, *68*, 221–24.

Vertical Integration of Successive Oligopolists

By M. L. GREENHUT AND H. OHTA*

Vertical integration of successive monopolists (with fixed production coefficients) has long been known to provide merging monopolists with greater profit and their customers with greater outputs at lower prices. We contended in our earlier papers that similar welfare attributes apply to mergers between monopolist input suppliers and Cournot-type oligopolists.[1] But what is the result when the input supplier is also an oligopolist? The present paper answers this question. It demonstrates, in particular, that when vertical integration of successive oligopolists is mutually profitable, industry output increases and product price is lowered. The welfare gain stemming from vertical integration is further shown to hold not only under Cournot oligopoly but a Stackelberg "leader-follower" type of oligopoly.

*Professor, Texas A&M University, and associate professor, Aoyama Gakuin University (visiting professor, University of Houston), respectively. We wish to thank T. Copp, S. Holmes, F. Ryan, and T. Saving for their helpful suggestions and critiques. This paper is based in part on research funded by the National Science Foundation.

[1]The possibility of perverse welfare effects resulting from vertical integration of firms subject to variable input proportions was considered initially by John Vernon and Daniel Graham, examined further by Richard Schmalensee, George Hay, Frederick Warren-Boulton, recently repeated by Martin Perry, and by John Haring and David Kaserman. However, one can hardly neglect the quantitative importance of the vast set of industries and integrations for which fixed proportions apply. For example, in the petroleum industry, the quantity of crude remains invariant from the recovery process to the shipping of crude from wells to refineries. This invariance also applies to the shipment of the refined products to dealers and their final distribution to consumers. In refining, a preselected method of converting the crude into a certain output of refined products is used. Simple substitution of another mineral for some of the crude cannot be effected without shutting down the refinery and changing the entire production process.

I. Independent Upstream-Downstream Oligopolists

Consider two vertically related activities, say in the field of energy. Let the upstream stage involve the combined operation of refining and shipping petroleum by n independent input suppliers to m independent distributor-dealers. Conceive of the product sold by the m downstream firms as involving homogeneous tankloads of gasoline. The total tankloads for sale q_L are defined to be in fixed proportion to the homogeneous inputs of gasoline, which, in turn, are received in tankwagon quantities q_w from the upstream suppliers. In effect we have

$$q_L = \alpha q_w \tag{1}$$

where α stands for the constant coefficient of production.

Conceive next of the market demand for the final product as involving negligible cross elasticities of demand. Let this demand be a uniquely decreasing function of market price, given by

$$\begin{aligned} p_L &= f(q_L) \qquad f' < 0 \\ &= f(\alpha q_w) \qquad \text{via (1)} \end{aligned} \tag{2}$$

Market demand must be equated with industry supply. This requirement establishes

$$q_L = \sum_{i=1}^{m} q_{Li} \tag{3}$$

where q_{Li} stands for the ith distributor's supply.

Profit for the ith distributor π_i can then be given by

$$\begin{aligned} \pi_i &= p_L q_{Li} - p_w q_{wi} \qquad i = 1,2,\ldots,m \\ &= (\alpha f - p_w) q_{wi} \qquad \text{via (1)} \end{aligned} \tag{4}$$

where p_w stands for the price of the gasoline tankwagon purchased by the ith firm.[2]

[2]Other costs (such as in distribution) are disregarded in this paper without loss of generality.

Assume the m distributors are perfect competitors in purchasing gasoline. At the same instance, assume for the moment they are Cournot-type oligopolists in retailing the gasoline. The first-order profit-maximizing conditions for these distributors requires

$$(5)\qquad \partial\pi_i/\partial q_{wi} = 0$$
$$\therefore\ \alpha(f + f'\alpha q_{wi}) = p_w \qquad i = 1,2,\ldots,m$$

where under perfect competition in buying, p_w is a parameter invariant to changes in the quantity purchased by the individual distributor.[3]

Equation (5) thus depicts the individual distributor's demand for gasoline in tankwagon quantities q_{wi} at market price p_w. The total market demand for gasoline tankwagons simply involves summing (5) for all $i = 1,2,\ldots,m$.[4] This aggregation establishes

$$(6)\qquad \alpha\Big(mf + \sum_{i=1}^{m} f'\alpha q_{wi}\Big) = mp_w$$
$$\alpha\Big(f + \frac{1}{m}\sum f'\alpha q_{wi}\Big) = p_w$$

Since market demand, q_w must equate with the market supply of the n upstream firms, we also obtain

$$(7)\qquad q_w = \sum_{j=1}^{n} q_{wj}$$

where q_{wj} stands for the jth firm's supply of tankwagons of gasoline. The aggregate upstream supply depends on the profits

$$(8)\qquad \pi_j = p_w q_{wj} - c_j q_{wj} \qquad j = 1,2,\ldots,n$$

where c_j is a constant unit (= marginal) cost of production. Without loss of generality, we are conceiving, in effect, of a two-stage industry with petroleum refining and shipment belonging to the primary (upstream) stage of production, and distributing the final product to the consumers serving as the second (downstream) stage.[5] Profit maximization by the upstream Cournot oligopolists simply requires

$$(9)\qquad \partial\pi_j/\partial q_{wj} = 0$$
$$\alpha\Big(g + \frac{1}{m}f''\alpha^2 q_w q_{wj} + \frac{m+1}{m}f'\alpha q_{wj}\Big) = c_j$$
$$j = 1,2,\ldots,n$$

where $g = f + [1/m]f'\alpha q_w$, which henceforth will be called the correspondent to f. Note further that (9) is based also on profit-maximizing equilibrium conditions for the downstream producers; equation (5), in effect, is contained in (9). Summing (9) over all j's then establishes

$$(10)\qquad \alpha\Big(g + \frac{1}{mn}f''\alpha^2 q_w^2 + \frac{m+1}{mn}f'\alpha q_w\Big) = \frac{1}{n}\sum_{j=1}^{n} c_j$$

The equilibrium output of gasoline (in tankwagons as well as tankload quantities) is determined uniquely by (10), provided the c_j's are known and f is well-behaved.[6] Equation (10) has therefore established the equilibrium conditions for two vertically related activities, where the upstream stage involves Cournot oligopoly in selling and the downstream stage is characterized by perfect competition in buying.

II. Vertical Integration of Successive Oligopolists

The question may now be answered whether or not industry supply increases when some firms in the related stages of production integrate vertically. To answer this question, we shall consider the two

[3]The price of gasoline tankloads, on the other hand, is expected to vary as each distributor alters his supply while conjecturing that other sellers' supplies are fixed. The term $\alpha f'\alpha q_{wi}$ in equation (5) stems from this Cournot condition.

[4]Remember, in passing, that the demand for tankwagons of gasoline is readily transformed back to, in fact derives from, the downstream market demand for gasoline *tankloads*.

[5]Note that c_j could have been considered as the market price in gasoline units of the petrol-converted oil if we had assumed an additional lower stage of production.

[6]By well-behaved f we mean a continuous, twice differentiable function which, in addition, yields a monotonically decreasing function with respect to q_{wi} on the left-hand side of (10).

cases discussed below:

Case 1: *Cournot Oligopoly*. Consider l horizontally independent downstream firms which integrate vertically with l horizontally independent upstream firms where $l \leq \min(m, n)$. The first-order profit-maximization conditions for these integrated firms is then

$$(5') \quad \alpha(f + f'\alpha q_{wi}) = c_i \qquad i = 1, 2, \ldots, l$$

where the c_i's are the marginal costs of the upstream firms.[7] These costs are independent of, and conceived to be lower than the p_w of equation (5). Except for this specification, equation (5′) is equivalent to (5).

Now, the marginal revenues provided on the left-hand side of (5) and (5′) are the same for each of the downstream firms regardless of whether or not they themselves integrate with an upstream supplier. Moreover, the profit-maximizing condition for the $m - l$ nonintegrated firms remains as given before by (5) for these $i = l + 1, \ldots, m$ firms. (These $m - l$ dealers can be conceived for simplicity to purchase their gasoline tankwagons from the $n - l$ independent (oligopolistic) refineries.) Aggregating (5′) and (5), respectively, over $i = 1, 2, \ldots, l$ and $i = l + 1, \ldots, m$ therefore establishes

$$(6') \quad \alpha\left(f + \frac{1}{l} f'\alpha q^l_w\right) = \frac{1}{l}\sum c_i, \qquad q^l_w = \sum_{i=1}^{l} q_{wi}$$

and

$$(6'') \quad \alpha\left(f + \frac{1}{m - l} f'\alpha q^m_w\right) = p_w, \qquad q^m_w = \sum_{i=l+1}^{m} q_{wi}$$

These two equations, respectively, provide the aggregated inputs of the l integrated and $m - l$ nonintegrated downstream producers. Note in particular that equation (6″) represents the market demand for the gasoline tankwagons in the perspective of the $n - l$ nonintegrated upstream firms. Profit maximization by these input suppliers involves

$$(9a) \quad \alpha\left(g^{\dagger} + \frac{1}{m - l} f''\alpha^2 q^m_w q_{wj} + \frac{m - l + 1}{m - l} f'\alpha q_{wj}\right) = c_j \qquad j = l + 1, \ldots, n$$

where $g^{\dagger} = f + [1/(m - l)]f'\alpha q^m_w$. Since profit maximization by the l vertically integrated refineries is already given by (5′), it follows that in order to derive the counterpart to (10), we simply have to sum (9a) over $j = l + 1, \ldots, n$ to obtain

$$(10a) \quad \alpha\left(g^{\dagger} + \frac{1}{(m - l)(n - l)} \cdot f''\alpha^2 q^m_w q^n_w + \frac{m - l + 1}{(m - l)(n - l)} f'\alpha q^n_w\right) = \frac{1}{n - l}\sum c_j \qquad q^n_w = \sum_{j=l+1}^{n} q_{wj}$$

Market equilibrium requires the additional equations

$$(11) \quad q^n_w = q^m_w$$

$$(12) \quad q_w = q^n_w + q^l_w$$

These equations, together with (6′), (6″), and (10a), can be solved simultaneously for the five endogenous variables, q_w, q^n_w, q^m_w, q^l_w, p_w, where the derived equilibrium input price p_w must exceed the marginal costs (c_j) of the independent upstream firms.

A significant conclusion derives from the requirement $p_w > c_j$. Combining (6′) and (6″) towards this end, we obtain

$$(13) \quad \alpha g = p_w - (1/m)\sum_{j=1}^{l}(p_w - c_j) < p_w$$

where the correspondent to f, to recall, is defined as $g = f + (1/m)f'\alpha q_w$. If, in contrast, no vertical integration has taken place at all, equation (6) applies, repeated below for convenience as

[7] Vertical integration per se may reduce the costs of production, c's. In addition, economies of scale may operate to reduce the c's since integration increases output. We will assume away all of these possibilities, and concentrate our attention on the economics of integration that are related directly to market structures.

$$\alpha g = p_w \tag{13'}$$

Identity of the left-hand side of (13) and (13′), as well as the condition (pursuant to fn. 6) that they are decreasing functions of q_w, are each well established above. However, the middle term of (13) is less than the right-hand side of (13′).[8] The equilibrium result q_w is, therefore, unambiguously greater under the conditions of equation (13) than that which underscores (13′). The supply (q_L as well as q_w) must, in other words, increase with vertical integration, and the final price p_L must decline in accordance with equation (2).[9]

Case 2: Stackelberg Oligopoly. Intrinsic to the foregoing argument was the basic assumption that the l firm(s) which integrate vertically with the l oligopolistic input supplier(s) would behave *with respect to the noncolluded firms as would the firms in Cournot's world of oligopoly.* This assumption is, however, not requisite to our basic welfare results. In fact, if it were not for possible antitrust prosecution, the firms which integrate vertically with input suppliers could be expected not only to identify the reaction functions of noncolluded firms, but to *lead them* accordingly. The same general final market solution given previously would nevertheless obtain, as demonstrated below.

Consider Stackelberg's leader-follower market, and let l final good producers collude vertically with input suppliers. These firms, we propose, take the nonintegrated dealer's reaction functions as data in fulfilling the requirements of Stackelberg's leader-follower oligopoly. Their profit-maximization conditions would therefore not be given by (5′) but by

$$\frac{d\pi_i}{dq_{wi}} = 0, \quad \alpha\left(f + f'\alpha q_{wi} \cdot \left[1 + \frac{dq_w^m}{dq_{wi}}\right]\right) = c_i \qquad i = 1,2,\ldots,l \tag{5''}$$

where dq_w^m/dq_{wi} stems from the reaction functions of the $(m - l)$ nonintegrated firms. These reaction functions, provided by (5), are repeated below as

$$\alpha(f + f'\alpha q_{wj}) = p_w, \qquad j = l+1,\ldots,m \tag{14}$$

Differentiating (14) with respect to q_{wi}, while holding *all other merged firms' supply* as well as p_w constant, generates

$$\alpha\left(f'\left[1 + \frac{dq_w^m}{dq_{wi}}\right] + f'\frac{dq_{wj}}{dq_{wi}} + f''\alpha q_{wj}\left[1 + \frac{dq_w^m}{dq_{wi}}\right]\right) = 0, \qquad j = l+1,\ldots,m \tag{15}$$

Aggregating for all j's and rearranging terms establishes

$$\frac{dq_w^m}{dq_{wi}} = \frac{f'}{f'(m - l + 1) + f''\alpha q_w^m} - 1 \tag{16}$$

Substituting (16) back into (15) yields

$$\alpha\left(f + \frac{f'^2\alpha q_{wi}}{f'(m - l + 1) + f''\alpha q_w^m}\right) = c_i \qquad i = 1,2,\ldots,l \tag{17}$$

which equation provides the profit-maximizing conditions for the l merged firms.

[8] This condition requires stable levels of P_w before and after vertical integration when l is small relative to m. However, such stability is not even needed as l approaches m, i.e., as more and more firms integrate vertically.

[9] Perry argued that vertical integration requires profit incentives among the merging firms. However, such merger does not require greater industry profits. Rather, additional mergers would be feasible if they increase the profits of the merging firms at the expense of previously merged or still remaining independent firms. To appreciate the above proposition, assume $\alpha = 1$, $f(q) = a - q$, and let $m = n = 2$. Then it can readily be shown that vertical integration increases the profit of the initial merged firms, i.e., where $l = 1$. Incentive exists accordingly for the integration. However, the profit for the remaining independent firms, and the industry profit as well, can be shown to decrease in the process. There exist incentives, in other words, for the excluded (or slowpoke) firms to integrate vertically to recover their lost profits. In fact, the final result with $l = 2$ is characterized by lower total industry profit than that which prevailed initially when no integration at all had occurred, i.e., when $l = 0$. Merged firms would now find the original state a better one. Can they go back to *their* garden of Eden? Not individually without simultaneous agreement.

This equation contrasts with (5′), the profit-maximizing equation for the $(m - l)$ independent firms. Combining (17) and (5′) for all firms produces the counterpart to (13), namely

$$(13'') \quad \alpha\left(f + \frac{1}{m} f'\left[\alpha q_w^m + \frac{f'}{[f'(m - l + 1) + f''\alpha q_w^m]} \alpha q_w^l\right]\right) = p_w - \frac{1}{m} \sum (p_w - c_i)$$

where the major parenthesis term of (13″) remains above the correspondent g whenever the major bracketed term is less than αq_w. The sufficient condition for this particular relation is $f'' \leq 0$, although even if $f'' > 0$, the left-hand side of the above formula would continue to lie above g so long as $f'/[f'(m - l + 1) + f''\alpha q_w^m]$ is always less than unity. Under these general (rather nonrestrictive) conditions on the shape of the market demand function f, comparison of (13″) with (13) indicates sharply that market equilibrium supply would be even greater under vertical collusion in a Stackelberg world than under vertical collusion in a Cournot world of oligopoly.

III. Conclusion

The basic thesis of this paper applies in general to oligopolistic industries in which fixed proportions apply to successive stages of production. We propose, accordingly, that for industries so characterized, integration should be allowed without concern over arbitrary concentration ratios. In reverse pattern, our purely micro-economic inquiry into the subject of size indicates, for example, that the breaking up of large oil companies in the United States, *ceteris paribus*, would tend to diminish output.

REFERENCES

A. Cournot, *Mathematical Principles of the Theory of Wealth*, trans. N. T. Bacon, New York 1927.

M. L. Greenhut and H. Ohta, "Related Market Conditions and Interindustrial Mergers," *Amer. Econ. Rev.*, June 1976, *66*, 257–77.

______ **and** ______, "Related Market Conditions and Interindustrial Mergers: Reply," *Amer. Econ. Rev.*, Mar. 1978, *68*, 228–30.

J. R. Haring and D. L. Kaserman, "Related Market Conditions and Interindustrial Mergers: Comment," *Amer. Econ. Rev.*, Mar. 1978, *68*, 225–27.

G. A. Hay, "An Economic Analysis of Vertical Integration," *Ind. Org. Rev.*, No. 3, 1973, *1*, 188–98.

F. Machlup and M. Taber, "Bilateral Monopoly, Successful Monopoly, and Vertical Integration," *Economica*, May 1960, *27*, 101–19.

M. K. Perry, "Vertical Integration of Successive Monopolists: Comment," *Amer. Econ. Rev.*, Mar. 1978, *68*, 221–24.

R. Schmalensee, "A Note on the Theory of Vertical Integration," *J. Polit. Econ.*, July/Aug. 1972, *80*, 442–49.

J. M. Vernon and D. A. Graham, "Profitability of Monopolization by Vertical Integration," *J. Polit. Econ.*, July/Aug. 1971, *79*, 924–25.

F. R. Warren-Boulton, "Vertical Control with Variable Proportions," *J. Polit. Econ.*, July/Aug. 1974, *82*, 783–801.

Reprinted from

THE AMERICAN ECONOMIC REVIEW

[34]

Price and Market Space Effects of Bank Mergers*

John Greenhut
Melvin, L. Greenhut
Hiroshi Ohta†

Abstract

Bank merger policy has only recently begun to focus attention on spatial *sub*markets within the market area of banks. Regulatory decisions have noted the locational distribution of banks. But even then classical (spaceless) microeconomic theory and common sense have, at best, been applied. The present paper attempts to establish a different approach for dealing with the subject. It utilizes various principles of spatial microeconomic theory, applying them directly. Shortcomings of predicating bank merger decisions on the classical (spaceless) principles of competition are stressed, and an alternative set of principles set forth.

I. Classical Economic Approach to Bank Merger Policy

Regulatory authorities and courts in the U.S. have relied almost exclusively on classical (spaceless) principles of competition within banking markets in evaluating the competitive effects of bank mergers and acquisitions. This approach has assumed that all banks within a relevant banking market are subject to similar economic forces as competitive actions initiated in one segment of the market have been observed to be transmitted quickly to banks in other market segments. Once the geographic boundaries of the relevant banking market are drawn, all banks within these boundaries are then treated

---

* This paper is a sharply revised version of a paper initially presented with W. H. Kelly at the 1977 Conference on Bank Structure and Competition of the Federal Reserve Bank of Chicago. We wish to thank those in the audience there and several others in recent years who, along with Ohta's additional inputs, encouraged the writing of this paper.

as homogeneous, distinguishable only by differences in relative sizes and presumed market power.[1]

The definition of geographic market is therefore the standard critical factor governing evaluation of competitive consequences of bank mergers. Most large banks in major metropolitan areas typically compete not only for local deposits and loans, but also for regional, national, and international accounts. The geographic scope of banking services varies widely depending on the type of services and class of customers. Nevertheless, the Supreme Court has repeatedly defined the relevant geographic market for antitrust purposes as the *local* market since local customers, such as individuals and small commercial businesses, have the fewest alternative sources of banking services. They stand to lose the most if a viable independent competitor is eliminated by merger.[2]

Regulatory agencies and courts have typically included a variety of factors in conceptualizing the " local banking market ". They include commuting patterns, highway and road systems, radio, TV, newspaper coverage, natural access barriers (such as rivers or lakes), and legal barriers (such as state laws governing branching). The derived local area presumably contains a given, similar set of economic forces. But no distinctions are entered on the basis of locations *within* the local banking market, as *in essence* it is assumed that

---

1) In Philadelphia National Bank (1963), the Supreme Court ruled that banks provide a unique " bundle of services " and are therefore in a separate and distinct line of commerce within the meaning of Section 7. The Court recently reaffirmed its position in Connecticut National Bank (1974), which case is especially significant since savings banks in Connecticut are authorized to issue NOW accounts and are probably closer to commercial banks in terms of kinds of services provided local customers than any other type of nonbank financial institution. This paper adopts the Supreme Court's position and assumes " commercial banking " to be the relevant line of commerce, thus not distinguishing among banks on the basis of product mix. The theory to be developed herein, however, which uses location as the basis for distinguishing between degrees of competition within local banking markets, would nevertheless be naturally extendable to competitive distinctions based on differences in product mix and to other definitions of line of commerce.

2) See, e.g., Philadelphia National Bank (1963), Connecticut National Bank (1974), Marine Bancorporation, Inc. (1974), US vs Virginia National Bankshares, Inc. (1982), and Southwest Mississippi Bank vs FDIC (1980).

since all banks in the local market are subject to the same economic forces, a competitive action initiated by any one bank within the market is soon transmitted throughout the market.[3]

Beyond defining the relevant local banking market, the classical competitive analysis has become little more than a numbers game with mergers being evaluated in terms of impact on market structure.[4] For example, in the case of a horizontal merger between two banks in the same local market, the competitive effect has usually been assessed solely on the basis of impact on market concentration as measured by concentration ratios and the combined market share of the merging banks. No effort is normally made to distinguish on the basis of locations of the individual—merging banks. In other words, the market is generally treated as a point in space.[5]

The spaceless concept generally applies to the several agencies evaluating bank mergers, excepting in part, as we shall discuss below, the Federal Reserve Board of Governors. Yet even under the same overall spaceless approach, differences apply to the evaluations by regulatory agencies of the

3) It is generally held that Ranally Metro Areas (RMA's) is a better approximations of this concept of local market than the Standard Metropolitan Statistical Areas (SMSA's) since the RMA does not conform to county lines and hence would exclude banks at the fringe of the county which are not readily accessible to downtown commuters.

4) Only recently have courts displayed a tendency to deviate from a strict structural market test of illegality according to Kirkpatrick and Stephen (1976).

5) In the case of so-called geographic extension mergers, some differences among banks within local markets have been drawn on the basis of location. In particular, location has been considered when the relevant local banking market involves a relatively large metropolitan area and the acquiring organization is a large statewide bank holding company that normally would not be expected to enter the market except in a downtown location where its expertise in wholesale banking could be applied. In such case, banks within the Central Business District have been distinguished from suburban banks in determining the number of viable alternatives. But though locations are therefore considered, the distinction has been based essentially on differences in product mix and customer orientation rather than on the concepts of spatial economic theory. See, for example, in the Federal Reserve Bulletin (February 1975), pp. 109–112, the order denying the acquisitions by Texas Commerce Bancshares, Inc., Houston, Texas of the Austin National Bank and Oak Hill National Bank, both of Austin, Texas.

effects of bank mergers. Thus, for example, Velk (1972) contended that the Justice Department has based its bank merger decisions on only the competitive impact, as measured by changes in concentration, while the competitive impact was considered to be the least important of seven aspects of the law in the view of bank supervisory agencies. He further observed that bank supervisory agencies and the Department of Justice also disagree on the nature of the competitive impact, with the Department generally defining a smaller relevant market than the supervisory agencies (Velk, p. 1102). In the U.S. vs First National Bank of Houston (1967) case, for example, the Department held the relevant market to be Harris County while the Federal Reserve authorities defined the market as the five county SMSA.

Eisenbeis (1975) in his examination of the competitive factor found the Department's interpretation to be much stricter than that of the agencies. In similar context, J. Sims (1975) had already stressed the fact that the Department of Justice follows strict guidelines, as set forth by the Department in its (1968) publication. Bank supervisors, on the other hand, he said, do not agree with the strict guidelines.

According to Leavitt (1975) the Board has made it clear that in matters of concentration it does not follow any arithmetic formula and has no predetermined level of concentration in mind. In similar key, Waxberg and Robinson (1965) have argued that the Department's strict reliance on concentration ratios and market shares contrasts sharply from the agencies' reliance on other factors.

There has also been disagreement among regulatory agencies as to the application and relevance of the potential competition doctrine. Leavitt (1975) indicates that the Fed. places more weight on the history of the banks and the state's branching restrictions than on the possible adverse potential competition effects. Baker (1973) and Sims (1975) propose that potential competition can be adversely effected when statewide concentration changes.

This paper contends that the basic classical approach errs in treating local banking markets as if they are spaceless. Consumers do distinguish between banks on the basis of relative convenience (transportation costs). And even though most banks view rival banks within their immediate service area as their " major " competitors, they still react—even if somewhat indirectly—to competitive actions initiated by banks located in more distant segments of the market. A chain oligopoly effect a la Chamberlinean theory (1935, Appendix C) actually applies which generates nonclassical results and relations.[6)]

The Federal Reserve Board of Governors has in a sense adopted this logic in denying several horizontal acquisitions by bank holding companies which, on the basis of their impact on market concentration, would have to be classified as *de minimis*. Unfortunately, we shall later see that in their applications they did not have the perspective of spatial competition and pricing which we shall contend is relevant. For the moment, however, it suffices to focus attention on only their use of location as a basis for evaluating bank merger effects. Thus when First International Bancshares, Inc. (" First International ") sought to acquire two Houston suburban banks—First State Bank of Bellaire (" Bellaire Bank ") and University State Bank (" University Bank ")—the Board considered their respective locations. It noted that though First International was the state's largest bank holding company, it ranked only fifth in the Houston SMSA banking market with about 3.0 percent of the market's deposits. Vital too was the affiliation of Bellaire Bank and University Bank through common stockholding. Together these banks controlled only 1.2 percent of the market's deposits, and approval of both applications would not have significantly increased First International's market share nor materially affected deposit concentration in the Houston market. However, Bellaire Bank and University Bank were located only four miles from each other and had significant service area overlap. The Board of Governors recognizing this fact decided to approve the acquisition of Bellaire Bank and deny the University Bank acquisition, thereby breaking up the previous ownership affiliation tie and enhancing competition in the immediate environs of the two banks.[7)]

6) In most of the major metropolitan banking markets, the boundaries of the market extend well beyond the service areas of all but the market's very largest banks.

7) See Federal Reserve Bulletin (Nov. 1973), pp. 813–815.

The Board differentiated again in mid 1974 on the basis of location when it denied one of two applications by First City Bancorporation of Texas ("First City"). First City, the largest banking organization in Houston and second largest in Texas, applied to acquire Meyerland Bank, a small suburban bank in the Southwest section of the Houston SMSA banking market. At the same time, First City applied to acquire Almeda-Genoa Bank, another small suburban bank in the Southeast portion of the market. While Meyerland Bank was about twice as large as Almeda-Genoa Bank on the basis of deposits, neither bank controlled as much as 0.2 percent of the market's deposits. The acquisition of Meyerland Bank would have had a virtually imperceptible impact on First City's market share or on overall market concentration. In denying acquisition of Meyerland Bank, while at the same time approving acquisition of the Almeda-Genoa Bank, the Board noted that First City had already made significant inroads into the rapidly growing Southwest quadrant of Houston. In contrast with the Almeda-Genoa case, there would be significant service area overlap between Meyerland Bank and other banking subsidiaries of First City previously established in the Meyerland submarket. The Board was therefore concerned that First City might obtain too much market power in one section of the market through its ownership of four banking subsidiaries serving the same submarket within the Houston SMSA banking market.[8)]

There are other isolated examples where location has been a critical variable in the decision by the Board of Governors as to whether or not to approve a bank holding company application. However, their "locational" approach has not been tied to space-microeconomic theory. Nor has it been adopted in any way by the courts or industrial organization economists.

---

8) As further proof that the Board was not concerned with overall market concentration, but was concerned with competition between banks having service-area overlap, note that it recently approved four other acquisitions by First International in the Houston SMSA banking market, which together are 26 percent larger in deposits than University Bank. Again, the new acquisitions involve banks which do not have overlapping service areas. See Federal Reserve Bulletin (July 1974), pp. 506–510.

They cling instead to classical economic theory without appeal to an alternative theory that would explain the impact on competitive behavior of differences in bank location within a local banking market. Our paper is an attempt towards this theoretical underpinning.

II. Applying Spatial Price Theory

Our spatial pricing model requires aggregation (integration) of demands of consumers located *throughout* a service area. This aggregation involves complications which can be minimized by a few simplifying assumptions.

Conceive of a local market consisting of two banks separated by a significantly-costly distance S. Denote the banks as A and B and focus attention on A by treating B as the distant seller. Assume further that buyers are dispersed evenly along a line joining banks A and B.

Now, the demand for banking services of an individual consumer can be given by the general demand curve

$$(1) \quad p = a - bq^x$$

Lengthy discussion of this demand form, which we will refer to as an " exponential " demand, may be found in various articles (Greenhut, Greenhut 1975; M. L. Greenhut and Ohta 1976; J. Greenhut 1977). Suffice it to point out at this time that the demand form encompasses a wide range of demands. When a, $b>0$ and $x=1$, for example, the demand is linear. A constantly elastic demand is obtained by letting $a=0$, $b<0$, and $x<0$, while a convex (from above) demand stems from $a, b>0$ and $x>1$. As one might infer from these examples, demands embodied in (1) range from the convex demand ($x>1$) to a linear demand ($x=1$) to concave demand ($0<x<1$) to an " extremely " concave demand—where a price intercept does not even exist—($b<0$ and $x<0$). The exponent x is the vital parameter, then, in determining the shape of the demand curve.[9]

9) Different elasticities (increasing, decreasing of varying rates, and constant elasticity) can be shown to apply to our demand function. For stable equilibrium results (i.e., avoiding positively sloped marginal revenues), x must be constrained to values greater than -1.

Fundamental to the analysis of price-competition relations in banking is the observation that banks do not generally discriminate among *local* buyers on the basis of location. Instead, they discriminate according to risk, size of transactions, etc. Banks, in other words, charge a unique mill price to consumers possessing identical financial characteristics irrespective of their proximity to the bank. In spatial economic terms, they price f.o.b. mill with the consumer bearing the transportation costs incurred in doing business at the bank. Of course, bank loans to householders, small businesses, etc., involve different characteristics, in effect constituting multi-product lines in which the cost of transportation, hence location will be seen to have varying effects. (By way of example, a big firm may be willing to bank at large distances and hence will view many alternative banks as sources of funds, with each alternative source appearing as if located at a point in space.) In general, however, we shall propose that if m denotes the mill price charged by the bank for a " unit of banking services," then the total price paid by the consumer located t " dollars " from the bank is $m+t$; and this holds whether or not t is large or small per unit of distance, as the distance cost will be significant in either case.[10] The exponential demand curve may thus be written as

$$(2a) \quad m+t=a-bq^{x},$$

10) For our purposes, space should be viewed from the standpoint of economic rather than geographic distance (or location), by which we mean if the individual regards a bank as more convenient than another, it is in effect located closer to him in his economic space. Spatial economic submarkets are thus disjoint even though their geographic service areas may overlap. And see (Devletoglou 1971). Indeed, because of commuting patterns, individuals may bank at locations distant from their residences. In effect, if we let n stand for the number of service areas in the local market, we could then conceive of each individual as being t_1 distance cost units from service area 1 (downtown perhaps), t_2 units from service area 2 (his residence), and so forth. Since we are constrained in depicting this idea to a 2 dimensional space, the best we can do is (1) regard a commuter as located in the service area (place of work or residence) within which he considers banking services to be most convenient, and (2) recognize that the individual could switch to the alternative service areas if it becomes relatively advantageous for him to do so.

or

(2b) $m=(a-t)-bq^x$.

where $a, b>0$ when $x>$ while $b<0$ is assumed when $0>x>-1$. Quantity demanded at mill price m is then given by

$$(3) \quad q=\left[\frac{1}{b}(a-t-m)\right]^{1/x}.$$

Equation (3) represents only the demand of the buyer located t "dollars" from the seller.[11] But t may vary from 0 at the bank's location to some maximum value, say T, at the boundary of the product's service area, where $T<a-m$. We further assume homogeneous demands and a uniform distribution of buyers along a linear market space. Total demand at price m, which involves aggregating (integrating) the individual quantities, then yields

$$(4) \quad Q=\int_0^T\left(\frac{a-m-t}{b}\right)^{1/x}dt=\frac{bx}{x+1}\left[\left(\frac{a-m}{b}\right)^{(x+1)/x}-\left(\frac{a-m-T}{b}\right)^{(x+1)/x}\right]$$

Profit maximization involves equating marginal revenue with marginal cost. The equality may be expressed by

$$(5) \quad m+Q\frac{dm}{dQ}=c \quad \text{or} \quad (m-c)\left(\frac{-dQ}{dm}\right)=Q.$$

where c denotes marginal cost, assumed to be constant. Utilizing the latter form of the profit maximizing rule provides the equilibrium conditions for $x=1$ and $x=-1/2$

$$(6a) \quad (m-c)\left(\frac{T}{b}\right)=\frac{T}{b}\left(a-m-\frac{T}{2}\right)$$

$$(6b) \quad (m-c)b^2\left[\frac{1}{(m-a)^2}-\frac{1}{(m-a+T)^2}\right]=b^2\left[\frac{1}{m-a}-\frac{1}{m-a-T}\right].$$

---

11) As suggested by footnote 10, the cost of transportation properly includes expenditures of time and energy in addition to those of dollars. We may think in money-dollar terms in all cases, however, by placing a price tag (on the basis of opportunity cost) for time *and* energy.

Solving for m provides the following profit maximizing mill price formulas[12)]

(7a) $m=\frac{1}{2}(a+c)-\frac{T}{4}$

(7b) $m=c+\sqrt{(c-a)T+(c-a)^2}$

Equations (7a) and (7b) uncover two important conditions:

1. An upward shift in the demand curve (i.e., an increase in the parameter a) results in a higher price when $x=1$, but a lower price when $x=-1/2$.
2. A decrease in size T of the market area raises price when $x=1$, but lowers it if $x=-1/2$.

These relationships will be considered in greater detail later in this section. For the present they are pointed out in order to emphasize the importance of examining demand curves with negative as well as positive x.

Derivation of Mill Price Formulas for Two Spatially Separated Banks

---

12) The steps leading from equation (6) to (7) are as follows. Divide (6a) by T/b, add m+c, and divide by 2 to obtain:

(i-a) $m-c=a-m-\frac{T}{2}$

(ii-a) $m=\frac{1}{2}(a+c)-\frac{T}{4}.$

To derive (7b) from (6b), combine the fractions of (6b) and divide by b^2, yielding

(i-b) $(m-c)\frac{(2m-2a+T)T}{(m-a)^2(m-a+T)^2}=\frac{T}{(m-a)(m-a+T)}.$

Then, multiply both sides of (i-b) by $(m-a)^2(m-a+T)^2$ and utilize the distributive property to establish respectively:

(ii-b) $(m-c)(2m-2a+T)=(p-a)(p-a+T)$

(iii-b) $m^2-2cp+(2ac-cT+aT-a)^2=0.$

Equation (iii-b) is quadratic with solution

(iv-b) $m=\frac{2c+\pm\sqrt{4c^2+4(cT-aT+a^2-2ac)}}{2}$

$=c\pm\sqrt{(c-a)T+(c-a)^2}$

$=c+\sqrt{(c-a)T+(c-a)^2}$ (since $m>c$).

Price and Market Space Effects of Bank Mergers

The pricing structure in a local market comprising banks A *and* B obtains directly from (7) provided that the market between A and B is separated at a given point T " dollars " from A, hence S-T " dollars " from B. Due to variances in the quality of services, consumers may be conceived to be willing to pay a ***premium*** of r per unit of banking services provided by B compared to A. Hence, if the spatial demand for A's services is given by

$$(8)\quad m_A=(a-t)-bq^x,$$

the demand for the services provided by the preferred bank B is

$$(9)\quad m_B=(a+r-t)-bq^x.$$

Also disparity in costs may be assumed by letting A's marginal cost (MC) equal c, and B's marginal cost equal $c-f$, where the parameter f denotes the greater efficiency of B compared to A when $f>0$. Given these additional relations, profit maximization by the banks requires the mill prices

$$(10a)\quad m_A=\frac{1}{2}(a+c)-\frac{T}{4}$$

$$(10b)\quad m_B=\frac{1}{2}(a+r+c-f)-\frac{S-T}{4}$$

under conditions of linear demand for A and B respectively. We alternatively obtain

$$(11a)\quad m_A=c+\sqrt{(c-a)T+(c-a)^2}$$

$$(11b)\quad m_B=(c-f)+\sqrt{(c-f-a-r)(S-T)+(c-f-a-r)^2}$$

for demands characterized by the negative exponential $x=-1/2$.

The key parameter in (10) and (11) is the boundary-distance-cost T, which provides the link between pricing in A's service area and pricing in B's. For example, if bank B were able to intensify its competitive impact by expanding its service area (reduce T), bank A's monopolized service area would be cut. *Competition exists among local banks because they share service area boundaries.* But note, the boundary separating the service areas of banks is not an arbitrary variable set by economic warfare between the two opposing parties, as in the case of national-political boundaries. Instead, assuming (as we did) that bankers consider their market areas as exogenous variables (which assumption we shall relax later), equilibrium results only when T attains the ***unique*** value given by the demand and cost parameters obtained below.

Recognize initially that a market boundary point(s) applies to the location(s) where the distant consumer(s) is (are) indifferent between A and B. An indifferent consumer, in other words, would just as readily travel T units to bank A and pay m_A for banking services as he would travel S-T units to bank B and pay m_B. Recall further our assumption that customers are willing to pay the premium r for bank B's services. The consumer at T is therefore indifferent between A and B if and only if we have

$$(12)\quad (m_A+r)+T=m_B+(S-T).$$

Now, combining either (12) with (10) or (11), where use of (10) or (11) depends upon the value of x, establishes unique ***equilibrium*** values for m_A, m_B *and* T—three equations and three unknowns. At any value of T other than that provided by the simultaneous solution of the three equations, an unstable state must obtain.

Let us proceed then to solve the simultaneous equations for the profit maximizing values of m_A, m_B, and T. Working with the linear demand first, we rewrite the equilibrium conditions

$$(13a)\quad m_A=\frac{1}{2}(a+c)-\frac{T}{4}$$

$$(13b)\quad m_B=\frac{1}{2}(a+r+c-f)-\frac{S-T}{4}$$

$$(13c)\quad m_A+T=m_B-r+(S-T).$$

Substituting (13a) and (13b) into (13c) yields

$$(14)\quad \frac{1}{2}(a+c)+\frac{3}{4}T=\frac{1}{2}(a-r+c-f)+\frac{3}{4}(S-T),$$

which when solved for T establishes the market boundary

$$(15)\quad \hat{T}=\frac{1}{2}S-\frac{1}{3}(r+f)$$

where the circumflex $\wedge$ denotes an equilibrium result. Profit maximizing mill prices may then be derived by substituting $\hat{T}$ into (13a) and (13b). We obtain

$$\text{(16a)} \quad \hat{m}_A = \frac{1}{2}(a+c) + \frac{1}{12}(r+f) - \frac{1}{8}S$$

$$\text{(16b)} \quad \hat{m}_B = \frac{1}{2}(a+c) + \frac{1}{12}(5r-7f) - \frac{1}{8}S.$$

The equilibrium values of $\hat{T}$ and m_A, specified respectively by (15) and (16a), yield the market boundary price

$$\text{(17)} \quad \hat{m}_A + \hat{T} = \frac{1}{2}(a+c) - \frac{1}{4}(r+f) + \frac{3}{8}S.$$

Figure 1 is constructed given these profit maximizing values. It depicts the equilibrium state of two adjacent service areas in each of which demand is assumed to be linear. The vertical axis of Figure 1 represents the total price (mill price plus transportation cost) paid by consumers located at different points in the market space. So an individual located at the same point as A pays only the mill price

$$\frac{a+c}{2} + \frac{r+f}{12} - \frac{S}{8},$$

while distant customers of A (e.g., those located in the direction of B) incur the transportation cost t_A. Once t_A exceeds

$$\frac{S}{2} - \frac{r+f}{3},$$

the consumer banks with B. Figure 1 thus depicts the total price-transportation cost schedules of banks A and B, with A servicing the left-hand portion of the space and B the right-hand.

It warrants emphasis that the entire market space is divided equally when sellers are identical (r and f equal 0). But if the distant seller operates more efficiently than his competitor ($f>0$), or if he offers a more highly valued product ($r>0$), he will gain control over a *larger share of the local market.* More specifically, if the distant bank B is superior to A (r and/or $f>0$), then

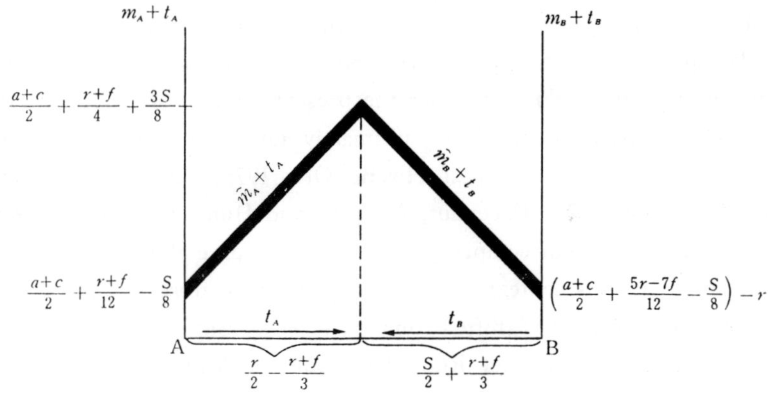

Figure 1 The Spatial Equilibrium State When Demand Is Linear

(18a) $\hat{T}<\frac{S}{2}$,

implying that less than half the local market is serviced by A. The opposite result holds true of course if A is the superior bank, for then r and/or $f<0$ which results in

(18b) $\hat{T}>\frac{S}{2}$

We are finally at the point where selected principles can be drawn. Recall initially our claim that the full scope of the spatial price-transmission process underscoring banking must be determined. Towards this end, we designated the cost and demand parameters which affect prices as c, f and a, r respectively. A change in a or c brings about identical changes in m_A and m_B. But these changes reflect forces that simultaneously affect all banks. The phenomenon we are interested in is a shift in the competitive balances among banks which ignite a series of price adjustments throughout the local market. Parameters a and c do not generate such a series, but r and f do. This fact explains why they were included in the model. If B's competitive strength increases, r and/or f increase, which forces A to react.

Now, we have already deduced above the impact of changes in r and/or f on $\hat{T}$. Among other things, we know that due to improvement in B's position, it can capture a larger share of the local market than before. A's market space is, accordingly, intruded upon by B. Does A retaliate? Does a pricewar ensue? No, not under the present model. As equation (16a) reveals, an increase in either r or f ultimately induces an *increase* in the mill price of A. (And see Greenhut, Hwang, Ohta 1975; Phlips 1976; Capozza and Van Order 1977; Greenhut, Norman and Hung 1987; Ohta 1988.) This is one paradox of competition in economic space alluded to earlier in our paper. In this context, Figure 2 depicts an increase in f in panel (i) as the mill price of A is shifted from m_A to m'_A. Similarly, the impact of a rise in r is shown in panel (ii). The important idea portrayed by Figure 2 is that *price changes are adversely transmitted throughout the local market whenever demand is linear.* Any improvement in one bank's competitive position enables it to *reduce* price and expand into a neighboring service area, which act however may surprisingly be met by an increase in price on the part of the distant bank. This particular result derives, in fact, from the general elasticity relation underscoring equation (3)$'$:

$$(3)' \quad ln\, q = \frac{1}{x}\; ln\, \frac{x}{b}(a-t-m)$$

$$\frac{1}{q}\frac{dq}{dm} = \frac{1}{x}\frac{b}{x(a-t-m)} - \frac{x}{b}$$

$$= -\frac{1}{x(a-t-m)}$$

$$\therefore \quad e_m \equiv -\frac{dq}{dm}\frac{m}{q} = \frac{m}{x(a-t-m)}$$

$$\therefore \quad \frac{\partial e_m}{\partial t} = \frac{m}{x(a-t-m)^2} \begin{matrix} >0, & x>0 \\ <0, & x<0 \end{matrix}$$

Thus, as transportation cost t increases, the individual demand q becomes increasingly more (less) elastic with respect to mill price m when demand is a positive (negative) exponential.

As the market area is expanded to include more and more distant points, the seller picks up buyers with increasingly more (less) elastic demand than

国際政経論集

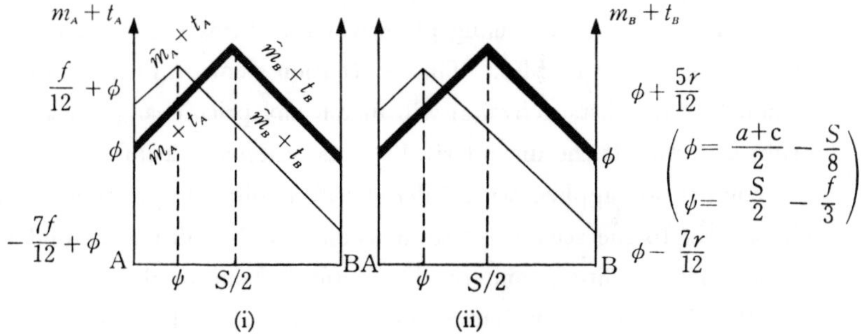

Figure 2 Competitive Effect Of Price Change When $x>0$

that of proximate buyers when $x>0$ ($x<0$). Aggregate demand accordingly becomes more and more elastic (inelastic) as successively more and more elastic (inelastic) individual demands are added to the total. Conversely, the impact of a distant competitor's intrusion (or new entry) on the original service area of a bank is to take away the most elastic (inelastic) demands in that bank's market space whenever demand is of the positive (negative) exponential form. The aggregate demand remaining, in turn, is less (more) elastic than it was before the change in competitive balance. This new elasticity causes prices to be *raised* (*lowered*). (Cf. Greenhut, *et al.* (1975, 1987); Ohta (1981, 1988).)

III. Widening the Scope of Spatial Price Theory

The spatial price theory introduced to this point in the paper broadens the scope of economic analysis in so far as concerns bank merger regulations. In particular, our theory has revealed the crucial role that the local market demand form plays in determining economic values over distance. (1) Can we conclude that a positive exponential demand, which *may* well characterize consumer wants for banking services, always brings about perverse price effects from spatial competition? (2) Can we conclude that bank mergers would—in general—be favorable under such conditions?

The answer to the first question is in the affirmative if firms are subject to the particular type of spatial competition implicitly assumed by us thus far in the paper. That spatial competition type is called Löschian competition, and is defined as taking place when all firms regard their market spaces as exogenous variables. This conception stems in turn from the assumption that the distant rival(s) will match any price change initiated by the subject firm. If the distant rival(s) acts otherwise, a different form of spatial competition applies, with different effects obtaining as shown below.

The answer to the second question would also be affirmative under the same Loschian conditions and the liquidation of one of the merged bank units. But the increased welfare resulting from greater distances and hence lower mill prices could, of course, be offset by the welfare loss incurred by customers in the neighborhood of the liquidated bank(s).[13] However for our objectives and needs, let us go beyond the alternatives provided by the Löschian model of spatial markets and evaluate results under an alternative model *as well as* price effects when the merger does *not* involve liquidating a facility.

Consider the framework initially set forth in Greenhut, Ohta, Scheidell (1972) rather than Lösch's spatial competition framework. In that model, a firm was assumed to regard its market space as *variable*. Only the rival's delivered price at and around a market boundary point (as determined by the mill price(s) which the subject firm and the rival firm(s) select) is conceived of as exogeneously given in that model. Alternatively phrased, a delivered price ceiling is taken as a datum in that model, not the mill price. What is the effect on bank merger policy of this particular spatial boundary point(s) assumption?

Take $p=p_0$ as the price ceiling at an as yet undetermined market boundary

13) There is a developing literature on the subject of welfare gains and losses over economic space. (E.g., see Holahan, W.L. (1975), Beckmann (1976), Greenhut, *et. al.* (1990); and also Anderson, de Palma and Thisse (1989). Present needs do not require any review or analysis along this line except to observe that a lower mill price does not by itself mean lower average delivered prices. In fact, it can be shown that it also does not mean an increasing "average consumers' surplus." The welfare gain from a lower mill price can easily be seen to be offset in some instances by a welfare loss among the customers in the neighborhood of the liquidated bank where delivered prices were, of course, originally the lowest, resolution of the matter depends on assumptions made.

point T; but conceive initially of it as having stemmed from Löschian competition, i.e., $T=T_0$ and $p_0=m_0+T_0$. Then any change in the subject firm's mill price m below *or* above the equilibrium price m_0 would generate a corresponding change in the rival's delivered price p at T_0. In that *alternative model*, the now assumed fixed ceiling price p_0 signifies that if p would in fact be lower than p_0 (or above it) at the old T_0 boundary point, the actual size of the subject firm's market area would be changed, either increased or decreased as the case be. The altered market space and new boundary would extend to the point where the price p approaches p_0. Thus the market boundary point T is a variable in the fixed p_0 model, being shifted further away from (or coming closer to) the subject firm as its mill price is lowered (raised).

It was shown (in Greenhut, Hwang, and Ohta 1975) that the elasticity of demand is higher in the fixed price ceiling model than it is under conditions of the Löschian fixed market area model *regardless of the form of the demand function*. It follows that the equilibrium price under the price ceiling type of spatial competition is *ceteris paribus* strictly less than would be the Löschian equilibrium price. It therefore follows that the perverse effect of spatial competition—a la Lösch—does *not* arise. More generally, the impact on mill price of the price ceiling type of competition is *always* to yield lower prices when a bank (firm) locates within the market space of another bank *at a distant point* from the established center, again *regardless of the form of the local demand function, ceteris paribus*. (And see Capozza and Van Order 1977.) The fixed ceiling price model accordingly provides the spatial analogue to classical price theory insofar as concerns the effect of entry *and* alternative production center (Greenhut, Hwang, and Ohta 1975).

The types of spatial (oligopolistic) competition evident above combine with the forms of market demands to play a decisive role in spatial pricing. Since banks are engaged in spatial competition, these same forces must be considered in evaluating bank mergers. Note that the foregoing analysis reveals greater underlying aggressiveness in one type of spatial competition (i.e., price ceiling type) vis a vis the other (i.e., the Löschian type of competition). Greater aggressiveness may also result in the liquidation of independent units via bank merger. Final results in any case remain favorable from the vantage point of the long run, as is indicated below.

Consider—in the last context—the path taken towards the zero-profit long-run state under the problem generating positive exponential demand that has been stressed thus far in this section of the paper. In the case of price ceiling type of competition, spatial entry (reduced distances) pushes delivered price schedules downward, while the opposite upward shift takes place under Löschian competition. Insofar as the mill price decreases monotonically as entry increases under the price ceiling type of competition, and the opposite relation applies to Löschian competition, the former competitive form must yield strictly lower prices over the entire market than would the latter. This result works regardless of whether or not a resulting bank merger involves the liquidation of a given facility. To see this last result, consider the following:

Let there be two connected banking centers at the end points of a line, by which we mean buyers at many locations between them could shift their trade readily from the one center to the other. Assume further that the two firms are subject to Löschian competition and enjoy windfall profits. So a third firm may enter, and we assume it locates at a point to the north of all buyers along that line at a site nearer than the original banks to the set of buyers located around the mid point of that line. (In effect, this new bank would be catering to the set of buyers who are located over the plain nearest its site.) Focus attention, however, on only the buyers distributed *near* to and *at* the midpoint of the line. If the subject entry occurred under Löschian competition, mill prices would go up *ceteris paribus* even while excess profits are wiped out by that entry. Suppose this did occur. The upshot would be that the original bankers find themselves squeezed. Hence they will tend to adopt a more aggressive price policy than previously marked their competition, in effect ending up with the price ceiling *type* of competition and lower prices.[14] The final result would then be either the take

14) Aggressive profit maximizing pricing over a landscape can take many forms which, in a general sense, are captured by our price ceiling. For example, see Gee (1985), Lederer and Hurter (1986), MacLeod, Norman and Thisse (1988).

over of the new bank (followed by liquidation) or (in the case of scale economies) continuance of the new facility with *desirable price effects* holding in either event.

We propose, accordingly, that the *differentia specifica* in models which generate the undesired Löschian competitive equilibrium results are 1) its derivation of relatively too many firms in a given market area, 2) charging comparatively high prices. We propose, however, that real world spatial price practices, and the development of competitive locations due to population growth will force a change from any moderate form of spatial competition to a more aggressive (price ceiling) type of competition, and that competition *may* lead to the merger of some units. But regardless of the merger, lower prices and more active spatial competition would have arisen.

Let us note finally in summary form that the location of a distant bank within the market space of another lowers prices under negative exponential demands regardless of the spatial model followed *and* whether or not the distant bank is an independent unit or a merged unit. Liquidation alone of that bank would produce bad price effects; but liquidation can be expected if and only if profits are found to be negative after the entry at a distance. And if negative, no entry was feasible. In contrast, price goes up under Löschian competition and positive exponential demands. And then if distant entry causes profits to become negative in the presence of rising mill prices, the price ceiling type of spatial competition along with its falling mill price effect is proposed as the likely replacement of Löschian competition. In turn, the distant bank disappears in time regardless of whether or not it had an independent existence. And last of all, if the distant entry still left positive profits, merger or independent status is non sequitur to the mill price effects, whether they were good or bad for the consumer.

IV. Conclusion

Our spatial micro-economic theory simply contends that only those mergers which generate higher mill prices in a market need be outlawed. It follows that if merged units collude with others to constrain entry, the projection of efficiency and lower prices for the space economy would fail to eventuate. Assuming away such conditions indicates that even just two firms (banks), *etc.* competing actively can provide the efficiency and zero profits equilibria which economists have long proposed as the guideline for the free enterprise economy. Mergers of banks should *in general* be allowed, provided the future entry of other banks remains likely at any competitive location, nearby or distant. We further propose that use of the concentration ratio (or related device) for measuring the dividing line between competition and monopoly is arbitrary and spurious (Benson and Greenhut, 1989). Most vitally, it is not scientifically established within the framework of classical spaceless theory. At the same instance, it is irrelevant to and misleading in the world of spatial realities (Phlips, 1977; Capozza and Van Order, 1978; and Ohta, 1980) which actually characterizes the banking industry.

† Authors are, respectively, Visiting Associate Professor, Arizona State University—West Campus; Abel Professor of Liberal Arts and Distinguished Professor of Economics, Texas A&M University, and Adjunct Distinguished Professor of Economics, University of Okayama; Professor of Economics, Aoyama Gakuin University, and Adjunct Professor of Economics, University of Houston.

REFERENCES

Anderson, S. P., de Palma, A. and Thisse, J. F., " Social Surplus and Profitability under Different Spatial Pricing Policies," CORE Discussion Paper #8910 (1989).

Baker, D. (1973), " Justice Department Standards " in R. Johnson, ed. *The Bank Holding Company 1973.* Dallas: Southern Methodist University Press, pp. 88–102.

Beckmann, W. (1976), " Spatial Price Policies Revisited," *Bell Journal of Economics*, 7, pp. 619–630.

Benson, B. and Greenhut, M. L. (1989) *The American Antitrust Laws in Theory and in Practice* (London: Gower Publishing Company).

Capozza, D. and Van Order, R. (1977) " Pricing Under Spatial Competition and Spatial Monopoly," *Econometrica*, 45, 6, pp. 1329–1338.

—— (1977), "A Simple Model of Spatial Competition," *Southern Economic J.*, 44, 2, pp. 361–367.

—— (1978), "A Generalized Model of Spatial Competition," *American Economic Review*, 65, 5, pp. 896–908.

Chamberlin, E. H. (1935), *Theory of Monopolistic Competition.* Cambridge, Mass: Harvard University Press.

Devletoglou, N. (1971), *Consumer Behavior.* London: Harper & Row.

Eisenbeis, R. (1975) " Differences in Federal Regulatory Agencies' Bank Merger Policies," *Journal of Money, Credit, and Banking*, 7, pp. 93–104.

Federal Reserve Bulletin, November 1973, pp. 813–815.

Federal Reserve Bulletin, July 1974, pp. 506–510.

Federal Reserve Bulletin, February, 1975, pp. 109–112.

Gee, J. M., (1985) " Competitive Pricing for a Spatial Industry." " *Oxford Economic Papers*, pp. 466–485.

Greenhut, John G. (1977), " On the Economic Advantages of Spatially Discriminatory Prices Compared with F.O.B. Prices ", *Southern Economic Journal*, 44, No. 1, pp. 161–166.

—— and Greenhut, M. L. (1975), " Spatial Price Discrimination, Competition, and Locational Effects ", *Economica*, 42, No. 168, pp. 401–419.

——, ——, and Ohta, H. (1990), " Regional Output and Price Effects of Spatial Price Discrimination," in *Festschrift*, K. Peschel ed. (Heidelberg: Springer Verlag)

Greenhut, M. L. (1956), *Plant Location in Theory and Practice*, Chapel Hill: University of North Carolina Press.

—— (1974), *A Theory of the Firm in Economic Space*, 2nd printing, Austin: Lone Star Publishing Co.

—— (1975), "A Theoretical Mapping From Perfect Competition to Imperfect Competition ", *Southern Economic Journal*, pp. 177–192.

——, Hwang, M. J. and Ohta, H. (1975), " Observations on the Shape and Relevance of the Spatial Demand Function," *Econometrica*, pp. 669–682.

——, Norman, G. and Hung, D. (1987), *The Economics of Imperfect Competition, A Spatial Approach*, Cambridge; Cambridge University Press.

—— and Ohta, H. (1975), *Theory of Spatial Pricing and market Areas*, Durham: Duke University Press.

—— and —— (1976), " Related Market Conditions and Interindustrial Merger," *American Economic Review*, pp. 267–277.

——, —— and Scheidell, J. (1972), "A Model of Market Areas Under Discriminatory Pricing," *Western Economic Journal*, pp. 402–413.

Holahan, W. L. (1975), " The Welfare Effects of Spatial Price Discrimination," *American Economic Review*," 65, pp. 495–503.

Kirkpatrick, M. W. and Stephen, P. M. (1976), " The Supreme Court and the ' New Economic Realism ' of Section 7 of the Clayton Act," *Southwestern Law Journal*, 30, pp. 821–837.

Leavitt, B. (1975), " Federal Reserve Holding Company Policies," in W. Baughm, ed., *Advanced Bank Holding Company Management Problems*, Dallas: Southern Methodist University Press, pp. 3–17.

Lederer, P. and Hurter, A. (1986), " Competition of Firms: Discriminatory Pricing and Location," *Econometrica*, pp. 623–640.

MacLoed, W. B., Norman, G. and Thisse, J. F. (1988), " Price Discrimination and Equilibrium in Monopolistic Competition," *International Journal of Industrial Organization*, pp. 429–466.

Price and Market Space Effects of Bank Mergers

Ohta, H. (1977), " On the Excess Capacity Controversy," *Economic Inquiry*, 15, pp. 153–165.

—— (1980), " Spatial Competition, Concentration, and Welfare," *Regional Science and Urban Economics*, 10, pp. 3–16.

—— (1981), " The Price Effects of Spatial Competition," *Review of Economic Studies*, 48, pp. 317–325.

—— (1988), *Spatial Price Theory of Imperfect Competition*, College Station: Texas A&M University Press.

Phlips, L. (1976), " Spatial Pricing and Competition," Commission of the European Communities, *Studies Competition-Approximation of Legislation Series*—Brussels.

——(1977), " Intertemporal Price Discrimination and Sticky Prices," presented at Summer Workshop, University of Warwick.

Sims, J. (1975), " Other Policy Developments: Justice Department Review," in W. Baughm, ed. *Advanced Bank Holding Company Management Problems*," Dallas: Southern Methodist University Press.

Southern Mississippi vs FDIC (1980) 499 F. Supp. I, II aff'd F. 2d 1013 (5th Cir. 1980).

U.S. v. Connecticut National Bank (1974) 418 U.S. 656

U.S. Department of Justice (1968), *Merger Guidlines*

U.S. v. First National Bank of Houston (1967) 386 U.S. 361

U.S. v. Marine Bancorporation, Inc. (1974) 418 U.S. 602

U.S. v. Philadelphia National Bank, (1963) 314 U.S. 321

U.S. v. Philadelphia National Bank (1969) 306 F. Supp. 1161 U.S. Supreme Court No. 1093, October Term, 1969.

U.S. v. Virginia National Bank Shares (1982), Bench Opinion by Judge Glen M. Williams, U.S. District Ct. Virginia.

Velk, T. (1972), "A Comparative Simulation of Decisions Under the Bank Merger Act," *Antitrust Bulletin*, 17, pp. 1083–1106.

Waxberg, S. and Robinson, S, (1965), " Chaos in Federal Regulation of Bank Mergers: A need for Legislative Revision," *Banking Law Journal*, 82, pp. 377–394.

Regional Science and Urban Economics 21 (1991) 127–134. North-Holland

Spatial discrimination, Bertrand vs. Cournot: Comment

M.L. Greenhut

Texas A&M University, College Station, TX 77843, USA
University of Oklahoma, Norman, OK 73019, USA

C.S. Lee

Soonchunhyang University, Seoul, South Korea

Y. Mansur

University of Oklahoma, Norman, OK 73019, USA

1. In an innovative paper in this journal which recognized the relationship between spatial pricing and industrial location, Hamilton, Thisse and Weskamp (1989) (henceforth HTW) derived the conclusions that Cournot quantity competition induces firms to agglomerate under conditions of low freight rates while Bertrand price competition promotes dispersion. In fact, HTW observed that Bertrand firms disperse almost perfectly when freight rates are sufficiently low. (By sufficiently low we mean that homogeneous duopolists located at opposite ends of a line market can still sell to the opposite market point at a delivered cost less than the monopoly price of the firm located at that end-point of the market.) Before setting forth our own extension of the HTW paper, a very brief summary of HTW's analytical framework appears in order.

2. The subject paper used standard space-economy assumptions, such as consumers being distributed uniformly along a line market indexed by $X \in [0, 1)$. The HTW framework centered on negatively sloping linear demands with unit intercept value, zero costs of production, and firms willing

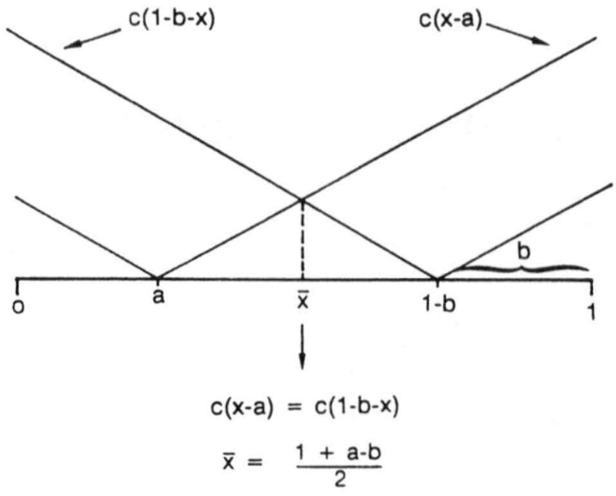

Fig. 1

to discriminate spatially in their prices.[1] The derived Bertrand locations and prices are given in fig. 1, where freight rates c are $\leqq 1/2$ (1/2 being the monopoly price at a monopolist's plant site). In the figure, a stands for firm 1's distance from the west end point of the line and b is the measured distance of firm 2 from the east end point of the line. As the freight rate rises above zero, the Bertrand locations are found to move slightly away from the first and third quartile sites, as in fig. 2. Meanwhile, the counterpart Cournot firms are found to agglomerate in the center of the line, their delivered price schedules exceeding those of the Bertrand firms at all market points. Profits of Cournot firms are greater than those of Bertrand firms under the aforenoted conditions.

It is, however, demonstrated that Bertrand profits rise as freight rates increase and Cournot profits decrease. In fact, for values of c falling approximately between 0.72 and 0.9, Bertrand profits began to exceed Cournot profits. The quantity-setting firms suffer lower profits under the subject freight costs, but are not yet induced to locate as the Bertrand firms. Would these firms continue to locate the same when transport rates are *still higher* compared to those noted above?

One additional set of HTW findings must be mentioned before answering the above question and others related to it. Specifically, while Cournot profits fell below Bertrand profits for freight rates in the 0.72–0.9 range, they began to approach Bertrand profits *and* to reach equality with them when $c \geqq 4$. These results point to the main problem: which of the two models best

[1]Willingness to price-discriminate at any point on the line market reflects the *spatial form of Bertrand*. That is to say, the subject firm charges as its price the delivered cost of its distant competitor on sales to buyers located in the proximity of the subject firm's plant.

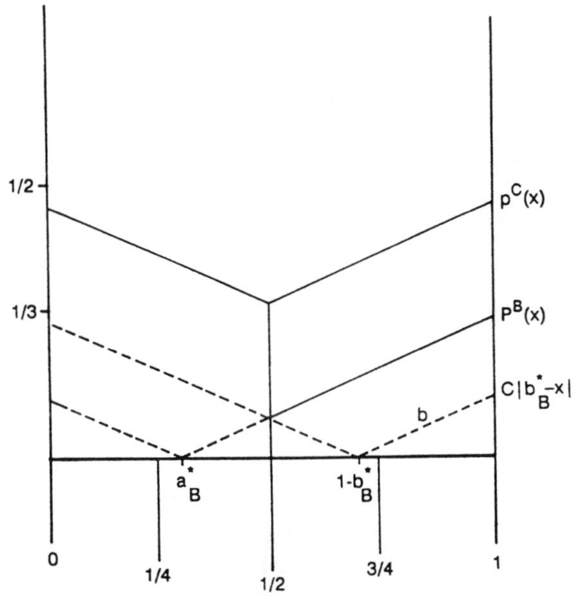

Fig. 2

characterizes spatial competition and location choice? It is to this subject matter that the following section is directed.

3. A large freight rate was traditionally claimed to disperse firms in standard location theory. Dispersion resulted in the theory because local monopolies become possible when cost of distance is great, ceteris paribus. On the other hand, a low freight rate was claimed to localize firms, ceteris paribus.

HTW found that Cournot quantity competition promoted agglomeration under conditions of a low freight rate because that rate would enable firms to compete for any market point. Apparently, the HTW result would also hold for three and more firms unless conjectural variations change.

The HTW analysis further indicated that Bertrand competition induces firms to disperse under the same low freight rate. This contrasting result with standard location theory followed the fact that Bertrand firms would undercut rival firms in establishing spatial monopoly locations. Each firm would take for its delivered price the higher delivered cost of the (distant) rival firm minus an epsilon. As pointed out by HTW, Bertrand firms locate to minimize their own transport cost. As the freight rate rises, the mark-ups

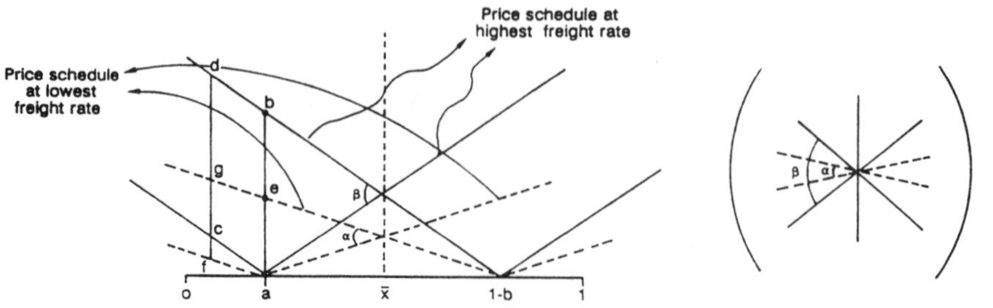

Fig. 3

and profits of Bertrand firms increase and their locations change slightly.[2] Unfortunately, however, for real world generalized significance, the 'discrimination' evident in this spatial variant of Bertrand pricing is likely to be considered predatory in nations such as the United States. The consequence is that not only does it become more likely that Bertrand *inclined* managers would disperse their firms towards profit maximizing (distributionally ideal) sites, but in doing this they would not follow the spatial variant of Bertrand pricing. Instead, they would adopt the classical profit maximizing, monopolistic-delivered price schedule, i.e., they would price locally at (1/2) the intercept price and add (1/2) the freight cost to each market point *when demands are linear and negative in slope.* Ideal dispersion should also hold for three or more firms. For any number of firms, *spatial* Bertrand pricing in many countries is neither a likely competitive conjecture nor would it be a likely reaction. Our rejection of it extends, however, beyond the antitrust laws of these countries, becoming fully general, as demonstrated below.

4. HTW found Bertrand profits increasing as freight rates increase over the $0<c\leqq 1/2$ range. The basic reason for this is that the higher profit mark-ups offset the decreased sales resulting from higher final good prices. (For example, compare *ab* with *ae*, and *cd* with *fg* for the firm at *a* in our fig. 3,

[2]Bertrand gains at higher freight rates point to a slight difference in their site selections compared to the firm which locates at a distance under base point pricing. The Bertrand firms minimize transport costs as HTW stressed; moreover, they add greater mark-ups at higher freight rates, their sales totals varying at each market point in direct proportion to demand conditions. Under base point pricing, the firm at a distance simply minimizes its transport costs throughout its market space, with its *allocated* share of total sales at each market point remaining a constant; whether freight rates are low or high, the distant firm's minimal transport cost location is unchanged. As will be stressed shortly in the text above, the same uniqueness in choice of a distant location does not apply strictly to Bertrand firms. See Greenhut (1956, Chapter 2 and Appendix V) for analysis of locations under base point pricing.

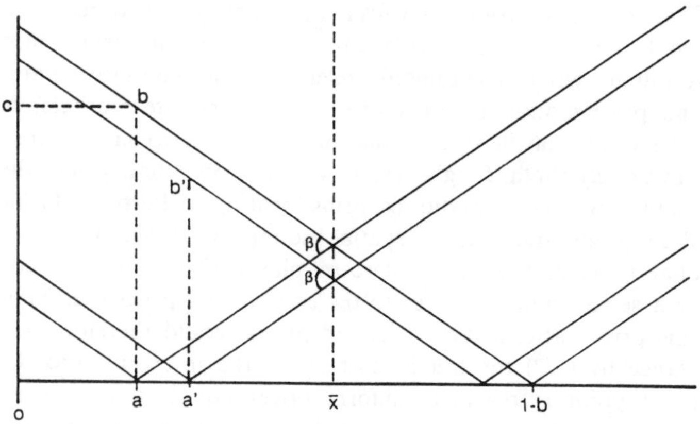

Fig. 4

the same holding for the firm at $1-b$). It therefore suffices for the case of $0<c\leqq 1/2$ to emphasize initially the significance of the mark-up in generating profits, and secondly to recall that the movement of firms to sites within the quartile points is in contrast to the classical expectations concerning higher freight rate impacts on location. We note for the low non-zero freight rate cases that HTW found the Bertrand firms moving towards the central site $\bar{x}$. (E.g., with $c\rightarrow 0$, $a=0.25$, whereas with $c=1/2$, $a=0.27$.) This movement towards $\bar{x}$ decreases the profit mark-up (compare $a'b'$ with ab in fig. 4), but is justified by the fact that the region $a\bar{x}$ is the area of greatest sales; as HTW stressed, the slight movement towards $\bar{x}$ therefore decreases total transportation cost. We note next in emphasis beyond HTW that the limit to the Bertrand localizing movement is quickly reached *because of the declining mark-ups*. In fact, in the extreme case of firms located at $\bar{x}$, the profit mark-up would be zero. It further follows from HTW that movements back to the quartile sites eventuate when freight rates are $\geqq 4$. This movement takes place because rates $\geqq 4$ would establish a completely monopolized market space for the dispersed firms.[3]

These basically clear-cut conclusions generate a rather fundamental set of questions whose answers provide a basically different perspective of Bertrand vs. Cournot 'price–location' theory. First of all, whether or not Bertrand firms disperse perfectly, would they not price-discriminate in the classical spatial profit maximizing pattern rather than pursue Bertrand price cut-

[3]Though not fundamental to the extension presented herein, it warrants mention that HTW also proposed full correspondence in locations by Cournot and Bertrand firms at freight rates $\geqq 4$.

ting?[4] That is to say, would two firms at dispersed locations act as if their prices had to descend to the delivered cost level of the distant firm? Would they not pursue what is commonly referred to as conscious parallelism of action and price monopolistically over their proximate markets? Moreover, even if sales from quartile or near quartile sites to peripheral points are ruled out by *extremely* high freight rates, we propose that given the defined demand and freight cost conditions, firms locating in Bertrand fashion would still tend to adopt the standard spatial monopoly delivered price: namely, a price equal to (1/2) the price intercept plus (1/2) the freight cost, and if necessary a set of uniform prices *to the very distant-peripheral buying points.* Under this price pattern, their delivered prices would therefore be increased with distance by (1/2) the freight cost up to the intercept price limit. After that market point is reached, uniform prices equal to the intercept price minus epsilon could be expected to apply up to the site(s) where the freight absorption necessary for a sale still to be profitable requires an effective net price equal to zero.[5]

5. We can best summarize the important facets of our extension by initially asking: How likely is it that either Cournot or Bertrand spatial competition per se really exists in practice? The logical extension of the HTW paper proposed in sections 3 and 4 suggests that the Bertrand form of spatial competition is the least likely to take place in practice. Even the Cournot model is unlikely, for as is generally the case with mathematical models in economics, the dynamics provided are beyond those which an individual can reasonably expect to prevail at any given moment in time [see Bresnahan (1988), in particular p. 941].

The above contentions do not deny, however, the strictly theoretical relevance of either model. In fact, one of the present writers has regularly utilized the Cournot model, and will continue to do so in order to demonstrate competitive impacts on prices and outputs. Furthermore, as the HTW paper suggests, the Cournot model may well characterize the price–location actions of firms in sales dominated competitive industries. In similar sense, the Bertrand price–location pair serves as a primer as to how firms subject to low freight rates may *initially view* an economic landscape.

As a conjectural primer, along with the preferences most of us have to avoid using the inverse demand function, the spatial Bertrand model is uniquely desirable. On the other hand, it is implicitly contradictory in

[4]In the context of Thisse and Vives (1988) a cooperative price policy would approach what we refer to as the classical form of spatial price discrimination.

[5]To the extent that *extremely* high freight rates suggest forthcoming entry, the location choice would involve movement closer together *or* further apart, with the delivered price schedule described above prevailing up to the time the entry took place.

proposing differentiated locations (and products) while still projecting substantial competitive price impacts. This combination (differentiated locations under conditions of substantial price competition) presumes that the firms would completely ignore their location monopoly advantages. Perhaps this is why Bertrand spatial price schedules do not in fact describe real-world situations.[6]

We propose accordingly that the Bertrand spatial variant must give way as a spatial competition model to other formulations. Oppositely, the Cournot model appears to mirror standard location theory by suggesting agglomeration under conditions of low freight rates and dispersion with independent spatial price discrimination under conditions of high freight rates. With modification, it could describe real-world situations [Greenhut (1981)]. If we recall the likely antitrust action in many countries against the Bertrand form of spatial pricing, we are left particularly with the conclusion that between the two, the Cournot model appears to warrant major consideration in spatial price–location microeconomics.

A special note on the long-run equilibrium

We proposed in our paper the likelihood of spatially separated firms following monopolistic pricing patterns rather than a Bertrand low delivered price schedule. Yet elsewhere, one of these authors along with others stressed a competitive oligopoly zero profit equilibrium in the long run [see Greenhut et al. (1987) and Greenhut and Lane (1989)]. Is that conclusion in contradiction to the present paper's rejection of Bertrand pricing? The answer is no, not at all. This paper's critique of Bertrand pricing by spatially dispersed firms actually has roots in (a) the assumption that locational differentiation can generate conscious parallelism of action in pricing: that is to say, a let-live maximax decision would prevail under locational dispersion rather than a Bertrand price cutting decision, and (b) the predatory nature of Bertrand pricing.[7] Most importantly, the spatial monopoly pricing we proposed in our paper would be short-run pricing at best. Profits over time would promote entry by a firm(s) proximate to one seller and/or between the sellers. This can be shown to cause the conceived of average revenue curve of the original duopolists either to break off over the lower portions of the curve if a Löschian or Cournot form of spatial competitive conjecture applies *or* to shift the entire schedule leftward under what has since been referred to as a Greenhut–Ohta conjecture [Greenhut et al. (1975)]. The effect in each

[6]See Greenhut (1981) where it was found that the delivered prices of real-world firms did not resemble Bertrand schedules.

[7]There exist under Bertrand pricing more proximate markets in which delivered prices would be higher than on sales to markets located at greater distances. This is a complete 'no–go' under antitrust laws such as those in the United States. See Benson and Greenhut (1989).

case would be to promote price reductions. Regardless of cost conditions and scale economies, the spatial distribution of demand, *and* the degree of behavioral uncertainty in the industry, a long-run zero economic profit equilibrium would eventuate in a spatial competitive economy, the same as it would in a spaceless oligopoly world. This zero economic profit equilibrium would have $3, 4, \ldots, n$ or even just 2 firms ultimately prevailing in the industry.

References

Benson, B. and M.L. Greenhut, 1989, The American antitrust laws in theory and practice (Gower, London).

Bresnahan, T.F., 1981, Duopoly models with consistent conjectures, American Economic Review 71, 934–945.

Greenhut, M.L., 1956, Plant location in theory and in practice (University of North Carolina Press, Chapel Hill, NC).

Greenhut, M.L., 1981, Spatial pricing in the USA, West Germany, and Japan, Economica 48, 79–86.

Greenhut, M.L., M. Hwang and H. Ohta, 1975, Observations on the shape and relevance of the spatial demand function, Econometrica 43, 669–682.

Greenhut, M.L., G. Norman and C.S. Hung, 1987, The economic theory of imperfect competition (Cambridge University Press, Cambridge).

Greenhut, M.L. and W.C. Lane, 1989, A determinate theory of oligopoly, The Manchester School, LVII, 3, 248–261.

Hamilton, J.H., J. Thisse and A. Weskamp, 1989, Spatial discrimination: Bertrand vs. Cournot in a model of location choice, Regional Science and Urban Economics 19, 87–102.

Thisse, J. and X. Vives, 1988, On the strategic choice of spatial price policy, American Economic Review 78, 122–137.

On the Basing-Point System

By BRUCE L. BENSON, MELVIN L. GREENHUT, AND GEORGE NORMAN*

Jacques F. Thisse and Xavier Vives observed in this journal (1988) that analysis of the base-point price (BPP) system "should consider its role as a coordinating and collusive device" (p. 12). This conclusion has much in common with that of Fritz Machlup (1952) and Clair Wilcox (1955) and provides a sharply contrasting thesis from that of David D. Haddock, who had contended in (1982) that BPP systems are competitive. However, Thisse and Vives (henceforth TV) were not specifically, or even primarily concerned with base-point pricing. Rather, they focused attention on noncooperative strategies in spatial markets, deriving several conclusions by approaching the choice of pricing policy from an explicitly strategic, game-theoretic viewpoint. While their results do imply that noncooperative base-point pricing is unlikely, they did not center attention on the conditions that must exist in order for a *competitive* base-point pricing system to arise.

The present paper extends TV's theoretical analysis by focusing exclusively on base-point pricing *and* by ascertaining the conditions that would be required for Haddock's noncooperative BPP system to arise. In particular, the initial part of this paper utilizes the TV framework to identify the necessary conditions for a noncooperative BPP system. The TV framework leads us to a different interpretation than Haddock proposed. The second part of this paper adds, however, to the contention that the system *could indeed have* competitive origins; but we shall observe that it limits such claim to certain highly restrictive conditions. This part of the paper also refers to the reality of BPP. A third and concluding section accounts for the "cooperative" use of the system when, in fact, other "collusive" delivered pricing systems that would be more profitable than BPP can be conceived of.

*Department of Economics, Florida State University, Tallahassee, FL 32306-2045; Department of Economics, Texas A&M University, College Station, TX 77843-4228 and adjunct, University of Oklahoma, Norman, OK 73019; and Department of Economics, The University of Leicester, Leicester, England LE1 7 RH.

I. Theory

For simplicity, assume that all consumers are identical, and are distributed over a line market in which there are two production sites I and II, with site I the lower-cost site (perhaps because of better access to raw materials). Assume that there are two firms, $i = I, II$ selling a homogeneous product, with firm i located at site i. Transport costs per unit of output from site i to consumer location x are given by a nonnegative, increasing function $t_i(|i-x|)$, where $|\cdot|$ is the distance norm, and $t_i(0) = 0$. Figure 1 (see also Haddock, Figure 1) illustrates such a case, with mc_i denoting marginal production cost at site i, and $m_i(x)$ denoting marginal cost of production and transportation from site i to consumer location x: $m_i(x) = mc_i + t_i(|i-x|)(i = I, II)$.

Define the monopoly price $p_i^M(x)$ that firm i would charge to consumers at x as the price that would maximize profit to firm i from consumers at x in the absence of any competition (this price is derived from the standard MR = MC condition). TV show that if the duopolists simultaneously choose their pricing policy and price, the noncooperative equilibrium pricing strategy $p_i^*(x)$ for firm i is

$$(1)\quad p_i^*(x) = \begin{cases} p_i^M(x) \text{ if } p_i^M(x) \le m_j(x) \\ m_j(x) \text{ if } p_i^M(x) > m_j(x), \\ \quad \text{and } m_i(x) \le m_j(x) \\ m_i(x) \text{ otherwise,} \end{cases}$$

584

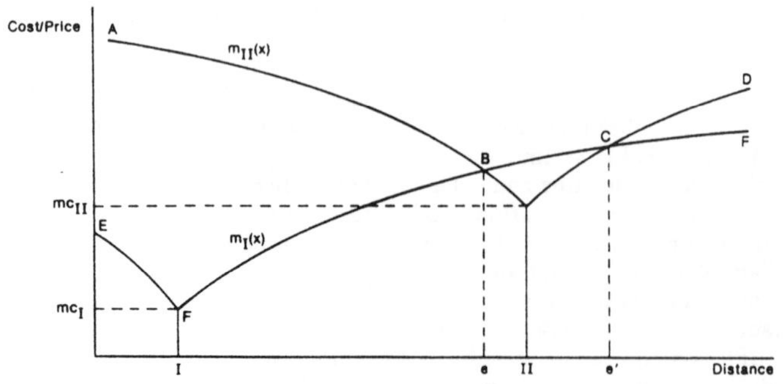

FIGURE 1

a form of price discrimination first discussed by Edgar M. Hoover (1937).[1] Assume without loss of generality that $p_i^M(x)$ everywhere exceed marginal cost of production and transportation for firm j ($j \neq i$). Then the price equilibrium is illustrated in Figure 1 by the lines AB, CD for firm I and BC for firm II. If the pricing game is a two-stage game, in which firms first choose a pricing policy and then compete in prices contingent on the chosen pricing policies, TV show again that the discriminatory policy of equation (1) is the unique (Nash) equilibrium outcome.

Is pricing policy (1) consistent with BPP? It is quite clear that firm II is following a BPP with site I as base, ***but firm I is also following BPP with site II as base***. In other words, the only equilibrium is a peculiar type of multiple BPP system in which consumers are charged a price less by the amount ε than the marginal costs plus freight of the second-lowest cost supplier.

Now consider what will arise if a second firm is introduced at site I: if, for example, the producer at site II has a second plant at site I. Using precisely the same argument, the resulting Nash equilibrium prices are now given by

$$(2) \qquad p_I^*(x) = m_I(x)$$

$$p_{II}^*(x) = \begin{Bmatrix} m_I(x) \text{ if } m_I(x) > m_{II}(x) \\ m_{II}(x) \text{ if } m_I(x) < m_{II}(x) \end{Bmatrix}.$$

These are illustrated in Figure 1 by the lines EFB and CF for the firms at site I and BC for the firm at site II. Pricing policy (2) is the policy derived by Haddock (although Haddock does so by requiring that production at site I be "competitive"): it is BPP with site I as base.[2]

II. Conditions for Competitive BPP

We can now identify the somewhat restrictive condition under which this policy emerges. For a single-base basing-point pricing system to be the outcome of a competitive process, it is necessary that production at the basing point be in some sense compe-

[1] This equilibrium assumes that individual demand is "well behaved," in that profit from consumers at x is quasi-concave in price.

[2] Recall that the pricing equilibria assume $p_i^M(x) > m_j(x)(j \neq i)$ for all x. Note that Haddock ignores the possibility that firm II (the local monopolist) could have a sufficiently strong monopoly advantage near site II as to be able, and so willing, to charge the monopoly price.

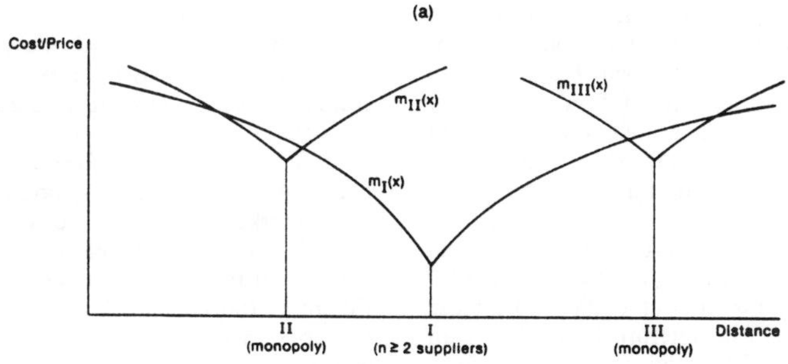

FIGURE 2. PANEL (a)

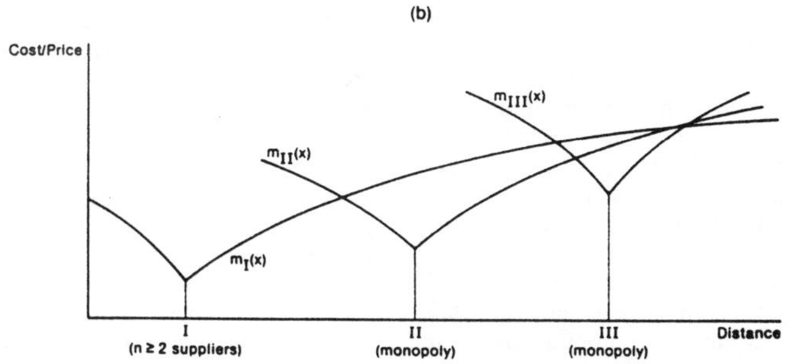

FIGURE 2. PANEL (b)

titive[3] *and production at distant sites be monopolized*. It is *further necessary that firms at the basing point* always *be either the lowest or the second-lowest cost suppliers to all consumers*. Extending the analysis, a single-base BPP system will also arise from the configuration of suppliers in Figure 2a, but not necessarily from the configuration in Figure 2b. Far from being competitive, the delivered price system in Figure 2a *derives from the exploitation of locational rents*!

A further peculiar result is readily evident with the BPP of equation (2). The low-cost producers just break even, but the high-cost nonbase-point firm that has a local monopoly position can earn supernormal profit or locational rents. Haddock's argument (p. 304) in this respect is in error. The locational rents arise because multiple-firm entry at the distant site is barred by a combination of demand and cost conditions. In particular, sufficient demand and revenues exist to generate returns for one firm that exceed opportunity costs, but entry of another firm would mean that both sellers incur economic losses. These conditions are exogeneous to the producer at the distant site. Such indivisibility has been discussed by Nicholas Kaldor (1935), Harold Demsetz (1964), and, more recently, B. Curtis Eaton and Richard G. Lipsey (1978).

One further concern of Haddock was to use BPP to present an efficiency argument for cross-hauling. But it is clear that cross-hauling does not require basing-point pricing. There is exactly the same form of cross-

[3]In the TV analysis, two competing producers will suffice.

hauling under the pricing equilibrium in equation (1), with firm *II* shipping to consumers to its left, and firm *I* shipping to consumers to the right of firm *II*. Simply put, differences in production costs and economies of long-haul transportation are sufficient to generate this kind of cross-hauling.[4]

In addition to the aforenoted theoretical criticisms, the idea of a competitive BPP system is further subject to the most basic criticism that it misinterprets the system. In particular, the BPP equilibrium under competitive conditions is justified on the grounds that it will allow the firm at site *II* to survive when f.o.b. pricing would not.[5] This result requires that firm *II* supply all demand in its natural market area: defined in Figure 1 as the area in which $m_{II}(x) < m_I(x)$ —region *ee′*. With such an assumption, BPP always generates greater total revenue than will f.o.b. pricing.[6] There will, therefore, exist some range of cost and demand conditions such that BPP will allow firm *II* to at least break even, while f.o.b. pricing will not. But this is not in the spirit of the BPP system. As Machlup (1949) states: "[the] basing-point technique of pricing makes it possible for any number of sellers, no matter where they are located and without any communication with each other, to quote identical delivered prices for any quantity of the product in standardized qualities and specifications" (p. 7).

Assume then that BPP leads to firm *II* sharing its market with the firms at site *I*. We know there must be at least two producers at site *I* for the subject BPP system to emerge. It follows that firm *II* can at the most expect only one-third of the total sales in the region *ee′* under the BPP system. By contrast, f.o.b. pricing will secure all demand for firm *II* in a region somewhat smaller than *ee′*. As Melvin L. Greenhut (1956, pp. 313, 314; 1970, Chapter 7) points out, once such market sharing is considered, f.o.b. pricing can dominate basing-point pricing and would if costs corresponded to those of Figure 1. Indeed, the classical form of spatial price discrimination by the distant firm, where its delivered price increases in *each direction* from its site, can dominate the f.o.b. pricing alternative; moreover, it would not appear to be predatory, as is the case for the systematic lowering of delivered prices in region *ee′* at some market points located at greater distances from the seller than others.

III. Conclusions

In order for a competitive simple basing-point price system to hold, it is necessary that a single firm located at a distance from a competitive production center exploit its local market power, collect locational rents, and alone sell over its dominated market space. This composite is a necessary condition; without its fulfillment, the *noncooperative* base-point price system would not exist. It follows in light of the requisite local market power at a distance that BPP is a noncompetitive system. Moreover, when such power exists, other delivered pricing forms will be used in the absence of collusion.

This paper thus contends that traditional views on the subject are more appropriate. (See Greenhut, 1956, Appendix V.) When base-point pricing is followed, it is attributable to (i) conscious parallelism of action, where some firms feel obliged (compelled) to adhere to the price schedule of others or (ii) stems from an outright collusive conspiracy whose design is to maximize profits *subject to* cartel policing and enforcement costs. Such costs are an intrinsic part of the system since a cartel must be organized and its agreement enforced in the presence of incentives to cheat. As many have pointed out (for example, Hoover, 1937, p. 190; Machlup, 1949, pp. 131–136; George

[4]Actually, even more extensive cross-hauling involving simultaneous supply of an area by two or more firms is easily explained with spatial competition models involving price discrimination (for example, John Greenhut and Melvin L. Greenhut, 1975). Base-point pricing is not a necessary condition for cross-hauling, or for freight absorption, so Haddock is clearly correct in emphasizing that these phenomena are not evidence of collusion. But significantly, they do not necessarily imply base-point pricing either.

[5]Actually, of course, the choice is more likely to involve discriminatory pricing than f.o.b. pricing.

[6]With trivial exception of some peculiar demand functions.

J. Stigler, 1979, pp. 1147–1148; Frederic M. Scherer, 1980, pp. 329–330), a base-point system is much less costly to police and enforce than are other spatial pricing arrangements. This helps explain its use instead of other organized delivered price systems that would be more profitable in the absence of policing and enforcement costs.

The fact that base-point pricing generates locational rents for distant firms also indicates why this system might characterize a cartel notwithstanding the existence of more profitable arrangements, such as f.o.b. pricing or spatial discriminatory pricing. These other more profitable systems may well induce competitive entry. It follows that if base-point pricing deters entry and in the process protects existing rents, it may actually be the most desirable arrangement that the cartel can adopt.

REFERENCES

Demsetz, Harold, "The Welfare Implications of Monopolistic Competition," *Economic Journal*, September 1964, *74*, 623–41.

Eaton, B. Curtis and Lipsey, Richard G., "Freedom of Entry and Existence of Pure Profit," *Economic Journal*, September 1978, *88*, 455–69.

Greenhut, John and Greenhut, Melvin L., "Spatial Price Discrimination, Competition and Locational Effects," *Economica*, November 1975, *42*, 401–19.

Greenhut, Melvin L., *Plant Location in Theory and in Practice*, Chapel Hill: University of North Carolina Press, 1956; 4th printing, Westport, CT: Greenwood Press, 1982.

———, *A Theory of the Firm in Economic Space*. New York: Appleton Century, 1970; 2nd printing, Austin, TX: Lone Star Publishing, 1974.

Haddock, David D., "Basing-Point Pricing; Competitive vs. Collusive Theories," *American Economic Review*, June 1982, *72*, 289–306.

Hoover, Edgar M., "Spatial Price Discrimination," *Review of Economic Studies*, 1937, *4*, 182–91.

Kaldor, Nicholas, "Market Imperfections and Excess Capacity," *Economica*, February 1935, *2*, 35–50.

Machlup, Fritz, *The Basing Point System: An Economic Analysis of a Controversial Pricing Practice*, Philadelphia: Blakiston, 1949.

———, *The Political Economy of Monopoly: Business, Labor and Government Policies*, Baltimore: Johns Hopkins University Press, 1952, esp. chs. 4 and 5.

Scherer, Frederic M., *Industrial Market Structure and Economic Performance*, Chicago: Rand McNally, 1980.

Stigler, George J., "A Theory of Delivered Price Systems," *American Economic Review*, December 1949, *39*, 1143–1159.

Thisse, Jacques F. and Vives, Xavier, "On the Strategic Choice of Spatial Price Policy," *American Economic Review*, March 1988, *78*, 122–37.

Wilcox, Clair, *Public Policies Toward Business*, Homewood, IL: Richard D. Irwin, 1955.

On the Basing-Point System: Reply

By BRUCE L. BENSON, MELVIN L. GREENHUT, AND GEORGE NORMAN*

David D. Haddock's (1990) contention is really that the Jacques F. Thisse and Xavier Vives (1988) and the Bruce L. Benson, Melvin L. Greenhut, and George Norman (1990) papers do not provide a collusive model that yields base-point pricing (BPP). He apparently believes his paper (1982) established competitive BPP and suggests (in 1990) that the collusive model and hard empirical work alone remain. However, no collusive model is required since it has already been well demonstrated in the literature on plant location and spatial price theory that firms at feasible distance locations from a production center would accept BPP only because they fear that to do otherwise would subject them to retaliatory actions by the larger, more powerful firms at the production center. Moreover, the paper by Thisse-Vives (1988, henceforth TV) and Benson-Greenhut-Norman (1990, henceforth BGN) indicated sufficiently that other systems would arise than Haddock's competitive BPP, especially since the restrictive conditions necessary for the latter militate against its use. Haddock, in fact, appears to accept these conditions in his references to Arthur R. Burns' proposals (1936) of *near*-base-point pricing (NBPP). Hard empirical analysis would indeed be in order in determining the extent of NBPP, not competitive BPP.

This paper responds to the above noted issues in three main sections. Section I briefly provides some historical data on the collusive uses of BPP for any future researcher who seeks empirically to uncover a true competitive BPP system. Most importantly from a theoretical standpoint, this section also explains why cartels will employ BPP notwithstanding the obvious and well-known thesis that other more profitable spatial pricing forms exist, *ceteris paribus*. Section II of this paper then distinguishes between profits and locational rents, in the process indicating in partial contradiction to Haddock (1990) that BPP does generate such rents. Though we have already contended that existing theory has demonstrated the use of different competitive forms of spatial pricing *and* locations under profit-maximizing conditions than competitive BPP, Section III of this paper provides specific basis for this contention as well as references. That same section discusses NBPP. To save space, we shall let the analysis on the subject of the TV (1988) and BGN (1990) papers stand by themselves, without repeat demonstrations or explanations of their results.

*Department of Economics, Florida State University, Tallahassee, FL 32306-2045; Department of Economics, Texas A&M University, College Station, TX 77843-4228, and adjunct, University of Oklahoma, Norman, OK 73091; and Department of Economics, The University of Leicester, Leicester, England LE1 7 RH. The authors wish to thank Tom Saving for a helpful suggestion.

I. What Is an Effective Cartel?

Haddock's references to weak or strong cartels and apparent suggestion (1990) that BPP would be used by weak cartels oversimplifies the subject. A cartel arises if it is able to cover the cost of organizing, and then survives if it establishes a sufficiently strong monitoring and enforcement (policing) system that is capable of limiting competition (for example, price competition, entry) to an acceptable level. Cartel costs vary with the characteristics of an industry (number of firms, geographic distribution of firms *and* consumers, etc.). When firms and consumers are geographically dispersed, organizational and policing costs tend to be high and the ability of the cartel to limit competition is lessened.

We echo many others when we suggest that BPP reduces policing costs for a geographically dispersed group. Haddock is not convinced by this argument. He contends that cheating will be detected more readily under f.o.b. pricing because prices (both f.o.b. and basing-point) are not easily observed. He proposes that effective monitoring must therefore involve observations of relative sales. He suggests that chiseling at a distance from a boundary "will create damning evidence" under f.o.b. pricing (1990, p. 959). We would propose, however, that prices are readily observed under many real basing-point pricing arrangements. Is Haddock suggesting that chiseling would not have been easily detected on the part of one or more of the eleven differentially located firms that offered cement to the U.S. government at the identical delivered prices of $3.286854 (*Aetna v. FTC*, 1946)? Or what of the ten sealed bids priced at $253,633.80 for reinforcing bars (*New York Times*, February 20, 1939), or the 59 steel pipe bids to the U.S. Navy Department, each for $6,001.83 (*Annual Report of the Attorney General*, 1937, pp. 37–38)? Or, consider the eight geographically dispersed cement companies that submitted bids to the Illinois Department of Highways for deliveries at 102 sites in 102 Illinois counties, every bid for every delivery being *identical* in price (*Congressional Record*, May 31, 1959, p. 7961).

The reason that basing-point prices are relatively easier to monitor is that they are determined by a simple formula that is known by every cartel member. For instance, between January 1982 and September 1983 there were three regional bases for the pricing of cement in England, and delivery increments were applied to every *5 miles of road*. These increments reflected haulage rate charges computed from a particular base point, *not the point of origin of the shipper*; these rates varied over time from 16p to 56p per ton per 5 miles of road. Prices certainly may not be readily observable under an f.o.b. system, but cooperative BPP makes them relatively more observable, and therefore reduces monitoring costs.

The fundamental feature of BPP that Haddock overlooks is that the main conspirators are typically localized at (near) the base point(s), and other spatially dispersed firms feel *obliged* to adhere completely to the system. A chiseler must be punished if caught, or there will be no effective deterrent to cheating. When chiseling under some organized type of pricing system other than BPP affects only a single firm located at a distant site, the incentives and ability of the cartel to retaliate and punish the transgressor are quite weak. This is particularly the case if the affected firm is small and not part of the main group of powerful conspirators. When chiseling impacts all cartel members, including the largest and most powerful, as would be the case under BPP, the potential for *and* likelihood of retaliation is much greater. This could conceivably induce, in some countries, the *pro*collusive type of antitrust action mentioned by Haddock; however, in a country such as the United States of the late twentieth century, any BPP cartel would be likely to pursue more subtle means of punishing a chiseler.

We contend that even if monitoring costs are no lower under a basing-point system than they are under some undefined, organized f.o.b. type of arrangement, *total* BPP cartel costs (which include enforcement as well as monitoring costs) will tend to be less. The imposition of credible punishment is an important part and cost of effective cartelization. For example, Clair Wilcox (1960) mentioned 49,000 pages of testimony along with 50,000 pages of exhibits on cement industry prices that were presented to the Federal Trade Commission. After also discussing the equally detailed documents on record concerning the steel industry, he went on to review penalties. Those imposed by the respective cartels on member firms that failed to adhere to the system were strikingly severe (pp. 280–81). He concluded that "If basing point pricing were a spontaneous outgrowth of natural causes, as some economists have argued, it would scarcely have been necessary to go to such lengths to ensure that its requirements be observed" (1960, p. 281).

Haddock is also incorrect when he suggests that sellers under BPP seem relatively more homogeneous to buyers than a cartel would wish (1990, p. 959). The fact of homogeneous output is exactly one reason why the system is desired by the large firms located at the base point. The steel, cement, and plywood firms that located at base points wanted *and took advantage of homogeneity* via a spatial delivered price that allowed them to maintain their markets over substantial distances. Haddock ignores an important aspect of many of these industries when he contends that a cartel would prefer geographic market division. As Wilcox (1960, p. 280) observed, changes in the geographic pattern of demand for steel (and presumably other construction material) took place rapidly in the United States. Thus, for these industries, producers' locations are fixed while consumers' are not.[1] When subject to geographic market division and f.o.b. pricing, firms would have to build new facilities to follow demand. This is not required as often under BPP since the large powerful firms under BPP can readily sell in new distant markets.[2]

II. Profits or Rents?

Haddock implies that cartelization must fulfill its objectives (for example, joint profit maximization, entry deterrence), or the cartel is ineffective. He refers to Ronald N. Johnson and Allen M. Parkman's (1983) demonstration that the cement industry did not earn supranormal profits, proposing this as evidence that any entry deterring efforts by the firms in the industry had to be ineffective. It would then seem to follow that any noncooperative, noncontrolled system could also be ineffective with respect to entry deterrence.[3] However, long-run rents in a true BPP system can appear in different form than higher net profits, while also resulting from entry deterring efforts. In particular, competition for prime locations would bid up the value of these sites. These locational rents would be capitalized as part of land values, rather than appearing regularly on P&L statements as high profits. More fundamentally, cement industry profits and individual firm profits are very different matters. This is especially the case because the distant small firm locates differently than a strictly competitive f.o.b. firm while, at the same instant, earning less under BPP than it otherwise would net (Melvin L. Greenhut, 1956). Finally, note that for risk-averse individuals, collusion that reduces the behavioral uncertainty inherent in noncooperative oligopoly could easily make the affected firms better off, even if nominal profits do not increase in any measurable way.

III. Conclusions: What in Fact Is Haddock's Noncooperative Spatial Pricing System?

Haddock's conclusions seem to agree with BGN that a true basing-point system would *not* exist under competitive conditions. Only its reflection would arise, with distant firms offering a modest discount.[4] He thus emphasizes what Burns (1936) called "near-base-point pricing," NBPP. If this is what Haddock means by competitive BPP, then

[1]BGN assume immobile consumers as well, but demonstrate that even in this case noncooperative pricing is very unlikely and market segmentation is the competitive result. In contrast, Haddock implies that market segmentation is strictly a collusive outcome.

[2]This is another consideration that would reinforce the TV (1988) conclusion that BPP becomes a relevant collusive practice.

[3]Haddock apparently accepts George J. Stigler's (1971) theory of economic regulation since he suggests that regulation and licensing may be a source of entry limits. According to this view, most regulatory actions provide cartel-like benefits for the regulated firms rather than benefiting consumers. Stigler's theory is based on the public choice paradigm in which bureaucrats and other public officials are driven by self-interest rather than public interest motives. Observe in this regard that the only examples of BPP which Haddock now appears to consider to be valid come from Europe "where the pricing structure is established and enforced through governmentally established bureaucracies" (1990, fn. 5). While we do not agree with Haddock that these are the only prime examples (for example, the federal milk order system in the United States has many basing-point characteristics), the fact that the most obvious examples arise in governmentally regulated settings reinforces the long-standing view that nongovernmentally imposed BPP is associated with cooperative rather than competitive behavior.

[4]A modest "discount" system could indeed prevail, and in a crude sense it often does in retailing where an uptown (suburban) department store *and* the uptown branches of downtown stores charge higher prices than the downtown price. Quite significantly, the differences in price correspond roughly to the time-distance "cost-saving" of suburban residents who shop at the stores located nearest them rather than having to go downtown.

there really is little disagreement between us except semantical. After all, competitive price discrimination, which just undercuts the base-point schedule, that is, NBPP, is precisely the noncooperative price equilibrium that arises in the BGN extension (1990) of the TV (1988) paper.

Competition in spatial markets, where both immobile buyers and sellers are spatially dispersed and transportation costs are significant, as modeled by Haddock (1982) and BGN (1990), leads naturally to a segmented market structure under which spatially separated firms, acting *independently*, would increase their profits by setting prices that undercut the distant rivals, *ceteris paribus*. It has, indeed, been well established in the literature on spatial price theory that freight-absorbing discriminatory pricing over a geographic space, as depicted by TV (1988) and BGN (1990), is the *natural pricing form* for noncooperative firms.[5] Certainly, demand elasticities can be expected on a priori grounds to differ at each buying site within a submarket (Edgar M. Hoover, 1936–37; Arthur F. Smithies, 1941; Greenhut, 1956). Note further that even the traditional view of f.o.b. pricing as a competitive process comes into question when invasion of another firm's submarket through price discrimination is considered (Greenhut, Norman, and Chao-shun Hung, 1987; Benson and Greenhut, 1989). Competitive spatial price discrimination enhances consumer welfare *relative* to a basing-point system, which welfare consequence is a rather clear theoretical prediction, not the unpredictable empirical issue suggested by Haddock.[6] Furthermore, BPP is a hybrid price system characterized by freight absorption and phantom freight, as all firms at sites other than the base point are obliged to price discriminate while those located at the base point price f.o.b. mill.

When a *true* basing-point pricing system arises, it is likely to have been imposed as a result of a cooperative process (Machlup, 1940; Stigler, 1949) under which the distant sellers feel obliged (coerced) to follow the established system (Greenhut, 1956; Wilcox, 1960). As such, it provides strong corroborative evidence of cooperative pricing, particularly when accompanied by organized enforcement efforts and punishment of those who cut price in violation of rate books, and so on. When Haddock's *quasi*-base-point price system arises, it is in the form of discounts offered to buyers located most proximate to a distant seller.

Two final issues warrant mention. (1) Haddock's statement (1990, p. 957) that "It seems peculiar to try to settle an essentially *empirical* issue through pure theory,..." (emphasis added) reveals a failure to appreciate the place of theory in understanding the world we live in. Specifically, what is the empirical issue? Surely not the issue of rivalrous versus collusive behavior. That issue is a purely theoretical one that can be resolved only through careful consideration of the theory of pricing behavior. A theoretical model explains the circumstances under which a firm will price f.o.b. or follow BPP. Then, and only then, does the empirical determination of the form of pricing, its circumstances *and* extent become relevant. (2) Based on theory, the reason for a distant firm's adherence to BPP requires just one restrictive condition: fear of the impacts that would follow from competitive pricing. On the other hand, the reasons why firms at the production center use BPP to protect rents rather than what otherwise would *appear* to be more profitable systems are the homogeneity/near homogeneity of their goods.

[5]For empirical evidence of this pricing *in* the United States, West Germany and Japan, see Greenhut (1981).

[6]Indeed, we find Haddock's discussion of welfare implications somewhat mystifying since the welfare benefits he discusses arise under NBPP (which is a form of spatial price discrimination) and BGN never suggested that such gains would be "modest." We are also surprised that Haddock turns to Austrian arguments to defend his position on competitive BPP that was originally based on a very non-Austrian static equilibrium model. Of course, producer surpluses are relevant, but the gains in consumer surplus from the breakdown of a basing-point system do not arise solely from a surplus transfer: the non-base point firm is also better off. Surely Haddock is not suggesting that BPP is acceptable because the base-point firms are better off even though consumers and distant firms lose out?

the simplicity of BPP, and the low costs in implementing, monitoring, and enforcing the system.

REFERENCES

Benson, Bruce L. and Greenhut, Melvin L., *American Antitrust Laws in Theory and in Practice*, Aldershot, England: Avebury, 1989.

______, ______, **and Norman, George,** "On the Basing-Point System," *American Economic Review*, September 1990, *80*, 584–88.

Burns, Arthur R., *The Decline of Competition*, New York: McGraw-Hill, 1936.

Greenhut, Melvin L., *Plant Location in Theory and Practice*, Chapel Hill: University of North Carolina Press, 1956; 4th printing, Westport, CN: Greenwood Press: 1982.

______, "Spatial Pricing in the U.S.A., West Germany and Japan," *Economica*, February 1981, *48*, 79–86.

______, **Norman, George and Hung, Chao-shun,** *The Economics of Imperfect Competition: A Spatial Approach*, Cambridge: Cambridge University Press, 1987.

Haddock, David D., "Basing-Point Pricing: Competitive vs. Collusive Theories," *American Economic Review*, June 1982, *72*, 289–306.

______, "On the Basing-Point System: Comment," *American Economic Review*, September 1990, *80*, 957–62.

Hoover, Edgar M., "Spatial Price Discrimination," *Review of Economic Studies*, 1936–37, *4*, 182–91.

Johnson, Ronald N. and Parkman, Allen M., "Spatial Monopoly, Non-zero Profits and Entry Deterrence: The Case of Cement," *Review of Economics and Statistics*, August 1983, *65*, 431–39.

Smithies, Arthur F., "Monopolistic Price Policy in a Spatial Market," *Econometrica*, January 1941, *9*, 63–73.

Stigler, George J., "A Theory of Delivered Price Systems," *American Economic Review*, December 1949, *39*, 1143–59.

______, "The Theory of Economic Regulation," *Bell Journal of Economics and Management Science*, Spring 1971, *2*, 3–21.

Thisse, Jacques F. and Vives, X., "On the Strategic Choice of Spatial Price Policy," *American Economic Review*, March 1988, *78*, 122–37.

Wilcox, Clair, *Public Policy Toward Business*, Rev. Ed., Homewood, IL: Richard D. Irwin, 1960.

***Aetna Portland Cement Co.* v. *FTC*,** 157 F. 2nd, 1946, Respondents Brief, p. 127.

***Annual Report of the Attorney General of the United States*,** Washington: U.S. Department of Justice, Office of the Attorney General, 1937.

***Congressional Record: Proceedings and Debates of the Congress*,** Vol. 105, Washington: USGPO, 1959.

***New York Times*,** February 20, 1939.

The Economic Journal, 101 (*May*, 1991), 539–556
Printed in Great Britain

BASING POINT PRICING AND PRODUCTION CONCENTRATION*

Jean B. Soper, George Norman, Melvin L. Greenhut and Bruce L. Benson

Basing point pricing is a delivered price system in which the price quoted for delivery of a commodity is the sum of the price quoted at a predetermined basing point plus the cost of transportation from the basing point to the point of delivery, whether or not the commodity is actually shipped from the basing point. Thus, a seller who is not located at the base site absorbs freight for shipments toward the base point and charges phantom freight on shipments away from the base point.

Basing-point pricing has been widely practiced throughout the world. For example, testimony of the Federal Trade Commission before the TNEC (1941, p. 33) alleged that industries in the United States which then or previously followed basing-point pricing included: lumber, iron and steel, pig iron, cement, lime, brick, asphalt, shingles and roofing, window glass, white lead, metal lath, building tile, floor tile, gypsum, plaster bolts, nuts and rivets, cast iron, soil pipe, range boilers, valves and fittings, sewer pipes, paper and paper products, salt, sugar, corn derivatives, industrial alcohol, linseed oil, fertilisers, chemicals, transportation equipment, and power cable.

Almost from its inception, economists have generally considered basing-point pricing to reflect a cartel or price leadership arrangement (Hoover, 1937; Stigler, 1949; Machlup, 1949) and such practices have been attacked under antitrust statutes; for example, *Aetna Portland Cement Co. vs. FTC*, 157 F. 2nd 533 (1946), *Triangle Conduit Cable Co. vs. FTC*, 168 F. 2nd 175, 7th Cir. (1948), *Cement Institute vs. FTC*, 157 F. 2nd 533 (1948). Nonetheless, basing-point pricing remains prevalent, particularly outside the United States. OPEC has used a Gulf-based price plus transport costs to determine the delivered prices of crude oil to most places in the world, Haddock (1982, p. 290), the pricing of cement in Great Britain and steel in Europe can be characterised as multi-base point systems: Greenhut (1987).

Recent attempts by, for example, Haddock (1982) to return to the theme that the basing-point system could be competitive and desirable have been challenged by Thisse and Vives (1988), and Benson *et al.* (1990) on the basis of recent advances in the analysis of pricing policy. Given, then, that we assume basing-point pricing to be a collusive device adopted by incumbent firms to impose some kind of price discipline on potential entrants – the price leadership point referred to above – important strategic and locational issues arise. In particular, a major concern of the early analysis of basing-point pricing was the effect such a pricing policy would have on location choice of entrant firms.

* We wish to thank two anonymous referees and an associate editor for very helpful comments and suggestions on earlier drafts. Remaining errors are the sole responsibility of the authors.

It was contended in the work, for example, of Machlup (1949) and Greenhut (1956) that basing-point pricing encourages concentrated production at or near the base point while discouraging entry at distant sites. Empirical support for this view derived from the work of Wilcox (1963) who noted that the growth of the Southern and Western United States was retarded by the Pittsburgh plus basing-point system in steel (p. 284). This contention was further supported by the relatively rapid expansion of steel production capacity in the South and West, in Detroit and Cleveland and along the Eastern seaboard after basing-point pricing was abandoned in July, 1948. Similarly, within three years of the 1948 *Cement Institute* antitrust decision, 52 new cement plants were started or planned in 28 states (Congressional Record, March 31, 1951, p. 4564).

This paper concentrates upon these locational issues, particularly in their effects on a new entrant. Specifically, a spatial model is developed which allows us to analyse the location choice of an entrant when that entrant *either* accepts the ruling basing-point pricing system *or* enters in price competition with the incumbent firms. The model sheds more analytic light on the claim noted above that basing-point pricing encourages more localisation of production than would otherwise occur. The specific conditions under which this claim is justified are identified but it is also shown that there will be cases in which basing-point pricing and competitive entrants will adopt *identical* locations.

The paper is organised as follows. Section I outlines the spatial model upon which the analysis is based. Price equilibrium under basing-point and competitive entry are analysed in Section II. Location choice for the two types of entrant is computed in Section III and Section IV compares location choice under competitive and basing-point entry for different values of the relevant parameters. The main conclusions are summarised in Section V.

I. THE MODEL

A very simple spatial model is used that is now familiar in the literature. The market area is assumed to be a bounded line, denoted by the interval $[0, Z]$, over which identical consumers are uniformly distributed at unit density. Two types of firms are assumed to exist in the market:

(i) A set B of firms that are coincidentally located at the single basing-point. B contains $n \geqslant 2$ firms. Without loss of generality we assume that the basing-point is the left-hand extremity of the market;

(ii) A potential entrant firm that is assumed to locate at some distance x to the right of the basing point, where x is a decision variable. The potential entrant is denoted by subscript x.[1]

[1] It might appear that this treatment of the firms in the market is somewhat restrictive for two reasons: (i) that the basing-point system may be a multiple basing-point system (we are grateful to an Associate Editor for raising this point), and (ii) that there may be more than one entrant. Consider (i). So long as the entrant is assumed to enter the market 'to the right' of the basing-point that is 'furthest to the right' in the market our analysis will go through essentially unaltered. All that needs to be considered, therefore, is entry between two basing-points. Intuition suggests that the entrant would be driven to a central location no matter the pricing system the entrant adopts. In addition, there is little sense in talking of greater or lesser production concentration in such a case: a move toward one of the basing points is, by definition, a move away from the other. Given the focus on pricing policy and location choice, it is more interesting to treat the entrant as coming into the periphery of the market. After all, this has long been considered the major potential threat

Both types of firm produce a homogeneous product. Individual demand for this product is assumed linear in delivered price and given for a consumer located at s by the normalised demand function:

$$q(s) = 1 - p(s) \quad (s \in [0, Z]) \tag{1}$$

where $q(s)$ is quantity demanded and $p(s)$ delivered price at s. The linear assumption eases computation but, as is well known from spatial price theory, Greenhut *et al.* (1987), can be taken as representative of a wide range of concave, or 'not too convex' demand forms.

Consumers buy from the firm offering the product at the lowest price. If the entrant *chooses* to follow the basing-point price *throughout a market segment* then demand in this area will be shared equally between the entrant and the basing-point firms. This is in the spirit of the historical justifications advanced in favour of basing-point pricing: it was (and is) claimed that basing-point pricing facilitates interpenetration of markets.

With competitive entry there may also be points where delivered prices from the basing-point and x are the same. Assume that price competition is Bertrand-at-every-point, at least for the entrant. So long as the basing-point firms' delivered price is greater than the entrant's costs at a particular market point, the entrant can undercut the basing-point firms and win that market. This is sometimes referred to as the ϵ-argument: the low-cost firm can undercut its competitor by ϵ, where ϵ is 'small'. It is assumed, therefore, that the left-hand boundary of the competitive entrant's market area is the market point at which the entrant's marginal production and transport costs just equal the basing-point firms' delivered price. This does *not* mean that the basing-point firms are necessarily passive actors in the competitive game with the entrant. Indeed, one of the issues to be considered below is the 'best' choice of price for the basing-point firms *given* that they anticipate the entry of a price-competing firm.

Production is assumed to be characterised by constant marginal costs which are normalised to zero at the basing-point. Locations distant from the basing-point suffer a production cost penalty: perhaps because the basing-point enjoys favourable access to production inputs. The cost penalty is assumed linear in distance and output. Thus marginal production costs at location x are given $Kx (K \geqslant 0)$. Note that the assumptions regarding the linearity of the market and the end-point location of the basing point allow reference to be made interchangeably to 'location x' and 'the firm (or consumer) distance x from the basing point'.

Transport is assumed linear in distance and quantity,[2] and given by t per

to a collusive basing-point system. There remain, of course, interesting strategic issues with respect to 'central' as opposed to 'peripheral' entry, but these are outside the scope of this paper. Reason (ii) also raises some interesting questions. Certainly, it would be possible to model multiple entry as a sequential process; see, for example, Prescott and Visscher (1977) and subsequent extensions. The qualitative conclusions on the location choice of a single entrant will, however, be essentially unaffected if the analysis is extended to allow for multiple entry. In other words, the additional insights that might come from allowing for multiple entry do not justify the increased analytic intractability such a generalisation necessitates.

[2] Nonlinear transport costs in distance could be considered but this severely complicates the analysis without affecting the qualitative conclusions.

unit, per unit distance. It will prove convenient to rewrite the production cost penalty by the substitution:

$$k = K/t; \quad Kx = ktx. \tag{2}$$

Note that demand and cost conditions imply that the right-hand boundary of the market is at most at distance $1/t$ from the basing point. In other words, the market area is some subset of the interval $[0, 1/t]$. Z is, therefore, either limited exogenously by natural geographic conditions to something less than $1/t$, or it is determined by the maximum delivered price a consumer is willing to pay.[3] In addition, for the potential entrant to be able to compete with the basing-point firms, a required restriction is that:

$$0 \leqslant k < 1. \tag{3}$$

$k > 1$ implies production costs at *any* non-base site exceed production costs at the base point plus transportation costs from the base point.

II. PRICE EQUILIBRIUM

In identifying price equilibrium in this spatial model, assume that the locations of the basing-point firms are fixed.

II.1. *The Incumbent B-firms*

Although the incumbent firms are assumed to collude on pricing *policy* – they adopt basing-point pricing which is, by definition, f.o.b. – there may still be competition between them on the *actual* base-point price: of course, in equilibrium all active B-firms will charge identical delivered prices. It appears, therefore, that price competition among the B-firms should be modelled as a repeated game. This is a complicated exercise much of the essence of which can be captured by parameterising price competition among the incumbents.[4] Given our demand structure, this is equivalent to assuming that the B-firms charge a mill price α, where:

(i) $\alpha = 0$ is equivalent to unrestricted price competition: the incumbents act as Bertrand competitors with marginal cost pricing the only Bertrand equilibrium for two or more B-type firms;

(ii) $\alpha = \alpha^*$ is equivalent to perfect collusion between the incumbents: where α^* remains to be determined (see below);

(iii) $0 < \alpha < \alpha^*$ can then be interpreted as being equivalent to different degrees of collusion between the incumbents.

The approach implicit in (iii) allows analysis of the impact on the entrant's location of different degrees of collusion among the incumbents: in essence, α is taken as exogenous. The perfect collusion case (ii) should be treated

[3] This implies, of course, that the entrant is constrained to supply only customers in $[0, Z]$ perhaps because it is constrained to operate within a particular basing-point area. In the formal analysis, the effect on location choice of imposing different limits on the market area is considered.

[4] We are grateful to an anonymous referee for suggesting the following argument. It is consistent with the Folk Theorem which suggests that many equilibria are possible in repeated price games: Friedman (1971); Tirole (1989).

somewhat differently. This case is equivalent to α being determined endogenously. The price charged by the incumbents will affect the location of the entrant and this will affect the post-entry profit of the incumbents. With perfect collusion between the incumbents there is an optimal price they should charge which need not – and with competitive entry typically will not – be the monopoly price. The optimal base-point price α^* is likely to be affected by:

(i) the number of incumbents;

(ii) the cost penalty incurred by the entrants; *and*

(iii) the pricing policy adopted by the entrant.

II.2. *A Competitive Entrant*

The potential competitive entrant in choosing whether to enter the market and the location at which it will enter anticipates the price equilibrium that will apply post-entry. The post-entry price equilibrium for *any* location choice $x \in [0, Z]$ of the entrant, denoted $p_x(.)$, can be described by direct application of the analysis of Thisse and Vives (1988), on the assumption that the entrant competes in price with the incumbents.

For any location choice $x > 0$, the entrant can profitably undercut the basing-point firms in the market interval $Z_x = (z, Z)$ (see Fig. 1) where z is defined by:

$$z: \alpha + tz = ktx + t(x-z) \Rightarrow z = x(1+k)/2 - \alpha/2t. \tag{4}$$

The entrant has monopoly pricing power – defined by $p_x^M(s) < \alpha + ts$ – for consumers in the interval $Z_x^M = (v, Z)$ where v is defined by:

$$v = \begin{cases} [(1-2\alpha)/t + x(1+k)]/3 & \text{for } v \leqslant x \\ (1-2\alpha)/t - (1-k)\,x & \text{for } v \geqslant x \end{cases} \tag{5}$$

and the optimal monopoly pricing policy for the entrant is the familiar '50 per cent freight absorption' policy:

$$p_x^M(s) = \tfrac{1}{2}(1+ktx) + \tfrac{1}{2}t|x-s|. \tag{6}$$

Note that $v < 1/t$ for $x > 0$. Hence the potential entrant always has monopoly pricing power for some nonempty set of consumers provided that the market area is sufficiently extensive, i.e. that $Z > v$.

Finally, profit to the entrant is concave in $p_x(s)$. Thus, if the entrant has a cost advantage at s, but no monopoly power, its profit maximising price is $\alpha + ts$ (the price charged by the basing-point firms).

The price equilibrium for the competitive entrant can now be stated:[5]

$$p_x^c(s) = \begin{cases} p_x^M(s) & \text{for } s \in Z_x^M \\ \alpha + ts & \text{for } s \in Z_x - Z_x^M \\ ktx + t|x-s| & \text{otherwise.} \end{cases} \tag{7}$$

[5] See Thisse and Vives (1988), Lederer and Hurter (1986), Gee (1976), and Hoover (1937). Our analysis is a slight variation on Thisse and Vives in that the incumbent firms are assumed not to respond to the entrant's price competition by changing α post-entry. Of course, the comments above regarding the endogenous choice of α imply that the incumbents may set prices optimally given that they know entry will occur.

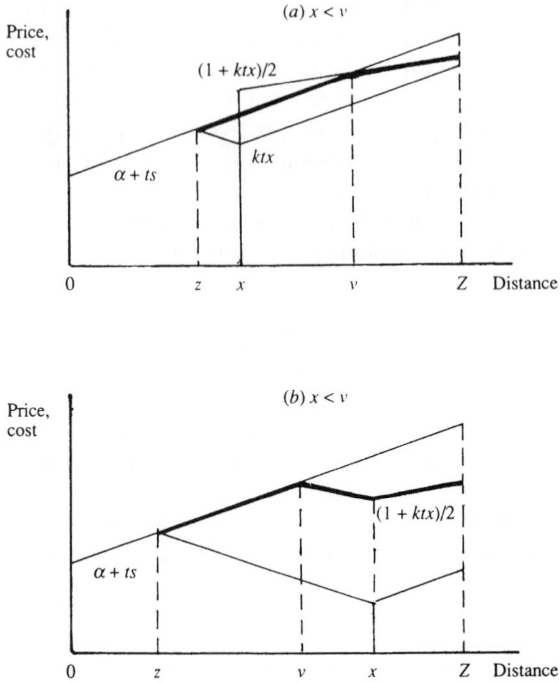

Fig. 1. Competitive (Nash) price equilibrium.

The market area for the entrant is the interval in which it can profitably undercut the incumbents. Demand for the entrant's product is:

$$q_x^c(s) = \begin{cases} 1 - p_x^c(s) & \text{for } s \in Z_x \\ 0 & \text{otherwise.} \end{cases} \tag{8}$$

The price equilibrium is illustrated by the heavy lines in Figs. 1 (*a*) and (*b*) for the entrant's market area.

The market area for the basing-point firms is $Z_b = (0, z)$. Since it is assumed that demand from consumers in Z_b is shared equally among these firms:

$$q_i^c(s) = (1 - \alpha - ts)/n \quad \text{for} \quad s \in Z_b \quad \text{and} \quad i \in B. \tag{9}$$

Z_x^M is nonempty for any location choice $x > 0$ provided only that $Z > v$, so the price equilibrium for the potential entrant is *not* basing-point pricing. There is a region (z, v) over which prices 'look like' basing-point prices, but in this region the entrant is able to use its cost advantage to secure a monopoly position.

II.3. *A Basing-Point Pricing Entrant*

Suppose that the entrant chooses (by threat or free will) to follow the basing-point pricing policy. Delivered price to the consumer location s is then:

$$p_x^b(s) = \alpha + ts \tag{10}$$

and the entrant will want to supply those consumers for whom $p_x^b(s) > ktx + t|x-s|$. This is just the market interval Z_x (see Fig. 1). But now the entrant shares demand in this interval with the basing-point firms. (Recall our discussion of basing-point pricing as a method of market interpenetration.) Demand for the entrant's product is

$$q_x^b(s) = \begin{cases} (1-\alpha-ts)/(n+1) & \text{for} \quad s \in Z_x \\ 0 & \text{otherwise.} \end{cases} \tag{11}$$

III. LOCATION CHOICE

No matter whether the entrant's pricing policy is the Nash equilibrium discriminatory policy (7) or the basing-point policy (11), the entrant firm's objective is to find the location x^* that will maximise its profit at the post-entry price equilibrium. Profit from location choice of x (gross of fixed costs) with pricing policy $\hat{p}_x(.) \in [p_x^c(.), p_x^b(.)]$ is

$$\pi[x, \hat{P}_x(.)] = \frac{1}{N}\int_{Z_x} [\hat{p}_x(s) - ktx - t|x-s|][1-\hat{p}_x(s)]\, ds, \tag{12}$$

where N is the number of firms supplying consumers in Z_x. With discriminatory pricing $N = 1$, while basing-point pricing implies $N = n+1$. The entrant is assumed to choose the location $x^*[\hat{p}_x(.)]$ that maximises profit under pricing policy $\hat{p}_x(.)$.

III.1. *Competitive (Nash Equilibrium) Pricing*

The profit equation is, from equation (7),

$$\pi[x, p_x^c(.)] = \int_z^v (\alpha + ts - ktx - t|x-s|)(1-\alpha-ts)\, ds$$
$$+ \int_v^Z [p_x^M(s) - ktx - t|x-s|][1-p_x^M(s)]\, ds, \tag{13}$$

where profit is written gross of fixed costs and z and v are given by equations (4) and (5) respectively. The first term is profit in the market area $Z_x - Z_x^M$, in which price is determined by delivered price from the basing-point, while the second term is profit in the market area Z_x^M in which the entrant has a monopoly position.

Given the assumed demand and cost conditions, the profit function (13) is a cubic in tx. The first order condition is a quadratic, the appropriate form of which depends on whether x is less than or greater than v, i.e. whether the optimal location is described by Fig. 1 (*a*) or (*b*) (recall equation (5)). We can write this quadratic in the form:

$$dt^2x^2 + etx + f = 0, \tag{14}$$

where the parameters d, e and f of the quadratic are determined by the relative values of v, x^* and Z: see below. Second order conditions then determine optimal location with competitive entry by the familiar equation:

$$tx_c^* = \frac{-e-\sqrt{(e^2-4df)}}{2d}. \tag{15}$$

Three cases must be considered in evaluating the solutions of (14) and (15):[6]

(i) $v < x_c^* < Z$: this is equivalent to the case illustrated in Fig. 1 (*b*). The values of d, e and f are:

$$\left.\begin{aligned} d &= 36k-5(1+k)^3, \\ e &= (8+2\alpha)(1+k)^2-24+12tZ(1-k)^2 \\ f &= (1+k)(\alpha^2-4\alpha-2)+12tZ(1-k)(1-tZ/2). \end{aligned}\right\} \quad v < x_c^* < Z, \tag{15a}$$

(ii) $x_c^* < v < Z$: this is the case illustrated in Fig. 1 (*a*) and assumes that the interval Z_x^M is non-empty. In other words, this case assumes that the entrant can charge the monopoly discriminatory price to some set of consumers. From equation (5), the condition $v < Z$ is equivalent to the constraint

$$x_c^* > (1-2\alpha-tZ)/t(1-k). \tag{16}$$

The direction of the inequality arises, as can be seen from Fig. 1 (*a*), since, if $x_c^* < v$ then a move to the left by the entrant (a move nearer to the basing-point) *increases* v and so *reduces* the market interval in which the entrant has a monopoly position.

In this case the values of d, e and f are:

$$\left.\begin{aligned} d &= 1+\tfrac{1}{4}(1-k)^3-\tfrac{1}{8}(1+k)^3, \\ e &= [\tfrac{1}{2}(1+k)^2-2](1-\alpha)+\tfrac{1}{4}(1+k)^2\alpha \\ &\quad -\tfrac{1}{2}(1-k)^2(1-2\alpha-tZ) \\ f &= \tfrac{1}{4}(1-k)(1-2\alpha)^2-\tfrac{1}{8}\alpha(1+k)(4-3\alpha) \\ &\quad +\tfrac{1}{2}tZ(1-k)(1-tZ/2). \end{aligned}\right\} \quad x^* < v < Z, \tag{15b}$$

(iii) $v \geqslant Z$: this is similar to the case in Fig. 1 (*a*), but now the entrant does not have a monopoly position anywhere. The second term in the profit equation (13) disappears and the appropriate values of d, e and f are:

$$\left.\begin{aligned} d &= 1-\tfrac{1}{8}(1+k)^3, \\ e &= [\tfrac{1}{2}(1+k)^2-2](1-\alpha)+\tfrac{1}{4}\alpha(1+k)^2, \\ f &= tZ(1-k)\left(1-\alpha-\frac{tZ}{2}\right)-\tfrac{1}{8}\alpha(1+k)(4-3\alpha). \end{aligned}\right\} \quad v \geqslant Z. \tag{15c}$$

[6] The relevant case is determined by the parameters α, k and Z. The optimal value of x^* is continuous across the boundaries defining these cases. Proof of the results presented below is tedious and can be obtained from the authors on request.

III.2. *Basing-Point Pricing*

If the entrant chooses to follow the basing-point price, the entrant's profit gross of fixed costs is given by:

$$\pi[x, p_x^b(.)] = \frac{1}{N}\int_z^Z (\alpha + ts - ktx - t|x-s|)(1-\alpha-ts)\,ds. \tag{17}$$

The first-order condition is again quadratic in tx, with solution (from the second-order conditions):

$$tx_b^* = \frac{-e-\sqrt{(e^2-4df)}}{2d} \tag{18}$$

where:

$$\left.\begin{aligned} d &= 1-\tfrac{1}{8}(1+k)^3 \\ e &= [\tfrac{1}{2}(1+k)^2-2](1-\alpha)+\tfrac{1}{4}\alpha(1+k)^2 \\ f &= tZ(1-k)(1-\alpha-tZ/2)-\tfrac{1}{8}\alpha(1+k)(4-3\alpha). \end{aligned}\right\} \tag{19}$$

IV. COMPARISON OF LOCATION CHOICE

Some limited analytic investigation is possible of equations (15*a–c*) and (19). It can be shown, for example, that an increase in the basing-point price α, in the cost penalty k, or a decrease in the market boundary Z encourages entry nearer to the basing-point – reduces x^* – no matter the pricing policy of the entrant. What is not so obvious is the impact of the entrant's pricing policy upon the entrant's location choice, or the comparative statics of this relative location choice. Numerical analysis is straightforward, however, and the discussion below presents the results of a number of such numerical simulations.

One preliminary remark is in order. It might be thought, from an examination of equations (15*a–c*) and (19), that location choice by the entrant is independent of the number of *B*-type firms. This is so, however, only if:

(i) the *B*-type firms are Bertrand competitors – in which case $\alpha = 0$; or

(ii) the degree of collusion as measured by α is exogenous, i.e. is independent of the number of incumbents, the impact of entry, *and* the pricing policy of the entrant.

If α is endogenous, then the optimal choice of α, as indicated above, is likely to be affected by the number of incumbents. There will, therefore, be an interaction between the number of incumbents and the entrant's location choice.

IV.1. α *Exogenous*

Location choice by a basing-point and competitive entrant are compared in Tables 1 and 2 for a number of different combinations of the parameters α, Z and k. Some brief comments are, perhaps, necessary on our choice of parameter range. This has been made in part for purely illustrative reasons, but there is also an important economic constraint on this range. The increased agglomeration induced by an increase in α, decrease in Z or increase in k results

Table 1

Optimal Location Choice with Different Values of Cost Penalty $k: Z = 0{\cdot}667$

	$k = 0$		$k = 0{\cdot}05$		$k = 0{\cdot}1$	
α	BP	CE	BP	CE	BP	CE
0·000	0·381	0·382	0·374	0·374	0·367	0·367
0·017	0·371	0·372	0·363	0·364	0·356	0·356
0·033	0·360	0·363	0·352	0·354	0·344	0·345
0·050	0·350	0·354	0·341	0·344	0·333	0·334
0·067	0·339	0·346	0·330	0·334	0·320	0·323
0·083	0·328	0·337	0·318	0·324	0·308	0·312
0·100	0·316	0·329	0·306	0·315	0·295	0·301
0·117	0·304	0·321	0·293	0·305	0·282	0·290
0·133	0·292	0·313	0·281	0·296	0·269	0·280
0·150	0·280	0·306	0·268	0·287	0·255	0·269
0·167	0·267	0·298	0·254	0·278	0·241	0·259
0·183	0·254	0·292	0·241	0·269	0·227	0·249
0·200	0·241	0·286	0·227	0·261	0·212	0·238
0·217	0·227	0·280	0·212	0·253	0·197	0·229
0·233	0·220	0·275	0·207	0·245	0·194	0·219
0·250	0·216	0·271	0·204	0·238	0·191	—
0·267	0·213	—	0·200	—	0·188	—
0·283	0·209	—	0·196	—	0·184	—
0·300	0·204	—	0·192	—	0·180	—

Note: BP denotes basing-point pricing entry and CE competitive entry.

Table 2

Optimal Location Choice with Different Values of Market Boundary $Z: k = 0{\cdot}05$

	$Z = 0{\cdot}667$		$Z = 0{\cdot}6$		$Z = 0{\cdot}1$	
α	BP	CE	BP	CE	BP	CE
0·000	0·374	0·374	0·346	0·346	0·299	0·299
0·017	0·363	0·364	0·336	0·336	0·290	0·290
0·033	0·352	0·354	0·326	0·326	0·281	0·281
0·050	0·341	0·344	0·316	0·316	0·272	0·272
0·067	0·330	0·334	0·306	0·306	0·263	0·263
0·083	0·318	0·324	0·295	0·296	0·253	0·253
0·100	0·306	0·315	0·284	0·285	0·244	0·244
0·117	0·293	0·305	0·273	0·275	0·234	0·234
0·133	0·281	0·296	0·261	0·266	0·224	0·224
0·150	0·268	0·287	0·249	0·256	0·214	0·214
0·167	0·254	0·278	0·237	0·246	0·203	0·203
0·183	0·241	0·269	0·225	0·237	0·192	0·193
0·200	0·227	0·261	0·212	0·227	0·185	—
0·217	0·212	0·253	0·202	0·218	0·183	—
0·233	0·207	0·245	0·199	—	0·182	—
0·250	0·204	0·238	0·197	—	0·180	—
0·267	0·200	—	0·194	—	0·178	—
0·283	0·196	—	0·191	—	0·176	—
0·300	0·192	—	0·188	—	0·174	—

Note: BP denotes basing-point pricing entry and CE competitive entry.

in the left hand boundary (z) of the entrant's market area approaching the basing-point. From equation (4) the entrant's market area will be the entire interval $[0, Z]$ for any (α, Z, k) combinations such that

$$(1+k)\, tx^*(\alpha, Z, k) - \alpha \leqslant 0. \tag{20}$$

With competitive entry, such (α, Z, k) combinations would result in the entrant capturing the entire market. We rule out such (α, Z, k) combinations by assumption, confining attention to parameter values in the set:[7]

$$\zeta(\alpha, Z, k) = \{\alpha, Z, k : (1+k)\, tx_c^*(\alpha, Z, k) - \alpha \geqslant 0\}. \tag{21}$$

As was indicated above, agglomeration is encouraged – the optimal location of the entrant moves towards the incumbents' site – with an increase in α, an increase in k and a decrease in Z. So far as relative location choice is concerned, the simulation results indicate that:

$$x_b^*(\alpha, Z, k) \leqslant x_c^*(\alpha, Z, k) \quad \text{for all } \alpha, Z, k. \tag{22}$$

The competitive entrant never locates nearer to the basing-point than does the basing-point pricing entrant. Basing-point pricing does, indeed, appear to support production agglomeration as Greenhut and Machlup suggested.

It is also clear from these simulations, however, that there are parameter combinations for which the two types of entrant will choose identical locations. Comparison of equations (15c) and (19) identifies the precise circumstances under which identical location choice arises: see also equation (16). For the two types of entrant to choose *different* locations the competitive entrant must have a monopoly pricing advantage with respect to some sub-set of consumers: this sub-set will, of course, be located at the right-most extremity of the market.

Fig. 2 and Table 3 illustrate these results. Feasible combinations of α and Z for any given cost penalty k are defined by three constraints:

(i) the demand constraint: $\alpha + tZ \leqslant 1$;

(ii) the monopoly pricing constraint: $\alpha \leqslant \alpha_m = \frac{1}{2} - tZ/4$ where α_m is the optimal monopoly price for the basing-point firms: see Greenhut *et al.* (1987, p. 118);

(iii) the market area constraint: $\alpha, Z \in \zeta(\alpha, Z, k)$ (recall equation (21)).

These constraints define the feasible region $OABC$ in Fig. 2.

We can also define the set:

$$\chi(\alpha, Z, k) = \{\alpha, Z, k : v(\alpha, Z, k) \geqslant Z\}. \tag{23}$$

For all (α, Z, k) combinations in $\chi(\alpha, Z, k)$ the competitive entrant has no monopoly pricing advantage anywhere and so adopts the identical location as would a basing-point pricing entrant. The set $\chi(\alpha, Z, k)$ is defined within the feasible set by the shaded area OAD in Fig. 2.

Only for (α, Z, k) combinations in the region $ABCD$ does the competitive entrant have a monopoly pricing advantage to a non-empty sub-set of consumers.

[7] No such complications arise with basing point entry since the entrant shares the market with the incumbents.

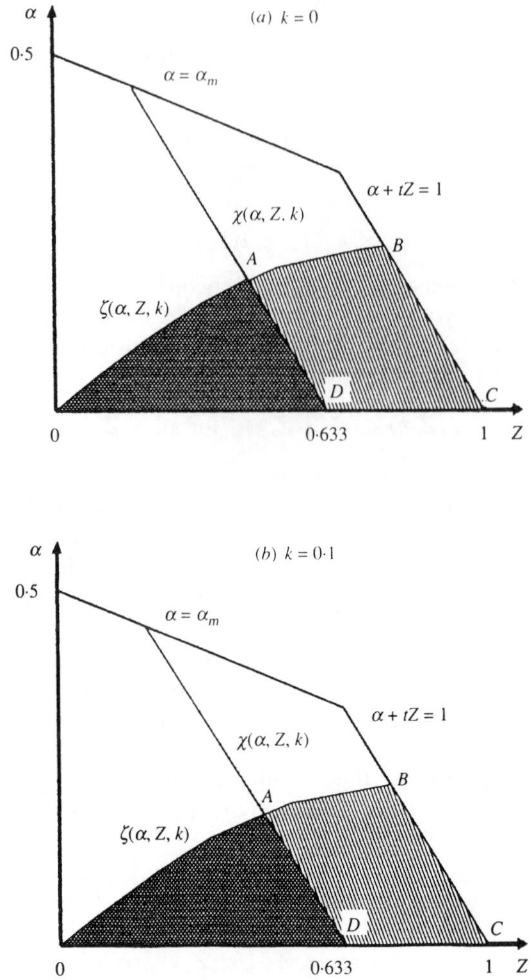

Fig. 2. Parameters generating coincident location.

The existence of such a sub-set of consumers is more likely the more extensive the market (the greater is Z), the lower the cost penalty (k) incurred by the entrant, and the higher the price (α) charged by the incumbent basing-point firms: in our interpretation of α made here, the greater the degree of collusion between the incumbent basing-point firms.

Machlup's conclusion that basing-point pricing leads to greater production concentration must, therefore, be qualified. This conclusion is much more likely to hold true in extensive market areas, where the incumbent firms hold off to at least some extent from price competition between themselves and where these firms enjoy no great production cost advantage with respect to new entrants.

Table 3
Boundaries of $\zeta(\alpha, Z, k)$ and $\chi(\alpha, Z, k)$

$\zeta(\alpha, Z, k)$ α	$k = 0$ Z	$k = 0{\cdot}05$ Z	$k = 0{\cdot}10$ Z
0·0	0·633	0·651	0·669
0·15	0·483	0·498	0·513
0·30	0·333	0·345	0·358
0·45	0·183	0·192	0·202
0·60	0·033	0·040	0·047

$\chi(\alpha, Z, k)$ α	$k = 0$ Z	$k = 0{\cdot}05$ Z	$k = 0{\cdot}10$ Z
0·0	0·0	0·0	0·0
0·05	0·103	0·103	0·104
0·10	0·214	0·216	0·218
0·15	0·343	0·346	0·351
0·20	0·517	0·527	0·541

IV.2. α *Endogenous*

The discussion of section IV.1 assumes that the incumbent basing-point firms adopt the same base-point price no matter the pricing policy of the entrant. It is difficult to maintain such an assumption once perfect collusion between the incumbents is allowed. There is a relationship between the incumbent firms' post-entry profit and the base-point price they adopt. This relationship identifies an optimal base-point price, α^*, that perfectly colluding incumbents should adopt. Recall that the entrant chooses the optimal location *given* the price level charged by the incumbents. Thus, the optimal base-point price α^* is identified on the assumption that the incumbents do not attempt to deter entry but do correctly anticipate the location the entrant will choose. Effectively, the incumbents are acting as leaders of a Stackelberg game.

Basing-Point-Pricing Entry

A complication arises if the entrant adopts basing-point pricing since the incumbents' profit/base price relationship can have two maxima. From our discussion in section IV.1, an increase in the base-point price induces the entrant to locate nearer to the base-point. But this implies that the left-hand boundary (z) of the entrant's market area will approach the basing-point, i.e. z will tend to zero. From equation (4) the entrant's market area will be the entire interval $[0, Z]$ for any base-point price which is such that

$$x_b^*(\alpha)(1+k)/2 - \alpha/2t \leqslant 0. \tag{24}$$

Define the base-point price α' as:

$$\alpha' : x_b^*(\alpha')(1+k)/2 - \alpha'/2t = 0. \tag{25}$$

For any base-point price greater than α' the base-point firm and the entrant share the total market, with each firm taking $1/(n+1)$ of total demand. Profit for the incumbents will increase as the base-point is increased above α' until the base-point price is raised to the monopoly price

$$\alpha_m^* = \tfrac{1}{2} - tZ/4. \tag{26}$$

For base-point prices less than $\alpha', z > 0$. The incumbents are sole suppliers in the interval $[0, z]$ and share with the entrant the interval $[z, Z]$. Profit to the incumbents is:

$$\pi_b^i = \frac{1}{n}\int_0^z \alpha(1-\alpha-tr)\,dr + \frac{1}{n+1}\int_z^Z \alpha(1-\alpha-tr)\,dr \quad (0 < \alpha < \alpha'). \tag{27}$$

A necessary condition for this profit function to have an internal maximum in the interval $[0, \alpha')$ is:

$$\frac{\partial \pi_b^i}{\partial \alpha} < 0 \quad \text{as} \quad z \to 0. \tag{28}$$

Differentiating (27) gives:

$$\frac{\partial \pi_b^i}{\partial \alpha} = \frac{1}{n}\int_0^Z (1-2\alpha-tr)\,dr + \frac{1}{n+1}\int_z^Z (1-2\alpha-tr)\,dr + \alpha(1-\alpha-tz)\frac{\partial z}{\partial \alpha}\left(\frac{1}{n}-\frac{1}{n+1}\right). \tag{29}$$

The first two terms are positive. They constitute the increase in profit arising from the price effect of the increase in the basing-point price. The third term is negative – since $\partial z/\partial \alpha < 0$. It is the reduction in profit arising from the market area effect of the increase in the basing-point price. Increasing the basing-point price reduces the market area in which the incumbents are the sole suppliers or, equivalently, increases the market area in which the incumbents must share demand with the entrant. Only if the market area effect dominates the price effect is condition (28) satisfied.

As z tends to zero, (29) simplifies to:

$$\left.\frac{\partial \pi_b^i}{\partial \alpha}\right|_{z\to 0} = \frac{1}{n+1}\left[\frac{2-4\alpha-tZ}{2} + \frac{\alpha(1-\alpha)}{n}\frac{\partial z}{\partial \alpha}\right]. \tag{30}$$

The first term is the (positive) price effect. It is smaller the more extensive is the market area and/or the nearer the basing-point price approaches to the monopoly price: see equation (26). The second term is the (negative) market area effect and is greater in absolute magnitude the smaller is the number of incumbent basing-point firms.

This can be put another way. Assume that the incumbents anticipate the entrant will follow the basing-point pricing scheme. Then perfect collusion among the incumbents is more likely to lead to the optimal basing-point price being the monopoly price of equation (26) the greater is the number of incumbents and the less extensive is the total market area.

Table 4

Optimal Basing Point Price (α_c^*) with Competitive Entry

Entrant's cost penalty (k)	Optimal basing point price (α_c^*)	
	$Z = 0{\cdot}667$	$Z = 0{\cdot}6$
0·00	0·1215	0·1093
0·01	0·1205	0·1088
0·02	0·1196	0·1084
0·03	0·1187	0·1079
0·04	0·1178	0·1074
0·05	0·1170	0·1069
0·06	0·1161	0·1064
0·07	0·1153	0·1059
0·08	0·1145	0·1054
0·09	0·1137	0·1049
α_b^*	0·3333	0·350

For the particular cases considered in this paper, condition (28) is not satisfied for any combination of parameter values, and the optimal, perfectly collusive base-point price is the monopoly price of equation (26).[8]

Nash Equilibrium Pricing Entrant

Similar ambiguities do not arise if the entrant competes on price with the incumbents. If the incumbents choose a base-point price equal to α'[9] then the entrant takes the whole market and the incumbents' profit falls to zero.

Table 4 identifies the optimal, perfectly collusive basing-point price with competitive entry. The optimal basing-point price is lower:

I. the greater the cost penalty incurred by the entrant;

II. the more constrained is the market area.

Comparison of Optimal Collusive Prices

Table 4 also provides for comparison the perfectly collusive basing-point price with basing point entry. In comparing the optimal basing-point price for different pricing policies of the entrant, assume initially that condition (28) is satisfied and, in addition, that the internal maximum is a global maximum. Then conditions I and II above also characterise the optimal basing-point price in the event of basing-point entry. There is, in addition, a third condition:

III. with basing-point entry, if there is an internal equilibrium the optimal basing-point price will be lower the fewer incumbents there are.

If condition (28) is not satisfied, equation (26) gives the optimal basing-point price for the incumbents in the event of basing point entry. In this event only condition II characterises the optimal basing point price (see Table 4).

Whether or not condition (28) holds, the incumbents' optimal basing point

[8] Preliminary investigations indicate that condition (28) would be satisfied by alternative specifications of, for example, the demand function.

[9] This value of α' will typically not be the same α' as would apply with basing-point entry.

price is always higher with basing point than with competitive entry, a conclusion that should not be surprising given the market sharing arrangements that characterise the former type of entry.

Some comments are, perhaps, in order as to why the number of incumbents may affect the optimal incumbent price with basing-point entry but not with competitive entry. Consider first competitive entry. The entrant takes *all* demand in its market area and the best the incumbents can do is choose α to maximise aggregate post-entry profits in their remaining market area. The resulting optimal value of α will be independent of the number of incumbents. By contrast, basing-point entry allows the incumbents to share demand with the entrant in the entrant's market area. Profit to each incumbent is then an $(n+1)$th share of profit in the entrant's market area and an nth share of the remaining market area. Aggregate profit to the incumbents is no longer independent of the number of incumbents. Hence, the optimal incumbent price (α^*) will be some function of the number of incumbents: provided always, of course, that this is not the monopoly price with basing-point entry.

Conditions I, II and III may appear to be counter-intuitive. I and II arise because an increase in the cost penalty incurred by entrants, or a reduction in the overall market area, will encourage the entrant to locate nearer to the incumbents for any given incumbent price level. This reduces the monopoly market area of the incumbents, and so encourages them to lower the base-point price in order to maintain sales and profitability, and in order to limit market penetration by the entrant.

So far as III is concerned, recall that the assumption that α is endogenous is equivalent to perfect collusion on the part of the incumbents. The greater the number of incumbents the less will be the impact of a basing-point entrant on their aggregate profitability: the entrant takes an $(n+1)$th share of demand in its market area. As a result, the greater the number of incumbents the nearer will the collusive, post-entry price approach the monopoly price.

Relative Location Choice

Now consider relative location choice with different types of entry. When α is endogenous, it is unlikely that basing-point pricing and competitive pricing will ever give rise to the same location choice by the entrant. The optimal price, α^*, charged by the perfectly collusive basing point firms is determined by the pricing policy of the entrant and, with basing-point entry, the number of incumbents. As we have seen, the expectation of basing point gives rise to a higher basing point price than will the expectation of competitive entry. This difference in basing-point price is sufficient to ensure that the expectation of competitive entry will lead to greater decentralisation of production than will expected basing-point entry. The degree of decentralisation of production decreases the lower the cost penalty of location choice distant from the basing-point and the less constrained is the market area. Nevertheless, even if the market area is sufficiently constrained to eliminate any monopoly pricing advantage for the entrant, there will still be a difference in location choice resulting from the pricing policy of the entrant. In other words, the traditional conclusion is correct *provided that* the incumbent basing-point firms collude perfectly in their choice of the basing-point price.

V. CONCLUSIONS

The contention that basing-point pricing encourages production concentration has long been part of received wisdom. What has not been appreciated are the precise conditions under which this received wisdom is, indeed, correct. It has been shown in this paper that two conditions are sufficient.

First, if there is imperfect collusion among basing-point firms, a basing-point entrant will locate nearer to the basing-point than a competitive entrant *only if* the competitive entrant has a monopoly pricing advantage with respect to a non-empty sub-set of the consumer market. The existence of such a sub-set of consumers is more likely in extensive market areas in which the incumbent firms enjoy no great production cost advantage with respect to new entrants and in which the incumbent firms hold off to at least some extent from price competition between themselves.

In the event of perfect price collusion among the incumbent basing-point firms, the expectation of basing-point entry will lead to a higher base-point price than will the expectation of competitive entry. Even if the market area is sufficiently small as to eliminate any monopoly pricing advantage for a competitive entrant, there will be a difference in location choice resulting from the anticipated pricing policy of the entrant. In other words, perfect collusion among the incumbent base-point firms is sufficient to generate concentrated production.

University of Leicester

Texas A&M University

Florida State University

Date of receipt of final typescript: August 1990

References

Benson, B., Greenhut, M. L. and Norman, G. (1990). 'On the basing point system.' *American Economic Review*, vol. 80, pp. 584–8.

Friedman, J. (1971). 'A noncooperative equilibrium for supergames.' *Review of Economic Studies*, vol. 28, pp. 1–12.

Gee, J. M. A. (1976). 'A model of location and industrial efficiency with free entry.' *Quarterly Journal of Economics*, vol. 90, pp. 557–74.

Greenhut, M. L. (1956). *Plant Location in Theory and Practice*, Chapel Hill: University of North Carolina Press.

—— (1987). 'Basing-point system.' In *The New Palgrave Dictionary of Economics* (ed. J. Eatwell, M. Milgate and P. Newman), London, Macmillan Press.

—— Norman, G. and Hung, C. S. (1987). *The Economics of Imperfect Competition: a spatial approach*. London: Cambridge University Press.

Haddock, D. D. (1982). 'Basing-point pricing: competitive vs. collusive theories.' *American Economic Review*, vol. 72, pp. 289–306.

Hoover, E. M. (1937). 'Spatial price discrimination.' *Review of Economic Studies*, vol. 4, pp. 182–91.

Lederer, P. and Hurter, A. P. (1986). 'Competition of firms: discriminatory pricing and location.' *Econometrica*, vol. 54, pp. 623–40.

Machlup, F. (1949). *The Basing Point System*. Philadelphia: The Blackiston Press.

Prescott, E. G. and Vischer, M. (1977). 'Sequential location among firms with foresight.' *Bell Journal of Economics*, vol. 8, pp. 378–93.
Stigler, G. (1949). 'A theory of delivered price systems.' *American Economic Review*, vol. 39, pp. 1143–59.
Thisse, J.-F. and Vives, X. (1988). 'On the strategic choice of spatial price policy.' *American Economic Review*, vol. 78, pp. 122–37.
Tirole, J. (1989). *The Theory of Industrial Organization*. Cambridge, Mass.: The MIT Press.
TNEC (1941). *Final Report and Recommendations*. Washington, D.C.: Government Printing Office.
Wilcox, C. (1963). *Public Policies Toward Business*, 6th. ed., Homewood Ill.: Richard D. Irwin.

Reprinted from THE SOUTHERN ECONOMIC JOURNAL
Vol. XXIV, No. 2, October, 1957
Printed in U.S.A.

FREE ENTRY AND THE TRADE MARK-TRADE NAME PROTECTION

MELVIN L. GREENHUT*

Florida State University

I. INTRODUCTION

Marks, Names, Patents, and Copyrights

The protection provided by trade mark and trade name is not nearly so strong as that which is gained under patent rights or copyrights. But marks and names do promote, although to a lesser degree than patents and copyrights, any tendency that may exist to gain monopoly control of markets. Recognition of these relations has governed both the cases in which patent right extension was sought through the device of trade marks and trade names and the cases which are purely of mark and name content. While this paper deals essentially with the latter category of problem, a further word or two about similarities between patents, copyrights, marks, and names is first in order.

The patent or copyright provides exclusive use over a period of years to a process or a creation. Under broad filing arrangements, the owner gains simple monopoly control; competition remains possible from only distant processes or quite different products. Mark and name rights, in their turn, exclude others from use of the same term of reference. Process or creation can be comparable just so long as words of end description appear to differ. Thus it is the law that the patent for cellophane enabled the E. I. duPont de Nemours Co. to exclude others from its production during the life of its right. But its attempt to prevent others after the patent expiration date from producing a like product *under the term cellophane* was denied in the courts. Cellophane, the Supreme Court said, means a new wood product, not an article of commerce that is unique to duPont. Neither mark nor name right exist in the word cellophane. The word cellophane is descriptive of the product not its origin.[1] Patents and copyrights protect process and creation; marks and names, *when found*, protect only the source.[2] When not found, not only may the product be copied but so too the name.

Assumptions And Objectives

This paper postulates that trade marks and trade names offer some monopoly control to their owners. These possessory rights in the hands of enterprises which are otherwise dominant in the national market (and in some cases in regional or

* The author wishes to acknowledge his thanks to the Southern Fellowship Fund for a grant which made this study possible. Also a debt of gratitude goes to Professor Frank Miller of the Washington University Law School for his helpful suggestions.

[1] DuPont Cellophane Co. v. Waxed Products Co., 304 U.S. 575 (1938).

[2] Scandinavia Belting Co. v. Asbestos and Rubber Works, 250 U.S. 644 (1919); Yale and Towne Mfg. Co. v. Ford, 203 F 707 (CCA 3d, 1913), and G. and C. Merriam Co. v. Syndicate Pub. Co., 237 U.S. 618 (1915).

local markets) serve to promote fewness in numbers. This paper assumes that free entry into markets is desirable, that restraints on entry, legal and noneconomic,[3] direct and indirect, should be kept to a minimum. Under its assumptions, the paper offers a standard of mark and name protection that is designed toward this end of free entry. It sets stage for the inquiry by examination in section II of the classes and types of mark and name cases. This demonstration of how widespread the mark and name exclusions have been manifests the need for discussion of this problem by the nation's economists as well as by its lawyers.

It is critical in a paper of this type which stresses the economic side of laws and adjudications not to be bogged down with legal technicalities. Yet at the same time, the intricate pattern and checker-board effect[4] of 48 state laws plus a federal law can be confusing. Readers may wonder which law, state or federal, common or statutory, is involved. This matter and the facts which determine the outcome are sufficiently complex to baffle often the lawyer much less the reader who is technically trained in other matters. It is hoped that the next few remarks will settle this problem for those who may have it arise during their reading of this paper.

Our interest in the present article is mainly in general law, and not in specific state laws or particular federal statutes. This general law which forms our focus is composed fundamentally of the common law.[5] Thus, little mention is made in this paper of the Lanham Act[6] or of any of the specific state statutes on the subject. We need note only that the Lanham Act provides for registration of marks partly in line with common law conceptions of what is a trade mark and partly outside of the common law pattern. Thus descriptive, geographical, and primarily surname words among others are registrable as marks in certain cases even though at common law they would not be trade marks. But distinctions of this type do not really concern us. Our emphasis and our terminology will be in accord with the concepts of the common law rather than any given statute. Significantly, for the purpose of this article, it suffices that the underlying philosophy of protection given by the Lanham Act appears to be in line with the general law interpretations which we later on will relate.[7]

The complex effect of 48 state laws, common and statutory, requires that we mention but briefly the importance of state law in this field of jurisprudence. Even where federal jurisdiction is exercised over a dispute, state law has generally been held to be applicable.[8] Only on the count of violating federal regis-

[3] We need not discuss here the question whether natural economic restraints on entry should be encouraged or not.

[4] See J. Sweeney's reference to the Klaxon Case and its checker-board effect in the Bulova Watch Co. v. Stolzberg, 69 F. Supp. 543 (D. Mass, 1947).

[5] In this respect it may be pointed out that the common law serves as the basis for interpretation of statutory law unless legislated specifically to the contrary.

[6] The Trade Mark Act of 1946, 15 U.S.C.A. §1051 et seq.

[7] And see *infra*, note 29, where J. Clark's dissenting interpretation of the Lanham Act will be seen to compare closely with the extreme of the general law that is described in section II of this paper.

[8] Erie R. Co. v. Tompkins, 304 U.S. 64 (1938); Pecheur Lozenge Co., Inc. v. National Candy Co., Inc., 315 U.S. 666, 667 (1941).

tration does national law always fill up the gaps left open by the statute in question.[9] When, however, federal jurisdiction is gained because of diversity of citizenship or on grounds of a cause substantially related to a federal claim, the relevant law is often held to be the local law.[10]

In many respects, the matter of applicable law is insignificant in practice. Often the issue is not raised and the parties rely on federal law.[11] Moreover, there may not be any real difference between the laws.[12] If any trend exists, one might expect that under section 45 of the Lanham Act some swing to federal law will come about. But this matter too is not of great import to the present paper. Our special interest here is in the fairly widespread pattern of cases which favor more and more protection rather than the old amount of protection. Whether or not this pattern is fully general can be disputed. The point, however, is largely academic to us and unimportant, though there is authority which stresses this trend and which points to the Lanham Act as one example of this bent.[13] In any case, this paper will contend that the protection given today is not desirable in any of its prevalent forms.

II. TYPES OF POACHING

Common Law Protection Of Mark And Name

At common law, protection was offered any tradesman who was subject to mark or name encroachment by another. This legal aid was supported by the impelling claim that the consumer interest above all other things must be protected, for, by the very nature of the economic theory of Adam Smith, was not the consumer the focal point of all business activity? Prevention of mark and name encroachment would eliminate possible source of confusion. Fair competition for the satisfaction of an informed consumer was the ultimate goal.

The idea of protecting consumers from deceptive practises of poachers was, however, more illusory than real.[14] It was not the end buyer of goods and services who was uppermost in the minds of judges, rather it was the property right of

[9] Time, Inc. v. Viobin Corp, 128 F. 2d 860 (CCA 7th, 1942); Mishawaka Rubber and Woblen Mfg. Co. v. S. S. Kresge Co., 316 U.S. 203 (1942).

[10] For the matter of jurisdiction, see Hurn v. Oursler, 289 U.S. 238 (1933); Armstrong Paint and Varnish Works v. Nu-Enamel Corp., 305 U.S. 315 (1938); and Musher Foundation, Inc. v. Alba Trading Co., 127 F. 2d 9 (2nd DDA, 1942). For applicable law see note 8 *supra*, and National Fruit Product Co. v. Dwinell-Wright Co., 47 F. Supp. 499 (D. Mass, 1942). To the partial contrary, see Bulova Watch Co. v. Stolzberg, *op. cit.*

[11] Kellogg Co. v. National Biscuit Co., 305 U.S. 111 (1938); Skinner Mfg. Co. v. General Foods Sales Co., 143 F. 2d 895 (CCA 8th, 1944).

[12] Safeway Stores, Inc. v. Sklar, 75 F. Supp 98 (E.D. Pa 1947); Gum, Inc. v. Gumakers of America, Inc., 136 F. 2d 957 (CCA 3d, 1943).

[13] See J. Clark's statements *infra* note 29. J. Clark leaves strong impression in this case that over the years the amount of protection has been increased. In this regard he appears not to be in argument with J. Hand. It is only on the matter of just how extreme is the protection that the Lanham Act provides that the dissent is sharp. But even here whether the Lanham Act limits protection to more than the case of confusion alone as J. Hand explains or to confusion by itself as J. Clark contends, this Act reflects a vast body of general law which carries protection to a rather forward position.

[14] See Judge Frank's "concurring opinion" in Standard Brands, Inc. v. Smidler, 151 F. 2d 34 (CCA 2d, 1945).

business men which attained primary consideration in the courts. It mattered not that the poacher of another's mark or name effected price reductions for the benefit of the consumer. Judicial protection repeatedly was extended to the party whose mark or name was taken, regardless of the extent of competition in the market.

Types Of Poaching

This idea of property right protection "above all else" amounts to ownership of a monopolistic privilege by the tradesman who is able to claim possessory rights to mark or name. By classifying into types the market situations in which this property right concept is applied, we can see readily that the mark and name protection in this country serves to foster that which the Sherman and Clayton Acts seek to prevent.

A. COPYING THE TRADE MARK AND TRADE NAME. The trade mark differs from the trade name in the following main respects. The trade mark at common law is an arbitrary and fanciful designation. Its owner gains recognition of the mark only if adopted prior to the use of the same mark by another. It must be conspicuously affixed to goods. It may be a word, letter, number, design, picture, or combination of these things. It cannot be a common or generic name for the goods or a geographical, personal, corporate, association, or descriptive name.[15]

The trade name at common law is not necessarily associated with goods. It may relate to services or the business itself. Affixation is therefore unnecessary and so too prior use. The use, in fact, may be secondary, tertiary, or even still later in point of time. What matters is whether the consumer recognizes the designation as representative of the subject firm. This identification sets up a secondary meaning at law which indicates that the trade name designation has gained special significance. Thus, even though it may have been a common or generic name, or a geographical or personal name, or even though it may be a corporate, association, or descriptive name, its use over time and the identification of the public has given the trade name unique reference to only the subject firm.[16] The main difference between common law trade mark and trade name, apart from such matters as fact proving and damages, is this time element distinction. The trade mark gains protection almost immediately;[17] the trade name achieves property right status only after long use.[18]

[15] See section 715, 3 Restatement, Torts.

[16] See section 716, 3 Restatement, Torts.

[17] Jantzen Knitting Mills v. West Coast Knitting Mills, 46 F. 2d 182 (1931); Clorox Chemical Co. v. Chlorit Mfg. Corp. 25 F. Supp. 702 (1938).

The Jantzen case explains most clearly and simply the basic requirements and distinctions of the trade mark. In that case, the court held that the design of the girl formed the trade mark, not the bathing suit worn by her. Expression is therefore given to the arbitrary. The swimming suit is merely instrumental. Nothing about the design describes the suit. At most, it is suggestive and not invalid as a trade-mark. This trade mark right takes place almost immediately.

[18] Kay Jewelry Co. of Chattanooga v. Morris, 26 Tenn. App. 285 (1942); John B. Stetson Co. v. Stephen L. Stetson Co., 85 F. 2d 586 (1936); Horlicks Malted Milk Corp. v. Horlick, 143 F. 2d 32 (1944).

Poaching of trade mark and trade name (and of corporate name[19]) takes place when another party adopts as its trade mark or trade name a designation which is confusingly similar to that of the tradesman who claims a property right.[20] This confusing similarity normally requires for proof an objective appraisal of points of likeness rather than of difference.[21] Furthermore, in the simplest instances, it takes place between competitors of the same goods in the same market.

(1) Competing Goods Sold In The Same Market. The easiest case to handle of mark or name poaching arises when a tradesman creates a product substantially identical to that of another and markets this good under close mark or name in the same sales area. Immediately the possibility of poaching exists. That which the plaintiff need establish is that his trade mark fulfills the requirements noted above or that his claim of a legally recognized trade name is valid by fact of compliance with the requirements listed above, or, of course, with any governing statute. The intent of the poacher is not a factor in these cases.[22] Confusion of consumers is the single extra element needed. In concert with legally recognized mark or name, confusion of consumers solidifies the plaintiff's claim in the case of competing goods sold in the same market. The combination warrants his protection against the intruder.

Consumer uncertainty in this case does not have to contain detrimental features in addition to that of the natural emotional disturbance caused by mark or name similarity.[23] Unfair intrusion on the mark or name of the plaintiff through confusion of product and source carries with it the diversion of trade that forms the basis for legal condemnation of the act of the poacher, innocent[24] or otherwise.[25] That the consumer may benefit through price reduction is irrelevant matter to the lawyer.

(2) Noncompeting Goods Sold In The Same Market. A more difficult problem field has been the case where the so-called poacher invades the claimed property right of another by copy of mark or name but without any trade being diverted from the original owner of mark or name. Nondiversion of trade arises when the

The Kay Jewelry case illustrates quite clearly the need for time in gaining the secondary meaning that forms the basis for a legal trade name. Thus, it was said that personal names, like other trade names, must become well established and recognized by previous use.

[19] Corporate name actually is part of the same general species of law as the trade name. Minor differences possibly exist in some jurisdictions in the award of damages.

[20] Section 728, 3 Restatement, Torts.

[21] Section 729, 3 Restatement, Torts.

[22] Section 717, 3 Restatement, Torts.

[23] In particular the federal trade commission has moved heavily in the direction of protecting a trade name against unfair practises even if consumers are misled to their pecuniary advantage. See Federal Trade Commission v. Algoma Lumber Co., 291 U. S. 67 (1934). And see Adolph Kastor and Bros., Inc. v. F.T.C., 138 F. 2d 824 (CCA 2d 1943), where the element of confusion alone was given possibly its strongest hand by the commission.

[24] Isador Straus v. Notaseme Hosiery Co., 240 U.S. 179 (1916); Hygeia Distilled Water Co. v. Consolidated Ice Co., 144 F. 139 (1906).

[25] Laurence Mfg. Co. v. Tennessee Mfg. Co., 138 U.S. 537 (1891); Elgin National Watch Co. v. Illinois Watch Case Co., 179 U.S. 665 (1900).

poacher produces a different good. In this event, the claimant of a monopoly right affirms only that his reputation must be protected. Likelihood of confusion of source of manufacture sets up by itself sufficient basis for protection.[26] The identification problem requires close relation between the products of the plaintiff and the products of the defendent.[27] Only then may real uncertainty develop. In certain jurisdictions, however, the doctrine has been carried to the extreme of granting protection even where the products were very remotely related to each other.[28]

The essential difficulty with these views is that the consumer economic interest has again been discarded. The question of consumer benefit or loss, apart from emotion, is not of matter in courts which require closely related products nor in courts which grant protection even when products are substantially dissimilar. Inferiority of product need not be proven,[29] nor even need intent to palm off be established.[30] It suffices sometimes that just slight basis for confusion exists to warrant protection of mark or name.[31] But, how far should monopoly rights be extended?[32] Should persuasive advertising of nothing more than name be fostered or should informative advertising of substance be protected?[33] Decision in favor

[26] Aunt Jemina Mills v. Rigney and Co., 247 F. 407 (CCA 2d 1917); Yale Electric Corp. v. Robertson, 26 F. 2d 972 (CCA 2d 1928).

See Kinnaird, "Goods of the Same Descriptive Properties," 35 *Ky. L. J.*, 330, 332, where the writer states that the more recent cases have been emphasizing confusion whereas earlier cases stressed the attempt "to palm off" for oneself the property right of another.

[27] California Fruit Growers Exch. v. Sunkist Baking Co., 166 F. 2d 97 (1948); S. C. Johnson and Son, Inc. v. Johnson, 116 G. 2d 427 (CCA 2d, 1940), and 175 F. 2d 176 (CCA 2d 1949).

[28] Tiffany and Co. v. Tiffany Productions, Inc., 147 Misc. 679, 264 N.Y. 459 (1932) . . . jewelry and motion pictures. Kroll Bro. Co. v. Rolls Royce Ltd., 126 F. 2d 495 (C.C.P.A. 1942) . . . baby carriages and automobiles. And see Wolff, "Non-Competing Goods in Trademark Law," 37 *Col. L. Rev.*, 582, 591 (1937), where it is said that some courts, being unable to find substantial damage to the plaintiff and not wanting to base protection on a property right, have made deception of source not only a test of unfair competition or trade mark infringement but an "independent and self sufficient *basis* of injunctive relief."

[29] Only in the "dissenting opinion" of Judge Frank in the Triangle Publications Inc. v. Rohrlich et. al., 167 F. 2d 969 (CCA 2d, 1948) does there exist a strong appeal to the question whether the product of the poacher is inferior or superior. Indeed, in the dissenting opinion of Judge Clark in the S. C. Johnson Case, *op. cit.*, we find that, in his interpretation of the *objective* of Congress in the Lanham Act, the opposite extreme was believed to be intended. According to Judge Clark, confusion alone, apart from close relation of products, should form the basis for protection.

[30] See Section 729, 3 Restatement, Torts.

[31] Callmann, "The "Sunkist" Decision: Trade Marks at the Crossroads," 38 *Trade Mark Rep.* 304, 308 (1949).

[32] Ford Motor Co. v. Ford Insecticide Corp., 69 F. Supp 395 (1947) . . . automobiles and fertilizers; Bulova Watch Co. v. Stolzberg, 69 F. Supp 543 (1947) . . . watches and shoes; Alfred Dunhill of London, Inc. v. Dunhill Shirt Shop, Inc., 3 F. Supp 487 (S. D. N. Y. 1929) . . . smoker's supplies and shirts; Lady Ester, Ltd. v. Flanzbaum, 44 F. Supp. 666 (D.R.I. 1942) . . . cosmetics and shoes.

[33] Brown, "Advertising and the Public Interest. Legal Protection of Trade Symbols," 57 *Yale L. J.* 1165. The essential theme of the paper is that advertising programs which encourage consumer purchase because the product is manufactured by "The" XYZ Co. impart little if any value to the consumer. In contrary manner, those advertising programs

of confusion alone or even in favor of confusion plus closely related goods favors the persuasive or selected name reference type of advertising; it enlarges monopolistic privileges. Decision requiring demonstration of inferiority of product in addition to source confusion and related goods serves to promote the informative or so-called primary advertising which stresses the content of the product.[34]

It is manifest that in time the situation of sales of noncompeting goods in the same market may, through the addition of new product lines by the original seller, become a case of sales of competing goods in the same market. This eventuality that the plaintiff may expand production to the poacher's field is especially probable when the original goods are in the same general line. It is because of this possibility that the lawyer who speaks of property rights in marks and names rather than just in terms of confusion of consumers is willing to extend the protection that is granted in the case of competing goods sold in the same market to the case of noncompeting goods sold in the same market. But the economist notes that if protection is not given the claimant of the property right at the time before his production of like goods takes place, the confusing similarity in name, territory, and then in goods that will arise upon plaintiff's expansion to the poacher's field may well lead to price competition. In contrast, if protection is granted, a price leadership "competition only in brand name" type of market tends to be promoted. More and more, the economist must wonder about the place of the consumer in this field of law.

(3) Same Goods Sold In Noncompeting Markets. The third main category in which protection may be found under the trade mark and trade name law is that of the case where goods are similar but market areas are different. In those cases, injunctions are readily given the owner of the mark or name just so long as there is strong possibility that the plaintiff may expand into the market area of the poacher.[35] Though intent is not an essential element of these cases,[36] many of the decisions have stressed the intent of the late comer.[37] In this way, these cases are somewhat distinguishable from those noted previously. Basically, however, the fundamental consideration appears to be the borrowing of another's reputation by way of confusion of source.[38] As in the case of noncompeting goods sold in the same market, where inferiority of product might be expected to be a main consideration, the fact is that it is not. Indeed, as in

which explain why this product is better than that one are said to be of the type that should be encouraged. Extreme protection of mark and name encourage the initial type of advertising; restricted protection would encourage the informative brand of advertising.

[34] *Ibid.*

[35] See Section 732, 3 Restatement, Torts.

[36] Brooks Bros. v. Brooks Clothing of California Ltd., 69 F. Supp 442 (1943).

[37] See Sweet Sixteen Co. v. Sweet "16" Shop, Inc., 16 F. 2d 920 (1926), where it is held that prior appropriation in a market area governs except where the mark or name was taken with design inimical to the interest of the other. Also see Ritz Carlton Hotel Co. v. Ritz Carlton Hotel Corp. 66 F. Supp 720 (1946) and United Drug Co. v. Rectanus Co., 248 U.S. 90 (1919). And see Gable, "Where and What a Trade-Mark Protects," 22 *Ill. L. Rev.* 379, 381 (1927).

[38] Stork Restaurant, Inc. v. Sahati, 166 F. 2d 348 (1948); Maison Prunier v. Prunier's Restaurant and Cafe, Inc., 288 N. Y. S. 529 (1936); Safeway Stores, Inc. v. Sklar, 75 F. Supp, 98 (E.D. Pa. 1947).

that situation, it may not even be relevant datum.[39] The policy in these cases appears to no small extent to be that the use of another's mark or name has a dilution effect by the very nature of the frequency of its appearance before the public; this alone seemingly warrants extension of monopolistic privileges.[40]

At a minimum, it might be suggested in contrast to the above described law that refusal to grant monopolistic protection, in all cases except where there prevails inferiority of product, would guaranty a more active base of competition in price throughout the nation. Also, it would promote informative and not persuasive advertising, as well as to cause an associated decrease in the amount of monopolistic privileges that are granted in this country. But more about effects after the remaining main forms of poaching are outlined.

B. COPYING THE PRODUCT. Though not perfectly in line with the emphasis of this paper, two situations closely related to that of the trade mark-trade name protection should be noted. These types of encroachment require the very brief examination which follows:

(1) Copying The Functional Part. Product duplication may take two forms: (a) copy of only the functional part of the good or (b) copy of the nonfunctional part of the good. Objection to product duplication in this country has been extended by our courts only to the latter type of copy. The reason for this restricted action lies in the obvious fact that complete duplication of absolutely nonessential parts of a good can scarcely by justified. But, where the features of the good that are copied are functional, that is, where they offer utility to the consumer, the duplication of the product does not arouse any sanction. Competition to its furthest point is justified in these cases, just so long as some necessary reason exists for the copy.[41] In contrast to the cases listed under (A), confusion of the public as to whether it is receiving the product actually expected is not so important in the legal treatment of this class of case as is the objective of gaining alternative sources of the good.[42]

(2) Repacking The Product. Unfair competition of the trade mark and trade name variety extends to those cases where well known goods are altered by a repackager and sold under guise of the original. Frequently amounting to adulteration of the original good, the holdings in these cases invariably permit representation of the name of the original producer with explanatory note of qualifying or modifying form.[43] This general type of decree has possibilities of

[39] See Food Fair Stores, Inc. v. Food Fair, Inc., 83 F. Supp 445 (D. Mass 1948), where a Massachusetts statute *designed* to place Massachusetts law in step with federal law emphasizes confusion alone.

[40] See Schechter, "The Rational Basis of Trademark Protection," 40 *Harv. L. Rev.* 813 (1927). He would do away with the requirement of similar descriptive properties or like requirements. He would stress the use of the mark alone as being wrong, especially when the mark is unique.

[41] Wesson v. Galef, 286 F. 621 (S.D.N.Y. 1922); J.C. Penny Co. v. H. D. Lee Mercantile Co., 129 F. 2d 949 (1941); Kellogg Co. v. National Biscuit Co., *op. cit.*

[42] Arinsworth v. Gill Glass and Fixture Co., 26 F. Supp. 183 (E.D. Pa 1938) . . . to do otherwise would be to extend monopoly to products not so inventive as to merit a patent.

[43] A. Bourjois and Co., Inc. v. Katzel, 260 U.S. 689 (1923); Prestonettes, Inc. v. Coty, 264 U. S. 359 (1924); Bourjois Inc. v. Hermida Laboratories, Inc., 106 F. 2d 174 (CCA 2d, 1939).

application to the trade mark and trade name deceptions examined above. Indeed, it forms the focal point of the solution to be suggested herein for the mark and name dilemma.

III. PROPOSALS

An Economico-Legal Basis For Trade Mark And Trade Name Protection

The vast body of the law of unfair competition that is related directly to encroachment of trade mark or trade name suggests the impossibility of a single simple standard that is applicable without adjustment to every conceivable case. But, the vastness of field and the range of cases does not make impossible the formulation of a general standard to serve as guide. Quite the contrary, the very contradiction between the monopoly busting anti-trust statutes and the monopoly promoting trade mark and trade name policy indicates need for formulation of a generic approach to the subject. Without much doubt, this approach has been lacking in the past.[44]

The encouragement of as much product and price competition as can be achieved constitutes central basis for the generic standard proposed here. This policy of encouragement signifies that absolute injunctions and monetary damage awards should be confined to cases of gross fraud and high inferiority of product. Malicious palming off of product or passing off of clearly inferior products must be frowned upon by any capitalistic society. This requirement of bad faith points up the overall moderation of the proposed standard. In cases of less than vicious palming off, that is, where the mark or name encroachment is innocently adopted or is adopted with single intent to gain immediate place in the market, mere confusion of source would not serve as basis for property right protection as is present the case (see especially Section II this paper, A (1), (2) or (3)). All that which the poacher would have to show in this event for nonsuit under the proposed standard is distinction of his designation to the satisfaction of the reasonably *prudent* buyer. His entry into the market is an economic need which a capitalistic society should encourage, not discourage.

The proposed standard reflects appreciation of the assumption that the present day policy of ready protection to mark and name means extension of monopoly privileges. It emphasizes the importance today of the distinction in titles; associatively, it recognizes the weight that present day policy gives to persuasive advertising rather than to informative advertising. These results are not deemed beneficial to a capitalistic society. A more active competition in price and an encouraged entry of rivals should serve as *the* goal. This objective would be approached by restricting trade mark and trade name protection to the situations cited in the general standard proposed above.

The fundamental element required by the general standard is the probability of economic loss to the plaintiff and related harm to the public because of the *inferiority of the poacher's product*. If such inferiority does not exist, the claimant

[44] See Brown, *op. cit.* And see Auerbach, "Quality Standards, Informative Labeling and Grade Labeling as Guides to Consumer Buying," 14 *L. and Contemp. Problems* 362 (1949).

of the monopoly right loses not in reputation. He suffers only diversion of trade from competition. He is forced to differentiate his product to the advantage of buyers of varying whims and fancies. He is obliged to explain and to emphasize the unique difference of his product over that of rivals. Most fundamental, he probably will be forced to resort to competitive pricing in endeavor to retain his custom.

Under the proposed generic standard, not only is a policy formulation gained which is in line with the general objectives of the anti-trust program, not only is competition in price encouraged as well as competition by actually differentiated products (and not by just fancied differences because of trade mark or name), but a certainty or definiteness in judicial attitude can also be attained.[45] This certainty will make possible the ready adoption of mark or name. The requirement of differentiation to the satisfaction of reasonably "discerning" buyers maintains need for careful consideration in the mark and name adoption. This stipulation is inextricably tied up with the provision that injury to the original user's reputation by way of clear inferiority of product will be enjoined absolutely and with damages. A few words in explanation of the underlying meaning of this combination is now in order.

The General Standard: Mark Or Name Qualification And Product Inferiority: Conclusion

The general standard envisioned adds up to a double standard which requires very slight mark or name qualification and acceptable levels of product performance.[46] Under the standard, any tradesman adopting the mark or name of another must distinguish it in such manner that the reasonably prudent buyer is immediately forewarned that perhaps there are two or more producers of like mark or name. This requirement of distinction reflects to an extent the protection usually accorded original producers of goods whose products are being repackaged.[47] Further, it reflects the trend of adjudications under section 5 of the Federal Trade Commission Act where words of distinction are often required.[48] The essential difference in the treatment of trade mark and name

[45] See In The Matter of Manhattan Brewing Company, 42 F.T.C. 226 (1946), for an example of confusion of judicial attitude in the general field of unfair competition.

[46] Contrast this standard with section 32 of the Lanham Act. *op. cit.* where clear distinction of mark appears intended.

[47] See Prestonettes Inc. v. Coty, *op. cit.*, and Bourjois Inc. v. Hermida Laboratories, *op. cit.* And see Champion Spark Plug Co. v. Sanders, 331 U. S. 125 (1947).

[48] See F.T.C. v. Good-Grape Co., 45 F. 2d 70 (CCA 6th 1930), where the trade name Good-Grape was permitted with the proviso of an added clause that the product is an imitation artificially colored and flavored. Also see Jacob Siegel Co. v. F.T.C., 327 U.S. 608 (1946), where the misleading term Alpacuna Coat was permitted provided it was specified that the coat contains no vicuna. And see In The Matter of Manhattan Brewing Company, *op. cit.*, where the modifying clause, made in the United States, was to be appended to the use of the names Canadian Ace Brand Beer or Canadian Ace Brand Ale. And see F.T.C. v. Royal Milling Co. et. al. 288 U.S. 212 (1933), where the appended remark, not grinders of wheat, was required to offset the misleading quality of the word Mill in the corporate name.

under the general standard proposed here as compared with the trend of prosecutions under the Federal Trade Commission Act is not in remedy, but in the form which the cases take that will require remedy.

The standard of protection for the public can be and should be raised in the mark and name cases so that rather than protect practically everyone, the unwary as well as the wary, only the reasonably prudent will stand in the position where protection from poaching of mark or name is in order.[49] Distinction in standards thus arises. In mark and name cases, protection is to extend from the reasonably prudent to the informed buyer (or the trained buyer). In unfair methods cases, protection extends (and is to extend) to all consumers; the words and points of explanation in those cases must be clear and emphatic for all.

Difference in standards for mark and name cases compared with the others complies with the fact that the situations which come under commission surveillance are frequently instances of misleading advertising. This form of competition justifies all-inclusive levels of protection; in turn, the extreme protection provided by the commission promotes price competition. In the mark and name kind of problem a different condition prevails. Price competition is promoted by giving the tradesman broad latitude in the adoption of his designation rather than by placing strict limitation thereon. The standard of distinction between the licit and illicit requires inclusion only of that poaching which would confuse the reasonably prudent type of buyer. Significantly, the slight distinction guaranteed to the claimant of the property right assures him the custom of the discriminating market. It also encourages the entry of rivals.

The mark or name qualification suggested by the standard of the reasonably prudent buyer obviously permits a more subtle expression of distinction than that which would exist in the case of a standard based on the unwary buyer. This kind of slight differentiation does not reduce sharply the value of a secondary use of mark or name. To the contrary, its value is left largely unaffected.

Under the proposed standard, a somewhat greater number of adoptions of established marks or names, with slight verbal-like differentiation, could be expected to take place than are arising under present law. Yet, at the same time, endless cases of copy would not arise. In those fields where similarity in mark or name is of advantage to new firms, close duplication in form will be promoted. Elsewhere, the trend to mark or name differentiation will continue unabated. The permission behind the copy would stand as that economico-legal factor which facilitates entry of new producers into the established markets which otherwise might seem impenetrable. It would serve as the factor which promotes

[49] Present mark and name cases do not distinguish between wary and unwary buyers The matter of confusion is not directed to certain classes of buyers but to all buyers. See especially California Fruit Growers Exch. v. Sunkist Baking Co., *op. cit.*, and S. C. Johnson and Son Inc. v. Johnson, *op. cit.*, note 31 *supra*, and the dissenting opinion of Judge Frank in Triangle Publications, Inc. v. Rohrlich et. al., 167 F. 2d 969 (1948). In the last reference, the discussion turns on cases where not a single buyer was shown to be misled. Significantly, J. Frank states that the exact number and type of buyers who should be confused to warrant action is never specified. He notes that quantitative standards are applied only for purposes of emphasis; they are not applied on a consistent basis in decision making.

competition in price and in primary advertising in place of price leadership, selected advertising, and competition in mark or name.

The policy of limiting the extension of monopolistic protection in mark and name can be expected to force the public to weigh its purchases with greater caution. It should play down the importance of mark or name. Especially in markets like that of drugs and cosmetics, there should arise more than in the past the tendency to emphasize price and basic qualities of products. Most important of all, the general enlightenment of the public on this matter should serve to lessen and not to increase the prevailing amount of confusion of source and product.

The proposed standard does not signify complete loss or destruction of the mark and name property rights. The standard simply means that the amount of protection at law is to be limited to the flagrant cases where the public is harmed. The staying of endless extension of monopolistic privileges by substitution of minimum amounts of mark and name protection is enough to guaranty the product heterogeneity that supports goodwill. The general *kind* of competition alone will be changed.

Besides serving to stimulate competitive potentialities of industry, the type of disclosure recommended in the general standard, through its tending to make the public somewhat more alert, has the advantage of minimizing the likelihood of confusion. Furthermore, the second stipulation of the standard that there should not be clear inferiority of product pre-warns any poacher that, if inclined to copy from another, he had best distinguish his product noticeably in price and name if it is of inferior variety, or else give it some unique aspects which will clearly distinguish the product from that of the tradesman whose mark or name is copied. Failure to do so gives rise to absolute injunction and to damages. The deterrent value of speedy clear-cut prosecution could reduce greatly such types of reputation damaging encroachments. In conclusion, and perhaps most important of all the advantages of the proposed standard, may I cite creation of certainty among jurists and the public at large that the policy of the law is to (a) encourage price and product competition as much as is possible, (b) discourage complete and unnecessary monopoly in mark or name, and (c) discourage copy with inferiority, or purely malicious copy. Such knowledge would clarify the rights and duties of business firms. It would lessen if not end the confusion that now exists.[50]

[50] See in particular S. C. Johnson and Son, Inc. v. Johnson, *op. cit.*, for admission of this present state of confusion.

Product differentiation and intensity and sensitivity of preferences

M.L. Greenhut, C.S. Lee and G. Norman

Abstract
Product differentiation can be seen as an attempt by producers to extract consumer surplus from the heterogeneous tastes of consumers. Analysis of product differentiation has, however, neglected the idea that consumers may differ not only by having heterogeneous preferences, but also in their intensity and sensitivity of preferences. If producers know the intensity/sensitivity class of their consumers, they can discriminate between them. This paper examines the pricing policies that result. It is shown that consumers with more intense/sensitive preferences need not always be charged higher prices. Relative prices between consumer classes will be determined by market conditions: in particular by the extent to which the market can support product variety, given the precise form of consumer demand and the conjectures held by firms with respect to their competitors' likely reactions to price changes.

1. Introduction

Product differentiation is treated, in general, as an attempt by producers to profit from the heterogeneous tastes of consumers. As a standardized example, there is differentiation within the airline industry according to departure times and speed of trip (number of stops *en route* to a certain destination). But this set of alternatives actually downplays a basic property of differentiated goods, namely the relationship of a class of goods to those products of competing industries and those within the industry. For example, typewriters provide something unique compared with other equipment which creates messages besides written messages. Most generally, then, a product variant competes not only with the products of other (closely related) industries, but also with other variants within the differentiated industry.

There is no reason to believe that consumers react identically to those factors that distinguish all differentiated industries. To illustrate: a 'busy' person who has a higher opportunity cost of time will appreciate a fast airline trip more than does a less busy person. Comparably, the busy individual tends to derive greater utility (at least relatively) from a fast airplane trip than the less busy person. In other words, we should allow for product differentiation not only with respect to consumers' 'most preferred' product variants, but also with respect to the *intensity* and *sensitivity* of preferences which consumers exhibit for particular product characteristics.

It is to these considerations that this paper is addressed. For simplicity in the subsequent discussion, our analysis of a differentiated product and industry is predicated on just two classes of consumers: those who besides being consumers differentiated by their heterogeneity of taste also have different levels of demand intensity and sensitivity with respect to the differentiated good. Accordingly, we investigate the underlying features of a differentiated industry whose sellers price discriminate between consumers according to their demand intensity/sensitivity.

The basic model on which our analysis is based is presented in Sections 2 and 3. We make more explicit in Section 4 what we mean by intensity and sensitivity of demand. In Section 5, the resulting equilibrium pricing policies are identified and discussed, and in Section 6 we discuss the effect of relaxing some of the assumptions made in constructing the model. Our main conclusions are outlined in Section 7.

2. Background literature

The theoretical framework of our analysis has much in common with recent analysis by, for example, Benson (1985), Ireland (1983), Lancaster (1979), Phlips (1984), Phlips and Thisse (1982), Salop (1979) and Schmalensee (1978). Typically, these models share the following assumptions regarding consumer preferences for the products of a differentiated industry:

(i) Consumers are distributed according to their preferences on the circumference of a circle of unit length, with a consumer's 'location' identifying that consumer's most preferred product variant.[1] The density of consumers is assumed to be uniform.

(ii) Each product variant occupies a unique position on the unit circle, defined by the product's characteristics.

(iii) Consumers buy exactly one unit of the differentiated product provided the product price plus the utility lost (a negative value) in obtaining that product compared to their ideal variant is less than a reservation price determined by the value of the outside (alternative) good.

(iv) All remaining income is spent on the outside good which, in turn, is competitively produced and available at a known parametric price.

(v) The fixed income of consumers is measured in terms of the outside good.

(vi) The utility loss incurred by consuming a non-ideal variant is analogous to a transportation cost, and given by:

$$UL = \delta|i - j| \tag{1}$$

where UL = utility loss

δ = the rate of utility loss per unit distance of characteristic space

i = the ideal variant for consumer i who is characterized by being at position i along the characteristic circle (line)

j = the actual variant.

The effective price of the product variant j to consumer i is therefore the price of the variant j plus $\delta|i - j|$.

3. A variation

The model analysed in this paper differs from the framework described previously in three important respects. First, demand for the differentiated good is assumed to be elastic, so that consumers may purchase more than one unit of the product variant.[2] Second, the rate of utility loss or *sensitivity* of demand is not constant across consumer lines. Third, we allow for differing *intensity* of demand towards the differentiated goods. We shall make clear below the formal distinction between intensity and sensitivity of preferences. Essentially, intensity of preferences reflects strength of preference for the most desired product variant, while sensitivity of preference relates to the rate of utility loss incurred in consuming a variant other than the most preferred variant.

In the last context, the proposal by Katz (1984) deserves mention. He classifies consumers over a characteristic space by their positions in the space and their sensitivity towards the quality offered by the product variant. He argues that people with high sensitivity have a higher utility loss in not being able to acquire and consume their ideal product variant. The consumer's utility function in his model does not include an outside good i.e., he considers the differentiated good only. It follows that the sensitivity of the consumer centres strictly on quality itself, not the relative quality of the differentiated good *vis-à-vis* the outside good. Katz assumes a sensitivity factor linear with respect to the utility lost. Then he conceives of greater sensitivity as if it were added distance from the supplier for a product variant that is not the ideal variant. It follows that the net demand of consumers who have a high sensitivity towards a particular product variant may be more or less than that of consumers whose sensitivity is lower: this two-sided condition applies since the sensitivity property has, itself, variable multiples with respect to the degree of dissatisfaction given by the available variant.

Let the utility function of consumers j be in the form $U(x_j, y, \theta)$, where x_j is the most preferred variant (for consumers j) and where the outside good y is the numeraire. Following traditional methods, the outside good y is assumed to form a separable utility function for good x: therefore $U_y > 0$, $U_{xy} = 0$, $U_x > 0$, and $U_{xx} < 0$. Furthermore, $U_{yy} = 0$ because y is the numeraire good and yields constant marginal utility, and θ in the utility function gives us a measure of the intensity of the consumer's taste for the most preferred product variant (a differentiated good). We assume that the intensity (θ) which characterizes consumer preferences is such that $U(x_j, y; \theta_1) > U(x_j, y; \theta_2)$ if $\theta_1 > \theta_2$.

Recall that y provides constant marginal utility regardless of the type of consumer. As a result, the utility function for consumer type θ_1 is not a simple monotonic transformation of the utility function of consumer type θ_2.[3] Rather, the constant marginal utility of the outside good y suggests that the marginal rate of substitution between product variant x and the outside good y is greater for type θ_1 consumers than for type θ_2 consumers.

Consumers cannot always get their most preferred good, i.e. the ideal product variant. For a complete representation of preference, we must specify preferences not only with respect to the numeraire (i.e., the outside good) but also with respect to other product variants. We specify the consumer preference structure over product variants by assuming that the utility loss per unit of non-ideal product variant per unit of distance in the characteristic space – the sensitivity of preferences – is $\delta(\theta)$ for a type θ consumer, and that $\delta(\theta)$ is invariant with respect to the amount of the product variant consumed. Then the only difference among consumers with respect to an ideal product variant and an available one located at z units of distance in the characteristic space from the ideal variant is $\delta(\theta)z$. The consumer would be indifferent as between the ideal product variant at price $P^*(=P_z + \delta(\theta)z)$ and the available product variant at price P_z.

We can define a compensation function:

$$h(z) = P^* / P_z = 1 + (\delta(\theta)z) / P_z \tag{2}$$

where h(z) is the factor that converts the given amount of the actual variant at distance z from the ideal product variant in such a way that the greater the distance of the product variant from the ideal variant, the greater is the compensation needed to make the consumer indifferent. Then $h_z > 0$ and $h(0) = 1$.

If the individual consumes x(z) units of a product variant located at distance z from the ideal variant, and if additional y units of the outside good are consumed, it follows by definition of the compensation function that the consumer's utility level is $U(x(z) / h(z), y; \theta)$. Since good y is assumed to form a separable utility function from good x, and since the marginal utility of income (or the marginal utility of the outside good y) is assumed to be unity, we can, without loss of generality, write the utility function as:

$$U(x(z)/h(z), y; \theta) = V(x(z)/h(z); \theta) + y. \tag{3}$$

The maximization problem given by (3) under a budget constraint requires a two-stage process, such as Pollak's (1971). In the first stage, the consumer decides on the allocation of his income between good y (the outside good) and the differentiated good, x(z). Since the outside good is treated as the numeraire for price and income, the budget constraint has the form $P_z x(z) + y = I$, where P_z is the price of the product variant x(z) and I is the consumer's income. The budget allocation decision is given by the maximization problem:

$$\text{Max } [V(x(z)/h(z); \theta) + y] \quad \text{s.t. } P_z x(z) + y = I. \tag{4}$$

The first order conditions (f.o.c.) are:

$$U_{x(z)} = (1/h(z)) V_{x(z)}(x(z); \theta) - \lambda P_z = 0 \tag{5}$$

$$U_y = 1 - \lambda = 0 \quad \text{and} \tag{6}$$

$$P_z x(z) + y = I \tag{7}$$

where λ (= 1) is the Lagrange multiplier, and where the f.o.c. provide the optimal bundle $(x^*(z), y^*)$.

The decision taken at the first stage can be illustrated by resorting to a conditional, indirect utility function:

$$\begin{aligned} IU &= V(x^*(z)/h(z);\theta) + y^* \\ &= V(x^*(z)/h(z);\theta) - P_z x^*(z) + I. \end{aligned} \tag{8}$$

The consumer will buy the amount $x^*(z)$ of the differentiated product if IU is greater than I. Otherwise, the consumer buys only the outside good. The demand function for the product variant x(z) is then given by:

$$x(z) = \text{Max}[x^*(z), 0]. \tag{9}$$

Each consumer executes the same maximization process for every product variant. In the second stage, the consumer selects the bundle yielding the highest IU.

4. The impact of the intensity and sensitivity factor

Following traditional economics, each consumer is assumed to be able to determine the optimal bundle and to consume a positive amount of the optimal product variant. We also assume that the optimal product variant and the intensity and sensitivity levels of consumers are x(z), θ and $\delta(\theta)$ respectively. From the f.o.c., the demand function for the product variant x(z) becomes:

$$x(z) = f(P_z h(z);\theta). \tag{10}$$

Since $h(z) = 1 + \delta(\theta)z/P_z$, the demand curve for product variant x(z) is:

$$x(z) = f(P_z + \delta(\theta)z{:}\theta). \tag{11}$$

This demand function describes the consumer's preference for the differentiated good completely. The equilibrium[4] prices of the product variants will be identical, so we have:

$$x(z) = f(P + \delta(\theta)z{:}\theta) = f(P, z{:}\theta),\ f_P < 0;\ f_z < 0, \tag{12}$$

given that we assume that θ and $\delta(\theta)$ are positively related. Hereafter, without loss of generality, we consider $\delta(\theta)$ a linear function of θ such that $\delta(\theta) = \alpha\theta$, with $\alpha > 0$. Then we can drop the parameter $\delta(\theta)$ from the function f( ).

Clearly, the demand curve is a decreasing function of price and the characteristic distance z. But f_θ may be positive or negative depending on the value of z: larger or smaller demands can be associated with a larger value of θ. This result is easily explained: if the value of z is small, the intensity of the consumer's taste for the ideal variant outweighs the sensitivity effect, i.e., the effect of utility loss caused by consuming a non-ideal variant, while the opposite holds for large values of z. Illustratively, high θ people (business people) derive more utility from a fast airline trip than do low θ people, but lose more utility when they move from their ideal variant (ideal departure time) to a non-ideal variant (a non-ideal departure time). Thus the net utility gain of high θ people is higher or lower than that of low θ people depending on the value of z.

Preferences for the ideal product variant have been assumed to be uniformly distributed over the circumference of the circle. This assumption guarantees symmetry in aggregate demands for alternative varieties of the differentiated product. Aggregate demand of type θ for the 'representative' product variant[5] is:

$$q(P,Z;\theta) = 2D\int_0^Z f(P,z;\theta)dz, \tag{13}$$

where D is the density of type θ consumers per unit distance along the circumference of the circle, and Z is the market radius. Note that $q_p < 0$, $q_Z > 0$. We assume for simplicity that D is invariant with θ; this, as we shall show below, involves no loss of generality.

Total market demand for the representative firm is:

$$Q(P,Z) = 2D[\int_0^Z f(P,z;\theta_1)dz + \int_0^Z f(P,z;\theta_2)dz] \tag{14}$$

where $Q_p < 0$, $Q_z > 0$.

5. Differentiated product demand curves and price policies

Following traditional analysis, we characterize producers by assuming:

(i) Each produces only one product variant, with the product's market space centred on the location of the product variant.
(ii) The cost function is $C = F + cQ$, i.e. it exhibits economies of scale.
(iii) Competitive entry into the market continues until expected profits of potential entrants vanish.[6]
(iv) Relocation cost is zero and firms are equally spaced in the equilibrium.

The demand curve for a product variant at distance z for type θ consumers is a function of the full price $P + \delta(\theta)z$. This is analogous to the delivered price in spatial economics and allows us to use the analysis of Greenhut, Hwang, Ohta (1975), Greenhut, Greenhut, Kelly (1977), Capozza, Van Order (1978) and Benson (1980) to analyse the representative firm's pricing policy.[7] A firm's competitive prices are determined by two factors: (1) the underlying individual demands the firm faces, and (2) the alternative behavioural assumptions governing how rivals react to the firm's price actions, i.e. the prevailing price conjectural variations.

With regard to the second factor, we assume for the moment what has come to be known in the spatial literature as Löschian price conjectural variation. The essential distinguishing feature of Löschian competition in this context is that each firm in the industry, in choosing its profit-maximizing price, treats its market space parametrically: this is equivalent to the assumption of price matching by competitors.[8] So far as the first factor is concerned, we know from the spatial literature (see

Greenhut, Norman, Hung (1987)) that pricing policy is crucially affected by the degree of convexity of the individual demand function.

Following Lovell (1970), we define the utility function for type θ consumers with respect to a product variant at distance z as:

$$U = \theta x - \frac{1}{k(k+1)} x^{k+1} + \delta(\theta) z x \quad (-1 < k < \infty;\ k \neq 0). \tag{15}$$

It is assumed that U_θ is positive for any positive value of x within the relevant range of z. Hence this utility function satisfies all of the properties we previously described in the paper. Of course, we assume that the parameters in (15) satisfy the condition $U_x > 0$. Utility maximization subject to the budget constraint $Px + y = I$ establishes the demand curve given by:

$$\begin{aligned} x &= f(P,\ z{:}\theta) \\ &= [k(\theta - (P + \delta(\theta) z))]^{1/k}, \end{aligned} \tag{16a}$$

where P is the price charged for the representative product variant.

The inverse demand function is:

$$(P + \delta(\theta)) z = \theta - x^k / k. \tag{16b}$$

It is well established that if $k > 0$ ($k < 0$), the demand curve (16a) is less convex (more convex) than a negative exponential.[9] For simplicity, we shall confine our attention to the cases of $k = 1$ for the less convex demand possibility and $k = -1/2$ for the more convex demand alternative. Then we have:[10]

$$x = \theta - P - \delta(\theta) z \quad \text{for less convex demand; } k = 1 \tag{17a}$$

$$x = [-\frac{1}{2}(\theta - P - \delta(\theta) z)]^{-2} \quad \text{for more convex demand; } k = -1/2. \tag{17b}$$

Thus the representative firm's aggregate demand by type θ consumers distributed over a known market radius Z is given by:

$$\begin{aligned} q(P, Z{:}\theta) &= 2D \int_0^Z (\theta - P - \delta(\theta) z) dz \\ &= 2D[\theta - P - \frac{\delta(\theta)}{2} Z] \quad (k = 1) \end{aligned} \tag{18a}$$

$$\begin{aligned} q(P, Z{:}\theta) &= 2D \int_0^Z [-1/2(\theta - P - \delta(\theta) z)]^{-2} dz \\ &= 8D\left[\frac{Z}{[(P - \theta)(P - \theta + \delta(\theta) Z)]}\right] \quad (k = -1/2). \end{aligned} \tag{18b}$$

The firm's optimal price for type θ consumers is:[11]

$$P(\theta, Z) = \frac{\theta}{2} + \frac{c}{2} - \frac{\delta(\theta)}{4}Z \quad (k = 1) \tag{19a}$$

$$P(\theta, Z) = c + [(c - \theta)\delta(\theta)Z + (c - \theta)^2]^{1/2} \quad (k = -1/2). \tag{19b}$$

How does the firm price discriminate among consumers characterized by different intensity and sensitivity of demand? What is the impact of reduced equilibrium market length (Z) due to new entry?

First consider the discriminatory price schedules that would stem from less convex demand – equation (19a). These are illustrated by the line, $P(\theta_1,Z)$ and $P(\theta_2,Z)$ in Figure 1. Two important points emerge from this Figure. First, there is a negative relationship between price and market radius. In other words, and anticipating our discussion below, competitive entry increases price in the case of less convex demand. This apparently perverse result has been extensively discussed elsewhere; see, for example, Greenhut (1956, pp. 82, 83), Greenhut, Greenhut, Kelly (1977), Benson (1980), Capozza, Van Order (1978) and Greenhut *et al.* (1985). It arises, essentially, since competitive entry, in reducing the market area of our representative differentiated product, competes away consumers with the highest individual demand elasticities and so reduces aggregate demand elasticity.

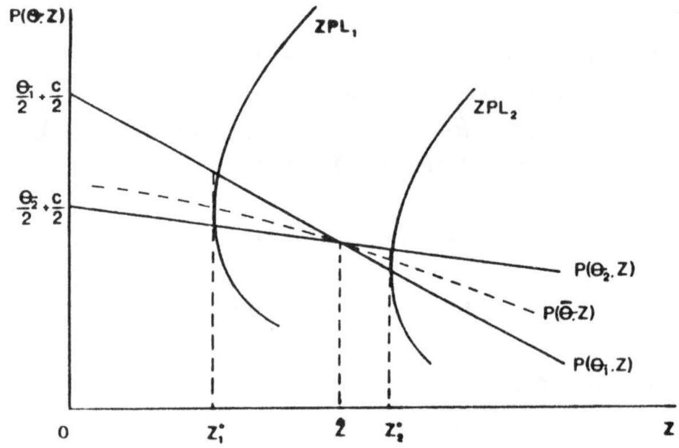

Figure 1 Pricing policy: less convex demand ($\theta_1 > \theta_2$)

The second point to emerge from Figure 1 is more important for our purposes. If market radius for the representative product is greater than Z, consumers with more intense and sensitive preferences will be charged *less* than consumers with less intense and sensitive preferences. This, perhaps surprising, outcome can be explained in a relatively straightforward way. Consumers' demand is determined by full price (P + δ(θ)Z); as we have noted, if individual demand is less convex, the elasticity of aggregate demand increases with market radius. Greater market radius is equivalent to the market containing fewer product variants, and so to consumers having to purchase a product that is, on average, located a greater 'distance' in a characteristic sense from the most preferred product. The consequent increase in aggregate demand elasticity is greater for consumers with high θ preference (type θ_1), implying that price for type θ_1 consumers will decrease more rapidly with increased market size (decreased product variety) than it will for type θ_2 consumers.

What, then, determines equilibrium market size? First, we define average product price paid by consumers of the representative brand:

$$\begin{aligned} P(\theta, Z) &= \frac{P(\theta_1, Z)q(P, Z; \theta_1) + P(\theta_2, Z)q(P, Z; \theta_2)}{q(P, Z; \theta_1) + q(P, Z; \theta_2)} \\ &= \frac{P(\theta_1, Z)q(P, Z; \theta_1) + P(\theta_2, Z)q(P, Z; \theta_2)}{Q(P, Z)} \end{aligned} \tag{20}$$

illustrated by the broken line in Figure 1. Next, we can write profit as:

$$\Pi(P, Z) = (P(\theta, Z) - c)Q(P, Z) - F \tag{21}$$

from which we can identify combinations of price and expected market radius at which a potential entrant would just break even ($\Pi(P, Z) = 0$). This locus is denoted (Capozza, Van Order (1978)) the *zero profit locus* (ZPL) and is illustrated in Figure 1. For given demand intensities and sensitivities, the position of the ZPL is determined by fixed costs and overall consumer density: the ZPL lies further to the left the lower are fixed costs and the greater is overall consumer density.[12] In other words, and as we would expect, product variety increases, *ceteris paribus*, the lower are fixed costs of entry and the greater is consumer density.

What if the basic demand curve is more convex than the negative exponential? The optimal pricing schedule, equation (19b), indicates that the product price $P(\theta, Z)$ increases as the equilibrium market radius increases. The reason for this is that, if individual demand is more convex than a negative exponential, competitive entry takes away the consumers with *lowest* individual demand elasticities, and hence increases the aggregate demand elasticity for the firm's good. It follows that price decreases as the firm's equilibrium market space decreases.

The equilibrium price schedules of equation (19b) are illustrated in Figure 2, together with the average price schedule and ZPL.

The slope of the product price schedule ($\partial P(\theta,Z)/\partial Z$) is steeper for high values of θ (i.e. θ_1) than for low θ values (i.e. θ_2). In other words, the equilibrium product price of the firm increases more rapidly with an increase in market radius the greater are the intensity and sensitivity of demand. It can be shown that the price schedules for type θ_1 and θ_2 consumers eventually cross each other.[13] In other words, with more convex demands and prices that discriminate with respect to intensity and sensitivity of demand, consumers with a high intensity/sensitivity pay a lower (higher) price than do consumers with a low intensity/sensitivity if the equilibrium market space is small (large), a result that is exactly opposite to that obtained for less convex demands but which can be explained on exactly the same basis.

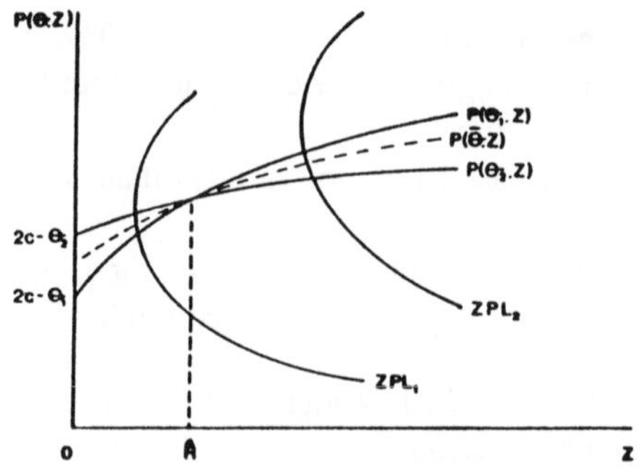

Figure 2 Pricing policy: more convex demand ($\theta_1 > \theta_2$)

6. Alternative assumptions

An obvious question to ask at this stage is whether our conclusions are merely the consequence of our assumptions with respect, in particular, to the form of the individual demand function and the firm's conjectural variations.

We could have worked instead with a rectangular demand function (Salop (1979)) such that consumers purchase exactly one unit of the differentiated product, provided its price is less than a known reservation price. It is easy to see in this case that the class of aggregate demand functions for the representative firm will be as in Figure 3.[14] The relative price charged to type θ_1 consumers depends upon average cost (given by c + F/2q) i.e. upon whether the market is capable of sustaining a greater or lesser degree of product variety.

Now consider the impact on product prices of assuming Bertrand–Nash conjectures. The resulting relationship between price and market size is given by equations (22) and illustrated in Figure 4 (see Capozza, Van Order (1978), Benson

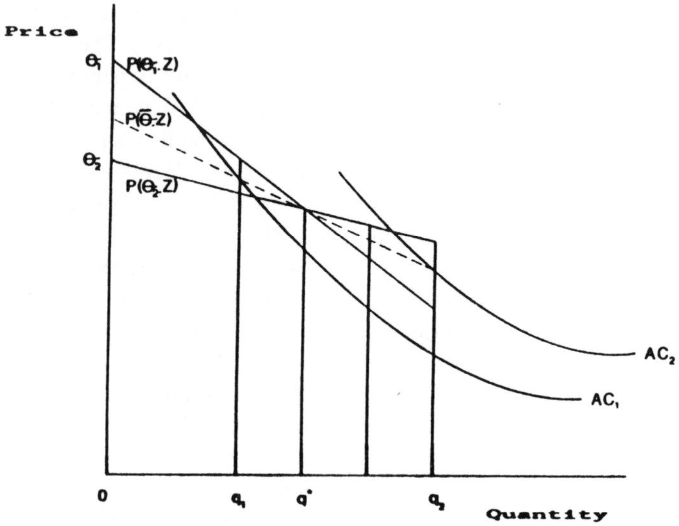

Figure 3 Pricing policy: rectangular demand ($\theta_1 > \theta_2$)

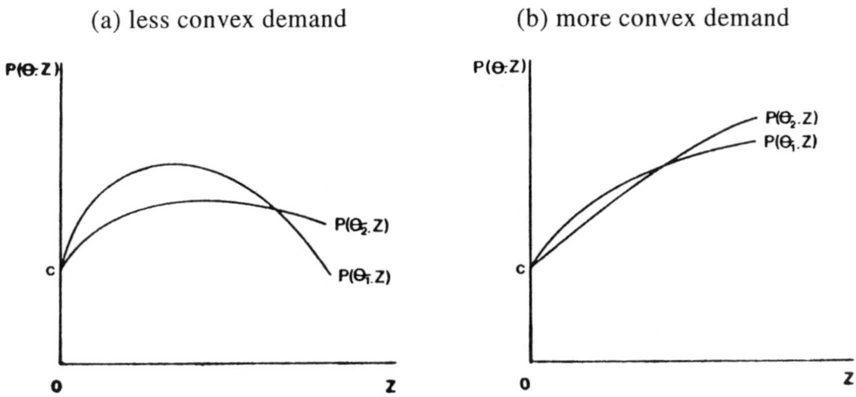

Figure 4 Pricing policy: Bertrand–Nash conjectures ($\theta_1 > \theta_2$)

(1980) and Greenhut, Norman, Hung (1987)): note that Bertrand–Nash conjecture is equivalent to Hotelling–Smithies conjecture in the spatial literature.

$$P(\theta, Z) = c + \frac{2\delta(\theta)Z(\theta - P(\theta, Z) - \delta(\theta)Z/2)}{(\theta - P(\theta, Z) + \delta(\theta)Z)} \quad (x = 1) \tag{22a}$$

$$P(\theta, Z) = c + \frac{2\delta(\theta)Z[(c - \theta)\delta(\theta)Z + (c - \theta)^2 - (P(\theta, Z) - c)^2]}{(P(\theta, Z) - \theta)^2} \quad (x = -1/2) \tag{22b}$$

With this conjecture, as market size falls (product variety increases), prices become approximately competitive.

As can be seen, and in contrast to the Löschian case, convexity of demand does not affect the problem of price discrimination between consumers with differing intensity/sensitivity of preferences. No matter whether individual demand is more or less convex, for 'small' market size, elasticity of aggregate demand decreases as market size increases. With Bertrand–Nash conjectures, a reduction in product price impacts aggregate demand in two ways: the *demand effect* on existing customers and the *competition effect* of additional demand expected to be won from competitors. At 'small' market size the competition effect dominates, no matter the convexity of demand, while an increase in market size reduces the proportionate importance of the competition effect. An increase in intensity of demand increases (reduces) aggregate demand elasticity if individual demand is less (more) convex. Increased sensitivity of demand may increase or decrease aggregate demand elasticity through the demand effect, but *always* reduces aggregate demand elasticity through the competition effect. At 'small' market size the latter effect is dominant no matter the convexity of demand.[15]

Thus with Bertrand–Nash conjectures the greater the degree of product variety capable of being sustained in the market, the more likely it is that consumers with greater intensity/sensitivity of preferences will be discriminated against.

One final point may be worth noting. The Bertrand–Nash result is, to some extent, a special case in that it is only with this conjecture that prices are approximately competitive at 'small' market size. With any other conjecture (Löschian, Cournot or rational, for example) price as $Z \to 0$ will be a function of θ and will take us back to the analysis of Figures 1 and 2.

7. Conclusion

Analysis of product differentiation has tended to neglect the idea that consumers may differ, not only by having heterogeneous preferences, but also by exhibiting differing intensity and sensitivity of preferences. If producers know the intensity/sensitivity class of their consumers, they can discriminate in price between them.

It is tempting to believe that consumers with more intense/sensitive preferences will be charged higher prices. This is shown to be the case, however, only where the market is capable of sustaining 'extensive' product variety *and* (except in the case of Bertrand–Nash conjectures on the part of competing firms) only when consumer preferences generate an individual demand function that is less convex than a negative exponential.

More convex individual demand may lead to consumers with more intense/sensitive preferences being charged less. Similarly, if the market is capable of supporting only a 'small' degree of product variety, perhaps because of high fixed production costs or low consumer density in the market, consumers with high intensity/sensitivity of preferences will be charged less than those with low intensity/sensitivity of preferences.

Notes

1. It will be noted that we confine our attention in this paper to horizontal product differentiation. See Sutton (1986) for a discussion of recent advances in vertical (quality) product differentiation.
2. We shall discuss below the effect of assuming a rectangular demand function of the type identified in (iii) above.
3. Let us assume that utility functions for type θ_1 and type θ_2 buyers are given by:

   $$U(x, y; \theta_1) = \theta_1 x - (1/2)x^2 + y$$

   $$U(x, y; \theta_2) = \theta_2 x - (1/2)x^2 + y.$$

   Then,

   $$[U_x(x, y; \theta_1)]/[U_y(x, y; \theta_1)] \neq [U_x(x, y; \theta_2)]/[U_y(x, y; \theta_2)],$$

   i.e. $(\theta_1 - x)/1 \neq (\theta_2 - x)/1$. Here U_x is assumed to be positive.
4. This assumes that equilibrium exists and is symmetric. See Novshek (1980) for a discussion of symmetric equilibria; also d'Aspremont *et al.* (1979) and Neven (1985) for a discussion of the existence of equilibrium.
5. Given that equilibrium is symmetric (see note 4), we need consider only a representative product variant.
6. See Eaton and Lipsey (1978).
7. Note that there is a one-to-one correspondence between the representative firm and the representative product variant.
8. This assumption has the advantage of significantly easing mathematical manipulation. We shall consider below the effects of assuming Bertrand–Nash conjectures.
9. The negative exponential demand function has the form $q = ae^{-bp}$.
10. Equations (17) with $z = 0$ is the basic demand curve, i.e. the demand curve for an ideal product variant. Note that θ is the price intercept for (17a) and the lower limit of the demand curve for (17b). Hence the higher values of θ are associated with larger demand.

11. Greenhut, Norman and Hung (1987) indicate that for (19b) to hold, it is necessary that $\theta > c$: otherwise infinite profit can be made by selling only to proximate consumers at price $P = \theta$.
12. An increase in the *proportion* of type θ_1 consumers would swivel the average price schedule clockwise. The ZPL would move to the left (right) if it originally lay to the left (right) of Z, leading to an overall increase (decrease) in product variety.
13. Proof is tedious but can be obtained from the authors on request.
14. See Salop (1979) and Norman (1985) for more details of the derivation of these demand curves. The kink in the demand curve assumes a symmetric equilibrium. Note also that since equilibrium will always be a 'kinked equilibrium', the comparative statics of the equilibrium will be perverse (see Salop for more detailed discussion). This should not be surprising since rectangular individual demand can be viewed as the extreme case of less convex demand.
15. Formally, as Z tends to zero, the slope of the price schedule $P(\theta, Z)$ tends to $2\delta(\theta)$.

References

C. d'Aspremont, J. Gabszewicz and J.-F. Thisse, "On Hotelling's 'Stability in Competition'", *Econometrica*, September 1979, **47** 1045–50.

B.L. Benson, "Löschian Competition under Alternative Demand Conditions", *American Economic Review*, December 1980, **70**, 1098–1105.

B.L. Benson, "Increasing Product Variety and Rising Prices: From Ready-to-Eat Cereals to Physicians' Services", Montana State University (mimeo), 1985.

D.R. Capozza and R. Van Order, "A Generalized Model of Spatial Competition", *American Economic Review*, December 1978, **68**, 896–908.

B.C. Eaton and R.G. Lipsey, "Freedom of Entry and Existence of Pure Profit", *Economic Journal*, September 1978, **88**, 455–69.

M.L. Greenhut, *Plant Location in Theory and in Practice*, Chapel Hill: University of North Carolina Press, 1956.

J. Greenhut, M.L. Greenhut and W.H. Kelly, "A Spatial–Theoretical Perspective for Bank Merger Regulations", 1977, Proceedings, Bank Structure and Competition, Federal Reserve Bank of Chicago.

M.L. Greenhut, C.S. Hung, G. Norman and C. Smithson, "An Anomaly in the Service Industry: The Effect of Entry on Fees", *Economic Journal*, March 1985, **95**, 169–77.

M.L. Greenhut, M. Hwang and H. Ohta, "Observations on the Shape and Relevance of Spatial Demand Function", *Econometrica*, July 1975, **43**, 669–82.

M.L. Greenhut, G. Norman and C.S. Hung, *The Economics of Imperfect Competition*, Cambridge: Cambridge University Press, 1987.

N. Ireland, "Monopolistic Competition and a Firm's Product Range", *International Journal of Industrial Organization*, September 1983, **1**, 239–52.

M.L. Katz, "Firm Specific Differentiation and Competition Among Multiproduct Firms", *Journal of Business*, University of Chicago, January 1984, **57**, s149–s166.

K. Lancaster, *Variety, Equity and Efficiency*, New York: Columbia University Press, 1979.

M.C. Lovell, "Product Differentiation and Market Structure", *Western Economic Journal*, January 1970, **8**, 120–43.

D. Neven, "Two Stage (Perfect) Equilibrium in Hotelling Model", *Journal of Industrial Economics*, March 1985, **33**, 317–25.

G. Norman, "Monopolistic Competition: Some Extensions from Spatial Competition", Washington University in St. Louis, Working Paper Series, Working Paper 79, April 1985.

W. Novshek, "Equilibrium in Simple Spatial (or Differentiated Product) Models", *Journal of Economic Theory*, August 1980, **22**, 313–26.

L. Phlips, *Economics of Price Discrimination*, Cambridge: Cambridge University Press, 1984.

L. Phlips and J.-F. Thisse (eds), Symposium on Spatial Competition and the Theory of Differentiated Markets, *Journal of Industrial Economics*, September/December 1982, **XXXI**.

R.A. Pollak, "Conditional Demand Functions and Implications of Separable Utility", *Southern Economic Journal*, April 1971, **37**, 423–33.

S. Salop, "Monopolistic Competition with Outside Goods", *The Bell Journal of Economics*, Spring 1979, **10**, 141–56.

R. Schmalensee, "Entry Deterrence in the Ready-to-Eat Breakfast Cereal Industry", *The Bell Journal of Economics*, Spring 1978, **9**, 305–27.

J. Sutton, "Vertical Product Differentiation: Some Basic Themes", *American Economic Review*, May 1986, **76**, 393–96.

The Economic Journal, **95** (*March* 1985), 169–177
Printed in Great Britain

AN ANOMALY IN THE SERVICE INDUSTRY: THE EFFECT OF ENTRY ON FEES

*M. L. Greenhut, C. S. Hung, G. Norman, and C. W. Smithson**

In the context of traditional microtheory, the entry of new firms into a competitive market is always expected to lower the price of the product being exchanged. However, several empirical investigations of the private health care industry in the United States have uncovered an apparently 'perverse' relation: As the number of health care providers in the market increases, the price of the health care service (the nominal fee) increases.

A statistically significant, positive relation between fees and health care provider density – e.g. physicians per capita – has been reported by Newhouse (1970), Fuchs and Kramer (1972), and Dyckman (1978). Indeed, Pauly and Satterthwaite (1980) asserted that 'the zero order correlation between physicians per capita and various measures of physician fees tends invariably to be positive.'

These empirical data spawned a number of analyses of the fees charged in private health care markets. Some researchers used competitive models (e.g. Feldstein (1970) and Fuchs and Kramer (1972)) and assumed health care providers to be price-takers. Most notable, however, are the papers which abandoned neoclassical theory and turned instead to 'targeted income/demand creation'. The idea that service providers are able to create demand was first introduced formally by Newhouse (1970) and subsequently expanded upon by Evans *et al.* (1973), Green (1978), Fuchs (1978), and Dyckman (1978). The notion was that health care providers have some 'target income'; and if the number of providers increases each provider can maintain income by advising patients to consume additional services (e.g. more diagnostic tests). The providers are able to 'create demand' and can increase the fee charged along the new demand curve.

Anderson *et al.* (1981) examined theoretically the concept of supplier-induced demand. As they demonstrated, supplier-induced demand can explain the observed positive relation between provider density and fees. However, such a model also yields additional predictions not borne out empirically (e.g. organised medicine would promote entry of new practitioners). Additional empirical evidence provided by Pauly and Satterthwaite (1981) also puts into question the validity of 'targeted income/demand creation'.

We propose to reconcile the empirical evidence with traditional microtheory. We utilise the 'full price' notion introduced by DeVany (1976); but our analysis goes beyond the implication that demand elasticity increases as more customer-supplied time is required. Our analysis also differs from Pauly and Satterthwaite's (1980; 1981) attempt at reconciliation via their theory of 'increasing

* We thank Michael B. Ormiston and Mark R. Fratrick for their helpful comments and critiques. We also wish to thank an anonymous referee and an associate editor for most helpful comments and suggestions.

monopoly' where increases in the number of sellers of a 'reputation' good makes search more costly and thereby increases price. Closer to our analysis is the full price model proposed by Anderson and Ormiston (1983).

Our approach has its foundations in spatial economics; but it should not be viewed as a spatial analysis. No assumptions are made about the location of the service providing firms – the physicians' offices. Neither do we require that customers – patients – go to the nearest provider. And, although we conceive illustratively of a uniform fee for a particular service, differentiated services (or skills of the providers) are well within the scope of this analysis. In fact, while we employ a modelling technique developed in a spatial context, its application here is due simply to the fact that it encompasses not only the (private) fee paid but also the other costs borne by the consumer in the form of customer-supplied time.

I. A NEOCLASSICAL APPROACH

Thus far, we have concentrated on the health care industry. However, our model is more general and would be applicable in any market in which the customer supplies a substantial amount of time – in particular, the service industries. Accordingly, consider a generalised service industry and define the full price of the service as

$$\pi = p(n, t) = n + wt, \tag{1}$$

where n is the nominal fee, w is the (per unit) value of customer-supplied time, and t is the amount of time supplied by the customer – time in service, waiting time, and commuting time.[1]

We assume that all consumers have identical demand functions and that the basic (individual) demand is a function of the full price. That is,

$$q(n, t) = f(\pi) = f[p(n, t)], \tag{2}$$

where $f' < 0$.

Note that the amount of time consumers will be required to provide depends strictly on the consumer's opportunity cost of time. While this appears to contradict the assumption of homogeneous demand, it actually does not. The model we propose – based on spatial price theory – encompasses the situation where two individuals can have identical tastes, income, and want for the service, can be situated at the same location, and also frequent the same service provider, but yet have substantially different values of time. So, wt varies among individuals with otherwise identical demands, since the opportunity cost of time differs. Therefore, the term wt is, accordingly, a counterpart to distance. (See Phlips, 1983.)

The elasticity of the individual demand curve with respect to the nominal fee is given by

$$\epsilon = -n\frac{f'[p(n, t)]}{f[p(n, t)]} = -n\frac{f'}{f}. \tag{3}$$

[1] This formulation is analogous to the concept of delivered price in spatial economics: π would be delivered price, n the mill price, w the transport cost per unit of distance, and t the distance.

We can characterise the basic (individual) demand function with respect to convexity using, as a benchmark, a negative exponential function: The demand function is a negative exponential if and only if $f'' = (f')^2/f$ – e.g. ae^{-bp}. The demand function is less convex than a negative exponential if and only if $f'' < (f')^2/f$. (Note that both linear and concave demand curves are less convex than a negative exponential and that constant elasticity demand functions are ruled out if demand is less convex than a negative exponential.) The demand function is more convex than a negative exponential if and only if $f'' > (f')^2/f$.[1]

With the negative exponential, $-f'/f$ is a constant with respect to $p(n, t)$. If the demand curve is less (more) convex than a negative exponential, $-f'/f$ is a monotonically increasing (decreasing) function of $p(n, t)$.[2] Furthermore, in our case, $p(n, t)$ is a linear function of time and it follows that[3]

$$\frac{d}{dt}\left\{-\frac{f'[p(n,t)]}{f[p(n,t)]}\right\} \gtreqless 0 \quad \text{as} \quad f''[p(n,t)] \lesseqgtr \frac{f'[p(n,t)]^2}{f[p(n,t)]}. \tag{4}$$

As demonstrated by Benson (1980) and Ohta (1981), using expressions (3) and (4), the following lemma can be established:

> If the basic demand function is less (more) convex than a negative exponential, the elasticity of the individual demand function with respect to the nominal fee is a monotonically increasing (decreasing) function of customer-supplied time. If the basic demand function is the negative exponential, elasticity is constant with respect to time.

That is, since $\partial\epsilon/\partial t = -n[\partial(f'/f)/\partial t]$,

$$\frac{\partial \epsilon}{\partial t} \gtreqless 0 \quad \text{as} \quad f'' \lesseqgtr \frac{(f')^2}{f}. \tag{5}$$

We next consider the way a particular firm believes its competitors will react to a change in nominal fee – i.e. the firm's price conjectural variation. Assume, for now, that the price conjectural variation is of the type referred to as Löschian competition. In essence, Löschian competition means that each seller

[1] In Greenhut *et al.* (1977), the function $p = a-(b/x)\,q^x$, with $b, p, q > 0$ and $x \neq 0$, was used. For relevant negative values of x (i.e. $-1 < x < 0$), this function is more convex than the negative exponential; for all positive values of x, it is less convex than the negative exponential. The two ranges yielded opposite pricing effects resulting from competition, a result entirely consistent with the analysis to follow.

[2] Consider:

$$\frac{d}{dp}\frac{-f'(p)}{f(p)} = \frac{-f''(p)f(p)+[f'(p)]^2}{[f(p)]^2}.$$

Since $f[p(t)]$ is strictly positive, it follows that the expression is greater than, equal to, or less than zero as

$$f''(p) \lesseqgtr \frac{[f'(p)]^2}{f(p)}.$$

[3] In this case,

$$\frac{d(-f'/f)}{dt} = \frac{[d(-f'/f)/dp]\,dp}{dt} = [d(-f'/f)/dp]\,w.$$

Since $w > 0$, the sign pattern established in the previous footnote is unchanged.

is aware of the prices charged by rivals and expects its rivals to duplicate any price change. For a service industry, Löschian competition is a meaningful paradigm, since the principal implication is simply that sellers expect their rivals to match any reduction in the nominal fee.

In the more traditional context of spatial economics, with a given number of firms in the market an equilibrium will result such that there exists some market radius, R, for each competitor. Löschian competition implies that this market radius is invariant to the mill price charged, m. Since any change in the mill price charged by one seller is expected to be matched exactly by its rivals, no firm can capture another's market area; so, $\partial R/\partial m = 0$.

In the context of our full price model, Löschian competition has an analogous interpretation. In the short run, the arrival rate of customers in conjunction with the number of service providers determines an equilibrium. This equilibrium is expressed in terms of the nominal fee charged and what we will refer to as the 'limit time', T. This equilibrium limit time reflects the maximum amount of time that the customer will actually be required to supply. (In a spatial context, this might be the commuting time of the firm's most distant consumer.) Under Löschian competition, this limit time is invariant to the nominal fee – i.e. $\partial T/\partial n = 0$. If any one firm were able to lower its nominal fee unilaterally, consumers would be willing to provide more time (e.g. wait longer in the appointment queue); so, the limit time for that firm would rise. But, if Löschian competition prevails, each seller expects its rivals to match any reduction in the nominal fee. And, if nominal fee reductions are matched, there will be no change in the limit time in the market. (The lower nominal fee would make the customers *willing* to supply more time; but if all firms reduced the nominal fee charged, the amount of time *actually required* of the customer will remain unchanged.) Since the sellers expect to be unable to capture each other's customers, a change in the nominal fee would not be expected to have any effect on the prevailing limit time in the market.

The aggregate demand function is given by

$$Q(n) = \int_0^T f(n+wt)\, dt. \tag{6}$$

Using Leibniz's formula, the elasticity of aggregate demand with respect to the nominal fee is

$$E = -n\int_0^T f'(n+wt)\, dt \bigg/ \int_0^T f(n+wt)\, dt - n\frac{\partial T}{\partial n}\frac{f(n+wT)}{\int_0^T f(n+wt)\, dt}. \tag{7}$$

If Löschian competition prevails, the second term of the right-hand expression is zero, since $\partial T/\partial n = 0$. Hence, for Löschian competition we can rewrite (7) as

$$E_L = \int_0^T \epsilon(t)\, \gamma(t, T)\, dt, \tag{8}$$

where
$$\gamma(t, T) = f(n+wt) \bigg/ \int_0^T f(n+wt)\, dt > 0 \tag{9}$$

and

$$\int_0^T \gamma(t, T)\, dt = 1. \tag{10}$$

From (8) it can be seen that the elasticity of the aggregate demand is the weighted average of the elasticities of the basic demands.

Now, applying Leibniz's formula to (8), we obtain

$$\frac{dE_L}{dT} = \int_0^T \epsilon(t)\, \gamma'(t, T)\, dt + \epsilon(T)\, \gamma(T, T), \tag{11}$$

where

$$\gamma'(t, T) = \partial\gamma(t, T)/\partial T < 0. \tag{12}$$

If we differentiate (10) further,

$$\int_0^T \gamma'(t, T) + \gamma(T, T) = 0. \tag{13}$$

Substituting (13) into (11) yields

$$\frac{dE_L(T)}{dT} = \int_0^T [\epsilon(t) - \epsilon(T)]\, \gamma'(t, T)\, dt. \tag{14}$$

In (14), note that $\epsilon(t) - \epsilon(T)$ is strictly negative (positive) for all t if $\partial\epsilon/\partial t$ is positive (negative). Hence, using the lemma established earlier, equation (14) implies that the aggregate demand elasticity is a monotonically increasing (decreasing) function of T, if the basic demand function is less (more) convex than a negative exponential. If the basic demand function is the negative exponential, the elasticity of the aggregate demand function is constant with respect to T.

With the entry of new firms into the market, the amount of required, customer-supplied time will be reduced – i.e. the entry of new firms will reduce waiting and/or commuting time. Hence, the limit time T will decline. Using this definition of competitive entry, we have established the following theorem:[1]

THEOREM. *If the basic demand function is less (more) convex than a negative exponential, competitive entry with Löschian competition lowers (raises) the demand elasticity for the firm's services with respect to its nominal price, n. If the basic demand function is a negative exponential, demand elasticity is unaffected by competitive entry.*

If the basic demand function is less convex than a negative exponential, the entry of new firms will result in a less elastic aggregate demand curve. Therefore, nominal fees will rise as additional service providers enter the market. More generally, with the entry of new firms, we can characterise the behaviour of the nominal fee, n, as follows:[2]

$$n \text{ will} \begin{Bmatrix} \text{rise} \\ \text{remain unchanged} \\ \text{fall} \end{Bmatrix} \quad \text{as} \quad f'' \lesseqgtr \frac{(f')}{f}. \tag{15}$$

[1] The argument contained in this theorem was presented intuitively by Benson (1980) and formally proved by Ohta (1981). Note the similarity of this theorem to the proposition made by Pauly and Satterthwaite (1981, p. 489) with respect to the impact of entry on the elasticity of the demand curve facing the service provider.

[2] This basic result was given in Greenhut *et al.* (1975). It has also been argued by Benson (1980 1982) and established by Ohta (1981).

Hence, it is not necessary to appeal to 'demand creation' or some form of market failure in order to reconcile the empirically observed positive relation between nominal fees and service provider density.[1] Considering full price, the initially surprising relation can be a natural outcome of a not particularly restrictive set of demand conditions and conjectural variations.

II. A CAVEAT: ALTERNATIVE CONJECTURAL VARIATIONS

To this point we have implicitly assumed that the level of entry into the market is sufficiently modest to allow Löschian conjectural variations to be maintained. However, if entry occurred on a larger scale, some of the underlying assumptions may be altered. In this section we will consider the outcome if large-scale entry induces the sellers to switch to another form of price conjectural variations.[2]

As indicated by (7), the competitor in a service (or spatial) market is subject to two price-behaviour determinants: (1) the demand effect associated with the basic demand convexity,

$$-n\int_0^T f'(n+wt)\,dt\bigg/\int_0^T f(n+wt)\,dt, \tag{16}$$

and (2) the competition effect stemming from the price conjectural variations of competitors,

$$-n(\partial T/\partial n)\,\left[f(n+wt)\bigg/\int_0^T f(n+wt)\,dt\right]. \tag{17}$$

The demand effect is the only factor determining the Löschian firm's price. However, both the demand and the competition effects apply under Hotelling/Smithies (H–S) or Greenhut/Ohta (G–O) conjectural variations. In the former case, each decision maker assumes that his competitors leave their nominal fees unchanged. Hence, a price reduction is expected to extend the firm's trading space. More specifically, $\partial T/\partial n = -\frac{1}{2}w$. In effect, the firm that cuts price expects to be able to substitute a reduction in the nominal fee, n, for a slightly greater T. (Were we to consider the market (distance) space of a health care provider, this effect might well be small; however, the effect on waiting time reflected in the second term on the right-hand side of (7) would be significant.) The result is that the H–S elasticity always exceeds the Löschian elasticity, $E_{HS} > E_L$. On the other hand, G–O conjectural variation entails a constant delivered price (full price) over all border-zone areas. (This paradigm may be less applicable to medical services, but may be quite applicable to services

[1] Newhouse *et al.* (1982) examined an allied issue, the physician's location decision. They found demand creation to be flawed both theoretically and empirically and that physician location behaviour conforms to the predictions of standard location theory.

[2] As a referee correctly noted, there is no evidence that different scales of entry necessarily lead to different behavioural conjectures. However, given that there is the possibility that Löschian competition cannot be maintained with massive entry, our objective was to note the limits on the conclusions we can draw. In more general terms, the reader might view Löschian competition as the benchmark case. This caveat is meant to demonstrate that other forms of price conjectures can alter the results, regardless of whether the change was due to entry or some other factor.

that are priced over zones.) The trading space extension resulting from a conjectured price reduction by the subject firm under this paradigm would be greater than that projected under H–S competition (i.e. $\partial T/\partial n = -1w$). As established by Greenhut *et al.* (1975), it follows that $E_{GO} > E_{HS}$.

The conjectured negativity of $\partial T/\partial n$ and the (increasing) negativity of the weighting function $[f(n+wt)/\int f(n+wt)\,dt]$ require that $E_{GO} > E_{HS} > E_L$. (See Ohta (1981).) Hence, the relation of the nominal fees under these three paradigms is $n_L > n_{HS} > n_{GO}$. It is manifest that the H–S and G–O firms react according to an imagined (expected) demand curve that is more elastic than the actual demand curve viewed by the Löschian firm.

Most importantly, the effect of competitive entry on nominal fees under H–S and G–O conjectural variations will differ from that which characterises Löschian competition. Under the H–S price conjectural variation, aggregate demand elasticity may rise, remain unchanged, or fall, depending on the impact of competitive entry on the demand effect as presented in equation (16). This effect will be determined in turn by the convexity of the individual demand function, as in equation (15). On the other hand, competitive entry will always increase aggregate demand elasticity through the competition effect presented in equation (17). And, since the denominator of (17) approaches zero as T falls, the competition effect can eventually outweigh the demand effect; so, nominal fees may fall.[1] Under the G–O price conjectural variation, the competition effect *always* outweighs the demand effect. Therefore entry will always lead to a greater elasticity and thereby lower nominal fees.

Thus, if the individual demand function is less convex than a negative exponential and if the degree of entry is modest, entry can lead to an increase in nominal fees. However, for service industries with low-cost entry, classical theory suggests that a change in conjectural variations from Löschian toward H–S (or G–O) competition is possible. If this change in conjectures occurs, competitive entry could be expected to lead, at least eventually, to a reduction in the nominal fee charged.

III. CONCLUDING REMARKS

We began with some empirical evidence from the health-care service industry: A positive relation has been found to exist between nominal fees charged and the density of the service providers. Interpreting this to mean that the entry of new firms raises the prices charged in a competitive market, much research has been devoted to nontraditional models of behaviour, particularly in the health-care markets.

We have used the techniques of spatial economics to demonstrate that this result is not inconsistent with neoclassical microtheory. In order to obtain

[1] As a referee noted, this is true only if costs are low enough that the zero profit equilibrium is reached before entry drives the system to the point where the competitive effect outweighs the demand effect. If there are high fixed costs – a situation that may be very relevant in the market for health care services – nominal fees could rise over the entire economically relevant range of T (T never approaches zero in this case even with H–S conjectures).

the apparently 'perverse' result, only three prime requirements must be fulfilled:

(1) demand is determined by full price rather than only the nominal fee,
(2) competition approximates the Löschian form,[1] and
(3) the individual demand functions are less convex than a negative exponential.

We propose that these requirements are much easier to accept than resorting to the idea of supplier-induced demand.

Following Greenhut (1956) and, more recently, Benson (1982), we can provide some intuitive justification. Were we to exclude time costs and concentrate only on nominal fees, it is apparent that entry into a competitive market would shift the supply curve out and reduce the fee charged. Considering full price, the entry of new firms does increase supply; but, the entry of new firms also affects the demand curve. As firms enter the market, the amount of customer-supplied time is reduced; so, there is also a change in demand elasticities. Herein lies one of the primary differences between analyses of nominal and full prices (or, between a spaceless analysis and a spatial world): Events that would affect *either* supply *or* demand in a nominal price (spaceless) world affect *both* supply *and* demand in a full price (spatial) world.

Note that our analysis does not suggest that the full price of the service will rise. If requirements (1)–(3) above are met, entry will raise the nominal fee but will lower the time cost component; so, the impact on full price is indeterminate. If the individual demand functions are more convex than or identical to a negative exponential, or alternatively, if H–S or G–O competition prevails and entry occurs, both the nominal fee and the full price will decline.

We are unaware of empirical evidence regarding the convexity of the demand for health care services. However, we propose that the demand for these services would, in general, be of the less convex type. This assertion is based on the view that uncertainty (e.g. uncertainty with respect to whether (1) treatment is needed and will be beneficial and (2) would best be performed by a particular physician) signifies greater elasticities at higher prices. Furthermore, the mathematical requirements for the applicability of the more convex demands are prohibitive. (As has been pointed out by Salop (1977) and others, consumers with high values of time may be charged a higher nominal fee if their demand is inelastic with respect to time cost. This relation would obtain for demands more convex than a negative exponential.)

The effect of entry under our model can easily be shown to diminish firms' profits and, unless there exists Löschian competition and demand curves that are less convex than a negative exponential, to increase consumer welfare. The former result stands opposite to that which would derive from theories of rising consumer ignorance, supplier-induced demand, increasing monopoly power, and the like. To be sure, if increasing specialisation (service variety) and

[1] Strict Löschian competition need not necessarily exist. As was indicated in the previous footnote, under certain conditions, H–S competition or some intermediate case would deliver the same results.

medical discoveries generate shifts in the demand curves over time, the firms' profit and consumer welfare effects would be positively correlated.

Texas A & M University
Florida Atlantic University
University of Leicester
Texas A & M University

Date of receipt of final transcript: June 1984

REFERENCES

Anderson, R. K., House, D. and Ormiston, M. B. (1981). 'A theory of physician behavior with supplier-induced demand.' *Southern Economic Journal*, vol. 48 (July), pp. 124–33.

—— and Ormiston, M. B. (1983). 'A full-pricing analysis of the owner-managed firm.' *Southern Economic Journal*, vol. 50 (July), pp. 57–70.

Benson, B. L. (1980). 'Löschian competition under alternative demand conditions.' *American Economic Review*, vol. 70 (December), pp. 1098–105.

—— (1982). 'The impact of entry at a distance on market demand.' *Review of Regional Studies*, vol. 10 (Fall), pp. 62–8.

Dyckman, Z. Y. (1978). *A Study of Physicians' Fees*. Washington, D.C.: Council on Wage and Price Stability.

DeVany, A. S. (1976). 'Uncertainty, waiting time, and capacity utilization: a stochastic theory of product quality.' *Journal of Political Economy*, vol. 84 (June), pp. 523–41.

Evans, R. G., Parish, E. M. A. and Sully, F. (1973). 'Medical productivity, scale effects, and demand creation.' *Canadian Journal of Economics*, vol. 6 (August), pp. 376–93.

Feldstein, M. S. (1970). 'The rising price of physicians' services.' *Review of Economics and Statistics*, vol. 52 (May), pp. 121–33.

Fuchs, V. R. (1978). 'The supply of surgeons and the demand for operations.' *Journal of Human Resources*, vol. 13 (Supplement), pp. 35–6.

—— and Kramer, M. J. (1972). *Determinants of Expenditures for Physicians' Services in the United States 1948–60*. (NBER Occasional Paper 117) Washington, D.C.: Department of H.E.W.

Green, J. (1978). 'Physician-induced demand for medical care.' *Journal of Human Resources*, vol. 13 (Supplement), pp. 21–34.

Greenhut, J. G., Greenhut, M. L. and Kelly, J. (1977). 'A spatial-theoretical perspective for bank merger regulations.' Proceedings Bank Structure and Competition, Federal Reserve Bank of Chicago.

Greenhut, M. L. (1956). *Plant Location in Theory and in Practice*. Chapel Hill: University of North Carolina Press and Westport, Connecticut: Greenwood Press, 1982.

—— Hwang, H. and Ohta, H. (1975). 'Observations on the shape and relevance of the spatial demand function.' *Econometrica*, vol. 43 (July), pp. 669–82.

Newhouse, J. P. (1970). 'A model of physician pricing.' *Southern Economic Journal*, vol. 37 (October), pp. 174–83.

—— Williams, A. P., Bennett, B. W. and Schwartz, W. B. (1982). 'Does the geographical distribution of physicians reflect market failure?' *Bell Journal of Economics*, vol. 13 (Autumn), pp. 493–505.

Ohta, H. (1981). 'The price effects of spatial competition.' *Review of Economic Studies*, vol. 48 (April), pp. 317–25.

Pauly, M. V. and Satterthwaite, M. A. (1980). 'The effect of provider supply on price.' In *The Target Income Hypothesis and Related Issues in Health Manpower Policy*. Washington, D.C.: U.S. Department of Health, Education and Welfare.

—— and —— (1981). 'The pricing of primary care physicians' services: a test of the role of consumer information.' *Bell Journal of Economics*, vol. 12 (Autumn), pp. 488–506.

Phlips, L. (1983). *The Economics of Price Discrimination*. Cambridge: Cambridge University Press.

Salop, S. (1977). 'The noisy monopolist: imperfect information, price dispersion, and price discrimination.' *Review of Economic Studies*, vol. 44 (October), pp. 393–406.

INTERNATIONAL JOURNAL
OF TRANSPORT ECONOMICS
Vol. XVIII - No. 1 - February 1991

FINANCIAL-ECONOMIC ASPECTS OF AIRLINE DEREGULATION (*)

JOHN GREENHUT
GEORGE NORMAN
M.L. GREENHUT (**)

ABSTRACT: A disturbing feature of *ex post* analysis of the effects of passenger transport service deregulation is a projected set of conflicting effects that deregulation could have on the pricing and frequency of airline services. The present paper uses an "address" model to uncover the conditions which would portend ambiguity in results. It then demonstrates that the relationship between post - and pre-deregulation fares and departure schedules depends on the regulatory environment, the type of oligopolistic rivalry, and the nature of consumer demand. It concludes that if post-deregulation entry conditions are sufficiently free, the discipline of the regulated environment will be broken to the benefit of consumers. In such a situation, our theory predicts a post-deregulation reduction in fares and an increase in departures, even given a possible increase in airline merges.

1. INTRODUCTION

Deregulation of air passenger transportation in the United States has been accompanied, and to an extent was anticipated, by several economic studies of its likely impacts on route structures, fares, and other aspects of service quality - see, for example, Meyer and Oster (1984), Meyer *et al* (1981), Douglas and Miller (1974). One apparently disturbing feature of the *ex post* analysis has been the weak and occasionally conflicting effects that deregulation initially had on the pricing of passenger transportation. There was, for

---

(*) *Final Version: July 1990*

(**) *J. Greenhut is affiliated with the Arizona State University; G. Norman, is at the University of Leicester; M.L. Greenhut is at Texas A & M University.*

example, little evidence of the sharp reduction in price that some analyst proposed would result from deregulation: see also Johnston (1987) for recent U.K. evidence.

This paper shows why such ambiguity in the impact of deregulation could have been expected. We also discuss some of the conditions that are necessary to resolve the ambiguity. The model on which our analysis is based is outlined in section 2. While this model is couched in terms of air transport it is equally applicable to passenger bus transportation. Thus our model could be applied to comment upon recent moves in the United Kingdom, for example, to deregulate city-based bus transportation systems.

Section 3 discusses long-run equilibrium in an unregulated passenger travel industry. In section 4 we compare this equilibrium with regulated equilibria under a number of different regulatory policies. Section 5 discusses the effects of relaxing particular assumptions, and the main theoretical conclusions are summarised in section 6. Section 7 records recent data applicable to the United States and then points to a combination theory which explains the data and allows us to comment upon the likely effects of the recent increase in merger activity in the deregulated industry.

2. THE MODEL

We take advantage of the formal similarity that exists between models of passenger transportation and "address" models of differentiation that have been developed in the specific contexts of product differentiation and spatial competition - Archibald *et al* (1986), Neven (1986). Assume accordingly that the transport route under consideration runs from a single source A to a single destination B, with no intermediate pick-up and set-down points (1). Travellers have access to two transport "industries", the first of which, the "inside" industry, is currently regulated but is a candidate for deregulation. The second, "outside" industry (Salop, 1979) produces alternative travel services under competitive conditions.

A traveller's "address" is given by her most preferred daily departure time t^*; the utility obtained from travelling at some other time t is given by a

(1) Intermediate stops can be handled without any change to the analysis: provided, of course, that competing carriers do not race to overtake each other!

utility function U(t*, t) such that:

$$U(t^*, t^*) > U(t^*, t) \text{ for } t \neq t^*. \quad [1]$$

The "market" over which travellers are distributed is assumed to be circular of length T - the 24 hours of a clock face (?) - in order to avoid end-point problems. Travellers are assumed to be evenly distributed over the market, according to their desired departure times t*, at density D (2).

The price paid by a traveller using the inside carrier consists of two parts: the fare paid to the carrier F, plus the value of the disutility incurred in having to travel at other than the most preferred time (see de Vany (1976), de Vany and Saving (1977) for a discussion of this concept of "full price"). In order to keep the analysis simple we impose a symmetry assumption that the value of time to a traveller is identical, whether this is time the traveller loses by having to travel "too early" or "too late". The value of the disutility is assumed linear in time and given by

$$UL = w|t^* - t| \quad (w > 0) \quad [2]$$

where w is the unit valuation of time (3).

The inside carrier will be used so long as the surplus obtained exceeds that of using the outside carrier: in other words, the existence of the outside carrier implies a maximum full price $\bar{s}$ above which the inside carrier will not be used.

Standard consumer analysis allows us to derive demand for the inside carrier's services as a function of the full price. Consider potential travellers time distance γ_i from departure i (flight or bus) for which the fare charged is F_i. Demand by these travellers for this departure can be represented:

$$q(F_i + w\gamma_i) = D.\hat{q}\,(F_i + w\gamma_i) \quad [3]$$

(2) We shall consider in Section 5 the effect of relaxing the uniform distribution assumption.

(3) We do not consider in this paper the important measurement problems that confront any attempt to put a valuation on time "lost" in this way.

where: (i) $\hat{q}(F_i + w\gamma_i) > 0$ if $F_i + w\gamma_i < F_j + w\gamma_j$ for all $j \neq i$ and $F_i + w\gamma_i < s$;
$= 0$ otherwise

(ii) $\hat{q}'() < 0$.

The individual demand function $\hat{q}()$ can be interpreted in one of two ways: (1) the proportion of travellers at "address" γi who will use the regulated carrier on a particular day, or (2) the number of trips these travellers will make over some defined period - e.g. week, month or year.

We shall consider in section 5 the effect on the analysis of assuming that the demand function is rectangular (Salop, 1979) i.e. each traveller makes exactly one trip per period provided the full price of an inside carrier is less than the reservation price. This will be shown to be a special case of the more general function in equation (3)

Aggregate demand for a particular departure i provided by an inside carrier is derived as in Figure 1 and given by:

$$Q_i(F_i) = \int_{Z-i}^{0} q(F_i + w\gamma)\, d\gamma + \int_{0}^{Z_i} q(F_i + w\gamma)\, d\gamma. \qquad [4]$$

where the "market boundaries" are given by:

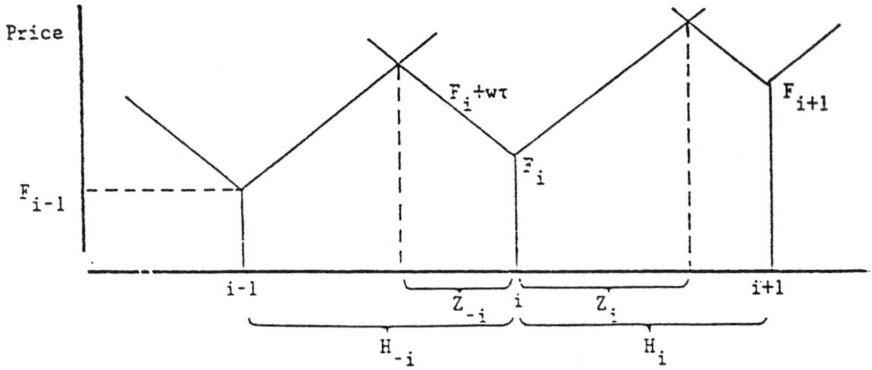

Figure 1: Market Boundaries

$$(Z_{-i} : F_i + wZ_{-i} = F_{i-1} + w(H_{-i} - Z_{-i})$$
$$(Z_i : F_i + wZ_i \;\; = F_{i+1} + w(H_i - Z_i) \qquad [5]$$

and H_{-i} and H_i are the respective headways between departure i and departures i-1 and i+1.

Assume that the costs for an individual departure are given by:

$$C(Q_i) = f + cQ_i \;\; (f, c \geq 0). \qquad [6]$$

That is, costs are identical throughout the market, exhibit economies of scale and consist of a fixed cost f plus constant marginal costs c. The cost structure (6) admittedly does not fully reflect cost conditions in the transportation industries. There is, however, evidence to suggest that it is close enough for smaller carriers to justify the analytical simplification and generalisation it gives us in the context of the ex post deregulation results described in section 6. Profit on an individual departure is readly specified then as:

$$\pi_i (F_i) = (F_i - c)\, Q_i\, (F_i) - f. \qquad [7]$$

A problem that characterizes address models is that, in general, there exists no Bertrand-Nash equilibrium in the joint price-location game implicit in these models - d'Aspremont *et al* (1979), Novshek (1980). Very simply, the aggregate demand function for departure i is not continuous in "location", i.e. departure time: if departure i approaches sufficiently closely, for example to departure i + 1 it will be able to undercut i + 1 and so appropriate (i + 1)'s total market.

A number of modifications to the competitive game and/or to the model's specification have been suggested in order to ensure existence of equilibrium - see Anderson (1986), de Palma *et al* (1986) for brief surveys. In particular, we can suggest a modification to the conjectures attributed by a carrier to its rivals - the neighbouring carriers. No matter what conjecture is held with respect to a general price cut - of which the Bertrand conjecture of no reaction is one example - if this price cut results in price undercutting a neighbour at that neighbour's location, the neighbour is conjectured immediately to react by cutting price to marginal cost. This "no mill price undercutting" (nmpu) conjecture has been analysed by, for example, Eaton (1972), (1976), Novshek

(1980), Kohlberg and Novshek (1982) in order to generate equilibrium in address models similar to that formulated in this paper.

There remains the question of the "shape" of the resulting nmpu equilibrium. We follow Salop (1979) and concentrate upon symmetric equilibria with all departures evenly spaced and charging identical fares (See Novshek, 1980). In consequence, we can considerably simplify equations (4) and (7) by considering the "representative departure", with headway (market area) H between itself and its neighbours, and charging fare F. Aggregate demand and profit for the representative departure are:

$$Q(F, H) = 2 \int_0^{H/2} q(F + w\gamma)\, d\gamma \qquad [4']$$

$$\pi(F, H) = (F - c)\, Q(F, H) - f. \qquad [7']$$

3. EQUILIBRIUM FOR THE UNREGULATED INDUSTRY

We consider first post-deregulation long-run equilibrium in the inside industry. In doing so we assume that the representative departure always has competitors as neighbours: thus market structure consists of $n \geq 2$ independent carriers, whose departures are interleaved.

The decision variable for competing carriers is the fare F: headway is determined endogenously. Price elasticity of aggregate demand for the representative departure is:

$$\eta(F, H) \underset{def}{=} - \frac{dQ}{dF} \cdot \frac{F}{Q} = \frac{F}{Q} \cdot \left[\frac{\partial Q}{\partial F} - \frac{1}{2} \frac{\partial Q}{\partial H} \frac{\partial H}{\partial F} \right] \qquad [8]$$

where elasticity is, by convention, represented as a positive number. This elasticity consists of two components: the first gives the change in demand from *existing* travellers, while the second gives the change in demand resulting from the expected change in the representative firm's market area. Profit for the representative departure is maximised at fare F* by the familiar pricing equation:

$$F^* \left[1 - \frac{1}{\eta (F^*, H)} \right] = c \qquad [9]$$

which holds for any headway H.

Headway H is determined in the unregulated environment by the entry of new carriers (or additional departures by existing carriers). We assume that the process of moving to the long-run equilibrium is characterised by zero relocation costs, i.e. the timetable is assumed flexible: a feature that appears to have characterised the early history of deregulated routes. Entry after deregulation will continue so long as excess profits can be made. Thus it would appear reasonable to assume that headway H is determined by the zero profit condition (4):

$$\pi \ (F, H) = (F - c) \ Q \ (F, H) - f = 0. \qquad [10]$$

Equilibrium in the unregulated industry is obtained by simultaneous solution of equations (9) and (10). The precise nature of this equilibrium and its comparative statics are crucially affected by two factors (Greenhut, Norman and Hung, 1987):

(i) The shape of the demand function (3): in particular whether it is more or less convex than the negative exponential function

$q = ae^{-bp}$ (a, b > 0).

(ii) The behavioural reaction of rival carriers implicit in the conjectural variation $\partial H/\partial F$ in equation (8): this indicates the extent to which the representative departure's market area is expected to increase as a result of a fare decrease. Two extreme cases can be identified:

---

(4) See Eaton and Lipsey (1978) and Capozza and van Order (1980), recalling the zero-relocation-cost assumption. There is, of course the complication implicit in the indivisibility of departures (Kaldor, 1935), Demsetz (1964)): excess profit may accrue with N departures, while losses are made with N + 1 departures. We shall assume equilibrium is characterised by sufficiently frequent departures as to make this complication unimportant.

(a) Bertrand-Nash (BN) : no price reaction by rivals, so that $\partial H/\partial F = -1/w$ (since the market area is two sided);

(b) Price-Matching (PM) : price changes are expected to be exactly matched by rivals so that $\partial H/\partial F = 0$.

It follows immediately that in a market with known headway, the elasticity of demand is an increasing function and the fare charged a decreasing function of the increase in market area $|\partial H/\partial F|$ that is expected to follow a reduction in the fare.

We make no attempt to choose between alternative specification of the demand function. This is a matter for empirical research, and while there may be suggestive evidence in favour of a concave (less convex) specification (Johnston, 1987) the evidence is too tentative to allow *a priori* choice in a paper of this type. Nor shall we choose between alternative conjectural variations. There remains the age-old oligopolistic problem of what is a "reasonable" conjecture, but this cannot be decided independently of the institutional setting. For example, BN may be reasonable in the airline industry given that incumbent carriers face charges of predatory pricing or complicity in pricing if they match too closely or quickly the pricing policies of entrants.

The resulting equilibria are illustrated in Figure 2 (see Greenhut, Norman, Hung, 1987), Part I for details of the derivation of this diagram): the pricing equation (9) is represented by the curves labelled 'F' and the entry equation (10) by the curve labelled $\pi = 0$. Fares are higher but flight frequencies greater (headways shorter) with PM conjectures than with BN conjectures (5). We shall not consider the comparative statics of the unregulated equilibria in this paper. It should be obvious from Figure 2(a) that these can be "perverse" in the less convex demand case. Two points are, however, worth noting. Firstly, the second term in the expression for price elasticity of aggregate demand (equation (8)) tends to infinity as H tends to zero - provided, of course, that $|\partial H/\partial F| \neq 0$. Thus so long as conjectures are not PM, sufficiently free entry will result in long-run equilibrium being approximately competitive. Secondly, the

(5) A similar model has been analysed by Foster and Golay (1986), but they consider only the linear demand case and, while stating that they adopt the nmpu conjecture, actually use the PM conjecture.

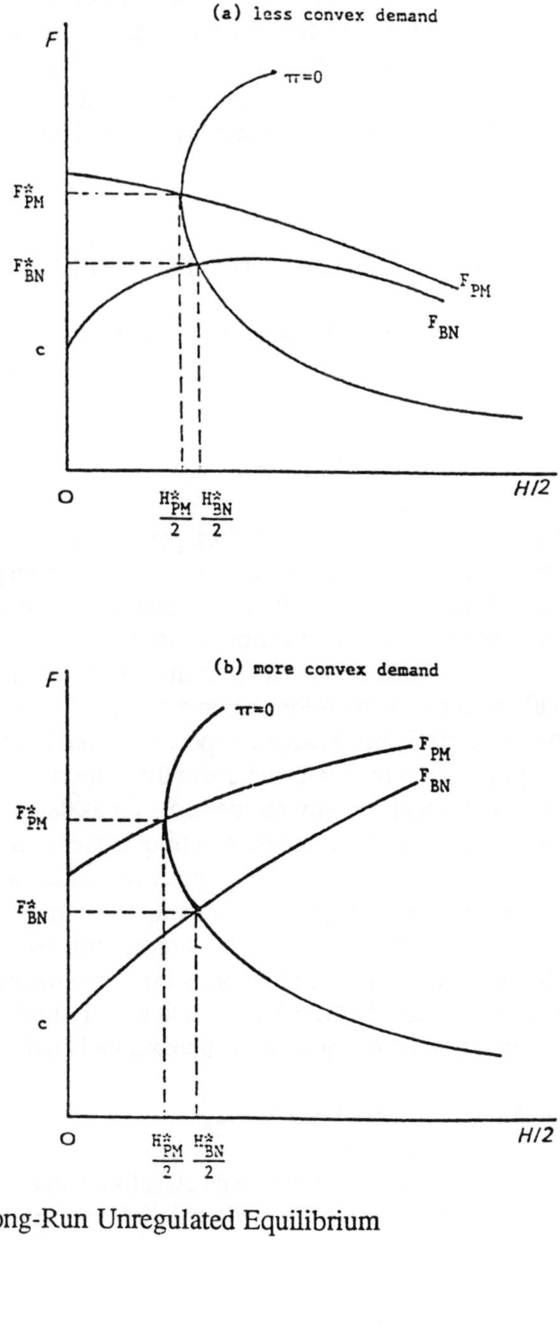

Figure 2: Long-Run Unregulated Equilibrium

greater the conjectural variation $|\partial H/\partial F|$ the nearer will the resulting price line lie to the PM price line: Cournot conjectures or rational conjectures generate such intermediate price lines. We concentrate throughout on comparing PM with BN conjectures: our qualitative conclusions generalise, of course, to the comparison of PM and any other conjecture intermediate to PM and BN.

4. REGULATED AND UNREGULATED EQUILIBRIA

The comparison of regulated and unregulated equilibria depends on the policies adopted by the regulatory authorities. Various policies might be considered.

4.1 *Policy I: Price Restraint/Free Entry*

Price restraint in the transport industries has, perhaps somewhat perversely, often taken the form of imposing either a *fixed* or a *minimum* price on carriers: as evidenced by recent attempts in the European Community to deregulate airline fares on particular intra-European routes.

The two restraints are equivalent so long as the minimum fare restraint is binding. We shall concentrate, therefore, upon a fixed fare restraint. Only if this is fixed above F^*_{PM} in Figure 3 can we expect an unambiguous reduction in fares post-deregulation, no matter the nature of the conjectures that competing firms hold in the unregulated environment. So far as departure frequencies are concerned, an unambiguous increase in frequencies will occur only if the regulated price is greater than $\dot{F}_2$. With a lower regulated price, departures will be more (less) frequent post-deregulation if carriers hold Price-Matching (Bertrand-Nash) conjectures. Very simply, for deregulation of a fixed-fare constraint to *guarantee* a reduction in fares and increase in departures frequencies, the regulated fare must be set at a "very high" level compared to the fares that will be charged in the unregulated environment.

4.2 *Policy II: Entry Restraint/Free Pricing*

It is tempting to argue that a restraint on entry is likely to create collusive conditions in the regulated industry. This will certainly be the case if entry is

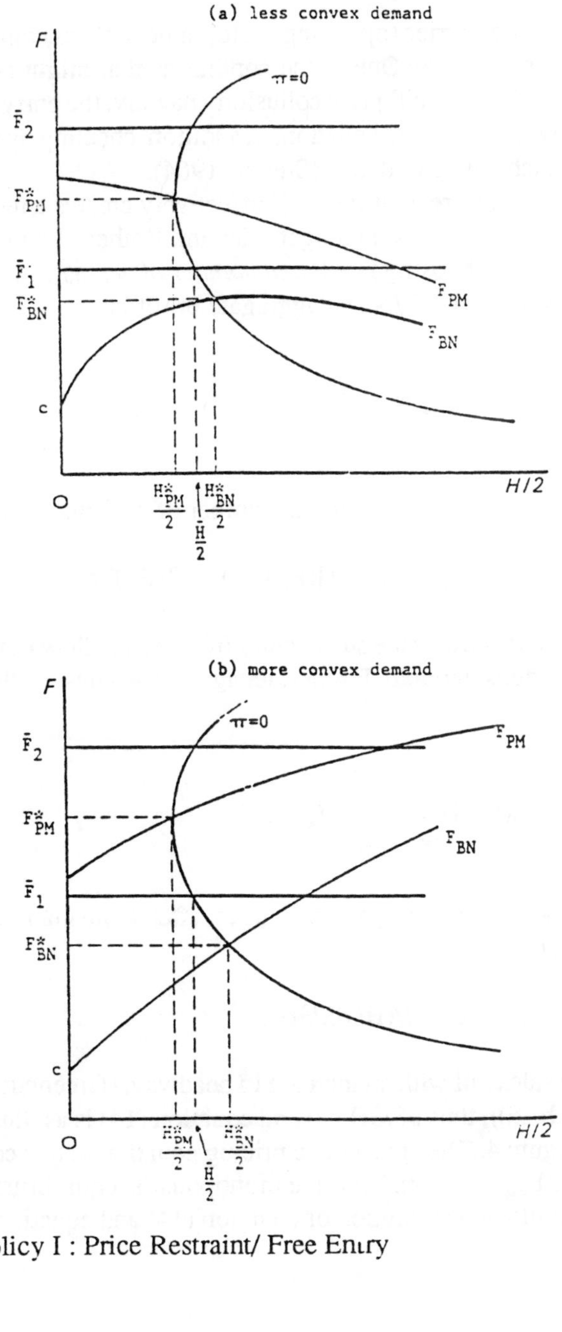

Figure 3: Policy I : Price Restraint/ Free Entry

confined to a single carrier (operating multiple departures) but is also likely with two or more carriers. One of the conditions that might be expected to break down tacit (or explicit) price collusion - namely, the entry of competing carriers - is now ruled out by regulation. In addition, cheating by regulated carriers will be much easier to detect (Stigler, 1964).

We assume, therefore, that Policy II effectively creates a monopoly . The zero profit condition (10) is no longer relevant. Rather, the monopolist will maximise profit by choosing fare F *and number of departures* N. With N departures, headway is H = T/N and aggregate profit is:

$$\Pi(F, H) = \frac{T}{H}\pi(F, H) = \frac{T}{H}(F - c)\, Q(F, H) - \frac{T}{H} f. \qquad [11]$$

Departures will be added up to the number of departures N at which:

$$\Pi(F, T/N - 1) < \Pi(F, T/N) > \Pi(F, T/N + 1) \qquad [12]$$

Assume that departures are sufficiently frequent to allow us to treat N, and so H, as a continuos variable. Further, let aggregate sales for the monopolist be denoted:

$$S(F, H) \underset{def}{=} \frac{T}{H} Q(F, H) \qquad [13]$$

Maximising (11) with respect to H gives, after some manipulation and use of equation (13):

$$F^* = c - Tf/(H^2\, \partial S/\partial H). \qquad [14]$$

Aggregate sales fall with an increase in headway, (Greenhut, Norman and Hung, 1987, ch. 20), thus $\partial S/\partial H < 0$ and equation (14) is as illustrated by the curve F_M in Figure 4. The appropriate pricing equation in this collusive environment is the F_{PM} equation. Thus the monopolist's equilibrium (F^*_M, H^*_M) is given by simultaneous solution of equation (14) and equation (9) with PM conjectures.

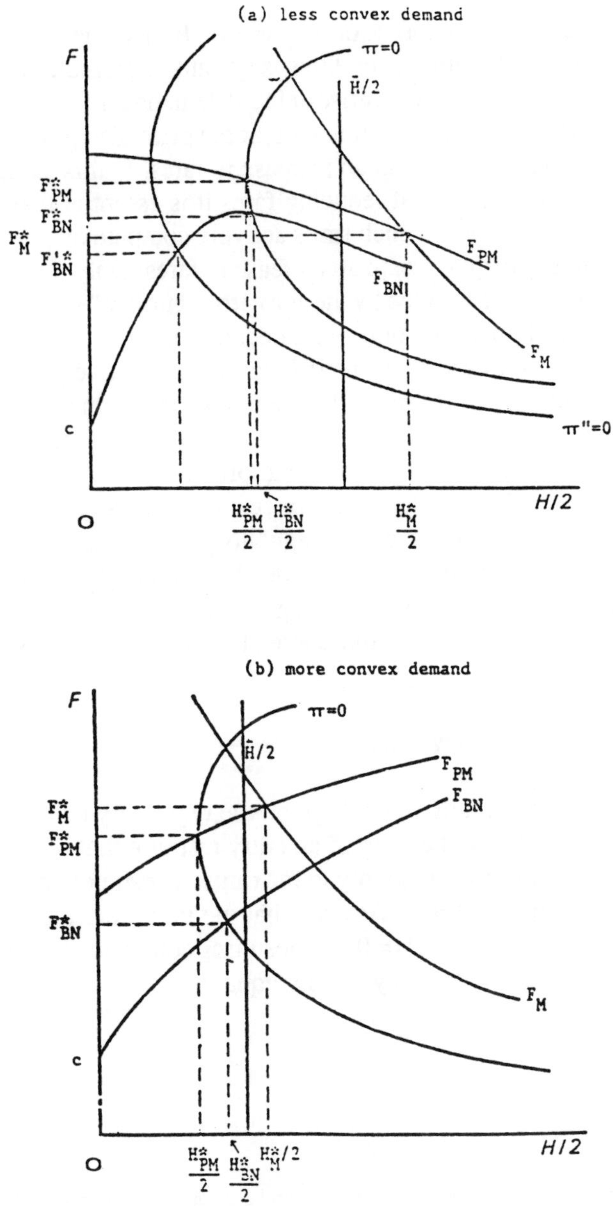

Figure 4: Entry Restraint/Free Pricing

The impact of deregulation on departures frequencies is unambiguous: headways fall. But the impact on fares is not at all clearcut. Fares will fall if demand is more convex, but may rise or fall if demand is more with less convex demand. In the latter case, a continuation of the price discipline implicit in the P.M. conjectures will result in an increase in fares. In this case, if deregulation is to have any chance of reducing fares it is essential that deregulation creates an environment in which firms actively compete on price. Even then, BN conjectures *may* give rise to an increase in fares. Only if entry conditions are relatively easy - as implied by the zero profit curve π'' in Figure 4 (a) - will deregulation lead unambiguously to a decrease in price. Fortunately, this is just the kind of condition that is likely to give rise to active price competition.

What would happen if Policy II were to take the form of a control on departure headways, i.e. control on the total number of departures? This might occur, for example, if the regulatory authorities were concerned with some measure of the quality of transport services or if, as was occasionally the case in the United States, there were a regulatory requirement to stop at a small city located between major origin and destination points. Policy can then be represented by a vertical line at the regulated headway, e.g. the line $\dot{H}/2$ in Figure 4 (6). Similar results to those already discussed in this section will be obtained.

4.3 *Policy III: Ramsey Prices*

Quality of service may figure high on the regulatory authorities' agenda. Thus policy might take the form of an entry restraint that requires the resulting monopoly or quasi-monopoly to maximise consumer surplus subject to a minimum profit constraint. Assume that the minimum profit constraint is $\Pi(F, H) = 0$, implying $\pi(F, H) = 0$. The resulting constrained optimisation problem will generate the Rasmey pricing equation:

(6) The reader is left to analyse the effects of relaxing a regulatory policy that controls *both* price and frequency. The total ambiguity of the effects of deregulation in this case should not be surprising.

$$F_R\left[1-\frac{1-\lambda}{\lambda}\cdot\frac{1}{\eta(F_R, H)}\right]=c \qquad [15]$$

where F_R is the Rasmey fare and λ is the Lagrange multiplier on the profit constraint. The price elasticity of demand is that generated by the PM conjecture. Comparison with equation (9) indicates that the Ramsey pricing schedule (15) lies below the PM schedule as in Figure 5. The precise position of the Ramsey schedule will be determined by the Lagrange multiplier λ; this requires a third equation - an amended optimal frequency curve F'_M (the dotted curve in Figure (5). Deregulation will increase prices and departure frequencies with PM conjectures, but will have ambiguous effects if the deregulated industry is characterised by BN conjectures. Once again, deregulation is more likely to decrease fares the easier are post-deregulation entry conditions.

5. ALTERNATIVE ASSUMPTIONS

The analysis of previous sections has assumed a relatively general specification of the demand function (7). We should, however, consider whether our results are changed in any fundamental sense if we assume demand is rectangular: travellers purchase exactly one trip so long as price is below the reservation price (Salop, 1979). It is shown elsewhere (Greenhut, Norman and Hung, 1986) that the rectangular demand function is a special case of less convex demand. The results derived above for the less convex case carry through to the rectangular case.

Of potentially greater importance is our assumption that consumers are uniformly spread over the market: that the distribution of most preferred departure times is uniform over the day. This assumption patently does not characterise many transport links: especially those with high volumes of business travellers.

(7) We have also ignored throughout this paper the possibility that demand is a function of quality of service as measured by load factors. It should be obvious that incorporating this feature makes demand less price elastic, thus raising all the price lines, and changing the zero profit line, but otherwise does not affect the analysis.

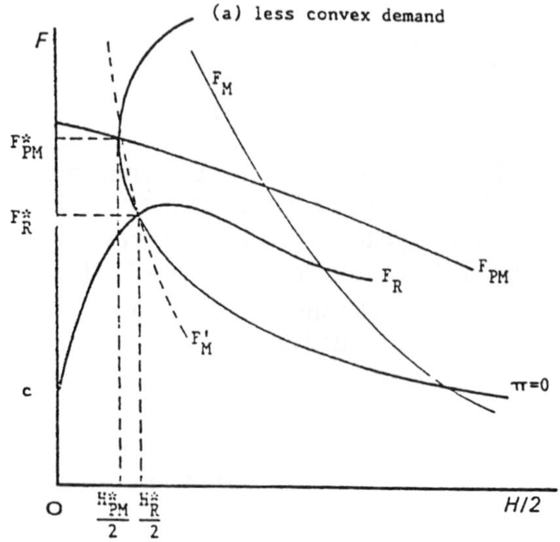

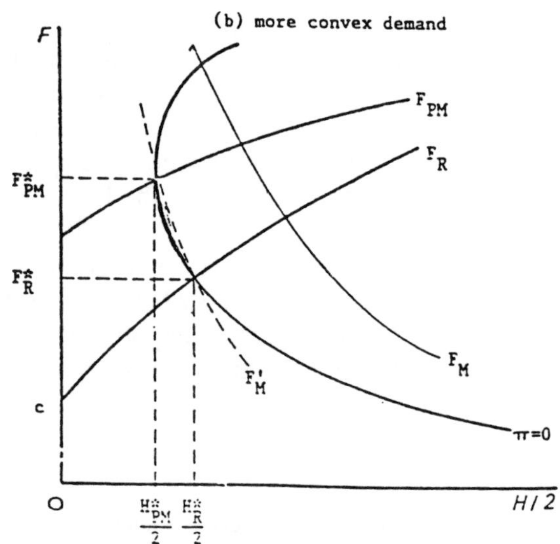

Figure 5: Policy III: Ramsey Pricing

A full analytic treatment of the non-uniform case would prove excessively complex, but a flavour of the resulting equilibria can easily be given. The zero profit condition (10) can be rewritten using equation (3):

$$\pi(F, H) : (F - c)\, \hat{Q}\, (F, H) - f/D = 0 \qquad [10`]$$

where $\hat{Q}$ (F, H) is travellers' demand normalised by consumer density : the zero profit condition will lie further to the left in the (H/2, F) plane the greater is the traveller density. By a similar argument, the monopolist's market headway equation (14) lies further to the left the greater is the traveller density.

As one might expect, post-deregulation departures will be more closely spaced in peak periods. Indeed, we could go further and hypothesise that post-deregulation entry is more likely to be confined initially to periods of high travel demand densities. Of course, the ambiguity with respect to the fare impact of deregulation remains, although there is some reason to expect that high travel demand densities, by facilitating easier entry, are more likely to generate fare reductions.

6. THEORETICAL CONCLUSIONS

The theoretical objectives of this paper have been three-fold. First, to indicate how address models of differentiation can be applied to the analysis of scheduling and pricing of passenger travel services. Second, to show that no *a priori* predictions *could* be made regarding the effects of deregulation of travel services. Post-deregulation fares would be higher or lower, and departure schedules more or less frequent than the pre-deregulation situation depending upon:

(i) the policy applied by the regulatory authorities;

(ii) the way in which oligopolistic rivalry is manifested post-deregulation; and

(iii) the nature of consumer demand for passenger travel.

Third, we wanted to identify conditions that would increase the possibility of fare reductions post-deregulation. These turn out to be remarkably simple. Competitive forces have to be sufficiently strong, and so entry conditions sufficiently easy as to break down the price discipline that might carry over from the regulated to the unregulated industry. Such price discipline is implicit in price matching conjectures and the consequent avoidance of price competition among rival carriers.

We now turn to a consideration of whether these conditions appear to apply to the United States of the nineteen-eighties. In particular, we are interested to determine whether the theories of sections 3-5 can explain the data.

7. RECENT DATA

The Civil Aeronautics Board (CAB) regulations in the United States (U.S.) applied to interstate air travel only. Thus, comparing the relationship between unregulated interstate fares with regulated interstate fares can be suggestive of those facets of our theory that are most likely to apply to the airline industry in the U.S.

7.1. *Fares*

The unregulated fare in the late nineteen-seventies on the 338-mile intrastate flight from Los Angeles to San Francisco was $ 18.75. Regulated fares on interstate flights of similar distance during the same period of time averaged between $ 37.96 and $ 38.89. The 239-mile unregulated Dallas to Houston fare was $ 23.15, while the regulated fare for the 236-mile flight from Las Vegas to Los Angeles was $ 28.70. Such differences understate the true advantage to consumers of unregulated flights because they do not take into account the evening and weekend discounted fares, such as the $ 13.89 discount applicable on flights between Dallas and Houston. In general, regulated interstate fares were typically between 50 and 125 per cent greater than unregulated intrastate fares on flights of similar distance (Adams and Block, 1986)).

A second method to evaluate empirically the theories in the paper is to look at fares before and after the Airline Deregulation Act of 1978. Figure 6 provides data on this point. At first glance, the figure appears to indicate mixed results. Real revenues, or fares, increased between 1978 and 1981 and then declined thereafter. Such a pattern of price changes is consistent with the story emerging from our model. Deregulation with the existing carriers may initially lead to price increases precisely because new entry has not occurred, but as competition in the deregulated industry develops, particularly in response to entry of new carriers, a downward pressure on price will be established: airline travel costs fell from 4.4 cents per mile in 1978 to 3.5 cents per mile in 1986. It might be thought that a more rational response by the existing carriers would have been to cut prices immediately in order to limit entry. Work on dynamic pricing by Gaskins (1971) and Norman and Nichols (1982) indicates, however, that such an attempt to limit entry may not maximise long-run profits when entry is unavoidable.

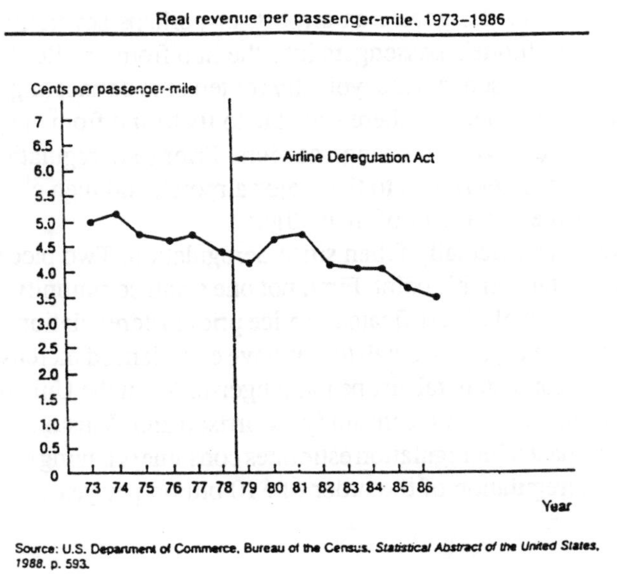

Figure 6: Real revenue per passenger-mile, 1973-1986

7.2 *Headways (Service)*

Equally important is whether the benefits in fare reduction happened to derive from reduced service, i.e. increases in H. Many people had feared that deregulation of the airlines would allow carriers to stop servicing the unprofitable, low-density markets in the U.S. But note, carriers in the regulated environment were rarely required to continue servicing unprofitable routes. In fact, between 1970 and 1975, the CAB permitted certified (regulated) carriers to reduce service to small communities in America by 25 per cent. Thus it would seem to be improper to criticize deregulation if it led to carriers doing what they had rarely been *disallowed* from doing prior to deregulation.

The facts are the complete reverse of the fears, the impact of deregulation on service availability having been positive. First of all, a substantial increase in the number of carriers has taken place since deregulation; the number of carriers more than tripled between 1978 and 1985. Deregulation also allowed the airlines to make greater use of hub-and-spoke operations. With hub-and-spoke, each carrier designates an airport, or perhaps several, as its hub(s). Then the carrier funnels passengers into the hub from smaller feeder routes. Once at the hub, passengers are typically routed onto connecting flights of the same carrier. Customers are therefore able to fly to and from very small communities without having to change carriers. Prior to deregulation, travellers had to take commuter flights to the major airports, and then change to a major carrier for the remainder of their flight.

Headways have actually fallen since deregulation. Two pieces of empirical evidence establish this point. First, not one small community which had even a minimum level of certificated service prior to deregulation has since lost that service. Actually, most small towns have experienced increases in weekly departures. Second, general airline passenger-miles in the United States have more than doubled (8). A recent study (Morrison and Winston, 1986) p. 1) of the overall impact of deregulation estimates consumers having enjoyed net benefits from deregulation of the order of $10 billion per year.

---

(8) U.S. Department of Commerce, Bureau of Census, *Statistical Abstract of the United States*, 1988, p. 593.

7.3 *Other Relevant Matters*

Two rather clear post-deregulation lessons should be set forth at this point. First, regulation should be used only when economic justification exists. Legitimate economic justification for regulation might be the existence of such conditions as (a) natural monopoly, (b) deficient information, and (c) poorly defined property rights.

The matter of natural monopoly is easily handled. Airline services are not intrinsically monopolistic. In fact, smaller carriers enjoy a cost advantage (Adams and Brock (*op. cit.*, p. 220). The successful entry of dozens of new, relatively small airlines since deregulation confirms this contention.

With respect to deficient information, as in the Pan Am disaster in England in 1988, the answer lies in the matter of safety regulation, not fares. What about property rights? When they are poorly defined, governments can have positive impacts through regulation. Clearly, no airline has a well-defined airspace property right. A legitimate role for government thus applies. But this is essentially limited to safety concerns, which remain a function of the FAA.

Second, it is often argued that regulation entails a regulatory agency being captured by the industry. This possibility, we shall see, ties up directly with the theories of sections 4 and 5 of our paper.

The outcome of the *capture theory* is the claim that a regulatory agency decides its policy on the basis of the interests of the firms in the regulated industry rather than those of the consumers. If such regulatory capture did take place within the regulated industry then it is highly likely that deregulation will be unambiguously beneficial. For this to be the case, entry to the regulated industry should have been restricted and fares controlled at near monopoly levels.

Consider the actual situation in the regulated industry. In the United States, the CAB was given authority both over the fares that could be charged and over entry into the airline market. If the airline were able to "capture" the CAB, higher fares without lost sales to new rivals could be expected. It is significant that the CAB consistently rejected requests by individual carriers to lower fares; indeed, in the 1950's they exhorted carriers to raise their fares and to eliminate the use of discount fares (Adams and Brock, *op. cit.*, p. 224).

In an unregulated environment, high fares would have served to attract new rivals. To be successful, the airlines had to have confidence that the CAB would also restrict entry. Although nearly 100 companies applied to enter the

American interstate airline industry between 1938 - 1978, not one was allowed to enter. (9).

A final financial facet of deregulation should be noted. Specifically, might we not expect financial advantages to result form mergers of newly established airlines, a concentration effect that would reverse the previous competitive outcome of increased departures at lower fares? In fact, Kilman, 1987 p. 1) concluded that airline competition had come full circle. For example, he noted that in the carefree days before deregulation in 1978, five big airlines handled most of the passenger traffic in and out of the Lambert - St. Louis International Airport. Then came decontrol, the air wars, and nine more airlines invading the market. *Now*, most of the traffic is handled by one carrier: Trans World Airlines. TWA today enjoys a degree of dominance that any airline would have envied prior to deregulation.

In similar context, more than 75 per cent of the traffic in Pittsburgh, Memphis, and Minneapolis is now handled by a single carrier. Over the nation as a whole, the four-firm concentration ratio in airlines has risen to 61 per cent. (See the Appendix for further details). We are not convinced, however, that such levels of concentration need be important (see Greenhut, Norman and Hung, 1987, Ch. 19), or that regulation is again needed to control mergers and enforce anti-trust guidelines. All that is necessary is that the unregulated environment encourages price competition and quality of service among competing carrier. To see this, note that, for example, the equilibrium identified in section 3 of this paper will be the same equilibrium whether it is characterised by N* competing carriers operating one flight each or 2 competing carriers operating N*/2 flights each.

7.4 *How Our Theory Accounts for the Ex Post Non-Regulatory Improvement*

The actual case of regulation in the United States involved a combination of the Policies we analysed in section 4. Specifically, consider the combined combination policy:

---

(9) "The Economic Report of the President", Washington, D.C., *Council of Economic Advisors*, January 1988, p. 202.

Policy IV: Price Restraint/Entry Restraint

This policy can be evaluated using the amended form of Figure 4 illustrated in Figure 7. The regulated industry is likely to act as a monopoly charging a constrained price (10). Profits are maximised by choosing the number of departures that will maximise the profit function of equation (11), subject to the price constraint $F = \dot{F}$. For any given fare, the profit maximising number of departures is given by equation (14), illustrated in Figure 7 by the curve F_M. The regulated equilibrium is, therefore, $(\dot{F}, \dot{H}/2)$. So long as the regulated fare is greater than F^*_{PM}, deregulation will decrease fares no matter the conjectures that characterise the unregulated industry, and so long as the regulated fare is greater than $\hat{F}_{BN}$ with less convex demand or F^*_{BN} with more convex demand, deregulation will lead to reduced prices provided that it also encourages active price competition and case of entry.

It is also probable that deregulation has resulted in increased departures.

In summary, regardless of the precise form of consumer demand, given that the regulated industry was characterised in the U.S. by Policy IV, the post-regulation conversion process strongly suggests lower fares, increased service departures, even with mergers of many new and old firms.

(10) That the price constraint is effective, i.e. that the monopolist cannot implement the profit maximising fare: headway combination, is implied by the discussion in section 7.3.

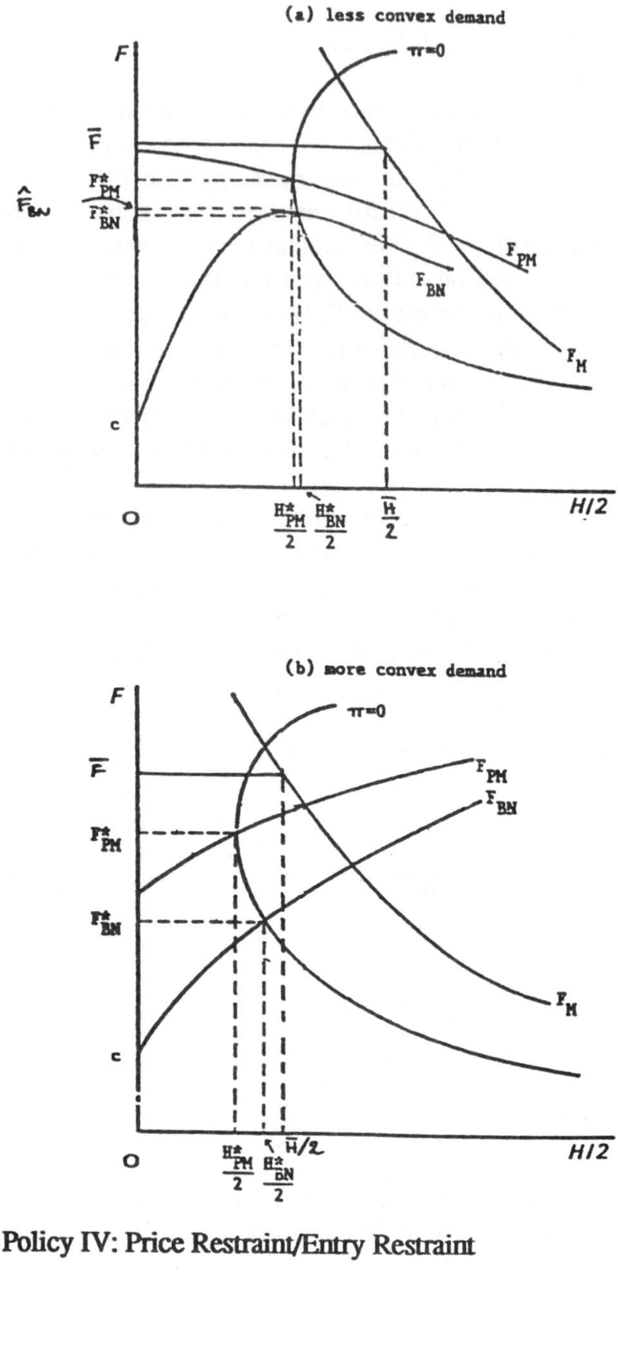

Figure 7: Policy IV: Price Restraint/Entry Restraint

APPENDIX: OLIGOPOLY AND COMPETITION

Gattuso (1) (who equates the word oligopoly with the cartel (or organised oligopoly) form) contends that those who claim deregulation of airlines in the United States is producing oligopolistic results are wrong. Instead, he contends that airlines in the USA are much more competitive today. He illustrates his contention by noting that "...in 1977 almost half of all passengers flew on routes where one carrier had 70 per cent or more of the market, last year only about 20 per cent did so". He admits that at certain major airports, one or two carriers have increased considerably the proportion of flights they provide. But he claims this is "...a natural consequence of the 'hub and spoke' system of routing..." (2). His basic conclusion is that airlines now serve more consumers with more flights at much lower costs. Moreover, he stresses that residents of smaller cities who were heralded as those most likely to suffer from deregulation have been the greatest beneficiaries. In substance, they are enjoying more frequent service and obtaining more work-stop destinations than would otherwise prevail. He proposes that if legal barriers to service by non-US carriers are reduced *and* more airports developed, even better results would obtain. As is predicted theoretically in the present paper, he too anticipates that deregulation would mean less competition and higher prices.

In maintaining the "hub and spoke" system after deregulation, many airlines merged, a condition which prompted the charge of increased oligopoly. (Henceforth, we shall employ the term organised oligopoly to indicate what Gattuso refers to simply as oligopoly (3). It is recognised that notwithstanding mergers, the national market shares of the major US carriers are presently very similar to those before deregulation (4). Gattuso emphasises the fact that what

(1) James L. Gattuso, "Status Report: Airline Competition and Concentration since Deregulation", *Backgrounder*, No. 717, June 1989, Washington: The Heritage Foundation.

(2) *Ibid*, p. 1. This system reduces the number of empty seats while increasing the frequency of flights to less travelled destinations. This was particularly true after the airline mergers which followed deregulation.

(3) And see F. Machlup, *The Economics of Sellers Competition*, (Baltimore: The John Hopkins Press, 1952) and M.L. Greenhut, *The Theory of the Firm in Economic Space*, (New York: Appleton Century Crofts, 1970; 2nd printing Austin: The Lone Star Press, 1974) for the distinction between competitive oligopoly and organised oligopoly.

(4) Gattuso, *op cit*, p. 3.

counts to any passenger is not the market share of an airline but the number of choices the individual has in flying from one point to another. The "... amount of competition on each of the 70,000 or so routes across the country" (5) is the important factor. Most germane to the theory advanced in this paper is the fact that in 1977, more than one in ten passengers flew on carriers with 100 per cent of the traffic on their route. In 1987, only 18 per cent did so" (6).

The explanation for the decreased concentration on routes, *given* the fact that overall market shares are today about the same as they were before deregulation, is simply that under the old system the Civil Aeronautics Board (CAB) in the US often gave protected positions to airlines; in contrast, deregulation allowed competitors to elbow their way into a route, thus decreasing concentration notwithstanding mergers.

All of the above is not to say that all airports are experiencing increased competition. As Maldutis (7) observed, percentages handled by one carrier increased substantially in St. Louis and Minneapolis. But Maldutis also found decreases elsewhere. Moreover, while the number of passengers per airline at a hub may yield an increased percentage, they are often merely connecting form one flight to another. Although airline concentration, as measured by airport traffic share, may have increased substantially since 1977 under the Herfindahl-Hirschman Index, concentration on routes to and from a hub is much lower than a decade ago (8). For all hub airports, airlines controlling a 70 per cent share or more of the passengers fell from 42 to about 32 per cent between 1980 and 1988 (9). Equally fundamental is the fact that fares over given distances are lower in the US the less frequent the number of flights since decreased frequency typifies the non-hub airport vis-a-vis the hub airports (10).

---

(5) *Loc cit.*

(6) *Loc cit.*

(7) Julius Maldutis, "Airline Competition at the 50 Largest U.S. Airports since Deregulation", New York, Salomon Bros. Inc., August 1987, pp. 22, 28.

(8) For example, almost 35 per cent of passengers going to or from St. Louis were on routes in which one carrier handled 90 per cent or more of the traffic while that percentage fell to 17 by 1988. See Gattuso, *op cit*, p. 5.

(9) Simat, Heilenson and Eichner, *Hub Operations: An Analysis of Airline Hub and Spoke Systems Since Deregulation*, Tables 4-11, New York, Salomon Bros. Inc., May 1988.

(10) Gattuso, *op cit*, p. 6 illustrates this by citing Cleveland which is a non-hub city in the US and which posts fewer flights at lower fares than Minneapolis-St. Paul, a hub city of the same size. Correspondingly, Dayton, a city half the size of Cleveland, offers as many departures as Cleveland.

REFERENCES

Adams, Walter and Brock, James W., 1986, *The Bigness Complex*, New York, Pantheon Books.

Anderson, S. P., 1986, "Equilibrium existence in the circle model of product differentiation" in Norman, G. (*ed*), *Spatial Pricing and Differentiation Markets*, Pion Press, London.

Archibald, G. C., Eaton, B. C. and Lipsey, R. G., 1986, "Address models of value theory", in Stiglitz, J. and Mathewson, G. F. (eds), *New Developements in the Analysis of Market Structure*, Macmillan Press, London.

Capozza, D. R. and van Order, R. 1980, "Unique equilibria, pure profits and efficiency in location models", *American Economic Review*, 70, pp. 1046-53.

d'Aspremont, C., Gabsczewicz, J. and Thisse, J. F., 1979, "On Hotelling's 'Stability in Competition' ", *Econometrica*, 47, pp. 1145-50.

Demsetz, H., 1964, "The welfare implications of monopolistic competition", *Economic Journal*, 74, pp. 623-41.

de Palma, A., Labbè, M. and Thisse, J. F., 1986, "On the existence of price equilibria under mill and uniform delivered price policies", in Norman, G. (ed) *Spatial Pricing and Differentiated Markets*, Pion Press, London.

De Vany, A. S., 1976, "Uncertainty, waiting time and capacity utilisation: a stochastic theory of product quality", *Journal of Political Economy*, 84, pp. 523-41.

De Vany, A. S. and Saving, T. R., 1977, "Product quality, uncertainty and regulation: the trucking industry", *American Economic Review*, 67, pp . 587-94.

Douglas, G. W. and Miller, J.C., 1974, *Economic Regulation of Domestic Air Transport: Theory and Policy*, The Brookings Institution, Washington D.C.

Eaton, B.C., 1972, "Spatial competition revisited", *Canadian Journal of Economics*, *5*, pp. 268-77.

Eaton, B.C., 1976, "Free entry in one-dimensional markets: pure profits and multiple equilibria", *Journal of Regional Science*, *16*, pp. 21-33.

Eaton, B.C. and Lipsey, R. G., 1978, "Freedom of entry and existence of pure profit", *Economic Journal*, 88, pp. 455-69.

Foster, C. and Golay, J., 1986, "Curious Old Practices and Equilibrium in Bus competition", *Journal of Transport Economics and Policy*, *XX*, pp. 191-216.

Greenhut, M. L., Norman, G. and Hung, C. S., 1986, "A general theory of pricing in a differentiated product industry", Discussion Paper No. 55, Department of Economics, University of Leicester.

Greenhut, M. L., Norman, G. and Hung, C. S., 1987, *The Economics of Imperfect Competition: a spatial approach*, Cambridge University Press, New York.

Johnston, P., 1987, "Airline deregulation and new entry: a case study of the London-Glasgow route", Working Paper No. 82, Department of Economics, University of Durham, England.

Kaldor, N., 1935, "Market imperfections and excess capacity", *Economica*, 2 pp. 35-50.

Kilman, Scott, 1987, "Growing Giants: An Unexpected Result of Airline Decontrol Is Return to Monopolies", *The Wall Street Journal*, 20 July, p.1.

Kohlberg, E. and Novshek, W., 1982, "Equilibrium in a simple price-location model", *Economic Letters*, 9 pp. 7-15.

Meyer, J. R. and Oster, C. V. (eds), 1981, *Airline Deregulation: the Early Experience*, Auburn House, Boston, Mass.

Meyer, J.R. and Oster, C.V., 1984, *Deregulation and the New Airline Entrepreneurs*, MIT Press, Cambridge, Mass.

Morrison, Steven and Winston, Clifford, 1986, *The Economic Effects of Airline Deregulation*, Brookings Institution, Washington D.C.

Neven, D., 1986 "'Address' models of differentiation", in Norman, G. (ed), *Spatial Pricing and Differentiated Markets*, Pion Press, London.

Novshek, W., 1980, "Equilibrium in simple spatial (or differentiated product) models", *Journal of Economic Theory*, 22 pp. 313-26.

Salop, S. C., 1979, "Monopolistic competition with outside goods", *Bell Journal of Economics*, 10 pp. 141-56.

Name index

Economists of the Twentieth Century

Monetarism and Macroeconomic Policy
Thomas Mayer

Studies in Fiscal Federalism
Wallace E. Oates

The World Economy in Perspective
Essays in International Trade and European Integration
Herbert Giersch

Towards a New Economics
Critical Essays on Ecology, Distribution and Other Themes
Kenneth E. Boulding

Studies in Positive and Normative Economics
Martin J. Bailey

The Collected Essays of Richard E. Quandt (2 volumes)
Richard E. Quandt

International Trade Theory and Policy
Selected Essays of W. Max Corden
W. Max Corden

Organization and Technology in Capitalist Development
William Lazonick

Studies in Human Capital
Collected Essays of Jacob Mincer, Volume 1
Jacob Mincer

Studies in Labor Supply
Collected Essays of Jacob Mincer, Volume 2
Jacob Mincer

Macroeconomics and Economic Policy
The Selected Essays of Assar Lindbeck, Volume I
Assar Lindbeck

The Welfare State
The Selected Essays of Assar Lindbeck, Volume II
Assar Lindbeck

Classical Economics, Public Expenditure and Growth
Walter Eltis

Money, Interest Rates and Inflation
Frederic S. Mishkin

The Public Choice Approach to Politics
Dennis C. Mueller

The Liberal Economic Order
Volume I Essays on International Economics
Volume II Money, Cycles and Related Themes
Gottfried Haberler
Edited by Anthony Y.C. Koo

Economic Growth and Business Cycles
Prices and the Process of Cyclical Development
Paolo Sylos Labini

International Adjustment, Money and Trade
Theory and Measurement for Economic Policy, Volume I
Herbert G. Grubel

International Capital and Service Flows
Theory and Measurement for Economic Policy, Volume II
Herbert G. Grubel

Unintended Effects of Government Policies
Theory and Measurement for Economic Policy, Volume III
Herbert G. Grubel

The Economics of Competitive Enterprise
Selected Essays of P.W.S. Andrews
Edited by Frederic S. Lee and Peter E. Earl

The Repressed Economy
Causes, Consequences, Reform
Deepak Lal

Economic Theory and Market Socialism
Selected Essays of Oskar Lange
Edited by Tadeusz Kowalik

Trade, Development and Political Economy
Selected Essays of Ronald Findlay
Ronald Findlay

General Equilibrium Theory
The Collected Essays of Takashi Negishi, Volume I
Takashi Negishi

The History of Economics
The Collected Essays of Takashi Negishi, Volume II
Takashi Negishi

Studies in Econometric Theory
The Collected Essays of Takeshi Amemiya
Takeshi Amemiya

Exchange Rates and the Monetary System
Selected Essays of Peter B. Kenen
Peter B. Kenen

Econometric Methods and Applications (2 volumes)
G.S. Maddala

National Accounting and Economic Theory
The Collected Papers of Dan Usher, Volume I
Dan Usher

Welfare Economics and Public Finance
The Collected Papers of Dan Usher, Volume II
Dan Usher

Economic Theory and Capitalist Society
The Selected Essays of Shigeto Tsuru, Volume I
Shigeto Tsuru

Methodology, Money and the Firm
The Collected Essays of D.P. O'Brien (2 volumes)
D.P. O'Brien

Economic Theory and Financial Policy
The Selected Essays of Jacques J. Polak (2 volumes)
Jacques J. Polak

Sturdy Econometrics
Edward E. Leamer

The Emergence of Economic Ideas
Essays in the History of Economics
Nathan Rosenberg

Productivity Change, Public Goods and Transaction Costs
Essays at the Boundaries of Microeconomics
Yoram Barzel

Reflections on Economic Development
The Selected Essays of Michael P. Todaro
Michael P. Todaro

The Economic Development of Modern Japan
The Selected Essays of Shigeto Tsuru, Volume II
Shigeto Tsuru

Money, Credit and Policy
Allan H. Meltzer

Macroeconomics and Monetary Theory
The Selected Essays of Meghnad Desai, Volume I
Meghnad Desai

Poverty, Famine and Economic Development
The Selected Essays of Meghnad Desai, Volume II
Meghnad Desai

Explaining the Economic Performance of Nations
Essays in Time and Space
Angus Maddison

Economic Doctrine and Method
Selected Papers of R.W. Clower
Robert W. Clower

Economic Theory and Reality
Selected Essays on their Disparity and Reconciliation
Tibor Scitovsky

Doing Economic Research
Essays on the Applied Methodology of Economics
Thomas Mayer

Institutions and Development Strategies
The Selected Essays of Irma Adelman, Volume I
Irma Adelman

Dynamics and Income Distribution
The Selected Essays of Irma Adelman, Volume II
Irma Adelman

The Economics of Growth and Development
Selected Essays of A.P. Thirlwall
A.P. Thirlwall

Theoretical and Applied Econometrics
The Selected Papers of Phoebus J. Dhrymes
Phoebus J. Dhrymes

Innovation, Technology and the Economy
The Selected Essays of Edwin Mansfield (2 volumes)
Edwin Mansfield

Economic Theory and Policy in Context
The Selected Essays of R.D. Collison Black
R.D. Collison Black

Location Economics
Theoretical Underpinnings and Applications
Melvin L. Greenhut

Spatial Microeconomics
Theoretical Underpinnings and Applications
Melvin L. Greenhut

Capitalism, Socialism and Post-Keynesianism
Selected Essays of G.C. Harcourt
G.C. Harcourt

Time Series Analysis and Macroeconometric Modelling
The Collected Papers of Kenneth F. Wallis
Kenneth F. Wallis

Foundations of Modern Econometrics
The Selected Essays of Ragnar Frisch (2 volumes)
Olav Bjerkholt

Growth, the Environment and the Distribution of Incomes
Essays by a Sceptical Optimist
Wilfred Beckerman